Edith

FIFTY FAVORITE OPERAS

FIFTY FAVORITE OPERAS

BY
PAUL ENGLAND

FROM
CHRISTOPH GLUCK
TO
RICHARD STRAUSS

BONANZA BOOKS
New York

Copyright © 1985 by Crown Publishers, Inc.
All rights reserved.

This 1985 edition is published by Bonanza Books,
distributed by Crown Publishers, Inc.,
One Park Avenue, New York, New York 10016.

Printed and Bound in the United States of America

Library of Congress Cataloging in Publication Data

England, Paul.
    Fifty favorite operas.

    Includes index.
    1. Operas—Stories, plots, etc. I. Title.
II. Title: 50 favorite operas.
MT95.E58 1985   782.1′3   85-12767

ISBN 0-517-481030
h g f e d c b a

TO

MY GOOD FRIEND

HARRY K. DICK

OF COLUMBIA UNIVERSITY

DEUS SIT PROPITIUS

CONTENTS

FOREWORD

Passion! What better word is there to describe opera? The vital core of opera *is* passion—sometimes violent, or joyful, loving, hateful, ecstatic, melancholic, vengeful; the gamut of emotions are exposed on the operatic stage and are transformed through the beauty of the music and the human voice. These emotions enter into an exalted state and, like everything else about opera, they are bigger than life. In opera, the ordinary becomes extraordinary.

Not only does passion reign on the operatic stage, but it also elicits as intense a response on the other side of the curtain. Opera audiences are known to erupt into wild outbursts—either giving performers wildly enthusiastic ovations and showering the stage with bouquets of flowers, or loudly hissing and booing and, even worse, throwing tomatoes and other "symbols of displeasure" onto the stage. Passion is returned with passion; indeed, the ardent devotion of some opera fans has stimulated the formation of cult-like groups around certain charismatic performers. It isn't difficult to understand how listeners can be awed by opera's grandeur and transported by the passions unfolding onstage.

Opera stands as one of the great cultural achievements of western civilization. It represents a glorious fusion of the arts, combining drama, music, dance, and the visual arts. No one art form can be discounted; opera requires each of its components to fulfill its essential role—anything less, and the opera suffers. Perhaps no one understood this better than Richard Wagner, who insisted that he did not compose opera as such but, rather, created *Gesamtkunstwerk* ("Total-artwork"). He meant by this a synthesis of poetry, music, drama, and spectacle, in which each element cooperatively subordinates itself to the total purpose. That total purpose—the music-drama (opera)—is not a mere "entertainment" but a profound and compelling work of art that elevates the listeners and resonates with our humanity.

Yet opera is pure artifice. If in the ordinary theater our disbelief must be willingly suspended in order to make the illusion of the play work, in opera that is no longer the question. We simply accept a world in which, among other things, people sing—beautifully—whether of love, of death, or murder, or whatever. Thus, Samuel Johnson had a valid point in defining opera as "an irrational entertainment." The late Kenneth Clark, the eminent British art historian, once asked, "What on earth has given opera its prestige in western civilization—a prestige that has outlasted so many different fashions and ways of thought?" He finds the answer in Dr. Johnson's definition: "... because it *is* irrational. 'What is too silly to be said may be sung,—well, yes; but what is too subtle to be said, or too deeply felt, or too revealing or too mysterious—these things can also be sung and only be sung."

Unusual for a rarefied pleasure (which it is oftentimes considered), opera today enjoys a flourishing and growing popularity. With the advent of modern technology, opera is able to reach millions of people around the world who would otherwise not be exposed to its splendor. The phonograph enabled opera to be brought into people's homes and, later, radio provided opera with a powerful and pervasive forum from which it attracted new listeners. More recently, the cinema and, especially, television have been instrumental in introducing opera to uninitiated audiences and converting many into fans.

Fifty Favorite Operas provides an ideal source of information for newcomers to opera or for regular opera-goers who wish to refresh their memories about opera plots, many of

ix

which are involved and seemingly convoluted. Paul England, who was a noted musicologist, has untangled these labyrinthine plots in lucid summaries that give insight into the dual aspects of music and drama, clearly defining the relationship between the action and the music. Each summary not only covers the libretto—or story—of the opera, but also incorporates a running commentary on the music, revealing all the highlights—arias, ensembles, overtures, and important orchestral passages. The narratives, written with verve and wit, are comprehensive without being overly technical and are in themselves enjoyable reading. Dates and places of first performances as well as other pertinent historical facts are included in each summary.

Intended as a popular guide to the opera, this book explores fifty operatic masterpieces, the majority of which are part of the standard repertory, though there are some that may be unfamiliar even to the aficionado. The operas, by Italian, German, French, and Russian composers, represent a wide range of styles from the eighteenth to the twentieth centuries. They are arranged in roughly chronological order to give the reader a sense of the development and historical continuity of the opera.

Opera comes, so to speak, in all shapes and sizes, and England's selection of operas reflects this great variety. Comedy and tragedy, grand spectacle and tender intimacy—all this and more can be found here. From the ebullient comedies of Rossini's *Il Barbiere di Siviglia* and Donizetti's *L'Elisire D'Amore* to the profound tragedies of Verdi's *Otello* and Wagner's *Tristan und Isolde*; from the intimacy of *La Boheme* to the spectacle of *Boris Godounov*; from the moral and social satire of *Le Nozze di Figaro* to the religious drama of *Parsifal* some of the greatest composers are represented here by what many consider to be their masterpieces.

One special feature of the book is the author's initial chapter, which presents a concise but broad and informative survey of opera that places it within a wide historical perspective. Opera's evolution is traced from its roots in the liturgy of the Church and its origins in the Renaissance to the twentieth-century operas of Richard Strauss.

Another valuable feature is the illuminating essay by Olin Downes that serves as the book's formal introduction. Downes, the renowned former *New York Times* music critic, offers insightful comments—especially helpful to the novice—on listening to opera.

This book will greatly aid the listener in the appreciation and enjoyment of opera. Were it possible for us to understand all that opera has to offer just by attending performances, books like this would be entirely unnecessary. However, that is not the case. The more one understands the stories, the reasons for the actions, the music, the arias, and so on, the more one will feel a greater sense of satisfaction and be able to appreciate what the creators of the operas had intended. However, one does not have to understand anything about the music or the story to experience the opera's emotional impact during a performance. Passion in opera speaks directly to the heart (who cannot fail to be moved by Mimi's death in *La Boheme*?) and, in a sense, one of the "miracles" of opera is its ability to produce, almost invariably, that emotional intensity. But no matter how essential that is, there are still other levels on which opera works; and unless we strive to penetrate them, we are missing a great deal. Reading this book is a first step in beginning to understand opera.

New York
1985

PAUL J. HOROWITZ

HOW TO LISTEN TO GRAND OPERA

By

OLIN DOWNES

THE impression is abroad that it is necessary to have technical knowledge of music in order to "understand" a great opera or symphony. This idea, which has frightened many people, is foreign to the spirit of art. A work of art is not a logarithm or a mystery for a chosen few, but a human expression. The great composers created from their experience for the men and women out in the wide world. Their object was the expression of feeling and beauty. It is true that certain professionals and routiniers would have us believe otherwise. They want to brand music, catalogue it, reduce to rules and formulas what will always be free and marvelous past the comprehending. It is a futile business, one that has no important results, save, perhaps, to temporarily obstruct or delay the common citizen's communion with the creative artist. The public, by and large, has a certain healthy instinct which the academicians cannot corrupt, and which, in the long run, brings recognition and love of what is fine. In the meantime the self-appointed high priests of the temple wonder why they are ignored, and complain that this public is incapable of appreciating "serious" music.

The French composer Debussy remarked that there is one music, which may exist in a waltz or a symphony. He might have extended the comparison to a fugue or a jazz ditty. Real music is careless of its outward garb, and may appear with much ceremony, or inhabit disreputable places. What is needed for its reception is an ordinarily capable pair of ears and human capacity for feeling.

Further requirements, to grasp its most profound meanings, are hospitality to greatness in the listener, and the quickening of aural perception, the refining of taste which experience of good music brings. These developments on the part of the individual are not dependent upon technical data. How a score is made is the business of the composer. The concern of the listener is not its machinery, but what it says.

Its message is particularly comprehensible in the field of opera, which is one of the more obvious and directly expressive of the media available to the composer. Purer musical forms, such as the instrumental sonata, quartet or symphony, are at once finer in facture and more elusive to the unaccustomed ear. By comparison with these forms opera is an open book for him who runs to read. Scenery and action are illustrative of text. The story is told by word as well as tone. Half a dozen arts that appeal to the eye as well as the ear are combined in the theatre, each intended to supplement the effect of the other, and the whole transfigured by the sovereign power of music. The symphonist must rely wholly upon tone for his expression, and follow laws that are traditional, however much he may vary their application. The opera composer has but one purpose, first and last, which is to project by the most forceful and intensive means in his power the emotions of the drama. He may use any technical device he pleases to accomplish this. He may adopt the rich symphonic method of a Wagner, or the seething, explosive style of a Mascagni. It is all one, so long as he achieves musical and dramatic unity and stirs the emotions of his audience. For him every rule, as such, is dispensable, and the straight line the shortest distance between two points! It is this directness of address, coupled with the universally intelligible methods of the theatre, which makes opera such a popular and readily comprehensible form of art.

Opera, then, is theatre and drama combined with music. Obviously the first step for anyone interested in it—whether musician or layman—should be to acquaint himself with the characters and the plot of the work to be presented on the stage. This is particularly necessary for those who speak only English, since very few of the important operas are written in that tongue, and the masterworks are seldom performed in translation. In other than English-speaking countries the publics are impatient of texts not understood. They insist upon knowing what the opera is about, without being compelled to secure a libretto or book of opera stories to give them that knowledge. In France or Germany or Italy operas by outlanders are customarily sung in the vernacular. In England and America there is a different situation, hence the usefulness of synopses and texts that are explanatory.

It is advisable, even in operas of the older and often dramatically absurd type, to understand every detail of the action and conversation. There are a few works of the old-fashioned type for which only a general outline of the plot is necessary. A listener to Donizetti's "Lucia di Lammermoor", or Bellini's "Sonnambula" needs little more than synopsis of the situations to enjoy the melodious airs and the florid vocalization so characteristic of their style and period. No particular study of drama is necessary to grasp the beauty of the famous "Lucia" sextet or the pyrotechnics—if that is the listener's taste—of the "Mad Scene", although even in this opera acquaintance with the text will do much to make the listener appreciate the real dignity and the aristocratic style of the two airs that Edgar of Ravenswood sings before he dies. Donizetti composed hastily, often superficially, but he had an admirable sense of musical line, and "Lucia" was composed primarily for the tenor—not the coloratura soprano! For such works as these identification of the characters and understanding of the main situations are the principal necessities. But this is not enough to get all they contain from such scores as that of Rossini's incomparable "Barber of Seville", or Donizetti's "Don Pasquale"—his comedy operas are far superior to the stilted "Lucia" style—or the operas of Verdi that come after "Ernani". Every moment and every remark on the stage should be understood, if the listener to the "Barber" is to enjoy to the full the sparkle and wit of the music, laugh as much as the composer and laugh with him. The music and text flash like quicksilver. The ensembles at the end of the first and second acts are sheer genius in their portrayal of individual character and sentiment, and the mastery with which the individual parts are welded together.

As for Verdi, the melodiousness of his earlier operas has often caused their emotional force and effectiveness to be overlooked. Consider, for example, the work that has been included by hostile criticism among his so-called "barrel-organ operas"—"Rigoletto". The music of this opera is in a large part familiar to the man in the street. Some of it is conventional and old-fashioned; most of it is astonishingly intense and even modern in accent. The great quartet of the last act is heard not only from the aforesaid barrel-organ, but from every brass band or other purveyor of the higher class of popular music. This "selection" always carries over, regardless of its significance in the theatre. But how much more it can mean when the situation that it interprets is realized. Here are four people singing in superb harmony, yet each one constitutes an independent dramatic element. The Duke is shown in his character of a careless voluptuary; Maddalena, the light o' love, is coquetting with him; Rigoletto is swearing vengeance, and Gilda agonizing over the perfidiousness of her lover. Each musical part, heard alone, expresses a different thing, and all combine in a passage of haunting beauty. It is worth while to realize these things, mirrored in the music. Less obvious, therefore more important to understand, is what is passing in the mind of Rigoletto as he appears in a dark street of Mantua, and squats, misshapen, in the gloom, and mutters of the curse which he himself invoked, and which he feels descending upon him. In this place Verdi uses two chords in the orchestra—the same two chords that Schubert uses with unforgettable effect in one of his songs —and they fall on the ear like a black shadow, with the word "maledizione"—"the curse". Rigoletto broods upon the peril of his daughter, dearer to him than life, and a flute breathes a phrase of her melody. There is the conversation between Rigoletto and the assassin Sparafucile, while a melody that is simple in the old Italian way but most ominous in the croon and shudder of the instrumentation creeps through the orchestra. And see Rigoletto, the buffoon, despair in his heart, skipping and clowning before the courtiers of the Duke, who have aided in the abduction of his daughter! The orchestra preludes his appearance, echoes faithfully his misery and his attempts at dissembling, until there is the sudden volcanic transition, with the desperate cry "mio figlio"—"my daughter." For Verdi, even in one simple chord, is an incorrigibly dramatic composer.

The score of Rigoletto is mentioned in certain details, as illustration of what even the more popular and readily appealing type of opera means and what dramatic music can convey. When one reaches the Wagnerian opera, or "music-drama", as Wagner most fittingly called it, a knowledge of every word of the text and the meaning of every situation is most desirable. It is not that the magnificent music will fail at the climaxes to reach the auditor to whom it becomes at all familiar. Once give rein to Wagner the musician, and the splendor of his genius is hardly escapable. Wagner also asks understanding of what his characters are thinking as well as doing—of what is transpiring deep within them, and the forces that surround them, and the clash with these forces that makes their experience. If these well-springs of their existence are known the music needs little explanation. Its root is the dramatic and philosophic idea, which rules the tonal conception. As the ear accustoms itself to the restless sea of tone, to the melodic phrases which sink deep in the current or rise magically to the surface, or subtly change their shapes, or combine, at the dictation of the stage, in some vast epic tumult— then the listener knows the potency of music and the resources of music-drama, and he feels Wagner, not as a composer of "chromatic harmony", "suspensions", "leading motives" and the rest of the rigmarole, but as the incredible master of tone that he was, and one of the great flaming spirits of his century. Memorize his motives and ticket their transformations; analyze his counterpoint and his instrumentation; peruse his scores— if this is possible, the more the better. Whatever promotes familiarity with the actual music is valuable. But not all the technical analysis or even score-reading in the world will in themselves bring home the poignancy of the moment when Tristan approaches to receive his fate at the hands of Isolde, or Wotan turns for a last embrace to Brunhilde his daughter, whom he, at command of a destiny he can no longer control, must bid eternal farewell.

These are things to be sought in opera: the beauty, the emotion, and not the mechanism of the music; the quality of the drama, and the relation between the music and the stage. There are, of course, operas and operas. Not all of them compass the greatness of Wagner or Verdi, or, let us say, Gluck, Mozart, Weber, Moussorgsky, Debussy at the height of their powers. It is not necessary that they should. It has been well said that the temple of art has many niches; its manifestations are as various as the creative impulses of the race. Important facts to realise are that the literature of opera contains pleasures of one kind or another for all persons of normal sensibilities; that art is not a technical affair but the unfoldment of wonderful things; and that in this field, above all others, there is unrestricted freedom to seek and find what oneself desires. This is the play-ground, the limitless place, for adventure and exploration. It is a realm of horizons and vistas greater than any that can be defined, and it is as accessible to those who have no special knowledge of its usages as to those who make these matters their particular occupation. This, indeed, is true of all arts, whether they are considered separately, or as they assemble to perform their ministrations in the lyric theatre.

FIFTY FAVORITE OPERAS

A SHORT HISTORICAL SUMMARY

ITALIAN Opera was the child of the Renaissance, conceived at the very end of the 16th century. The earliest opera that has come down to us is called *Euridice,* and was produced at Florence in 1600; Rinuccini was the author of the words, for which Peri and Caccini wrote the music.

They did not call their work opera, but 'drama for music'; their object was to write a play on a classical subject which could be sung throughout in what they called 'speaking music,' or recitative, this being, as they believed, the manner in which the ancient Greek Tragedy had been performed. It is interesting to note that though this experiment, like the whole of the Renaissance, was a protest against ecclesiastical tradition, the only existing model for their guidance was the plain-song of the Church liturgy.

Although their attempt to find the perfect fusion between sense and sound did not succeed, this idea has never ceased to be the inspiration of the noblest achievements in opera, as well as the guiding principle of its great reformers. "Take care of the sense and the sounds will take care of themselves" is a homely maxim, but one very necessary for opera-makers to bear in mind; its general neglect has invariably resulted in a period of decay.

The singers in *Euridice* were accompanied by four instruments; when, only seven years later (1607), Monteverde produced an opera on the same subject, entitled *Orfeo,* he increased the number to forty, thus early raising the still vexed problem of the relative importance of the singers and the orchestra. With Monteverde, too, the rather austere lines of the recitative began to put forth little blossoms of melody which were not long in attaining an almost too luxurious growth.

It must be remembered that for the first forty years opera was an affair solely of Courts and palaces; the first public opera house was opened in 1637 at Venice, which now became the centre for these exhibitions, and a place of pilgrimage for the whole of fashionable Europe.

Among the visitors to this primitive Bayreuth in 1645 was the famous diarist John Evelyn, who writes as follows:

"This night we went to the opera, where comedies and other plays were represented in recitative music by the most excellent musicians, vocal and instrumental, with variety of scenes painted and contrived with no less art of perfection, and with machines for flying in the aire, and other wonderful motions; taken altogether it is one of the most magnificent and expensive diversions the wit of man can invent."

After extolling the splendour of the production Evelyn goes on to speak of the performers: "Anna Rencia, a Roman, and reputed the best treble of women; but there was an eunuch who in my opinion surpassed her; also a Genovese that sang an incomparable base. They held us by the eyes and ears till two in the morning."

He refers again to "the famous Anna Rencia, whom we invited to a fish dinner after four daies in Lent, when they had given over at the theatre. Accompanied with an eunuch whom she brought with her, she entertained us with rare music, both of them singing to an harpsichord." We feel sure that Pepys would have added, "and all merry."

In this lively peep into the fashionable life of Venice in 1645 we see already established certain main features of

2

the operatic world which have not changed with the centuries. Opera has generally been "a magnificent and expensive diversion," and although the 'eunuch,' or male soprano, has disappeared,[1] it has always had its Anna Rencia, with her taste for little supper-parties on off-nights. But at that time the harmful necessary prima donna, at once the glory and the bane of Italian Opera, was still in the bud—the next century was to witness her dazzling efflorescence.

It is interesting to note that, at this period, while the music was often left in manuscript, the 'book,' on the contrary, was invariably printed; this was evidently in response to popular demand, the extent of which may be inferred from the following facts. As the performances were given at night, in a dimly lighted theatre, the keen opera-goer would bring his own candle with him in order to follow the words, and librettos still exist in which the singed leaves and dropped wax clinging to the pages bear witness to the interest they once inspired, and raise more than a suspicion that even in those days the singers were not always articulate.

With the rapid growth of public support for opera the demand for spectacle, sensation, and frivolity gradually gained the upper hand; considerations of dramatic propriety were thrust aside, and by the end of the century the decay of the libretto was fairly complete. The music, too, had suffered changes; popular melodies of all kinds were introduced without justification; the chorus, which had grown to some degree of importance, now disappeared, and an opera consisted practically of one long chain of vocal solos. It was along these lines that Italian Opera was to move unchallenged till far into the 18th century.

While noting the general decadence that now set in, we

[1] The last to be heard in England was Velluti, in 1825.

must not forget that this very period witnessed the first, and possibly the fairest, flowering of that entrancing melody which was to become the peculiar glory of the Italian school. The works of such masters as Scarlatti, Cesti, Caldara, have long been shelved because of their lack of dramatic vitality, yet they abound in airs of a serene and noble beauty which have never since been surpassed.

With the 18th century the corruption went on apace. It was the age of the great singers; it witnessed the development of a vocal perfection almost unthinkable in our own day, and the consequent tyranny of the prima donna and the *castrato*. Operas were written simply as a medium for vocal display, and the patrons were apparently content to have it so. When Handel established Italian Opera in London in 1711 the wits as well as the public were not slow to make fun of its obvious absurdities; the amusing articles of Addison and Steele in the *Spectator* and *Tatler* on the zoölogical element, so popular in Italy, the (human) bears and lions, the "pretty warbling choir" of real birds let loose in the theatre, make excellent reading. But the chief cause of objection was, doubtless, the employment of a foreign language on the stage, and the strongest protest against this new exotic form of entertainment was the production in 1728 of the mock-heroic *Beggar's Opera,* the words by John Gay, the music consisting largely of popular songs and dance tunes, arranged by Dr. Pepusch. This ran for sixty-two nights, and was the begetter of any number of so-called ballad-operas of a similar type.

However, the rising tide of Italian Opera was not to be checked; although Handel, after a thirty years' fight with opposition and intrigue, left the operatic field in 1740, the works of his rivals, Porpora and Buononcini, of Hasse, Sacchini, Galuppi, and other half-forgotten

4

composers, continued to find favour with the fashionable world. All the great singers flocked to London, where they enjoyed the same idolatry and stirred up the same strife as elsewhere; in fact, the history of opera for the better part of a century is largely a chronicle of the doings of these Madames and Signors, whose vocal feats as reported would seem incredible had we not the music to convince us, with passage after passage of difficulties which would prove insurmountable to any singer of the present day.

The operas of that time are, like the singers, gone beyond recall; they served their turn by demonstrating the perfection to which the human voice, as a musical instrument, may aspire; dramatically they can scarcely be said to have existed. We must make an exception perhaps in the case of Handel, whose virile genius and true dramatic instinct could infuse life even into the flabby material in which he had to work. There is a definite movement just now, both in this country and in Germany, in favour of a revival of Handelian opera; should it succeed it would mean a welcome swing of the pendulum toward a higher standard of vocal perfection.

Meanwhile France and Germany had dealt with the problem of opera, each in her own way. Into both countries the new entertainment from Italy had been introduced before 1650, with very different results. In the north of Germany several attempts had been made to establish a native opera, or at least to have opera sung to German words, yet in spite of the enormous reputation of Reinhard Keiser, who was working with Handel at Hamburg about 1700, and is credited with over a hundred German operas, the national movement collapsed, and by 1730 the whole of musical Germany was Italianized, and Vienna was on the way to become the chief seat of Italian Opera in all Europe.

In France things had gone very differently. When
G. B. Lulli—generally known as Lully—was brought as a
boy from Florence to the Court of Louis XIV, he found
a sort of native opera already established, in spite of
several early attempts to introduce the Italian style. The
French variety had been developed from the earlier ballet
with its song and dance, and it was by devoting himself
to this brand of music that Lully won the favour of the
Grand Monarch, who was passionately fond of dancing
and would himself condescend to appear in the Court
spectacles. Later, with the poet Quinault for his librettist, he produced a series of grand operas (1672-87)
exactly suited to the pseudo-classical taste of the age.
Far severer in style than the already decadent Italian
School, with greater regard for just expression, these
works would weary us by the formal dullness of their
librettos; but they mark a great advance in the handling
of the orchestra, and the form of overture devised by
Lully served as a model for nearly every composer until
the arrival of Gluck.

J. P. Rameau (1683-1764), Lully's successor, best
known to us by his harpsichord pieces, was a genius who,
with a finer sense for drama and a profounder knowledge
of harmony, made a more solid contribution toward the
formation of a national type of opera. Yet both Lully
and Rameau are little more than names to-day; their
works lie buried under the faded verbiage of the librettos,
where everything is as 'calm and critical' as Mrs. Jarley's
waxworks. But the "low punches" to which that lady
objected have in them a vitality which has outlived all
waxwork shows, and it is interesting to note that a certain little comic opera introduced to Paris in 1752 by a
troupe of Italians, with far-reaching results, is still alive
in Italy to-day, and was only recently heard with delight
in England. We refer to Pergolesi's dainty intermezzo,

6

La Serva Padrona, which, written as long ago as 1733, may claim to be the oldest operatic work that still survives. Its interest in connexion with the French Opera lies in the fact that, like *The Beggar's Opera* in England, its immense popularity in Paris signified a revolt against the 'classical' opera of the time. J. J. Rousseau followed it up with *Le Devin du Village,* a work of similar calibre, which remained high in popular favour for nearly eighty years. Moreover, the growing taste for this lighter form of entertainment led to the establishment in 1762 of a definite house for *Opéra Comique,* a term which has come to include many a masterpiece that is far from 'comic' in character.

This same year, 1762, is still more memorable for the triumph of the first great reformer, Gluck (1715-87). A Bohemian by birth, he had studied in Italy, and produced his first Italian opera in 1741. Four years later he was in London, where he met Handel, by whom he seems to have been deeply impressed. That he was considered somewhat of a revolutionary so early as 1756 is plain from the remarks of Metastasio, his librettist, on the production of a new opera at Vienna. "The drama," says the poet, "is my *Re Pastore,* set by Gluck, a Bohemian composer, whose spirit, noise, and extravagance have supplied the place of music in many theatres of Europe." These remarks from the man who dominated Italian Opera for the greater part of the 18th century take us at once to the root of the matter.

Gluck, disgusted at the stagnant state of the Opera, saw clearly that any reform had to start with the libretto, which must be a 'drama for music,' and not merely, as it had come to be, a patchwork of elegant verses made to suit the requirements of the singer rather than the composer. There is no doubt that the 'poets' and singers had long since entered into a conspiracy which had reduced Italian Opera to little more than a concert of vocal music combined with spectacle; dramatic truth and sincerity of expression were set aside—the essential task of the librettist was to provide a series of neat quatrains, mere commonplaces of sentiment or morality, which would serve the composer for the number of airs, of varied character, allocated by rigid convention to each of the singers. The ability to supply this unworthy material had been developed to such a diabolical pitch of perfection by one man that he seems to have got the business entirely into his own hands; this was the Metastasio referred to above, who reigned for over fifty years (1730-82) as Court poet at Vienna. His reputation and authority were so unquestioned that a 'book' by this great man was considered essential to the success of any opera; most of his works were set by several different composers, some as many as thirty times over. Gluck in his earlier career had been obliged, like the rest, to put up with the Metastasian libretto, but as his plans for reform expanded, he realized that the old man of the sea must be got rid of before anything could be done. Happily he found in the poet R. Calzabigi a reformer as enthusiastic as himself; the result of their collaboration was the opera *Orfeo,* which is generally regarded as the oldest work in the repertory. In it we see recovered some of the principles, though not the methods, of the founders of Opera in 1600, while its serene loveliness is a nearer approach to the true classic spirit than is to be found in any product of the actual Renaissance period. *Orfeo* makes many an opera of the following century look faded by comparison, and itself, one thinks, can never grow old. It has for its subject one of the great immortal truths, that love can triumph over death; musically it excludes the elements of decay by insisting on two vital principles; that nothing is to be admitted which does not

8

spring directly from the dramatic situation, and that the quality of sensuous beauty must always be given its lawful prominence.

Orfeo was produced in Vienna in 1762, and was followed by two other works, *Alceste* and *Paride ed Elena,* in both of which Calzabigi collaborated. Gluck then moved to Paris, where his new doctrines found a readier acceptance than in Southern Europe. It was there that the celebrated rivalry between him and Piccinni ran its course, resulting in the conversion of the latter, who continued to compose classical operas on the Gluck model after that composer's death.

But the day for such themes was almost over—the stale fumes of the Renaissance were rolling away; a brisker, gayer atmosphere had been brought to Paris by the 'Bouffons' with their dainty little *Serva Padrona,* and the new house for *Opéra Comique* had given fresh incentive to men like Monsigny, D'Alayrac, and Grétry, who exercised their genius or talent on subjects of light romance or fantastic comedy.

In Italy, too, the comedy element shone brightly in the operas of Cimarosa (1749-1801), whose *Matrimonio Segreto* still keeps the stage, and Paisiello (1741-1816), whose reputation was to be dimmed only by the brilliance of Rossini. But this is to run on too fast; we must return to Vienna to assist at the rising of the splendid star that was to preside over the birth of real German Opera —the incomparable Mozart (1756-91), whose masterpieces, with the exception of *Don Giovanni,* were all produced in that city.

Not that Mozart can be classed as distinctively German; while he excelled Gluck in the ability to express emotion or sum up a dramatic situation by the simplest possible means, he could be as florid as Porpora when he chose, and he had all the southern gaiety of Cimarosa.

Three of his greatest works, *Figaro, Don Giovanni,* and *Così fan tutte,* are classed with *opera buffa,* while his serious opera *La Clemenza di Tito* was written for one of Metastasio's frozen librettos, and suffered in consequence. So much for the Italian side ; on the other hand his delightful little *Singspiel* (song-play), *Die Entführung aus dem Serail,* was written to German words, and *Die Zauberflöte* may be considered the first real German opera.

But, German or Italian, gay or serious, Mozart's dramatic music differs from any other in a certain constant quality of pure loveliness; it matters not what subject is presented to him, he will clothe it in its appropriate mantle of music, and the result is invariably a thing of beauty, glowing with "the light that never was on land or sea." Within the last decade three of his operas, *The Magic Flute* (*Die Zauberflöte*), *Figaro,* and *The Seraglio* (*Die Entführung*), have become for the first time widely known in this country; as a result we have an ever-growing number of opera-goers who are prepared to swear that over all composers Mozart is king—and who can blame them for so excellent a choice?

With the production in 1814 of Beethoven's *Fidelio,* the first work of which it may be said that the interest lies mainly in the orchestra, Vienna ceases to be the central seat of opera—we must look to Italy and to Paris for some time to come.

Rossini (1792-1868) and Meyerbeer (1791-1864) are the two figures that dominate the operatic world from 1820 to 1870, roughly speaking. Their earlier successes were made in Italy, but both migrated later to Paris, and brought about that fusion of the French and Italian schools which lasted until the influence of Wagner began to make itself felt.

Rossini's masterpiece *Il Barbiere di Siviglia* was produced at Rome in 1816. Although an interval of thirty years separates this work from Mozart's *Figaro* (1786) the transition does not seem so very abrupt; both are comic masterpieces in their varying degrees, and in each case the libretto is taken from one of Beaumarchais' great twin comedies. Yet in their musical effect the two operas are poles apart; while Mozart delights and satisfies with a great variety of well-graduated *nuances,* Rossini excites and dazzles by an unceasing flood of brilliance.

The Barber is the gayest of operas; it is also the most florid. Gluck's reforms had made but little impression in Italy, and Rossini was all on the side of the singers; no composer has ever understood them better, none has written so sympathetically for every class of voice. The grace and sparkle of his music proved irresistible, and he and his successors, Bellini and Donizetti, dominated the world of opera completely for more than half a century. The result was the emergence of a number of exceptional singers whose enormous influence constituted a real danger to operatic progress. Pasta, Malibran, Grisi, Piccolomini, Alboni, Lind, Patti, and, of men, Mario, Rubini, Tamburini, Lablache, are names worthy of all honour in their own sphere ; but there can be no doubt that the public idolatry with which they were surrounded was largely responsible for the artistic decline of what we now call 'old-fashioned Italian Opera,' and delayed the progress of the coming great reform.

Il Barbiere has never lost its hold ; the part of Rosina remains to this day the chosen battle-horse of any singer who wishes to assert her claim to be a *prima donna assoluta.* We may be thankful that it is so—this work, when rightly sung, can never fail to charm; one cannot help wishing that Rossini had given us another *Barber,* instead of being betrayed by the rivalry of Meyerbeer into writing *Guillaume Tell* in order to meet the grandiose demands of the Paris opera house.

Giacomo Meyerbeer (actually Jakob Beer) is one of those temporarily important figures in musical history whom it is impossible to ignore, and not easy to praise. A fellow-student with Weber under the Abbé Vogler, he began by writing Italian Opera in the manner of Rossini, whose rival he eventually became. In 1826 he settled in Paris, where all his best-known works were produced—*Robert le Diable* (1831), *Les Huguenots* (1836), *Le Prophète* (1849), *Dinorah* (1859), *L'Africaine* (1865). The prodigious success of *Robert* installed Meyerbeer as the autocrat of the Paris Grand Opera practically for the rest of his life. The reason for that success is well suggested by the writer of the article "Meyerbeer" in Grove's Dictionary: "With this strange picturesque medley all were pleased, for in it each found something to suit his taste." This is perhaps as far as commendation can go in Meyerbeer's case; brilliantly gifted, of astonishing industry, with every advantage of education and experience, he seems to have been utterly devoid of a musical conscience. Weber had tried in vain to influence him for good; Wagner's high ideals and absolute sincerity made no appeal to him. To quote again from Grove: "Meyerbeer's music now belongs to the past, and there is little chance of it ever coming into fashion again. . . . He strove to please his public, and he had his reward."

In spite of the fact that his style is an inorganic composition of various schools, Meyerbeer is sometimes referred to as the Father of Modern French Opera; it would be interesting to learn which of his many brilliant successors has ever acknowledged his parentage. Apologists are not lacking among his critics, but Wagner's well-known contemptuous estimate will probably stand in future histories. Not all Meyerbeer's prodigious cleverness and *flair* for effect could make up for his obvious lack of sincerity—and what must Wagner, the poet, have thought of a man who could stoop to such subjects as *Robert le Diable* and *Dinorah?*

It is difficult to realize that MM. Barbier and Carré, who were responsible for the latter piece of imbecility, could also supply, and in the same year (1859), the 'book' for Gounod's *Faust,* surely one of the best that any composer ever had to work on. Thanks to its excellence, Gounod was able to produce that fine and original work which entitles him, and not Meyerbeer, to be regarded as the originator of the modern French school developed by A. Thomas, Saint-Saëns, Delibes, and Massenet.

But Paris was not destined to occupy much longer that paramount position which the influence of Gluck, Rossini, and Meyerbeer had gained for her; toward the middle of the century a power had arisen in Germany which was to challenge the attention of the musical world by upsetting all previous operatic standards.

Any notice of Wagner as the Great Reformer must be preceded by a reverential tribute to his precursor, Carl Maria von Weber (1786-1826), whose *Der Freischütz,* produced at Berlin in 1821, remains, with the exception of *Die Meistersinger,* the most intensely national opera that Germany possesses. It is now generally acknowledged that in this work of high genius Weber has anticipated, by intuition, many of the ideas which Wagner afterward developed with such marvellous results. But Weber worked from sheer inspiration rather than from any conscious theory, and in his other two operas, *Euryanthe* and *Oberon,* squandered his lovely music on such worthless librettos that both works are practically lost to the theatre. However, *Der Freischütz* remains, still fresh and fair, and though only a *Singspiel,* the most perfect operatic embodiment of the old German spirit of Romance.

This same spirit was no small part of the inspiration of Richard Wagner (1813-83) whose daring originality had made its mark within a quarter of a century after Weber's death.

Der fliegende Holländer was produced at Dresden in 1843, *Tannhäuser* in 1845, and *Lohengrin* at Weimar in 1850. Although these works only partially embody those theories which later on were to transform 'opera' into 'music-drama,' the new seed was sprouting in them, plain for all to see. The insistence on dramatic continuity, the rejection of the old cramping melodic formulas, of show-pieces or ornament of any kind merely for its own sake, the important part assigned to the orchestra in the unfolding of the story, the guiding-themes as a clue to the underlying emotions—all these things clearly portend a revolt against established traditions. Moreover, the glowing genius of Wagner, more precious than all his theories, was already present in its youthful vigour; nothing had ever been heard remotely approaching, in descriptive power, the overtures to *The Flying Dutchman* and *Tannhäuser,* while the visionary beauties of *Lohengrin* served to bring all heaven before the eyes of many who had never previously looked to the opera house for such an experience.

The librettos alone were a revelation. Hitherto the 'opera-books' had been, for the majority, a negligible quantity, or for the more thoughtful a thing to be regarded with contemptuous tolerance; there was in them no respect for dramatic probability, no standard of literary decency; with hardly an exception they were intellectually disreputable. But here were skilfully constructed dramas of great interest, written in a literary style that did no discredit to the high romantic nature of the subject; it seemed almost a misnomer to apply the word 'libretto' to works like these. Wagner, like Gluck, had realized that no reform was possible that did not begin with the words; in his ideal 'drama for music' words and music were co-important, inseparable, and, if possible, should spring both from the same imagination; fortunately he possessed a poetic faculty sufficient for the needs of his musical genius, and we see the result in such homogeneous creations as *Tannhäuser, Die Meistersinger,* and *Parsifal.*

This revolution in the 'book' of the opera created a new class of opera-goers; the *intelligentsia* could now enter the temple of the lyric drama and still preserve their self-respect. As time went on and the cult of Wagner became almost a religion it cannot be said that the attitude of these highly intelligent worshippers was altogether a healthy one. Fascinated and led astray by the composer's insistence on the philosophical importance of his music-dramas, the Perfect Wagnerite came to regard a visit to the opera rather as an intellectual exercise than an artistic enjoyment; *The Ring* in particular was looked upon as a sort of guide to the Higher Wisdom, and books have been written about it that can only be classed with the literature of the Great Pyramid and the Bacon-Shakespeare controversy.

But all this is merely amusing in retrospect; Wagner's nebulous philosophy has long ceased to be of interest, even some of his art theories have been given decent burial, but the splendour of his music remains undimmed, and the reforms which he carried through are perhaps the most far-reaching and at the same time the most valuable that were ever effected in any field of art. It is open to question whether in some cases Wagner did not allow his theories to obscure the brightness of his genius. *The Ring,* for instance, once so blindly worshipped, is now seen, as a music-drama, to be founded on too complex a basis; people are no longer interested in the elaborate mythological pantomime which does duty for drama, nor in the truths which it is supposed to symbolize. But the gorgeous music still entrances, and many are of opinion that this will survive among the treasures of the symphony concert when the work is no longer to be seen in the theatre. Already the tendency is to give performances of single sections of *The Ring* rather than of the complete cycle in its colossal entirety.

There remain the three unquestioned masterpieces in which plot, poetry, and music must remain for ever inseparable—*Tristan* (1865), *Parsifal* (1882), and, above all, *Die Meistersinger* (1868), which for mellow wisdom of conception combined with exquisite beauty of expression occupies a place in Wagner's works comparable to that of *The Tempest* among the plays of Shakespeare, and which, moreover, is full of just the sane and kindly humour which we find in Shakespearian comedy.

At the very time that Wagner was tearing up the past by the roots and changing the whole operatic outlook, another composer, still working in the long-established formulas, was infusing new life into the old Italian Opera. Giuseppe Verdi (1813-1901) is the only composer whose fame is commensurate with that of Wagner in the musical history of their time. Born in the same year as the German master, he had written several operas while Donizetti was still alive; he survived Wagner by eighteen years, and in his last opera, *Falstaff,* written at the age of eighty, he showed that he had assimilated what was best in the Reformer's methods, while retaining all his old melodious charm, and revealing for the first time a rich vein of delicate humour.

But the peculiar genius of Verdi is seen at its best in

the works which belong to the middle period of his long career. His first vital opera, *Rigoletto*, was produced in 1851 (a year after *Lohengrin*); this was succeeded by *Il Trovatore* and *La Traviata*, both in 1853; *La Forza del Destino* followed in 1862, and *Aïda*, the crowning achievement, in 1871.

Verdi brought into Italian grand opera the much needed elements of strength and sincerity. Rossini's natural genius had found its true expression in comedy; Bellini's delicate flutings were sufficient for *La Sonnambula*, but hardly for such a subject as *Norma;* Donizetti had written excellent comic opera, but his attempts at the grand style are merely weak and pretentious—we feel that, like Meyerbeer, who for our purpose may well be classed among the Italians, he is merely making up music according to a popular receipt.

But Verdi, in his maturer work, is always unquestionably sincere; his principle seems to have been: "Look in thy heart and write!" The libretto may be crude melodrama, the situations absurd, but Verdi manages to seize and alchemize them, and the result is a spontaneous outpouring of lovely and appropriate melody. His 'tunes,' as they are often called in derision, are sometimes blatant and banal, but seldom weak or sentimental—at their best they possess a certain glamour which belongs to the region of pure romance. Although in his latest operas Verdi shows himself in perfect sympathy with the modern principle which demands that the orchestra shall have its full share in the musical interpretation, it is as a master of dramatic vocal melody that Verdi occupies the high place assigned to him.

Among later Italian composers the best known are Ponchielli (1834-86), Mascagni (1863-), Leoncavallo (1858-1919), and Puccini (1853-1925). The first three are all one-opera men; the rightful heir to Verdi's throne has not yet appeared.

Although Wagner's reforms may be said to have renewed the face of the operatic world, it has not been found possible to accept his principles in their entirety—composers in every country have adopted such features as appealed most to their individual genius. One of the earliest to profit by the new light was Bizet (1838-75), whose *Carmen,* produced in the year of the composer's death, was actually condemned at the time for being too Wagnerian; it has long since taken its place among the masterpieces of dramatic music—not strictly to be classed with 'music-drama,' it stands, with *Aïda,* on the bridge which separates the old world from the new.

The next French composer to make a striking success in the Wagnerian manner was Charpentier (1860-   ) with his opera *Louise* (1900), a work which conforms to Wagner's counsel of perfection that words and music should be the work of a single brain. The subject, it is true, is thoroughly un-Wagnerian, for *Louise,* described as a 'musical Romance,' is actually a realistic picture of modern Parisian life, farced with a certain amount of dubious ethical propaganda which has undoubtedly contributed largely to the popularity of the work.

In complete contrast to *Louise* is *Pelléas et Mélisande* (1907), by Debussy (1862-1918). Maeterlinck's poem, in which we seem to catch the echoes from some dim region "out of space, out of time," offered the composer exactly the right material for the exercise of his extraordinary genius. In his handling of it Debussy seems to reach backward as well as forward; while exactly preserving Wagner's principle of dramatic continuity he goes far beyond 'the Master' in novel and audacious harmonic combinations; at the same time, in the almost complete fusion of words and music, *Pelléas* comes nearer to the

18

original intentions of the Florentine founders of 1600 than any opera that has yet been written.

In Germany the composer who has followed the Wagnerian model most closely and with the greatest success is Engelbert Humperdinck (1858-1921), who in *Hänsel und Gretel* has given us one of the loveliest of operas, worthy to stand beside *Der Freischütz* as an inspiration drawn from the traditional romance and mystery of the German forest.

Richard Strauss (1864-   ), the most significant composer who has appeared since the death of Wagner, and one of the greatest symphonists of all time, certainly laid himself open in his earlier works, *Salome* (1905) and *Elektra* (1909), to the charge of putting "the statue in the orchestra" and a most unsightly "pedestal on the stage." He seems, however, to have found his true measure in *Der Rosenkavalier* (1911), a brilliant piece of satirical humour which makes a deeper impression with every hearing. It is to be noted as of good omen for the future that this, the latest opera of first-class importance, recalls, in some of its most delightful moments, the sweetness and gaiety of Mozart; should the composer continue to develop this happy side of his genius, he may yet give us an opera worthy to take its place in the great line of musical comedies, with *Falstaff*, *The Mastersingers*, *The Barber of Seville*, and *Figaro*. This would indeed be a welcome turn of the tide—the world of opera is ripe for such a change. We have had enough of noisy sensation, of morbid psychology, of a too frank eroticism; nothing is more to be desired, for our present need, than a revival of comic opera in the grand style, and the rise of a school of composers prepared to maintain, with the Poet Laureate, that

> Howsoe'er man hug his care
> The best of his art is gay.

ORFEO ED EURIDICE

Music by GLUCK. *Words by* CALZABIGI.
Vienna, 1762; *London,* 1770; *New York,* 1863.

IT is one of the happiest of chances that what is generally regarded as the oldest opera in the repertory should bear the name of Orpheus, the legendary singer, minstrel, magician—the symbol through all ages of the power of music. As Dryden has told us:

> Orpheus could lead the savage race,
> And trees uprooted left their place,
> Sequacious of the lyre;

but his fame derives its greatest lustre from those songs which

> Drew iron tears down Pluto's cheek,
> And made Hell grant what love did seek,

and the classic story of Orpheus and Eurydice has been the inspiration of musicians for close on four centuries.

With the very earliest experiments we are not here concerned, but the first real Italian opera, or drama for music, was the *Euridice* of Peri and Caccini, produced at Florence in 1600. In those early days the subject was treated again and again, and generally under the title of *Orfeo*.

At the end of the 17th century, when opera had already departed sadly from its first ideals, a version was put forward in which the motive was oddly altered by turning Orpheus into a '*galant' uomo,*' so that Eurydice dies, not from the traditional snake-bite, but from jealousy!

Several settings of the legend were produced in Gluck's

20

lifetime, notably one by Bertoni, an air from which was sometimes introduced into Gluck's opera. Haydn wrote an *Orfeo* specially for London in 1794—the last of the serious versions. Sixty years later Offenbach's *Orphée aux Enfers,* an *opéra bouffe* produced at Paris in 1858, was for some time the delight of the Second Empire. Today Gluck's *Orfeo* still holds its place in the repertory, where the pure gold of its quality makes too many of its companion operas seem like tarnished Brummagem by comparison.

As the success of Gluck's opera depends almost entirely on the personality of a single artist its revivals must always be comparatively infrequent. The most famous Orfeo of the last century was the famous contralto Pauline Viardot-Garcia, for whom Berlioz rearranged the part; she played the rôle in the Paris revival of 1859 for one hundred and fifty nights in succession, and repeated her triumph at Covent Garden the following year. Within living memory the two most notable revivals in London have been one for Giulia Ravogli in 1890, and another for Marie Brema in 1898.

The short and simple fable is unfolded in four principal Scenes, the division into Acts varying with the several revivals.

Scene I. The curtain rises on a vale in Thessaly, where Eurydice, but lately dead, lies buried. Nymphs and shepherds, her former companions, pay the solemn rite of mourning at her tomb; there is a sad procession, and the strewing of flowers, while they call on the departed, if she still can hear them, to give some sign of her presence. Above the subdued and sombre strains of the chorus rises the poignant cry of Orpheus, the bereaved lover—*"Euridice! Euridice!"* He bids them leave him to his grief. Alone with the dead, he invokes her dear shade in a passionate recitative, and calls the trees, the streams, all nature, to testify to his undying love. In a short, plaintive melody thrice repeated he finds what comfort he may in talking with Echo, who at least makes music of the beloved's name. At last his growing passion moves him to resolve on the greatest of all adventures; he himself will go down to Hades, down to the underworld, to claim his bride and bring her back to earth—such love as his, he feels, must move even the Stygian realms to pity.

Nor does love fail him—Amor, the God of Love, appears; the gods have heard his cries and approve his courage. "Go, then, with thy lyre," says Amor, "to the gates of Hades; thy songs, thy mighty love, shall surely prevail even with those awful Powers." But one condition the gods impose. "In leading home thy lost Eurydice, thou mayst indeed speak with her—*but thou shalt not look upon her*—if thou dost, her life and thine are forfeit. Go, and joyfully obey the will of heaven!"

But even in his first outburst of joy and thankfulness Orpheus foresees the failure that threatens him; how is it possible to hold his love once more in his arms, yet not to look at her? How shall he bear it? What will she think? Yet the gods must be obeyed—and love will surely triumph over all.

[The recitative in which Orpheus expresses these feelings should rightly end the Scene; but the singer's requirements induced Gluck to add a long and unusually elaborate song for the Paris production of 1774, since when it has been the frequent custom to substitute an air from another of Gluck's operas, or by another composer, *e.g.*, Bertoni; but it is better to omit the number altogether.]

Scene II. The entrance to Hades, the kingdom of the dead—darkness and Stygian fumes and dreadful gleams from subterranean fires. The Furies, snake-tressed monsters, who guard those gates, are already aware of some strange influence, and stir uneasily; as Orpheus approaches they spring fiercely forward to challenge him in harsh and gloomy chorus, with the clash of brazen cymbals. "What impious mortal dares invade the realms of Erebus? Here none may enter but by the gods' permission!" As the singer preludes on his lyre they break into a frenzied dance, while the horrid bark of three-headed Cerberus mingles with their cries of defiance. Still Orpheus holds his ground, trusting to the charm of song and lyre to move even the powers of Hell to pity. At first, to all his pleadings, their only answer is a thunderous "No!" reiterated thirteen times at intervals with tremendous effect. Nothing daunted, the hero urges the claims of his own transcendent sorrows: "I fear not the tortures of Hell!" he sings. "Yourselves would count them little, could ye but know the pangs of a bereaved lover!"

When even the power of song has failed, the mighty name of love prevails. The spell begins to work; strange feelings of compassion stir in those monstrous forms; their angry voices sink gradually into an almost wistful softness; slowly the awful gates roll back, and Orpheus passes through unharmed into the underworld.

[It is hardly possible to give any idea in words of the music to this short but perfect Scene; the tense, picturesque action, the contrast of contending passions, are depicted with an economy and restraint without a parallel, and the result is the most vivid embodiment possible of the poetic conception; but this can only be realized by seeing and hearing it performed as the composer intended.]

Scene III. Short and simple as this opera is, it profits more than almost any other by the effect of striking contrasts. After the gloom and terror of the last Scene we pass to the golden calm of the Elysian Fields. The short introductory minuet strikes at once a note of serene beauty which reigns unbroken. The following chorus, with soprano solo—sometimes sung by a "Blessed Spirit," sometimes assigned to Eurydice—is full of a tender grace which the flute obbligato helps to invest with a "something afar from the sphere of our sorrow."

But the climax of beauty is achieved in the next number: *Che puro ciel! Che chiaro sol!* Here we have such a musical picture as has never been surpassed; by purely orchestral means Gluck has rapt us into the very heart of Elysium; here are the light, the airs, the streams, of Paradise—they are no earthly trees on which those birds are singing. In this number Gluck is at the height of his inspiration, and the illusion of musical description can go no farther.

[The composer's masterly employment of the woodwind is here the most notable feature of the instrumentation; as with the flute in the previous number, so here he gets his most poignant effect with a solo oboe.]

Even Orpheus, on entering this abode of bliss, yields to its tranquil spell; his first melodious phrases are well attuned to the peace and beauty that flood the scene. But soon the old yearning stirs within him; parted from love, beauty itself is void of recompense—he can have no peace until his quest is accomplished. A chorus of invisible spirits breathes consolation, and tells him that his reward is close at hand. After another of those delicious ballets which in Gluck never seem intrusive Eurydice appears, in glowing beauty, attended by her sister-spirits.

"Fear not to leave us," so they sing, "and to return to earth! Thy husband claims thee—and where love is, there is Elysium!"

So Orpheus and his Eurydice are once more united.

Scene IV. We are still in the underworld, but in another region; the difficult earthward journey has begun.

Orpheus, who knows too well the danger of delay, is impatient to regain the upper air; in his haste he has even released his hold on the beloved's hand, and presses onward, exhorting her to follow.

But the trial is too severe for poor Eurydice. "How can he bear to leave my side so soon! His words are few and cold, and not one glance of love! What can it mean! Am I so changed? Am I no longer fair? Go then!" she cries, "return to earth without me! What happiness awaits me there, now thou hast ceased to love me?" Torn by anguish and suspicion, Eurydice will move no farther.

Orpheus, distracted, still urges her to follow—but he does not turn, his glance is still averted from her. "Look on me once, beloved!" she pleads. He dares not—and he despairs of making her understand his reason. In impassioned song and dialogue the unequal contest goes on —but her tears, her reproaches, her entreaties, are too strong for even a hero's resolutions—he turns, he clasps her in his arms, he looks into her eyes with all the hunger of love and even as he does so, she droops and fails in his embrace; she is withdrawn from his mortal vision, and is once more his lost Eurydice.

Then follows that famous solo which, it would seem, age cannot wither nor custom stale. *Che farò senza Euridice* is the dear possession of many thousands who have never seen the opera, and know nothing of Gluck but this one air. From the dramatic point of view the accompanied recitative which precedes it is a still finer inspiration, an intenser expression of tragic passion. This second cruel parting from his love is more than Orpheus can bear; in desperation he is about to stab himself, when his guardian God of Love again appears and averts the fatal stroke. The hero's trial is over, his faithful love has moved the gods again to pity. Eurydice is restored to him, and the earthward journey is resumed to the strains of a triumphant march. After a succession of dances the scene is changed. We are on earth once more, in the temple of Love, whose praises are sung in a short mellifluous trio. The dances are then resumed, and finally culminate in a long, elaborate, and very spirited *chaconne*.

Exquisitely graceful as Gluck's ballet-music always is, there is certainly too much of it in the Paris version of *Orfeo,* the one usually performed. Gluck himself made a stand against the dramatic impropriety of transferring the courtly dances of the 18th century to the Elysian Fields and the vales of Thessaly; but the traditions of the ballet overruled all other considerations, and the Vestris family, that long line of famous dancers, was just then in the ascendant: "Monsieur Gluck," said Papa Vestris at a rehearsal of *Orfeo,* "I want a *chaconne* here, if you please!" *"Chaconne! Chaconne!"* cried Gluck, "this is a Greek drama! Do you suppose the Greeks knew anything about *chaconnes?"* "Did they not?" replied Vestris, with lifted eyebrows; "then they are much to be pitied!" But the dancer got his *chaconne* as we have seen.

Nor was this the only concession that Gluck had to make against his better judgment; for the Paris production (1774) he was obliged to assign the rôle of Orfeo, written for a male contralto, to a tenor, a change unfavourable to the musical effect, besides necessitating incidentally the introduction of inappropriate alterations and additions. In the original exponent of the part, Guadagni, the composer was exceptionally fortunate. This admirable singer had been in London in 1745, and was specially chosen by Handel to sing the alto parts in *Samson* and the *Messiah*. He seems to have been specially devoted to the dramatic side of his art, and in

26

the course of his frequent visits to England he became the friend and pupil of Garrick. Indeed, his reverence for dramatic propriety has earned him a reputation unique, one supposes, in the annals of the stage—it is said that he never gave an encore, and even refused to return to the scene in acknowledgment of the loudest applause. By persisting in this course "he so greatly offended individuals and the opera audience in general that at length he never appeared without being hissed." Nevertheless, he continued a great favourite in London, where he played Orfeo in 1770. It is worthy of note that this remarkable man reaped further laurels in a very different field; he was known as "the best billiard-player in Europe." Such a combination of talents has probably been equalled only in the French composer Philidor (1726-95), whose musical reputation was almost eclipsed by his fame as a chess-player.

DIE ENTFÜHRUNG AUS DEM SERAIL

Music by MOZART. *Words by* BRETZNER.
Vienna, 1782; *London,* 1827.

THIS little opera, more generally known as *Il Seraglio,* can be made one of the most delightful of entertainments; the fresh and homely humour of it intrigues us from the start, the sentiment fortunately fails to move us, except to enjoyment of the music. As to the words, it is said that Mozart himself had a large share in them. It may be; in any case they serve their turn well enough for the musical setting, and for the conduct of the simplest of plots.

Picturesqueness of scene is secured by giving the little play a Turkish setting—the palace of the Pasha Selim, on the shores of the Bosphorus. Here Costanze, a noble lady who has been carried off by pirates, is held captive in the harem, together with her maid Blonde, and Pedrillo, the droll, faithful servant of Costanze's *fiancé* Belmonte. Costanze, pining for her absent lover, is embarrassed by the attentions of the Pasha, while little Blonde is plagued by those of old Osmin, the surly gardener—who is, moreover, the Pasha's right-hand man and the great comic figure of the piece. Pedrillo manages to introduce Belmonte into the palace, and together they plan an escape which nearly succeeds, when Osmin intercepts the elopers and drags them bound before the Pasha Selim. In the course of conversation it comes out that Belmonte's father once did the Pasha some tremendous wrong, which would seem to call for even severer punishment than the

28

immediate circumstances demand. Selim, however, is every inch a gentleman, and sees his chance here for a show of splendid magnanimity. He, who, in spite of his ardent passion for the fair Costanze, has never tried to force her to his will, now resigns her to Belmonte, the son of his bitterest enemy, grants them a free pardon, and provides all with a safe passage to their native land.

Act I. In the grounds of the Pasha Selim's palace, part of which gleams white through the trees, while the waves of the Bosphorus sparkle blue in the background. Enter Belmonte, devoured by all a lover's impatience. Though he has managed to find his way to the place of Costanze's captivity, he is at his wits' end how to communicate with his beloved. He has just time for a plaintive little air, *Hier soll ich dich denn sehen,* when approaching footsteps send him into hiding.

It is Osmin who enters—a magnificent figure of fun, with his surly humour and huge bass voice, "that can sing both high and low." (The part was written for a certain Ludwig Fischer, who had a compass of two octaves and a half.) The old man, with a basket on his arm, mounts a ladder that stands against a fig-tree, and sings grotesquely as he gathers the fruit. He seems to have the harem rather on his mind; women *will* be women—even his little Blonde gives him a lot of trouble —and he has a life's experience behind him, which he sums up in the song, *Wer ein Liebchen hat gefunden*:

> When a maiden takes your fancy,
> And you want her for your own,
> Be a hero in your wooing,
> Always kissing, always cooing,
> Never leave the girl alone![1]

Belmonte, who has just found his way into the palace

---

[1] These extracts from the English version are printed by kind permission of Messrs Boosey and Co., Ltd.

grounds, interrupts him: "Hey, friend! is this the Pasha Selim's house?" Osmin eyes him sourly, but deigns no answer; he goes on with his song:

> But when once she's safely landed,
>   Lock the door and turn the key!
> For you'll find the charming creature
> Has a restless, roving nature,
>   Far too fond of liberty!

The two men soon go at it hammer-and-tongs in a lively duet, in which Belmonte is driven off the stage. The arrival of Pedrillo and his cool request for figs rouse Osmin to still greater fury. His longish solo, *Solche hergelauf'ne Laffen* is a masterpiece in the *buffo* style; he gets almost inarticulate toward the end, as he enumerates the things he would like to do to Pedrillo, if only he got the chance:

> Hang you first! Draw and quarter!
> Souse you next in boiling water!
> On a spit then I'd pin you!
> Last of all I'd take and skin you!

A spirited chorus of janissaries, together with the ladies of the harem, welcomes the arrival of Pasha Selim in his state barge, from which he gallantly hands the lovely captive-heroine on to the stage.

"Still drooping, fair Costanze?" he questions. "Still in tears?"

Alas, yes! it is the poor girl's fate to move weeping through the opera, as a foil to so much gaiety! However, her first air, *Ach, ich liebte,* affords at least some consolation (to a prima donna) by being extremely florid and extremely high, a remark which is still more applicable to the great solo allotted to the heroine (*Martern aller Arten*) in Act II. The part was, in fact, written for an exceptionally high soprano, Aloysia Weber, Mozart's first love, subsequently his sister-in-law, and sister to the Mme Hofer who 'created' the rôle of the Queen of Night in *The Magic Flute*. However, Costanze's song (of devotion to her lost love) touches the heart of Selim, who vows never to put constraint upon one so tender and so true.

Pedrillo, meanwhile, has persuaded the Pasha to take Belmonte into his service as architect, and the scene closes with a merry knockabout trio, *Marsch, marsch, marsch!* in which Osmin tries to stop Belmonte and Pedrillo from going into the palace, but is himself overpowered and rolled in the dust, while the pair make a triumphant entry.

Act II. We begin with a lively quarrel between Osmin and Blonde, daintiest of soubrettes, who, "as a freeborn English woman," flatly declines to take her orders from any heathen Turk—least of all an elderly one! Blonde's music throughout absolutely sparkles with gaiety and high spirits, and in their duet, *Ich gehe, doch rath' ich es dir,* the way in which she flaunts the old fellow, mocks his manner, and leaves him gasping with amazement at her audacity, is quite delicious. Osmin being thoroughly routed, Pedrillo enters to tell Blonde of the brightening of their prospects—of Belmonte's admission to the palace, and their plans for escaping that very night. Blonde breaks out into an exuberant little song, *Welche Wonne, welche Lust!* which obviously calls for an accompanying dance, and is perhaps the most captivating solo in the opera.

Costanze, meanwhile, is well provided for in the great air, *Martern aller Arten,* one of the most exacting pieces of *coloratura* in the soprano repertory; this outburst is occasioned by the Pasha informing Costanze that his patience will not last for ever, and that she really must reconsider her position. But the fun is resumed in a rollicking duet, *Vivat Bacchus!* in which Pedrillo plies

Osmin with unaccustomed drink and so puts him *hors de combat*. Belmonte, Costanze, Blonde, and Pedrillo now join in the quartet of rejoicing which ends the Act. Any possible monotony of mood is cunningly broken by the introduction, in the middle of this number, of one of those inevitable little tussles between the sexes. Belmonte and Pedrillo are both struck by a horrid suspicion that their respective mistresses may not have been *quite* so firm against the temptations of the harem as they vow they have been. This is too much for the patience of the fair ones; Costanze, of course, is soon in tears; Blonde promptly boxes Pedrillo's ears—

> (Me, forsooth, to be suspected
> With an ugly waddling Turk!),

and the men are quickly brought to their senses.

Act III. The escape is planned for midnight. As the hour draws near, Belmonte invokes the God of Love to aid him, in a suave Mozartian air, with much Italian ornamentation, *Ich baue ganz auf deine Stärke.* But all in vain! Osmin and the guard are on the watch, cut off the fugitives, and bind them fast to await the coming of the Pasha, while the old ruffian bursts out into an almost fiendish song of triumph, *Ha! wie will ich trumphiren!* a song which with its compass of two octaves and its strenuous hammering on the high notes must remain the admiration and despair of all but exceptional basses. In a long and pathetic duet Costanze and Belmonte resign themselves to their fate, but the entrance of Selim with his halo of magnanimity and a free pardon for everybody brings the play to an end with a chorus of gratitude, the departure of the happy lovers for their fatherland, and the popular collapse of that old windbag, Osmin.

"The Escape from the Seraglio," to give the title its

true English meaning, may well be considered as the beginning of the German School of Opera; it breaks away from Italian traditions in many particulars, chiefly in the attempt to secure a closer union of words and music, and the introduction of a large amount of spoken dialogue, a novelty in an operatic work of any importance. Its form is actually that of the *Singspiel*, a category which includes *The Magic Flute*, Weber's *Freischütz*, and even Beethoven's *Fidelio*. Although there are certain conventional Italian airs in *Seraglio*, these must be counted as its weakness; its strength lies in the sweet simplicity of some of its tunes, the sprightly gaiety of others, and the rich humour to be found in the concerted pieces and throughout the whole part of Osmin. This little opera is of a thoroughly intimate *genre*, and can be given properly only in a small theatre. Until recently it has not had a fair chance in England because of a tasteless 'arrangement'—say, rather, distortion—produced nearly a hundred years ago at Covent Garden, with "original additions" by one Kramer. It was successfully revived, however, in England about fifteen years ago in its original purity, and with a new English libretto, and is now a well-established favourite, while Osmin's first song, "When a maiden takes your fancy," has become one of the most popular *buffo* songs in the concert-room.

LE NOZZE DI FIGARO

Music by MOZART. *Words by* DA PONTE, *from* BEAUMARCHAIS. *Vienna,* 1786; *London,* 1812; *New York,* 1823.

THIS is an opera which, owing to the delicious gaiety of many of the scenes, the charm of certain of the characters, and, above all, the ever-present enchantment of Mozart's music, it is possible to enjoy to a great extent without any real understanding of the plot. It would be a mistake, however, to go no farther, for the music is so illustrative of the drama that our enjoyment is doubled when we are able to appreciate how subtly Mozart has moulded it to every changing mood and to every twist and turn of the rapid action. Some knowledge at least is necessary of Beaumarchais' two great comedies, *Le Mariage de Figaro,* from which this opera is taken, and its predecessor in point of time, *Le Barbier de Séville,* so familiar to all opera-goers in connexion with Rossini's *Barbiere.* It is essential, for instance, to bear in mind that the Count and Countess of Mozart's creation are the Almaviva and Rosina of the earlier play (and of Rossini's opera), that poor Rosina has been long neglected by her roving husband, and that Figaro is no longer a mere 'barber,' but a valet, and the actual rival of his master in love.

A writer at the beginning of this century described the 'book' of *Figaro* as "a moral blister"; a fantastical comedy of intrigue would seem perhaps a truer description. In Beaumarchais' play, *Le Mariage de Figaro,* upon which da Ponte based his libretto—and which was said to have had its share in hastening the French Revolution—there are, of course, darker undertones and

34

threads of serious interest, but he must have a morbid mind indeed who can discover anything in the words and action of the opera but the most delightful flummery, touched here and there with tender sentiment.

The scene is laid appropriately in a castle in Spain, and the persons of the drama may be said to act accordingly. The chief characters are not the Count and Countess, but his valet Figaro and her maid Susanna. The two are about to get married, and Figaro has good reason to be anxious about the Count's unwelcome attentions to Susanna, his plans to prevent their marriage, and his purpose to revive certain seigneurial privileges, of a kind which would certainly come as a shock to our modern ways of thinking. The maid and the valet, who are very much in love, combine with the neglected Countess to defeat the Count's designs, and incidentally by a public exposure to shame him into a better way of life. The plan is entirely successful; we enjoy the rake's discomfiture, even if we cannot put much faith in his permanent reformation.

The under-plot is concerned with the intrigues of a rather farcical duenna, Marcellina, who, at the outset, is bent on marrying Figaro herself, a plan in which she is backed up by the Count and old Bartolo, for whom she keeps house; but no one who has any acquaintance with the stage devices of that period will be in the least surprised to learn how "the unexpected discovery that Figaro is her son leads to a generally happy *dénouement!*"

So much for the 'moral blister'! In the midst of this unsubstantial but very complicated plot, a' every corner we find lurking that pearl of all operatic Pages, the delightful Cherubino, the roguish, sentimental youngster, standing, but with no reluctant feet, on the threshold of manhood. Whatever can be alleged against the Chérubin of Beaumarchais, Mozart's Cherubino must not be so aspersed; he is a figure of purest fantasy, and a sheer delight.

Act I. After an overture which promises nothing but gaiety the curtain rises on a piquant situation. Figaro is measuring the walls of a large apartment, while Susanna, before the looking-glass, is making herself more than usually attractive by trying on the bridal wreath and veil. "Fifteen! Eighteen!" sings Figaro, with his footrule; "Yes, 'tis really sweet and dainty," sings Susanna to herself in the glass. It is their wedding eve; the Count has kindly given them this fine room for their own. "Just between the Count's room and the Countess's—so handy!" says the simple Figaro. "Handy! yes—for the Count!" replies Susanna; "*you* can use it if you like— *I* won't have it!" She then tells him certain facts which make him fairly caper with rage and break into the jolly air *Se vuol ballare*:

> Let me but catch you here,
>   My pretty master,
>   Straight to disaster
>   I'll lead you a dance! [1]

And so Figaro dances off.

Enter that cattish duenna Marcellina with Bartolo, who is very willing to help her in catching Figaro. Susanna re-enters, and, in a sprightly duet, each lady, while 'making politeness' at the door, tells the other what she thinks of her (*Via resti servita*):

> MAR. I bow to my lady
>   So dainty and fine!
> SUS. Nay, nay, ma'am, believe me,
>   The honour is mine!
> MAR. Now pray go before me!
> SUS. No, no! 'tis for you!

MAR. I'm not so uncivil——
SUS. I know what is due!
MAR. The bride of the moment!
SUS. A lady—though plain!
MAR. The Count's little fancy!
SUS. The doxy of Spain!
MAR. Your innocence——
SUS.   Dignity!
MAR. Your influence——
SUS.   Your age!
MAR. (By heaven, I could throttle her!
       I'm bursting with rage!)

With every sentence the ladies bow and curtsy with
ever greater politeness, until Susanna's last shot—"Your
age!" drives Marcellina from the field.

Now comes Cherubino, almost in tears; the Count
has caught him flirting with the gardener's daughter,
Barberina—(Fanchette in Beaumarchais' comedy)—and
has dismissed him from the castle. Never again will he
see his dear Susanna—no, nor the Countess either! He
is equally in love with both, it seems—nay, with all the
women in the world, as his delicious solo so well sets
forth (*Non so più cosa son, cosa faccio*):

Yes, it's true! I don't know what I'm doing!
Such a fever within me is brewing!
Every maiden I meet makes me flutter,
Any fair one can set me on fire!

It is necessary to record that in this scene Cherubino
contrives to snatch from Susanna a ribbon belonging to
the Countess, and gives her in exchange a little song he
has composed, and which he hopes Susanna will sing to
her mistress; for this is the *Voi che sapete* which the Page
sings himself in the Second Act.

Suddenly the Count's voice is heard outside, and the
plot immediately thickens in a way which demands our
closest attention. Cherubino, in a fright, hides behind
the big armchair. The Count, who has come to beg

Susanna for a rendezvous, has not got far with his gallantry when the voice of Basilio, the music-master, makes him jump. The Count, of course, must not be found in Susanna's room (least of all by Basilio, who has a serpent's tongue)—he will hide behind the armchair; just in the nick of time Cherubino slips round to the seat of the chair and is covered up by Susanna.

Enter Basilio, to tease Susanna, who hates him, with the most scandalous insinuations about Cherubino and herself—"and as for the Page and her ladyship the Countess—well, everybody is saying——" "*What* is everybody saying?" thunders the Count, springing up from behind the chair. The trio *Cosa sento!* paints the general confusion, in the course of which Cherubino is naturally dragged from his lurking-place. The Count acts promptly; there is a commission vacant in his regiment, Cherubino shall have it, and he must be off at once. Susanna and the Countess are both a little sorry, but Figaro thinks it fine fun, and nobly has Mozart provided for his mood: there is surely not an opera house the world over that has not been 'brought down' by *Non più andrai,* the most admirable example of robust humour to be found in the whole range of vocal music.

> So, Sir Page, your vagaries are over!
> Far too long you've been living in clover,
> Till at last they've begun to discover
> That you're turning the house out of doors![1]

How gaily he mocks the airs and graces of the lad, pulls his curls, tweaks off his feathered cap! Ah, life's a very different thing in the army!

> You'll forget your parlour dances
> When the sweltering line advances.
> Over mountains! through the river!
> First you sweat and then you shiver!

[1] These four incomparable lines are by the late W. H. Bellamy; it would be sacrilege to substitute any other version.

Up you get and on you blunder,
Trumpets blare and cannons thunder,
While the shots come whizzing round you
Till you wish yourself away!
Cherubino's all for glory!
He's the boy to win the day!

Act II. In contrast to the lightness and gaiety of the First Act a deeper note is sounded on the second rise of the curtain. The Countess, alone in her apartments, a pathetic figure of neglected love, voices her sorrow in the cavatina, *Porgi amor qualche ristoro.* This is a crystal stream of Mozartian melody, "pouring unto us from the heaven's brink."

Plaintive as are the words, the music soars above all earthly melancholy; whether the song is dramatically appropriate may be questioned—we are more than content to accept it as a perfect piece of abstract beauty.

But soon all is once more in movement. Susanna comes to talk with her mistress, and the entrance of Figaro promises further plots and intrigues.

It is well to notice the way in which the stage is set for this Scene: the room has a closet, a curtained recess, two doors, and a window; all of which prepare us for a certain liveliness of action.

Figaro has a plan for diverting the Count from opposing the coming nuptials. "Our only hope of defeating his lordship," he says, "is to turn the tables upon him—keep his thoughts away from other people's wives by making him apprehensive about his own!" With this object he has sent him an anonymous letter warning him that the Countess has an assignation with a gallant in the park that very evening. That will give him something to think about! Meanwhile, Susanna must promise to grant the Count his wished-for rendezvous at the same time and place. "But surely," says the Countess, "you will not let Susanna do that!" "Not exactly!" he answers; "Cherubino shall go, disguised, in her place!"

So Sir Page is not yet off to the wars! He enters now, and after all this dialogue of intrigue his little song is welcome, *Voi che sapete*—who does not know it?

> One feeling moves me,
> All else above—
> Tell me, fair ladies,
> Can this be love?

Susanna proceeds gaily to dress the youngster in the garments he is to wear as her substitute that evening. The chatter and laughter are at their height when an angry knock is heard at the door, which Susanna had locked in view of the 'trying on.' It is the Count— heavens! and Cherubino, only half dressed, in the Countess's chamber! He flies into the bedroom and bolts the door behind him; Susanna hides behind the curtains of the recess. The Countess lets in her furious lord, full of suspicion, with Figaro's letter in his hand. A chair is overturned in the bedroom. "Only Susanna!" says her ladyship. The Count demands entry, to see for himself; the Countess bars the way; the door is locked, she says, and shall not be opened. The Count goes in search of a hammer to break it down, and takes the Countess with him. Cherubino opens the door, kisses his Susanna good-bye, and jumps through the window into the garden, while Susanna takes his place in the bedroom. Re-enter the Count and her ladyship; and then begins one of those long and elaborate finales—*Esci omai, garzon malnato*—which Mozart had a special genius for devising.

So far as the music is concerned, movement succeeds movement in sprightly variety, and with admirable clearness; not so the plot, however, in which no less than eight persons are involved. The complications are so numerous and so tangled that it is impossible to recount them in detail. The chief effect is made by the entrance of Marcellina, Bartolo, and Basilio, who present to the Count an alleged contract of marriage between Figaro and Marcellina, and demand that justice be done to the aggrieved duenna. The Count, of course, is privy to this conspiracy, and promises to have the matter tried before the court. Mention must be made of the episodic entry of the gardener, old Antonio, with a damaged pot of choice carnations. Someone—Cherubino, of course—had jumped on to them from the Countess's bedroom window that very morning! But even this awkward incident is explained away by the ready wit of Figaro and Susanna, who swear that the jumper was none other than Figaro himself.

Act III. *Scene* I opens with a short dialogue very essential to the plot, in which the Countess tells Susanna that she has determined to go herself to the rendezvous with the Count, who, taking her for Susanna, will thus be detected in paying lawful attentions to his own wife! Then follows one of the loveliest and best-known numbers of the opera, the duet *Crudel, perchè finora,* in which Susanna agrees to meet the Count that evening in the park. The music exactly illustrates both the amorous ardour of the Count and the delicious coquetry of Susanna, and blends them together into a flawless whole. [It is very well worth while to compare the duet with the equally well-known *Là ci darem* in *Don Giovanni,* and to note the subtle and perfectly appropriate differences in the method of treatment.]

The following showy air for the Count, *Vedrò mentr'io sospiro,* expressive of jealousy and rage against Figaro, is perhaps the least interesting number in the whole opera; dramatically it has hardly any justification, and might well be omitted, as it is most obviously 'written in' to gratify the demands of the singer. At the same time, it makes a most effective piece for the concert-room, where it has always been a great favourite.

Now enters Marcellina with her supporters, Basilio and old Bartolo, together with Don Curzio, the stuttering lawyer who is to decide on the claims against Figaro. "The defendant must either pay the plaintiff the sum demanded or marry her this very day," says Don Curzio. The second alternative, however, is soon ruled out by the discovery that Figaro—who has "a strawberry mark on his left arm!"—is the long-lost son of Marcellina and Bartolo! A short but pregnant sestet follows in which many things happen. Figaro is welcomed by his new-found parents; Susanna enters just in time to see him embracing Marcellina, and, under a misapprehension, boxes his ears; but an explanation follows and the usual 'happy *dénouement*' is greatly assisted by the bag of gold with which Susanna discharges Figaro's obligation to Marcellina; how she came by it was her own secret— and the Count's!

Scene II. The scene now changes to the Countess's apartment and we have in quick succession two of the loveliest lyrical numbers of the opera—the great air *Dove sono i bei momenti,* similar in sentiment (but very different in musical form) to the *Porgi amor* of the previous Act—and what is perhaps musically the most enchanting of all Mozart's duets, *Sull'aria,* in which Susanna writes, at the Countess's dictation, a letter to the Count fixing the exact spot for their rendezvous.

[This letter, it is important to remark in view of subsequent developments, they secure not with a seal, but a *pin.*]

Now to the strains of a robust march the wedding procession enters, and Figaro and Susanna with much ceremony receive the blessing of their master and mistress. A stately *fandango* is then danced, and a short chorus sung in praise of the Count, who invites them all to the grand festivities of the evening.

Kindly note the *pin* again! Susanna has managed to pass her letter to the Count, who pricks his finger with the pin; Figaro observes this, but without suspecting Susanna.

Act IV. *Scene* i. A room in the Castle.

A careful study of the short scene with which this Act opens is absolutely essential for the understanding of the tangled *imbroglio* which is to follow. It begins with a dainty miniature of an air for Barberina, the gardener's daughter: *L'ho perduto*. The girl is looking for a pin— the one with which Susanna had 'sealed' her note to the Count, and which she had entrusted to Barberina to take back to her as an acknowledgment of its receipt. Figaro enters and learns all the circumstances from the unsuspecting child; he hastily concludes that Susanna is faithless to him after all, and intends to yield that evening to the Count's solicitations; stung to a fury of jealousy, he denounces the entire race of women in the song *Aprite un po' quegl'occhi*:

> These are your so-called goddesses
>   That claim your whole devotion,
> Whose very skirts and bodices
>   You worship from afar!
>   *I'll* tell you what they are!
> They're vampires that cling to you
>   With poisonous breath,
> They're sirens that sing to you
>   And lure you to death!
>
>   .   .   .
>
> They vex us and grieve us,
>   They always deceive us,
> And then at the last
>   In the lurch they will leave us!

A perfect tornado of abuse is this song, and a wonderful piece of musical ingenuity.

Scene 11. In the park, under the pine-trees, where the final entanglement is to be knit and unravelled.

Susanna has heard from Marcellina of Figaro's unwarranted suspicions; she is very angry, and determined to make him smart for it: "One gentleman coming to make love to me, and another to spy upon me! Well, I'm ready for both of them!"

She takes her seat in one of the arbours in the dim and perfumed garden; she knows that Figaro will be lurking near; she is masked and dominoed. Indeed, the whole atmosphere on the stage, as in the orchestra, is one of masks and dominoes and moonlight, were it not that even moonlight would be too indiscreet for the conduct of the intrigue that is to follow.

It is late evening and the moon has not yet risen. It is the very hour of love, and Susanna sings such a love-song as was never heard before and has never since been equalled, *Deh vieni, non tardar*. It would be ungrateful to suggest that the mood of the music is far too exalted for the situation—no situation could be worthy of it, for it is no earthly music.

> In heaven there shines no star, the moon is hidden—
> Now all the world to love's high feast is bidden.
> Then come, no more delay, my heart's dear treasure!
> Here, where the darkness broods, we'll take our pleasure.

Alas that such a piece of "linkèd sweetness long drawn out" should do worse than "waste its sweetness on the desert air"! It exactly fulfils Susanna's intention by confirming the suspicions of the listening Figaro, who regards it as the genuine expression of Susanna's passion for the Count—and determines on an instant revenge.

With the arrival of the Count, the Countess, and Cherubino, we plunge at once into such a game of cross-purposes as is rarely to be found even in the *imbroglio* of

44

an 18th-century comedy of intrigue. Not only have we the confusion of masks and dominoes, but even the voices must lend themselves to the deception while the Countess plays Susanna to the Count and Susanna passes herself off on Figaro as the Countess.

When Figaro finds out the truth, and the lovers are reconciled, Susanna still keeps up her disguise in order that together they may enact a little love-scene for the benefit of the Count, who discovers his wife, as he supposes, actually encouraging the attentions of his own valet. This is too much: the Count calls loudly for his people to arrest Figaro, the stage is crowded with the complete *personnel* of the piece (not omitting even the gardener Antonio and the stuttering Don Curzio), and the *dénouement* is swiftly reached. The supposed Countess is revealed as Susanna, the supposed Susanna as the Countess; Figaro is innocent; the Count is guilty enough in intention, but through the ready wit of the two women is landed in a purely farcical situation, being detected in making proposals of gallantry to his own wife! So fast and furious are the complications of this last and most elaborate scene that it is almost a relief to reach the final tag:

> To this day of dire confusion,
> Queer adventure, fond illusion,
> Let us make a gay conclusion
> With a merry wedding ball!

All now are happily provided for: old Bartolo does his duty by Marcellina, Cherubino concentrates on Barberina, the Countess, the long-suffering Rosina, gives Count Almaviva another chance, and, best of all, Figaro, the one-time Barber of Seville, is free at last to marry his faithful Susanna.

A word as to the libretto of *Figaro*. It is laid out

effectively for musical setting, its lyrics are generally graceful and often most ingenious; nevertheless, it is a failure owing to the fact that da Ponte, the author, tried to do too much. Successfully to compress the contents of Beaumarchais' long and witty comedy within the cramping limits of a four-act opera is manifestly impossible—it is certainly astonishing to find how little, even of the less important quality, has been omitted, yet the result is still but a baffling confusion. The opera, we must remember, was produced when the play was only two years old, and was in everybody's mouth, so that nearly all who listened to da Ponte's version were already familiar with the original, and such familiarity is essential if we wish to understand the action of the opera. Even were the dialogue clearly heard and understood, that would not be enough, as so much of the development is carried on obscurely in the concerted pieces and finales. The earlier English versions, indeed, were so unsatisfactory that people tacitly agreed to leave them alone and enjoy the glorious music for its own sake; they were content to admire the outstanding characters, Figaro, Susanna, Cherubino, to wonder what on earth the other mysterious figures, Bartolo, Basilio, Barberina, etc., were doing on the stage, and, by the time the dense *imbroglio* of the fourth Act began, to give the whole thing up as a bad job. As if these unhelpful English versions were not hindrance enough to the understanding of the plot, it became too often the custom to make senseless 'cuts,' which entirely destroyed such thin threads of continuity as existed. At last in 1915 a version was prepared by Sir Thomas Beecham for his original Opera Company, in which, by the judicious readjustment of certain scenes, and the introduction of much additional dialogue from Beaumarchais' comedy the whole becomes an intelligible and delightful frolic. Played in this way it immediately caught the public taste, with the result that what was once a collection of 'favourite airs' for old-fashioned lovers of music has now become one of the most popular entertainments for general enjoyment.

DON GIOVANNI

Music by MOZART. *Words by* DA PONTE.
Prague, 1787; *London,* 1817; *New York,* 1826.

OF all operas *Don Giovanni* would seem to have the best chance of what mortals call immortality; there is certainly no other about which musical as well as popular opinion is so unanimous. Hailed as a masterpiece on its first production, its reputation has steadily increased in the course of nearly one hundred and forty years; Beethoven (frowning on the subject of the libretto) kept a portion of the score beside him for study and admiration, Rossini knelt in reverence before the autographed original in Viardot-Garcia's possession; Wagner's enthusiasm for it increased with his own development, and Gounod, on the occasion of its centenary, wrote the most splendid panegyric that any composer has ever penned of another's work. It is still an inexhaustible treasure-house of ideas for musical students of to-day, and it is probable that, as the late H. E. Krehbiel prophesied, when the next great Master shall arise, he will be found to be a descendant not of the Titan Wagner, but of the 'divine Mozart' who wrote *Don Giovanni*.

Da Ponte, the librettist of *Figaro,* has served Mozart only fairly well in this second collaboration. The subject was not new; the story of the Libertine and the Statue that came to supper had been familiar for at least two centuries. Both Molière and Corneille had been attracted by it—the English laureate Shadwell had used it in *The Libertine Destroyed* (1676)—Gluck had written a ballet round it. Da Ponte's 'book,' *Il dissoluto punito: ossia il Don Giovanni,* is taken directly from a Spanish version called *El Coñvidado de Piedra* ("The Stone Guest"). The scene is laid in Seville, and the producer who wishes to get the right atmosphere would do well to seek his inspirations in the grim, occasionally *macabre,* humour of the Spanish painter Goya.

With one exception, every person in the opera is a distinct piece of careful characterization. We have the reckless, all-conquering libertine, Don Giovanni, whose only virtues are his persistent gaiety and his indomitable courage; Donna Anna, a haughty and tragic figure, inconsolable for the loss of her father the Commendatore (who is killed in the first Scene, and reappears as the spectral statue in the last); Donna Elvira, the too credulous victim of the Don's fascinations; Zerlina, the rustic coquette, with her boorish lover Masetto; lastly, Leporello, the Don's droll dog of a valet, always a coward, always grumbling, but still attached to his master. The only 'wooden' figure is Don Ottavio, the *fiancé* of Donna Anna, to whom Mozart has assigned by way of compensation two of the loveliest tenor songs ever written.

It is difficult to place Mozart's masterpiece in any particular category—the original label of *dramma giocoso* or *opera buffa* is obviously inadequate; in fact *Don Giovanni* as an opera stands alone, though the libretto in its naïve blending of supernatural horror with scenes of gaiety and even low comedy reminds us somewhat of Horace Walpole's *Castle of Otranto* and must have seemed just such a daring innovation. The serious element is confined almost entirely to the beginning and to the end of the opera. In the opening Scene the dissolute 'hero' kills in a duel the father of a noble Spanish lady whom he has insulted; retribution is deferred until the final Scene, when the spectre of the slain man appears in the banquet hall to shatter the revelry, and drag the unrepentant libertine away to that place of torment where the worm dieth not and the fire is not quenched.

The greater part of the opera is given up to further amorous adventures of the incorrigible Don Giovanni, and the ineffectual attempts on the part of his victims to bring him to justice; the rather loosely knit scenes are treated almost entirely in a spirit of comedy, and their dramatic value is not very great, but the entire opera is made glorious by the radiant atmosphere of beauty with which Mozart's music has invested it.

Act I. *Scene* 1. We are introduced to our libertine hero in an unlucky moment; the all-conquering Don Giovanni has made a sad mistake for once. The scene is a court in the palace of the Commandant of Seville; it is past midnight, and Leporello, drowsing in a corner, is tired of waiting for his master, busied with amorous adventure inside. The *buffo* music of Leporello's opening air, *Notte e giorno faticar,* soon passes to dramatic excitement as two figures hurry from the palace—Don Giovanni, concealing his face with ample cloak and downdrawn hat, and a lady clinging to him, in frantic endeavour to tear his disguise away; it is Donna Anna, the Commandant's daughter, whom the insatiable Don had hoped to add to his list of conquests. The lady is furious, and her indignant cries soon bring her father to her assistance; he forces Don Giovanni to a duel, in which the elder man is slain; Donna Anna, who has not succeeded in discovering the identity of her insulter, has gone in search of further aid.

[Attention should be given to the music of this short scene, in which the swift action and the varying emotions are most vividly expressed with a marvellous economy of means.]

The lady now returns with Don Ottavio, her affianced

lover, to lament her father's death in heart-rending phrases; in the agitated duet *Fuggi, crudele!* the two swear to devote themselves to the detection and punishment of the murderer.

Scene II. Outside the walls of Seville. Leporello, as is his habit, is engaged in lecturing his master on his evil ways, when the sound of footsteps sends them both into hiding. Enter a lady in distress—it is Elvira, an old flame of the Don's, not long deserted; in the vigorous trio *Ah, chi mi dice mai* she pours out her indignation against her betrayer, while Leporello and his master make their characteristic comments. Don Giovanni, not recognizing the voice, steps forward, eager to console the lady ("Console! that's good!" says Leporello. "How many hundreds has he 'consoled' already!"); to his confusion she discovers his identity, but before she has exhausted her reproaches he manages to slip away, leaving his servant to do such 'consoling' as he may. Leporello's method is certainly an odd one. "Madame," says he, "you are not the first whom my master has used in such fashion—nor will you be the last! Permit me to give you some account of the fair ones, not a few, whom he has already honoured with his attentions!" Then follows the famous *Madamina!* perhaps the most amazing example of unctuous humour to be found in Mozart. Drawing a formidable parchment from his pocket, Leporello proceeds to rattle off a sort of catalogue, illustrated by his own gestures and grimaces, of his master's amorous exploits. The number of his conquests is certainly prodigious. In Italy alone they amount to 640; Germany, France, Turkey, all contribute, the last a mere trifle of 90; Spain, of course, comes out on top with a glorious total of 1003! Duchesses and real princesses, country damsels, city ma'amselles—fair or swarthy, tall or tiny—he has 'consoled' them all with an impartial benevolence; true, he prefers the plump in winter, reserving the slender for the summer heat, and—but there is no need to go farther into Leporello's lively description! The song is, in fact, a piece of extravagant clowning which the alchemy of Mozart's genius has transformed for us into delicious gaiety, a thing of pure delight. It must be confessed that it is hardly calculated to console the poor forsaken lady. However, in order that our sympathies may be still further enlisted on her side, it has become the custom to let her bring down the curtain on the fine air (No. 25), transferred from Act II, *Mi tradì quell'alma ingrata,* in which the fair Elvira expresses her willingness to pardon the dear rogue and give him yet another trial.

Scene III. A scene of rustic gaiety in a village not far from Don Giovanni's palace. It is the wedding day of Zerlina and Masetto; the peasants are all assembled for the festivities, and the radiant bride is exhorting the maidens to follow her example and make the best use of their time (*Giovinette che fate all' amore*). The Don, who enters with Leporello, casts an approving eye on the dancing beauty, and grasps at once the possibilities of the situation. With a courtier's affability he approaches and invites them all to consider his palace and gardens as their own for that day; Leporello is told off to conduct them thither, while, in spite of Masetto's protest, Zerlina is persuaded to stay behind with her new admirer. Indeed, the wide-awake coquette offers little resistance to the Don's advances, and, by the time the bewitching duet *Là ci darem la mano* is finished, is quite willing to accompany him to the neighbouring summer-house—but for the arrival of the indignant Elvira, who, taking in the situation at a glance, warns the peasant girl of Don Giovanni's real intentions and leads her off to a place of safety.

52

Enter Donna Anna in deep mourning, leaning on Ottavio's arm; they are still looking for the man who slew her father, and are about to enlist the Don's aid when Elvira returns and tries to make them realize the true state of affairs. In the quartet which follows, *Non ti fidar, o misera,* Elvira's excited protestations are admirably contrasted with Don Giovanni's subtle insinuations that the poor lady is mad, and the hesitation of the other two in coming to a decision. As the baffled woman makes a despairing exit, the Don follows, in pretended anxiety for her safety; in bidding the others a courteous *au revoir,* something in his voice awakens Donna Anna to the truth at last—there goes the wretch who insulted her, the slayer of her father! She declaims her fierce longing for vengeance in the superb aria *Or sai chi l' onore,* probably the severest test for a dramatic soprano to be found in any of Mozart's operas. Admirable is the contrast afforded by Ottavio's song of sympathy, *Dalla sua pace,* one of those restful oases of serene beauty to which all true Mozartians look forward with especial delight. Ottavio having retired, Leporello appears, followed by his master; the former has cleverly disposed of Elvira—the coast is clear, the guests already assembled. Don Giovanni gives orders for the most lavish entertainment and bids Leporello take care that the wine gets well into the dancers' heads. Leporello, indeed, is expected to act as master of the ceremonies, the Don having certain private affairs on hand that will keep him fully occupied. In *Fin ch'han dal vino,* a perfect tornado of a song, the very incarnation of devil-may-care gaiety, the incorrigible rake gleefully anticipates the coming revels, in the course of which he hopes to add another score to the already prodigious roll of his conquests.

Scene IV. The garden-front of Don Giovanni's country house; through the rose-covered colonnades, the open

53

doors and windows, we see a vista of brilliantly lighted halls and galleries; in the grounds is a summer pavilion, and groups of trees, favourably disposed for amorous hide-and-seek; the scene is plainly set for one of those elaborate *finales* of complicated action in which Mozart fairly revelled. But first he gives us one of those heavenly simplicities of his which make a universal appeal: if any melody may be said to be "not for an age but for all time," surely it is Zerlina's song of *Batti, batti, o bel Masetto.* The bridegroom is naturally aggrieved at the young woman's behaviour in the previous Scene. "Encouraging his lordship in that way!" he grumbles. "Hussy! I've a very good mind to give you the beating you deserve!" But Zerlina knows better: at once her arms are round the sulky neck, and all her cajoleries brought into play: "Beat me, then, dearest, if it please you! See, here I stand, as meek as any lamb! Strike me, pull my hair out, do your worst! And then when all is over, I will kneel at your feet and kiss the dear hands of the only man I love!" But it is Masetto, of course, who is beaten: at the first sign of his relenting she seizes those 'dear hands' and sings and dances him once more into subjection.

Don Giovanni now appears, followed by a crowd of peasants gaily decked for the masquerade; as they pass into the ballroom the Don again attempts to detain Zerlina, but Masetto interposes, and all three go in together. The musicians are already striking up—we hear snatches of a minuet with which we shall soon become familiar—when three masked figures in sombre dominoes make an impressive entry. Leporello, spying them from a balcony, invites them to the dance; they accept, but, before entering, advance to the footlights and, removing their masks, reveal themselves as Donna Anna, Donna Elvira, and Don Ottavio; they are searching for the slayer of the Commendatore, and unite in a fervent prayer that heaven will protect the innocent and punish the guilty.

[This trio, *Protegga il giusto cielo,* is a splendid instance of Mozart's power of expressing essential grandeur in a little space; though only twenty bars in length, the music leaves an ineffaceable impression of solemn beauty of which one never tires.]

Scene v. We are at last inside the palace, where the revels are in full swing. If Don Giovanni has made lavish provision for his guests of food and wine, Mozart has been even more prodigal in the matter of dance-music. No less than three small orchestras are placed in the various apartments; one is playing a gavotte, another a 'German,' the third a minuet—surely the most famous minuet in the world—all three blending in satisfying harmony, clear and unconfused.

Confusion enough, however, is soon astir among the actors. Don Giovanni, who has Zerlina for partner in the gavotte, manages to steer her toward a private apartment, into which he drags her and locks the door behind them. Loud cries for assistance are shortly heard, and the dancing stops, as Ottavio and his two companions hurry to the spot; the door is forced, and Zerlina rushes out, disordered and terrified—the truth is plain to all. Leporello slips into the room to warn his master, who promptly drags him back into the company and denounces him as the villain who has insulted Zerlina! The Don's guilt, however, is too evident; Donna Anna and her party are resolute in their attack, and the general anger grows hot against the shameless libertine. A violent storm in the orchestra, thunder and lightning 'off,' proclaim the consenting wrath of heaven, and it almost seems as if the villain's career were ended; but cool courage, our 'hero's' greatest quality, comes once more to his aid, and the curtain falls on Don Giovanni, sword in hand, clearing his way through the ranks of his enraged assailants.

Act II. The closest attention is needed for the understanding of the Scenes that are now to follow; if the complex situations are of no great assistance to the drama, they at least give rise to an almost continuous succession of musical masterpieces such as Mozart himself has never surpassed.

Scene I. We begin with a delightful little patter duet, *Eh, via buffone!* in which Leporello, really scared by his recent experiences, seeks once again to break away from his dare-devil master, but is soon brought to heel by the clink of a purse of gold. Don Giovanni, undaunted, nay, in the highest spirits, is bent on fresh gallantries. The two are standing at nightfall in the spacious square where Donna Elvira has her mansion. Has Leporello noticed the lady's bewitching little chambermaid? Well, his master's heart is already on fire for her, and he means to begin the siege at once! as a preliminary it will be advisable for him to change cloak and hat with Leporello—little chambermaids have grown so shy, lately, of dashing gentlemen!

No sooner is the change effected—and little does poor Leporello dream of all the woes this disguise will bring upon him!—than a high casement is flung open, and Elvira leans out to sigh her sorrows to the evening breeze; her heart, it seems, is still heavy for her faithless lover. The opportunity is too good to be lost; pushing Leporello into the moonlight and crouching down behind him, he protests to the lady, in melting accents, his sincere penitence, his renewed devotion.

[In the trio *Ah, taci, ingiusto core!* Elvira's music is of an exquisite beauty which is apt to suffer in performance from the *buffo* extravagances of the other two. It should

56

be noted that the shameless Don, in his appeal to the lady, 'tries on' some of the phrases from the serenade that he is shortly to sing to her maid.]

Elvira's foolish heart succumbs once more to that seductive voice; without more ado she descends and flies to her former lover, as she supposes, though it is Leporello, of course, who receives the poor lady in his willing arms. "Dear love," she says, "behold me all on fire for you!" "And I," says Leporello, "am already burnt to ashes!"

His master, impatient to have the coast clear, scares them away with uncouth cries, and, taking his mandoline, sings the serenade *Deh vieni alla finestra,* with which he hopes to melt the heart of the pretty chambermaid.

[Although the English versions and analyses of the opera assume that the serenade is intended for Zerlina, whom Elvira, they say, has taken into her household, there is no warrant for this idea in the original, and it is more reasonable to assume that Don Giovanni is tracking down a new victim.]

Hardly is the song over when Masetto enters with a band of peasants armed with muskets and searching for the villain Don. That gentleman, secure in the disguise of Leporello, is quite ready to assist in so worthy a cause; giving elaborate directions as to how they may best find the object of their search, he gets rid of them all except Masetto, whom he detains for a little private conversation. Under pretence of anxiety for his safety he inquires as to the sufficiency of the weapons he carries; Masetto hands them over for inspection, and thus disarmed is suddenly seized by the indignant Don, beaten black and blue, and flung into the ditch. This broadly farcical scene is rounded off in true Mozartian fashion; attracted by poor Masetto's groans, Zerlina hastens to the spot, and sings a song so sweet as to make Masetto,

57

or any lover, think lightly of his pain. Certain it is that *Vedrai, carino* has brought a healing balm to many thousands of hearers, and will continue to do so while music still has power to soothe.

Scene II. In the twilight *imbroglio* of this Scene it is Leporello who is the central figure; all the characters, with the exception of Don Giovanni, find their way by night, for operatic reasons, to a spacious courtyard of Donna Anna's—formerly the Commandant's palace— most unfortunately for Leporello, but with the happiest musical results; the sestet *Sola, sola in buio loco,* is one of the outstanding glories of Mozartian opera.

The first to appear are Leporello and Elvira, seeking refuge from their late alarms; he, of course, is still play- ing the part of his master, and is soon to reap the bitter consequences of such an impersonation. He soon man- ages to lose Elvira in the darkness, and is just about to make his escape when the door he is trying opens, and Donna Anna enters, leaning on Don Ottavio's arm. His second attempt is even more disastrous, as he runs right into Masetto, Zerlina, and all the peasants in hot pursuit of the wicked Don, whom they now imagine they have caught at last. The torches they carry throw a damning light upon the fine hat and mantle; the others join in the attack, and Leporello, in some danger of his life, finds it best to cast off his disguise, fall at their feet, and claim their pity as another victim of Don Giovanni's treachery. But many accounts have to be settled, and Leporello soon finds that he must answer for his master's misdeeds as well as his own. Zerlina begins it: "So you," she screams, "are the ruffian who beat my Masetto black and blue!" "And you," cries Elvira, "are the base villain who so shamefully tricked me!" ("I wonder," thinks Lepor- ello, "which is the better actor—my master or I?") Don Ottavio, too, is on the point of arresting him for being on the premises for an unlawful purpose when Masetto, armed with a stout cudgel, and smarting with the memory of his sores, interposes and claims the privilege of dealing with the culprit out of hand. Leporello, however, contrives to gain time with some clever patter, and finally gives them all the slip. Don Ottavio is now given another chance to emerge from his insignificance, and brings down the curtain on *Il mio tesoro,* that supreme test of the lyric tenor, a song which enjoys the same unquestioned supremacy in the realm of classical opera as does the Prize Song from *The Mastersingers* in the modern world of music-drama.

[A short scene that follows between Zerlina and Leporello comes rather as an anti-climax, and is generally omitted; the grand aria for Elvira (*Mi tradì quell'alma ingrata*) which follows here as No. 25 is usually transferred, as has been noted, to an earlier place in the opera.]

Scene III. Pale moonlight floods the space in front of Seville Cathedral; in the middle of the square gleams an equestrian statue of marble, fresh from the sculptor's hand, to the memory of Don Pedro, the murdered Commandant—it dominates the scene and prepares us for the fantastic terrors that are to come. It is not long past midnight; Don Giovanni, still dressed as Leporello, enters, fresh from some discreditable adventure which he describes with gusto to his servant. They are carrying on their ribald dialogue in the usual *recitativo secco* when suddenly, to the accompaniment of sombre chords from the orchestra, an awful voice is heard: "Laugh on until the dawn! Then—no more laughter!" Leporello's heart sinks within him—his master, angry but unafraid, noisily challenges the unseen speaker. Again comes the awful monotone: "Be silent, thou madman! Leave the dead to their slumbers!" There can be no longer any doubt; it is the statue that is speaking. Leporello is now half dead with fright; his master, on the other hand, breaks out into boisterous mirth: "Tell the old dotard," he says to Leporello, "that I invite him to sup with me this very night!" When the trembling wretch has stammered out this message, the statue seems to bend its marble head. Don Giovanni is still unimpressed; swaggering up to the Commandant he looks him full in the face: "Speak, old man, if you are able! Say, will you sup with me to-night?" Once more that awful voice is heard—and with the one word "Yes!" Don Giovanni's doom is sealed.

[The action is delayed at this point by the interpolation of a long solo for Donna Anna, *Non mi dir, amato bene,* one of Mozart's elaborate concert arias in the Italian manner; it has little to do with the drama, but it is a most welcome refreshment to prepare us for the grotesque horrors of the closing scene.]

Finale. Although Don Giovanni had gone straight home with Leporello, intending to prepare for the entertainment of his strange expected guest, he would seem to have thought little more of the matter; for in the sumptuous hall on which the curtain rises we find him (to quote the stage directions) "seated at the table, surrounded by several young and beautiful women, who jointly partake of the banquet with him."

The scene is of the gayest; the musicians in the gallery play a selection from operas popular at the time, by composers whose very names are now almost forgotten. Leporello, guzzling furtively in the intervals of service, knows all the tunes, and nods approval more especially when the band strikes up *Non più andrai* from *Figaro,* the favourite opera of the day.

Even now, when the sands are nearly run, one last

chance of repentance is offered to the hardened libertine; Elvira, of all persons the least expected—Elvira who has never ceased to love the worthless Don, and is gifted now it would seem with some prophetic instinct of his coming fate—bursts into the room and flings herself at his feet. She pleads not for herself, but for him, passionately imploring him to forsake his evil ways before it is too late. But all in vain; the wretched man is deaf to such appeals —mockery and insult are all he gives for answer. Indignant, broken-hearted, she leaves the room—but only to turn back with shrieks of horror and to make her escape through another door. The guests and musicians all follow her in wild disorder—horror is in the air! Don Giovanni, angry but undismayed, sends Leporello to inquire into the cause of the panic. There comes a cry more terrible than Elvira's, as the wretched valet staggers back into the room and babbles of what he has seen and heard: "The Marble Man, señor—as white as death! If you could only see him—and hear him, as he comes down the corridor, *thump! thump! thump!*" Even as he speaks a loud knocking is heard—Don Giovanni pushes Leporello aside and opens the door. There stands the invited guest, the Man of Stone, who has come to supper; on horseback no longer, heavily, step by step, he advances into the room—*thump! lump! thump! lump!*

Even now Don Giovanni retains a perfect composure; he receives his guest with courtesy, and gives orders for his entertainment. But this visitor is from another world —he would have his host remember that all earthly things are over and done with. "I am here," he says, "to invite thee to *my* dwelling—to bid thee sup with *me!* Say—wilt thou come?" Don Giovanni's courage has never failed him yet; "I fear thee not," he says, "nor hell, nor heaven! And I will come to supper!" "Then," says the Marble Man, "give me thy hand in pledge!"

The haughty Don stretches out a hand of flesh, and a hand of stone closes upon it in the grip of death. The libertine has lost his hold of earth, the wildest terror seizes him, but his pride is still unbroken. "Repent! Repent!" thunders the awful voice of the Stone Guest. "Never!" shrieks the captive, as he writhes and struggles vainly to get free.

But there is a term to Heaven's forbearance; the last offer of mercy has been rejected, the messenger can stay no longer. The stony fingers are relaxed, the Man of Stone has vanished; hell opens, and through the belching flames Don Giovanni is seen struggling to the last, desperately struggling with the fiends who drag the unrepentant libertine down to his doom of torment without end.

DIE ZAUBERFLÖTE

Music by MOZART. *Words by* SCHIKANEDER.
Vienna, 1791; *London,* 1816; *New York,* 1833.

A BAD libretto has generally proved fatal even to
a great composer; too often it has dragged his
music down to an early grave. *Die Zauberflöte*
is the glittering exception; not only is it well in its
second century, but to-day, in England at least, it seems
to have acquired a new vitality, and has become a popular
'draw': no one but Mozart has ever achieved so great a
triumph with such a heavy handicap. Dr. Johnson said
of Richardson's *Pamela* that anyone who tried to read it
for the sake of the story would be likely to cut his throat,
and surely the man who goes to see *The Magic Flute* for
the sake of the dramatic interest might be forgiven any
rash act before the performance was ended. Fortunately
the music saves us from any such risks; it raises us to a
state of ecstasy where dramatic propriety and the logical
sequence of events are of no account whatever; we are
quite content to lay common sense aside so long as we
can breathe in the rarer atmosphere of absolute beauty.
However, for our present purpose, the plot must be
faced; let us handle it boldly, "nothing extenuate, nor set
down aught in malice."

The action takes place either in temples—Egypto-
Masonic—or in the groves that surround them. Sarastro, as High Priest of Isis, is of course entitled to his
temple; the Queen of Night (Astrafiammante) also has
one, and three ladies to do her bidding, whose names in
the Italian version are Aretusa, Iperatusa, and Egle.
There is a blackamoor called Monostatos, the bird-

63

catcher Papageno, dressed all in feathers, and a withered old woman who, later on, for the bird-catcher's benefit, is turned into the young and lovely Papagena. In addition to these remarkable personages we have Tamino, a prince, Pamina, daughter of the Queen of Night, three Genii, two Men in Armour, two Priests, and an Orator.

The plot, which employs so formidable an array of fantastic characters, may be told in a few lines. Sarastro, the embodiment of lofty wisdom, has removed Pamina from the evil guidance of her mother, the Queen of Night, and keeps her guarded in his temple, where she is trained in the ways of virtue. The Queen persuades Tamino to attempt her abduction, promising him Pamina in marriage as his reward. Tamino, however, on meeting with Sarastro, comes at once under his influence, and chooses to remain in the Temple of Isis, where he and Pamina successfully pass through the ordeals essential for initiation into the Mysteries, and are at last united. This very simple action is complicated by a number of queer episodes which apparently have little to do with the plot, though some of them provide a 'comic relief' which is very welcome.

Act I. Outside the temple of the Queen of Night. Enter Tamino, pursued by a serpent—so runs the first stage direction! The unhappy youth falls fainting to the ground, while three Ladies, attendants on the Queen, come from the temple, armed with spears, and destroy the 'monster.' At once enamoured of Tamino's manly beauty they join in the sprightliest of trios, in which each expresses her determination to remain and tend the unconscious prince; but as they seem unable to agree on this matter, all three re-enter the temple together.

Tamino recovers from his swoon, and has only just time to ask himself where he is when a merry tooting is heard, and Papageno, the bird-man, appears—the quaintest figure, in his gay dress of feathers, and playing on his pan-pipes as he sings *Der Vogelfänger bin ich ja!* a jolly air which sets all heads wagging to the rhythm.

In the spoken dialogue which follows, Papageno boasts that it was he who slew the serpent—a lie which brings its swift punishment, as the ladies are quickly on the spot once more with gifts from the Queen; to Tamino she sends a portrait of her daughter, Pamina, while for Papageno there is a golden padlock with which they effectually shut his mouth, adding insult to injury by their advice "not to drink too much!"

Tamino at once falls in love with Pamina's beauty, which he praises in the sweetest of arias, *Dies Bildniss ist bezaubernd schön,* when mysterious strains proclaim the coming of the dreaded Queen of Night. This character is perhaps the most baffling in the whole range of opera—impossible to act, almost impossible to sing. The part was written—dropped in, we might say—for Josepha Weber (Madame Hofer), Mozart's sister-in-law and cousin to the composer of *Der Freischütz,* a coloratura soprano with an incredibly high voice; it consists of two airs, which require a working-compass of over two octaves and a volume of voice quite incompatible with their extravagant range. The Queen's aria, *O zittre nicht,* has a lovely *andante* deploring the loss of her daughter, followed by an elaborate *bravura* section in which she urges Tamino to bring Pamina back to her.

She vanishes, and the Ladies appear once more, remove Papageno's padlock, and tell him to attend Tamino on his quest; they also furnish him with a little set of chiming bells, and Tamino with a golden flute, both instruments of power, to help them in time of trouble—and for their further comfort promise them the assistance of three Genii to guide them on their way.

[The quintet *H'm! h'm! h'm!* has not a dull moment

in it; it is a succession of artless little melodies, sweet and gay, first cousins to the folk-song, which exercise an inexplicable fascination; even with moderately good performers this number can never fail of its effect.]

Scene II. We are now introduced to the queerest character of the drama, Monostatos, a blackamoor, who resides in Sarastro's palace and is referred to as 'Chief of the Slaves.' Perhaps we should regard him as the comic villain of the piece, in contrast to Papageno, who is the pure and simple clown. We find Monostatos in a room of the temple, forcing his attentions on Pamina; as she repulses him, she is bound in chains by two black slaves and swoons with fright. At this moment Papageno appears in his gaudy plumage; he has never seen a black man before, and never in his life has Monostatos seen a man who looks so like a monstrous parrot. Each believes the other to be the Devil, and the little scene of comic terror that ensues compensates for the apparent irrelevancy of the incident. But something better is to follow. Papageno turns to Pamina, who has awakened from her swoon, and persuades her to join him in a search for Tamino. The duet which follows, *Bei Männern welche Liebe fühlen,* dear to our ancestors as "The Manly Heart," belongs to that realm of serene unearthly sweetness to which Mozart alone of all composers can admit us.

The *finale* of this Act is a not very coherent medley of incidents which take place in the grove before the Temple of Isis. The three Genii lead in Tamino, and leave him to seek admittance at one of the three doors confronting him. His first two attempts are repulsed by voices from within, but as he approaches the central door a Priest comes forth; he informs him that Pamina is safe, and that, with patience and obedience, he may hope to see her that very day. Tamino, remembering his magic flute,

66

begins to play on it, in the hope of bringing his beloved to his side—with what surprising results may be gathered from the stage directions: "Various birds of every hue and plumage appear amongst the branches of the trees, and carol in concert to his music; various wild beasts, apes, etc., also appear, and draw round Tamino, soothed and charmed by the magic spell of his flute." Toward the conclusion of his lovely air *Wie stark ist nicht dein Zauberton!* he hears Papageno's pan-pipes not far away and hurries off to seek him. The bird-man immediately enters with Pamina, and is quickly followed by Monostatos with his black slaves, still bent on carrying off the lady. Fortunately Papageno bethinks him of his ring-o'-bells, which he sets chiming with remarkable results. At the very first sound Monostatos and his sooty fellows drop their chains and their villainy at the same time, and stand rooted to the ground, while a smile of ecstatic delight spreads over their features; then the music takes them in their feet, and with arms upraised and uncouth gestures they dance in time to the bird-man's rhythmic jingle; like another Pied Piper he draws them after him across the stage, and, having got rid of them in the wings, he and Pamina in a duet of entrancing simplicity bring to an end a delicious little scene that is all too short.

A march and chorus behind the scenes herald the approach of Sarastro. From the depth of the grove comes a long procession of Priests and Priestesses with wreaths and baskets, cats and crocodiles, and all the symbolic pomp attendant on the rites of Isis; these form in double line and sing a solemn chorus to welcome the even more impressive procession that follows, in the midst of which Sarastro is seen, standing in a slave-drawn chariot, "magnificently attired; a wreath of laurel is on his brow, and in his right hand he holds a long, golden wand with the emblem of the Sun at its top." Pamina instantly throws herself at his feet to implore pardon for having left the temple in order to escape from Monostatos' persecution. Sarastro at once reassures her; he knows the secret of her heart, and approves her choice of Tamino. At this juncture Monostatos, leading Tamino in chains, enters; he expects praise from Sarastro for his zealous capture, but, to his surprise, hears himself condemned to be soundly bastinadoed. Meanwhile Tamino and Pamina have recognized each other at sight, and are happy in their first embrace. Sarastro now proposes to depart, and bids Pamina mount beside him in the chariot, while Tamino and, oddly enough, Papageno also, are given into the hands of the Priests to be veiled and vested for the rite of initiation.

Act II. A forecourt in the Temple of Isis. A dim vista of columns, sphinxes, pyramids—mysterious rumblings underground, and thunder in the distance—all these are meant to attune our minds to solemn mood. Far more effectual are the two musical numbers with which the Act opens, a march and a solo for bass (*O Isis und Osiris*), which can best be described by the cheapened word 'sublime.'

Looking down the long lines of white-robed Priests, each with lighted torch and silver trumpet, we see the High Priest, Sarastro, mysterious lord of wisdom and of love; he tells them of Tamino, the new postulant for initiation into the rites of the temple—he is virtuous, discreet, benevolent, in all ways worthy of admission—here all raise their silver trumpets and, by three long, sonorous blasts, signify their approval.

Further, the gods have ordained that Pamina too shall enter on her probation, so that the two may be in the end united. The wonderful song *O Isis und Osiris* is a prayer to those deities that the young pair may be strengthened for the coming ordeals or, should they perish, may pass to the realms of everlasting light.

Sarastro having retired, Tamino and Papageno are brought in, to be instructed by the Priests: silence is the first duty enjoined on them; the second, to be on their guard against the wiles of women. Left to themselves, they are put to an instant test; the Queen of Night's three Ladies rise out of the ground, to Papageno's great dismay, and prophesy dire misfortune to both should they remain in the temple. Tamino is proof against all temptations and disobedience, and manages to keep the bird-man's terrors within bounds; the Ladies vanish at the sound of threatening voices from the temple, from which the Priests appear, who veil Tamino and his clown-companion, and lead them off for further instruction.

Changes of scene now follow with such kaleidoscopic frequency that an exact chronicle would be tedious, especially as much depends on the judgment, or the resources, of the particular producer; it is sufficient to say that the action takes place either in the temple of Isis or in the grove surrounding it.

On a flowery bank, flooded with moonlight, Pamina is discovered asleep by Monostatos, who, after a rather unconvincing solo, *Alles fühlt der Liebe Freuden,* proceeds to take advantage of the situation; he is about to steal a kiss from the unconscious girl when, to the accompaniment of thunder and lightning, the Queen of Night rises through the earth, and the blackamoor slinks into hiding. On learning from her daughter that Tamino is determined to become an Initiate in the temple, the enraged Queen lays a solemn charge on Pamina to slay Sarastro, and recover from him the golden Symbol of the Sun which had once been in her possession, and on which all his power depends; for this purpose she thrusts a dagger into the amazed Pamina's hands, sets off such a series of vocal crackers as never before were heard, and vanishes as she had come.

[The *bravura* air *Der Hölle Rache* is certainly the most exacting in the repertory; not only is the voice kept throughout at an abnormally high pitch, but the character of the piece calls for such a forcible delivery as is rarely at the command of a *soprano sfogato*; so seldom, indeed, is a satisfactory performance achieved that one is inclined to ask whether it would not be better to cut it out altogether, as unworthy to keep company with some of the loveliest and most vocal music that even Mozart ever wrote.]

Monostatos now comes out of hiding and, snatching the dagger from Pamina's hand, threatens to stab her if she will not yield to his wishes, but is put to flight by the timely arrival of Sarastro. Pamina, assuming that he is aware of the Queen's evil design, pleads for her mother. Sarastro assures her that his way is to return only good for evil, and soothes her with his majestic song *In diesen heil' gen Hallen.*

Another change of scene allows of some more fooling on the part of Papageno, this time with the old woman who is destined later to become his youthful bride. The three Genii next arrive, with a banquet ready spread, Tamino's flute, and Papageno's bells—a sign that their real ordeal is about to begin.

[These Genii are described in some editions as Boys; if any doubt could exist as to the essential spirituality of their nature, it would at once be dispelled by the little trio: *Seid uns zum zweitenmal willkommen.* Like many other happy little tunes throughout this opera, it gives one the impression of having been made up, just for fun, in "the nurseries of heaven."]

Pamina now makes a joyous entry, only to find herself repulsed, as she imagines, by Tamino, whose recent vow forbids him to acknowledge her greeting by word or look. The broken-hearted girl, unaware of the reason for his attitude, pours out her sorrow in an air, *Ach, ich fühl' es,* which floats above the heights of beauty, and at the same time is full of a pathos which has no parallel in Mozartian opera. It was Sontag, an incomparable exponent of the part, who used to say: "A Pamina who in this air cannot move the public to tears has no idea of Mozart."

We now get a rather bewildering succession of short scenes. In a crypt of the temple, lit by the fires of many altars, Sarastro and all the Priests are assembled in solemn conclave; Tamino is led in, "clothed in a long garment of pure white, girt about at the waist with a plain gold fillet, a chaplet of roses on his brow"—ready for the rite of initiation which is about to be performed. Pamina is also introduced, to take farewell of her beloved, though Sarastro cheers her with hints that they will meet again; leading them both by the hand, and followed by the long succession of Priests, he passes into the innermost recesses of the temple, and the brazen gates close behind them.

After these impressive proceedings it is rather a shock to find the irrepressible Papageno intruding, quite unabashed, among such strange surroundings. It is well to note, however, that this queer parrot-fellow is not without some claim to our consideration; if Sarastro represents the higher wisdom, Papageno may well stand for the rare quality of common sense. In a previous dialogue, when a Priest asks him whether he too does not yearn to follow Tamino in the pursuit of truth and wisdom, he replies that he has no desire to meddle with what does not concern him; his real business is with meat, drink, and sleep—yes, and a buxom little wife would ensure his best attention. So on the present occasion when the Priest sternly reminds him that he has forfeited his chances of attaining to the higher life, Papageno stands firm—he does not in the least regret his decision; what he really sighs for is a glass of good wine. This is immediately provided, and inspires him with a most rollicking, amorous ditty, *Ein Mädchen oder Weibchen,* in which he shakes his magic bells with delightful effect. The old woman again appears, but changes at once into the young maiden of his desires, who is, however, snatched away from him at his first approach, for no intelligible reason.

In another garden scene the Genii again appear, just in time to prevent Pamina from using her mother's dagger on herself in her despair at Tamino's fancied desertion; they are able to assure her that he is still faithful to her, and lead her away happy in the prospect of a joyful reunion.

We now come to the great business of the ordeal by fire and water through which the lovers must pass in order to achieve their union and obtain admission to the kingdom of light and love.

The original stage directions are so terrific and so little followed in modern times that it will be best to quote them in a curtailed version. "The stage represents a wild and gloomy region at the foot of a black and rocky mountain . . . vast caverns are perceived stretching far into the interior . . . dim flashes of sulphurous light flash forth from these caverns . . . a ruddy glare may be seen within, which gradually increases. On the left, an opening in the precipice is closed by a pair of massive and lofty iron gates, over which an inscription is carved on the face of the rock, the characters thereof seeming to emit a phosphorescent light; a similar gate on the right." From the latter gate Tamino is led forth by "the two Guardians of the Threshold, men of gigantic stature, clad

in full black armour; from their helmets a flame of ruddy
fire is blazing"; the tips of their spears also "send forth
a ruddy glow." These imposing personages draw Tamino's attention to "the characters of living fire over the
opposite gates." The words of the inscription are:

> Who dares the varied storms of yon dark realm to weather,
> Made pure by fire, by water, earth, and ether,
> Shall soar triumphant, conqueror o'er sin and death,
> To heav'n, as angel-priest of our true faith.
> If at her shrine the suppliant humbly kneel,
> To him shall Isis then her mysteries reveal.

[This duet, for tenor and bass, *Der welcher wandert
diese Strasse,* gives occasion for some of the noblest music
in the opera. Mozart has employed, for the vocal theme,
a fine old German choral, solemn, suave, and broad, and
has woven for it an orchestral accompaniment of such
cunning beauty, in striking contrast to the previous
temple music, that we ask ourselves if this is not rather
the great Bach himself.]

Pamina now enters, determined to follow her beloved
through fire, through water, through the very gates of
death. After a duet of rapturous reunion, followed by a
magnificent contrapuntal quartet in which the Guardians
join, the great gates on the left are thrown open and—
but here we must have recourse again to the formal stage
directions: "Tamino takes his flute, Pamina clings to
his arm. . . . Eddies of flame rush from the caverns,
which are rent asunder as with an explosion, burning
lava pouring down on all sides, etc., etc. In the midst
of this elemental strife Tamino, playing manfully on the
flute, and Pamina, clinging to him, are seen to pass."
Successful and undaunted, the pair are the next minute
"perceived buffeting with the billows of a foaming and
impetuous torrent, still clinging to each other, Tamino
steadily playing his flute: after being nearly torn asunder

by the force of the waves, they are finally cast on the rocky shore."

The scene immediately changes to the inmost sanctuary of the temple, where Sarastro is ready at the altar to bless the brave and faithful lovers.

The short chorus of triumph which follows should certainly be the end of the opera; but Papageno and Papagena have not yet had their scene together, and there is also the Queen of Night to be disposed of. Mozart would seem to have had a special affection for his quaint parrot-man; even at this late hour he chooses to provide him and his partner with page after page of delicious foolery, musically as fresh and charming as anything that has gone before.

First, Papageno enters in despair; he has lost his Papagena—what has he to live for now? So he resolves on a most prudent attempt at suicide. Standing on a largish stone at the foot of a tree, he throws a rope over the branch above, adjusts it loosely round his neck, and is about to kick the stone away—with not so much as the risk of a sprained ankle—when the good Genii come to his relief, and advise him rather to have recourse to his magic bells. At the first peal his pretty Poll is at his side, and in a lively duet the two resolve to go into partnership, with unlimited power to add to their number.

Now for the baleful Queen of Night! In a cavern immediately beneath the inmost shrine of the temple she is discovered, with her three Ladies and the black Monostatos, putting the finishing touches to some fiendish plot which shall involve Sarastro, the temple, and all within it in final and irrevocable ruin. But the Powers of Darkness have had their day, and Sarastro must now assert his power. The conspirators "are interrupted by a loud succession of peals of thunder from within the rocks, and the rushing sound as of mighty waters; the rocks rapidly surround and close in upon them as they strive to fly"—and the opera ends, as it was bound to do, in the Temple of Isis with Sarastro's blessing of the triumphant lovers, and a final chorus in praise of Wisdom, Truth, and Virtue.

The reader who has had the patience to plough through the above mass of confused happenings may be surprised to hear that anyone should be found to take it seriously; yet many have done so; in fact it would require quite a long shelf to hold all that has been written about the 'inner meaning' of *Die Zauberflöte*. Without going deeply into the matter, it seems worth while to examine the origin of this strange affair. Emanuel Schikaneder, a friend of Mozart who ran a small theatre in Vienna, approached the composer with a libretto of a comic opera which he had taken from a fantastic Eastern tale, *Lulu or the Magic Flute*. A low-comedy actor, he had elaborated the part of Papageno for himself, and as Mozart's sister-in-law, Mme Hofer, was engaged at his theatre, the part of the Queen of Night was specially designed for her peculiar talent. However, before the opera was ready, a musical version of the same story was produced at a rival theatre with great success, and there was nothing for it but to change the character of Schikaneder's libretto.

The question of Freemasonry was very much in evidence at that time, owing to the repressive measures taken against it by the Emperor Leopold and his Empress Maria Theresa, and it seemed to Schikaneder that this material might be worked up into a popular attraction for the theatre; he and Mozart both being Freemasons, it was easy enough to devise the temple scenes and the final business of the ordeal, which contrast so strangely with the flimsy texture of the original fairy-tale. There seems to have been little attempt to blend the two elements, and the result is a scarcely intelligible succession of loosely related incidents. Those who insist on the cryptic significance of the piece inform us that Sarastro stands for Freemasonry, as the guardian of all truth and wisdom, Monostatos for the Clerical Party, Papageno for the lusty Viennese *bourgeoisie,* and the baleful Queen of Night for the great Maria Theresa. This is interesting, but does not reconcile us to the tedious folly of the action, which is a jumble of contradictions, confusions, and sheer buffoonery, all the more irritating when contrasted with the dignified solemnity of the temple scenes; as Mr. Krehbiel puts it, the best way to regard *The Magic Flute* is as "a sort of Christmas pantomime which Mozart has glorified by his music."

FIDELIO

Music by BEETHOVEN. *Words by* BOUILLY, *and others.*
Vienna, 1st version 1805, *2nd version* 1814; *London,* 1832;
New York, 1839.

ALTHOUGH Beethoven's only opera is rather a tradition than an experience with opera-goers of to-day, it has a brilliant record of success behind it. Before the coming of Wagner not only was it regarded by serious musicians as the fine flower of German lyric drama—and even the Perfect Wagnerite allowed that *Fidelio* had certain claims to consideration —but the enthusiasm with which it was received by the public was quite extraordinary. During the period of its greatest popularity, in the first half of the last century, it was not unusual to repeat the Prisoners' Chorus, and the whole of the *finale* to the second Act. On one occasion, we read, "the splendid overture was also performed twice; indeed, owing to the multitude of encores, the audience might almost as well have waited to the end, and insisted on a repetition of the whole opera." Further, in the dungeon scene, "loud and excessive applause drowned the music, and testified the delight of the house."

There is no fear of any such demonstrations, so strange a mingling of good and bad taste, at the present day; musicians will always welcome the infrequent revivals of an interesting classic, but its hold on the public is not likely to be renewed. The truth is that *Fidelio,* in spite of its profound musicianship and its many noble qualities, has aged considerably. To make the inevitable comparison, the simplicities of Weber's *Der Freischütz* convey a much fresher, more vital impression of beauty to-day than all the heroic pretensions and wonderful symphonic achievements of *Fidelio*. If Weber, as he has recorded, strove for "nothing save truthfulness of expression, passion, and delineation of character," Beethoven's aim was assuredly not less noble; nevertheless, in writing for the voice he not seldom fails to reach it. For instance, in the famous quartet *Mir ist so wunderbar,* where four separate emotions call for expression, the composer employs the form of the 'canon,' which obliges each person to repeat the same melody, note for note, a method which scarcely lends itself to "delineation of character." So throughout the opera; while the grandeur of the conception is often apparent, and the orchestra rises to heights of dramatic significance hitherto unparalleled, the vocal writing frequently fails in right expression, owing to the cramping rigidity of the conventional forms employed. It is the work of a giant unable wholly to shake off the chains that bind him. However high we may rate Beethoven's symphonic genius, we must recognize that, in writing for the voice, he had not Mozart's gift of making beauty smile upon us even through narrowing prison bars.

Fidelio, oder die eheliche Liebe is the accepted title of this opera, in spite of Beethoven's preference for the alternative *Leonore,* which is the real name of the heroine. Produced at Vienna in 1805, during the French occupation of that city, it was a failure, and, though revived in the following year, was withdrawn after a few performances. Not till 1814 did it start on a successful career, when it was put on at the Kärnthnerthor theatre, with a greatly improved libretto. The part of Leonore was sung by Mme Milder-Hauptmann, for whom it had been written nine years previously. This lady, whose good gifts seem to have been all on the

78

heroic scale—"You have a voice as big as a house, my child!" was old Haydn's remark—complained, nevertheless, of the too strenuous nature of her music, and actually succeeded in getting Beethoven to alter certain passages which she declared to be ruinous to the voice. If, with Wagner's heroines in mind, we are inclined to smile at such a protest, it cannot be denied that the part of Leonore makes exceptional demands on both actress and singer; the difficulty of finding an artist worthy of the work goes far to account for the infrequency of its revivals.

Schröder-Devrient, who followed Milder-Hauptmann in the part (and lived to satisfy Wagner by her impersonations of his earlier heroines) was probably its greatest exponent. Malibran sang it (in English) in the 'thirties, her sister Viardot-Garcia somewhat later; Johanna Wagner, Sophie Cruvelli (German in spite of her name), Lilli Lehmann, Marianne Brandt, are all remembered as distinguished representatives of a part which yields to none in dramatic dignity. One of the most memorable performances was at Her Majesty's in 1851, the year of the Great Exhibition, when Cruvelli played the heroine and Sims Reeves the part of Florestan, while a number of prominent artists, including such names as Lablache and Gardoni, did homage to the great composer by appearing in the Prisoners' Chorus at the end of Act I. More than this, however, was needed to atone for the outrage committed by interspersing Beethoven's music with recitatives composed for the occasion by Balfe, the begetter of *The Bohemian Girl*.

Technically, *Fidelio* does not come under the category of Grand Opera; like *The Magic Flute, Il Seraglio,* and *Der Freischütz,* it ranks as a *Singspiel,* or *Opéra Comique, i.e.,* an operatic work in which music and spoken dialogue are intermingled. The 'book' as we now have it is the work of many hands; based on a French original by Bouilly, a well-known librettist of the time, it was adapted in the first instance by Sonnleithner (Kotzebue's theatrical successor in Vienna), reduced later by von Breuning from three Acts to two, and finally revised by Treitschke in 1814 with excellent results. The story, as its sub-title shows, is one of wifely devotion. The heroine Leonore is the wife of Don Florestan, a noble Spaniard, who has been seized by a political opponent, Don Pizarro, and thrown into the foul dungeon of a castle near Seville, where he has languished for two years before the action of the piece begins. Although he is reported to have died, Leonore, suspicious of the truth, has disguised herself as a youth, Fidelio by name, and entered the service of old Rocco the jailer, whose confidence she has contrived to gain. From him she has heard much of a mysterious prisoner who is confined in the deepest dungeon of all, and treated with ever-increasing severity—only lately has his ration of bread and water been cut down to starvation point, and the very straw on which he lay been taken from him; it is plain that nothing less than his death is aimed at. Leonore, convinced of the prisoner's identity, schemes how she may yet save her husband's life. She induces Rocco, who is growing feeble, to let her help him in his arduous duties in connexion with the many cells he has to visit daily. There is no time to lose. Pizarro, as she hears, has that very morning received a letter from Don Fernando, the Minister of the Interior, announcing his speedy arrival—he has heard reports of undue severity and other irregularities in the management of the prison, and is coming himself to inquire into the matter. Pizarro, panic-stricken, resolves to make an end of Florestan and to remove all traces of his existence; he

80

orders Rocco to despatch him at once; but this the old man refuses to do, so the Governor is driven to act as his own executioner. Leonore, who has overheard their conversation, determines to prevent the murder even at the cost of her own life. [Here comes the great scena *Abscheulicher!* so well known on the concert-platform.] The first Act ends effectively in the celebrated Chorus of Prisoners, who are allowed for a brief space to breathe the fresh air of the garden, only to be driven back again by Pizarro's orders to their dismal cells below.

The second Act shows us the dungeon in which the wretched Florestan is confined—a place of unimaginable horror, in the remotest depths of the foundations. Although Rocco declines to be the prisoner's murderer, he consents to dig his grave, and in this task Fidelio is to help him. As the two enter the dungeon, which is lit only by a solitary feeble lamp, they can hardly recognize the prisoner, seated on a block of stone, loaded with fetters, and chained to an iron ring fastened in the masonry of a massive column.

Near at hand are the ruins of a long-disused cistern, now choked with rubbish, in which Pizarro has decided to conceal the body of the murdered man; it is Leonore's task to assist Rocco in preparing it for that purpose. In the short pauses of her heavy toil she is able to satisfy herself that the wretched being she sees before her, wasted with misery and only half alive, is really Florestan, her own beloved husband.

Pizarro enters, eager to despatch his old enemy without delay, as he fears every moment to hear the signal announcing the approach of Don Fernando, who comes to judgment. Advancing on his victim, he is just about to strike when Leonore, the supposed Fidelio, rushes in between them; with the cry "First kill his wife!" she takes her stand in front of her dear husband, to live or die with him.

In spite of his astonishment and confusion the villain thrusts her roughly aside and is about to deal the fatal blow when Leonore again interposes with a loaded pistol pointed at Pizarro's forehead, and at the same moment is heard from the battlements of the castle the solemn trumpet-call which announces the coming of the Minister.

[This, of course, is the great moment of the opera, and grandly has the composer treated it; the trumpet-call is the fitting climax to one of the most dramatic scenes in the whole range of musical drama.]

Don Fernando, after a hasty investigation of the true state of affairs, soon brings matters to a happy issue; the villainous Pizarro is led away to receive his just punishment, and Florestan, in whom Fernando recognizes an old friend, is at once set free, the actual loosing of his chains being allotted to the heroic wife who alone is worthy of so high an office. The prisoners are released and brought once more into the light, and the opera closes with a chorus of rejoicing, and of praise for Leonore—well named 'Fidelio'—the glorious example of wifely devotion.

Besides the characters already mentioned, two others are introduced with the object of lightening the gloom which broods rather heavily over the entire performance —Marcellina, the jailer's daughter, in love with the imaginary youth Fidelio, and Jacquino, the turnkey, in love with Marcellina. But *Fidelio* is actually a one-part opera; its successful revival must always depend upon the rare occurrence of an ideal Leonore, an artist with the 'Give me the dagger' method of a Sara Siddons, and "a voice as big as a house."

Beethoven wrote no less than four different overtures

for this work, the first three being known as "Leonore," 1, 2, and 3; "Leonore No. 3" has always been a great favourite in the concert-room, where the "Overture to *Fidelio*," which always precedes the opera, is also frequently heard.

IL BARBIERE DI SIVIGLIA

Music by ROSSINI. *Words by* STERBINI, *from* BEAUMARCHAIS.
Rome, 1816; London, 1813; New York, 1819.

ALTHOUGH present - day opinion is sharply divided as to the value of Rossini's comic masterpiece, and it would be rash to prophesy how long it may continue to hold its rather precarious place in the repertory, historically it must always be considered as of first-class interest. In *Il Barbiere* not only did Rossini introduce new effects both vocal and instrumental, surpassing in brilliance anything that had gone before, but he also finally abolished the method of the old *recitativo secco* (dry recitative), with its thin chords on the keyed instrument, in favour of a full orchestral accompaniment throughout. Moreover, for an opera which is well over its century, *Il Barbiere* is brought curiously close to our own times by reason of its connexion with a great line of singers whose actual personal influence still lingers among us. In 1906 there died in London, at the age of 101, Manuel Garcia, the world-famous teacher of singing, some of whose pupils are still carrying on the great tradition in our midst. This Garcia was the son of a still more famous father. Manuel del Popolo Vicente Garcia was the original Almaviva in the first production of *Il Barbiere* at Rome in 1816, and repeated his performance at the first New York performance in Italian in 1825, when his son, Manuel, aged 20, sang the part of Figaro, while the Rosina was his daughter Maria, who, as Mme Malibran, was destined in the few short years of her career to prove herself perhaps the greatest genius that ever appeared in

84

opera. It is not easy to realize that a man who took a prominent part in this historic performance died in London just twenty years ago.

The first night of *Il Barbiere* (Rome, 5th January, 1816) was a fiasco of the loudest; the noise began with the Count's first solo and reached its climax with the second Act, very little of which got across the footlights. The opposition came chiefly from the partisans of the great Paisiello, a composer of the former generation, whose opera on the same subject had been immensely popular with the Italians for close on fifty years. Rossini had foreseen the difficulty; he had written a flattering letter to the aged *maestro,* and received a civil reply; moreover, he had named his work *Almaviva, ossia l'inutile precauzione* in order to disavow any idea of competition with the accepted masterpiece, Paisiello's *Barbiere di Siviglia.* But, ironically enough, his own precautions proved of no avail. Happily, the first-night failure did not greatly disturb the genial composer; he made a few prudent alterations in the score, and by the end of the week the new *Barbiere* had triumphed, and Rossini was the darling of the Roman public.

Apart from the prejudice in favour of Paisiello, one of the objections to the new opera was that the voices were overpowered by the instrumentation. The charge was no new one; it had been brought against Gluck more than half a century ago, and at the first performance of Hadyn's *Creation* in 1797 did not the soprano complain that this was "the first time she had ever been asked to accompany an orchestra"? In Rossini's case the suggestion was ridiculous; he worshipped the voice as the loveliest of all instruments, and no composer has ever handled it more tenderly. At the same time, he was most exacting in his demands on the singers; he was the first to try to curb their excessive passion for ornamentation by writing out all florid passages in full, and insisting, as far as he was able, that they should sing nothing but what was set down. One would have thought that Rossini's original *fioriture* would suffice for the most exuberant of prima donnas, yet when Adelina Patti, soon after her *début,* sang *Una voce poco fa* to the aged *maestro,* she did so disguise the air in a network of new embroideries as to provoke his gentle sarcasm: "That's a very pretty song, my child! Who composed it?"

Il Barbiere is, in fact, the most persistently florid opera in existence; should anyone suppose that *Una voce* is an exceptional show-piece, let him examine the music of Almaviva (tenor), Figaro (baritone), and Bartolo (bass); each of these parts abounds in florid passages demanding a quite exceptional agility—indeed, for sheer *bravura,* Almaviva eclipses Rosina, and is, musically, the dominant rôle in the opera. It is doubtful whether it would be possible at the present day, in any of the leading opera houses, to give a really worthy performance of *Il Barbiere* as Rossini wrote it.

The music for Rosina, it should be noted, was written originally for contralto, or low mezzo, a type of voice which Rossini was the first to bring into prominence; the part, however, passed into the hands of the high soprano with results that can only be deplored; *Il Barbiere* in our day is revived only occasionally and for the sake of the popular prima donna of the hour, and in too many cases means little more than *Una voce* and the interpolated display in the Lesson Scene. This is a thousand pities; for *Il Barbiere,* if properly given, is not only a feast of gay, delicious music, but manages also to convey a fair amount of the spirit of Beaumarchais' brilliant comedy from which it is derived.

The well-known overture has a queer history attached

to it; originally written for a serious opera on a classical subject (*Aureliano*), it had served, later, as an introduction to *Elizabeth, Queen of England;* it would seem, however, to have found its proper place in *The Barber,* where its rather jiggety melodies are a fit preparation for the scenes of impossible gaiety which follow. The truth is that Rossini never troubled much about the dramatic propriety of his music—his creed seems to have been that a really good tune could be made to fit any situation.

To the present generation Mozart's *Marriage of Figaro* is probably better known than Rossini's *Barber of Seville;* anyone familiar only with the first opera may feel slightly confused on making acquaintance with the second, as in both works we meet the same characters— Figaro, the Count Almaviva, Rosina (the Countess), Dr. Bartolo, Basilio — under very different circumstances. We must bear in mind that the dramatic action of *The Barber* precedes that of *Figaro.* Rossini shows us the wooing and winning of Rosina, the ward of Bartolo, by the Count Almaviva with the assistance of Figaro the Barber; in Mozart's opera, Figaro (now the Count's valet) is intriguing to secure his own matrimonial happiness, which his master is most ungratefully striving to destroy; Rosina, now the Countess, plays the rôle of the neglected wife; the characters of Bartolo and Basilio are much the same in both operas, though the old Doctor naturally looms larger in *The Barber* as the guardian and prospective husband of Rosina. The vocal differences are interesting; Almaviva, the florid tenor of *The Barber,* appears as a baritone in *Figaro; Figaro,* the volatile baritone of Rossini, is a *basso-cantante* with Mozart, who treats Basilio, another Rossinian baritone, as a light tenor.

Act I. *Scene* I. A street in Seville, flooded with

early morning sunlight. Here lives old Doctor Bartolo with his pretty young ward Rosina, whom he intends soon to make his wife. Her room looks on the street, but the shutters are still closed when Count Almaviva appears with his band of music, to waken the lady with a gentle *aubade*. [This effective number, *Ecco ridente il cielo,* like the overture, had already done duty in two previous operas.] The Count dismisses the musicians, but with such a liberal reward that they refuse to go till they have sung a noisy chorus of gratitude; finally the Count and his servant, Fiorello, have to drive them off the stage.

Now that all is quiet, Rosina appears on the balcony, only to be frightened back again by the thrumming of a guitar; Almaviva too goes into hiding. Indeed, the empty stage is hardly big enough to hold the important personage who now advances—Figaro, the pride of Seville, the barber of quality, prince of all barbers, blood-letters, plotters and go-betweens. "Room for the city's factotum!" (*Largo al factotum*) sings this agreeable rattle in a breathless patter-song which for sheer high spirits has no rival in opera.

The Count recognizes in Figaro an old acquaintance who had been useful to him in Madrid, their native city; it was there that Almaviva had first seen the lady of the balcony, whom he had followed to Seville, and who is, as he supposes, old Bartolo's daughter. Figaro enlightens him—he happens to be intimate with that household, where he is "barber, perruquier, chirurgeon, botanist, and horse-doctor"—Rosina is not Bartolo's daughter, but his ward.

At this moment the young lady reappears on the balcony—oh, so modest and demure!—with the suspicious Doctor at her heels.

What is that paper she holds in her hand? Merely a

ballad from the latest musical piece, *The Futile Precaution;* the Doctor knows it, of course? The Doctor does not; he disapproves of all poetry and playgoing, at any rate for young ladies. In her surprise at his ignorance Rosina lets the paper flutter from her hand to the street below—how careless!—and will the good Doctor kindly fetch it for her?

As soon as his back is turned, the minx signals to the waiting Count (whom she knows well enough by sight) to pick up the dropped note. When Bartolo finds it already gone—"It must have been the wind!" she says innocently. The old man is not so sure; but his business calls him abroad, and he bustles off, after giving strict orders to admit no one in his absence, with the exception of Basilio, the music-master.

Rosina's note assures the Count that she is not indifferent to him—if only she knew his name and his station! Could he not manage to convey such information in a little ballad sung beneath her window? Taking Figaro's guitar, the Count replies in the air *Se il mio nome saper voi bramate;* his name, he tells her, is Lindoro; he has no riches, nothing but a faithful heart, on fire for her alone. This greatly delights Rosina, who, at the end of the second stanza, begins a reply, when the loud slamming of a door alarms her, and she is seen no more.

[Rossini's music here is fresh and charming, but anyone who will take the trouble to look up the corresponding air (*Saper vorreste*) in Paisiello's superannuated *Barbiere* will have to confess that the older work loses nothing by comparison.]

Almaviva is now more on fire than ever, and gladly listens to Figaro's proposals for forwarding his suit: a company of soldiers has just come to town; the Count must disguise himself as a trooper, and present himself at Bartolo's house with a billeting order, which is bound to procure him a lodging in the house of his beloved. The Count at once recognizes a master-mind in Figaro, agrees to reward him liberally, and requires his address for future emergencies. Figaro gives it to him in several pages of music—his *Numero quindici* is the climax of the long and rollicking duet which ends the first Scene.

Scene II. Rosina's boudoir; the embroidery frame, the music-stand, tell us of her accomplishments, while the stout jalousies of the balcony, securely locked, suggest old Bartolo's opinion of her true character. Further, on a little writing-table, please notice that there are only five sheets of paper! The sixth, written and folded, is in the hands of Rosina, as she enters for her opening air. *Una voce poco fa*, like *Ombra leggiera*, and the Mad Scene from *Lucia*, is one of the half-dozen examples of old-fashioned florid Italian opera which every light soprano is still expected to have on her list, and is perhaps the one which produces the greatest effect with the least expenditure of energy. In it Rosina expresses her resolve to risk all for her dear 'Lindoro'; if her guardian tries to coerce her, let him look out!—"for," sings the charming rogue, "I can be a regular viper when I choose!"

She seals the note she has written to her lover; how shall she send it? She thinks naturally of Figaro, who enters at this moment, but has to fly at the approach of Bartolo. The old man's tantrums fairly drive Rosina from the room, and, on Basilio's entry, he announces his resolve to marry his ward the very next day. Basilio quite approves, especially as he has just heard that Count Almaviva (whom Bartolo has long suspected) is now in Seville; however, Basilio has a plan—he will spread such slanderous reports about him that the Count will have to fly the city. The singing-master is an adept in this art; in the famous "Calumny" song (*La Calonnia*) he pictures the progress of a slander from a tiny whispering breeze that grows and grows in force until at last it bursts in a furious tempest that brings the victim down in ruin.

Figaro and Rosina now have the stage once more to themselves; he tells her of her guardian's determination to marry her on the morrow, and, at the same time, assures her of Lindoro's devotion. There is no time to be lost; Figaro undertakes to deliver Rosina's letter and assures her that he will contrive a meeting between the lovers without delay. Bartolo returns to find Rosina with her fingers inky, the pen ruined, and one sheet of paper missing; to his angry questions she returns such fantastic answers that he flies into a passion, and ends the scene with such an elaborate specimen of florid patter, *A un dottor della mia sorte,* as is frankly beyond the skill of our modern basses.

Now begins the amazing *finale,* dramatically not too well constructed, but musically a sustained effort of mingled humour and brilliancy hard to parallel.

The Count, disguised as a trooper rather the worse for drink, forces his way noisily into Bartolo's presence, and waves his billeting-order in his face; their angry altercation brings Rosina quickly on the scene, with whom the Count at once manages to establish an understanding, and drops a note for her, which she conceals under her handkerchief. The Doctor, who has been searching for a paper which exempts him from all billeting, turns just in time to see the manœuvre, and, in a fury, orders the trooper out of the house. Figaro now enters and endeavours to prevent an actual struggle, for the Count is rather carried away by the part he is playing, and is inclined to overdo it. Just as the turmoil is at its height a knocking is heard, and the Civil Guard enters, to inquire the reason of the row; Bartolo orders them to arrest the trooper, which they are about to do, when the latter, managing to take the officer aside, shows him the insignia of his nobility. The effect is magical; instead of arresting him, the officer steps back and salutes; the rest are struck dumb with amazement. Old Bartolo, in particular, seems turned to stone, and the fine *largo* which follows, *Freddo ed immobile,* is of the same duration as the Doctor's stupefaction, which ends in a violent sneeze, the result of some snuff considerately administered by Figaro. In spite of this incident, 'cold and immovable' they all remain through eighty more pages of closely constructed *ensemble,* of which a noticeable feature is a broad melody of thirty bars (*Mi par d'esser colla testa*) sung by all the voices in unison or in octaves, and repeated later on in a higher key. The musical interest is well sustained to the end, but the whole *finale* is of such interminable length that it is doubtful if it will ever be heard again in its entirety.

Act II. The farther we proceed in this opera the more must we regret that Rossini's original title, *Almaviva, or the Useless Precaution,* has not been retained, for, whether as Lindoro, the drunken soldier, or the singing-master of the coming scene, Count Almaviva is by far the most prominent personage in the play: Barber Figaro may be the inspirer of the complicated intrigue, but the Count is always the protagonist. His music, too, naturally outshines all the rest, written as it was for Manuel del Popolo Vicente Garcia, one of the most remarkable tenors of that or any other period; if we examine, for instance, the close of the present Act, we shall find it little more than a series of florid solos for Almaviva, of an almost incredible brilliance, while Rosina's vocal claims are practically ignored. However, for more than half a century their positions have been reversed—the Count has dwindled, and Rosina has demanded all the limelight; people go to *Il Barbiere* to hear Mme Melbazzini in the Lesson Scene.

The Doctor is alone in Rosina's boudoir, when Almaviva appears, this time in the dress of a cathedral chorister; Alonzo is his name, he says, and he is Basilio's pupil; his master is ill, and has sent him in his place to give Rosina her singing-lesson. Bartolo is at first not too ready to agree to this, but 'Alonzo' has hit on a cunning device for persuading him—he has found, he says, a letter from Rosina to 'Lindoro'; in the course of the lesson he proposes to inform her of his discovery in such a way as to arouse her suspicions of her lover's honour. Bartolo approves the idea, pockets the letter, and brings Rosina into the room to have her lesson.

As everyone knows, this scene is the prima donna's playground; at her master's request for a song she sings what she likes, with no regard for dramatic propriety, and adds just as many encores as she feels inclined to. We do not propose to trace the origin and development of the custom; it would be tedious to compile a list of the "airs with variations," the "vocal waltzes," in which different prima donnas have 'fancied themselves,' or to note that Mme A. always finishes with "Robin Adair," while Mme B. prefers "Home, sweet home!" A prima donna, as experience teaches us, if once given her head, is *capable de tout*. Catalani, for instance, might well have introduced *Non più andrai*, the bass air from *Figaro*, into this scene—it was one of her favourite *tours de force*; and was there not a favourite 'Marguerite' in the last century who made a point of singing "Nearer, my God, to Thee!" in the Church Scene in Gounod's *Faust?*

Rosina having sung herself out at last, it is old Bartolo's turn; after obliging with an old-fashioned love-song, he follows it up with an old-fashioned fling, but stops short on finding that Figaro is mimicking his absurd capers behind his back. The Barber has come to shave the Doctor, who bids him fetch the soap-dish, and hands him his bunch of keys for the purpose; Figaro takes the opportunity to detach the key of the balcony shutters—(" 'Tis the newest one!" whispers Rosina). His search for the soap-dish results in a loud crash of falling china, which sends old Bartolo hurrying to the spot, leaving the lovers time for the long-wished-for *tête-à-tête,* in which they have just time to plan an elopement for that night. Bartolo and Figaro return, and the shaving is about to begin when all are amazed by the entrance of Basilio, apparently in perfect health, and with no knowledge of any pupil by the name of Alonzo! Figaro rises to the occasion; with his practised eye he sees at once that Basilio is undoubtedly very ill—in fact he is suffering from scarlet fever! Old Bartolo takes alarm at this, Basilio's protests are useless, and he is hustled from the room. The shaving at last begins in earnest, and the two lovers are thereby enabled to carry on a conversation in a low voice; but the Count, forgetting the situation, raises his voice too high, and some remarks to Rosina about 'disguises' serve to kindle the old man's worst suspicions. In a towering passion he drives 'Alonzo' and Figaro from the house, and proceeds to show Rosina her own letter to 'Lindoro,' with a scandalous account of how it came into his possession; indignant at what she considers proof of her lover's faithlessness, she volunteers to marry her guardian the next morning, and leaves the room in tears.

Act III. Midnight was the hour appointed for Rosina's elopement with her 'Lindoro'; well, she will be ready, but only to load him with reproaches, to show him "what a regular viper she can be when she chooses!"

To prepare us for a stormy scene Rossini has written

an orchestral *tempesta* which, if not very convincing, makes an effective background for the entrance of the two conspirators, the Count and Figaro. Hardly have the balcony-shutters been thrown back, and the pair stept softly into the room, when Rosina confronts them in a blaze of indignation. 'Lindoro,' however, has little difficulty in clearing up the misunderstanding; he throws off his cloak, and reveals himself as that glittering personage the Count Almaviva. Their mutual rapture is expressed in a duet, *Ah quel colpo!* of so excessively florid a character that even Figaro, who himself is no stranger to such vagaries, is compelled to cut in with a mocking imitation. But, looking from the window, he sees two figures with lanterns approaching the house—there is no time to be lost—the three prepare to descend from the balcony.

[Here comes the famous trio, *Zitti, zitti!*—a trivial little tune, but so daintily handled that it rarely fails of its encore.]

Alas! there is no escape that way—someone has removed the ladder! The arrival of Basilio and the Notary with the marriage-contract for Bartolo and his ward Rosina seems to threaten complete disaster—but Figaro's assurance carries all before it. He takes instant possession of the Notary, introducing himself as the uncle of Rosina, who is about to be married to the Count Almaviva. Is the contract sealed? Very good; then let us proceed to the signing. No use for the astonished Basilio to protest—the Count holds him up with a pistol in one hand and a valuable ring in the other—Basilio chooses the ring. Old Bartolo—it was he who discovered the telltale ladder!—now bursts into the room with an officer of the guard to arrest the burglars; but as it is obviously impossible to arrest the Count Almaviva on such a charge, and as the marriage-contract between him and Rosina is already signed, there is nothing for it but a general reconciliation. The Doctor, while cheated of his Rosina, is somewhat consoled by her dowry, which the Count places in his hands, and is left to reflect on the singularly appropriate title of "the new opera, *The Useless Precaution*."

We have given the plot of this opera in all the detail of the original for the better information of the reader, but he must not expect to find it in exact correspondence with any present-day performance. Even more than Mozart's *Figaro*, Rossini's *Barber* is usually cut so clumsily as to make it almost unintelligible. The sad truth is that it is impossible to-day to find a full cast capable of doing justice to the exceedingly florid music; we must wait for a great revival of the art of singing, and a corresponding change in public taste, before we can hope for a worthy performance of *Il Barbiere* in its entirety.

DER FREISCHÜTZ

Music by WEBER. *Words by* F. KIND.
Berlin, 1821; *London,* 1824; *New York,* 1825.

FEW masterpieces interest us from so many points
of view as *Der Freischütz;* it is the first purely
German, the first purely romantic opera; it anticipates the Wagnerian reforms in a truly remarkable manner; its delicious music, with something of the heavenly
candour of Mozart about it, appeals alike to musicians
and the laity. Finally we are attracted irresistibly by
the figure of Weber the composer; the contrast between
the wildness of his earlier days and the serene happiness
of his married life, his heroic struggle with disease, his
pathetic death in the very flush of his English triumph,
his burial in a London grave—these things cannot fail
to arouse our sympathies.

Weber's letters from London during the last weeks of
his life are good reading. He had come to London to
conduct his *Oberon,* specially composed for this country,
and was the guest of Sir George Smart in Portland
Place; although it is to be feared that the raw climate
tried the poor consumptive severely, he found the social
atmosphere invariably genial. "The people are really
too kind to me," he writes to his wife (5th March,
1826). "No king had ever more done for him out of
love; I may almost say they carry me in their arms."
Of his reception by the public he speaks in sheer astonishment: "Smart led me to my place, and what followed
baffles description. . . . The calling, shouting, and waving of handkerchiefs throughout the whole house seemed
to have no end; nobody can call to mind a parallel

enthusiasm." Again: "Are these your 'cold English' of whom I have been told so often? Their enthusiasm is incredible." This from one who, as the composer of *Der Freischütz,* had been for five years the musical idol of Europe is no slight testimony to the warmth of a London audience a hundred years ago.

Carl Maria von Weber was buried in the Catholic Church of St Mary Moorfields (21st June, 1826), but those who wish to lay a wreath upon his tomb must direct their steps elsewhere. In 1844 the composer's body was removed to the family vault at Dresden, where the musical arrangements for its solemn reception and re-interment were fittingly entrusted to the reverent care of Richard Wagner.

Der Freischütz is a romantic opera in the true sense of that term; the supernatural incidents in the action, as tiresome as such things usually are, though redeemed in this case by the glamour of the music, merely contribute to the general effect—it is the lighting-up of common things that makes Weber's opera the enchanting master-piece we know. The dark mysterious forest for a background, the

> Plaint of the horn, where it moaneth
> Deep in the heart of the woods,

the lusty huntsmen, the simple, joyous woodlanders with song and dance and drinking under the tavern lime-tree —these sights and sounds of common day Weber, with the help of a not unskilful librettist, has flooded with the light of true romance, that "light that never was on land or sea." Both music and book are full of that atmosphere of natural magic, that deeply rooted forest-feeling begotten of song and legend and lovely fancy, that made Old Germany, every whit as much as Italy, "the land of Romance." As Teutonic as *Die Meistersinger von*

98

Nürnberg, Der Freischütz makes even a more universal appeal, and by its very simplicity may outlast the more elaborate structure of Wagner's creation. The title itself presents a difficulty; it is impossible to translate the word *Freischütz,* and hard even to explain it; "The Free-shooter," *Le franc archer, Il franco arciero,* fail to give the real meaning, and *Robin des Bois,* the title of the first Paris version (1824), merely shelves the problem. The most one can say is that a *Freischütz* is one who shoots with magic bullets that never fail to hit the mark, and, at the same time, are sure to bring disaster on him who uses them.

The well-known overture invites inevitable comparisons with that of *Tannhaüser;* far shorter and simpler, it is hardly less successful than the later work in foreshadowing the action of the drama. In the opening section the delicious melody for the horns sets us in the fragrant heart of the sunlit forest, a shrine of peace and beauty; but even there an evil power intrudes, the clouds gather, and with a change to the minor we pass into an atmosphere of wild tumult. We are conscious of the awful figure of Zamiel, the Demon Hunter, walking in darkness and exercising his unseen influence over the young ranger; we hear Max's despairing cries, and all the clash and horror of the Incantation Scene is rising around us, when the sunshine is restored with the entrance of the *allegro* from Agathe's great *scena* in Act I—the *motif* of exultant love—and after some tussle between this and the darker themes the overture ends, like that of *Tannhäuser,* with the victory of Love, the triumph of Good over Evil.

The plot is simple enough. The scene is laid in Bohemia, but this localization is of slight importance—it is enough that we are in the heart of a woodland country; the late Mr Krehbiel hits the mark when he says of this opera: "Instead of shining with the light of Florentine Courts, it glows with the rays of the setting sun filtered through the foliage of the Black Forest." Agathe, the daughter of Cuno, Head Ranger to Prince Ottokar, is betrothed to the young forester Max, Cuno's favourite pupil; Caspar, his senior, and a rejected suitor of Agathe, is bent on revenge. Caspar is the villain of the piece—he is in league with the Powers of Darkness; he has sold himself to Zamiel, the Demon Hunter, whom to encounter is death, as he rides with his hellhounds at midnight through the forest. Under the spell of Zamiel, Max, who has long been the finest shot for miles around, finds himself deprived of all his powers; for weeks he has brought home neither fur nor feather from his forest walks, and not a single prize from the *Schützenfeste* (shooting-competitions), of which he was formerly the champion. As the time approaches for the most important event of all, the contest in the presence of the Prince himself, of which the reward is the succession to the Head Rangership, together with the hand of Agathe, Max becomes desperate, and Caspar is not slow to seize his opportunity. After convincing Max of the efficiency of a Magic Bullet (*Freikugel*) which he has in his possession, he persuades him to meet him at midnight in the Wolfs Schlucht (Wolf's Glen)—for only there, in the moon's eclipse, and by the aid of Zamiel, can such infallible bullets be procured. At the hour appointed, with every possible accompaniment of a rather grotesque *diablerie,* the deed is done; seven bullets are cast, six of which are guaranteed to hit the mark designed by their possessor, but the seventh (a fact of which Max is kept in ignorance) obeys the guiding hand of Zamiel alone— where he will, there it finds its billet. Meanwhile Agathe, though quietly preparing for her approaching wedding, is not without her misgivings and forebodings;

these have been confirmed by the Hermit of the Forest, a sage greatly revered for his holy life, who has always had a fatherly regard for the girl. On a recent visit he had warned her of some unseen danger that threatened, and given her a knot of consecrated roses, powerful to protect her in the hour of peril.

On the day of the great shooting-match, when the decisive trial is to be brought off, Caspar is present in the certain hope of witnessing his rival's destruction; he is persuaded that Zamiel is prepared to accept the soul of Max in exchange for his own, and his time for discharging his debt is almost up.

He climbs into a high tree to watch the event. Agathe has not yet arrived when the Prince orders the trials to begin and requests Max to aim at a white dove just flying past. Max fires—at the same moment Agathe enters and apparently receives the shot, as she falls senseless to the ground. It is soon realized, however, that it is Caspar who has been mortally wounded; Zamiel appears, to claim his soul, and the wretched man dies with curses on his lips.

Meanwhile the venerable Hermit—whose roses have done their part in shielding the innocent girl—comes forward from his cave to restore the unconscious Agathe and to champion the cause of Max, with whom the Prince is inclined to deal sternly on account of his traffic with the Devil. All join in the Hermit's plea for mercy, and it is finally agreed that the young forester's recovered integrity shall be put to the test of a year's probation, at the end of which he is to be rewarded with the post of Head Ranger and the hand of the faithful Agathe.

Act I. The open space in front of a village tavern, on the edge of a forest; groups of huntsmen and country folk are watching a shooting-match, which is just coming to an end. As the curtain rises, Kilian, a strapping young peasant, has just succeeded in bringing down the stuffed bird attached to the star which forms the centre of the target, and is rewarded by a noisy chorus of congratulation. A procession is formed, of men and maidens arm-in-arm, to conduct Kilian in triumph round the village; only Max, once the champion, who has failed completely on this occasion, sits at a table, his head on his arm, in solitary dejection. As the procession comes his way, Kilian stops to jeer at him, and to demand the homage due to the victor. His song, *Schau' der Herr mich an als König,* backed by the cackling laughter of the chorus, gives a capital impression of rough country banter—mischievous rather than ill-natured, for Kilian is a genial boor at heart. But it is too much for Max— he, a self-respecting forester, to be jeered at by a common peasant lad, and, alas, with reason! He hurls himself furiously upon his tormentor, and the peasants close in on them in an endeavour to rescue their man, when Cuno, the Head Ranger, arrives on the scene, with Caspar and others in attendance. Grieved to hear of Max's repeated failures, he bids him take heart and summon all his powers, for the morrow is the day of the decisive Trial Shot, on which depends the succession to the post of Ranger, and the hand of Agathe, to both of which Cuno hopes to see his favourite establish his title.

The long and tedious dialogue which follows, chiefly concerned with the legend connected with the Trial Shot, serves at any rate to develop the character of the treacherous Caspar, who frequently mutters the name of Zamiel, his familiar demon, and otherwise betrays his villainous nature.

In the trio and chorus, *O diese Sonne,* in which Max gives way to his despondent mood, all express their sympathy, and try to cheer him, with the exception of Cas-

par, whose harsh voice takes on a very different colour.
Very characteristic of the composer is the melodious
choral passage, *O lass Hoffnung,* in the accompaniment
of which he employs horns and bassoons with delicious
effect, after which the huntsmen's voices make a lusty
entrance, and work up a joyous *finale,* in which they hail
the bride and bridegroom of the morrow.

On Cuno's departure the village band strikes up the
simplest of waltzes, in which all take part except Max.
The light is fading now; and the dancers disappear,
some to the tavern, some to the forest ways, leaving Max
to his despondency. His great *scena* that follows is an
alternation of light and shadow; after the first gloomy
outburst, *Nein, länger trag' ich nicht die Qualen,* he
passes to the lovely melody *Durch die Wälder, durch die
Auen,* in which he recalls his former happy days, the careless life of the forester, and the bliss of returning at
nightfall to the welcome of Agathe's smile.

[Flutes and clarinets here combine to give that out-
door feeling, that atmosphere of sunshine in woodland
glades, which we find again in *Euryanthe* and in many
of the songs, and which seems to have been Weber's
peculiar secret.]

The sky now grows dark and threatening and in the
orchestra the drums give gloomy warning. In the background, invisible to Max, appears the gigantic figure of
Zamiel, the demon of the forest, "clothed" (according to
the stage directions) "in dark green, with a mantle of
fiery red; a large hat adorned with a plume overshadows
his terrible countenance." Under the influence of his
presence Max relapses into his former despondency, but
Zamiel's stay is short, and the young lover indulges in a
delicious reverie of Agathe watching from her window
for his coming. Zamiel again returns to plague Max
still more sorely, and at the concluding movement

Max expresses his abandonment to utter despair. "Are we the sport of idle Fate? Is there no God in heaven?" is his bitter cry.

In this dangerous mood he is found by Caspar; he, by contrast, is all roaring jollity, calls for drink in which Max must join him, and sings a capital tavern song in praise of Wine, Women, and Cards: *Hier im ird'schen Jammerthal.* The words are hardly to his hearer's mood:

> Wine, be thou my ABC!
> Woman, my divinity!
> Cards and dice, my Bible!

Max, however, cannot refuse to drink with him, and Caspar manages from time to time to drop something into his comrade's glass, calling at the same time upon Zamiel in a hollow whisper.

The drugged wine is taking effect upon Max, who rises to go home, but Caspar finds a way to keep him. How can he venture to face his sweetheart in such a sorry state, with a long tale of ill-luck, and no hope for the morrow? Still, all this may be remedied—there are ways and means—he, Caspar, knows a thing or two!

Max is incredulous of any sudden retrieving of his fortune, until the other gives him proof that his is no idle talk. "Here!" says Caspar, "take my rifle, and aim at yonder eagle!" It is nearly dark, the bird is far out of range, a mere speck in the clouds; yet, in the apathy of desperation, Max fires, and a huge golden eagle falls dead at his feet. Max knows it was an impossible shot; incredulous no longer, he allows himself to be persuaded to share in the secret powers which Caspar undoubtedly possesses. He will meet him at midnight in the Wolf's Glen for the casting of the Magic Bullets; but it must be that very night, for the moon is then in eclipse, and only under such conditions, Caspar explains, can the infernal traffic be carried on.

Max, with the eagle's plume stuck proudly in his hat, goes off to bid Agathe good-night, while Caspar ends the scene with a song of fiendish triumph over his rival's approaching destruction: *Der Hölle Netz' hat dich umgarnt.*

Act II. A spacious and rather 'romantic' chamber in what had formerly been a princely hunting-lodge; there are faded tapestries, antlers, and other sporting trophies, an altar in a curtained recess, heavy furniture black with age. But though the setting may savour of a mouldering past, the two occupants of the room afford a delightful contrast to it; these are Agathe, old Cuno's daughter, Max's affianced bride, and Aennchen, her young cousin, a piece of demure roguery—"just husband-high." Agathe's bridal dress is lying on a table, and Aennchen's spinning-wheel stands idle. Each of the girls is somewhat oddly occupied; Agathe is tying a bandage round her forehead, which has been bleeding, and her cousin is rehanging a large picture which has fallen from the wall and evidently been the cause of Agathe's injury. It is a portrait of one of Cuno's ancestors, and Agathe is inclined to look upon its fall as an evil omen, but young Aennchen will listen to no such talk—she is all for laughing dull care away. The contrasted characters of the pair are admirably displayed in the pretty duet *Schelm! halt fest!* Agathe, even on her bridal eve, cannot shake off a presentiment of coming disaster, her broad, sombre phrases standing out strongly against Aennchen's rippling gaiety, which sparkles as brightly in the passage *Grillen sind mir böse Gäste.* Still livelier is her solo *Kommt ein schlanker Bursch gezogen,* in which she declares herself quite ready to say "Yes!" when her turn comes. This short scene has a peculiar and unique charm; it is a *genre* painting, a domestic interior, that would scarcely have seemed old-fashioned in the Germany of thirty years ago.

After Aennchen's exit, Agathe begins her famous scena, *Leise, leise,* which, for so many amateurs, is the great attraction of the opera.

It is past her time for retiring, but her anxiety for Max will not let her rest; she must go to the window to watch until he comes. As she draws aside the curtain, the room is flooded by the light of the full moon which has just risen over forest and mountains, all clearly seen, though in the farther distance the sullen gathering clouds portend a thunderstorm. Awestruck at the majesty of the sight, she kneels beside the altar and prays for heaven's protection. This simple melody of sixteen bars (*Leise, leise*), must surely be known to thousands who have never heard of *Der Freischütz,* through its introduction into the religious services of various denominations, where, however out of place, it seems to satisfy the demands of popular piety. From Agathe's lips the air is appropriate and beautiful, though it must yield in musical value to the following section, *Alles pflegt schon längst der Ruh.* She has flung back the lattice and leans out, all eyes and ears for the faintest sign of her lover's approach; there is no sound but the rustle of the beech-woods, the sighing pines, the tinkling of the falling rill, and all these are brought close to us, through the medium of the orchestra, in a way that is wholly magical.

At last! a horn's low note—a hurrying step—'tis Max! and in his hat, as she fondly thinks, the sign of victory that augurs all good for the morrow. Heaven opens wide before Agathe's eyes, and she pours out her joy and thankfulness in the fiery *allegro vivace* which forms the chief theme of the overture, *All' meine Pulse schlagen.* It might be well, musically, if the scene ended

106

here; but a final trio is demanded, and develops naturally enough out of the situation. Agathe's perfect happiness is soon clouded over by Max's agitated manner, and his announcement that he must shortly leave her, to bring home a stag which he has left lying in the Wolf's Glen. The mention of this ill-reputed spot renews Agathe's worst forebodings, and the final number is divided between her entreaties to Max to remain at home, his insistent plea of necessity, and Aennchen's lively endeavours to put everything in as favourable a light as possible.

Scene II. The Wolf's Glen: the Incantation.

It is difficult to give a just impression of this Scene in mere words; the amazing music baffles description, while the trivialities of the libretto hardly invite it.

The hour is midnight, the place the depths of a tremendous gorge, with waterfalls, and twisted pines and blasted oaks, fantastically lit by the stray beams from the full moon just above. We have skulls and crossbones, owls and ravens, ghostly apparitions of the living and the dead—all the tawdry paraphernalia of the cheap supernaturalism so popular in Germany at the time.

We begin with a dismal hooting of spectral owls—the stage directions go so far as to demand one specially large owl with fiery eyes, which open and shut at rhythmic intervals—while invisible demons chant the following words in monotone:

> Moon's milk fell upon the weed—
>   (*Uhui! uhui!*)
> Now the spider's web doth bleed—
>   (*Uhui! uhui!*)
> Ere another eve succeed—
>   (*Uhui! uhui!*)
> Dies the bride, a stricken reed—
>   (*Uhui! uhui!*).

Caspar, with the conventional magic rites, calls upon Zamiel to appear; he tells how Max has fallen into the snare, and bargains with the Demon to accept the young man's soul in exchange for his own—for Caspar had long since sold himself to Zamiel, and his time for fulfilling the pact is nearly come. Zamiel apparently agrees to the proposal and vanishes.

Max is now seen on the crazy wooden bridge that spans the height of the ravine, hesitating whether to descend. The ghost of his mother, the phantasm of Agathe, appear and try to turn him from this dreadful project, but Caspar, with the aid of Zamiel, lures him down to the depths, and the casting of the Magic Bullets begins. To the accompaniment of rending boughs, screaming night-fowl, corpse-fires, and will-o'-the-wisps, the unhallowed work proceeds, with ever-increasing tumult and uproar of the elements—two thunderstorms are demanded by the librettist!—until, with the sixth bullet, the earth seems to rock, the gates of Hell to open, and the Wild Huntsman with spectral hounds and horses is seen galloping through the sky; at the casting of the fatal seventh, Zamiel again appears, towers threateningly over Max, and vanishes. Both men are thrown violently to the ground, where Caspar lies senseless, but Max, who has contrived to make the sign of the Cross at Zamiel's approach, is seen to raise himself upright as the curtain falls.

With only this stale and unprofitable material to work in, Weber's imagination has produced a symphonic masterpiece of weird fantasy, which suggests far more than a merely physical horror. How much Wagner owed to this earlier master of romance is becoming more and more fully recognized as time goes on, and nowhere are the germs of the great reformer's ideas more clearly traceable than in this Incantation Scene in the Wolf's Glen.

Act III. After an orchestral *intermezzo*—on the theme of the famous Huntsmen's Chorus, which for more than half a century was the obsession of every man, woman, and child who could hum, strum, or whistle —the action is resumed in Agathe's chamber in the Forester's Lodge. She is in a simple dress of white trimmed with the green ribbons which befit a huntsman's bride; on the little altar the Hermit's white roses have a conspicuous place.

Her rather hymn-like melody, *Und ob die Wolke sie verhülle,* breathes a spirit of hope and trustful resignation, but she is still unable to shake off her forebodings, which have been confirmed by her dreams of last night. The lively Aennchen, to whom she confides her fears, laughs them all away, and, in a delightful mock 'romanza,' *Einst träumte meiner sel'gen Base,* relates her own experience of a frightful apparition with fiery eyes and clanking chains, which turned out to be nothing worse than—"Nero the watch-dog!"

The bridesmaids now enter to finish the adorning of the bride; the little tune they sing, *Wir winden dir den Jungfernkranz,* was known for a long time as "The Bridal Chorus" *par excellence,* until the statelier march in *Lohengrin* came to supplant it. Poor Agathe!—evil omens still pursue her. The ancestral portrait of old Cuno has again fallen from the wall during last night's storm, and, worst of all, when the box which should contain the bridal-wreath is opened, it is found to contain a funeral wreath instead. However, the Hermit's roses are obviously destined for this special purpose, and, after a wreath has been hastily twined, the bridesmaids repeat their song, though in subdued tones, and the orchestra closes in the minor key as the little procession leaves the house.

Scene II. The concluding Scene of the Trial Shot is one of rather crowded incidents and of no special musical interest except for the Huntsmen's Chorus, which is now fully developed in the opening number. The stage represents a green expanse, with a mountainous background, where the whole countryside is assembled to witness the exciting contest. Prince Ottokar's pavilion occupies one side of the scene; on the other are long tables set for the foresters and huntsmen, and feasting and drinking are the general order of the day. The Prince rises from his daïs to hasten the conclusion of the business in hand; Max has already acquitted himself well and won his approval—but one shot now remains to establish him in the position of Head Ranger. The Prince bids him aim at a white dove that is flying from tree to tree; Max fires with the last Magic Bullet in his possession, the Fatal Seventh. At that instant Agathe arrives on the scene, and apparently receives the shot, falling senseless to the ground. It is soon seen, however, that it is not Agathe, but the villain Caspar who has got his death wound—for it was Zamiel who directed the shot, and over the sinless maiden he had no power. Caspar's body comes tumbling from the high tree to which he had climbed in the hope of witnessing Agathe's death by her lover's hand; Zamiel, invisible to all but his victim, comes to claim Caspar's soul, while his body is dragged off to be thrown into the Wolf's Glen.

Agathe has now revived, in time to hear her lover's contrite confession of his entanglement in the snares of Zamiel and his possession of the Magic Bullets. The Prince, horrified by what he considers such unpardonable wickedness, banishes Max for ever from his realms, nor will he listen to the entreaties of Agathe, Aennchen, and the old Cuno. But the venerable Hermit now comes forth from his cave and dominates the situation; it is against the will of Heaven, he says, that one solitary lapse on the part of a youth so brave and honest should be so severely punished; Max must have another chance. Ottokar agrees; the culprit shall be put on a year's probation, at the end of which time he may look to attain his heart's desire. Agathe and Max are jubilant at the prospect of their now assured happiness, and the opera ends with a chorus based on the motive of Exultant Love —the *allegro* of the overture—wedded to words which celebrate the unfailing power of virtue and enjoin submission in all things to the will of God.

GUILLAUME TELL

Music by ROSSINI. *Words by* JOUY *and* BIS.
Paris, 1829; *London,* 1830; *New York,* 1857.

IT must be confessed that the interest of this opera
for our day is largely historical. If Rossini is to
maintain a place in the repertory, it will be through
the florid elegance and sparkling gaiety of *Il Barbiere,*
the most perfect expression of his peculiar talent and
purely Italian in style; *Tell,* on the other hand, must be
classed with the French School, to which the composer
belonged by adoption only. In *La Gazza Ladra* and *La
Cenerentola* he had given us very suitable companions to
Il Barbiere, and although he had written serious operas
as well, *Tancredi, Otello,* and *Semiramide,* these were
every whit as Italian in conception and treatment as the
lighter works from his pen.

However, in the thirteen years that elapsed between
The Barber and *Tell,* Paris had become, or was rapidly
becoming, the centre of operatic activities; Rossini seems
to have discerned the rising star of Meyerbeer upon the
horizon, and judged that the time was come for him to
compose a 'grand' opera in the French manner. The
production of *Guillaume Tell* in 1829 served to raise the
composer higher than ever in public esteem, and he had
arranged to write four other works of a similar character, when the revolution of 1830 and the subsequent
change in the French dynasty upset all his plans, and
drove him into exile.

During this period Rossini may possibly have come to
doubt whether he was quite the man to write the 'serious'
opera which the future seemed to demand. Whatever

his reason, he composed no more for the stage—in fact during the thirty-two years of life that still remained to him his only important production was the completed version of the famous *Stabat Mater,* a work so little 'serious' in character that it was found possible in the eighteen-sixties to utilize it for an admirable set of quadrilles, where the luscious tunes seem less out of place than when forced into connexion with the grave Latin stanzas for which they were originally written.

But although *Tell* was brilliantly successful on its first performance, it was seen to be far too lengthy. Its five Acts were cut down to three, and finally left at four; nor was it long before it became the custom in Paris to present a single Act of the opera in conjunction with some other work. In England it was treated with greater reverence; till well into the 'sixties it was regarded as Rossini's masterpiece and, with the exception of *Fidelio,* the finest example of dramatic opera in existence. But not all its picturesque setting, nor even the novelty and brilliance of its orchestration, can convince us to-day that, as an opera, *Tell* is anything but a clumsy and long-winded affair.

The composer was unfortunate in his libretto. The rather colourless story of William Tell, undistinguished except for the incident of the perilous shot at the apple, hardly lends itself to operatic treatment. The practised hand of Scribe perhaps might have succeeded in pulling it together, but the two obscure librettists (MM. Jouy and Bis) to whom it was entrusted could make nothing of it—the plot, as we have it, is flat and amorphous.

The scenario has every advantage of the picturesque, in the lakes and mountains of Switzerland, with its fishers, herds, and hunters—the historical background, too, is of interest, showing the struggles of Helvetia in the 13th century to throw off the Austrian yoke. The opening Scene promises well; we have the familiar figure of the young and ardent patriot, Arnold, opposed to the cruel tyrant, Gessler, yet in love with that tyrant's daughter, Mathilde, and we scent the inevitable conflict between love and duty. So far, so good. But the trouble is that Arnold, though the *primo tenore*, is not the real hero, and that William Tell, who of course occupies that position, is unfortunately prevented from marrying the heroine, being already provided with a shadowy wife, Hedwige, and a puppet son, Jemmy. The result is that our sympathies are divided and our minds confused. For a successful intrigue it would be necessary to make Tell a single man, and to marry him to Mathilde after shooting the apple from her head instead of Jemmy's. The purists, it is true, might possibly kick at such a variant of a time-honoured legend; and there is the still graver objection that no prima donna would ever consent to marry a mere baritone, however heroic.

The overture to *William Tell* still holds an honoured place in the repertory of the concert-hall, but can only make its full effect when heard as an introduction to the opera. It is a beautiful example of descriptive music; we see the placid waters of the lake, we breathe the pure mountain air, we hear the call of the shepherd on the heights, the sound of the sheep-bells; then comes the storm, only to yield again to returning calm, and the rhythmic gallop of a hunting party ends the scene.

Act I offers but poor dramatic fare. The scene is by the lake of Lucerne; such a chance for Swiss music was not to be missed, and Rossini has stuffed his score with choruses and dances of peasants, shepherds, and fishermen, with the sounds of hunters in the distance. Much is made of a village festival at which several couples go through a ceremony of betrothal. Old Melcthal, the venerable patriarch of the village, who blesses the affianced pairs, is vexed that his son Arnold (also re-

114

ferred to as Melcthal, to our confusion) has not yet made
up his mind to enter into the 'bonds of Hymen.' The
unhappy tenor, who dares not let his secret be suspected,
finds what consolation he may in acquainting the audience,
in a series of asides, with his passion for Mathilde, the
daughter of the hated tyrant Gessler. As the heroine
does not appear at all in this Act, these asides are the only
means Arnold has of informing us of the truth, and it is
this necessity which accounts for the interminable duet
between him and Tell, in which the future liberator of
his country urges Arnold to join him in his effort to throw
off the yoke of the oppressor. To Tell's fiery pleadings
he gives but a lukewarm response—"all," as he is careful
to keep us informed, "on account of Matilda," for
Arnold, of course, is a sturdy patriot at heart.

We are half-way through the Act before anything
happens. At last the stagnation is ended by the entrance
of Leuthold, a shepherd, breathless and exhausted, his
dagger still dripping with blood. His only daughter had
been abducted by one of Gessler's soldiers—he has killed
him, and is fleeing from the wrath of his pursuers. His
only chance of escape is to reach the opposite shore of
the lake: who will row him across? No one, it seems,
not even the most experienced boatman, will venture on
so perilous a journey in the face of the storm that is
gathering. Gessler's men are already heard approaching,
when Tell himself arrives and at once offers to take the
risk of the crossing. As he hurries the hunted man into
the boat and rows swiftly away, the villagers sink on their
knees in one of those stage prayers which Rossini had
already done so much to popularize.

If this particular example is not quite so spell-binding
as its famous predecessor in *Moses in Egypt*, it certainly
makes an effective contribution to a picturesque and
vigorous *finale*.

The fugitives are already out of reach when the soldiers arrive, led by Rudolph, furious at Leuthold's escape. He at once demands the name of the other man in the boat. Not only will no one give it him, but the venerable Melcthal comes boldly forward to denounce the blustering Rudolph to his face, and is immediately seized, to be led before Gessler, at whose hands he is little likely to find mercy.

Act II is also singularly devoid of dramatic interest. The scene is in the deep heart of a forest where Mathilde has come to await her lover. After an irrelevant huntsmen's chorus, our heroine sings the best-known solo in the opera, *Sombres forêts,* an air hardly distinguished, except for its comparative freedom from Rossini's usual florid ornamentation. On Arnold's arrival she joins him in a duet of tedious length, at the end of which she is driven into hiding by the sound of voices—it is Tell and his fellow-patriot Walter Furst, who have been witnesses to the lovers' hurried parting. They both upbraid Arnold for his want of patriotism in dallying with the tyrant's daughter at a time when his country needs his aid in the struggle for freedom. In the course of an interminable trio Tell informs Arnold that his father, the venerable Melcthal, has been put to death by Gessler's orders; he is now thoroughly roused to a sense of his position—Mathilde is no more for him, he must live and die for Switzerland alone. All the patriots of the Three Cantons now assemble on the stage, and in what is known as the Conspirators' Chorus call heaven to witness that they will never cease to fight till Switzerland is delivered from the foreign yoke.

Act III. We now come to the famous incident of Tell and the apple, which so long passed for history, but has now been relegated to the category of sun-myths.

Before we get to action, however, we must have a farewell interview between Arnold and Mathilde. We cannot help feeling that up to this point the prima donna has been rather unhandsomely dealt with, but some compensation is now made her in the long solo, *Pour notre amour,* a vigorous affair with some bold flights of *coloratura,* enabling the lady to display a compass of two good octaves.

We now pass to the big scene of the opera. We are in the market-place of Altdorf, where Gessler has arranged to celebrate the centenary of the Austrian occupation of Switzerland, and so enable the natives to express their thankfulness for all the benefits derived from that happy event. This, of course, gives admirable opportunity for the inevitable ballet, with Tyrolese choruses, and military evolutions on the part of the Austrian soldiers. (It is worthy of note that on the first night of *Tell* the great Taglioni herself led the dancing.)

A prominent feature of the spectacle is a hat fixed on the top of a pole which Gessler has set up as a symbol of the imperial power, to which all are obliged to do homage. Tell alone refuses to make the required obeisance. He is at once arrested and condemned to imprisonment, together with the boy Jemmy. The tyrant, however, realizing that he can wound Tell still more grievously through his affection for his son, offers to release the latter on one condition—Tell, the famous archer, must give an exhibition of his skill by shooting at an apple placed on Jemmy's head. He is in honour bound to accept the challenge, and Gessler confidently expects to see the son's death brought about by his own father. After performing the perilous feat, Tell, in embracing his son, lets drop a second arrow to the ground; on being questioned as to its purpose, he boldly confesses that it was intended for Gessler, in case the first one had done its deadly work. He is again arrested and doomed to end his days in the dungeons of Kussnach ("a prey to hungry reptiles," as Gessler pleasantly assures him). Jemmy is condemned to a similar fate, but on this point the tyrant yields to the unanimous pleadings of peasants and soldiers, and more especially to those of Mathilde, who takes the boy into her safe-keeping until she can restore him to his mother.

Act IV. With the commanding figure of William Tell to dominate the opera, it is no easy matter to provide sufficient opportunities of vocal display for Arnold, who, if not the hero, is at least the *primo tenore*. However, now that Tell is safe in prison, the tenor is temporarily promoted to the place of First Patriot. We find him revisiting the deserted house on the shores of the lake, so rich in memories of childhood. The thought of his murdered father fills him with bitter grief, and in the andante *Asile héréditaire* he takes his last farewell—henceforth his life must be his country's, and revenge his only business. Cries of "Vengeance! Vengeance!" announce the arrival of a band of armed insurgents, who acquaint Arnold with Tell's arrest, and call on him to lead them at once against the tyrant; he responds in the martial air *Amis! Amis!* which as a show-piece for a really robust tenor is comparable only to *Di quella pira* in *Il Trovatore*.

Hedwige now enters, distracted at the fate of her husband, whom she looks upon as lost, but the unexpected return of their son Jemmy, accompanied by Mathilde, brings her some comfort, besides allowing for a trio for three sopranos: *Je rends à votre amour*. Tell, meanwhile, has managed somehow to escape from his chains, and is now seen on the lake in a boat struggling to reach the shore. The voyage is a perilous one, for a hurricane is raging. However, after another of Rossini's celebrated prayers, and some pages of storm music, our hero gains the shore and stands once more among his own people, the determined liberator of his beloved land. Jemmy hands his father his bow and arrow, and Gessler the tyrant arrives on the scene only to receive the last convincing proof of Tell's unerring aim. The tyrant falls, Helvetia is freed from the foreign yoke, and all unite in a song of thanksgiving for the triumph of liberty.

Such is the story of the opera when extended over four Acts. There is fortunately a condensed version in which the Swiss insurgents pour on to the stage immediately after the incident of the apple, despatch the tyrant, and so bring matters to a conclusion at the end of Act III.

The last performance of *Guillaume Tell* at Covent Garden was in 1889; it is hardly likely that it will again find its way into the repertory. If in the future we are called upon to drink to "the immortal memory of Rossini," we shall surely couple it with the name of that enchanting opera *Il Barbiere di Siviglia*.

LA SONNAMBULA

Music by BELLINI. *Words by* ROMANI.
Milan, 1831 ; *London,* 1831 ; *New York,* 1835.

IT has long been a fashion, not altogether wise, to
sneer at *La Sonnambula,* that long-cherished idol of
the early Victorians; it is doubtful if any opera
remained so long at the height of popularity to fall at
last so low in the general esteem. Yet this work has so
many excellent qualities that the modern attitude toward
it can only partially be justified. So great a man, so
opposite a genius as Wagner, was always ready to recognize Bellini's extraordinary gift of melody, and in *La
Sonnambula* we have that melody in rich abundance, sweet
and crystal-clear. The libretto, too, has conspicuous
merits; a simple story is unfolded in a natural forthright
manner, with no unnecessary padding, and offering just
the right opportunities for Bellini's peculiar and limited
talents—in fact the whole has a definite artistic value,
although the conventions in which it was begotten have
long since passed away; the opera of *La Sonnambula*
is just a pleasing pastoral, commendably free from the
customary operatic extravagance of incident.

Act I. *Scene* 1. A hamlet in a picturesque valley of
Italian Switzerland; a handful of houses, a considerable
hostelry, an old water-mill, with mountains for the background. The villagers are excited over the approaching
nuptials of Amina, the popular village beauty, and Elvino,
a young farmer of the neighbourhood. [Bellini's
choruses are never his strong point, and these peasants do
not get beyond "Long live Amina! Tra-la-la-la-la!" to
the thinnest of accompaniments.] Lisa, the young

120

hostess of the tavern, the only unsympathetic character in the piece, now enters, and in a showy but colourless air, *Tutto è gioja,* gives us to understand that Elvino's affections were once hers, and that, in consequence, she is not well-disposed toward Amina, his present *fiancée.* The attentions of Alessio, the young peasant to whom she is actually betrothed, merely irritate her, especially as he is the leader of the choral demonstration in honour of Amina, who now appears, in all the bloom of youth and innocence.

The history of opera is no bad guide to the changing psychology of the centuries. For the England of 1831, Amina, the spotless village maiden, established a type which exactly answered to the 'ideals' of the coming Victorian epoch. It took a quarter of a century to prepare for the acceptance of the frail Violetta in Verdi's *Traviata,* and a complete revolution in the moral outlook was necessary before the morbid horror of *Salome* could become the rage of two continents. Enter, then, from the mill Amina, the guileless orphan, with Teresa, her foster-mother. With the very first notes she sings the charm of Bellini begins to work; he has peculiarly the art of natural, graceful recitative, every phrase of which produces its effect. Amina's first air, *Come per me sereno,* and the following caballeta, *Sovra il sen,* expresses perfectly, within their own conventions, the innocent joy of a young girl in love, under the serene Italian sky. Moreover, no music that was ever written shows a more perfect knowledge of the capacities of the voice as a medium of æsthetic beauty; so long as we have singers equal to the task, so long shall we listen gladly to the joys and sorrows of Amina as Bellini has conceived them in song.

Now comes the Notary, to draw up the contract of espousals; Elvino follows with the ring for Amina's finger, and a posy of flowers which she slips into her bosom. Their flowing duet, *Prendi l'annel,* is followed by an 'ecstasy' solo for the soprano, *Ah, vorrei trovar parola,* which may have served Verdi as a model in more than one similar situation.

So far the soprano and tenor, supported by a feeble chorus, have managed to sustain the whole interest; now with some bustle of importance enters the baritone, a distinguished stranger, who asks the way to the Castle—he is actually the Count Rodolfo, the long-absent lord. His air, *Vi ravviso,* for a long time perhaps the most popular number in the whole opera, has lost its savour for us to-day; it seems to lack the true Bellinian glamour which still surrounds so much of Amina's music.

Evening is falling; it is too late for the Count to proceed on his journey—indeed, it is better that all should retire to rest, for this is the hour when the dreaded spectre which haunts the valley is wont to appear. The credulous villagers tell us all about it in a chorus, *A fosco cielo,* which gave a new thrill of mystery to the audiences of that day.

The Count resolves to put up at the village inn; before retiring, however, he finds time to show his admiration for the pretty Amina, so pointedly indeed as to arouse Elvino's jealousy, and the Scene ends with one of Bellini's most graceful duets, *Son geloso del zeffiro errante,* too often omitted in performance.

Act II. The bedroom in the inn prepared for the reception of the Count—a full moon shines in through a large wide-open window. Lisa, the comely and flirtatious hostess, enters to wish his lordship pleasant dreams, and is only too willing to prolong her stay, when a sudden noise drives her into hiding. Then at the window appears "a tall figure all in white"—is it the spectre? No, 'tis Amina, the spotless heroine, walking in her sleep. Her mind filled with the thought of her Elvino, she advances into the room, imagining, as her snatches of song confess, that she is even then approaching the altar with her lover at her side. She sinks in slumber on the bed, the picture of virginal purity. Lisa, rejoicing at what she construes as a scandal, now makes her escape, dropping a tell-tale handkerchief as she goes. The Count, awed by the presence of innocence, takes his departure, leaving Amina to sleep in peace.

The spiteful Lisa loses no time in seizing her opportunity; she goes in search of Elvino and Teresa, who, with a crowd of villagers, enter the room to find Amina in her unfortunate situation. Appearances are too strong for her; no one believes her protestations of innocence, least of all Elvino, who casts her from him, leaving her fainting in her mother's arms. The duet *D'un pensiero,* with the broad sweep of its phrases, makes excellent material for the well-wrought *finale,* and comes perhaps as near to passion as the conventionalities of the form will allow.

Act III. *Scene* I. On the way to the Castle, whither the villagers are going to intercede with the Count in favour of Amina. Enter Elvino, to pour forth his sorrows in the much extolled *Tutto è sciolto* which, as a contemporary critic writes, in the manner of his time, is "an effusion which nor can the audience hear nor the vocal histrionic express without being suffused in tears!" Without going so far as that, we may allow that the melody is truly 'affecting,' in the Victorian idiom, and, given a tenor with the right *timbre,* could never fail to suggest a lover's melancholy. High praise, too, must be given to Elvino's second solo, the vigorous *Ah, perchè non posso odiarti* [literally, "Ah, why can I not hate thee!" but known, wherever English is spoken, by the idiotic title "Still so gently o'er me stealing"]. It must be mentioned that the latter air is called forth by Amina (supported, of course, by her foster-mother Teresa), who pleads for a reconciliation. Elvino, however, is still furious; he snatches the betrothal ring from her finger, and leaves her once more to faint in Teresa's arms. This Scene is Elvino's great opportunity; no tenor who could do justice to the two numbers alluded to could fail to have the world at his feet in a very short time. Unfortunately, the extraordinarily high *tessitura* employed, in which the high B, C♯ and even D, are of constant recurrence, makes the adventure an impossible one for all but quite exceptional voices.

Scene II. The water-mill is here the chief feature of the stage setting; it must be old and dilapidated, with a big wheel, a rushing torrent, stone steps, crumbling and slippery, and a 'trick' bridge of wood so rotten that one of its planks is ready to give way any moment. Elvino has returned to his old love Lisa, and they are actually on their way to the church when the Count stops them. He upbraids Elvino for his base suspicions of Amina, which, he declares, are without the slightest foundation; Amina has never wavered in her love and truth. He then expounds the nature of somnambulism; how its victims are led to do the most extraordinary things while under its influence, of which they have no recollection in their waking hours; Amina, he declares, is a somnambulist, and, therefore, not responsible for her actions of the previous night. They are all incredulous, but convincing proof of the Count's statements is immediately forthcoming. From an upper chamber of the mill comes Amina, robed in white, holding a lamp in her hand—the unnatural fixity of her gaze shows that she is in the sleepwalker's trance. To the horror of the onlookers she ventures on the crazy bridge that spans the foaming stream; a plank gives way beneath her, the lamp falls

124

from her hand; miraculously guarded, as it seems, she
continues her perilous course, down the uneven moss-
grown stairway, until she stands safe among her neighbours, unconscious of their presence. Poor Amina! why
should her life be preserved? What has she to live for
now? Elvino is gone for ever; even the ring he placed
on her finger is no longer there. And the flowers he
gave her? She draws the posy from her bosom—alas,
they are withered, and no tears of hers can bring them
back to life. Warned by the Count, the much-moved
villagers do not dare to disturb her, until the penitent
Elvino—for Lisa's treachery has now been revealed—
gently replaces the precious ring; the chorus can no
longer refrain from shouting their favourite *Viva
Amina,* as the happy heroine wakes to find her lover
kneeling at her feet, her mother at her side, and all the
world once more a place of perfect bliss!

This last Scene has inspired Bellini with music of such
direct and poignant expression as is found nowhere else
in the opera. Amina's air, *Ah non credea mirarti,* remains one of the best examples of true pathos to be found
in the entire range of Italian opera; it possesses that
peculiar elegiac quality in which Bellini excelled, and it
owes nothing to vocal ornament, which is appropriately
reserved for the brilliant rondo *Ah non giunge,* which
ends the opera in a shower of fireworks.

It is easy to understand the enormous popularity of this
Scene with early Victorian audiences. It appealed, in
the first place, to the sentiment, the 'sensibility,' of the
age, and, secondly, to the growing interest in popular
science of all kinds. Somnambulism was just coming up
as a subject for popular discussion among frivolous and
serious alike; a proof of this is found in an early edition
of this opera, the preface of which has some columns
devoted to an exposition of this strange abnormality,

illustrated by anecdotes and a whole string of references to learned medical treatises in English and Latin.

La Sonnambula, produced at Milan in 1831, was heard in London the same year, and two years later was given at Drury Lane, in English, with Malibran as Amina. Never has any English version of an Italian opera achieved such a popular success; a knowledge of it spread throughout the length and breadth of the country, and about the time of the Great Exhibition of 1851 there were few persons with any pretensions to gentility who could not hum the tunes of "Still so gently," "As I view," and "Do not mingle." Since not many people now alive can be acquainted with the quality of the 'lyrics' concealed behind these titles, it may be of interest, in view of their amazing ineptitude, to give some quotations from them; they should make us a little less dissatisfied with the English versions of the present day, which, whatever their faults, will certainly not suffer by the comparison.

ELVINO. Still so gently o'er me stealing,
    Mem'ry will bring back the feeling,
    Spite of all my grief, revealing
     That I dearly love thee still.
    Though some other swain may charm thee,
    Ah, no other e'er can warm me,
    Yet, ne'er fear, I will not harm thee,
     False one, no! I love thee still.
     . . . .

THE COUNT. As I view these scenes so charming
    With dear remembrance my heart is warming
    Of days long vanished. Oh, my heart is filled
     with pain,
    Finding objects that yet remain
    While those days come not again.
    Maid, those bright eyes my heart impressing
    Fill my breast with thoughts distressing
    By recalling an earthly blessing
     Long since dead and pass'd away.
    She was like thee, e'er Death oppressing
     Sank her beauties in decay.

AMINA.   Do not mingle one human feeling
             With the rapture o'er each sense stealing;
             See these tributes to me revealing
             My Elvino true to love.

There has hardly been a prima donna since 1831 who has not endeavoured to make the part of Amina 'her own.' The original exponent, strangely enough, was Pasta, whose reputation is more usually associated with such tragic rôles as Medea and Norma. Malibran followed her immediately, then Sontag, Persiani, and Grisi; in 1842 came Jenny Lind, and effaced all previous impressions, at least so far as England and America were concerned. It would be tedious to extend the list, but it is interesting to know that on the statue of Bellini in Naples the three singers who have been thought most worthy of association with the part are Pasta, Malibran, and Emma Nevada.

NORMA

Music by BELLINI. *Words by* ROMANI.
Milan, 1831; *London,* 1833; *New York,* 1841.

WHATEVER we may think of the music of *Norma* there is no denying the strength of the libretto. It is a drama of conflict on the highest plane of tragedy; against a background of warring Gauls and Romans we have the struggle of tremendous passions, of love opposed to patriotism, of pity conquering hate, of jealousy yielding to maternal instinct.

The action takes place in Gaul during the Roman occupation in the first century B.C. Norma, a priestess of the Druids, and regarded by them as an inspired prophetess, has, unknown to anyone, broken her vow of chastity for the sake of Pollione, the Roman proconsul, to whom she has borne two children; wearying of her, he has formed a new connexion with Adalgisa, a young virgin attached to the temple.

Act I. *Scene* 1. For the opening Scene we may imagine a reconstruction of Stonehenge as it was 2000 years ago, taking care to supply a huge oak thick with mistletoe, and, suspended near, the shield of Irminsul, God of War, whose brazen clang is the signal that calls the warriors to arms. A procession of priests enters, headed by Oroveso the Arch-Druid; he is impatient for action; too long have they borne the insufferable tyranny of the Roman invader; it is time to beat on the sacred shield and rouse the tribes to fury. But that solemn act only Norma, the high-priestess, can perform; Oroveso, her father, bids them all return at the rising of the moon, when Norma shall be there. Pollione, the Roman governor, now enters to tell us, or rather his centurion Flavio, of his new passion for Adalgisa. Flavio warns him of his danger should he be caught in the sacred precincts, and he retires after hurling defiance at the priesthood in the bold allegro *Mi protegge, mi difende.*

The Druids return singing a solemn chant to the accompaniment of the famous march which still holds its own among such compositions. When all are assembled, Norma should enter with superb effect, in flowing white, the golden sickle in her hand with which to cut the sacred mistletoe. She is priestess, prophetess, and their ruler: let them put aside their foolish clamour for rebellion; the power of Rome indeed must be broken, but the time is not yet.

The full moon floods the scene as Norma cuts the mystic branch, while she sings the great aria, *Casta diva,* to the chaste Queen of Heaven, and the sequel, *Ah bello a me ritorno,* in which she laments for Pollione's love grown cold.

The rite being over, and all departed, Adalgisa takes the stage to ask pardon of the gods for her guilty passion from which she cannot free herself. She is soon joined by Pollione, who in a long duet persuades her against her conscience to fly with him to Rome.

Scene II. Here in her private dwelling we see Norma, no longer the awe-inspiring prophetess, but a tender mother with a bleeding heart. Her children are with her—hers and Pollione's—but they can comfort her no longer; she fears that their father is about to abandon her and them, and what then will be their fate? Sadly she sends them from her presence, and turns to welcome one who, like herself, is in sore need of consolation. It is Adalgisa, who, conscience-stricken, has come to seek counsel of Norma, her dearest friend, of whose relations with Pollione she is of course ignorant; to her she confesses her fault, and asks to be released from her vow. The priestess, moved to instant sympathy by an experience so like her own, gives her ready absolution, when Pollione appears upon the scene, and the true state of affairs is revealed, Norma's love turns to hate, and Adalgisa is so horrified at Pollione's treachery that she resolves to give up her lover, and remain faithful to the friend who has shown her a mother's tenderness.

Act II opens with Norma's half-hearted attempt to kill her children, in her mad desire for revenge; her mother-love, however, prevails against the evil impulse, and she commits them to the care of Adalgisa, whom she advises to trust her happiness to Pollione and to follow him to Rome; for herself, she declares, death is the only refuge. But Adalgisa's infatuation is over—she has resolved to end her life in the service of the Temple; Norma's happiness, she feels, may be restored by Pollione's return to his first love, and she herself will go to him and persuade him to his true duty.

The last Scene is a court in the temple, where Norma is waiting for news of Adalgisa's success. The messenger returns, to tell her the worst; Pollione refuses to give up Adalgisa—nay, should she persist in flying from him, he will drag her from the very precincts of the Temple. On hearing this, Norma is roused to the wildest fury— Pollione, and Rome with him, shall be made to suffer for this insulting threat. Hastening to the tree where hangs the brazen shield of Irminsul she strikes three times thereon, and at that sound the Druids all assemble. War, she tells them, is now the will of the gods—war against the Romans, fierce and determined. At the same moment a tumult is heard without—some Roman has actually dared to pollute the sacred groves with his presence; it is Pollione, who has fulfilled his threat to Adalgisa. He is brought in and condemned to instant

130

death; indeed, his intrusion is almost welcome, as it supplies the human victim that must be sacrificed in order to ensure the success of the expedition.

And Norma's is the hand that must strike the blow. But at the last her old affection wakes again within her —she tries to save him; if he will but give up Adalgisa his life shall be spared. But Pollione refuses life on such terms, and Norma, in despair, resolves to end her sufferings by death. The gods, she announces, have chosen another victim for the sacrifice, a virgin priestess of the Temple, who has broken her vows, and brought disgrace upon her country and her father; the punishment is death by fire. Amazed and wrathful, the Druids demand her name—"It is I—Norma!" comes the terrible reply. Her father, Oroveso, incredulous, joins with the others in imploring her to take back her words. But no— "Norma cannot lie!" Unfaltering, exalted by her purpose of atonement, she ascends the sacrificial pile—and by her side is Pollione, awake at last to the lofty nature of the woman he has wronged, and rejoicing to share in the only expiation which holds for both the hope of a future reunion.

Such is the 'book' that Felice Romani, the skilful librettist of *La Sonnambula,* prepared for Bellini as a successor to that simple pastoral. That the young composer was overweighted by so tragic a subject is not surprising; we certainly find a considerable advance in breadth of treatment as compared with the earlier opera —there is a spirited March of Druids at the outset, and a rousing chorus, a call to battle, in Act II—but Bellini could not command the note of tragedy, and the music moves too often with a stilted mechanical swing. On the other hand, in the purely lyrical passages the true Bellini triumphs as before; he is at his very best in Norma's lovely prayer to the rising moon, *Casta diva,* her scene with the slumbering children, *Teneri figli,* and the duet for Norma and Adalgisa, *Mira, o Norma!* Granted that there are tunes in *Norma* that a self-respecting barrel-organ might kick at, nevertheless it contains so much melodic beauty, to say nothing of the dramatic interest, that an occasional revival of the opera will always be welcome not only to opera-goers, but to all save the most narrow-minded of musical *connoisseurs.* The one indispensable condition is a really strong cast; the three chief parts require singers of exceptional gifts, while the heroine must be not only a perfect mistress of *il bel canto,* but also a tragic actress of a high order; it is small wonder, then, that for many years *Norma* has been practically out of the repertory.

The opera started on its career with every advantage. In the previous year Bellini had made an enormous success with *La Sonnambula,* the leading part in which was designed especially for Mme Pasta, one of the greatest actresses of the time, from whom even those of the 'legitimate' stage did not disdain to learn. In the rôle of the Druid priestess Pasta found a part far worthier of her tragic powers and gave a performance that was one of the sensations of the time. But even a perfect Norma is handicapped unless supported by the right Adalgisa, and here, too, Bellini was equally fortunate; in the first production this rôle was assigned to no less an artist than Giulia Grisi, who was soon to succeed to Pasta's laurels in the part of the heroine, and to remain the ideal Norma for close on a quarter of a century. [During Grisi's reign Mario was the accepted Pollione, and the great Lablache did not despise the small part of Oroveso.] Pauline Viardot-Garcia, Johanna Wagner, Adelaide Kemble, were all notable Normas; Sontag, Jenny Lind, great singers both, were hardly equipped by nature for such heroic flights. The second half of the 19th century produced no distinguished representatives of the part until Mme Lilli Lehmann, quite late in her career, chose to demonstrate that one of the greatest interpreters of Wagnerian heroines could be equally great in 'old-fashioned Italian opera.' The performance of *Norma* at Covent Garden in 1899, with Mme Lehmann in the title-part and Mme Giulia Ravogli as Adalgisa was as near an approach to the standard of the original production as can be hoped for. Each of these ladies was vocally superb, while Mme Lehmann was a rare combination of all that is best in both the German and Italian schools. After a long course of Wagner, she revelled in a part which, while providing full scope for the tragic actress, allowed her a whole evening of that pure Italian singing her devotion to which she had never lost. Of especial value in this rôle was her remarkable faculty of clothing the most elaborate florid passages with a dramatic significance which completely hid their apparent banality; so intensely did she apply herself to the task that she—an artist who hardly knew what fatigue meant—confessed that a single performance of *Norma* tried her more than all three evenings of Brünnhilde in *The Ring*. These are the words of an exceptional artist, but their general application would bring about a much-to-be-desired reform in the operatic performances of to-day; let every aspirant to Wagnerian honours first school herself to sing the part of Norma—she will then find that, vocally, Isolde, Kundry, Brünnhilde, are mere child's play by comparison.

L'ELISIR D'AMORE

Music by DONIZETTI. *Words by* ROMANI.
Milan, 1832; London, 1836; New York, 1883.

WHEN Donizetti was asked whether he believed the story that Rossini took thirteen days
to write *The Barber of Seville*, he replied:
"Very likely—Rossini is such a lazy fellow!" Truly, at
the rate at which Donizetti composed—the last Act of
La Favorita, which ranks among his best work, was
written in a single night—a fortnight may well have
seemed a long time to spend on any opera. He must
have written habitually at a furious pace; his first opera
was produced at the age of twenty, and in the quarter of
a century of activity that remained to him he added sixty
more to his credit.

But the composer's power of invention was not robust
enough for such a strain—we find him often spinning too
slight a thread. The writer of the article in Grove remarks that "of Donizetti's operas at least two-thirds are
quite unknown in England"; he would be considered a
specialist to-day, we imagine, who could name even ten
of them. Besides the three or four works which may be
said to have a place in the repertory, the names of a few
others are remembered by certain melodious numbers
which still survive. *O mio Fernando* may be said to have
outlived the opera *La Favorita* in which it occurs, as *Don
Pasquale* has bequeathed to us the delicious serenade
Com' è gentil, and *Convien partir* will probably be heard
when *La Fille du Régiment* is laid aside. *L'Elisir
d'Amore* also has its popular attraction with the lovely
tenor romance *Una furtiva lagrima,* but is by no means

dependent on it, as the entire opera is essentially attractive. *L'Elisir* was written early in Donizetti's career, when he was strongly influenced by Rossini, and much of the music is delightfully reminiscent of that great master's gayest manner, while Dulcamara, the quack doctor, is one of the great *buffo* figures in Italian opera, worthy to rank with Rossini's Figaro and Mozart's Osmin.

This Dulcamara is the centre of the rather flimsy little plot. Adina, the heroine, a capable young woman who farms her own land, has two suitors, Nemorino, a diffident young farmer, who does but sigh for her, and Belcore the sergeant, who courts her boldly. The latter seems likely to carry all before him, when the arrival of the great Doctor Dulcamara alters the probable course of events; Nemorino obtains from him a love-potion warranted to make any girl his willing slave; under its influence Adina gives her hand to the young farmer, Belcore cheerfully accepts the situation, every girl in the village lays in a bottle of the magic draught, and Dulcamara's reputation is made for ever.

Act I. *Scene* 1. The scene is in the garden belonging to Adina's comfortable homestead; it is high noon and harvest-time, and the reapers are resting in the shade. The lady is reading, and chuckling over her book. Challenged by the others, she tells them that it is an old romance called *Tristan and Iseult*: "Just listen! Tristan is in love with the lady, who will have nothing to do with him; he therefore procures a certain elixir [*l'elisir d'amore*], drinks it, and Iseult at once falls into his arms! Now, isn't that delightful!" Very; all the girls would like to know where such useful draughts can be obtained; so would Nemorino, who has been lurking and listening, not daring to come forward.

[The reader will notice that we have here a curious variation of the usual tradition of the love-philtre; as a

135

rule the potion must be mixed with the drink of the one whose love it is desired to gain, whereas in this case it is drunk by the rejected lover and endows him with the power of inspiring love. The reason probably is that this scheme fits in best with the development of our innocent little story.]

Martial music now prepares us for the entrance of the gallant sergeant Belcore and his men. The son of Mars has no use for love-philtres—he believes in simpler methods; he is of opinion that he can "put the come-ther" upon any woman he chooses, in double-quick time. Just now his object is the very wide-awake Adina. Without hesitation he marches smartly up to her, presents his bouquet, and after a few *roulades* in the true Rossinian manner, lays siege to her heart in a fine bold melody, *Più tempo, oh Dio, non perdere,* in which he urges the lady to waste no more time since, as he points out, she is bound to yield at last. This theme serves as material for the *ensemble* that follows, in which Adina keeps him well in hand—she herself declines to be hurried, but will take time to think it over.

The sergeant having withdrawn his men for refreshment, the timid Nemorino comes out of his retirement and begs a word with her. Now though Adina's heart secretly inclines toward this too modest wooer, she finds his long face and woebegone speeches a little tedious. "If you can't stop sighing," she tells him, "would it not be better to go right away for a time? Go and visit that sick old uncle of yours—if you don't hurry up he may die before you get there, and you'll find yourself cut off with a shilling! Then, of course, *you'll* die—of hunger!" "Better die of hunger than of love!" is the desperate retort. "Well," she says coldly, "I'm sorry—but *I* can't love you!" "Why?" asks the fatuous young man. It takes Adina several pages of elegant filigree-work

136

to explain her reasons—and even then poor Nemorino is not satisfied.

Scene II. Now the fun begins in earnest. The village square is empty when the curtain rises, but the blare of a trumpet brings the women out of the houses and the men from their labour. The advancing trumpeter is but the herald of a truly imposing spectacle; on the stage there rolls a golden chariot, only less dazzling than the magnificent and spanking personage who stands upright in it with an air of lordly patronage for all the world. This is the great Doctor Dulcamara, most picturesque, most genial of all stage quacks and charlatans.

[The colossal Luigi Lablache, who created the part, seems to have set a standard of perfection which no one since has ever approached; a superb presence, an unctuous humour, a perfect method applied to perhaps the finest bass voice on record, all these combined to make that wonderful artist unique in this as in many other parts.]

The Doctor's hands and pockets are full of little phials and boxes, the virtues of which he extols in the long patter-song *Udite, o rustici,* a piece of Rossinian gaiety, only comparable with that master's *Largo al factotum* or *Miei rampolli feminini.* Have you toothache, heart-ache, wrinkles? Here is an ointment that will banish them for ever! And here, still greater marvel, is the universal remedy that will cure all diseases, dry a widow's tears, and make an old man young and lusty! As for the price—well, everyone knows that Dulcamara's Grand Specific is worth a guinea a bottle, but to them, his own dear countrymen, the price is half a crown!

When the grateful peasants have departed, well satisfied with their treasures, Nemorino seizes the opportunity; has the Doctor perchance any of that patent fluid that Sir Tristan used in order to bring Madame Iseult to reason—the elixir of love? The Doctor beams with satisfaction—why, he himself is the distiller and sole proprietor of that magic potion! [The lively duet *Obbligato!* exactly expresses Nemorino's joy at his good fortune and Dulcamara's opinion of him as the silliest pigeon he has ever plucked!] The amorous youth puts down his last coin for a flask of formidable size with which he is eager to experiment at once. "Certainly!" says the benevolent Doctor, "drink it now! But remember it will not take effect till to-morrow, by which time," he confides to the audience, "I shall be far enough away!" After another delightful duet, *Va, mortale fortunato,* Nemorino is left alone to try what effect the elixir will have on himself. The first draught delights him, the second excites him; by the time he has drunk it all he feels a new man—and no wonder, since, as the Doctor has informed us in an undertone, the famous elixir is just a bottle of good red wine!

Adina enters—she can scarcely believe her eyes: this is never Nemorino, this laughing, singing, rollicking loon! Their duet, *Esulti pur la barbara,* sung for the most part 'aside,' allows sufficient musical dialogue for Nemorino to assure the lady that he has taken her advice to heart; no more sighing for him—he feels quite jolly already!— and to-morrow—"Well, to-morrow," he says, "you will see!" "Yes!" retorts Adina, now thoroughly nettled, "we *will* see!" The opportune entrance of Belcore determines her course of action. She is all smiles and complaisance for the newcomer, and, as the sergeant is out for victory, in less than five minutes he has asked her to name the day. "Say a week from now!" says Adina, with her eye on Nemorino, to see how he will take it. To her discomfiture, and Belcore's indignation, her once bashful adorer does nothing but chuckle to himself, or laugh aloud, to think how the tables will be turned to-morrow, when the elixir has begun to work its magic on Adina.

But alas! how easily things go wrong! A messenger arrives with despatches: marching orders for to-morrow morning—and the wedding indefinitely postponed! Nemorino, well pleased at this new turn of affairs, is still chuckling, when Belcore forces the pace and carries all before him: after all, why should they wait? Why not get married to-day? Adina assents to the proposal with the greater alacrity as she notices the astonishing effect it has on Nemorino. The poor fellow almost collapses; he sees all his hopes vanish in a moment—the elixir he knows will not take effect until to-morrow, and by that time Adina will be another's! He implores her not to act so rashly—to wait until the morning! But the lady is obdurate; Nemorino's assumed indifference has wounded her pride, and she will make him smart for it.

All through this scene we are left in doubt whether Adina may not be using the sergeant merely as a blind, in order to bring the young farmer back to his old allegiance. However, the hour for the wedding is fixed, the neighbours bidden to the feast, and the curtain falls on the distracted Nemorino, jeered at by all and calling wildly on the Doctor to come to his aid.

[The closing quartet and chorus are a worthy climax to an Act the music of which is consistently graceful and exhilarating; in the elaborate middle section, *Adina credimi*, and the delicious final frolic, *Fra lieti contenti*, we see how admirable was Donizetti's talent so long as he confined himself to his proper sphere of comic opera.]

Act II. *Scene* 1. The preparations for the wedding have begun already; there is some jolly feasting at the tables in the big farmhouse kitchen, and Belcore's men are making a jolly noise on their brass instruments. The only personage not there is Nemorino, and it is significant that Adina's first words are an expression of regret at his absence. Dulcamara, of course, is in his element; he earns our gratitude by introducing a really captivating little duet—a *barcarolle* he calls it—in which he induces his fair hostess to join him; it is only just out, he says, as he produces the music from his pocket and hands her her part, and we are all the more delighted when we find that Adina, who is certainly one of the most attractive of light-opera heroines, includes among her many gifts the ability to sing at sight.

On the arrival of the Notary all leave the room except Dulcamara, who calmly goes on with his feasting. Nemorino enters in desperate plight: much good the elixir has done him! What's the use of winning Adina's love to-morrow if she is married to someone else to-day? Can't the Doctor do something? Certainly! Nemorino has only to take another bottle, and the charm will begin to work in half an hour. "That," adds the Doctor for our benefit, "gives me plenty of time to get away!"

This is good hearing, only Nemorino has no money—well, the Doctor has to go back to his inn, so Nemorino must raise the money and bring it to him there in a quarter of an hour.

Belcore enters most opportunely—Nemorino tells him his need, though not the reason for it. The sergeant, eager to get him out of the way, advises him to enlist for a soldier, and put money in his pocket that way. Nemorino agrees, signs the paper, and the two go off together.

Scene II. We begin with a really humorous little chorus for female voices.

The girls in the square are evidently much excited. Such a piece of news! "Can it be possible?" " 'Tis all nonsense, I believe!" "No indeed, 'tis true!" "But what is it?" "Well—not a word to anyone!—but they told me at the shop that—but you're sure you won't let

140

it go any farther? Then I'll whisper it: Nemorino's old uncle is dead, so now he's a millionaire, the richest man for miles around! But—silence—here he comes!"

Nemorino has just finished the second bottle of elixir, and is so absorbed in analysing its effects that he has no eyes for anything else; he suddenly wakes to find himself the centre of attraction for a bevy of village beauties, all bowing and curtsying and eyeing him with unmistakable meaning. And the things he hears them say! "Oh, isn't he a darling!" "So modest and amiable!" "And what a gentlemanly air!"

Nemorino, who has heard nothing of his rise to fortune, is taken aback for a moment—then he remembers: of course, it's all the result of that elixir—bravo Dulcamara! And as he is now beginning to feel all the better for so much good wine, he is quite ready for the good time coming, and lets himself be dragged off to the dance, where he seems likely to have more partners than he can conveniently do with.

Now of this very lively scene—and it must be said that the conduct of the girls, especially of a minx named Giannetta, is rather scandalous—Adina has been a pained and horrified spectator. Nemorino, then, is really indifferent to her—her approaching marriage with Belcore is nothing to him! This discovery—and perhaps the fact that she has never before seen him in so favourable a light—serves to fan to a flame the love that has long smouldered in her heart. Resentment is forgotten—the tables are turned indeed—she is now a suppliant for love, to whom Nemorino can dictate his terms.

But still she cannot understand why all the girls in the village have suddenly gone mad about him! When the others have danced off the stage, Dulcamara (who knows all about that uncle) condescends to enlighten her. She has read of the magic philtre by means of which Sir

Tristan gained the love of the lady Iseult? Well, he, Dulcamara, is the only living man who has the secret— he has given the elixir to Nemorino, and this is the result! All the girls on fire for him! "But," inquires Adina, "has he made his choice yet?" "I think so," says the cunning Doctor, "when he came to beg me for the potion, he certainly mentioned someone for whom he was dying—and he must have been in deadly earnest, for I know he enlisted for a soldier just to get the money to pay me for it!"

Adina is now all remorse and tenderness—the faithful, noble fellow, how can she have wronged him so! The Doctor's heart is touched: "Ah, my dear," he says, "it's a bottle of my elixir would do you a world of good —so be advised, and take it!"

Adina is now all smiles again—but no elixir for her! Like Mozart's Zerlina she prefers to rely upon her own fascinations. Her unpretentious little air *Una tenera occhiatina* has a winning archness about it that should appeal to all light sopranos.

> With a tender look I'll charm him,
> With a tear or sigh disarm him.
>
> Never a man was yet so mulish
>   That I could not make him yield;
> Nemorino's fate's decided
>   When Adina takes the field!

He would be a bold man who should suggest to the tenor that his solo, *Una furtiva lagrima,* were better omitted; in any case the suggestion should be made with a wink of the eye, for though the graceful number is a mere sop to the singer, and dramatically indefensible, it is generally 'the hit of the evening,' and its popularity on the concert platform seems inexhaustible.

Adina's course is not yet all plain sailing. To make

sure of Nemorino she takes the very sensible step of
secretly buying him out of the army, but when she waves
the document triumphantly in his face, the wretch pretends not to understand her motive. "To a rejected
suitor like me," he cries, "of what use is liberty? Better
to die on the field of glory than stay at home and die of
love!" [He has said something very like this before,
we remember.]

But Adina has her way. When Belcore enters a few
minutes later he finds the pair in each other's arms, and,
rightly concluding that he is no longer wanted there,
marches cheerfully off to fresh conquests.

Dulcamara, we may be sure, improves the occasion:
the blissful lovers owe it all to him, and, mark you, what
his elixir has done for them it can do for the rest of them
—so be in time! be in time! be in time! In a few
minutes his entire stock is sold out, and the magnificent
creature, mounting his golden chariot, departs, as he
came, in a blaze of glory.

So ends this sparkling little opera, which all lovers of
true musical comedy should pray to see revived, not at
one of the big houses, with star performers, but put on
for a run at some little theatre, where it could be played
in the intimate manner that it demands.

LUCREZIA BORGIA

Music by DONIZETTI. *Words by* ROMANI.
Milan, 1834; *London,* 1839; *New York,* 1847.

*L*UCREZIA BORGIA, produced at Milan in 1834, was first seen in London, at Her Majesty's Theatre, in 1839, and at once established itself in popular favour. It would seem that the moral vigilance of that period was somewhat lax in comparison with the standards of 1854, when *La Traviata* found all the forces of virtue ranged against her, for it must be admitted that the story of the earlier opera is open to far more serious objections. There are few names in history so infamous as that of Lucrezia Borgia, most shameless member of a shameless house. It is true she has not wanted for apologists, but Victor Hugo, author of the drama from which the opera is taken, was not of their number; his play is as unpleasant as his 'romantic' pen could make it, and although Romani, the librettist, has toned down many a flagrant detail of the French original, much of the unpleasantness still remains.

The opera is described as being in a Prologue and two Acts, but the three parts are of equal length, and the action continuous. The first Scene is laid in Venice, where, in a moonlit garden, some young gentlemen-at-arms are revelling on the eve of their departure for Ferrara, on a mission to the Duke, Don Alfonso d'Este, fourth husband of Lucrezia Borgia. One of the revellers, Gennaro, falls asleep, and the rest retire. A masked female arrives in a gondola, dismisses her attendant, and, unmasking, breaks out into lyrical admiration of the slumbering youth; in the last line of her long and sickly song she mentions the fact that she is his mother, and proceeds to wake him with a kiss.

The awakened youth takes fire at once at the sight of this lady, as fair as she is kind. "Whom perceive I?" he cries in rapture, only to be repulsed by a coy "Oh! leave me, Sir!"

What follows is best given in the delicious English version of 1850:

HE.   Nay, nay, my gentle creature,
        I long to learn ev'ry feature!
        To Beauty ne'er I blind me!
SHE. Gennaro! can this be possible!
        Your breast for *me* doth warm?
        Speak candidly!
HE.   Then, by my knighthood, I love thee!
SHE. (*aside*). Too joyous!

But Gennaro is the soul of honour: "I must tell you," he says—

       There is a prior selection
       To whom I owe more affection!

He refers, it seems, to his mother—whom he has never seen—little dreaming that it is she with whom he is speaking! This ineffably silly scene is interrupted by the return of Gennaro's companions. The lady hastens to replace her mask—"To fly doth behove me!" she remarks ("struggling to free herself from Gennaro"). But it is too late—she is recognized, and they approach her each in turn with a mocking reverence. "Madam!" says the first, "my name is Maffio Orsini! you poisoned my brother!" "You murdered my uncle," says the second, "and stole his estate!" "And what did you not do to my nephew!" cries a third. Then, all together:

> She is wanton—a faithless betrayer!
> An incestuous night-loving slayer!
> Nature, owning abortion so hideous,
> Stands convulsed at the awful offence!

Meanwhile the indignant would-be lover of the lady is preparing to do battle for her honour, when Orsini tears the mask from her face and reveals the dreadful truth: "Look on her!" he cries, " 'tis the Borgia!"

Gennaro "dashes her from him with horror and detestation," the others hurry him from the scene, and Lucrezia is left alone, in tears and rage, to think out some dark scheme of vengeance.

The scene is transferred to Ferrara. Gennaro, after some late festivities, is saying farewell to his friends at the door of his house which faces the Ducal Palace. Charged by them, in jest, with cherishing a passion for the lovely, if infamous, Lucrezia, he proceeds to show his detestation of the lady in practical fashion. On one of the palace gates is a heraldic shield bearing the word

BORGIA

in raised letters; with his sword the young man strikes off the initial 'B,' leaving the horrid word

ORGIA

for all to jeer at. This ingenious insult is immediately punished. The Duke has long suspected his wife of being infatuated with Gennaro, and seizes this opportunity to have him arrested on the spot.

The next day Lucrezia, informed of the outrage but ignorant of its author, demands the instant punishment of the culprit; and the Duke gladly swears an oath, at her request, that he shall die before the day is ended. Gennaro is brought into the presence. Lucrezia, beside herself with remorse and fear when she sees how she has

146

been trapped, pleads desperately for his life; the Duke is inexorable, but, after Gennaro has been led out to prepare for death, tells his wife she may choose whether the culprit shall die by the sword or by poison—she decides on the latter. The prisoner is brought back; the Duke informs him that, in response to his wife's entreaties, he has resolved to pardon him, and pleasantly invites him to drink a parting cup before he goes. Two flagons stand ready, the silver and the gold—from the one the Duke and Duchess are served—the other holds the wine of the Borgias, the wine of death. From this the Duchess is made to fill a goblet and present it with her own hands to Gennaro, who unsuspectingly drinks it off. The Duke at once leaves the room with a smile of satisfaction on his face—for one who has drunk the wine of the Borgias is not likely to trouble him much longer. Lucrezia, however, is in possession of a remedy known only to herself; hastily revealing the truth, she makes Gennaro swallow the antidote, and assists him to escape by a secret door in the wall of the audience chamber.

Act II. Anyone who loves to sup on horrors might do worse than look in—already well fortified by a good dinner—on the last Act of *Lucrezia*. Dramatically it is not without merit of a certain kind—the action is swift, the contrasts undeniably effective; sensation can hardly go farther than the closing scene. The music is vigorous and full of garish colour; moreover, it includes the dashing 'brindisi,' *Il segreto per esse felice*, with which everyone is familiar.

Lucrezia has not forgotten her discomfiture of the opening scene; she has waited some time for her revenge, and now an operatic providence has placed her assailants in her power.

Still at Ferrara, we are invited to a midnight banquet

(the third in the opera) at the palace of the Princess Negroni, a close friend of the Borgia. Lucrezia's enemies, five in number, are all present, as well as Gennaro, who has accompanied his friend Orsini, a fact of which his infatuated mother is ignorant. A too boisterous incident in the revels has driven the ladies from the room; the men settle down to the serious business of drinking, and a special flagon of 'wine of Syracuse' is sent up for their better entertainment—it is, of course, the Borgian wine, the wine of death. Under its rousing influence Maffio Orsini—the gallant young captain who, for musical reasons, must be impersonated by a lady with a rich contralto—volunteers the drinking-song to which reference has been made, a reckless effusion in which we are exhorted to care not a hang for the morrow, so long as we're jolly to-night.

The noisy chorus which follows is killed by the tolling of a funeral bell—but the dare-devil Orsini still goes on. As the second verse proceeds the lamps are seen to grow gradually dimmer, until at the end but few are left alight; yet the stage is filled with a strange unfestal glare as the great doors of the banqueting-hall are slowly parted, to reveal a large apartment, hung all with black, and lit by the inverted torches that speak of death.

A procession of monks, black-robed and hooded to the eyes, advances slowly, chanting a mournful Latin psalm, and lines both sides of the hall, while a third rank is drawn across the far end of the inner chamber. The terror-stricken revellers attempt to escape, but find that every door is locked.

Now through the torchlight gloom is seen advancing with tragic stalk a woman's figure, trailing the sombre robes of death, a smile of awful triumph on her face as she salutes her victims: "Yes! look on me! 'Tis I, the Borgia! In Venice, Sirs, you entertained me finely—

148

now in Ferrara I return your kindness! I trust the Borgia's wine was to your liking!" At a sign from her the monks in the background, the Black Penitents that guard the secret of the inner chamber fall back on either side and disclose—shades of Mrs Radcliffe, Monk Lewis, and Maria Monk!—five coffins raised upon a platform, draped in black and set round with funeral tapers. Lucrezia is watching her wretched victims— already the poison has begun to work. "Gentlemen!" she says, "I see you have drunk deep! you may desire to slumber—see where your beds await you!"

But the Borgia has reckoned amiss. "Madame!" a clear voice cries behind her, "there are but five! Is there no resting-place for me?" She turns to find herself confronted with Gennaro, whose presence at the banquet she has never suspected. With a cry of horror the wretched woman bids the monks hurry her drooping, staggering victims from the room. The folding doors are shut; she is alone with the dying Gennaro.

[At this point the librettist has very wisely shied at the text from which he was working; those who wish to shudder, or laugh, at the impossible horrors of the original are referred to *Lucrèce Borgia*, the drama by Victor Hugo.]

A few drops of the precious antidote still remain; Lucrezia frantically implores Gennaro to swallow it in time, but he refuses to survive his comrades. Weak as he now is, the piteous farewells of his bosom friend Orsini, heard from the inner room, rouse him to fury; he seizes a knife and is about to rid the world of this monstrous woman when Lucrezia, driven to bay at last, reveals a part, at least, of her terrible secret: "Stay!" she cries, "thou darest not slay a Borgia, for thou thyself art one! Gennaro! dear Gennaro! *I am thy mother!*"

With this disclosure the horrors of the past seem all forgotten; Gennaro finds some strange consolation in dying in the arms of even such a mother, and Lucrezia, allowing herself time for a last *cabaletta,* falls dead upon his body.

Of the music as a whole there is little to be said; it is largely of the rocking-horse order, and generally undistinguished; the waltz tunes, marches, *boleros,* and *cabalettas* in which it abounds make excellent pianoforte duets for schoolroom practice. One number, Orsini's drinking-song (*Il segreto per esse felice*), is still an effective contralto solo for the concert platform.

Lucrezia, in short, belongs to "the palmy days of opera," the 'forties and 'fifties of the Victorian era, when the favourite singers of the day carried all before them. And this opera was well served: Mario chose it for his London *début;* Grisi, Brambilla, Tamburini, Lablache, and, later, the luscious Alboni, all seem to have revelled in the showy melodies and thrilling situations it offers. Titiens was probably the greatest interpreter of the name part, and sang it with superb effect a few days before her death. It was revived for Caruso not so long ago in New York, and there seems no reason why some exceptionally gifted soprano who fancies herself in the part of the lurid heroine should not bring *Lucrezia Borgia* once more into temporary popularity.

LUCIA DI LAMMERMOOR

Music by DONIZETTI. *Words by* CAMMARANO.
Naples, 1835; *London,* 1838; *New York,* 1845.

APART from the fact that our Queens of Song seem still to find in the part of Lucia an irresistible opportunity for vocal display, it is difficult to see why this opera retains its place in the repertory. The Waverley Novels, stripped of their atmosphere and their rich Scottish humour, are but dry bones at the best, and *The Bride of Lammermoor* emerges badly from the skeletonizing process. Scott's piteous romance of poor Lucy Ashton and the Master of Ravenswood, as treated by Donizetti's librettist, Cammarano, becomes a chronicle of gloom unrelieved by any lighter touches; a commonplace plot moves heavily through three Acts to the accompaniment of music that is at once pretentious and undistinguished; the various persons of the drama hardly admit of characterization, and Donizetti has attempted none, but, for the delight of amateurs of *il bel canto,* there is always the limelit heroine with her boundless prodigality of trills and *roulades,* vainly attempting to conceal the poverty of the melody under a tangle of trumpery ornament.

To the general public *Lucia* means the Mad Scene with its flute obbligato; the soprano romance, *Regnava nel silenzio,* the tenor solo, *Fra poco a me ricovero,* are to be found in all 'operatic albums,' and the sextet, *Chi me frena,* had an immense reputation until the advent of *Rigoletto,* with its famous quartet, *Un dì se ben rammentomi,* gave the *cognoscenti* something more deserving of their enthusiasm.

That the action is supposed to take place in Scotland just at the close of the seventeenth century need send no one to his Scottish history nor even to Scott's novel; this puppet drama is played in the shadowy region of operatic convention, which has scant relation to place or period.

Act I. There is little doing in the first Act. In the opening Scene we gather that there is an ancient feud between two noble families—that Enrico, who is in difficulties, ascribes all his bad luck to Edgardo, whom he hates accordingly. In order to repair his fallen fortunes Enrico has arranged to give his sister Lucia in marriage to the wealthy Arturo, before consulting her wishes in the matter, and is naturally furious on learning from his retainers that she has already given her heart to the hated Edgardo.

[It may be as well to explain that 'Enrico' stands for Sir Henry Ashton, 'Edgardo' for the Master of Ravenswood, 'Arturo' for Lord Arthur Bucklaw, while 'Lucia' is Lucy Ashton, the Bride of Lammermoor.]

Scene II shows us the moonlit garden and the fountain where Lucia is waiting for her lover; an elaborate solo on the harp forms an appropriate prelude to Lucia's air, *Regnava nel silenzio,* in which she relates how she had lately seen a spectral form appear beside the fountain which, to mark the occasion, had run with blood—an evil omen, thinks Lucia. And, indeed, ill news is on the way. Edgardo enters, only to tell her that they must part at once—he leaves for France that night; in a long duet they plight their solemn troth, and say farewell. [The sugary waltz-tune, *Verranno a te sull'aura,* must be noticed; it is usual to refer to it as one of the 'gems' of the opera.]

Act II. We do not get far in this Act before we discover that Enrico is a black-hearted fellow, as are also

Normanno, his henchman, and Raimondo, his chaplain: the three have conspired to wreck the happiness of poor Lucia.

Edgardo has now been for some months in France; he has never failed to write regularly to his affianced bride, but not a single letter has reached her—all· have been intercepted by her brother Enrico. Still worse, that gentleman has not hesitated to forge a letter showing that her lover has been faithless to his vows. Thus armed, and with the ready help of Raimondo, he works upon the heart of the unhappy girl until she has abandoned all hope, and then tells her that he himself is on the brink of ruin from which she alone can save him by an immediate marriage with Arturo. Lucia's consent is at last wrung from her. Arturo arrives, the guests assemble (to the music of a choral march, *Per te d'immenso giubilo,* which is first cousin to the first Druids' chorus in *Norma*), the marriage-contract is produced, and Lucia has just signed it when Edgardo makes a dramatic entry, in time to confound the guilty, but too late to save the wretched lovers from their doom.

All are paralysed for the moment—"Edgardo! oh thunderbolt!" is Lucia's strange remark—and the great sextet *Chi mi frena?* begins.

Those who are familiar with the quartet in *Rigoletto* are not likely to be greatly impressed by this composition for six voices, only three of which attain to individual importance. The music throws little light on the situation, but from the words we gather that Lucia's stony despair admits not even the relief of tears, that Edgardo is torn between love and a desire for revenge, while Enrico is a prey to late remorse—Normanno, Raimondo, and Alisa (Lucia's *confidante*) serve merely to fill in the harmonies.

The sextet over, Edgardo's wrath against the treacherous Enrico seems likely to get the better of him, when the chaplain, Raimondo, comes suddenly into the lime-light; after cautioning Edgardo against the wickedness of harbouring revenge—he even quotes Scripture for his purpose—he proceeds to convince him of the hope-lessness of his case by drawing his attention to Lucia's signature on the contract of marriage.

Edgardo, in a frenzy, flings his engagement ring at Lucia's feet, and demands his own in return; he then requests to be butchered immediately, in order that Lucia may have the pleasure of trampling on his bleeding corpse on her way to the altar with Arturo.

The six solo voices are now "supported by the entire strength of the company," and the result is one of Doni-zetti's most substantial *finales,* conventional and rather colourless, but undeniably effective.

Act III opens with a stormy scene between Edgardo and Enrico; in a long hammer-and-tongs duet they express a mutual desire for each other's blood, and arrange for the inevitable duel, which the Master of Ravenswood insists shall be fought among the tombs of his ancestors.

A jubilant chorus of retainers is interrupted by Rai-mondo, who breaks the awful news—Lucia's reason has given way, and she has murdered poor Arturo in their bridal chamber!

The heroine now wanders on to the scene to show us that, whatever the state of her mind may be, she has her voice under perfect control. The meanderings of dis-traught maidens, on the lyric stage at least, are apt to run on much the same lines both in matter and method, and Lucia, in her Mad Scene, has points of resemblance with sleep-walking Amina, Dinorah with her shadow, and Marguerite in prison.

In the opening andante, *Il dolce suono,* she imagines herself once more in the moonlit garden waiting for Edgardo [the orchestral reference to her earlier solo, *Verranno a te sull'aura,* anticipates Gounod's masterly use of this device in the Prison Scene in *Faust*], but the phantom rises from the fountain, as of old, and puts the dream to flight. Now, like Amina, she is standing with her beloved at the altar (*Ardon l'incensi*) and life henceforth is to be a heaven on earth. [It is at this point that the flute obbligato is introduced with such happy effect.] But the entrance of Enrico recalls the signing of the marriage-contract, and its awful consequences; again, in fancy, Edgardo stands before her, but only to denounce and cast her off for ever, and poor Lucia exhausts herself in a piteous appeal for forgiveness. At last in the aria *Spargi d'amaro pianto* she resigns herself to the approach of death; Enrico will mourn over her ashes, while she, in heaven, will pray or their swift reunion.

It is a pity that the opera cannot end here—but Edgardo, of course, has to be provided for. To the tomb of his ancestors he comes in the last Scene, not, however, to fight the intended duel; before Enrico can arrive he hears of Lucia's death and puts an end to his own existence, impatient to join his beloved in the skies (*Fra poco a me ricovero*).

It is difficult to say much in favour of *Lucia* as an opera, and easy enough to laugh at the Mad Scene, but, after all, ours is not an age that can afford to discourage such vocal exhibitions; there are not many sopranos to-day who can do justice to its extremely difficult passages, and, should the tradition wholly die out, it would be a real calamity for the singer's art. The prima donna who in the great air from *L'Étoile du Nord,* in *Ombra leggiera* from *Dinorah,* or in the Mad Scene from *Lucia* can triumphantly assert her claim to rival the competing flautist, deserves all possible praise, since she reminds us of what we are too apt to forget—that the human voice is æsthetically the most beautiful, and may be made the most perfect, of all instruments.

LA FILLE DU REGIMENT

Music by DONIZETTI. *Words by* BAYARD *and* ST GEORGES.
Paris, 1840; *New Orleans,* 1843; *London,* 1847.

LA FILLE DU RÉGIMENT, better known to us
in the Italian, *La Figlia del Reggimento,* was
written in 1840, toward the end of the composer's career; like most of his work it strikes our modern
ears as painfully thin, such musical interest as it possesses being confined to the popular numbers *Ciascun lo
dice, Convien partir,* and the *Rat-a-plan* Chorus.

The libretto is of little merit, but it had the advantage
of introducing a new type to the operatic stage in Marie,
the *vivandière,* and a certain piquancy is introduced by
placing the heroine in two well-contrasted settings—the
freedom of camp life, and the old-fashioned proprieties
of the castle. At the same time, it must be confessed
that the 'book' is naïve to the verge of banality; the
fact that it is so emphatically *pour les jeunes filles* has
undoubtedly contributed largely to its popularity in
England.

The part of Marie was a favourite with a succession
of prima donnas in the Victorian era, Jenny Lind being
the most illustrious example; but it is hardly likely in the
present century to appeal to any artist of the first rank.

Act I. The scene is a valley in the Austrian Tyrol,
which at the time is in the occupation of Napoleon's
army. There has evidently been a skirmish in the neighbourhood just before the rise of the curtain, for we find
a chorus of ladies on their knees, entreating heaven to
protect them against the foe, and a ridiculous Countess
in a fainting condition, being supported to a seat by

157

her servant, Ortensio; she is evidently a prey to war's alarms, and hints darkly to Ortensio of terrible experiences in the past. But, the last shot fired, and the danger over for the present, the Countess retires to a cottage, while the frightened peasants gather together and break out into a chorus of "Tra-la-la!" according to the well-known custom of their country.

Sulpizio, a French sergeant, now swaggers in to tell how the Tyrolese took to their heels; and close behind him comes Marie, the pride, the pet, the Daughter of the Regiment. The regiment is her official father, so to speak, but she regards each man in it as her particular papa, more especially the sergeant, who found her, a mere infant, abandoned on the field of battle, and has brought her up in the lap of the army. And in her duet with Sulpizio she knows plainly that she takes after her father—or fathers; she is all for "allonging and marshonging"—"Plan-rat-a-plan!" comes as naturally to her lips as does "Tra-la-la!" to those of the Tyrolean peasant.

Still, there are other things to be thought about; as Sulpizio reminds her, she is getting a big girl now and it is time she got married; she has the whole regiment to choose from, and hardly a man of them but would be glad to exchange his paternity for a tenderer relationship. Pardon!—but she has chosen already, and *not* from the regiment! He is just a young Tyrolese, Tonio by name, who recently saved her from falling over a precipice.

A noise without—and on come the soldiers, dragging Tonio with them; he is suspected of spying, and must die the death. Marie's explanations, however, soon alter their attitude; a friends of hers is a friend of theirs; so they must clink glasses together, and, as the rum goes round, the Daughter of the Regiment shall sing them the song they love best to hear, *Ciascun lo dice,* a catchy, spirited tune in praise of "the glorious Twenty-first." The drums are heard beating the roll-call, and the soldiers march off, taking Tonio with them. He manages to give them the slip, however, and in less than no time is back at Marie's side for his share in a love-duet of unsophisticated but not ungraceful humour. The sergeant, indignant at finding him there, puts a stop to all further philandering by the blunt declaration that none but a soldier of the glorious Twenty-first may aspire to the hand of the Daughter of the Regiment. Tonio accepts the decision, but is of opinion that the obstacle is not insurmountable, and retires to see what can be done.

Now re-enters the Countess, still in a highly nervous condition, to beg a military escort to see her safe to her Castle of Birkenfeld; the name awakens memories in Sulpizio's mind in connexion with the finding of Marie; a paper found on her at the time, and now produced by the sergeant, establishes the fact of her aristocratic birth, and the Countess claims her as her niece. "I trust," adds the stately dame, "that Marie has been educated as becomes a lady!" "Oh, perfectly!" says the sergeant, "her manners are most correct!" At this instant the voice of the young 'lady' is heard behind the scenes, swearing like the little trooper that she is: *"Parbleu! Morbleu! Corbleu!"*—a whole string of horrid oaths! The shocked Countess, however, makes the best of it, and hurries her reluctant niece away, to instruct her in the responsibilities of her new position.

The soldiers once more crowd the stage. After the popular noise of the famous *Rat-a-plan* Chorus has died away, Tonio reappears, with the French colours in his cap, and succeeds in convincing Marie's assembled 'fathers' that he is now as eligible a suitor for her hand

as any other man—besides, she happens to prefer him,
so there's an end of it! The brave fellows take the
philosophical view:

> Then she has selected!
> 'Tis most unexpected!
> But yet, if she loves him,
> She *must* be his wife!

But Tonio's dream of happiness is shattered by the
return of Marie, in the custody of the Countess; the
Daughter of the Regiment is on her way to the Castle
of Birkenfeld, to assume her rightful position in high
society; she must leave her low associations behind her,
and try to forget that she was ever the humble comrade
of "a brutal and licentious soldiery." Such at least is
the Countess's view. But Marie feels differently; with
a breaking heart she prepares to take farewell of her
dear companions, in music worthy of the pathetic situation. *Convien partir* is one of those really lovely and
significant melodies with which Donizetti occasionally
surprises us; it stands side by side with *O mio Fernando*
(*La Favorita*) and *Una furtiva lagrima* (*L'Elisir
d'Amore*), and is likely to live long after the opera has
ceased to be performed.

The interest is well sustained in the short *finale* that
ends the Act. With tears in her voice and on her cheek,
Marie takes leave of them one by one—Pietro, Matio,
dear old Tomasso—Sulpizio she embraces fondly, to the
scandal of her aunt; as for Tonio, well, they part to
meet again. The chorus meanwhile console themselves
by consigning the Countess to the care of the Devil for
robbing them of their treasure; they present arms as
Marie passes through their ranks, and as the curtain
falls Tonio is seen to tear the French ribbon from his
cap and trample it underfoot.

Act II. We find Marie unhappy amid the luxurious

160

surroundings, the old-fashioned etiquette, of the Castle of Birkenfeld. She is being trained in the elegant accomplishments—to dance the minuet, to sing the 'classical' compositions beloved by the Countess; worst of all, she is to be married to the Duke of Crakenthorpe without delay. Her only comfort is that old Sulpizio, the sergeant—for reasons purely operatic, apparently—is still allowed to attend her.

The Countess enters, in a gorgeous toilette, to perfect Marie in a song with which she is to charm the company that evening, a *canzonetta* by the *maestro* Caffariello. While the former Daughter of the Regiment sings, to the Countess's accompaniment, of the loves of Venus and the woes of Philomela, Sulpizio sits gloomily by, exchanging sympathetic asides with Marie on the dullness of such stuff compared with the jolly camp-songs they sang together in happier days. At last, when the Countess requires her niece to "sing like a nightingale" the limits of endurance are reached; carried away by a flood of old associations, they throw etiquette to the winds, and break out into the rowdy *Rat-a-plan*, "allonging and marshonging," up and down the room to the disgust of the dignified old lady, who goes out in high dudgeon. The sergeant, too, is fetched away to speak with a wounded soldier, who is waiting for him outside—some ruse of Tonio's, he suspects. Left to herself, Marie sings of her constant longing for her old companions of the army; she has just ended on the theme of her air in Act I (*Convien partir*) when the roll of approaching drums rouses her to a wild enthusiasm, as the boys of the Twenty-first pour on to the stage for a joyful reunion. Tonio, of course, with a wounded arm, is among them, and—the rest having retired for refreshment—he, Marie, and the sergeant join a really spirited trio, *Stretti insiem tutti tre,* which well deserves attention. This is the last point of interest in the very huddled finale. The Countess confesses to Sulpizio that she is actually Marie's mother, and proceeds to use her maternal influence to hurry on her daughter's wedding with the Duke. However, the regiment, headed by Tonio, returns to enter a vigorous protest against any such coercion, and quite prepared to enforce their 'paternal' claims by direct action, if necessary. Fortunately the Countess, moved by her daughter's grief and Tonio's obvious devotion, consents to their union; she joins their hands amid general cheers, and a patriotic chorus, *Salvezza alla Francia!* led by Marie, brings down the curtain, and assures us that the Daughter of the Regiment will always remain faithful to her adopted fatherland.

LES HUGUENOTS

Music by MEYERBEER. *Words by* SCRIBE *and* DESCHAMPS.
Paris, 1836; *London,* 1842; *New York,* 1850.

THE name of Meyerbeer means little more to the present generation than three popular vocal pieces, *Nobil signor, O mon fils,* and *Ombra leggiera;* yet each of the operas from which these are taken —*Les Huguenots, Le Prophète,* and *Dinorah* respectively—was a prime favourite with the public up to the end of the last century—the first-named was given as late as 1912 at Covent Garden, and at the Metropolitan Opera House, New York, in 1918. Should there come a Meyerbeer revival, the choice would probably fall on this opera.

Yet it is doubtful if *Les Huguenots* would ever regain its former popularity in England. It belongs to an age of grandiosity quite alien to our own; it makes no strong emotional appeal; as a spectacle it has been superseded by *Aïda;* and, musically, it certainly does not contain the seed of immortality. On the other hand, there is no denying its strong superficial attractions; those who demand the pomp of Courts, marching soldiers, brawling mobs, duels, bells, and cannonades will find here all they want. The piece is like some crowded historical canvas, showily painted. Showy, too, is the music—showy and vastly clever, but having too often that ring of insincerity with which so much of Meyerbeer's work is chargeable. The best plea, perhaps, that can be urged for its retention in the repertory is that it furnishes an almost unique opportunity for vocal display; for its adequate performance it demands no less than six singers of the first rank, thoroughly schooled in all the brilliance and elegance of style which seems essential to this opera. This, it need hardly be remarked, is at the same time a formidable obstacle to its revival. At the Metropolitan Opera House, New York, in the winter of 1894, *Les Hugue-nots* was given with Melba, Nordica, Scalchi, Maurel, Plançon, and the two De Reszkes. An impresario who can get together a cast like that may put on *Les Hugue-nots* any time he likes with a fair certainty of being able to run it for just so long as his singers hold out.

The first thing that strikes us about this opera is that there is altogether too much of it—that the five Acts are crowded with too much noise, too much *bravura,* too much plotting, too many improbable incidents, with the actual Massacre of St Bartholomew's Day as an over-whelming *finale.* At first we are inclined to grumble at a plot which seems to require almost as much prepara-tory study as *The Ring* itself; but, soon or late, we come to see that the whole thing resolves itself into the tortu-ous love-story of Raoul and Valentine, shown up against a highly coloured historical background.

Raoul de Nangis is a Huguenot gentleman, Valentine the daughter of a Catholic noble, the Count St. Bris. The lady is betrothed to the Duke de Nevers, a Catholic like herself; but Marguerite de Valois, who, though a Catholic, is espoused to the Protestant Henry of Navarre, is anxious to reconcile the two political-reli-gious parties, and so determines to break Valentine's engagement with Nevers, and marry her to Raoul instead. This is the situation when the play begins. The Scene is in Touraine, the year 1572, and, for the benefit of readers with a theological bias, it may be well to state that all the characters are Catholic, with the exception of the Huguenot Raoul de Nangis, and Marcel, his grim old Puritan retainer.

Act I. The short Prelude, an ingenious setting of the Lutheran chorale *Ein' feste Burg,* serves rather to emphasize the title of the opera than as a key to its contents. With the rise of the curtain, it is true, there is just a little talk of both religion and politics—the great names of Medici, Coligny, and Calvin are mentioned—but we soon pass to lighter topics. The Count de Nevers is entertaining his brothers-in-arms at a banquet, to which they cannot sit down before the arrival of an expected stranger, Raoul de Nangis, whom, although a Huguenot, he is desirous of treating with special courtesy; there is a movement in the Catholic party toward an agreement with the Protestants, and Raoul is necessary for their purpose. The young Huguenot on his entry proves to be as comely a figure as any in the room, and breathes quite freely in the atmosphere of gallantry that prevails. To pass the time it is suggested that each hot young lover shall reveal the secret of his heart. As for Nevers, he confesses that his is already plighted in earnest—no more amorous adventures for him! Raoul too, it appears, is very much in love, but with little more than a fleeting vision, a "phantom of delight"; in the romance *Plus blanche que la blanche hermine,* he tells us how he rescued, lately, a lady fair from insult, how she raised her veil, gave him one smile and left him, and how henceforth he is her slave for evermore. While a merry toast is being drunk in Raoul's honour, a booming bass breaks in upon their chorus—it is his old servant Marcel, a fanatical Huguenot who, shocked to see his master thus consorting with the ungodly, strikes up the Lutheran chant of the Prelude (*Ein' feste Burg*) as a protection against the Powers of Evil. The amused company hear him out to the end and even clamour for more. The grim old Puritan relaxes so far as to give them a longer and far livelier performance; this is the famous *Piff! Paff!* a fine rollicking ditty in spite of its ferocious sentiments, "Down with the Pope, and a plague on all women!"

This outburst against femininity is, very fittingly, the cue that brings the first woman on the scene. A veiled lady passes across the back of the stage, attended by a servant who presently summons Nevers to wait on his mistress. Here is an adventure indeed to the taste of the jolly company! After their host has left the room their curiosity rises to a pitch where manners are forgotten—they crowd eagerly to the window, and there, in the garden, is the loveliest of ladies in earnest conversation with the young Count. They are so enthusiastic about her beauty that even Raoul is tempted to take a look. The next moment he regrets his action, for there, in close communication with Nevers, is the fair one of whom he has already told us. The others, whom of course he takes into his confidence, must have their laugh at him in a gay little chorus, but this time they, as well as Raoul, have read the situation wrongly. The audience, however, are not left longer in the dark. Nevers is seen in the corridor to take a most respectful farewell of the lady; then, managing to evade his guests, he comes to the footlights and lets us into the secret. The lady is or was his *fiancée,* and a maid of honour to Marguerite de Valois, Queen of Navarre; at her royal mistress's command she has come to ask Nevers to release her from her engagement, for reasons of state. "To this," says Nevers, "I am bound, as a gentleman, to consent; at the same time, I must say, I am infernally annoyed" or, in the politer language of the English version:

As a courteous knight I my promise engage,
But I secretly burn with direst rage.

[Here we have an excellent example of the difficulties
presented by the ordinary opera libretto; this explanation by Nevers is absolutely necessary to the understanding of the plot, yet, conveyed as it is in a single page of
dry recitative, it is almost sure to pass unnoticed by the
audience.]

Nevers now turns again to his guests, who have
scarcely time to rally him over his supposed new conquest when they are interrupted by a new arrival. This
is a page, a glittering, impressive, and, as we shall soon
find, far too florid page. His name is Urbain. [Urbain
started his career as a high soprano, but when, in 1844,
the luscious-voiced Alboni ("Venus-contralto," as Walt
Whitman calls her) took a fancy to the music, Meyerbeer rearranged it to suit her voice, since when most of
the great contraltos have revelled in the part.]

To Urbain is assigned the best-known number in the
opera, generally referred to as *Nobil signor,* which are
the first words of the Italian version of the recitative.
The air, made so pretentious by its trills, *roulades,* and
cadenzas, has but the slightest dramatic significance; it
merely tells us that the page is the bearer of a letter from
a great lady to one of the present company. Nevers
naturally concludes that he is the man; but no, the letter
is for le Sieur Raoul de Nangis, who reads it aloud for
our benefit. The lady's request is a strange one: Raoul,
after allowing himself to be blindfolded, is to be conducted by Urbain into her presence; as to who she is,
and what her object may be, not a word is said. The
young man's amazement on reading the letter changes
to utter bewilderment at finding himself the centre of
extravagant interest—the others crowd around him with
most obsequious congratulations on his good fortune;

love and luxury, power and glory, all these, they hint, are henceforth his for the taking. The only discordant voice is that of old Marcel, who scents the world, the flesh, and the Devil in such irregular doings, and bawls out a few staves of a *Te Deum* to keep the enemy at bay. The explanation of the company's change of attitude toward Raoul is simple enough; Nevers and the others have seen the seal and signature of the letter, and have recognized them for those of the greatest lady in the land.

The young Huguenot is led submissively away by the giddy page. This is the second time since the rise of the curtain that he has found himself involved in mystery; first came the affair of the veiled lady in the garden, and now we have this strange summons from the fair unknown, who is evidently accustomed to be obeyed. The audience are left almost equally in the dark as to the real significance of the two incidents; however, we have only to wait for the explanation till the next Act, when we shall find them to be intimately connected.

Act II. This is often played as the second Scene of Act I, but even by itself it is rather a formidable affair when given in its entirety. It deals with Raoul's interview with the sender of the letter—who is no less a person than Marguerite de Valois, Queen of Navarre—his introduction to Valentine, the bride she has selected for him, his violent rejection of the alliance, and the consequent quarrel between him and the lady's father, the proud St Bris. The dramatic content, it will be seen, is not large in itself, but the Act is considerably inflated by show pieces for the solo voices and other music of a purely decorative nature.

We begin with a long and brilliant *scena* for Marguerite de Valois. The scene is in the garden of her castle of Chenonceaux; seated in her pavilion by the riverside, revelling in the beauty of a perfect day in her own fair land of Touraine, she sings the praises of nature and the joys of life and love, *O beau pays de la Touraine!* It is plain that the gloomy band of Puritans will find no favour at her Court. Echoing her lively mood, her ladies furnish a graceful harmonic background for the vocal fireworks of their mistress, who ends with an air of a more vigorous character, *À ce mot tout s'anime.* Urbain the page is, of course, in attendance. In this Scene he finds ample opportunity to show himself a true descendant of his more famous predecessor Cherubino; he is in love with every one of the maids of honour, and with his royal mistress most of all.

And here comes another fair one with whom he falls in love at first sight. This is the veiled lady whom we saw in Nevers' garden, sent thither, we remember, by the royal command. Her name, we learn, is Valentine, daughter of the Count de St Bris. She has but a short interview with the Queen, who tells her of the project she has formed for marrying her to Raoul. Valentine offers no objection, and retires to prepare herself for her prospective bridegroom, to whom we may assume her to be, in elegant Victorian language, 'not indifferent.'

Here follows what is generally known as the Bathing Chorus. The ladies of the Court retire to a shady grove close to the river bank and entertain us pleasantly with song and dance; the amount of actual bathing permitted depends, of course, upon the taste and discretion of the management. In any case, the Queen does well in banishing from such a scene the amorous page who is caught lurking in the bushes; the next moment, however, he is here again to announce the arrival of a young nobleman; the ladies need not fear him—his eyes are safely bandaged! This, of course, is Raoul, for whose admittance the Queen at once gives orders. Meanwhile the irrepressible Urbain takes the stage with a lively solo (written in for Alboni), "No, no, no, no!" in which he relates the sensation caused among the villagers by the sight of a cavalier with bandaged eyes being led through the streets to the castle by the Queen's own page—how the boys made fun of him, while the girls pelted him with flowers! Urbain paints so vivid a picture that the ladies are all curiosity to see this mysterious personage. On his entry they move on tiptoe around the blindfolded man, peering into his face and singing, or whispering, a really dainty and effective little duet, *Le Voilà!*; they can scarcely tear themselves away even when the Queen arrives and orders all to leave the room.

Raoul and Marguerite de Valois are now alone. The long duet *Beauté divine! Enchanteresse!* is little more than an elaborate and graceful vocal exercise for two gifted singers; the musical texture, a thing of shreds and patches, is scarcely adequate even for the expression of the artificial sentiment. Raoul is dazzled by the gracious beauty of his royal mistress, who is by no means indifferent to the charm of his youthful ardour. Words and music alike are mere tinsel, and not too well put together. After the Queen has explained her reasons for summoning Raoul to her presence and prepared him for the meeting with Valentine, on whom he is supposed never to have set eyes before, we pass to matter more worthy of Meyerbeer's peculiar talent.

To the strains of what is described as a minuet, though sadly lacking in the grace which we usually associate with that measure, her Majesty's subjects assemble to do her homage; Catholics and Protestants in about equal numbers, they give occasion for one of those crowded scenes which the composer so loved to handle. After the Queen has introduced Raoul to the company she requires that all shall in her presence swear an oath to keep the peace and lay the foundation of an enduring friendship. With lamb-like submission, though with voices of thunder, the Huguenots and their inveterate foes, the Catholics, with hands upraised to heaven, proceed to take the solemn oath demanded of them: "By the faith of our fathers, by the honour of our swords, by the fealty to our King, by the God of all truth, we swear to keep the bond of everlasting peace and friendship!"

Amidst the tremendous volume of sound one dissentient voice has no effect; we must search the printed page to find how carefully that stout old Protestant, Marcel, while keeping time with the rest, contrives to alter the words so as to satisfy his conscience—courtiers may swear their souls away, but Marcel is not one of them: "Neither friendship nor peace will I swear," he sings, "and may God turn my master from the error of his ways!"

All this hard choral swearing is perhaps more noisy than convincing, and we are grateful for the relief of even a short unaccompanied passage quietly sung; but, once started on his sonorous career, Meyerbeer was always ready to go from strength to strength—the *ensemble* with which the Act concludes almost wipes out the impression of the one from which we are just recovering. Truth to tell, there is good reason here for sound and fury. The business of the oath concluded, Marguerite proceeds to bring Raoul face to face, for the first time as she supposes, with his future bride. The Queen's hopes are centred in this union, and she has no misgivings as to the issue of their meeting; like the *"jeune et brave Dunois"* of a later Queen's imagining, Raoul is "bravest of the brave," while Valentine is "fairest of the fair"—surely they were made for one another! Valentine enters on the arm of her father, the haughty

171

St Bris. Raoul starts back in horror. In the lovely vision before him he recognizes one whom he has already seen on two occasions—she is the maiden in distress whom he had succoured and who had become for a time the idol of his dreams, but, alas, she is also the veiled madame whose compromising visit to Nevers had meant for Raoul such a rude awakening. He turns away with a sneer: "What! ally myself with her! Never!"

No wonder if "most things twinkled after that!" In the general uproar that follows we distinguish the indignant amazement of the Queen, the despair of Valentine, the furious wrath of St Bris and Nevers, and the bewilderment of the chorus, who sing throughout in a sustained *fortissimo*. The outraged father is for taking instant vengeance on Raoul for this gross insult, and it needs all the Queen's authority to make them postpone the inevitable conflict. A welcome touch of character is added by old Marcel, who throughout the tumult consoles himself by calling good Dr Luther to his aid, and in the pauses of the chorus is allowed to bawl out snatches of *Ein' feste Burg* without attracting the least attention.

Act III. The scene is the *Pré-aux-clercs* in the late 16th century—a good opportunity for the presentment of old Paris with the glamour of the Middle Ages still hanging about her. But let no one look for the atmosphere of Hugo's romances—we must try, too, to forget the wonderful pictures of mediæval life in Wagner's *Mastersingers*. Meyerbeer has no such magician's wand. The result of his collaboration with Scribe in this opera has been compared to Shakespearean drama, and to the novels of Sir Walter Scott; it reminds us rather of the puppet-plays for which, as children, we used to cut out the coloured figures and mount them on cardboard.

However, we have here a brave array of puppets, a

rich background, plenty of action, and more than enough of noise. The essentials for the stage setting are as large an open space as possible, a church on one side, and a tavern on the other.

It must be understood that, as a set-off to Raoul's contemptuous rejection of Valentine, it has been decided to marry her at once to Nevers, her former *fiancé;* it is already the evening of the day which has been chosen for the ceremony.

First to fill the stage are a crowd of citizens, who inform us that this is a day for feasting, a fact confirmed by the noisy groups of Huguenot soldiers seated round the tavern—roaring fellows, who drink to the health of Coligny, and down with the Catholics! [Another famous "*Rat-a-plan* Chorus," in which the singers clap their hands in time to their vocal imitation of the drum.] In contrast to this boisterous outburst comes a procession of Catholic ladies chanting an *Ave Maria* on their way to the church, where Valentine and her father are passing the time previous to the nuptial ceremony which is to take place, apparently, about midnight. The Protestants do their best to drown the gentler voices with their *rat-a-plan,* to the great indignation of the populace, who are only prevented from falling on them by the opportune arrival of a troop of gipsies, introduced solely for the purpose of the ballet which follows.

When the stage is clear again, St Bris, with an attendant, appears from the church and is met by Marcel, who brings a letter from his master, Raoul, challenging St Bris to mortal combat, at short notice, and in that very place. Having signified his acceptance, St Bris consults with his friend how best to secure the death of Raoul, by fair means or foul; it is agreed that should fortune favour the young Huguenot in the duel there shall be those lurking near who will quickly despatch him.

The curfew now rings out and sends all Paris hurrying home to bed. The stage is empty and nearly dark.

Out of the darkness emerge two figures—Valentine, who comes from the church in deep distress, and Marcel, determined to be within his master's call in the hour of peril. In the interminable duet that follows, *Dans la nuit où seul je veille* (which might well be passed over in silence so far as its musical interest is concerned), Valentine tells Marcel of the trap that is being laid for Raoul, the details of which she has overheard; she also confesses that her love is all given to the young Huguenot, for whom she is prepared to die should need arise. She re-enters the church, and Marcel lurks in the shadow, as the combatants Raoul and St Bris arrive on the scene, each with his brace of seconds. With Marcel in the background, all six of them advance to the footlights and join in the admired septet *En mon bon droit j'ai confiance,* in which they swear by all that is holy to conduct the affair in strict accordance with the code of honour, "Each for himself, and God for all!" It is plain, however, that certain of these gentlemen do protest too much, for Marcel presently detects no less than three armed men stealthily approaching, prepared to lend most dishonourable assistance to the cause of St Bris. The faithful old servant starts up in their path, and things begin to look ominous both for him and his master, when from within the tavern is heard the rousing *Rat-a-plan!* of the Huguenot soldiers, to which Marcel replies with a stentorian version of his favourite Lutheran chorale. In quick response, his comrades pour out of the tavern, followed by a band of Catholic students, also warmed with drink. Women of both parties spring up from somewhere to join in the fray, and a most lively struggle is in progress when the arrival of the Queen brings all to their senses.

The remainder of the Act is kaleidoscopic. St Bris and Marcel both lay their different accounts of the quarrel before the Queen, each accusing the other side of treachery, when the old Huguenot produces his chief witness in the person of Valentine, who again comes forward from the church. Valentine it was who overheard the plot and revealed it to Marcel! But why? In whose interest? Amid the general astonishment the Queen, with an amazing lack of discretion, proceeds to tell Raoul the truth—or at least a part of it; Valentine's visit to Nevers, she hints, originated in her own wish to break off an engagement which she detested—Raoul has always been the choice of her heart. This disclosure, however flattering to Raoul, comes rather late to afford him much consolation. It is followed immediately by the arrival of the lucky man, Nevers; he comes in a gorgeously illuminated state barge to bear Valentine away to the scene of their midnight nuptials. Here, of course, is all the material for a colossal *finale*. In addition to the usual orchestra there is a band of music on board, both of which support, or possibly drown, the huge body of singers in one of the most blatant of choruses, as the bridal procession is formed and passes on to the barge. The tumult of the mob is by no means ended, and Huguenots and Catholics are still hard at it till the very fall of the curtain, breathing out threatenings and slaughter one against the other, in sad contrast to the peace and friendship they had sworn at the beginning of the Act.

Act IV. This is the best-esteemed Act in the opera, largely on account of the impressive Scene known as "The Blessing of the Poniards," and was often chosen to form part of those mixed programmes which we associate with state and gala performances. We are in Nevers' castle, to which he has brought home his not too willing bride. Poor Valentine opens with a *romance* (for which a long recitative is sometimes substituted) concerned with her love for Raoul and her struggle to drive his image from her heart. Raoul, made reckless by the Queen's revelation of the truth, promptly appears on the scene, merely, as he says, to see her once again and then to die. His wish seems likely to be fulfilled without delay, as the voice of St Bris is heard without. Valentine has just time to hide her lover behind the curtain when her father, Nevers, and a number of their adherents enter the room. St Bris would have his daughter retire, but Nevers obtains permission for her to stay —perhaps with a view to the effective assistance she is able to lend in the coming *ensemble*.

Neither here nor throughout the Scene does the music suggest the horror of the purpose for which they have met together—nothing less than to plot the extermination of all the Huguenots in Paris that very night, the Eve of St Bartholomew. One voice alone is raised in protest—Nevers will never consent to stain his ancestral sword by such ignoble butchery! He is promptly arrested and led away. St Bris is left to work up the feelings of the others: the evils that affect the realm, the dangers that threaten the Royal House, the plots and conspiracies that are everywhere afoot, all are the work of that accursed band of heretics, the Huguenots! It is time to make an end, to wipe them from the face of the earth! Are all agreed? They are agreed; it is the King's command—it is the will of Heaven!

St Bris then proceeds to allot to each man his place and share in the coming massacre. Coligny, the leader of the Huguenots, must be the first to fall; afterward, all must assemble at the Tour de Nesle; the signal will be the tolling of the great bell of St Germain.

176

For such a holy enterprise one thing, of course, is needed—the sanction of Holy Church. All swords are drawn and solemnly blest by three monks who, led vocally by St Bris, proceed to work the others up to a state of frenzy by their bloodthirsty exhortations:

> Holy and sacred swords, receive Heaven's
> blessing!
> Eternal wreaths of glory
> Shall deck the warrior's brow
> Who now, great Heaven, before thee
> Shall make the impious bow!
> No pity for them show!
> Let none escape your vengeance!
> Our swords shall lay them low!
> 'Tis Heaven wills it so!

[So much for the black villainy of the Monastic Orders! As a companion picture old opera-goers may recall the renegade nuns whose restless phantoms figure in the churchyard ballet in *Robert le Diable*.]

After St Bris has distributed the white badges marked with a cross by which his party may be recognized, the entire chorus line up to the footlights, brandish their swords, and give vent to their feelings in a 'barbaric *yawp*' to which we feel a war-dance would be the appropriate accompaniment: "Strike them down and show no quarter! Let not one of them escape!"

> So shall we gain the grace of Heaven
> And all our sins shall be forgiven!

The monks, in giving a final blessing, implore them to go softly; they even exhort each other to silence with the words:

> Whisper low! Not a word,
> Not a breath should be heard!

But all in vain—the holy zeal within them burns too fiercely for restraint; once more do they return to the footlights and rend the air with a mighty shout of "Heaven's will be done!"

Such is the famous Scene which so impressed our forefathers; it belongs frankly to the 'palmy days' of Italian opera, when the immense chandelier with its blaze of cut-glass lustres that hung from the roof of Covent Garden Theatre seemed like the presiding spirit of the place. The situation is effective, if absurd, and, with adequate performers, must always make a sensation through mere violence and volume of sound, but, musically, it would be difficult to find its defender at the present day; we feel that here, at least, Meyerbeer deserves the hardest things that have been said of him.

Happily the Act does not end here, and the duet that follows between Raoul and Valentine is the one number in the opera which musicians have agreed to praise, *Oh ciel, où courez-vous?* It is of great length and of supreme dramatic importance, as it is not only the *finale* of an Act, but constitutes the end of the opera as usually played. As soon as the stage is clear Raoul comes from his hiding-place and rushes to the door, but is stopped by Valentine, who uses every persuasion to prevent his going. His situation is a terrible one—he burns to fly to his comrades and warn them of the coming disaster—even now it may be too late—and here is Valentine, his one and only love, imploring him to stay. The conflict between love and duty could hardly be more poignantly presented. Duty holds her own, and Raoul makes another attempt to go, when Valentine throws herself in front of the door: "Nay, nay! not to thy death! Or, if thou diest, I will die with thee! For know, Raoul, I love thee!" To Raoul at last has come, if only for a brief moment, the realization of his dream of love, and he abandons himself to it wholly.

[The long section *Tu l'as dit, oui, tu m'aimes!* con-

178

tains perhaps the best melody Meyerbeer ever wrote, of
a kind which finds an echo in Gounod and Saint-Saëns.]

Valentine's distress is intense—she is conscious of the
guilty nature of her love, and is torn by anxiety for her
beloved's safety; Raoul is lost in an ecstasy, and for
the time has no other thought but her. The awakening comes with the ominous booming of the slaughter.
Already the flames light up the Scene; Raoul sees in
imagination the Seine run red with blood, the dead
bodies of his comrades on every side. There is but one
place for him, beside his own people, to fight and die
with them. Valentine has fainted; commending her to
God's protection, he leaps from the balcony into the
raging fury of the streets.

In order to bring the opera within reasonable limits
it is customary to end it with this dramatic climax, in
which case a vigorous fusillade following on our hero's
disappearance gives us to understand that he has fallen
in the cause of duty; lovers of sensation, however, will
find it well worth their while to make themselves
acquainted with the still more exciting finish provided in
the next Act.

Act V. In certain respects this short Act is the best
of the five. The necessity for cramming such an amount
of incident into so small a space seems to have had a
salutary effect upon the composer; there is no time for
prolixity, there is no need for mere musical noise amid
the rattle of musketry and the cries of the wounded;
even the melody, always Meyerbeer's weakest point,
seems to flow more easily under the increased pressure of
events.

There are two Scenes: the first at the Tour de Nesle,
where the Huguenots are celebrating the festivities in
honour of the royal marriage. The music of a minuet is
interrupted by that booming bell, the meaning of which

is already known. They pause for a moment in wonder, but resume their dancing to a livelier measure. Suddenly Raoul makes a wild entry, an awful figure, his clothes all stained with blood. He tells them the dreadful news; he has seen Coligny slain, his house destroyed; a general slaughter is in progress, that spares neither man, woman, nor child. His heroic call to vengeance and the frenzied response are the more effective from not being unduly prolonged.

The scene changes to the cloisters of a church to which many of the Huguenots have fled for shelter. The cold-blooded massacre is in full swing, the tumult comes ever nearer and nearer. Raoul now appears, with Marcel; the two are about to rush into the thick of the *mêlée* when Valentine appears, and struggles desperately to keep her lover at her side. She knows of a certain method by which he may be saved—if only he will let her bind this white scarf round his arm, as a sign that he is a good Catholic! But no—never will Raoul abjure his faith! Besides, why should he wish to live? Valentine, wedded to Nevers, can never be his. But here Marcel intervenes with the welcome information that Valentine no longer has a husband—Nevers has just died a hero's death in a successful effort to save the old Huguenot's life! The lady promptly grasps the situation; she is now free—she will become a Protestant and marry Raoul, if only to die in his arms. If anything could surprise us now, it might be the fact that Marcel is called upon to play the part of priest and to pronounce a marriage blessing, to which a fictitious dignity is lent by the chanting of the Lutheran hymn by the wretched fugitives in the church. The assassins have by this time broken in, and are at their brutal work; snatches of the hymn are still heard amid the gunfire and the shrieks of the dying, until the silence tells us that the grim work is completed.

Here Marcel, wrought to the height of religious ecstasy, has a vision in which he sees the souls of the victims ascending straightway to their reward in heaven; Valentine and Raoul join him in what is perhaps the most melodious number in the opera. Raoul next receives a mortal wound, and is being helped away by Marcel and Valentine when they are met by a small band of the enemy and the challenge "Who goes there?" "Huguenots!" gasps the dying man, while Marcel repeats the word in a shout of defiance. Then comes the order: "In the King's name—fire!" "Great Heavens!" exclaims Valentine, "it is my father's voice!" But it is too late—the shots ring out—and St Bris finds that he has added to his list of victims Raoul, Marcel, and his own daughter, Valentine.

"Room for the Queen!"—it is Urbain's voice we hear—and the *tableau* is completed by the arrival of Marguerite de Valois, Queen of Navarre, returning from the ballroom to her palace. She recognizes the dying Valentine, and, overcome with horror, raises her hand as a signal to stop the carnage, as the curtain falls.

MARTHA

Music by FLOTOW. *Words by* VERNOY *and* ST GEORGES.
Vienna, 1847; New York, 1852; London, 1858.

MARTHA, after enjoying an enormous popularity for over half a century, has fallen into undeserved neglect in England, the last performance at Covent Garden dating as far back as 1896; in New York, however, it still keeps its place in the repertory, and there seems to be no reason why a London revival should not succeed, if given in a smaller theatre and in the intimate manner which it demands. The music, though it makes no great pretensions, is consistently graceful and melodious, and notably free from the commonplace padding which bores us in many a more ambitious work of the period. Moreover, it has the advantage of a thoroughly amusing libretto which goes its easy way unimpeded by complications or obscurities of any kind. Approached from the proper point of view, *Martha* is a delightful entertainment, and only an incorrigible 'highbrow' will shrug a contemptuous shoulder at it.

The story, like the music, is of the slightest texture and clear as daylight; it needs no preliminary analysis. The time is early in the 18th century, and the scene is Richmond, near London.

Act I. The Lady Harriet Durham is maid-of-honour to Queen Anne; she is young, she is lovely, she is a reigning toast—yet she has come already to the conclusion that life is a hollow sham and has nothing more to offer. True, the world of London is at her feet, but crowded cities have lost their charm for her; amid all the splendours of the Court she

> Sighs for a park, but, when a park she sees,
> At once she cries: "Oh odious, odious trees!"

We make her acquaintance first in a pleasant apartment in the royal palace of Richmond, where the Court is in residence. Poets have sung the praise of Richmond Park, but the Lady Harriet finds the trees here more than ordinarily odious; her spirits are at their lowest ebb, yet she knows not what she lacks. Nancy, her confidential waiting-maid, shrewdly guesses that it may be love. Love? Oh dear no! Of lovers she has enough and to spare, and they are all more odious, if possible, than the trees.

Sir Tristan de Mickleford, who now enters, is one of them; too elderly, perhaps, to be taken seriously, he is, nevertheless, her most devoted swain, and his mistress's sad condition causes him great distress. He is there to serve her—will her ladyship go with him to the donkey-races? Or to see some cockfighting? Her ladyship will do nothing of the sort; at the same time, the absurd airs and graces of the foppish old beau cause her to break into a hearty fit of laughter, which Sir Tristan takes as a favourable sign. Certainly the Lady Harriet seems more inclined to shake off her fit of the vapours, and laughter, fortunately, is in the air; it floats in through the open window, mingled with a melodious chorus of fresh young voices. These are the country wenches from miles around on their way to the Mop Fair at Richmond. A Mop Fair, Nancy explains, is a sort of festal gathering at which servants of every kind assemble, once a year, and take their stand in the market-place, to be hired by those farmers and their wives who are in need of such commodities. The girls, it is plain, look upon it all as a great joke—their gaiety is so infectious that the Lady Harriet forgets all about her own blighted existence. How bright the world is looking! What lovely weather! What fun it would be to dress up in peasant guise and go with these merry wenches to Richmond Fair to take their chance of getting a comfortable place and good wages for the next twelve months! Nay, but they must act without delay: "Nancy, fetch me the peasant costumes we wore at the Queen's rout last week. Good—quite becoming! Now let me think—we must change our names, of course; I will be Martha! Nancy, I shall call you Julia [or Betsy in some versions]—and you, Sir Tristan, will be just plain John!" The stiff old courtier protests loudly against so wild a scheme, but to no purpose—the girls are now fully possessed with the idea. A little conscious, but charming in their peasant garb, they proceed to practise a rustic dance, into which they drag the gouty old beau, and the curtain falls on poor Sir Tristan exhausted and breathless from his exertions, and the two girls in fits of laughter at the uncouth gambols of their victim.

With *Scene* II we are in the thick of Richmond Fair. The opening chorus of farmers and their wives is soon reinforced by the voices of the servants in the lively melody we have already heard; but before the actual business of the hiring begins we make the acquaintance of two young farmers, obviously of the better class. Plunket, a baritone, is of the robust order, Lionel, as befits a tenor, is of finer mould, with a certain air of distinction that hardly belongs to his station. Their duet, which contains one of the best-known airs, *Solo, profugo, reletto,* lets us partly into the secret. Lionel, we learn, is Plunket's foster-brother; as an infant he had been confined to the care of Plunket's mother by a mysterious stranger, of whom nothing had since been heard; he had, however, left behind him a ring, with instructions that his son, if ever he find himself in danger or difficulty, should forward it to the Queen, on whose favour he might confidently rely. Up to now Lionel has had no occasion to test the virtue of the ring, nor has he any desire for royal patronage; the Court does not attract him; he and Plunket are the best of friends, and well content to spend their days in the peace of the country. Alas, the destroyers of that peace are already close at hand!

Now the pompous old sheriff comes puffing on to the scene. "Silence! in the name of the Queen!" while he reads out the conditions of the statute by virtue of which the Fair is held. For a few minutes the Mollies and the Dollies keep as quiet as mice and listen to the proclamation; all must clearly understand that when once a maid has pledged herself to service by taking the first instalment of her wages, the earnest-money, in her hand, there can be no drawing back—she is bound to her master or mistress until the year is out. Are they all agreed? Very well—then let the girls step forward and show their paces! The sheriff seems to know them all by name; he calls on

> Kitty Bell and Liddy Well,
> And Nelly Box and Sally Cox

to state what each can do; after hearing a recital of her qualifications he fixes the amount of wages to which she is entitled, and some lucky farmer hastens to secure the treasure. Business is brisk, the girls go off like hot cakes, and the chorus ends with a general hubbub of eager bargaining, and the passing of money from hand to hand.

But here come the disturbers of our rural happiness. The rustic dance of the previous Scene is played as Martha and Julia, demurest of rustic beauties, come jigging on, with the wretched Sir Tristan still in tow. Fine mistress and smart maid are hardly convincing in their peasant guise, while their elegant escort is thoroughly out of place as plain John. His uneasiness is greatly increased by the Lady Harriet's evident delight in their adventure, and her determination to make the most of it; in his opinion nothing but trouble can come of it, and he is impatient to get them away. But the poor gentleman may as well keep quiet, for now comes young Cupid to take a hand in the game, and to move the puppets as he will. Lionel and Plunket are quick to note the new arrivals, and only too ready to make acquaintance with two such dainty rogues; here indeed is a new variety of serving-maid, and one exactly to their taste. Nor are the girls altogether displeased by the admiring glances of two such comely and presentable young fellows, though they are hardly prepared for the suddenness with which events are moving. After a short preliminary skirmish, and almost before they realize what is happening, they have taken the earnest-money and find themselves engaged for a whole year as servants to the two young farmers—ten pounds a year for each, beer found, and pudding on Sundays! They refuse, of course, to take the matter seriously and are anxious now to get away as soon as possible. But it is too late—the gold pieces are in their hands; the young men will not take the money back, and the sheriff's authority is appealed to. His verdict is final:

> Once the coin is in your keeping
> You must serve the twelvemonth out!

These words, chanted in a solemn monotone, are repeated by the chorus, and finally by Lady Harriet-Martha and Miss Nancy-Julia, with ludicrous effect.

Sir Tristan, of course, is in a terrible taking, but quite

186

unable to render aid; since his arrival he has been a helpless victim in the hands of the merry country wenches, who find him an excellent butt for their mischievous pranks; they now close round him and hold him prisoner while Lady Harriet and her companion are bundled into a wagon with the two young men and driven off to scrape the pots and pans in a farmhouse kitchen.

This Scene is quite admirable as an example of much action packed into a small space without suffering confusion in the process; the sequence of incidents is perfectly clear and intelligible, while the music, of the lightest possible texture, is graceful and melodious, free from banality, and entirely suitable to the subject. Would that many a more pretentious opera were so genuinely entertaining!

Act II. Pretty as a picture, the present Act contains little of dramatic importance, and will not detain us long.

Having got their fair baggages safely home, the two young men are not long in discovering that they have two rather queer customers to deal with. On being shown their own room, these newly hired 'servants' are for shutting the door at once and retiring for the night! What! there is work to be done first! But they know very little about domestic duties—and, besides, they are much too tired. Plunket is inclined to resent such independent behaviour, but Lionel is too tender-hearted not to yield at the sight of beauty in distress. To let them down lightly he proposes that they shall start with a little spinning. Here again they profess their ignorance, so the young men undertake to instruct them—after all, to sit beside a pretty girl and guide her hand on wheel and spindle is no unpleasant way of passing the time. So the 'Spinning Quartet,' *Presto, presto, andiam!* runs on harmoniously, even hilariously after a time, for the girls cannot long restrain their laughter at the young

187

men's clumsy attempts at what they themselves, of course, understand perfectly well, and their tittering sounds pleasantly against Plunket's *Br'm! br'm! br'm!* as he bends solemnly to his task.

At last the lively Julia grows restive, kicks the wheel over, and makes for the door with Plunket in hot pursuit. We are now ready for a duet of sentiment between the other two.

The susceptible Lionel has had time to fall head-over-ears in love with his charming pupil, who can hardly be said to have kept him at a distance. Her instinct tells her that here is a young man who would not be out of place in polite circles, and toward whom she may allow herself to unbend without loss of dignity. When she frankly confesses that she would much sooner play than work, and that she dearly loves a hearty laugh, Lionel finds himself in perfect agreement; work is certainly not to be expected from such a pretty creature—but will she not delight him with just one little song? After some coquetry with a flower she is wearing, of which, of course, he gets possession, Martha obliges with "The last rose of summer," and the young man's fate is sealed. Toward the end of the second verse he strikes in harmoniously, and there follows a love-duet, tender and spirited, which would doubtless receive the praise it deserves were it attributed to a better-esteemed composer.

They are noisily interrupted by Plunket with the saucy Julia in his grasp. That lively young woman seems to have led him a dance all round the house, upsetting the furniture, breaking the crockery, spilling the wine; now, however, he has her fast and—— But here the clock obligingly strikes twelve, and with perfect propriety the young men leave the girls to themselves, after an amicable "Good-night!" quartet.

The Lady Harriet and her companion both agree that,

come what may, they must get out of it and at once—but how? There is a stealthy tap at the window—Sir Tristan to the rescue! He has a carriage waiting outside, and the three drive off before their ill-used masters get wind of their intentions. Lionel is in despair at the loss of his Martha, but the irate Plunket vows he will have the law on them, and the neighbours, roused by the noise, and tempted by the offer of a reward, set out at once in pursuit of the fair runaways.

Act III. Sufficient time has elapsed for the young people to have reflected well upon their recent adventure, and we are now to see its effect upon the heart of each. Plunket, on whom the curtain rises, seems, as we should expect, his usual robust self; we find him drinking with some jolly farmers under the trees in Richmond Park, where the Queen and her Court go a-hunting to-day.

[His drinking song in praise of good old ale—though the Italian version, wishing to be ultra-English, calls it porter—is well worthy of notice; it is far less noisy than such things are apt to be, and attracts by a certain Mozartian simplicity.]

The hunting-chorus which follows is largely in the hands of a bevy of charming young Dianas with their bows and arrows and Cupid's darts. When our once merry little Nancy ('Julia' now no longer) enters pensively to an *andante* in the minor key, we feel that here is something amiss; however, her aria, *Esser mesto il mio cor,* speaks of nothing worse than what we might call a 'pleasing pain,' and soon passes into a gay polka to remind us that, in spite of its Queen Anne label, *Martha* belongs emphatically to the age when that rather plebeian measure was all the fashion.

But here is Plunket bent on making trouble; he has recognized this smart young woman as the runaway 'Julia,' and would insist on her returning with him to work out her time in his service. This, of course, she has no intention of doing; she promptly summons the fair huntresses to her aid, and with drawn bowstrings they drive the astonished young farmer off the stage. Now Lionel wanders on, the picture of a lovesick swain. After a few bars of "The last rose of summer," of fragrant memory, he sings the best-known air in the opera, *M'appari tutt' amor;* its universal popularity is now a thing of the past, though "Emma Parry," as it was once affectionately referred to, is still a favourite, we believe, in certain circles.

The lady of his heart is not long in appearing, but to his passionate avowals she dare not respond; although absence has taught her how much she loves him, she cannot bring herself to stoop to one whom she believes to be so far beneath her. Stung by her contemptuous reply, Lionel attempts to assert his rights as her lawful master, a piece of folly which leads to his arrest by Sir Tristan's orders. The musical interest culminates in a melodious and well-built quintet, *Ah! chè a te perdoni Iddio,* and the announcement of the Queen's approach gives Lionel the opportunity of placing in her hands, through Plunket's agency, the ring which is to end all his troubles.

Act IV. This is one of those last Acts in which much has to be done in too short a space, and the music suffers in consequence. Lionel's troubles, it would seem, are by no means over; the ring, it is true, has worked a great improvement in his fortunes—it has proved him to be the son and heir of the late Earl of Derby, whose title and estate he now inherits. But he is unable to realize his position—his mistress's coldness, nay, her treachery as he conceives it, has turned his brain. Poor Lady Harriet, too, is quite distracted; her love for Lionel has naturally increased now that she is free to indulge it, and she is torn with remorse when she sees the sad effects of her former cruelty.

Such is the situation when the two are brought together again in the long duet with which this scene is chiefly concerned. Lady Harriet hopes to restore the young man's reason by an open avowal of her affection, but the result is very different from what she had expected. Lionel's darkened mind is obsessed by one idea only, his mistress's heartless conduct. She pleads repentance, implores forgiveness, in vain—he is obdurate—even "The last rose of summer" fails to move him, even her frank offer of her hand in marriage. Lionel only loads her with reproaches, and rushes from the stage, leaving the poor lady tearful, humbled, but still in love.

The *dénouement* is as happy as it is unexpected. By a change of scene we find ourselves in a part of Lady Harriet's private grounds where a merry throng are doing their best to reproduce an exact presentment of the Richmond Mop Fair in Act I. Here are the chattering wenches waiting to be hired, here are the farmers and their wives, here is the sheriff with the contracts ready for signing. And here, gently led on by the faithful Plunket, comes our sad lover, wasting in despair. The well-remembered spectacle, the familiar sounds that greet him, work like a spell through heart and brain; the evil spirit is banished and Lionel is himself once more. This time the Lady Harriet's wit has served her well—she stands expectant of her reward. The noisy chorus are silent, while Plunket, assuming the part of the sheriff, strolls up to the once haughty beauty: "Well, my girl, and what can *you* do?" Not much, it seems—and yet enough! the only service she can render is that of love, to one master only, her Lionel—and to him while life shall last. Lionel needs no further hint; he cares not whether her name be Martha or Harriet, so long as he may hold her in his arms. Meanwhile Plunket has no difficulty in engaging Nancy on similar terms; all join in a hearty rendering of "The last rose of summer," and we leave the theatre with that agreeable melody lingering in our memory.

DER FLIEGENDE HOLLÄNDER

Words and Music by WAGNER.
Dresden, 1843; *London,* 1870; *New York,* 1877.

THE 2nd January, 1843, is the most portentous date in the history of modern opera—it marks the production, at Dresden, of *Der fliegende Holländer,* and in this work the real Wagner emerges for the first time. Henceforth the reign of Italian 'opera' is threatened, the very word is discredited, and 'music-drama' is shortly to be the accepted term in musical circles.

The overture alone must have been an unmistakable herald of the coming change; who that had ears to hear could fail to realize that this was something entirely new —a new atmosphere, new horizons, a new-created world? As the opera unfolds we are conscious that the composer is still bound by the fetters of many old conventions— there are set pieces, inflexible melodies that distort the textual meaning, concessions to the singers—yet the work throughout is felt to be pulsing with new life-blood. Again and again we see the working of the two great principles which underlie all that is valuable in Wagner's subsequent reforms, and which he enunciates so plainly with reference to his *Tristan und Isolde*: (1) that the mere melody must in all cases be subservient to the words, must be prescribed by the tissue of the text; and (2) that the substratum, the basis of everything, is to be found in the orchestral music.

The amazing developments of Wagner's genius in his later works have naturally thrown this early opera into the background—it is performed only too rarely at the present day; yet it contains moments of sheer inspiration which are unsurpassed by anything the master ever wrote, and it is permissible to suppose that, for the sake of these, *The Flying Dutchman* may still be acceptable to a future generation no longer patient of the cumbersome machinery of *The Ring*.

The story of *Der fliegende Holländer* is based on the age-long legend of the Wandering Jew, or rather on Heine's variant of it, from which Wagner's libretto was directly adapted. In both versions the central figure of the legend is condemned, for some transgression, to bear the burden of this mortal life for countless generations—to wander, an outcast on earth, until the end of time. The Wandering Jew had mocked the Saviour on his way to crucifixion; to the later story a more trivial and fantastic turn is given. A Dutch sea-captain, prevented by adverse winds from rounding the Cape, swears a fearful oath that he will not give in though he has to sail the seas for evermore; Satan hears, and condemns the wretched man to the fate he had so rashly invoked—the sea shall be his place of torment until the Judgment Day.

To this motive, common to both stories, Heine added a new element, on which Wagner was quick to seize—the redeeming power of a woman's love. Once in seven years the Dutchman was allowed to come to land in the search for a woman who would be faithful unto death. This idea was one of Wagner's most constant obsessions; it finds its happiest expression in *Tannhäuser,* and students of *The Ring* will know how large a part it plays in the psychology of that elaborate structure. In *The Dutchman* it is the dominating force of the plot, assuming dimensions which somewhat disturb the proportion of the drama and the probability of its incidents. Nevertheless, Wagner has given us a libretto of absorbing dramatic interest, of swift action, and well-balanced situations, in which the two chief characters at least are no mere stage-puppets, but living, passionate creatures, with power to move our deepest sympathies.

The symphonic poem which forms the overture presents a magnificent impression of a vessel storm-tossed upon an angry sea; we hear the whistling of the wind through the cordage of the straining ship, the wild cries of the sailors at their strenuous work, and always the tumultuous voice of the ocean:

> The hiss and roll of the rising, the crash of the falling wave.

From all this din and turmoil two arresting and well-contrasted themes emerge—the grim curse-motive attendant upon the Dutchman, and the suave and lovely melody which typifies Senta's devotion, the love that is faithful unto death. In this respect the overture has affinity with that of *Tannhäuser,* where the theme of the Pilgrims' Chorus struggles with the wild insistence of the Venusberg music and eventually triumphs, as does the Senta motive in this, the earlier, opera.

Act I. From a rockbound shore we look out over a wide expanse of stormy sea; foul weather off the coast of Norway has driven Daland, a sea-captain on his homeward voyage, to seek shelter in a little bay some miles distant from his own port. His ship lies anchored close to land; her captain has gone ashore to get his bearings, while the sailors shout and sing as they haul at the ropes. Daland comes on board, and, satisfied that the storm is passing, sends his crew below to take some rest, and retires to his cabin, leaving the ship in the steersman's care. The young sailor, overworn by long watches, tries to fight off sleep with a song, *Durch Gewitter und Sturm,* a lovely piece of spontaneous melody, comparable to the young shepherd's song in *Tannhäuser,* "Dame Holda came from the dark hillside." Before the second verse is ended he is asleep. The storm rolls up again, the air grows darker and more eerie; the curse-motive is heard in the orchestra, and a ship looms out of the mist, the sails blood-red, the masts as black as night. She casts anchor close to Daland's vessel; in silence and without a sound the spectral seamen furl the sails; her captain, the Flying Dutchman, goes ashore. Once more the term of seven years is ended—once more begins the hopeless quest for the maiden whose love shall bring the wanderer rest at last. In the long declamatory scena, *Wie oft im Meeres tiefsten Schlund,* he tells of his never-ceasing search for death. No seas will drown him, no natural force, no human hand, can end his misery. And yet one hope remains—even the Accursed One's torment must end when earth itself shall pass away.

> Day of destruction! Judgment Day!
>   When shall thy morning dawn for me?
> Thou trumpet, sound the crash of doom
>   At whose dread blast the stars shall flee!
> When at the last the dead shall rise,
> Then death shall close my weary eyes.
> Ye planets, fall from heaven's dome!
> Endless oblivion, take me home! [1]

And from the hold of the phantom vessel comes the echo, in tones of unutterable anguish:

> Endless oblivion, take us home!

Daland now comes up from his cabin, to find the steersman asleep and the strange vessel anchored within call of his own. To his loud hail the Dutchman answers only after a long silence, but the two are soon on friendly terms. In one of those overlong and tedious duets into

[1] These extracts are taken, by kind permission, from the English version by Paul England, published by Messrs Adolph Fürstner, Berlin. W.10 (copyright, 1895, by Adolph Fürstner).

which Wagner was so often betrayed, Daland explains his situation, and the Dutchman, learning that his home is near at hand, begs the favour of his hospitality if only for a single night; furthermore, on hearing that Daland has a daughter he at once proposes for her hand. In order to further this strange proposal he bids his men bring from his ship a chest of jewels, of such splendour and in such profusion that the dazzled father is ready to consent to whatever the stranger may demand. The storm is over now; the sweet south wind springs up; Daland will hoist the sails at once and make for home. The Dutchman, for the sake of his o'erwearied crew, pleads for a few hours' delay; he will follow soon. In joyful mood the Norwegian sailors put out once more to sea, raising their voices all together in the steersman's tender song of the homecoming:

> On the wings of the storm, from distant lands,
>   Belovèd, home I fly!
> From the billows that break on southern strands,
>   Belovèd, here am I!
>
> Dear maiden, bless the good south wind
>   That hurries me home to thee!
> Blow, blow, ye breezes, warm and kind;
>   My true love doth wait for me!

Act II. The orchestral prelude to this Act is little more than a repetition of the melody we have just heard from the sailors at the end of Act I. To the audience of 1843 this must have seemed a piece of audacious unconventionality—yet no happier way of linking the two Acts could be imagined. The song tells of the seaman's longing for the girl he has left behind him, and the curtain now rises on a group of these very maidens, who sit at home and dream of their absent sweethearts' return. The scene is the great hall in Daland's house, where the girls are seated at their spinning, under the watchful eye

197

of old Mary, who keeps the house in perfect order. Fresh and homely is the ditty they are singing as the wheels fly round—*Summ' und brumm', mein gutes Rädchen*:

> Twirl and whirl, my spindle, gaily!
> Merry, merry wheel, spin on!
> For the flax must dwindle daily
> Till our winter's task be done.
> My lover sails the ocean foam,
> And thinks of her who sits at home.
> Then fly, good spindle, fast and free—
> Ah! couldst thou blow him home to me!

Dame Mary urges them to greater diligence; the men will soon be home with their pockets full of money—no one like a sailor to pick up the good red gold!—and it is the busiest spinster who gets the finest present.

There is one, however, who does not spin. Senta, the daughter of the house, sits apart and in another world; on the wall toward which her chair is turned hangs a portrait on which her eyes and all her thoughts are fixed. It is a face that moves to pity and terror, a face pallid and drawn with pain—the hungry lips, the sunken eyes with their hopeless appeal, framed in a tangle of long, black hair—the face of a doomed and haunted man. From childhood Senta has known that picture on the wall; too early did she learn the story attached to it, the legend of the Flying Dutchman. The horror, the pity of it, have filled her soul; the presence of the picture in her father's house leads her to imagine that some member of her family ages ago may have betrayed the unhappy man by breaking troth with him; she has become obsessed by one idea, that she herself was born to be the maiden faithful unto death who shall deliver the Dutchman from the curse of existence.

Sunk in such musings, Senta can have no share in the happy business, the lively chatter, of those round her.

198

Old Mary scolds her, and the maidens tease; fie! to fall in love with a picture, and that, too, when she has a lover of her own! What will Erik say when he finds it out? Why, he will shoot his rival—from the wall! So the tittering chaff goes on, till Senta can bear it no longer; she begs them to stop the whirring wheels for a time; perhaps Mary will relate once more the woeful legend of the picture on the wall. But Mary bridles indignantly. The Flying Dutchman! Heaven forbid that she should meddle with any such wickedness! Then Senta herself will sing the ballad. The maidens leave their spinning and gather round her; only Mary keeps her place and still spins on; but by the end of the first verse she too is carried away by the passion which the young girl puts into the piteous narrative, and her wheel stands idle. The restless tides of ocean, the voices of the storm, are heard in the orchestra as Senta begins the ballad of the Flying Dutchman, *Traft ihr das Schiff im Meere an.*

> Say, hast thou seen the phantom ship,
>   Its blood-red sails, its ebon mast,
> Upon the deck the ghostly man,
>   His long hair streaming to the blast?
> Hui!—so pipes the wind!—yo-ho-hey!
> Hui!—how shrill it sings!—yo-ho-hey!
> Like an arrow the ship flieth on, never resting for aye!

Then comes the delicious refrain heard already in the overture as the motive of faithful love:

> Yet might a woman's hand the doomèd man deliver,
> Could he but find on earth one heart that loves for ever.
> Ah, where and when, pallid wand'rer, wilt thou meet her?
> Pray ye with me, that heaven may send her to him soon!

> The wind was wild, the sea was wroth,
>   As once he strove to clear the bay;
> The baffled seaman swore an oath:
>   "I will not rest till Judgment Day!"
>   And Satan heard
>   The fatal word—
> He is doomed o'er the ocean to roam, never resting for aye!

As the song proceeds Senta's excitement increases, until toward the end of the third verse she sinks back exhausted in her chair, and the girls, with hushed voices, take up the refrain:

> Ah, weary wanderer, where is she that shall deliver?
> When wilt thou find the maid whose love shall last for ever?

Like one inspired, Senta springs to her feet, and gives the answer:

> Mine be the faithful love that shall redeem him!
> Yea, though for him my life be given,
> Through me shall he find grace with heaven!

[Senta's *aria*, as a combination of dramatic intensity and melodic beauty against the richly wrought orchestral background, is something altogether new in opera. The slow movement with which each stanza ends foretells clearly the great melodist who was to give us the Prize Song and its companion pieces in *The Mastersingers*. On the other hand, the immaturity of Wagner's judgment at this period is nowhere more apparent than in the short conventional *cadenza* with which Senta closes her final outburst; so accustomed has the listener become to absolute dramatic sincerity in the music of this opera that this slight concession to vocalistic tradition strikes us with almost painful surprise.]

Mary and her companions are aghast at Senta's wild outburst; not less horrified is Erik, who enters in time to hear her last utterance. But the news he brings of the arrival of Daland's ship turns their thoughts in another direction; the girls are beside themselves with excitement, and would be flying off at once to the quay, but Mary insists on their staying at home to help in her lavish preparations for the hungry seamen who will soon be clamouring for food and drink. The bustling chorus

200

DER FLIEGENDE HOLLÄNDER

(*presto possibile*) *Das Schiffvolk kommt mit leeren Magen* is a very acceptable little comedy interlude at this point.

The duet which follows between Senta and Erik can hardly be said to have much musical value; Erik, the tenor, the timid lover, is but a shadowy figure, for whom Wagner was content to write conventional music. Dramatically, however, the scene is an interesting experiment. Erik, never too sure of Senta's affection, and troubled by her fanciful devotion to the portrait on the wall, urges her to hurry on their wedding while her father is at home. Senta is little inclined to listen to his pleadings—her sympathy is wholly with the Ghostly Man. She leads Erik to the portrait, and bids him contemplate the awful suffering written there. "What are *your* sufferings matched with his?" she cries. Her lover, in deep despondency, is moved to tell her of a dream he had last night; and here we have an excellent example of Wagner's power of dramatic invention. Senta, leaning back in her armchair, with closed eyes, passes (as Wagner puts it) "into a magnetic sleep, in which she seems to live in the dream which Erik relates." He tells how in his sleep he had seen a ship come sailing in; how two men came ashore, the one her father, the other—ah! Senta sees him too, his long, black cloak, his face so deathly pale! She stirs and speaks in her trance while Erik tells how, as the two men approached the house, he saw Senta come out to greet her father, but fall instead at the stranger's feet!

SENTA. [*speaking in her trance*]. He raised me up!
ERIK.   Upon his breast,
As in a happy dream, you lay.
Your burning lips to his were pressed.
SENTA. And then——
ERIK.   With him you sailed away!

Senta, now fully awake, springs to her feet, a wild-eyed prophetess of doom:

> For me he calls! To him I go!
> His fate is mine, for weal or woe!

In horror and despair Erik rushes from the room. Senta sinks into a reverie; with her eyes upon the picture she sings very softly the refrain of the Ballad. Then the door opens, and there before her stands the Flying Dutchman—no picture, but a living man. He advances slowly into the room; Senta, after one loud cry, stands rooted to the spot; Daland remains by the door, unheeded, until he forces himself upon his daughter's notice. He is naturally in a merry mood, and full of his plans for the advantageous match he is bent on making between the two. He acquaints Senta at once with the stranger's proposal, shows her rings and bracelets as a foretaste of the wealth that may be hers, and hopes that the next day will see them safely married. As neither Senta nor the Dutchman has spoken a word as yet, but remain motionless, gazing fixedly on each other, Daland concludes that they wish to be alone, and leaves the room in some vexation. The scene that follows is frankly tedious in action. Still motionless and on opposite sides of the stage, they have a long duet, and the Dutchman a solo, both of which are treated as 'asides.' Not till the situation has become intolerable do they move at last toward each other, at the section *Wirst du des Vaters Wahl nicht schelten.*

Senta is now assured that the dream of her life is near its fulfilment; hope flames up once more in the Wanderer's breast, and the two link their destinies in one for evermore.

Daland makes a welcome re-entry; the orchestra hints of the feast which the returned sailors are impatiently expecting; their captain is delighted to find that he will be able to add to the general gaiety by the announcement of his daughter's betrothal, and a short trio brings the Act to a cheerful ending.

Act III. For the undeniable dullness of much of Act II the Act before us makes rich amends; it is full of colour and movement; the interest, whether dramatic or musical, never flags.

The scene shows us a little bay with the two ships at anchor under the rugged cliff and Daland's house near the shore. It is a starry night; the Norwegian vessel is gaily illuminated for the expected feast, and the sailors are all on deck, singing and dancing; but the other shows no light: no form is seen: no sound is heard. Before the rise of the curtain the orchestra has given us part of the rousing Sailors' Chorus, "Steersman, leave the watch!"; it is a joy to hear it again in all its full sonorousness as the seamen stamp it out upon the deck.

From Daland's house come the maidens with store of wine and food for both the crews; they go first to the Dutchmen's ship and hail them from the shore—no light is shown, no sound is heard—there is a long, uncanny silence. It may be that the storm-tossed mariners are still asleep—the girls challenge them in a cheery dance measure, the Norwegians joining in with mock seriousness:

> 'Tis waste of breath! The men are dead!
> They have no need for wine or bread;
> They sing no song, they make no sign;
> In all their ship no light doth shine.

For a little while the lively interchange goes on, the sailors growing more and more hilarious, the maidens more uneasy; their loudest call is answered only by a longer silence than before, and in no dramatic work do we remember a silence so impressive. Their spirit fails them; truly it seems as if these men were dead! Overcome by a feeling of unaccountable horror (in which the audience can hardly help sharing), they turn away from the ship of death, leave their baskets with the Norwegian sailors, and hurry back to the house. The men, on the other hand, have been growing ever noisier in their mirth; now that they are well supplied with wine and good cheer their jollity breaks loose; they clank their wine-cups, roar a mighty chorus, and shout a challenge to their neighbours in the darkened ship.

And the challenge is answered. For some time the 'cellos and basses in the orchestra have been hinting at the growing unrest of ocean and the rising of the storm-wind; the Sailors' Chorus is ended; the dance is just beginning, but is stopped by a terrific crash in the orchestra, and the voices of fiends rather than men give out the curse-motive on a wild "Jo-ho-hoe! Jo-ho-ho-hoe!" All eyes are turned to the Phantom Ship, where a blue light flares at the mast-head, revealing for the first time the forms and faces of the spectral crew. Around their ship the sea is in wild commotion, the tempest howls and whistles through the rigging, in horrible contrast to the calm which prevails elsewhere. Higher and shriller than the wind ring the fiend-like voices as they defy the storm, and jeer at their accursed captain's idle quest.

The Norwegian sailors, at first struck dumb by what they see and hear, try to gain fresh courage by a renewal of their jovial song, straining their voices in a vain attempt to drown the pandemonium from the neighbouring vessel; but gradually overcome by terror they leave the deck, making the sign of the Cross as they go below. A wild burst of fiendish laughter seems the end of everything—the storm ceases, the sea is calm again; darkness and silence once more resume their reign over the doomed ship. Thus ends a scene which for tense dramatic interest, for truth of musical expression, has rarely been equalled; never has the device of contrast been more effectively employed; as for the element of supernatural horror, the scene of the Wolf's Glen in Weber's *Der Freischütz* had hitherto been the standard—we have only to compare that scene with the present to realize what new worlds Wagner had already conquered.

With the entrance of the miserable Erik we sink to a much lower plane—indeed, Wagner's musical treatment of this character would almost suggest that he was, at times, of the same opinion as his friend von Bülow, who declared a tenor to be "not a man, but a disease [*eine Krankheit*]." In this case, however, he is very necessary to the drama, which now hurries to its close.

The broken-hearted Erik has learnt from Senta that she can never be his; as they come from the house together he is reminding her that not so long ago she had promised to be his for ever; Senta is inclined to dispute this, but Erik makes out a fairly good case for his assertion in the anæmic solo *Willst jenes Tags du nicht dich mehr entsinnen.*

Alas! The Dutchman, who has approached them unseen, hears enough to convince him that Senta has been false to her former lover—then how can he hope she will prove true to him? Once more he sees his hope of salvation vanish: once more the ocean claims him for its own. To sea! To sea! With a despairing cry, "Senta! farewell! Lost, lost for evermore!" he turns his face seaward, and pipes the order to his men to roist the sails. Senta clings to him, and swears he is mistaken, but she has yet to learn the whole truth from his lips. It is compassion for her that bids him leave her: to swear eternal truth to him, and then to break that oath, would mean that she must share his awful fate—"Lost, lost for evermore!" That oath she has not yet sworn before

Almighty God, so she may yet escape. Tearing himself away, the Dutchman hastens aboard his ship, while the curse-motive is already heard as the horrible crew haul at the ropes. Daland and Mary rush from the house and try to drag Senta back, but with the strength of madness she breaks from them and mounts the highest cliff; with arms outstretched toward the Dutchman's ship she cries:

Behold me! faithful unto death!

Immediately the Dutchman's ship with its howling crew sinks beneath a boiling sea; but beyond the whirlpool and the tossing waves are seen the figures of Senta and the Flying Dutchman, united now for evermore, and soaring heavenward in the red light of the rising sun.

TANNHÄUSER

Words and Music by WAGNER.
Dresden, 1845; *New York,* 1859; *London,* 1876.

OF all Wagner's operas *Tannhäuser* is the one best known to the general musical public, as distinguished from the regular opera-goer; for forty years the overture has been a favourite stock piece with every orchestra in the world, the two vocal numbers *Dich, theure Halle* and *O du mein holder Abendstern* have been done to death in the concert-room, while the famous March and the Pilgrims' Chorus have even found their way into instruction-books. It must be confessed that these extracts (with the exception of the overture) are but slightly imbued with the true essence of Wagner—the thorough Wagnerian, indeed, is apt to deplore their existence; but they have done incalculable service by inducing countless thousands to make themselves acquainted with an opera which, with the possible exception of *Die Meistersinger,* enjoys a more solid popularity than any other of the composer's works. One chief reason for this is, beyond doubt, the attractive nature of the almost flawless libretto; it deals with what we might call Wagner's favourite theme, a woman's devotion, and the redeeming power of love. The story has all the advantage of a picturesque mediæval setting, and is unfolded in a perfectly natural sequence of events, without gaps or obscurities; there are numerous massive *ensembles* and scenes of spectacular splendour, for which the music makes noble provision; and, finally, in the purely lyrical passages, Wagner's verses are well worthy of the lovely melodies to which he has allied them.

The interesting nature of the plot and the sympathetic appeal of the chief characters may be gathered from the following synopsis: [1]

"Among the Singers attached to the Court of Hermann, Landgrave of Thuringia, at the beginning of the thirteenth century, were Tannhäuser and Wolfram, both of knightly rank. Both were in love with Elizabeth, the Landgrave's niece, whose heart secretly inclined to Tannhäuser. A year before the action of the drama begins, Tannhäuser, in a fit of anger and unrest, had left the Landgrave's castle on the Wartburg. Wandering on the slopes of the Hörselberg, or the Hill of Venus, in the recesses of which the goddess held her Court, he had fallen to her wiles, and for a whole year had dwelt at her side, bound fast by all the sensual pleasures that her power could command. Wearying at length of this unnatural existence, and moved by the memories of his earthly life, he contrives to break the spell and escape from her thrall. On waking from his trance, he finds himself in a valley in front of the Wartburg, the Landgrave Hermann's castle. Here he is discovered by the Landgrave and his nobles, and is persuaded to rejoin the Court by Wolfram's assurance that Elizabeth still loves him.

"To celebrate his return, the Landgrave lets proclaim a Tournament of Song, to which especial dignity is given by the promise that Elizabeth herself shall award the prize. The theme proposed to the assembled singers is the Nature of Love. Tannhäuser, in the course of his song, is brought again under the unholy sway of Venus, and after wildly chanting the praises of sensual love, boasts that he himself has dwelt in Venus' Hill. The nobles, incensed at this outrage, draw their swords on

[1] This synopsis and the subsequent quotations are given by kind permission of Messrs Boosey and Co.

208

Tannhäuser and are about to kill him, when Elizabeth throws herself in front of him and pleads for his life, in order that he may yet work out his redemption. The Landgrave consents, on the condition that Tannhäuser shall leave the country and go on a pilgrimage of penance. Crushed with remorse, he sets out for Rome. Elizabeth, left desolate, though tenderly guarded by Wolfram, watches anxiously day by day for the return of the Pilgrims in whose company Tannhäuser has departed. At length they come—but he is not among them. Broken-hearted, she withdraws from the world, to spend her life in prayers for his salvation.

"Tannhäuser at length comes back from Rome. To Wolfram he relates the story of his pilgrimage, and the failure of his appeal to the Pope; sooner shall green leaves grow on the Papal Staff (such was the doom pronounced) than he, Tannhäuser, shall find forgiveness. Mad with despair, he seeks once more the entrance to the Hill of Venus, and the goddess herself comes forth, to lure him in, while Wolfram struggles to prevent his going. At this moment a funeral chant is heard from the Wartburg and a procession descends, bearing the body of Elizabeth. Venus and her train are vanquished, and disappear. At the same time a band of pilgrims enter the valley, bringing tidings from Rome of the miracle that has been wrought—the Pope's Staff has put forth green leaves. Elizabeth's prayers have been heard. With a last cry, 'Holy Elizabeth, pray for me!' the ransomed Tannhäuser falls dead beside her bier."

There is no overture which sets forth so plainly, so succinctly, the drama subsequently to be unfolded as does the overture to *Tannhäuser*. There are two main themes, two broad and striking melodies in admirable contrast—the solemn chant of the Pilgrims and the bold, trenchant song of Tannhäuser in praise of Venus; in addition to these, we have a medley of 'motives' from the Venusberg revels, a wild orgy of sensuous excitement, which is finally quenched by the growing solemnity of the Pilgrims' Chorus. In this wonderful tone-picture we apprehend clearly the old struggle between "Sacred and Profane Love," in which the former triumphs—and this, briefly, is the argument of the drama.

Act I. The first Scene, known as 'The Bacchanal,' exists in two different forms—the original version produced at Dresden, 1845, and the Paris production of 1861. For the latter, Wagner, in order to comply with the inexorable traditions of the *Grand Opéra,* wrote a quantity of additional ballet-music, and greatly elaborated his original scheme; when this version is given, the curtain rises while the overture is still in progress, and there is no break in the continuity. In this country, however, the older form is usually adhered to; the overture is brought to a formal close, and the ballet is confined to very moderate dimensions.

Scene I. We are in the Hill of Venus, the Court of the Queen of Love, and the abode of all sensual pleasures. Around a blue lake stretching to the back of the stage are grottoes, groves, and wooded slopes, peopled with nymphs and fauns, dryads and satyrs, disposed in amorous couples. The whole scene is bathed in a rosy light, while a Bacchic dance goes on, rising at times to furious disorder. From the far end of the lake is heard the sirens' lovely song:

> Dream through the hours
> Here in these bowers,
> Till on your slumbers
> Bright visions thronging
> Fill you with rapture,
> Calm every longing.

A sense of languor steals over all—the dancers slacken; a dense mist rolls down the heights and hides the general scene, thus concentrating our attention on the figures of Venus and Tannhäuser in the foreground, the goddess reclining on a couch, with her arms around the neck of the kneeling man. Tannhäuser is in no mood to answer her caresses; he is wearied of her soft ways, of all the endless pleasures her realm can offer; he longs for the old familiar joys of earth—in his ears is ever a sound of bells from village steeples. Venus questions him anxiously—what is it he lacks? "The sunshine, the moonlight, the kindly stars of heaven! The grass that clothes the meadows—the nightingale, that sings when May is blooming! Ah—am I doomed never to see them more?" The goddess reproaches him for his ingratitude—how has she failed him? He replies in the great lyric outburst *Dir tön' ich Lob*—one of the two chief themes of the overture. Nay, the Queen of Love has not failed him, she has been only too bounteous in her favours; it is the weakness of his own mortal nature which makes him turn from pleasures such as only immortals can long endure:

> To scenes of earth I long to flee!
> Ah, Queen and Goddess, set me free!

Venus' answer is to put forth even more powerful enchantments than before. The soft, sensuous music of the Bacchanal stirs again in the orchestra—the climax of voluptuous excitement has not yet been reached; in strains of exquisite seductiveness she invites him to still greater blisses:

> Belovèd, come! See yonder bower
> With rosy vapours perfumed sweet;
> A god might rest for ever blest
> In such a fragrant, cool retreat!

With festal joy we'll mark our bond's renewing,
Love's raptures to their farthest bounds pursuing.
Shrink not till her most secret rites are done!
Come! and with love's own goddess mingle into one!

And from far away is heard again the Sirens' Chorus:
"Dream through the hours!"

For the third time, and with ever-increasing ardour,
Tannhäuser repeats his song in Venus' praise; but his
resolve is taken—to earth he must return! Venus, baffled, rises in rage and despair: "Go then," she cries,
"madman and traitor! After long years of friendless
wandering on earth, outcast and broken, thou wilt return
to me, craving for pardon at my hands! But of this be
sure—Heaven's pardon thou wilt never find! For thee
there is no salvation!"

"Heaven's pardon!" cries the knight. "Yes! that
indeed I hope to find—through the Blessed Mary's
intercession!" At the invocation of that name of power,
the goddess with a cry of anguish, vanishes, and the
whole scene is for a moment plunged in darkness.

Scene II. When the stage is again visible, Tannhäuser
seems not to have changed his position, but the scene
around him is changed indeed. Instead of the unnatural
glow and glamour of the secret cave, we have the green
earth flooded with sunshine, and the clear blue of heaven
over us; instead of the wild, voluptuous music and the
rush of frenzied dancers, the sound of sheep-bells and
the solitary figure of a young shepherd piping from a
rocky height. We are in a lovely valley of the Wartburg, with the castle soaring in the background, and the
Hörselberg, the Hill of Venus, seen dimly in the distance.
In the foreground is a shrine and image of the Blessed
Virgin.

The young shepherd has a delicious unaccompanied
song, *Frau Holda kam aus dem Berg hervor,* the signifi-

212

cance of which is not generally understood. In old Teutonic mythology Holda is the beneficent Goddess of the Spring with all its regenerating powers; Goddess of Love is she too, but far removed from that Venus "whose habitation is in the dark places of the earth and whose favours are a curse." The shepherd's song, then, expresses "a pure and natural delight in the manifestation of the Great Power which Tannhäuser apprehended only in its corruption."

> Queen Holda came from the warm hillside
> To roam where flowers were springing;
> Sweet airs were wafted far and wide—
> Ah! sweetly the birds were singing!
> A soft dream on my eyelids lay,
> And as I woke at break of day
> The sun shone bright around me.
>
> Now on my pipe I merrily play,
> For May is here, the lovely May!

But the shepherd's pleasant piping soon gives way to graver sounds, the solemn chant of a band of Pilgrims who are seen descending from the Wartburg. Their song is not the triumphant Pilgrims' Chorus heard in the overture, but a humble prayer for guidance:

> To Thee I turn, O Saviour blest,
> In Thee the Pilgrim's hope doth rest;
> And thou, O Virgin, pure and sweet,
> In mercy guide the Pilgrim's feet!

The shepherd boy waves them a greeting as he goes his way: "God speed to Rome! Pray for my sinful soul's salvation!" Tannhäuser, deeply moved, sinks in prayer before the shrine; with contrite heart he follows the penitential words of the chant:

> Borne down beneath this load of sin,
> In heavy chains my soul is lying,
> Nor peace nor rest I seek to win,
> But gladly walk in pain and sighing.

Shaken with sobs, the knight lies prostrate on the ground as the song of the Pilgrims dies away.

A different music now comes from the heights, the music of the chase, horn answering horn in various keys, as a party of green-clad huntsmen make their way down from the Wartburg; it is the Landgrave and his minstrel-knights, Tannhäuser's old companions. The noise of distant and approaching horns is like a fresh burst of sunshine, and prepares us for a *finale,* cheerful, vigorous, and animated in the highest degree.

It is long since Tannhäuser, in a fit of anger, had forsaken the Landgrave's Court, and all are glad to welcome back their most brilliant singer. But it is Wolfram, his dearest friend in former times, who takes the lead here; he is the first to recognize the kneeling figure, and when Tannhäuser, who has not yet shaken off the evil influences of his late experience, declines their invitation to return to his fellows, and begs them to leave him to his lonely fate, it is Wolfram who finds a way to win him back.

In the old days the two comrades had both been suitors for the hand of Elizabeth, the Landgrave's niece, who was accustomed to grace with her presence the singers' contests in the great Hall of Song in the Wartburg; it was known that her heart had inclined to Tannhäuser, and now Wolfram, with noble unselfishness, tells his friend how, after his departure, the maiden had grown pale and listless, and withdrawn herself altogether from the minstrels' gatherings; only Tannhäuser's return, he says, could bring back the colour to Elizabeth's cheek, and its former glory to the Hall of Song. [The lovely melody of this narration, *Wär's Zauber, wär' es reine Macht,* is repeated by the orchestra and the men's voices with fine effect.]

The mention of Elizabeth's name works an instant

change in Tannhäuser; the evil spell is now entirely lifted, pure love once more resumes its sway, and his way lies open to that earthly Paradise from which he has so long been exiled. He breaks out in a jubilant song of thankfulness: *Ha! jetzt erkenne ich sie wieder!*

> Now once again thy charm comes o'er me,
> Thou wondrous world from which I fled!
> How fair thy meadows gleam before me,
> How bright the boundless skies outspread!
> 'Tis spring! A thousand tuneful voices
> My lightened soul to gladness stir,
> Enraptured all my heart rejoices
> And cries aloud: "To her! To her!"

The Landgrave and his minstrel-knights join a lusty septet, to which the horns soon lend their music; more huntsmen crowd the stage with hounds and horses, and the curtain falls on a typical presentment of the picturesque out-of-door life of the Middle Ages.

Act II. The Minstrels' Hall in the Wartburg, with windows overlooking the valley of the previous Scene. Almost the whole of the Act is taken up with the splendid Tournament of Song which the Landgrave has commanded in order to celebrate Tannhäuser's return to the scene of his former triumphs; the three opening numbers, while necessary to the action, can hardly be said to have any great musical interest, although one of them, "Elizabeth's Greeting," as it is usually called, has been done to death on the concert platform more ruthlessly perhaps than any other Wagnerian excerpt. The scene is empty when the curtain rises, but Elizabeth soon makes an ecstatic entry with arms extended in greeting to the "Dear Hall of Song" (*Dich, theure Halle*) where she had spent so many happy hours. Her rhapsody of joy and thanksgiving for Tannhäuser's return is scarcely ended when that knight, escorted by the unselfish Wolfram, appears in the gallery, and hurries down to cast himself impetuously at Elizabeth's feet. He wins from the young girl a frank confession of her love in the passage *Der Sänger klugen Weise,* and they join in a long-drawn out duet, *Gepriesen sei die Stunde,* inevitably reminiscent of the *allegro* of Agathe's great scene in Weber's *Der Freischütz.* Tannhäuser goes off in an ecstasy of new-awakened happiness, stopping on the way to embrace the long-suffering Wolfram, who has been the means of restoring him to life and love.

The Landgrave now appears, and after some words of tender encouragement to his blushing niece—"My guardian, my second father!" she calls him—escorts her to her place on the high daïs from which they are to watch the brilliant pageant which now begins. To the strains of the famous March the company assembles; glittering knight and gorgeous lady in long succession pass, with due obeisance, before the Presence, and are escorted to their seats, until the whole hall is filled with the flower of Thuringia, and a full-throated chorus, *Freudig begrüssen wir die edle Halle,* goes up in praise of Landgrave Hermann, noblest patron of the glorious art of song.

When all are seated, the competing singers, six in number, enter, and are ushered by four pages to their places. The Landgrave now rises, and, after a courteous reference to Tannhäuser's return, announces the subject on which the minstrels are to exercise their art: Love is the theme, its nature and begetting. The victor is free to name his own reward, and Elizabeth's gracious bestowal will enhance the value of the prize. And so the contest opens. Order of precedence is determined by lot; six scrolls, each containing the style and title of one of the minstrels, are handed to Elizabeth; she draws one, and the pages call out the first name: "Wolfram of Eschinbach, begin thou!"

216

TANNHÄUSER

Although Wolfram's solo, *Blick' ich umher,* has little of
the melodious charm of the famous "Star of Eve" in
Act III, it resembles it in the vague mediæval allegory of
the words; Elizabeth is his

> One bright star that shineth
> Lone in her splendour, though the rest be fair;

there is also a silver fountain leaping heavenward, and
that is love; but star and fountain are equally unap-
proachable, for the devout lover may only worship from
afar.

> Oh, ne'er may I profane that well's pure water,
> Nor stain with impious hand that silver flood!
> In lowly devotion I kneel before it,
> Contented there to shed my heart's last blood.

Toward the end of the song Tannhäuser has shown
some not unnatural signs of impatience, and now rises,
half in protest. He, too, knows that fountain and does
it homage; but not for him is Wolfram's cold restraint—
he must approach and taste it.

> In fullest draughts I drink of rapture
> Where never doubt or dearth prevails,
> For none can quench that fount immortal,
> Which, like my longing, never fails.
> So, that my thirst may last for ever,
> Drink I these waters, day by day.

This, declares Tannhäuser, is "love's most perfect
way." Elizabeth, under the spell of her beloved's voice,
thinks so too; she begins to applaud, but is checked by
the chilly silence of all around her; it is plain that trouble is brewing. Walther von der Vogelweide (the poet
whom that other Walter in *The Mastersingers* acknowledged as his teacher) rises in support of Wolfram; continuing the imagery of the two previous songs, he administers a grave rebuke to Tannhäuser:

> The holy fount that Wolfram honours,
>   I, too, have watched its waters flow;
> But what its sacred stream concealeth,
>   That, Heinrich, thou canst never know!
> Then, for thy guidance, let me teach thee,
>   That holy fount is virtue's shrine.
>
> .   .   .   .   .
>
> Wouldst thou possess its charm, yet not destroy it,
> Then must thy soul, and not thy sense, enjoy it.

Tannhäuser is merely irritated by such cold-blooded moralizing: "Thou doest love a grievous wrong," he declares;

> The world itself would fall in ruin
> Were men to heed thy frigid song.

Far different is his own ideal of love; the stars of heaven we may regard with awe-struck reverence:

> But that which seems to crave caresses,
> Which to our heart and sense appeals,
> And, in our own familiar likeness,
> Into our bosom gently steals,
> Let us enjoy with fullest pleasure,
> For by enjoyment love I measure!

During this song the orchestra portrays clearly the dangerous excitement that is already rising in Tannhäuser's breast and influencing those around him. The rugged Biterolf, oldest of the minstrel knights, leaps angrily from his seat and pours forth his indignation upon the frivolous blasphemer, who answers him with scorn and insult. The nobles side eagerly with Biterolf, and an actual fray seems imminent, when Wolfram restores calm by a melodious appeal to the Star of Love to guide their judgment, *Dir, hohe Liebe*. But by this time Tannhäuser is once more completely under the influence of his evil past; scarcely allowing Wolfram to finish, he rises in wildest ecstasy and sings the praises of the heathen goddess in the very strains with which her sensuous charms had inspired him in her own unhallowed cave.

> Hail, gracious goddess! Fount of every pleasure!
> Thy mighty power shall still be sung by me!

Then, as a last outrage, in the face of all that noble and God-fearing company, he flings the fearful challenge:

> Faint-hearted! would ye taste love's keenest raptures,
> Away! swift to the Hill of Venus haste!

The assembly breaks up in horror and confusion; the knights and minstrels gather round the Landgrave in excited consultation; the ladies leave the hall—all but Elizabeth, who, like the rest, has risen, and, shaken with emotion, supports herself against a pillar of the throne. At the other extremity of the stage stands Tannhäuser, a solitary figure, still gloating over the unholy visions he had conjured up. The Landgrave and his courtiers decide on instant vengeance; Tannhäuser, who, by his own confession, has leagued himself with the Powers of Evil, is no longer fit to live. All, even Wolfram, draw their swords and are closing round the doomed man when, to their utter amazement, Elizabeth rushes forward to his rescue. "Back! back! from him!" she cries, and takes her stand in front of her fallen idol, a perfect picture of heroic love:

> Strike here! I care not—if it be your will!
> What were the deepest wound your swords could give me
> Matched with the deadly thrust that he hath dealt my heart!

Astonished, horror-struck, they can only suppose the unhappy girl to have lost her reason; again they close in upon their victim; but Elizabeth, strong in faith, in love, in spotless purity, controls their fury—she speaks like one inspired:

Who, then, are ye that ye should be his judges?
Would ye destroy his only hope of heaven?
Do ye not know God loves the sinner too?

Why should they seek his death? He has done *them*
no harm! But let them think what he has done to *her*—

> the maid, whose lovely spring-time
> Is blighted, ne'er to bloom again.

Yet she can forgive him, pity him, pray for him. In a
strain of infinite tenderness, *Ich fleh' für ihn,* she pours
forth her appeal:

> I plead for him! Let not his life be taken!
> By long repentance let his soul be tried,
> Till faith returning shall new hope awaken—
> Even for him Christ, our Redeemer, died!

Such love as hers is sure of victory; anger softens,
desire for vengeance dies away—it is the voice of
Heaven that they hear. A calmer spirit spreads among
them—Tannhäuser alone is in the throes of a fearful
agitation: "Woe, woe is me for mine offences!" cries
the unhappy man, torn with remorse and near to despair.
For him there is no present balm of healing, no hope of
earthly pardon; only one way remains, and that the
Landgrave shows him: "We thrust thee from our Court,
thou wretched, sin-polluted man! With us thou canst
no longer look for shelter! Yet, though we reject thee,
one hope still is thine. Hear, then, what thou shalt do!"

The orchestra here gives out the theme of the Penitent Pilgrims in Act I; another such band, the Landgrave
relates, are even now in the valley, on their way to
Rome; Tannhäuser must join them, in the hope of working out his own salvation.

> To Rome thou now must journey
> In lowly pilgrim's dress,
> There kneel in dust and ashes,
> And all thy guilt confess.

Beseech him who hath power
Through God to pardon sin,
But never turn thou homeward
If thou no pardon win!

In a massive and elaborate *finale* the conductor must exercise all his powers of control if, through a full orchestra and an excited and high-pitched male chorus, we are to hear the two solo voices which dominate the situation—Tannhäuser's poignant cries of contrition, and, above all, the broad melody in which Elizabeth offers her life, her all, to Heaven, if only her beloved may find salvation. As if in answer to her prayer the Pilgrims' Hymn is heard in the valley far below—

O blessèd who in faith endure!
Their sin shall find redemption sure!

Even Tannhäuser's face is lit up with a glow of newly kindled hope; he hastens to join the train of penitents, while all the rest call after him, in the words of the young shepherd in the first Act—

To Rome! God speed! To Rome!

Act III. The orchestral introduction, labelled "Tannhäuser's Pilgrimage," is built up of four principal themes. With two of these we are familiar, the chant of the Penitent Pilgrims, and Elizabeth's appeal, "I plead for him"; to these are added two new motives, one in throbbing phrases of broken semiquavers which well express Tannhäuser's contrite heart, his "tears and heavy sighing"—the other a broad ecclesiastical melody in six-four time, symbolical of the pomp and ritual of the Vatican. The grave and sombre atmosphere thus created is thrice disturbed by the rapid upward rush of whirring violins, with which we are familiar from the overture, suggesting the tumult of earthly passions ever striving for the mastery. It would be difficult to imagine a more complete epitome of the experiences of the penitent whose return from Rome we are expecting.

The curtain rises on the lovely valley we remember at the end of the first Act. At the Virgin's shrine where Tannhäuser then knelt, Elizabeth lies prostrate in prayer. It is late autumn, and the evening is fast closing in.

Wolfram is seen descending by a woodland path, but stops half-way at the sight of Elizabeth—each evening at the same hour he finds her there:

> The wound deep in her breast still burning,
> For him she prays with ceaseless yearning,
> Pleading with Heaven by night and day.
> O perfect love, that nought can slay!

Long indeed has seemed the time since Tannhäuser left her in the spring of the year; all through the summer she has possessed her soul in patience, but now the fall of the leaf tells her that the return of the Pilgrims is close at hand; each day raises her hopes and renews her fears —will he return with them?

Scarcely has Wolfram ended his soliloquy when he hears the sound of voices chanting far away:

> It is the joyful chorus
> That tells of happy souls by grace absolved.

Elizabeth, too, hears it and takes her stand where she can listen and watch. As the sounds draw nearer we recognize the opening theme of the overture, the noble song of hope and love triumphant, now heard for the first time in full choral splendour as the singers come in sight.

> The grace of God to the sinner is given,
> He too shall dwell with the blessed in heaven,
> Nor death nor hell can him dismay,
> Therefore we'll praise our God alway!

Weary, bowed, and travel-stained, but with faces radiant with joy, the Pilgrims crowd upon the scene—Elizabeth scans each group as it passes, with painful and ever-growing anxiety. Alas! the face she looks for is not there—henceforth she is to look no more on earthly things. When the Pilgrims' Song has died away, the broken-hearted maid falls on her knees and to the Virgin-Mother a virgin's prayer ascends:

> Let me but share thy sweet protection
> And humbly kneel before thy throne,
> Not for myself a boon to win,
> Only to plead for his great sin.

When at last she rouses from her trance-like state, Wolfram approaches in the hope of accompanying her homeward. Elizabeth makes a courteous gesture of thanks, but gently shakes her head and points to heaven, henceforth her only care. Slowly she climbs the winding path that leads upward to the Wartburg; Wolfram watches her until she is lost to sight among the trees. He too seems to pass into Elizabeth's visionary region; after preluding softly for some time upon his harp, he sings the famous "Star of Eve," of which the widespread popularity is due, in a great measure, to the atmosphere of vague 'mysticism' that surrounds it.

> Like death's grim shadow, darkness round me hovers;
> A misty veil the sombre valley covers;
> The spirit that would soar to yonder height
> Doth shrink in dread before that awful flight.
>
> There shinest thou, the fairest star in heaven,
> Whose gentle beams to mortal eyes are given;
> Before thy radiance night's dim terrors fail,
> For thou dost point my pathway through the vale.
>
> O pure and tender star of eve,
> Sweet is the comfort thou dost give!
> This faithful heart's unheeded sigh
> Bear to her when she shall pass thee by—

When, borne aloft on angel pinions,
Her soul shall enter heaven's dominions.

[The above, though not a literal translation, fairly
renders the spirit of the original words, the meaning of
which is by no means too clear. The actual evening star
has just risen over the heights of the Wartburg, and to it
Wolfram addresses his romance, at the same time iden-
tifying it with the "Star of Love" of which he has
already sung, and also with Elizabeth herself, "the fairest star in heaven." In the last six words he seems to
foretell the approaching release of her spirit from its
earthly prison, and its flight to heaven:

This faithful heart's unheeded sigh
Bear to her *when she shall pass thee by.*]

Wolfram's musings are interrupted by the entrance of
a wild figure in tattered dress, supporting himself painfully on a pilgrim's staff; he is horrified to recognize
Tannhäuser, whose life is forfeit should he be found here,
his guilt still unforgiven—and this man's looks speak not
of peace and pardon. But Tannhäuser is beyond all
such consideration—his one object in returning is to find
once more the entrance to the Hill of Venus, the only
refuge left for such as he.

Wolfram questions him. Yes—he has made the pilgrimage to Rome, the sincerest penitent of them all,
outdoing his fellows in acts of mortification:

When through the green and pleasant meads they wandered,
On stones and thorns I trod with naked feet;
When others sought the fountain's cooling waters,
I only drank the summer's parching heat.

At Rome he, like the others, did penance in the dust.

A thousand souls confessed their guilt, and shriven,
A thousand joyful pilgrims went their way.

But Tannhäuser was not among them—for guilt such

as his there was no forgiveness. These were the awful terms in which the Holy Father had pronounced his doom:

> Since thou in Venus' Hill hast dwelt
> Thy soul is lost beyond recall.
> As on this staff that here I hold
> Never again a leaf shall grow,
> So from the fiery pangs of hell
> Redemption thou can'st never know.

Mad with despair he had fled from Rome and hurried back, longing once more to taste those unhallowed joys which are now his only solace. In spite of Wolfram's horrified remonstrance, Tannhäuser proceeds to invoke the goddess in the very strains which she had used in Act I to bind him closer to her side, "Beloved, come! See yonder bower." The wild music of the Bacchanal is heard in the orchestra, the old seductive themes are repeated, the Sirens' Song, the dance of nymphs and satyrs. Now the scene is filled with wreaths of rosy mist, through which the forms of the hellish revellers are dimly discerned. At last Venus herself is clearly seen, in her most voluptuous attitude, eager to welcome back her truant lover, who listens greedily to the honied voice he so well remembers.

> Say, does the cruel world reject thee?
> Then shall my loving arms protect thee!

A violent struggle now begins between Tannhäuser and Wolfram, who seeks by force to drag him away from the awful peril. But Tannhäuser's resolve is taken:

> My soul can never find salvation,
> So be her love my consolation!

Venus redoubles her allurements and seems sure of her triumph, when Wolfram, as on a former occasion, employs once more the word of power: "Elizabeth!"

225

The music of that name on Wolfram's lips seems to break the spell of evil; with a cry of despair the goddess vanishes; Tannhäuser, freed for ever from her power, turns with a new rapture in his face to Wolfram, as the sound of pious voices is heard descending from the Wartburg; Wolfram explains their meaning to him in the solemn words:

> Thine angel pleads for thee at God's right hand!
> Her prayer is heard! Heinrich, thou art forgiven!

By this time the magical vapours have dispersed, to make way for the ruddy blaze of torches, as a funeral train, escorting the body of Elizabeth, winds slowly toward the valley. A great burst of song proclaims the triumph of her whose mighty love was faithful unto death, whose patient suffering and ceaseless prayer have won salvation for the man she loved.

> Oh blessed soul, that hath out-soared
>   This pious virgin's earthly frame!
> Thine is the faithful's just reward,
>   Joys that the saints alone can claim.

Tannhäuser's strength is nearly spent—he lies exhausted in the arms of Wolfram, who, as the procession passes, bids them set down the bier; to this he leads the dying man, who sinks gently down beside the dead Elizabeth, his arms extended across her body: "Blessed Elizabeth, pray for me!"—and with the words he dies.

The valley is flooded with the red light of morning as a belated train of pilgrims comes in sight, jubilant with the news they bring from Rome. God's mercy is over all His works! After Tannhäuser's departure from the Holy City, the miracle, too great for mortal man to credit, had actually happened:

226

TANNHÄUSER

The withered staff the Pope did bear
Hath blown in leafage fresh and fair;
So he whom toils of hell did bind,
Mercy and pardon yet shall find.

With God all things are possible—and the opera closes as it began with the great choral melody which speaks of pity and pardon, infinite and eternal.

LOHENGRIN

Words and Music by WAGNER.
Weimar, 1850; New York, 1871; London, 1875.

WAGNER had finished *Tannhäuser* in 1844;
the following year he started work on
Lohengrin, and the opera was completed in
1847. But although the two works are separated by such
a short interval of time, *Lohengrin* shows an enormous
advance on its predecessor. Wagner's genius was maturing rapidly, and in this work we can distinguish most
of the chief characteristics of his later style.

The story is the very old one of the Mysterious Lover
whose name must not be known, the vow of obedience
exacted from the Beloved, and the disaster that ensues
from her breaking of that vow at the prompting of
jealous advisers.

Act I takes place on the banks of the Scheldt, near
Antwerp. King Henry is seated under the Judgment
Oak, surrounded by his Saxon nobles. He is the one
historical character in the piece, being that Henry who
was called 'The Fowler,' and became celebrated for his
successful wars against the wild tribes of the Hungarians.
Opposite him are the nobles of Brabant, headed by
Frederick of Telramund and his wife Ortrud. Henry
has come to summon the Brabantine levies to join him
in his proposed campaign against the Hungarians. But
he finds there is a dispute to be settled first—Frederick
explains it. The late Duke of Brabant had appointed
Frederick guardian of his children, Elsa and Gottfried;
one day Elsa returned alone from the forest, where she
had been wandering with her brother, with a tale of how

228

she had lost him in the wood. Further search failed to discover the missing boy, and Frederick now accuses Elsa of fratricide, and claims the dukedom for himself and Ortrud. The King is horrified at this indictment, and demands that Elsa shall be summoned to answer it. She comes timidly forward, but is at first too much overcome to speak. When she finds her voice it is not to defend herself, but to describe a vision she has seen of a knight in shining armour who was sent by Heaven in answer to her prayers.

The great song generally known as "Elsa's Dream" is justly famous. Opening with a feeling of quiet and restraint, the music gradually grows richer as Elsa's excitement increases, till at last, kindling to ecstasy, she stakes all on her faith in Providence, and hurls her challenge at Frederick:

> That Knight be my defender!
> He shall my champion be!

But Frederick is unmoved—he honestly believes in the justice of his cause, and is prepared to uphold it in single combat against any knight. Let Elsa produce her champion! At the King's command the trumpets are sounded—twice—but no one appears. Already the judgment of Heaven seems to have been given against her, and she has fallen on her knees in fervent prayer, when in the far distance, visible only to those by the river bank, a wonderful sight is seen. A knight appears, in silver armour, as in Elsa's dream, and standing in a boat drawn by a swan. Rapidly he approaches and at length steps ashore amid the acclamations of the astonished people. Dismissing the swan with a few gentle words of farewell, he makes his obeisance to the King, and announces that he has been sent by God to defend a slandered maiden. Then, turning to Elsa, he offers himself as her champion. Should she accept him and should he conquer in the ensuing combat, he will be suitor for her hand as well. But let her understand clearly—she must trust him absolutely and whatever befalls, she must never ask his name.

To these proposals, and the condition that goes with them, Elsa gladly gives her assent. The lists are prepared, the King makes an impressive appeal to God to defend the right, the people echoing his words, and the fight begins. It is of short duration; Lohengrin soon fells Frederick to the earth. His victory is hailed by a shout from the people and an ecstatic song of rapture from Elsa, and all unite in a somewhat conventional *finale,* singing the praises of the victor. Ortrud joins in with threats of vengeance, and even Frederick so far recovers himself as to bewail his defeat in lusty tones.

Act II. The citadel of Antwerp; at the back are the men's apartments, on the left are the women's; on the right is the Cathedral. It is deep night, and in the darkness we can hardly distinguish the figures of Ortrud and Frederick, seated on the Cathedral steps and listening in bitterness of heart to the sounds of revelry proceeding from the men's quarters. The scene that follows is wholly admirable and is a worthy foretaste of Wagner's later triumphs. To fierce and sombre music Frederick upbraids Ortrud with being the cause of his downfall—it was her definite statement that Elsa was guilty which led him into levelling his accusation and thereby to that disastrous fight. Now he is a ruined man, his honour lost, himself an outcast in the land he had hoped to rule. Ortrud has been proved false by the judgment of God. "God!" cries Ortrud. "No, it was not by His help that Lohengrin's victory was won; on the contrary, it was by the power of sorcery." Even now it is not too late for them to repair their shattered fortunes. If they can only work on the impressionable Elsa and induce her to ask Lohengrin the fatal question, the spell will be broken. And failing that, there is still another hope. Those whose might is drawn from sorcery lose their strength if a portion of their body, be it ever so small, is cut from them. Could they contrive that Lohengrin should receive the slightest wound, his magic power would be destroyed. Frederick is doubtful at first, but Ortrud ends by convincing him.

Here there comes a change in the music, as though a cloud were passing from the face of the moon. Elsa appears on the balcony above them, and all oblivious of their presence whispers to the night the secret of her love, in the lovely number known as "Elsa's Song to the Breezes." At sight of her, Ortrud hastily bids Frederick withdraw and herself calls Elsa by name. It does not take her long to work on the girl's sympathy and persuade her to descend and admit her. Freely she forgives Ortrud all the wrongs she has suffered—she will win her pardon, and Frederick's too, from Lohengrin and the King. The crafty Ortrud is full of humble thanks, but, even as she pours out her gratitude, she begins her task of poisoning the young girl's mind. How can she repay Elsa? Never! But at least she can be near to support her when trouble comes. For come it will! The magic which brought Lohengrin to her aid will some day take him from her in the same way. As the two women go in together Frederick emerges from his hiding-place, and in a short monologue rejoices in his wife's success. Then, as day begins to dawn, he conceals himself again behind a buttress of the Cathedral.

Signs of life soon begin to show themselves in the citadel, and the nobles and people gradually assemble for the forthcoming ceremony, the marriage of Elsa and Lohengrin. After a chorus a herald appears and announces the

King's decree. Frederick is banished and Lohengrin shall rule in his stead as Guardian of Brabant; his wedding with Elsa is to be celebrated immediately. Another chorus follows, in the course of which it happens that four of Frederick's old adherents find themselves near the buttress. Frederick shows himself, tells them he will soon prove Lohengrin an imposter, and invokes their aid. The episode is over in a moment, and Frederick retires once more, just as Elsa and her train appear from the castle on the way to the Cathedral. But an interruption occurs. Elsa has reached the very steps of the sacred building when Ortrud comes forward and confronts her. Publicly she taunts her with neither knowing the name of her husband-to-be, nor the source of his supernatural power. Lohengrin appears with the King, and reduces Ortrud to silence with a few sharp and contemptuous words. But now Frederick reveals himself, and directly challenges Lohengrin. If he is truly sent by God let him reveal his name! Lohengrin scornfully refuses—his worth is well known, for he has proved it by his deeds. The people assure him of their confidence, but in the tumult Frederick and Ortrud have found their way to Elsa's side and are whispering their slanders in her ears, and again Lohengrin is forced to rebuke them before he turns with his bride and enters the Cathedral.

Act III opens with an orchestral Introduction which is one of the finest things in the work as well as one of the most popular. After this "superb, full-blooded epithalamium" (to quote Mr Ernest Newman) the curtain rises on the bridal chamber. Lohengrin is led in by the men at one door, Elsa by the women at the other, to the strains of the Bridal March. It is difficult to praise this number, however one may wish to do so. One can sympathize with Wagner's desire for simplicity here, but for once his instinct is at fault, and he has only succeeded in being banal. The poverty of the piece is the more apparent owing to its being placed between the magnificent introduction just referred to and a love-scene which, in spite of certain weaknesses, is a worthy predecessor to those in *Siegfried* and *Tristan*.

At first no shadow mars the rapture of the pair. It is only when Lohengrin caressingly murmurs Elsa's name that the first signs of the approaching tragedy are seen. Elsa complains that she is unable to utter her husband's name in reply, and in spite of all Lohengrin's attempts to calm her, or to change the subject, her agitation steadily increases; Ortrud's poison has done its work. In vain he assures her that his secret is no shameful one—his race and station are among the noblest. This only adds to her alarm. If he has given up all this for her he may some day be tempted to return to it. In a hysterical vision she sees the swan approaching down the river, drawing the fatal boat. All remonstrance is useless, and in an access of terror she breaks her vow and utters the forbidden question: "Whence comest thou? Where is thy home? Tell me thy name!"

Hardly are the irrevocable words spoken when Frederick rushes in with drawn sword, accompanied by his four associates. Elsa has just time to hand her husband his sword before they are upon him. With a single blow he strikes Frederick dead. The other four, seeing their leader fall, give up the fight and sink on their knees. He bids them take up the body and bear it to the King. Then summoning Elsa's ladies he instructs them to attend to their mistress, who has fainted. Let them prepare her also to appear before her sovereign.

The scene quickly changes to the banks of the Scheldt as seen in Act I. In the early dawn the nobles and their retinues are slowly gathering. The King himself arrives and greets the assembled army. But he misses its leader:

Lohengrin is absent. At this moment the four conspirators enter with the shrouded body of Frederick. They are followed almost immediately by Elsa, pale with fear, and almost fainting. Finally a general stir heralds the approach of Lohengrin. He comes forward, clad in full armour, and in answer to the acclamations of King and people replies shortly that he cannot lead them forth to victory. Briefly he recounts the circumstances of Frederick's death, and receives their assurance that he was justified in slaying him. Then sorrowfully he reveals how Elsa, fallen a victim to the plots of Ortrud, has broken her vow and demanded to know his name and origin. With that demand he must now comply. To the strains of solemn music, mostly based on the Grail-motive, he tells of the Castle of Montsalvat and the wondrous cup it holds; of the Knights of the Grail, who, invincible under its protection, go forth to distant lands to fight for God and the right, and of how their might depends upon their keeping secret their name and origin —once that is known, straightway they must return home. Such a knight is he. It was the Grail that sent him, and, obedient to its laws, he must now go back to Montsalvat. "My father Parsifal reigns there in glory; his knight am I, and Lohengrin my name!"

This narrative, with its splendid music, is as familiar on the concert platform as on the stage. His story told, Lohengrin returns to Elsa and gently reproaches her for her lack of faith. She begs him to remain and forgive her, for without him life to her will be impossible. The King and the people second her petition: let Lohengrin stay and lead them forth to battle. But the knight is adamant—he must not heed their prayers.

The swan is seen approaching. He greets it sorrowfully, and lingers to take yet one more farewell of Elsa. Could she but have remained one year faithful to her oath, then by the power of the Grail he could have restored to her her brother now held in enchantment.

He is going sadly to the bank when suddenly Ortrud appears, with an air of triumph. Yes, Lohengrin must go indeed, but let the foolish Elsa learn who it is that in the form of a swan is dragging him away. It is her brother Gottfried, turned into this shape by Ortrud's own enchantments! But the departing knight has heard. He falls on his knees in prayer, and the dove of the Grail hovers over him. The swan sinks, and in its place there rises a beautiful youth, who comes gravely forward and makes obeisance to the King. It is Gottfried of Brabant, and he hastens to his sister's side. Ortrud falls with a shriek, while Elsa, momentarily forgetful of her own trouble, welcomes her long-lost brother. Suddenly she remembers Lohengrin, and turns to the bank; but he is already far away upstream, standing in his boat that is now drawn by the holy dove. With a stricken cry, "My husband!" she falls lifeless in her brother's arms.

The Prelude to *Lohengrin* is Wagner at his best. It is constructed on a single theme, that of the Grail. This is first heard *pianissimo* on the violins alone, in their highest register, the effect being ethereal in the extreme. Slowly as it draws nearer the vision gains clearness and solidity; the violins are joined first by the wood-wind, and next by the horns, 'cellos, and basses; lastly the brass takes up the theme *fortissimo*—the radiance is overwhelming. But immediately it begins to fade, the instruments are gradually withdrawn, and the piece ends in the remote atmosphere of the commencement. It is a beautiful epitome of the whole opera.

The music of *Lohengrin* as a whole shows us Wagner in a state of transition. He seldom achieves the richness

235

and sustained inspiration of the works of his full maturity, although at times he comes very near to doing so (notably in the Prelude, the scene between Ortrud and Frederick in Act II, the Introduction to Act III, and the love-scene that follows). Nor has he yet completely succeeded in freeing himself from the conventionalities of the type of opera which it was his ambition to supplant (the very use of the words 'Romantic Opera' in the title, in place of the later 'Music-drama,' is significant in this connexion). The bad old tradition is reflected in the amount of chorus work, which is out of all proportion to the dramatic importance of the chorus, and is a serious blemish, especially as the music for these concerted pieces is sometimes (though not always) of an almost perfunctory kind. The *finale* to Act I is a case in point. The whole cast, principals and chorus, join in an elaborate and lengthy *ensemble,* although no one has anything of real importance to say, either dramatically or musically, and the singers are soon reduced to the old and wretched device of repeating their words over and over again in order to keep going at all. We notice, too, here and in other places, a certain rhythmic squareness, a clumsy rigidity of phrase, which seriously interferes with the flow of the music. This weakness is, however, far less obvious in *Lohengrin* than in any of Wagner's previous works, and there are long stretches that are completely free from it. But perhaps the most remarkable thing about the opera is the treatment of the orchestra. Here a tremendous advance has been made. The old dummy accompaniment has been finally exorcised, and in its place we see already the beginnings of that wonderful wordless commentary that delights us in *Tristan* and *The Ring*. Occasionally the instruments fade into the background for a moment, becoming a mere support for the voices, but far more often they are playing independent and interesting

parts of their own. The *leit-motifs,* too, are more numerous and more characteristic than in any previous
work; there is one for the Grail, one for Lohengrin, one
for the question Elsa must not ask, and several more besides. The composer has not yet developed them into the
marvellous system of his later years, but the elements of
that system have at any rate been isolated. *Lohengrin,*
in fact, contains practically all the constituents of Wagner's mature style; the parts have been assembled and
the first tentative model of the future 'Music-drama' has
been constructed. But the machine does not yet run quite
smoothly; certain improvements of detail are necessary, and the general standard of the workmanship must
be of a still higher order before complete success can be
achieved. Wagner realized this, and for the next few
years he wrote no music of importance, devoting himself
to literary work, while his great conception was slowly
ripening in his mind. When, in 1852, he set to work on
The Rhinegold, the rich results of the long period of
gestation were immediately apparent, and with the completion of that work in 1854 the creation of the new
art-form was definitely accomplished.

RIGOLETTO

Music by VERDI. *Words by* PIAVE, *from* VICTOR HUGO'S
"*Le Roi s'amuse.*"
Venice, 1851; *London,* 1853; *New York,* 1857.

MANY causes contribute to make *Rigoletto* one
of the most memorable of operas; it has a
plot unsurpassed for thrilling interest; musically it is Verdi's greatest achievement before *Aïda*; its
leading part is assigned to a baritone, and contains some
of the finest dramatic music ever written for that voice;
finally, it has the distinction of having been prohibited
in its original form owing to the alleged anti-monarchial
tendencies of its story.

Victor Hugo's drama, *Le Roi s'amuse,* from which
Piave's libretto was taken, was produced in Paris in 1832:
the story of its immediate withdrawal belongs, like the
first night of *Hernani,* to the political and literary history
of France during the Romantic Movement. Though it
was not till 1851 that Verdi's opera was offered for production at the Fenice Theatre, Venice, similar objections
were raised; permission was refused to the performance
of the original version, but by changing the scene from
France to Italy the difficulty was overcome. Hugo's
French king was transformed into a Duke of Mantua,
and Triboulet the jester became Rigoletto. *La Maledizione* (The Curse) was the title under which it was first
performed. Following Hugo's conception, Verdi has put
all his strength and sympathy into the tragic figure of the
hunchback; but two other parts (Gilda and the Duke)
are so well provided for that a favourite prima donna or
the tenor of the hour will sometimes contrive to have the

production so faked that their own vocal displays become the centre of attraction, greatly to the disturbance of the artistic balance. Moreover, the rôle of Rigoletto demands such a combination of dramatic and vocal endowments that worthy revivals of this fine opera are unfortunately rare.

The story is woven around a strong and fiercely passionate nature warped by physical deformity and the degrading influence of his surroundings. Poor Rigoletto, the despised hunchback with something of a lion's nature, is the paid ape of the profligate Duke of Mantua; grotesque with cap, bells, and bauble, he affords fine sport for the idle courtiers, on whom he often revenges himself by lashing them with his stinging wit. The Duke, who lives only for the seduction of women, finds him invaluable for his own evil purposes; embittered by misfortune, fouled by association, Rigoletto has become the willing tool of his master, and even finds pleasure in the ruin and anguish he helps to spread. His insolent indifference to the sufferings of others calls down on him a father's righteous curse, the fulfilment of which is the theme of the opera.

For there is another side of Rigoletto's nature which is unsuspected by the heartless nobles of the Court. In his youth, poor, wretched, misshapen as he was, a woman's faithful love had raised him to the height of happiness, only to be plunged into deeper misery than before by her early death. But consolation still remained in the little daughter his dying wife had left him, and to whom all the devotion of his passionate nature was transferred. After accepting his position at the ducal Court, in his anxiety to keep the young girl far from that ribald company, yet always within his reach, he had placed her in the care of a seemingly faithful servant, with orders never to let her stir abroad unless attended, and always to keep her from the public eye; even his own visits to her were made in strictest secrecy.

When the drama opens, Gilda is in the first bloom of lovely girlhood—but the plot for her ruin is already on foot. The Duke has often noticed her on her way to Mass, and his looks of open admiration have awakened love in her innocent breast. His courtiers contrive to carry her off and place her in the Duke's power. Rigoletto, enraged and broken-hearted, succeeds in recovering his daughter, and, after learning the truth from her lips, resolves to take a swift revenge. He hires an assassin to lure the Duke to a house of ill repute on the outskirts of the city; at midnight, after the deed is done, he will visit the murderer, pay him his reward, and himself dispose of the victim's body. Gilda has confessed that she still loves the Duke; in order to break her infatuation, her father takes her with him to the place before the time appointed, that she may be convinced of the baseness of the Duke's true character. Outside the dwelling he leaves her for a time. In the utter darkness of the scene Gilda, still faithful to the Duke, contrives to receive the assassin's blow, and to die the death that was designed for her lover. Rigoletto soon returns, and is carrying off the sack that contains, as he supposes, the body of his enemy, when the groans of a dying woman reveal the awful truth—it is his own daughter, Gilda, slain by the assassin whom he himself had hired.

Act I. There is no overture. After the orchestra has sounded some thirty bars of solemn warning, the curtain rises on the frivolities of the wanton Court of Mantua. The small orchestra on the stage, the succession of gay dance tunes, can scarcely fail to recall the similar scene in *Don Giovanni*; the delicate minuet in particular is not unworthy of its great original.

There is much intrigue in the first few pages. The

Duke has no secrets from his courtiers; after referring to
his latest conquest, the young girl he has met so often
on her way to Mass (none other than Gilda, the jester's
daughter), he draws their attention to the beauty of the
Countess Ceprano, and proceeds to make love to her
under her husband's very eyes. [His air *Quest' o quella*
is a delightful insistence on the virtues of infidelity.]

Rigoletto now comes forward to insult the Count in
his most offensive manner; even the Duke has to tell
him that he goes too far, and Ceprano engages the courtiers to join him in a scheme to avenge themselves on the
common enemy—a scheme suggested by the recent discovery that the hunchback himself pays secret visits to
one whom they suppose to be his mistress.

But Rigoletto is soon to arouse an even more terrible
spirit of vengeance. Struggling with the retainers, a man,
grey-haired but vigorous, forces his way into the hall. "I
say the Duke *shall* hear me!" he thunders out. It is the
aged Count Monterone, whose daughter the Duke has
recently dishonoured. His indignant denunciations are
cut short by the hunchback, who swaggers to the front:

"Let *me* answer him!" With every insult that tone
and gesture can convey, he mocks the broken-hearted
father to his face: "What folly is this!" he sneers—
"your daughter's honour gone? Well, why make so
great an outcry over such a trifle?"

With these words Rigoletto invites his own destruction
—Heaven itself will not suffer an outrage such as this.
The aged Monterone becomes an instrument of fate:
awful in his fury he calls down Heaven's wrath upon
them both—living or dead he will not cease until his
vengeance be accomplished. "Shame on you, tyrant," he
cries to the Duke, "who can set your mongrel on a dying
lion! And for you"—turning to the cowering hunchback
—"vilest of creatures, who can make sport of a father's

anguish—for you, what punishment can suffice? God's curse go with you for evermore!"

As Monterone is led away to execution, Rigoletto lies writhing on the ground, a father, justly stricken by a father's curse.

Scene 11. The short Scene that follows, with its admirable terseness of expression, is a triumph for both librettist and composer.

Rigoletto, his tell-tale form concealed as well as may be in a heavy cloak, is making his way cautiously, after nightfall, to the house where his daughter is kept secluded. He is gloomy with a sense of coming disaster: "That old man laid his curse on me!" he mutters—and its power is even now at work.

The orchestra begins an oddly sinister theme which persists throughout the dialogue. A stealthy footstep and a few low words; it is Sparafucile who accosts him, an assassin who may be hired to rid any man of his enemy. "You too," he says to Rigoletto, "may need my aid, for you have a mistress" (pointing to Gilda's house) "and—a rival!"

Rigoletto's fears increase; he inquires further of the man and his methods. He lives outside the city walls with his sister Maddalena; it is her part to lure the victims to their dwelling—Sparafucile's dagger is swift and sure. Though the hunchback has no need of him at present, he will do well to remember.

With the ending of this short dialogue the preparations for the drama are complete. The Duke, we know, is hot in pursuit of Gilda, not guessing her to be the hunchback's daughter; Count Ceprano, whom Rigoletto has made his enemy, will, in his desire for revenge, unconsciously assist the Duke to gain his ends; by his heartless insolence toward Monterone, Gilda's father has incurred an outraged father's curse; and in Sparafucile we see the agent who is to bring that curse to its terrible fulfilment.

We have by this time seen the worst of Rigoletto; for the rest of the opera he is a pathetic figure to whom we can hardly refuse our sympathy.

His fine soliloquy, *Pari siamo,* a dramatic outburst of convincing sincerity, goes far beyond anything that has yet been done in Italian Opera. It is the lament of the melancholy buffoon who is paid to make laughter for others while his own heart is aching—an idea that has been handled since by more than one composer, though never so finely. In this case there is a tragic fierceness in the music, perfectly in keeping with Rigoletto's character; he despises himself and his surroundings, he curses the corrupt tyrants whom he has to serve—if he is vile, it is they who have made him so. And all the while he is haunted by an awful memory—

That old man laid his curse on me!

Forcing all gloomy thoughts aside he unlocks the door that opens on the courtyard of his daughter's dwelling, and Gilda flutters gaily down the stairway to be folded to her father's breast. Now indeed is Rigoletto a changed man, all gentleness and love; there are few pages in opera more gracious than this duet between father and daughter. Gilda asked him to speak of her mother. In a solo of poignant pathos, *Deh! non parlar al misero,* he laments his angel and her early death, and thanks God for the daughter left to fill her place in his heart.

But his fears again awake—suppose someone should discover his secret, and rob him of his only treasure—is Gilda careful of her father's command never to go beyond the garden walls? Does she never go into the town? "Only to Mass!" Hardly satisfied, he summons Giovanna, the servant, and recommends the strictest watchfulness in the lovely air *Ah veglia, o donna, questo fiore*. Alarmed by the sound of footsteps, he leaves his daughter for a moment, and the Duke slips in unnoticed by the garden door. After Rigoletto's departure he discovers himself to Gilda, who has known him hitherto only by sight; he is a poor student, he tells her, Gualtier Maldé by name, and has long been her worshipper. The young girl listens entranced, for she too has long been in love with his handsome face. In the midst of their impassioned duet, *E il sol dell' anima*, Giovanna warns them that someone is coming. The Duke tears himself away, leaving Gilda to a delicious meditation on her lover's name: Gualtier Maldé! was ever melody so sweet! The song *Caro nome* well deserves its universal popularity; it is a true and fresh expression of a young girl's first experience of the mystery of love, and the florid graces with which it is overlaid, so far from being superfluous, form an essential part of its charm. [It should be mentioned that the concluding shake on the E above the stave is not due to Verdi; it is a foolish tradition, like the high C in Manrico's song in *Il Trovatore,* and might very well be discontinued.]

The short remainder of this Act contains an amount of rapid action that is not easy for the audience to follow. Gilda has retired; the night is dark, but by the air of guarded lanterns is seen a group of men, cloaked and masked, outside the wall of Gilda's house, next to which is the Ceprano palace—it is Ceprano himself, with other courtiers, coming to carry out their threat of vengeance on the savage jester by abducting his supposed mistress. Rigoletto himself, for some unexplained reason, comes on the scene, suspicious and alarmed; Ceprano hides; the others hasten to explain that they have come to carry off the Countess for the Duke's pleasure, in accordance with the hunchback's own suggestion. He falls into the snare,

244

and offers to assist them. Provided with a mask, secured
by a handkerchief so that he is prevented from using his
eyes, he is set to hold the ladder by which the others scale
the wall. Placed as he is, he can hardly hear a woman's
stifled call for help, or the stealthy steps of the conspirators as they escape with their victim through the courtyard. Alarmed at last by the silence, Rigoletto tears the
bandage from his eyes and hurries to the door of Gilda's
dwelling—it is open, and there on the pavement is a scarf
that only Gilda can have dropped. The awful truth is
plain; it is Gilda, his own daughter, who is now in the
hands of the shameless courtiers, and he, her own father,
has assisted in her abduction. He enters the house,
rushes wildly, vainly, from room to room, and staggers
out again, only to fall to the ground with the terrible
cry:

A father's curse is on my head!

Act II. The opera would certainly gain in dignity and
consistency by the omission of the first number of this
Act; the Duke's solo, *Parmi veder le lagrime,* is an unworthy concession to the exacting vanity of tenors.
Having revisited Gilda's house and found it empty, his
Grace concludes that she has been stolen from him by
some rival gallant; he proceeds to lament her loss and to
shed the tear of sensibility, but his avowals that Gilda
is the guiding star of his existence, for whose sake he intends to turn over a new leaf, do not convince us—they
are merely a blot on the picture of an otherwise consistent
blackguard. Verdi has certainly made good use of the
opportunity for an air of sentiment, but the chorus, in
which his courtiers enlighten him as to the actual situation, is in his worst 'conspirator' manner. However,
brave amends are made in what follows. It would be
difficult to overestimate the mastery with which the great

composer has managed to convey the complex emotions of the next scene, especially when we consider how inadequate for such expression were the cramping formulas in which he worked.

Rigoletto, ignorant of the sequel to last night's villainy, swaggers in among the courtiers, desperately trying to keep up his usual manner of careless insolence, while his heart is racked with fear and anguish. The courtiers observe his feverish anxiety, and play upon it; for a time he can get nothing from them; when at last some chance words assure him beyond all doubt that Gilda is actually in the power of the Duke, his control gives way. Telling them that it is his daughter, not his mistress, whom he is seeking, he struggles madly to get through the doors that lead to the Duke's apartments; but all his efforts are in vain, and he exhausts himself in a furious outburst against the whole race of courtiers and their infamous lives. Finally his rugged spirit breaks down altogether—with trembling voice and humble gestures he goes from one to the other imploring their pity, their pardon for his insults of the past—if only they will let him pass, to save his daughter while there may yet be time!

At this crisis Gilda herself enters the hall, to hide her shame in Rigoletto's sheltering arms. The courtiers retire; the frightened girl pours out her pitiful tale, and receives her father's pardon and his blessing. [Gilda's opening solo, *Tutte le feste al tempio*, and Rigoletto's pathetic outburst, *Piangi, piangi, fanciulla*, are noticeable episodes in this long and finely sustained duet.]

A dramatic interruption is here made by Monterone, who is being led to execution; pausing to hurl one last curse on the Duke, who is still apparently untouched by his former imprecations, he is suddenly confronted by Rigoletto, who, too late repentant of his own misdeeds, bids Monterone have no misgivings as to the Duke's future—he, Rigoletto, will see that justice is done. The scene ends with another duet for father and daughter, he breathing vengeance against the Duke, she, still tender to her first lover, imploring Rigoletto to have mercy on him.

Act III. The last Act of *Rigoletto*, like that of *Il Trovatore,* is one of the outstanding triumphs of Verdi's genius; masterly throughout, it contains one of the most famous solos, and unquestionably the finest quartet, to be found in the whole range of Italian Opera. Indeed, although he treats the vocal part as always of first importance and never stints the flow of suave or brilliant melody, Verdi has here made such progress in avoiding set forms and in employing the orchestra as a means of dramatic and picturesque expression that we feel we are no longer dealing with 'Italian Opera' in the olden sense; although *Rigoletto* precedes *Aïda* by twenty years, it may fairly be considered as the composer's first excursion into the domain of modern music-drama.

The action takes place in the riverside cottage outside the town, where Sparafucile, the assassin, lives with his sister Maddalena. The scene is so set as to allow us a view of the interior as well as of what goes on outside.

Under cover of the dark and heavy summer night Rigoletto has brought his daughter here to convince her of her lover's infamy; they stand concealed outside the door of the house, where they can see through the window.

"And you still love this man?" the father asks.

"Ah, yes!"

"Oh piteous folly of ·a woman's heart! And if I prove him false to you—would you still love him?"

Gilda is not to be moved: "Nay, but he loves me dearly!"

Rigoletto leads her near the window; there is the Duke in rough soldier's dress; while Maddalena and her brother prepare for his entertainment, he sings the famous air, of which, in its place, one can never tire, *La donna è mobile.*

> Women are all the same—
> Never believe them!
> Love them and leave them—
> That's how to play the game!

Now comes the great quartet, *Un dì se ben rammentomi.* Inside is the amorous Duke with Maddalena on his knee—outside, poor Gilda and her indignant father.

We begin with the libertine's practised gallantries and the coquettish repulses of Maddalena, who is well able to keep him at a distance so long as it suits her. Then comes the Duke's solo, *Bella figila dell'amore,* of an entrancing elegance, which well bears repetition in the closely woven quartet that now follows, in which each voice is of about equal importance to the dramatic effect. Above the seductive melody for the tenor soar the piercing soprano notes which tell of Gilda's anguish; mingled with these are Maddalena's boisterous gaiety, and Rigoletto's stern demand for vengeance.

After the quartet the drama runs swiftly to its awful end. The recitative which follows must be carefully noted. Rigoletto bids his daughter set out at once, alone, for Verona, in the man's dress he has provided for her; he will join her later. He then hands to Sparafucile half of the price agreed upon—the remainder to be paid when he returns at midnight, to find the murder done. The assassin's custom is to sew the victim's body in a sack, and throw it in the river close at hand—but this last ceremony Rigoletto reserves for his own satisfaction. "Tell me his name!" says the assassin. "His name is Villainy, and mine—Revenge!" is Rigoletto's answer as he departs.

A storm is gathering—the most effective storm in

248

Italian Opera until this amazing composer surpassed it thirty-six years later in his *Otello*. The Duke resolves to stay the night, and is shown to an upper chamber, where he is heard singing snatches of his wanton ballad as he lies down to rest:

Women are all the same!

. . . .

Love them and leave them!

It is plain that the gathering storm is close at hand—in this last grim scene the elements assume almost the importance of *dramatis personæ;* in the moaning wind at least there is an actual human cry, as the effect is produced by an invisible chorus, whose voices, through closed lips, rise and fall in chromatic thirds; the part of the lightning (as vivid in the orchestra as on the stage) is to show us poor Gilda, who has crept back in her male attire, cowering against the wall, lashed by the rain which seems furiously to demand admission to the evil house. Through chinks in the boarding Gilda can see and hear all that goes on inside.

Sparafucile is handling a large sack, which he bids Maddalena repair for the safe conveyance of its lifeless burden; but the caresses of the handsome Duke have awakened some feeling of tenderness in the woman's heart, and she beseeches her brother to spare his life. Sparafucile is greedy for the ten ducats that Rigoletto has still to pay him, and which he will not get if the Duke escape. "Then," says Maddalena, "kill the hunchback!" But the assassin's code of honour will not allow him to murder one of his own clients. However, as Maddalena becomes more urgent, he makes a slight concession: supposing, before the hour of midnight, some traveller, seeking shelter from the storm, should knock at their door, his murdered body shall fill the sack instead of the Duke's.

Gilda, who has followed their talk with growing terror, has now taken her resolve. What hope is there, on such a night as this, of any wanderer near the lonely spot? She herself will be the victim. She thanks God that, although her lover has betrayed her, she is allowed to give her life for his. She knocks at the door. All light is extinguished in the cottage—the practised hand of Sparafucile needs no such guide—and the victim's stifled cries are scarcely heard amid the crashes of the thunder. The tempest is now in all its fury; it rages for some considerable time in the orchestra before Rigoletto returns, impatient to enjoy the full flavour of his vengeance.

Sparafucile is at the door to receive the price of blood; at his feet lies Rigoletto's share of the awful compact. With hideous joy he proceeds to drag the body toward the river bank—he must even stop on the way to gloat over his murdered enemy. "Here then," he cries, "here lies my master, the betrayer of my daughter, the all-powerful tyrant, dead at my feet—and I, his poor despised buffoon, shall pitch him like any dead dog into the river, a sack for his only covering."

The storm is passing over; the wind has dropped, but the lightning still flashes from time to time. A well-known voice cuts short the hunchback's triumph:

> Women are all the same—
> Never believe them!

Rigoletto turns his head to see the Duke step out, alert and strong, from his bedroom window on to the city wall, and walk homeward, singing!

Frantically he tears the sack's mouth apart—Gilda is not quite dead—there is still time to ask her father's forgiveness, "For," she whispers, "I loved him too well

250

—and for him I chose to die. Father! your pity, your pardon, for him as for me!"

But it is Rigoletto who has most need of pardon—who but he had mocked at Monterone's anguish? He recalls the outraged father's curse, and can but recognize the justice of its fulfilment.

IL TROVATORE

Music by VERDI. *Words by* CAMMARANO.
Rome, 1853; London, 1855; New York, 1855.

IT is merely a parrot-cry that insists on the unique absurdity of the plot of *Il Trovatore;* compared with that of many another opera—say *Robert le Diable* or *Dinorah*—the libretto is a masterpiece of sane lucidity and dramatic inevitableness. It is true that you cannot expect to understand *Trovatore* on the first visit without a little previous study of the 'book,' but that is no uncommon case—what about *Figaro?* How about *The Ring?* No; as sheer melodrama the plot of "The Troubadour, or the Gipsy's Vengeance," is good and strong—we must admit that "the statements is interesting but tough," as Huckleberry Finn remarked of a very different work. The chief difficulty in keeping hold of the thread of the drama in performance lies in the fact that so much that is necessary for us to follow is packed into a couple of narratives (one by quite a subordinate character), and these are poured out in a flow of such fascinating melody that our attention is distracted from their logical contents.

Yet the story of *Il Trovatore* must be mastered if we would properly enjoy the music, which is far more closely wedded to the dramatic development than is generally supposed. Of course, when we find the soprano labelled Leonora, the tenor Manrico, the old seneschal Ferrando, and the *confidante* Inez, we prepare at once for a drama of incident rather than of character; nevertheless, the play contains one of the strongest personalities in the whole of opera—the aged gipsy Azucena, a true figure of tragedy and one of Verdi's greatest triumphs in musical characterization.

Many years before the opening of the drama, Azucena had seen her mother burnt at the stake on a charge of having by witchcraft caused the illness of one of the Count di Luna's infant sons. The girl, herself a mother, had, in her frenzy of grief and hate, stolen the sickly child and flung it on to the still flaming pyre in which her mother had just perished; such, at least, was her intention, but, actually, it was her own child whom, in the blindness of her rage, she had snatched from the cradle where the two infants slept side by side, and had sent to such an awful death. So far her efforts of revenge have recoiled upon herself; but the stolen child remains in her hands—she flies with him to the mountains of Biscaglia, her old home, where she brings him up as her son, to be used as the instrument of her vengeance in the future.

When the play opens, the old Count di Luna has long been dead, and his son, succeeding, imagines himself the last of his race. Meanwhile Fate and Azucena have so contrived that Manrico, the Count's unsuspected brother, has become his bitter opponent in feudal warfare and his rival in love. At the Court of the Princess of Aragon, to which the Count is attached, dwells the lovely Leonora, whom he designs to marry; she, however, has been captivated by the gallant figure of Manrico, the troubadour, famous alike for song and knightly prowess, at whose triumph in the tournament she has herself assisted. As Manrico is in the service of the Prince of Biscaglia, the enemy of the Count, the two brothers are in perpetual conflict and from a double motive. Manrico at last succeeds in carrying Leonora off to his own castle, where he is just about "to lead her to the altar" when the news arrives that Azucena, his supposed mother, has fallen into the Count's hands, and has been condemned to the flames. He rushes off to her rescue, only to be captured by the Count's men and thrown into prison.

Leonora returns to the Count and offers to yield to his wishes if he will set Manrico free; but in order to escape from her promise she takes poison and dies in the arms of her true love. The Count, baffled and furious, orders Manrico to instant death by fire. As the flames of the pyre in the castle leap high around the victim and throw their glare on the dungeon walls, the Count drags Azucena to the iron grating of the cell: "See!" he cries, "that is thy son!" "Nay!" comes the awful answer, *"that is thy brother!"* The gipsy's revenge is accomplished—she falls dead at the Count di Luna's feet.

Act I. Terraces and gardens of the castle of Aliaferia, where Leonora and the Count di Luna both reside, in attendance on the Court of Aragon. A moonlit night, with flying clouds. Soldiers are on guard, to prevent the expected intrusion of the Troubadour, whose nocturnal serenades of late have made the Count uneasy. Ferrando, an old retainer, tells once again the old story of the mysterious fate of the Count's infant brother, the gipsy-mother's fiery death, and the escape of the daughter. Even now some malevolent influence lingers round the place; the spirit of the old witch has been seen by many in the form of a gigantic owl, fluttering round the battlements, and shrieking horribly at dead of night. The midnight bell now sounds, and Ferrando and his listeners retire.

[In this short but significant scene Verdi begins at once to batter our ears with his too persistent dance rhythms; Ferrando's long narration, *Abbietta zingara,* is in mazurka form, while the reference to the spectral owl, *Sull'orlo dei tetti,* in which the chorus join, has the effect of a tarantella, though written in three-four time; never-

254

theless, these materials, if properly handled on the stage as well as in the orchestra, produce an undeniable, if crude, effect of mystery and terror.]

Now Leonora, in white satin, and attended by Inez, her *confidante*, floats down the marble steps into the moonlit garden, and soon transports us to a region

Where moonlight and music and feeling are one.

She expects her Troubadour, Manrico; meanwhile Inez must have the story of their first meeting at the tourney, and of his serenades beneath her window. [Her solo, *Tacea la notte placida*, is the first of the many exquisite melodies in this opera which exalt so beautifully the spirit of the early days of the romantic movement, as expressed in Byron, Mrs. Radcliffe, and certain of the tales of Edgar Allan Poe.] Inez warns her against cherishing "so perilous a flame," to which the soprano replies in the inevitable *cabaletta* which had to follow the *andante*, according to the operatic formula of the time.

They retire to Leonora's apartments, beneath the windows of which the enamoured Count di Luna now appears. He cannot sleep for love of Leonora, whose heart he hopes this very hour to move to pity. Barely has he time for his short recitative when a distant harp is heard, preluding to a thrilling melody, such as only a troubadour could sing, *Deserto sulla terra*. Leonora too has heard it, and comes rushing on to the scene just as Manrico enters. Confused by the uncertain light, she throws herself most unfortunately into the arms of the Count, to Manrico's natural indignation. [This seems a quite unnecessary complication, which merely serves to perplex the spectator.] A few bars, however, suffice to put the matter right, and the two lovers enjoy a whole page of mutual rapture before the Count finds voice to interrupt them. In a tempestuous *allegro assai mosso, agita-*

tissimo (*Di geloso amor sprezzato*), he pours out his furious jealousy, and demands Manrico's blood; the Troubadour's haughty defiance and the shrill pleadings of Leonora make up a perfect whirlwind of a trio which lasts to the end of the Act, leaving, if not the singers exhausted, the audience breathless with excitement. Leonora falls senseless to the ground, while tenor and baritone prepare for what promises to be a mortal combat.

Such is the first Act, effective, swift, and simple. We have already had a feast of melody, in three of the composer's most characteristic manners: the true romantic beauty of Leonora's opening solo and Manrico's song behind the scenes; the rather incongruous dance tunes of Ferrando's legend; and the amazing, almost brutal, energy of the Count's jealous outburst in the concluding trio. Yet each of these models will be improved upon as the opera proceeds.

Act II. *Scene* 1. We are now to make the acquaintance of the one great personage of the play, the gipsy Azucena. The scene is a gipsy encampment; the men are busy at the forge, the maidens dancing to their tinkling tambourines; all is life and gaiety, musically crude and highly coloured. The famous Anvil Chorus, to which the men beat time with their blacksmiths' hammers, runs its noisy course. The song, the dancing, cease, to be succeeded by music of a very different order.

Azucena has been cowering over a fire of logs, seeing, hearing, nothing of what goes on around her. Sunk in her brooding sorrow, bowed and withered not so much by age as by the awful experience of her girlhood, she lives for one thing only—revenge. It is true she has a mother's love for Manrico, whom she has reared from infancy to manhood, but even him she would sacrifice on the altar of her vengeance. Now she rises, a dark, menacing figure, under the influence of some terrible emotion; without prelude or preparation she begins her air *Stride la vampa*—'Azucena's Fire-song' would be its best description. Softly at first, as if her reverie by the camp-fire had not yet been broken, she paints the scene of her mother's awful fate: she sees her in rags, barefoot, bareheaded, her grey hair fallen about her shoulders, dragged to the stake amid the jeers and howls of the pitiless mob. The first part of the song is given with a tense and ominous quiet, but as the fire is kindled at the stake and the flames leap high around the victim, so does the voice gather strength and rise to a cry of agony. By the end of the second verse Azucena is exhausted, and has just sufficient strength for the *Mi vendica!* which was her mother's last utterance, and is her own life's one object.

The gipsies are now on the move, but Azucena remains, to explain to Manrico the meaning of her appeal for vengeance. In what is musically one of the finest numbers of the opera she describes how her mother in her death-agony bequeathed to her daughter the awful duty of revenge. She then goes on to reveal her own dreadful secret—how having stolen the old Count di Luna's son, intending to throw him into the flames, she finds that in her blind fury she has sacrificed her own child instead.

Here, it must be noted, we have the weakest link in the dramatic chain. Manrico draws the only possible conclusion from Azucena's narrative—that, as she never had more than one child, he cannot be her son. Her only reply to his challenge is that, in her excitement, she has told her tale amiss! Yes, he is her son! Has she not been to him the tenderest of mothers? So it is he who must take up her cause and the task of vengeance imposed upon her. "*Mi vendica! Mi vendica!*" she reiterates. The Count must be made to suffer for his father's crime.

She urges Manrico to a keener sense of this duty—did he not lately, when the Count was in his power, refrain from his advantage? What moved him to act thus?

Manrico's reply is one of the curiosities of the opera—a point which probably very few have noticed. His air, *Mal reggendo,* is a striking melody, yet of the vaguest significance, and the general attitude is to accept it, without further question, as one of those haunting tunes with which Verdi, at this period, could scarcely help plastering his score. The words, however, are full of quite unexpected interest; they relate how Manrico, when the Count lay prostrate at his feet, and his sword was poised for the fatal blow, was turned from his purpose by a voice from heaven saying to him, "Forbear to strike!" This subtle touch of psychology, suggesting a secret affinity between the two brothers, is rather surprising in an opera of the period and calibre of *Il Trovatore.*

Just as Azucena is spurring him on to greater ruthlessness in the future, a messenger arrives with the tidings that his presence is needed in two places—the Prince of Biscaglia has appointed him to the defence of a certain fortress, and Leonora, deceived by a false report of his death, is on the eve of entering a convent, there to take the veil. No need now to urge the Troubadour to action —he is on fire to be gone. But Azucena becomes all tenderness and apprehension; she cannot bear to let him go—and it is only after a lengthy duet that he succeeds in tearing himself away.

[Azucena's music all through this Scene is worthy of the closest attention; it shows an advance in the direction of 'music-drama' beyond anything yet achieved in Italian opera. The air *Stride la vampa,* which may be regarded as the central point of interest in the opera, is treated in a strikingly original manner; without any recitative to

258

introduce it—the usual "Where am I?" "O day of horror!" or "Well, I will tell you"—it cuts straight into
the scene of noisy gaiety with compelling effect; the
melody is given to the orchestra later on, quite in the
Wagnerian manner, and is introduced with still greater
point into the Prison Scene at the end.

But far finer music is to be found in the scena that
follows, *Condotta er' ella in ceppi,* in which Azucena re-
constructs the tragedy of her mother's death, and her
own fatal mistake; here the vocal phrases, broad and
melodious as they are, serve admirably to conduct the
narrative, while the independent figures in the orchestra
suggest most vividly the tragic idea of the aged gipsy,
dragging herself wearily through life under a burden too
great for her to bear; the long, low notes of the concluding bars, *Sul capo mio le chiome sento drizzarsi ancor,*
sung in the contralto's deepest tones, leave an impression
of hopeless misery not easily forgotten.]

Scene 11. Moonlight in the convent grounds. The
Count, who has heard of Leonora's intention of retiring
from the world, is determined to prevent her; he has
come, with his retainers, just in time. He sings of his
passion in the famous *Il balen del suo sorriso,* which,
under the title of 'The Tempest of the Heart,' was the
delight, or torment, of generations of Victorians. The
convent bell is heard, and a chanted chorale; the Count's
men stealthily prepare for action. From the chapel come
the nuns in procession to receive Leonora, who arrives,
attended by Inez; just as the convent gates are about to
close on her for ever, the Count steps forward to claim
her—and at the same moment Manrico and his men
arrive, with a similar purpose. Leonora flies to the arms
of her lover, whom she had supposed to be dead. Her
song of ecstasy, *Deggio e posso crederlo,* permits the
most interesting material for the *finale,* in which the

chorus of soldiers, retainers, and religious lend but feeble support; it is made plain, however, that Manrico's party is the stronger, and Leonora passes without a struggle into his possession. The heroine is allowed to end the Scene, *sola,* with a four-bar repetition of the loveliest phrases of her song of ecstasy.

Act III. *Scene* 1. An armed camp near the fortress of Castellor in the Biscaglia territory. The Count is besieging the castle, to which Manrico has brought Leonora. The Soldiers' Chorus with which the Scene opens is, of all such compositions, perhaps the most blatant and banal—though ample amends will soon be made. The Count enters, deploring his loss, and threatening swift revenge on his rival; on the morrow Castellor shall fall, and Leonora shall be his. A tumult in the orchestra heralds the noisy entrance of a band of soldiers, dragging in the unhappy Azucena, on whom they have just laid hands. To the Count and old Ferrando a gipsy is always an object of suspicion—the family legend is never forgotten.

Azucena, on being questioned, admits she is from Biscaglia, a hostile territory; on closer scrutiny Ferrando discovers, or decides, that she is the very gipsy who stole the Count's infant brother. The Count, of course, accepts his word, and when Azucena in her despair cries out: "Manrico, my son! why art thou not here to help me!" the discovery that the mother of his rival is in his hands rouses him to greater fury. Azucena must die the fiery death! The old woman makes a brave struggle for freedom, but is bound fast and dragged away, calling down the curse of heaven on the Count and her tormentors.

[In this short but very dramatic Scene, Azucena's music again creates the right atmosphere, that of the weary, desolate woman driven on to her doom. In spite

260

of its set, monotonous rhythm, the solo *Giorni poveri vivea* has a sombre sense of tragedy, as have also the rest of her broken phrases, while the frenzied vigour of her curse, *Deh! rallentate barbari!* seems almost to break its formal fetters, and works up the *finale* to a perfectly appropriate climax.]

Scene 11. This Scene, which passes inside the fortress of Castellor, consists virtually of but two solos, one of which is among the loveliest, the other the most sensational, in the entire opera. The lovers are about to be joined in marriage, but even now Leonora cannot quite shake off her fears of the dangers that surround them. Manrico bids his bride put all her trust in love: whether on earth or in heaven, no power can separate them—they are eternally united. [This is the meaning of the suave and finely developed air, *Ah sì, ben mio,* which for sheer melodic beauty Verdi himself has rarely surpassed.] This is followed by the sound of the organ, and a most effective passage for the two voices, which is too often omitted. They are on their way to the chapel when a breathless messenger breaks in on them with the dreadful tidings that Azucena has been captured by the Count di Luna's men, and is in instant danger of being burnt at the stake. There is not a moment to be lost—Manrico takes leave of his weeping bride, and expresses his passionate desire for his foster-mother's release in the famous *Di quella pira,* which calls for robuster vocal chords and a more heroic style of delivery than any other tenor solo in the whole of Italian Opera. For the wholly unnecessary parade of the high C, which is now universally expected at the end of the second verse, the vanity of tenors, and not Verdi, is responsible; he finishes the Scene with the aid of a male chorus, an arrangement in every way more satisfactory.

Act IV. Even if *Il Trovatore* should disappear from the repertory, it seems probable that the last Act would still survive; it is a compact masterpiece, in which lyric beauty and dramatic significance are closely blended, and seventy years of continuous popularity have failed to dispel, or even to diminish, its glamour of romance.

Scene 1. Outside the castle of Aliaferia. Manrico, in his attempt to rescue Azucena, has himself been taken prisoner; he and his foster-mother lie in the same dungeon awaiting execution.

Leonora, accompanied by one of Manrico's men from Castellor, is here; she has come inspired by one fixed purpose, to save the Troubadour's life even at the cost of her own. To the Count she will give her promise, if necessary, but herself, never! "Here," she says, raising the hand on which is a ring which conceals a deadly poison, "here is my sure protection!"

Turning toward the tower in which she knows Manrico to be confined, she pours forth her soul in a gush of warm and tender melody. *D'amor sull'ali rosee* far surpasses even her first air, *Tacea la notte,* as an example of romantic beauty. Hardly is it finished when the choir in the chapel are heard chanting the *Miserere,* the penitential psalm which implores mercy for the parting soul. "Have mercy, O Lord, on the souls of them that are so soon to leave this world! Let them not fall into the pit of darkness!"

[It is this simple chorus which has given this Scene the popular name of 'The Miserere,' now often misapplied to the great tenor solo which is to follow.]

All Leonora's terrors are aroused by these funereal sounds; in the poignant, broken phrases which follow we may hear her sobs, and count the very beatings of her heart.

Now from the tower floats down Manrico's pathetic

farewell to life and Leonora, *Ah, chè la morte*—short, simple, and of flawless outline, it is probably the nearest approach to an 'immortal' melody that is to be found in Italian Opera. Of rare intrinsic beauty, its effect on the stage is prepared and heightened by every circumstance. With the initial advantage of being sung by an invisible tenor, its broad phrases in the major key, breaking in upon the heart-rending sobs of the heroine, come as a complete surprise, and seem to lend a touch of resignation, if not of hope, even to her despair, while it gains enormously by mingling with Leonora's fervent responses, and the sombre strains of the religious choir. But even removed from its setting, and divested of all these advantages, sung in the concert-room or played on a barrel-organ, the melody of *Ah, chè la morte* never fails to cast its spell upon those who hear it—it seems to be made of the same imperishable stuff as Gluck's *Che farò senza Euridice* and Handel's *Largo in G.*

The Count enters, and in the long and exciting duet which follows Leonora has a hard struggle for the life of the Troubadour. Her first plea—"Slay me—but set him free!"—serves only to increase the fury of her rejected suitor, but he yields at last on her offering herself as the reward of his clemency; on condition that she marries the Count, she is to be allowed even to visit Manrico in his cell and be the bearer of his pardon. Leonora breaks into an ecstasy of rejoicing at this, and in the midst of her *roulades* finds opportunity to drain, unnoticed, the poison from the fatal ring.

Scene 11. A dungeon in the tower of the castle. Azucena is lying on her wretched bed, but cannot sleep. Manrico tries to comfort her, but in vain—the gipsy already feels the hand of death upon her, and her only hope is that she may die before they come to drag her away to execution. Always before her eyes is the horror of the blazing pyre, and her mother's agony repeated. [The fire-*motif* is here introduced in the orchestra with admirable effect.] She works herself up to a frenzy of terror, and sinks once more exhausted on the bed. Manrico takes his lute and soothes her to a calmer mood; between waking and sleeping she sees again in vision the hills of her native land, to which they both will surely soon return; and so she sinks to slumber. [The music of this scene—*Sì, la stanchezza* and *Ai nostri monti*—in its touching pathos, gained by the simplest of means, is more than worthy to stand side by side with the *Miserere* music, only it can hardly bear separation from its dramatic surroundings.]

Leonora enters, and the end follows swiftly. After the first rapture of meeting, her good tidings only awaken Manrico's suspicions; on what terms has she purchased his freedom? Guessing at only half the truth, he casts her from him, with reproaches for her infidelity. But the poison has nearly finished its work, and Leonora sinks into the arms of her repentant lover. The Count enters, discovers how he has been tricked, and orders Manrico to instant execution. Azucena awakes to find Leonora dead and Manrico gone. She grasps the truth —the moment for revelation has come, but it is too late. The Count drags Azucena to the grating of the cell to see Manrico already in his death-agony: "See! yonder is thy son!" "Nay! thy own brother!" is the terrible answer. With the cry "Mother! thou art avenged!" she sinks lifeless to the ground; the Count is left alone, to bear the burden of the gipsy's curse.

LA TRAVIATA

Music by VERDI. *Words by* PIAVE.
Venice, 1853; *London,* 1856; *New York,* 1856.

ALTHOUGH *La Traviata* is perhaps the most faded of all Verdi's surviving operas, containing few numbers of outstanding beauty, and several that show the composer at his worst, nevertheless its production must rank among the most important events in the history of the lyric drama. It marks a definite advance in Verdi's musical development, and introduces an entirely new *genre* of subjects capable of operatic treatment.

Its vigorous survival—and it is doubtful if even *Il Trovatore* enjoys so great a popularity at the present time—is due to two causes, one being the irresistible attraction it has always had for the prima donna, the other the genuine human interest of the story. Yet this story was in the beginning a fruitful source of trouble. The libretto is based on the French play *La Dame aux Camélias,* by the younger Dumas, written in 1849, but not produced till 1852 owing to the objections raised by the licensing authority of Paris. In this country the Lord Chamberlain absolutely refused to sanction any English version of the play, and when in 1856 *La Traviata* managed somehow to evade his vigilance and make a triumphant appearance at Her Majesty's Theatre it raised a storm of protest. Clergymen thundered at it from the pulpit, the *Times* denounced its "foul and hideous horrors," but the public found it neither foul nor horrifying, and with the enchanting Piccolomini as the heroine it drew crowded houses at each performance.

So widespread was the interest excited that even those pious persons who were loudest in their condemnation managed to satisfy their curiosity and their conscience by attending the concert performances of the work given at Exeter Hall, the stronghold of Puritanical principles. The situation is well summed up in Albert Smith's satirical comment:

> The chance won't come again to us, the world's regenerators,
> To hear improper music, and not in the vile theayters;
> The *Times* condemned its playhouse form, but—bless our
> happy land!—
> What's sin in the Haymarket is religion in the Strand!

An actual acquaintance with the opera soon convinced all sensible people that such prejudices were unjustifiable; *La Traviata* might be called silly or sentimental, hectic or in bad taste, but immoral it certainly was not.

Nevertheless Verdi's new opera was a daring experiment: not only does it mark the first intrusion of psychological problems into the lyric drama; it is also the first to deal with contemporary society in modern dress. This innovation was so little to the taste of an Italian audience on its first production (Venice, 1853) that the opera was a complete failure; but on its revival in the following year it was put back into the Louis-Quatorze period, and at once started on its successful career. This concession to convention, however, was soon dropped, and the opera is generally played, in accordance with Verdi's original intention, with the setting which Dumas' realistic drama demands. This is undoubtedly the proper treatment, for the atmosphere of *La Traviata* is unmistakably that of Paris in 1850. Another plan for which there is much to be said is to dress the piece according to the fashion actually in vogue at the time of the particular revival; whichever method is adopted, the opera retains its almost unique privilege of enabling the prima donna to wear all the diamonds her heart can desire without any risk of overdressing the part.

La Traviata, indeed, calls aloud for diamonds, emeralds, rubies—any jewellery you like, with the possible exception of pearls—dealing as it does with all the glitter of the fashionable *demi-monde* at a period when Paris might with truth be called 'the gay city.' The subject, considered so daring in its day, but seeming so hackneyed in our eyes by reason of its wearisome iteration on the stage, is the reformation of a courtesan through the influence of a genuine passion, and her sacrifice of wealth, happines, her newly acquired self-respect, everything, to the fancied interests of the man she loves. The story, so admirably handled by the younger Dumas, has been condensed by Piave, the librettist, into a well-knit play in which the pathetic figure of the consumptive heroine makes a strong emotional appeal.

Act I opens with a supper-party in the *salons* of the beautiful and notorious Violetta Valéry. The conduct of this scene, with the constant *va-et-vient* of the guests, the short phrases of vocal conversation, and the continuous brilliancy of the orchestral background, reminds us of the opening scene in *Rigoletto.* There, it will be remembered, the Duke, the *primo tenore,* emerges from the crowd to sing his first solo; here a still greater sacrifice of operatic convention is made, as the prima donna has no *aria d'entrata,* but is 'discovered' among her guests, and joins at once in the general conversation.

Violetta is the leader of the revels; an admirable hostess, she is constantly contriving some new pleasure, some fresh excitement, for the company. But from the very outset it is obvious that her intimate friends—Flora Bervoix and Gaston de Letorières—are anxious that she should not overtax her strength, for, as we learn, she has only just recovered from a severe illness, and her cough still troubles her. Gaston, in introducing his young friend Alfredo Germont as a new admirer, mentions that the latter has called every day of her illness to make inquiries. Violetta is evidently touched by this, though she treats it lightly, and laughingly holds such conduct up as a model to the Baron Douphol, who, though an old acquaintance, had paid her no such attentions.

Alfredo, in fact, has worshipped *"la belle Valéry"* for many months in secret, though they had never met before; his youth and ardour could hardly fail to move the poor *demi-mondaine,* who from time to time had allowed herself to dream of some such faithful lover. She calls for more champagne, fills his glass with her own hands, and demands in return a song in praise of the good wine. Alfredo then sings the song generally known as the 'brindisi,' *Libiamo ne' lieti calici.* Violetta adds a second verse, and the two voices in unison are supported by all the rest in a brilliant *ensemble.*

The strains of a waltz are now heard from an adjoining room, and Violetta will have all join in the dance. She herself is preparing to lead the way when a sudden faintness stops her. She insists, however, that her guests shall not lose their pleasure, which she hopes to share with them in a little while.

Left to herself, the poor girl begins to suspect the true nature of her complaint. Dragging herself to the mirror, she gazes, horrified, at what she sees there. The deathly pallor, the hectic spot, the wasted muscles of the throat, all warn her that the hand of consumption is laid upon her. However, the actual faintness has passed, and she turns back to the room—to find Alfredo at her side. Touched by her obvious frailty, he urges his chivalrous passion, his desire to protect her, to remove her from the perilous conditions of her present existence. Violetta, half incredulous, laughs at what she assumes to be a sudden fancy—how long, pray, has he loved her? From the moment when first he saw her—'twas then that the true meaning of love was first revealed to him.

This dialogue has been carried on to the accompaniment of the gay waltz music in the adjoining room; now the music stops as Alfredo begins his solo, *Un dì felice,* the second section of which should be specially noted:

> *Ah quell' amor ch'è il palpito*
> *Dell'universo intero,*
> *Misterioso altero,*
> *Croce e delizia al cor!*

> Ah Love, mysterious ecstasy
> By every heart confessed!
> Thou strange, delicious mingling
> Of rapture and unrest!

These words are set to a haunting melody which Violetta uses, with even finer effect, in her great *scena* which ends the Act. Violetta still keeps him at a distance; against his impassioned love-song she throws off some playful passages of brilliant *coloratura*—she warns him that he would do wisely to forget her.

The intrusion of Gaston for a moment seems to draw them more closely together; on his departure Violetta, in softened mood, gives Alfred a flower, which he has permission to bring back to her as soon as it is withered. "To-morrow then!" cries the enraptured lover, and departs full of joyful anticipation.

The guests now troop in to take a noisy farewell. It is plain that Violetta's absence has not damped their gaiety, but the red light of dawn is already paling the candles, and warns them that day is the time for slumber.

Violetta, left alone, begins her great scena, *Ah fors' è lui,* in which she debates the choice, which seems at last to offer, between her present way of life and one that promises a happiness that she has never known.

The situation is finely conceived. The light of day begins to stream in through the half-curtained windows, shaming the guttering tapers, the gilded mirrors, the tumbled luxury of the apartments. Of all her flattering friends not one has stayed behind; she is alone—but her new lover has just left her with the promise of a speedy return, and new hope has sprung up in her heart. Old memories now awaken—how, in her innocent girlhood, she had dreamed sometimes of a perfect union with the ideal lover who should offer her a life's devotion—was this her lover come at last?

Softly, timidly almost, she begins her song, as if afraid to drive the lovely dream away; but her voice gathers strength and passion as she glides into the melody she has heard so lately from Alfredo's lips—she repeats his very words:

> Ah Love, mysterious ecstasy
> By every heart confessed!
> Thou strange, delicious mingling
> Of rapture and unrest!

By the time Violetta has finished her second stanza we have to acknowledge that *Ah fors' è lui* is one of Verdi's most successful creations—the melody has a quite peculiar charm of its own, exactly appropriate to the character and situation to which it is assigned. We can only wonder, regretfully, remembering *Aïda,* what the composer might have made of it in the later stages of his development.

But she awakes from her dream; she, the practised courtesan, hardened in all the sordid shifts of her world, fighting her friendless way through "the crowded desert that men call Paris"—what has she to do with dreams of a better life and of an honest man's fidelity? 'Tis

270

folly! Abandoning herself to a reckless despair, she breaks out into an elaborate air of forced gaiety, *Sempre libera degg' io*—a composition far exceeding the 'brindisi' in brilliance. Her only way is to plunge yet deeper into the pleasure of the hour, and drown all tender memories, all foolish aspirations, in a constant whirl of ever fresh excitements—true love is not for her.

Only the voice of Alfredo outside her window, still singing of that mysterious power that moves the universe, allows us to hope that Violetta may yet attain to her heart's desire.

Act II. Scene 1. Violetta's country house, where she and Alfredo have been established for some months. It is within an easy carriage-drive of Paris, but the gay city rarely sees them now; they have passed from the first flush of passion into that serener stage where the mere sharing of a common life is sufficient for their perfect happiness. Violetta has found her dreams come true; it is to Alfredo she owes her redemption, her second birth, and richly has she repaid him. In his air, *Di miei bollenti spiriti,* he sings of how her tender, gracious influence has calmed the turbulence of his youthful passions and brought him into the tranquil haven of love. Alas, both are living in a false security; they

> Have not raised the veil to see
> If still their heaven be lit above.

The entrance of Violetta's companion, Annina, is accompanied by an ominous restlessness in the orchestra; she has just returned from Paris, and her explanations, in answer to Alfredo's questioning, are sufficient to rouse him from his dream of peace. The visit to the city was made at Violetta's request, with the object of raising money, by the sale of her property, to meet her current expenses. In the absorption of his present happiness Alfredo has failed to realize that the upkeep of their establishment has been borne by Violetta alone. Hitherto she had depended on the lavish generosity of her many admirers; now that these supplies have long been cut off she is at her wits' end to find the necessary funds; unwilling to apply to Alfredo, she had commissioned Annina, under a pledge of secrecy, to arrange for the sale of horses, carriages, valuables of all sorts, in order to replenish her purse. Alfredo is now fully awake to his dishonourable position; filled with shame and remorse, he determines to hurry off to Paris, unknown to Violetta, in order to raise the necessary money and stop the sale of her property.

Violetta now enters the room; she is no longer the painted, bediamonded *demi-mondaine* of the first Act, but a gracious, gentle figure, glowing with quiet happiness, and with at least the appearance of radiant health. Her first inquiry is for Alfredo; on learning that he has left the house she turns to her correspondence. There she finds a note from Flora Bervoix, her old acquaintance, inviting her to some festivity at her house that evening. She shakes her head with a quiet smile—such gaieties are no longer to her liking, and never again will she enter such society.

But destiny is implacable; moreover, there is much to be done in one short Scene, and the librettist is in a hurry. Violetta has just given the servant permission to admit, as she supposes, the man of business whom she is expecting when, on raising her head, she finds herself confronted with Alfredo's father, whom she now sees for the first time.

The elder Germont (an operatic *père noble* of the most tedious kind) has come prepared to curse, to threaten, to insist on an instant separation of the lovers, but Violetta's air and manner convince him of his mistake; this is not the woman he had expected to find. Still, his errand must be accomplished. Divining the nobler strain in her nature, he makes a subtle appeal to her generosity. He has a daughter—*Pura siccome un angelo* —a young girl just on the threshold of happiness; she is betrothed to the man she loves, but social conventions make it impossible for them to marry so long as the scandal of Alfredo's connexion with Violetta continues. Can she endure to blight this young girl's life? Will she not sacrifice herself for the sake of Alfredo's sister—nay, for Alfredo's sake, whose future prospects are gravely injured by this present *liaison?* Let her consider her own future also; to-day she is beautiful, she is young —though Alfredo is younger still; when her charms begin to wither, what other hold is she likely to have upon him? Would it not be better to part from him now, and leave a fragrant memory behind her? Violetta has listened in terrible distress to the elder Germont's arguments, struggling with all her might against their convincing logic. As he proceeds, his respect, his pity, increase; he feels toward her some of the compassion which he claims for his own daughter, and it is to the tender earnestness of his pleading that she yields at last. "Tell your daughter," she says, "that to ensure her happiness another woman has sacrificed her last hope on earth. I will leave Alfredo this very day, and, in order that he may not follow me, he shall be made to believe that I am faithless to him, though God is my witness my love is his and his alone for evermore. I feel I have not long to live. When I am dead promise that you will tell him the true story of my sacrifice." Full of gratitude the father takes his leave, after pressing to his heart the woman whom he would gladly have welcomed as his daughter had Fate allowed.

"Heaven give me strength to endure to the end!" is Violetta's cry when left alone. Alas, she does not yet know the fearful nature of the trial that awaits her. Her intention was to leave the house before Alfredo's return, and so escape the intolerable torture of a last farewell. She writes a note to Flora, accepting her invitation, and is planning the letter to her lover when Alfredo enters the room. He questions her as to what she is doing, but hardly waits for an answer, and even fails to notice her agitation; he has troubles of his own. His father has written him a stern letter to demand an interview, and he expects him at any moment. Ignorant of the scene which has just taken place, he sets his hope on the influence that Violetta's charm is sure to have over the elder Germont. "Ah!" he says, looking fondly at his beloved, "how he will love you when he sees you!"

This is almost more than Violetta can bear. His father must not find her there—she must retire, she says, for a time; on her return she will throw herself at his father's feet—he will forgive them—they will live henceforth happy for ever in their perfect love. Happy for ever! As she says these words the tears are streaming down her cheeks. She clings to Alfredo, repeating, with a feverish insistence, the question, "You do love me, Alfredo? You truly, truly love me?" Ah, how truly, how dearly! But why does she weep? " 'Twas only a passing cloud! Now I am calm again—see! I can smile at you, Alfredo! In a little while I will return to find you here—here, among the flowers! We will make our peace with your father, and no one, nothing, shall ever come between us!" Acting her part out bravely to the end, the broken-hearted girl takes, as she supposes, her last farewell.

[The closing passage of this Scene is perhaps the most affecting in the opera; the dramatic situation finds its direct and natural expression in the simplicity of the words and the poignant melody to which they are allied:

Amami, Alfredo, quanto io t'amo!
Addio!
Love me, beloved, as I love thee, for ever!
And now, farewell!

Words and music may seem bald on paper, but no one who has heard them rightly sung can ever forget the cry of the heart which they convey.]

Alfredo has had but a little while to ponder happily on the depth of Violetta's devotion when Fate knocks at the door—a messenger with a note entrusted to him by a lady in a carriage, on the road to Paris. It is in Violetta's handwriting; he opens it—and in a moment his world has fallen in ruins around him. She has gone— she, who seemed to live only in his love, has left him, to return to her old associates, her old way of living— her love for him was merely a passing fancy. The blow is too heavy. Alfredo staggers and falls—into his father's arms, who has entered unobserved. Tenderly condoling with his son, the elder Germont uses every argument to induce him to return home with him—home to the fair land of Provence, where skies are brighter and hearts more true. His father's love, the family honour, the warm welcome that awaits him—to all these considerations the younger man is deaf; his grief has already turned to raging jealousy; he suspects the Baron Douphol of being the cause of Violetta's desertion. Vengeance is now his only thought. Finding Flora's invitation for that evening on Violetta's writing-table, he concludes at once that she will go there to meet his rival. He hurries off to Paris to prepare for his revenge, and the distracted father follows him.

[It is obvious that the librettist has attempted too much in this short Scene; the action is so hurried that it misses its proper effect; *e.g.,* the interval between Violetta's adieu to Alfredo and his receipt of the letter which transforms the tenderest of lovers into a jealous madman is far too short—we are not convinced. Verdi must have found his task one of great difficulty; he seems divided between his own desire to write music that shall preserve the dramatic continuity and the necessity of providing his singers, and the public, with the conventional arias which he knew they would expect of him. These, unfortunately, are among the worst specimens of their kind; Alfredo's two solos may be passed over in silence, but the air for the 'heavy father'—*Di Provenza, il mar, il sol*—really provokes comment as being the most exasperating jingle that ever masqueraded as a pathetic melody. On the other hand, Violetta's music makes fair amends; her part preserves as much dramatic consistency as is possible in the circumstances; no florid passages are admitted, her two short-set melodies, *Non sapete* and *Dite alla giovine,* are not inappropriate to their sentiments, while her farewell is, as we have said, a masterpiece of expression.]

Scene 11. This being the second drawing-room Scene in the play—for Flora Bervoix has thrown open her *salons* to the gay world of Paris—Verdi has taken care to avoid any monotonous repetition of the musical atmosphere of Act I. Consequently we find Flora entertaining her guests with a masquerade—first come the Zingari (with a little byplay of fortune-telling), then a chorus of Spanish matadors. There is no ball-room dancing, the gaming-tables being the chief object of interest on the stage. Alfredo is the first to arrive, then Violetta escorted by the Baron Douphol; the latter, enraged at the sight of his rival, roughly warns Violetta against holding any intercourse with him, and the poor girl bitterly repents of her imprudence. (Her pathetic phrase

276

Ah, perchè venni incauta? although a stage 'aside,' is heard more than once above the other voices as the action proceeds.)

Alfredo seats himself at a gaming-table—his amazing run of luck draws the attention of the whole assembly. The Baron challenges him to play, Alfredo's luck still holds, and it is plain that the passions of both are rising high, when the announcement of supper separates them for a time, but not before Alfredo has promised to give Douphol full satisfaction on some future occasion, by which all understand that a duel is intended. Dreading the consequences to Alfredo, Violetta contrives to keep him with her when the other guests have gone to supper. She implores him to leave the house at once and so avoid further trouble; he will agree on one condition only— that she will accompany him. With a breaking heart, but strong in her resolution, she refuses—she has given her promise to another, who has a better right. "To whom?" he asks. "To the Baron Douphol." "Then," he persists, "you love him?" "Yes," replies Violetta, *splendide mendax,* a heroine indeed at this moment, "I love him!"

Beside himself with fury, Alfredo calls the astonished guests from the supper-room. He tells them the story of his long association with Violetta, of how he was led into allowing her to bear all the expenses of their establishment, of her subsequent desertion, of which they are all aware, and announces his intention of at once discharging the humiliating obligation. "And here," he cries, "I call you all to witness that I have made reparation in full!" With these words he flings the heavy purse containing the whole of his evening's winnings at Violetta's feet.

A general chorus of execration is heard—not one in the assembly but is shocked and disgusted at this wanton outrage. Loudest in his indignation is the elder Germont, who denounces his son's conduct as unworthy of his house; Alfredo, his fury dead within him, is stricken with shame and remorse; and above all the storm of the elaborate *ensemble* is heard the cry of Violetta, heartbroken at Alfredo's cruelty; yet even that cannot shake her faithful devotion—she is his, and his only, till death and beyond the grave.

[This Scene suffers, like the preceding, from the attempt to crowd too much into a short period. We become aware, too, of something amiss in the psychology. It is difficult to account for the unanimous outburst of sympathy with Violetta and of strong indignation against Alfredo for denouncing his late mistress; only in the elder Germont, who knows the truth of the affair, is such indignation explicable; to the others Violetta's sudden desertion of her devoted lover, apparently from mere caprice, must seem altogether blameworthy, while the behaviour of Alfredo, who believes himself to have been basely deceived, is natural and excusable. Admirers of Verdi may find their comfort in the elaborate and effective *finale* which he has managed to construct out of so unsatisfactory a situation.]

Act III. The tranquil beauty of the orchestral prelude—of a refinement quite remarkable for this stage of Verdi's development—prepares us for the quiet close of poor Violetta's stormy day. She has been for some time a prisoner in her modest Paris apartment—far gone in consumption, she is but a shadow of her former self, and death is nearer than she imagines.

In all respects she is a changed woman; she has made her peace with God, and awaits the end with resignation, grateful for the careful ministrations of her faithful Annina and the good doctor Grenvil. When the scene opens, her room is still curtained for the night,

278

but at her request Annina lets in the daylight. The streets are ringing with songs and mirthful cries; it is the Carnival, as Annina reminds her. Violetta's instant thought is for the many poor who will go hungry in the midst of so much feasting; she bids Annina take half the contents of her purse for distribution among them. The doctor enters, and tries to cheer her with promises of a speedy convalescence—but to Annina he whispers that her mistress has but a few hours to live. Left to herself, Violetta looks over the morning's correspondence.

The love-motive, *Ah, quell'amor,* is heard in the orchestra as she opens a letter from the elder Germont: "The duel was fought, the Baron wounded, but not seriously—Alfredo was obliged to leave the country. I have since written to him, telling him the full story of the noble sacrifice you made for his sake. Bravely have you kept your promise to me! Alfredo is hastening back to plead for your forgiveness—and I shall come with him. Only get well, and enjoy the happiness you so richly deserve."

Sweet comfort indeed—but it comes too late. Violetta drags herself to her mirror—one look is enough: she sees the shadow of approaching death. At the thought of her lover's return the longing for life awakes once more within her—but she knows it cannot be; farewell now to those false visions of recovery, farewell to all earthly hope; Alfredo will not come in time; she must die the lonely death allotted to those of her class—no cross, no springing flowers, will mark her grave. May God have mercy on the soul of the poor 'Traviata,' and give her rest at last!

[This solo, *Addio del passato,* ranks with Violetta's *Amami Alfredo,* in Act I, as an admirable example of true melodic expression—it has the ring of absolute sincerity. Even the fetters of the metrical form are less rigid than usual, and may easily be loosened by a skilful artist; sung throughout in a sustained *mezza voce* it makes an appeal of infinite pathos—it is the very dirge of perished hope.]

After the relief of a gay chorus from the revellers in the street Annina enters in great excitement—is her mistress well enough to hear some good news? Ah, Violetta needs no further hint—the door opens, and she is once more in the heaven of her beloved's arms.

The remainder of the Act is practically a duet between the two. In the first flush of joy Violetta seems to drink new life with every breath—even Alfredo is for a while deceived. They make plans for the future; they will leave Paris at once and live again the quiet country life in which they found such happiness.

[The duet *Parigi, o cara,* is one of the most popular numbers in the opera; it has, however, worn badly, and is singularly unfortunate in inviting comparison with the lovely *Ai nostri monti* in *Il Trovatore,* of which it might almost pass for a parody.]

Violetta is eager to take advantage of her recovered energies; she will go out—they will go together to church, to thank God for their reunion—but the effort is too much for her; she falls back, exhausted, and the doctor is sent for. Again she gathers some feverish strength, enough for the passionate protest against her cruel fate: *O Dio! morir si giovane!*—to die so young, and when happiness seemed once more within her grasp!

However, when the doctor comes he finds her calm and resigned, and the arrival of the elder Germont adds much to her contentment—in Alfredo's arms, and with his father reconciled to their union, she can smile in the face of Death.

Her last act is to give Alfredo a miniature of herself,

280

radiant with youth and health; he in turn is to give it, with her blessing, to the imaginary bride, more virtuous, but not more loving, to whom she commends his future.

Once more the throbbing violins whisper the love-motive *Ah, quell'amor*—so softly it hardly seems of earthly origin; as if in answer to the call, Violetta rises to her full height; with outstretched arms she utters a last cry, not of agony, but of joy and triumph, as her soul escapes from the prison of this mortal life.

Indeed, Violetta has made a good end, and no one will feel inclined to think harshly of the poor 'Traviata'; when contrasted with many of the 'heroines,' erotic, neurotic, exotic, that have been exploited on the operatic stage in recent years, she stands out as a shining example of faithful devotion and heroic self-sacrifice.

UN BALLO IN MASCHERA

Music by Verdi. *Words by* Somma, *adapted from* Scribe's
"Gustave III."
Rome, 1859; *London,* 1861; *New York,* 1861.

A LONG chapter might profitably be written on the libretto of this opera, coupled with reflections on the curiously elastic and elusive nature of librettos in general. Many a musically fine opera has failed, or fallen into neglect, owing to the insipid or incoherent quality of the text; some, making preliminary shipwreck, have been successfully refloated after a drastic revision of the 'book,' while certain old-established favourites, though still surviving, find the burden of a bad libretto ever a greater handicap as the years go on.

Among the last we may include Verdi's *Un Ballo in Maschera.* Although unusually well served by his librettists on the whole, our composer was peculiarly unfortunate in one respect. The subjects chosen by him were constantly bringing him into conflict with the political authorities, so that opera after opera was in danger of being 'choused' on the very eve of production. In every case Verdi contrived to win the day, but only by the sacrifice of certain situations in the drama, or by changing the scene, the period, and the names of the characters. In the cases of *I Lombardi* (1843), *Ernani* (1844), *Rigoletto* (1851), *I Vespri Siciliani* (1855), not one of these but had a tough struggle with the political authorities, while the titles of the two last operas had to be changed before the Austrian police would permit their production in Italy.

But the climax was reached with the work which we

are now considering. Its original title was *Gustavo III*, as it dealt with the historic incident of the King of Sweden's assassination at a masked ball in 1792. The opera was actually in rehearsal for production at Naples, in 1853, when the news of the attempted assassination of Napoleon III by Orsini decided the authorities to forbid the stage presentation of a similar incident. Verdi was told that he must either adapt his music to an entirely different libretto or withdraw it altogether. As he flatly refused to make such an alteration, the opera was withdrawn, to the intense indignation of the people. Verdi was immensely popular by this time, and the young Italy of the day nearly caused a riot by their processions through the streets of Naples; the name of 'Verdi' inscribed on their banners was well understood to represent the initial letters of Vittorio Emanuele, Re D'Italia, on whom they built their hopes of a free and united Italy.

When *Un Ballo in Maschera* was produced the following year, not at Naples but at Rome, Verdi had seen his way to altering, not the plot, but the period and place of his drama. The scene was now laid in Boston, Massachusetts, at the end of the 17th century, and the victim of assassination was the English nobleman who acted as Governor of that town. Oddly enough, this arrangement appears to have satisfied all political requirements, and the opera won an immediate success, which was repeated two years later in Paris, in London, and in New York. In the French version, *Le bal masqué,* the scene is changed from Boston to Naples, where the rather lurid happenings certainly seem more at home. However, we shall base our description on the Italian version, which is the one usually given.

Here is the outline of the story. Richard (Riccardo), Count of Warwick and Governor of Boston, is in love with Adelia, the wife of Renato, a Creole, his secretary and devoted friend; she returns his love in secret, but tries to check her inclination, as she is a true wife in intention. Circumstances, however, force them to an avowal of their mutual passion, and Renato discovers what he believes to be their guilty secret; at a masked ball given at the Governor's house he plunges his dagger into the heart of Riccardo, who lives just long enough to proclaim Adelia's innocence, and to pardon his assassin.

This simple plot is set forth in picturesque and melo-dramatic fashion; the result of its association with Puritan Boston in its early days may be imagined. The height of wild incongruity is reached when the English Governor, on the occasion of his visit to a negro sorceress named Ulrica, is made to express his feeling in a Venetian barcarole.

Happily the day of the purely fatuous type of libretto was nearly over. The year of *Un Ballo* saw the produc-tion of a far crazier specimen in Meyerbeer's *Dinorah*, but it also gave us the excellent 'book' of Gounod's *Faust*, the work of MM. Barbier and Carré,[1] since when there has been no lapse into sheer inanity. It is some-what astonishing, however, to reflect that in 1859 *Lohen-grin* had been nine, and *Tannhäuser* fourteen, years be-fore the public.

Act I. And so the curtain rises on a scene that hardly prepares us for the highly coloured events that are to follow. We are in Puritan Boston, say, in the year seventeen hundred. The good townsfolk are assembled in the audience chamber of Government House awaiting the appearance of their popular Governor, Riccardo, Count of Warwick. The suavity of their opening chorus is mingled with the ominous mutterings of two gentle-men of colour—Sam and Tom by name—on whom it

[1] It is only fair to add that these busy collaborators were also respon-sible for the absurdities of *Dinorah*.

would be well for us to keep an eye, so plainly does their music suggest the whisperings and tiptoeings which mark the stage conspirator.

On the entrance of Riccardo the Governor, we learn that a masked ball is arranged for the next day; a list of the invitations is submitted by Oscar (Edgar, in some versions), a particularly sprightly page, whose graceful share in the opera is among the chief causes of its success. The first name to meet Riccardo's eye is that of Adelia, the wife of his friend Renato, and he at once breaks into a rapturous avowal of his love for the lady in the aria *La rivedrò nell'estasi.*

The chorus having retired, Renato enters, full of affectionate anxiety for his friend and chief, whose life, he tells him, is threatened by a conspiracy in his own household. In spite of Renato's earnest exhortation, *Alla vita che t'arride,* Riccardo laughs all such fears away, and turns to receive the Lord High Judge who comes to demand the banishment of Ulrica, the black witch and prophetess, whose activities he regards as a danger to the city of Boston. Here Oscar the (soprano) page gets his (or her) first opportunity, as he pleads Ulrica's cause in a sparkling cavatina, *Volta la terrea,* which has the double effect of delighting the audience and of influencing the Governor in Ulrica's favour. He is determined to look into the matter himself, and as the chorus have by this time meandered back to the stage, he invites them all to meet him at the witch's hovel that afternoon. They express their pleasure at the prospect in a lively chorus, in which the sinister voices of Tom and Sam are hardly noticed, though it is plain that they are busy as ever with their black designs.

Scene II. Though it is difficult to take the libretto of *Un Ballo* seriously, it is possible to say a good word for the picturesqueness of the *scenario* and the varied interest of the action. After the rather hasty exposition of the opening Scene, which owes its attraction largely to three frankly popular tunes, so characteristic of the composer at this period, we pass to the highly fantastic atmosphere of the black witch's dwelling. The rich and sombre colouring of the short orchestral introduction prepares us for the apparition of Ulrica, a figure of dread, intent on the magic brew that is simmering in her cauldron. There are few finer opportunities for a real mezzo-contralto—with an easy command, be it noted, of more than two octaves—than the opening Invocation, *Ré del abisso, affrettati*. A chorus of women has but little to sing, and Riccardo only a couple of bars as he passes, disguised, across the stage into hiding.

The prophetess is now prepared for the exercise of her powers. Her first client is Silvano, a sailor, in the service of the Governor. Ulrica dismisses him curtly with promises of speedy good fortune, which Riccardo, who has heard all, hastens to fulfil by placing, unobserved, a purse of money and the warrant for a commission in the man's pocket.

Adelia now enters, to seek, not prophecy, but counsel and help in her affliction. She, Renato's true-hearted wife, is the victim of an unlawful love for Riccardo, the Governor and her husband's friend—she can have no peace unless Ulrica will find a way to rid her of this obsession. The sorceress has her remedy pat; in the short solo *Della città all'occaso* she gives Adelia her instructions. On the confines of the town, under the gibbet where the bones of malefactors dangle to the wind, there grows a plant the leaves of which can bring oblivion; this plant Adelia herself must gather, at midnight, and alone. The listening Riccardo thus learns for the first time that his passion is returned, and determines to meet his beloved at midnight in the appointed place. Adelia having left by a secret door, the Governor's friends arrive on the scene, together with the sinister couple, Tom and Sam, and, of course, the sprightly page whose high soprano is given every opportunity in the *ensembles* that follow.

All are anxious to put the prophetess' pretensions to the test. The disguised Riccardo in light-hearted mood leads off with an almost rollicking number, in the form of a barcarole, *Di' tu se fedele.* But the sibyl assumes her sternest aspect; taking Riccardo's hand, she foretells his awful fate—he is to die, and soon. "In battle, doubtless?" asks the scoffer. "Nay!" she answers, "by the hand of a friend!" Still unconvinced, Riccardo begins a lively quintet *È scherzo ed è follia,* which must rank among the very best of Verdi's concerted pieces.

But cannot the witch, he asks, describe this destined minister of fate? "Know then," she says, "'twill be the man whose hand you next shall take in yours!" More than ever convinced of the imposture, Riccardo laughingly offers his hand to any or all of the familiar company who surround him, but none will dare to take it. At this moment Renato enters the room and seizes the Governor's hand in the warm grasp of friendship. The tension is relaxed, Riccardo's identity is revealed, and Ulrica's gloomy prophecies are all forgotten. The Act is brought to an effective close by the device of bringing Silvano back, with a troop of friends, bent on finding the Governor and thanking him for his generous favours. We are thus provided with a largely augmented chorus to join in the hymn of praise, *O figlio d'Inghilterra,* which seems to augur nothing but a happy future for their well-beloved ruler. Only Tom and Sam know better.

Act II. Although *Un Ballo* was written five years after *La Traviata,* on which it is in some respects a great advance, the later opera contains some clear echoes of the earlier. The prelude and opening scene before us irresistibly recall the last Act of *La Traviata,* with its tender melancholy and its attempts to reach a certain atmosphere of spirituality.

Adelia, alone at the foot of the gibbet at the ghostly hour, is hardly equal to the strain of her varying emotions. She is loth now to accept the gift of oblivion that she had craved—the beloved's image once torn from her heart, what has she left to live for? As she still hesitates, the bell tolls for midnight; she yields to the terror of the place and the hour; she peoples the darkness with the phantoms of her brain; she sinks on her knees in a fervent prayer for Heaven's protection—she rises and finds herself confronted, not by a phantom, but by Riccardo, the beloved. Too late now to pluck the herb of oblivion!

The long love-duet which follows contains much that is stereotyped and banal, but is worked up to a vigorous climax, and the arrival of Renato gives occasion for a trio of the highest interest. From this point it is almost impossible on a first hearing to grasp the details of motive and action, yet these require careful attention. Renato has come in hot haste to tell the Governor that the rebels of whom he has warned him are even now in pursuit and will assuredly take him if he lingers. He, Renato, has overheard their conversation in passing—they know where Riccardo is, and will be here immediately. Renato, of course, has no suspicion of the identity of Adelia, who is heavily veiled. In the most admirable section of the trio, both she and her husband urge Riccardo to instant flight. He is at first unwilling to leave Adelia, but at last consents, on the perilous condition that Renato shall promise to escort the lady back to safety without speaking to her or attempting in any way to discover her identity. This the guileless Renato swears to do, and Riccardo hurries away.

The conspirators rush boisterously on to the scene, headed by Tom and Sam. In their disappointment at finding the Governor flown they are inclined to insult the lady, and are about to do violence to Renato when Adelia interposes and, in so doing, lets fall her veil and discovers her identity. This is the tensest moment of the drama, and Verdi has handled it in most original fashion. Adelia's despair and Renato's broken heart find, of course, some immediate musical relief, but their full expression must wait till the next Act for their proper development. Meanwhile the tragedy is overlaid with comedy by Sam, Tom, and their followers, who are delighted with what they regard as a piquant situation. Adelia's cries of distress and the broken phrases of Renato are accompanied by a laughing chorus from the rough band of rebels. This is interrupted for a time by a short dialogue in which Renato hints at his intention of joining their conspiracy, but is again renewed after he has left the stage with Adelia.

They give free vent to their ribald humour:

> To spread the scandal we shall not fail!
> How tongues will wag when they hear the tale!

and the scene ends with the chuckles and guffaws of Tom, Sam, and their companions—surely the merriest band of conspirators to be found in all Italian Opera.

Act III. We now come to the great scene between Renato and Adelia, which contains the most famous number in the opera. *Un Ballo* is noted throughout for its *ensembles* rather than its solos, which are too often of the showy, conventional pattern, but the present situation has inspired Verdi with music of a very different order. Renato, in the fury which has succeeded to the first numbness of grief, is resolved that death, and by his hand, is the only punishment for the wife whom he believes faithless. Adelia's indignant protestations of innocence are all in vain, but one last request he can hardly refuse her— that she may take farewell of her little child. [This touching solo, *Morrò, ma prima in grazia*, with its lovely cello obbligato reminds us inevitably of the softened Violetta in the last Act of *La Traviata*.]

Renato's reply to Adelia's petition is the noble *scena* well known to every concert-goer as *Eri tu*. It may be well to give a fairly close translation of the Italian text in order to show the material on which Verdi had to work.

"Rise, then!" says Renato to the kneeling woman; "I will allow thee to see thy child once more. To yonder chamber go—and there in darkness and in silence hide thy blushes and my shame." With her departure his mood changes. "Nay, not on her, not on a poor weak woman, must my revenge be taken!" Here he strides up to a portrait of Riccardo that hangs on the wall. "'Tis thy blood—*thy* blood, thou traitor, that must wipe out this insult! For 'tis thou who didst sully the whiteness of this innocent soul," etc., etc. Poor stuff, indeed, to inspire a composer; yet Verdi has contrived to use it for the basis of a little masterpiece of lyric beauty and dramatic sincerity; love, hate, and a broken heart, all are here expressed with a truth that is marvellous when we consider the poverty of the text as well as the cramping musical formulas by which the composer was still bound.

The tension is relieved by the arrival of our comic conspirators. Although they come in answer to a summons from Renato, they can scarcely believe his assurance that he desires to join them in their plot to assassinate the Governor; but, once convinced, it only remains to decide who is to have the honour of striking the fatal blow. [It is rather sad, after the excellent quality of the previous scene, to be confronted with the blatant trio *Dunque l'onta di tutti sol una,* a piece of cheap conspirator-music which Verdi might have written twenty years before with an easier conscience.] They agree to refer the matter to chance, and the lots are already prepared, when Adelia reappears, and Renato resolves that her hand shall draw the fatal number from the urn; to his great delight he finds himself the chosen man.

The page, who may always be relied upon to lighten a too strenuous situation, now enters with invitations from the Governor to the masked ball on the following evening, and the scene ends with one of those well-written and significant *ensembles* that are the peculiar glory of this opera.

The materials for the last scene—the masked ball and the assassination—naturally do not admit of much expansion, but the librettist has shown no small ingenuity in providing some variety of incident. First of all we get what we may call a whitewashing solo for Riccardo. The device is not new; admirers of *Rigoletto* will recall a similar number at the beginning of the second Act of that opera. The rascally Duke, after plotting the abduction of Gilda and discovering that someone has been before him, is provided with a pathetic soliloquy in which he professes himself heartbroken at the loss of her for whose sake, he assures us, he was prepared to turn over a new leaf and live cleanly ever after. Certainly no one ever believed in the Duke's repentance, nor are we prepared to accept our Riccardo as an entirely virtuous person. However, as sympathy has to be worked up for a *primo tenore* who is about to perish, we find him in a virtuous mood. The orchestra is playing the melody of his aria in the first Act, *La rivedrò nell'estasi,* while he makes up his mind not only to see Adelia no more, but also to ship her and her husband off to England, and thus remove temptation from his path. Having signed, after some hesitation, the document that secures Renato an honourable appointment in that far-off island, he takes, in imagination, his last farewell of his beloved—*Ma se m'è forza perderti*. As he prepares to join the dancers, Oscar meets him with an anonymous letter (from Adelia, of course) which warns him that an attempt will be made that very evening on his life. But the Governor will run all risks save that of being thought a coward; assuming mask and domino, he mingles with the general throng.

Renato now enters with his fellow-conspirators, Sam and Tom, all three in similar disguise. They are afraid at first that the Governor will not be present; Oscar, however, assures them that his master is in the rooms, though he refuses to give them any clue to his identity. His roguish little song, *Saper vorreste,* sounds the last note of personal gaiety possible in the face of the tragedy so near at hand. The inevitable love-duet between Adelia and Riccardo is woven into the measures of a graceful mazurka, but the emotion of the lovers is well brought out in the vocal parts. Adelia implores him to fly while there is yet time—the enemy may strike at any moment. Riccardo is obstinate as he is fearless; he feels he cannot tear himself away; but he nerves himself to tell her of his resolve, and how he has arranged for her return to England. "And now," he sings, "the hour has come for me to leave you—take, then, my last farewell!"

A madman rushes in between them: "And thou, too, take this last farewell from me!" thunders Renato, as he stabs Riccardo to the heart. His victim, of course, lives long enough to forgive his assassin, to vouch for Adelia's unspotted innocence, and, as a proof of his own noble intentions, to hand over to her the papers that will secure her husband's position in England. With tender fare-wells for all, not omitting his "beloved America," Ric-cardo, Count of Warwick and Governor of Boston, breathes his last amid the sobs of a grief-stricken people and in something rather like the odour of sanctity.

FAUST

Music by GOUNOD. *Words by* BARBIER *and* CARRÉ.
Paris, 1859; *London,* 1863; *New York,* 1863.

THE subject-matter of Gounod's *Faust* makes probably a more universal appeal than that of any other opera, so a few words on the reason may not be out of place.

Though *Faust* may be considered as the last of the supernatural-romantic librettos, it is certain that the human interest contained in it is the strongest element of its attraction. It would be easy to maintain that the hero—if we may use the term—is the Devil himself, in the guise of Mephistopheles, yet the deepest impressions that remain with us are not of the supernatural; it is the poignant human tragedy of Marguerite that moves us, her innocent girlishness, the awful consequences of her betrayal, her unwavering fidelity to her lover, and her final redemption through the power of love. Vividly, too, do we realize the typical figures that surround her —Valentine, the rough soldier-brother, Siebel, her boyish lover, even the slight comedy-sketch of old Martha, all these appear to us as actual human beings, though placed in a romantic setting. Faust, on the other hand, is, dramatically, rather a shadowy character, except in the first Act, and Mephistopheles, although he dominates the play, a towering figure of evil, is so skilfully handled that he is able to take his place, for the most part, among the human personalities with hardly a touch of the grotesque absurdity which ruins most of the operas into which a supernatural element is introduced. It is finally the tragedy of Marguerite that enthrals us: the

294

Germans do well to call the opera not *Faust* but *Margarete,* since of the spirit of Goethe's masterpiece there is hardly a trace. The psychology of Gounod's Marguerite is the invention of the librettists and the composer rather than of the great German philosopher. In any case the result is admirable; *Faust* is one of the few operas which, while touching our deepest emotions, sets us at the same time pondering over the eternal truths of life and death.

Act I. The place is Nuremberg, the time the Middle Ages; Faust is in his study. Though it is long past midnight, the aged scholar is still poring over his parchments or examining his crucibles. But even these have ceased to interest him; he is tired of life, of a life misspent in a struggle to solve, by all means lawful and unlawful, the riddle of the universe, the secret of the soul of man. The secret of his own soul is shown us plainly in the gloomy, heavily dragging phrases of the orchestra: this man is weary to the verge of despair.

The gloom is broken by the sound of cheerful voices from without. Faust flings back the curtain from the window—a new day is dawning, another day to be endured! The labourers go gaily to the fields, singing their songs of joy—the earth is fair, the skies are blue, praise God for all! These sights and sounds of innocent happiness are too much for Faust: for him life has nothing more to offer; he will die, by his own hand. Into a crystal goblet he pours a swiftly working poison, and is about to drain it, when the joyful voices of simple men rise once more in chorus: "The earth is fair, and life is sweet—praise God for all!" Roused to fury, the old man breaks out into a terrible cursing; he curses all things, human and divine; Heaven holds no hope for him—yet he knows on whom to call! "Satan! Satan! Appear!"

295

A crash and a flash! and into the room steps a courteous stranger, richly dressed, with plumed *chapeau,* and a sword at his side—the Devil himself, in fact, but with horns and hoofs well out of sight. Even Faust, versed as he is in the Black Art, recoils at first. "Begone!" he cries. But the Devil knows his own. "Ask what you will," he says, "I will give it into your hands! Speak! Is it riches—power—or glory?" "All these I despise!" Faust answers. " 'Tis pleasure I long for—and youth, to enjoy it!"

Nothing easier! He has only to sign his name to a certain little roll of parchment: Faust shall taste again all the joys of youth and life, and on earth the Devil will be his most obedient slave; but, after death—well, things will be very different down below!

As the wretched man still hesitates, the Tempter plays his strongest card. "Behold!" he cries, "where youth and beauty await thee!" Through clouds of enchanted vapour there appears a vision of Marguerite in all her innocent loveliness; she is seated at her spinning, and the sound of her wheel mingles, in the orchestra, with the seductive phrases of the great love-duet of the third Act. Faust hesitates no longer—the fatal deed is signed; he casts off the burden of old age, and emerges a handsome, gallant stripling, ready for all the delights that life and the Devil can offer him. They mingle their voices in a repetition of Faust's earlier confessions of his desires: *Je veux le plaisir—*

> 'Tis youth that I long for,
> The beauty of woman,
> Her ardent caresses,
> The love in her eyes!

and the pair go off arm-in-arm in quest of Marguerite.

The music of this Act is well on the way toward "the music of the future," as the term was understood in those

296

days and long afterward; that is to say, in place of set airs and formal closes, the action is carried on mostly in a sort of melodious recitative—you may call it *'melos'* if you choose—helped by an orchestral accompaniment of high dramatic significance. We find very few real 'tunes,' and these are quite appropriate to the situation, *e.g.,* the snatches of the Peasants' Chorus 'off,' and Faust's impetuous expression of his love-longings in the air *Je veux le plaisir*, that is so aptly repeated for the closing duet. In addition to this the orchestra introduces, during the vision of Marguerite, the broad melody of the great love-duet of Act III.

A word as to the overture. After a short introduction, highly expressive of the scene on which the curtain rises, we pass abruptly to a bold and arresting melody, the significance of which is not apparent. This form of the overture dates from the production of the opera at Her Majesty's Theatre in 1864, in an English version, and the melody in question is the first part of the famous air "Even bravest heart may swell"—better known as *Dio possente*—which was written for Charles Santley, the original English exponent of Valentine; "*Avant de quitter ces lieux*" is the first line of the French text.

Act II. A fair in full swing in the market-place. This lively scene is the choristers' opportunity; seldom indeed are the different sections of an operatic chorus given such a chance of separate distinction. First the basses, the thirsty students, the swaggering soldiers, all equally bent on deep potations and amorous adventure; next, the richly dressed burghers, the old men with their high-pitched cackle, content to sit apart and watch the game of life go on around them.

Now come the young sopranos, giddy and tittering, quite ready to meet their gallants half-way, be they soldiers or students; last of all the contraltos, not so young as they used to be, and shocked at the forwardness of their younger sisters.

Each of these groups has its own individual share of music and action, and finally they all combine in a masterly blending of the various characterizations. The climax is reached in a hand-to-hand scuffle between the younger and the elder women, in which the men also take part, and the crowd surges off the stage, to make room for Valentine, Marguerite's soldier-brother, Wagner, his comrade-in-arms, and the boyish Siebel. Valentine, who is off to the wars, is distressed at leaving Marguerite at an age when a brother's protection is most needed. He hangs round his neck a sacred medal which she has given him for a talisman in the hour of danger, and commends her to the care of Heaven in the famous air *Dio possente*, already referred to.

Siebel is allowed only a few bars in which to constitute himself Marguerite's watchful guardian, and Wagner bids them brush all such gloomy thoughts aside, for *"Toujours gai"* is the soldier's motto. He starts a lively song, but is cut off, after only a few bars, by the entrance of Mephistopheles, who at once dominates the scene. With a certain air of insolent courtesy, he proposes to entertain them with a song of his own—it is the song of the Golden Calf, (*Le veau d'or*); Gold is the lord of rich and poor—monarchs and people all adore him! There is but one god, Gold—and Beelzebub is his servant! Beelzebub, or Mephistopheles, the Master of Evil, stands there in the midst of them, and sways them all to his mood. In this song Gounod was inspired to write as fine a piece of grotesque *diablerie* as is to be found in any opera; the brutal, assertive melody, the weird chromatic changes in the harmony, the reiteration of the buzzing figure for the strings—was not Beelzebub the Lord of Flies?—all combine to produce an impression that is absolutely original and unique. When properly rendered the effect of this number is nothing less than terrifying.

Mephistopheles now proceeds to assert his uncanny influence in various ways. He seizes Siebel's hand, to tell his fortune; knowing the secret of his devotion, he banters him. "Strange, indeed! Henceforth each flower you pluck shall wither—so no more love-posies for Marguerite!" Grumbling at the wine they offer him, with his magic art and a flash of red fire he conjures a rare vintage from an empty cask, and drinks to the health of Marguerite. Valentine, angry at the introduction of his sister's name, challenges him to a duel—but the soldier's well-tempered blade is not proof against Satanic power— it snaps in twain. The people, now thoroughly aroused, and led by Valentine, advance on Mephistopheles with their sword-hilts held aloft, thus confronting the Prince of Darkness with the sign of the Cross. Against that sign not Hell itself has power; writhe as he may within the charmed circle, Mephistopheles cannot break through until they retire.

[The musical treatment of this scene is a striking example of economy; the rough vigour of the first short chorus, the solemnity of the second, based on the ecclesiastical chant intoned by Valentine, produce an overwhelming effect by the simplest means and in the shortest time.]

Faust now joins Mephistopheles; the orchestra, by its reference to the youth-and-pleasure motive of Act I, shows us what is passing in his mind— he is all impatience to see in the flesh the maiden of his vision. Nor has he long to wait. To the strains of the gayest and lightest of waltzes the stage is filled with a crowd of revellers, who sing what may best be described as a vocal accompaniment to the dance-rhythms, with a delicious effect of spontaneity. At last she comes—the damsel of the spinning-wheel! There is a lull in the dance—the crowd make way as Marguerite appears, with downcast eyes, and attended by old Martha, who, since the mother's death, has been her not too judicious guardian. In a moment Faust is at her side: "Pardon if I presume, O fair and gentle lady! Will you not take my arm and let me walk with you?" "Nay, Sir, I am no lady—you must not call me fair—nor do I need an arm to help me on my way!" And Marguerite is gone. Nothing could be simpler, nothing more commonplace than these words, yet Gounod's genius has clothed them in the light of romance. This short passage makes an ineffaceable impression, commensurate with its dramatic importance; if dialogue is to be carried on in measured melody, it could not be better done than in this instance.

In this chance meeting of a moment poor Marguerite's fate is decided; while Faust's ardour is only increased by the modesty of her refusal, Mephistopheles jeers at him for a timid wooer, and urges him to instant pursuit. Meanwhile the chorus resume their dance with a new zest, and the Scene ends, as it began, in a whirl of gaiety.

Act III. This is the lovely Garden Scene which after nearly three-quarters of a century still keeps its colour and its fragrance. The short but striking prelude seems to tell us whose garden it is; the time is evening, toward the moth-hour, the dew is gathering, and the air is filled with

A rosemary odour, commingled with pansies—
With rue, and the beautiful Puritan pansies.

And a yet more poignant perfume hovers there, ready soon to descend and fill all the scene with a sense of enchantment. Marguerite's modest dwelling is just shown, with its low windows and little porch; there is another door opening through the high garden-wall into

300

the street; and a small statue of the Virgin under a wooden canopy, with a shell for holy water.

The peaceful prelude changes to a livelier measure as Siebel enters from the street; it is his boyish delight each evening to place a nosegay near her door for Marguerite's acceptance, and then retire—for he is one who worships from afar. Ah—what is this! The flowers are withered in his grasp, as the Dark Stranger had foretold—undaunted, he dips his fingers in the holy water at the shrine where his beloved comes each evening to pray. Thus armed, he tries again. Joy! the curse is lifted, and full of triumph he plucks another posy for his offering.

[Siebel's Flower Song, *Faites-lui mes aveux,* one of the most hackneyed of airs, still keeps its fresh perfume; its effect on the stage is often marred by the custom of assigning the part to a heavy voice, in view of the sustained *legato* of the song in Act IV, *Si le bonheur.* But this Flower Song must be light and buoyant as a butterfly.]

Mephistopheles now enters with Faust, who seems at once to yield to the influence of the tranquil surroundings; he would be alone—and so Mephistopheles leaves him, after sarcastically calling attention to Siebel's innocent posy. Faust's better nature is in the ascendant, he feels he is in the presence of something pure and holy; this is the shrine that holds his beloved; the trees, the flowers, the humble cottage—oh! what peace, what wealth is hidden here!

[*Salut, demeure chaste et pure,* as a piece of expressive lyric beauty, is unsurpassed by any tenor solo in French opera; it demands the most perfect *bel canto* for its right delivery, and a fine bowing for the lovely violin obbligato.]

Mephistopheles returns with a casket of jewels, which he places at Marguerite's door, side by side with Siebel's freshly gathered flowers. Sounds are heard from the cottage, and the two intruders retire.

Marguerite enters; her thoughts are all of yesterday's meeting at the fair; who could he have been? Ah, if she only knew his name! With a sigh she seats herself at the spinning-wheel.

Gounod has avoided any 'spinning-wheel' music here; the interest lies in the song that Marguerite sings of the King of Thule, whose love was "faithful to the grave," a melody of rare beauty, with a sound as old as the hills. She is not thinking of the song, or its meaning—she sings mechanically, breaking off now and then to refer to the one subject which absorbs her: "His air was so courteous, his words were so kind. 'Tis only noble lords who speak like that."

She leaves her wheel; she takes up Siebel's humble bouquet—and drops it, for she has seen the glittering casket, and the spell of the 'Calf of Gold' begins its subtle work. Trembling and eager she takes out the incredible treasure of diamonds and pearls, she decks herself in necklace, rings, and bracelets—mirror in hand, she laughs to see herself so lovely—she is no longer Marguerite, but "a king's daughter, to whom all must do reverence."

Such is the theme of the famous Jewel Song, *Ah, je ris*; it is just a brilliant vocal waltz, a form which has been much abused, but which in this place seems very proper for the outpouring of a young girl's innocent vanity, and the natural pleasure she finds in her own beauty for the sake of the beloved.

The quartet that follows is a masterly blending of liveliness and tender romance. A vein of comedy is skilfully introduced in the absurd coquetries of old Martha with the Prince of Darkness, who seems to her the Perfect Gentleman. Mephistopheles brings the news of her husband's death, whereupon she loses no time in trying to capture him for her 'second.' Her ridiculous advances and the Devil's sarcastic encouragement are vividly reflected in the music, and make a capital foil for the love-passages between Faust and Marguerite. Arm-in-arm the two couples wander through the garden, twice the four voices are blended with wonderful effect in short lyric passages of restful beauty. Faust's passion grows with the rising moon, and Marguerite in her guileless innocence cannot help responding.

Mephistopheles, having shaken off his partner, has the stage to himself; in a brief but powerful number in which the orchestra is the predominant musical agent, he lays his evil spell upon the garden, and calls upon the demons of earth and air to put forth all their powers for the seduction of innocence—of the innocent pair, we may almost say, since Faust is for the present under the influence of Marguerite, his better angel.

The great love-duet begins—the loftiest expression in the older operatic form of sublimated sensuous passion: the heights of lyrical beauty are reached in the two movements, *Laisse-moi contempler ton visage* and *O nuit d'amour!*

The two are alone in the moonlit garden; it is late, and Marguerite wishes to retire to rest, but Faust detains her, and she, like him, "could say good-night until to-morrow." But her lover's rising passion frightens the innocent girl, and she breaks away from his too ardent embrace: "To-morrow!" she pleads, "till to-morrow!"—and Faust is once more subdued by her virginal purity; he lets her go, with one last avowal of their love, and the cottage door closes upon her. But Mephistopheles will not let his prey escape him; he hurries to his side, to jeer at such a futile wooing. Faust still struggles to free himself, but the Tempter holds him fast, and points to Marguerite's window, which slowly opens. The girl leans out into the cool of the night—in the first ecstasy of love, she feels herself a part of all the loveliness around her; all things seem to whisper her own delicious secret: "He loves me!" And to-morrow—"Oh, happy dawn, hasten thy coming, and bring him back to me!" Her wish is hardly uttered before Faust has her in his arms, and Mephistopheles ends the scene with a peal of fiendish laughter.

Act IV. The two big episodes in this Act are the Death of Valentine and the Church Scene; this is the order in which Gounod designed them, though the former more spectacular Scene, with its Soldiers' Chorus, is often saved for the end. In any case the Act should open with a short scene between Marguerite and Siebel at the public fountain; the poor girl's betrayal and desertion are by this time known to all, and her former companions, as they pass by on the other side, jeer at her with mocking songs of "The lord who loved and rode away." Forsaken by all, she can still rely on the boyish devotion of Siebel, which he now expresses in the familiar ballad, *Si le bonheur* (written specially for the English production of 1864).

But Marguerite will hear no word against Faust; she still loves him, and expects his return; she will go to church now, to pray for him—and for their child. Shouts and cheering and the measured tramp of feet announce the return of the soldiers. [Here comes the famous Soldiers' Chorus, as noisy and as effective a piece of stage-music as may be found in opera.]

Valentine enters, all impatience to see his sister once more; to his questions as to her welfare Siebel returns such dubious and evasive answers that the soldier's suspicions are at once aroused, nor are they quieted by the arrival of Faust and his diabolical companion. Valen-

304

tine conceals himself. Faust is conscience-stricken and depressed, but the Tempter is in his gayest mood; under the garden-wall of Marguerite's cottage he sings a mocking serenade, *Vous qui faites l'endormie,* which bears unmistakable reference to her misfortune. Valentine at once guesses the truth, and, furious with indignation, challenges one of the two to mortal combat. [Here follows the famous trio, in the course of which Valentine throws away his sister's sacred talisman, and thus delivers himself wholly into Satan's power.] Faust and Valentine fight, the latter is mortally wounded, and Mephistopheles hurries his companion away.

The neighbours, led by old Martha, come running to the spot—it is night and they have their lanterns—they raise the wounded man and render what little aid they can, when Marguerite, distracted with grief, rushes to his side, only to be met by repulse and reproaches: it is her sin, her shame, that have brought about his death— a life of infamy is all that now remains to her. In spite of her piteous entreaties he casts her off, and, though all beg him to have mercy, he curses her again and again: "In heaven, perchance, thou mayest find pardon, but on earth—be thou accursed!"—and with these words he dies.

It is impossible to deny the theatrical effectiveness of this Scene and the sincerity of its musical treatment, but it must be admitted that the death agony is too long drawn out; nevertheless, it is one of the greatest of opportunities for a dramatic singer, and there are very few operatic baritones who do not desire to die the death of Valentine.

The Church Scene. This should be a side-chapel in some vast cathedral, remote from the choir and the organ which dominates the music of the Scene. The brokenhearted Marguerite prostrates herself before the altar, in a piteous appeal to the Divine clemency. At once the Tempter is at her side—visible to the audience, he is invisible to her—he will not suffer her to pray! A whirring as of leathern wings is heard from the orchestra —the name of Marguerite is howled by demon voices; blended with the solemn roll of the organ are heard the Archfiend's jeering words. He recalls those days of girlish innocence when the angels hovered round her as she knelt, and bore her prayers to heaven; those days are gone for ever: " 'Tis hell that now awaits thee! Eternal ruin! Eternal pain!"

The cathedral walls are shaken by the full blast of the organ as the choir gives out the tremendous words of the *Dies iræ*, the old Latin hymn for the burial of the dead:

> Day of wrath, oh day of mourning!
> See, the last dread fires are burning,
> All the world to ashes turning.

Her anguish increased tenfold by the religious chant, she pours out her soul in a long and fervent prayer; but it is the Tempter's hour—he stands before her now in visible form, and thunders out the awful words: "Marguerite! thy soul is lost—lost for evermore!" With a wild cry of terror she falls to the ground, and the people coming out of church find her senseless on the chapel floor.

Act V. The Prison Scene. Faust's desertion, Valentine's death, and the constant assaults of the Tempter have turned Marguerite's brain; in a moment of frenzy she has destroyed her own child, and is now in prison awaiting execution.

The chromatic wailing of the prelude is interrupted by the sound of galloping hoofs; Mephistopheles has come, with Faust, in the hope of securing Marguerite's soul as well as that of her lover; should he succeed, the horses that wait in the courtyard below will bear all three straight to the Bottomless Pit. He has put the jailer to sleep, he has the keys of the prison—but the dawn is near and they must be gone ere it is light. Faust awakens Marguerite from her troubled slumber. Ah, how sweet sounds the voice of the beloved! She gazes in ecstasy on the dear familiar face—once more she is in his arms! But her mind is wandering—she is back once more in her cottage garden, nay, in love's enchanted garden of myrtles and roses; Faust, too, is swept away by the flood of old emotions, and they seem to live again those first hours of ecstasy. Marguerite recalls the very words of their first chance meeting, and the orchestra plays the broad melody from the love-duet, *O nuit d'amour*. Her lover has indeed come back to her—for the time he is wholly hers once more.

Alas! the dawn is here, the fatal hour is close at hand; wild with fear for his beloved's safety, Faust urges their instant flight, but some instinct seems to fight with her desire to go with him—her guardian angel holds her back. "It is too late!" she cries; "here must I stay and wait for death! Farewell, beloved!"

Now Mephistopheles will permit no more delay: "Hasten! Hasten!" he commands, "you and I at least must be gone. Come, and leave her to her fate!"

Marguerite at last awakens to realities—she sees the Archfiend stand before her, dreadful and menacing—in terror she turns for aid, not to her lover, but to Heaven. *Anges purs! Anges radieux!*—three times, with ever-soaring voice and ever-increasing exaltation, she calls on the heavenly powers to protect her and guide her home. Her prayer is answered; as Mephistopheles hurries his victim, Faust, away upon his last awful journey, a celestial chorus is heard, and angels come to earth to bear the pardoned soul of Marguerite to Heaven.

ROMÉO ET JULIETTE

Music by GOUNOD. *Words by* BARBIER *and* CARRÉ, *from*
SHAKESPEARE
Paris, 1867; London, 1867; New York, 1867.

THERE is, or was, a legend to the effect that
Gounod, the composer of *Roméo et Juliette, La
Reine de Saba, Cinq-Mars,* etc., did not write
Faust, the opera that made his reputation; the man who
was capable of that masterpiece would never have followed it up by works so vastly inferior; *Faust* was the
work of some obscure genius whom Gounod bribed to
remain in the background, while he himself took the
credit. This absurd story is obviously a malicious invention, yet it suggests a not unjust estimate of the composer's work as a whole. No other Gounod opera can
stand worthily beside *Faust;* written nearly three-quarters
of a century ago, it still remains one of the most popular
operas all the world over, and, hackneyed as it is, its
freshness comes as a perpetual surprise. Outside of
Paris, where it is still a favourite, *Roméo* languishes
rather sadly, if indeed it ever had much independent
vitality. It is a deliberate attempt to repeat the success
of *Faust* on the lines of the old model, and the inevitable
comparison is too damaging to the later work. Moreover, the libretto can hardly be said to favour such treatment; the deathless lovers lend themselves well to the
scheme, but there is no dramatic equivalent for Mephistopheles or Valentine, the Nurse has not old Martha's
happy touches of comedy, while, to supply the place of
Siebel, a new character, Stephano, had to be added to the
dramatis personæ of Shakespeare. In the love-scenes, of

course, Gounod could hardly fail; if the duets for Romeo and Juliet have not the real ecstasy we find in *Faust,* they are still full of that sensuous charm which the composer had almost always at command. But throughout the score the constant recurrence of methods, forms, and devices which we remember as having been used more successfully in the older and greater work is apt to weary us.

This opera must always depend more than others on interpreters of the two leading parts; there have been many favourite Juliets, but by those who had the good fortune to hear him the late Jean de Reszké will always be remembered as the one and only Romeo.

Act I. A short symphony is followed by an unaccompanied choral Prologue, during which the curtain is raised to show us, in a dim light, the chief characters of the drama, who recite the gist of the plot, much as Shakespeare gives it at the beginning of his play. After another short orchestral passage, based on the theme which precedes the Scene in Juliet's chamber, the opera begins with the festivities in the house of Capulet. Juliet soon appears on her father's arm, and in a brilliant waltz-measure gives us a foretaste of the more elaborate show-piece with which she is always associated. After some dancing, and a good deal of singing for old Capulet, who for musical reasons is given an undue dramatic prominence throughout the opera, the stage is emptied for the arrival of Romeo and his friends. For Mercutio's sake a musical version of the Queen Mab speech is dragged in by the heels; at the start it sounds suspiciously like a pale parody of Mephistopheles' "Calf of Gold" but develops into an agreeable patter-song, and serves at least to lend variety. Juliet's popular waltz-song, *Dans ce rêve qui m'enivre,* is but a disappointing reminder of Marguerite's Jewel Song, and suffers badly by the comparison. But the first meeting of the lovers has inspired Gounod with a really charming duet; this 'madrigal,' as he fitly calls it—*Ange adorable*—is not too unworthy of the honied conceits of Shakespeare's famous lines: "If I profane with my unworthy hand," etc.

Another line in the play, "My grave is like to prove my marriage bed," has been turned to good account; it is made the occasion for a very effective *adagio* passage in the orchestra, during which Juliet, who has just learnt that her lover belongs to the hated house of Montague, gives way to a presentiment of coming misfortune. After this welcome point of repose the Act ends with more vocalism for old Capulet and the resumption of the dance.

Act II. The Balcony Scene. Conscious of the difficulty in sustaining the requisite lyric ecstasy for even a short Act's duration, Gounod has been at some pains to ensure variety. Not much of Shakespeare's text is utilized, but the mocking chorus of Mercutio and his friends outside enables Romeo, who is safe within the garden, to give point to the line, "He jests at scars who never felt a wound." The famous passage "But soft! what light through yonder window breaks?" has produced nothing better than a rather commonplace cavatina, *Ah, lève-toi, soleil!*

After the first colloquy, carried on in a melodious recitative, contrast is obtained by the intrusion of Capulet's servants, led by Gregory; they have found the ladder by which Romeo entered the garden, and suspect a Montague to be somewhere in hiding. The Nurse (Gertrude) reassures them, and they depart after a little good-night chorus.

The long love-duet is then resumed and runs a rather undistinguished course; its climax is reached at the words:

Parting is such sweet sorrow
That I could say good-night until to-morrow!

a piece of cloying melody, well calculated to melt the hearts of the average audience. To the singers, of course, the whole Act is a blissful holiday; but the musician with memories of the Garden Scene in *Faust* must always feel a little sad.

Act III. There are two Scenes, of which the first, in Friar Laurence's cell, is a sorry bid for popular applause. How effectively Gounod could combine the organ with his orchestra we know from the Church Scene in *Faust;* some faint echo of that great and genuine success has been attempted, at the cost of adding some business for which Shakespeare is not responsible. In the play, when the lovers seek the friar's counsel, that worthy man takes them with him to find the priest who shall make them man and wife; in the opera he plays the priest himself, and goes through the form of a mock-marriage in his own cell. Juliet has brought the Nurse with her, so all is ready for the grand quartet, and with the aid of the organ we are treated to an absurd piece of sentimental religiosity which it is hard to bear with patience.

Scene 11, a street in Verona, is given over to duels and general brawling. Here, too, the librettists have had recourse to their own invention; in order to avoid monotony, and also to secure a soprano for the *ensembles*, they introduce a new character in Stephano, Romeo's page. His graceful canzonet, *Que fais-tu, blanche tourterelle,* is meant as a provocation to Gregory, the Capulets' servant, who is quite ready to teach the stripling a lesson, when the serious combatants arrive on the scene, and events follow exactly in the order of the play. The fiery Tybalt challenges Romeo, who at first refuses, for Juliet's sake, to fight him; Mercutio takes up the challenge and is slain; Romeo then kills Tybalt; there are two short *ensembles,* in which the quarrel becomes general; lastly, the Duke of Verona appears and sentences Romeo to banishment. There is really nothing in the Scene that calls for musical comment.

Act IV. Gounod's masterpiece is known in Germany not as *Faust,* but as *Margarete,* owing to the prevalent feeling that the opera is merely a perversion of part of Goethe's great philosophic drama. An Englishman may be pardoned for raising a similar objection to the operatic treatment of the exquisite Scene in Juliet's chamber.

> Wilt thou be gone? It is not yet near day.
> It was the nightingale, and not the lark,
> That pierced the fearful hollow of thine ear.

For us that is the inevitable opening. In Gounod's score, before these lines are reached, we have a long duet in sickly thirds, of an intolerable sentimentality, set to such words as, *Nuit d'hyménée, O douce nuit d'amour!* and though the sweet dispute about the lark and nightingale does indeed exalt the music to some show of passion, it soon relapses into the commonplace.

After the parting, Juliet's father enters, with Friar Laurence, to bid his daughter throw off her mourning for Tybalt and prepare without delay for her wedding with the Count Paris. As soon as he is gone, she turns for help to the Friar, who gives her the potion that will save her from that hateful union, and in the long solo *Buvez donc ce breuvage*—most grateful music for a *basso cantante*—explains to her its nature and the manner of its action.

Scene II. The wedding festivities. A processional march leads to an elaborate choral Epithalamium, chiefly unaccompanied. To this succeeds the ballet, with a chorus that reminds us pleasantly enough of the *Kermesse* in *Faust.* Room is then made for a grave solo in which old Capulet endeavours to cheer his drooping daughter.

312

The orchestra prepares us for what is coming by repeating the ominous throbbing phrases of the *adagio* in the first *finale*. Juliet secretly drinks the potion and falls in a deathlike swoon.

Act V. The tomb of the Capulets. This last scene had, of course, to be altered in accordance with operatic requirements; there must be a final duet for the lovers, and, consequently, Romeo is not allowed to die before Juliet has recovered from her trance.

After the orchestra has played a simple chorale by way of intermezzo, there is a short explanatory scene for Friar Laurence, and then another instrumental piece entitled, with but slight justification, 'Juliet's Sleep.' Perhaps the best of the music is the broad *andante* to which Romeo sings the equivalent of Shakespeare's words:

> Death, that hath sucked the honey of thy breath,
> Hath had no power yet upon thy beauty;
> Thou art not conquered!

This motive has been already used on two occasions, at the end of the Prologue and again in the Scene in Juliet's chamber; it seems intended to indicate that Romeo and Juliet were united in those true nuptials over which Death has no power.

The duet for the lovers is an exasperating imitation of the last Scene in *Faust,* only here it is the tenor, not the soprano, who wanders in his wits. Romeo, forgetting that he has taken the fatal poison, urges Juliet to fly with him, and, as he grows weaker, repeats, in the very manner of Marguerite, some snatches of the Scene of the bridal chamber. Juliet stabs herself, and the two breathe their last prayer in unison.

Gounod's is not the only setting of Shakespeare's tragedy; Zingarelli wrote a *Romeo* as far back as 1796, and an opera by Bellini on the same theme, entitled *I Capuleti ed i Montecchi,* composed in 1830, had a long career of success. There is a touch of irony in the fact that Wagner's niece, Johanna, who had created the character of Elizabeth in her uncle's *Tannhäuser* in 1845, chose for her London début in 1856 the part of Romeo in Bellini's opera.

But *Romeo and Juliet* as a libretto is no longer possible; with *Tristan* to set the standard, no composer will care again to handle a subject which must depend for its interest on a prolonged love-duet.

TRISTAN UND ISOLDE

Words and Music by WAGNER.
Munich, 1865; *London,* 1882; *New York,* 1886.

T HE tale of the unhappy loves of Tristan and
Isolde is one of the great stories of the world.
Whence it came it is hard to say, but it was a
well-known and popular subject among the singers and
poets of the Middle Ages.   Sir Thomas Malory devotes
to it a large part of his *Morte d'Arthur,* and in modern
times it has been treated in verse by Matthew Arnold,
Tennyson, and Swinburne.   Debussy is said to have used
it as the basis of an opera (hitherto unpublished) that he
left incomplete at his death, and as recently as 1924 it
appeared again as *The Queen of Cornwall,* a play
written by our veteran author Thomas Hardy, and set to
music by Rutland Boughton.

Wagner's version differs from all these in being much
simpler.   The original legend covers a considerable period
of time and includes a large number of characters, and
modern writers, while exercising their right of selection,
have used the pruning-knife with moderation.   Not so
Wagner.   He had been at work for some years on *The
Ring,* weaving and reweaving those intricate threads, and
now he was tired of complication.   He was still an exile,
too, and there seemed little chance of persuading anyone
to produce his Tetralogy, even if he succeeded in finishing
it.   The longing to cut himself free, to let the keen, fresh
wind of a single strong emotion blow through him and
kindle the spark of his genius to a flame again, grew ever
stronger.   Already he had cast his eyes on the story of
Tristan and Isolde and seen in it the one strong motive

that he was looking for. But something was still needed to drive him to the decisive step, and this was eventually provided by a curious incident. It was in the summer of 1857 that he received a visit one morning at his house at Zurich from a stranger who turned out to be an emissary from the Emperor of Brazil. The Emperor desired him to write an opera for the theatre at Rio, and offered him his own terms. Wagner was surprised, no doubt, but he accepted the commission, laid aside the unfinished score of *Siegfried* and set to work. By the time the new opera was ready in 1859 the Brazilian proposal had evaporated into thin air, but it may be doubted whether the composer wasted much time in vain lamentations. He had written *Tristan and Isolde* more to satisfy an inner need of his being than for any other reason. Performance might be delayed, but the score was there, and he knew it was his masterpiece.

Just as there are people who can be loved or hated but never ignored, so there are works of art that it is impossible to pass by with a polite indifference. *Tristan and Isolde* is one of these. It owes its magnetic power to a happy combination of qualities; not only is Wagner's inspiration more sustained here than in any other of his works, not only is his mastery of his medium complete and absolute, but there flows through these pages a singleness of purpose, an intense concentration of thought on a single idea, that are surely unique in operatic music. The composer has but one theme here, the passionate love that sweeps his two principal characters to ruin and death. Before the surge of this immense force everything else has to give way. The story has been lopped of everything but its bare essentials by a ruthless hand whose one object was to make of it a fit channel for the conveyance of this fiery flood. And magnificently he has succeeded. There is no break in *Tristan,* no digression. From the

316

first note to the moment when the curtain falls at the end of the Third Act it is all of a piece. In the whole of nature there is nothing with which to compare it, save the sea; there, and there only, as one watches the waves ceaselessly breaking on a rock-bound coast, does one find the same restlessness, the same infinite variety, and the same inflexible purpose.

With the very beginning of the Prelude Wagner goes straight to the heart of his subject. Out of the silence of the darkened theatre there float the yearning notes of the 'cellos; above them a bitter-sweet discord on the wood-wind dissolves into a sigh. It is the very voice of desire made audible, and it gathers strength as the music proceeds, till at length a climax is reached in which the pent-up forces seem to exhaust themselves. But as the storm of passion dies away the same troubled harmonies emerge once again and persist till the rising of the curtain.

They are a fit emblem of the emotions raging in Isolde's bosom. There she lies upon a couch, attended by her lady, Brangäne, who vainly endeavours to calm the storm of anger and resentment by which her mistress is overwhelmed. The scene is on the deck of a ship—the ship that is bearing the Irish Princess to King Mark of Cornwall as his promised bride—but the two women are alone in "a tent-like apartment" that has been erected to shield them from the eyes of the crew. We hear the song of a sailor from the mast above. Isolde imagines that it contains a slighting reference to herself and breaks out into a fit of rage which Brangäne is powerless to control. But her outburst soon exhausts her, she cries for air, and, the curtain being flung back, Tristan and his friend and follower, Kurwenal, stand revealed among the sailors. Isolde regards Tristan gloomily, while the music harping on the love-*motif* betrays the inward trend of her thoughts. Presently she speaks: why does he not approach her? Ah, well she knows the reason! Loving her as he does, he dares not face her now that he is bearing her away to a loveless marriage. But as his future Queen she can command him, and she sends Brangäne to bid him present himself before her.

Tristan's evasive answers compel the girl to lay emphasis on the strict imperative which the message contains. This rouses the faithful Kurwenal, and in rough words he tells her that his master owes obedience to no Irish Princess.

Brangäne can only return to her mistress, close the curtains, and report the failure of her mission. Isolde's stroke has failed; it has only served to make clear the ignominy of her position. Now she will tell Brangäne how it has all come about.

Not so long ago Morold, Ireland's bravest knight and Isolde's betrothed, was sent to Cornwall to collect the tribute which Mark had failed to pay. He was slain in battle by Tristan and his head sent insolently back in place of the tax he had come for. But Tristan did not emerge scathless from the encounter. Sorely stricken he sought the aid of Isolde, whose skill in the art of healing was well known, concealing his identity under the name of 'Tantris.' She soon saw through his disguise, and her first impulse was to slay him and avenge Morold. But, touched by his helplessness, and also (though she does not admit it) smitten with love, she spared him, healed his wounds, and allowed him to return home. This is how he repays her! This is his knightly honour! He reappears in Ireland as envoy of a victorious Cornwall to claim her as bride for the elderly King Mark! And Ireland, helpless before Tristan's might, must needs submit. Why did she hesitate when his life lay in her hands? It is her own disgrace that her weakness has compassed!

Again Brangäne endeavours to soothe her. Cornwall,

318

after all, is a goodly kingdom—and should King Mark prove cold, there is a spell that will bind him to her. Isolde, roused by this reference to her mother's magic arts, bids Brangäne bring her a certain casket that contains various potions. Yes, this holds the solution to her difficulties! But it is not the love-draught she selects. Vengeance is what she desires, vengeance for Morold, vengeance for her own injuries—the poison-draught alone will serve her need!

Cries from the sailors indicate that their destination is near, and Kurwenal appears to bid Isolde prepare for the landing. She sends him back with a fresh message for Tristan: she will not prepare for the landing nor let him lead her to King Mark unless he now presents himself and craves her forgiveness for the slight she feels he has put upon her. Alone again with Brangäne, she bids the reluctant girl prepare the fatal potion. Her instructions are scarcely given when Kurwenal returns and announces, "Sir Tristan!"

Tristan enters, to music whose repressed, concentrated force is eloquently expressive of the intense self-control that he is exerting. Isolde tells him why she has sent for him. Blood lies between them—the blood of Morold. To her falls the task of vengeance. The knight in answer draws his sword, and, holding it by the blade, quietly offers it to her. Let her spirit not fail her a second time. But this is not what she wants. She tells him to sheathe his weapon. She may not slay King Mark's most valiant servant. Let them drink atonement. He has guessed what lies behind this proposal, but he accepts death as the only way out of the intolerable situation. Seizing the cup which Brangäne brings forward he drinks deep. Isolde does likewise.

But Brangäne, shrinking from her mistress's awful command, has disobeyed. It is not the poison-draught that she has prepared, but the love-potion! Tristan and Isolde stand silent, awaiting death.

But soon the spell begins to work. Reluctantly, but irresistibly, they are drawn toward one another; a moment later they are in each other's arms. Oblivious to the shouts of the sailors, who have cast anchor and are now momentarily expecting the arrival of the King, they join in a song of rapture. Brangäne puts Isolde's cloak around her mistress as she falls on Tristan's breast. Kurwenal enters and goes to Tristan. The curtain falls with the lovers still lost in each other and the trumpets blaring forth their welcome to Mark.

Act II. The bulk of the Second Act consists of the glorious duet which forms the glowing centre-piece of the whole work. This defies any attempt at description in cold prose, but the events which surround it must be briefly narrated. An impassioned Prelude, in which the strains of the love-*motif* are blended with others depicting the calm beauty of the summer night, prepares us for the scene that follows. The stage represents the garden of the royal castle; on the left one sees the exterior of Isolde's chamber, over the door of which a blazing torch is fixed, for it is night. The King has arranged a hunting party, moved thereto by the knight Melot, and to the sound of horns the hunters canter by. Brangäne at the door watches them pass. Soon she is joined by Isolde, and together they listen to the notes of the receding horns, which are gradually swallowed up in the murmurs of the fragrant night.

Isolde, who has seized the opportunity of Mark's absence to arrange a meeting with Tristan, exhibits signs of the utmost impatience; she longs to summon her lover, and it is with the greatest difficulty that Brangäne restrains her till the hunters have got well away into the forest. The girl is uneasy: let Isolde beware of Melot!

This midnight hunt may be a device of his to entrap Tristan and the Queen.

But Isolde derides her suspicions, proclaims her complete confidence, and after a rapturous pæan in praise of Love, seizes the torch from the door and hurls it to the ground, where it is extinguished.

This is the signal for Tristan. In terrible excitement she awaits him. When he does not immediately appear she takes her scarf in her hand and waves it with ever-increasing urging. At length she catches sight of him and then, as he enters, rushes toward him and falls into his arms. After the frantic rapture of their first embrace the turmoil in the orchestra subsides and there follows that wonderful outpouring of lyric ecstasy, unique and supreme even among Wagner's works—the love-duet. Throughout its multitude of varying moods there runs the crimson thread of passion, unifying and colouring everything, while the orchestra, full-throated, untiring, exultant, envelops all in such a flood of inspired melody as the world has not heard the like of before or since. From time to time the voice of Brangäne is heard from the tower above, whither she has gone to watch, warning them that the night is swiftly passing and dawn draws near. But this does not interrupt the flow of the music. At length, in an elation that grows ever greater, they rise from the flowery bank on which they have sunk, and now, as the crisis approaches, their exaltation reaches a pitch at which the world seems to fall away, and they are left alone in a brimming, pulsating universe of pure emotion.

It is here, at the very climax of their ecstasy, that disaster overtakes them, sudden and overwhelming. Brangäne shrieks, Kurwenal rushes in with drawn sword crying, "Save yourself, Tristan!" and in a moment the stage is full of armed men. The hunt has returned!

In the grey light of dawn Melot, delighted with the success of his plot, turns to Mark for thanks.

But Mark is overcome with grief. It is not so much the faithlessness of his Queen that wounds him as the thought that it is Tristan, the friend whom he has regarded as the very soul of honour, who has betrayed him. With sad dignity he reproaches him. How has it happened? What fearful spell is at work? Tristan, whose demeanour has expressed increasing shame, raises sympathetic eyes to his King. But he may not answer his question. His resolve taken, he turns to Isolde. To a wonderful echo of the love-music he asks her, dare she accompany him to the dim region of night whither he is going, where no cold dawn breaks the everlasting gloom. In perfect trust she signifies her readiness to follow him whither he will. Suddenly he addresses Melot and taunts him with his treachery. Swords are quickly drawn and Tristan rushes at his enemy. But as he gets within reach he deliberately lowers his guard, allowing Melot's blade to pierce his breast, and falls back into the arms of Kurwenal.

Act III takes us to Careol on the cost of Brittany. Tristan lies sorely wounded and unconscious in the garden of his ancestral castle, watched over by the devoted Kurwenal. Everything around breathes an atmosphere of decay, for the place has been left uncared for during its master's long absence in Cornwall, and is now falling into ruin. The beautiful and pathetic Prelude contains a new version of the love-*motif*, gloomy and sad, expressive of the fate that has overtaken Tristan. In the distance are heard the notes of the shepherd's pipe playing a wild and haunting *ranz des vaches*. The player appears and asks Kurwenal for news of his master. It is little enough that he can tell him—Tristan is still unconscious. But no sooner has the shepherd departed than the sick

322

man stirs and opens his eyes—he asks where he is and how he came there. Kurwenal tells him: he is in Careol, whither the speaker himself has brought him. And now a messenger has gone to Cornwall—soon he will return, and with him Isolde. She it was who cured the wound that Morold inflicted; her skill will suffice this time also. At the mention of Isolde, Tristan rouses himself from his lethargy. The sad notes of the shepherd's pipe check for a moment his growing excitement, but soon it rises again, till at last the memory of the fatal draught causes him to break out into terrible cursings, at the end of which he falls back, unconscious once more.

For a moment Kurwenal fears he is dead. But his heart still beats—he revives in a calmer mood; a soothing vision of Isolde floats before his fevered imagination. Then, his agitation returning, he seems to see the ship approaching with his love on board. Kurwenal is holding him down by force when again the pipe is heard. But this time it is a new and joyous strain that we hear—the ship has been sighted! Still half delirious, Tristan cries out with growing vehemence. Kurwenal is sent off to help Isolde ashore, and once more the music surges toward a climax. It is reached as Isolde hastens breathlessly in. Tristan, who, risen from his couch, has been staggering wildly about the stage, falls into her arms and sinks slowly to the ground. Opening his dying eyes, still filled with unquestionable longing, he murmurs the one word "Isolde!" and expires. Despairingly she endeavours to revive him, but in vain, and at length, realizing that he has passed beyond the reach alike of her skill and of her love, she falls senseless on his body.

At this juncture the shepherd arrives in a state of great alarm. He tells Kurwenal (who has entered during the scene just described) that another ship is fast approaching. Kurwenal casts a look seaward, and, uttering a fearful oath, summons all to help him defend the castle. It is Mark and Melot who are upon them. A moment later Brangäne's voice is heard, and Melot appears in the gateway—with a shout of rage Kurwenal hurls himself upon him and strikes him down. But Mark and his men are close behind, and Kurwenal, fighting furiously to the last, is overborne. Mortally wounded, he staggers back and falls. He has just strength enough to crawl to Tristan's body and kiss his dead hand before his spirit follows that of his beloved master.

Mark gazes around him. He has heard the whole story now, and, rejoicing to know that Tristan was not deliberately guilty, but rather the victim of forces outside his control, he has come with forgiveness in his heart, inspired by a noble wish to unite the lovers at last. But he has come too late. Tristan is dead.

And now Isolde, who has remained unconscious of everything that has been going on around her, raises her head and looks at her lover. To her clouded eyes he seems to live again, and on a final flood of passionate adoration and surrender her soul, too, floats out to whatever lies beyond. It is the matchless *Liebestod,* crowning this drama of love with the sublime majesty of death.

Wagner was conscious that in *Tristan and Isolde* he had risen to heights which it was unlikely any man could reach twice in a lifetime. It was as magnificent an embodiment of his ideal as he was likely to achieve, and by it he took his stand. If judgment is to be passed on him, this is the work that must represent his case. There can be little hesitation about the verdict. Even the critics are almost unanimous. Weaknesses indeed they have claimed to discover in this as in all other products of human endeavour, and these we can leave them to discuss. But for us and for them the opera remains the supreme expression of a mind that saw more clearly and felt more deeply than it is given to other men to see and feel. Had Wagner written nothing else than this it would be sufficient to ensure his immortality. For Beauty does not grow old, and as long as music has power to move the hearts of men so long will *Tristan and Isolde* survive to bear witness to the mighty genius of its creator.

DIE MEISTERSINGER VON NÜRNBERG

Words and Music by WAGNER.
Munich, 1868; London, 1882; New York, 1885.

THE genial character of *The Mastersingers* gives it a unique position among Wagner's works. Putting aside his philosophic symbolism and all his mythological paraphernalia, he is content to wander happily about the streets of 16th-century Nuremberg, enjoying the freshness of the air and taking life as he finds it. No doubt Mr. Ernest Newman is right in attributing this change of attitude to a natural reaction from the somewhat hectic passion of *Tristan,* but a further explanation may be found in the composer's altered circumstances. It was while he was at work upon *The Mastersingers* that the ban of exile, which had so long embittered his life, was raised, and by the time the opera was finished in 1867 he was already basking in the favour of his new and generous patron, the King of Bavaria.

Happiness is notoriously popular, and it is little wonder this sunny masterpiece secured for itself a speedy production and an enduring reputation. A masterpiece it certainly is, a gem of such pure water and dazzling lustre that even in the Wagnerian treasure-house there is none to match it, save *Tristan* alone. It is needless to enter into a sterile discussion of the relative merits of these two works—of either of them we may say with Hans Sachs,

> Yet what could gauge its greatness?
> A measure no mortal hath seen.

326

The very completeness of both achievements renders comparison impossible.

But alike though they are in sureness of execution and imaginative splendour, they are poles apart in almost every other respect. We feel the difference with the very first phrase of the Prelude to *The Mastersingers,* which creates an atmosphere whose grateful freshness never comes to revive the passion-laden hearts of the immortal lovers. It is an entirely new country that we are exploring now, and by the time the curtain rises on the Church of St. Catherine in Nuremberg we have already breathed a plentiful supply of this exhilarating air into our lungs, and are ready and eager for the adventure.

Immediately in front of us we see the open space of the choir of the church, while on the left is the end of the nave with the last few rows of seats. In one of these (for a service is in progress) sits Eva, the daughter of Pogner the goldsmith, with her maid Magdalene, while leaning against a pillar at some distance away is Walther von Stolzing, a young knight, whose ardent glances quickly betray the secret of his heart. The congregation are singing a Chorale to the accompaniment of the organ, while the knight's perturbation is admirably conveyed by the orchestra, which fills the long pauses between the lines of the hymn with eager phrases, including some fragmentary hints of the immortal Prize Song. The ceremony ended, the congregation begins to disperse. Walther succeeds in intercepting Eva, an excuse is found for getting rid of Magdalene for a moment, and during her absence the knight asks his question: Is Eva betrothed? But Magdalene has already returned and it is she that makes answer, Eva interrupting her at intervals:

> MAG. The answer you would have, Sir Knight,
> No single word can give aright.

> For though betrothed is Eva held——
> EVA. No man hath yet the bridegroom beheld!
> MAG. None knows in truth the bridegroom's name,
> Until to-morrow shall sound his fame,
> When a Mastersinger the prize hath won——
> EVA. And him the bride herself will crown!

Walther is a stranger to Nuremberg, and this reply naturally leaves him more bewildered than ever. But now there enters David, a young apprentice in love with Magdalene, and to him is entrusted the task of enlightening the knight. Magdalene hurries Eva away, and the stage is filled by a crowd of apprentices who have come to prepare for the meeting of the Mastersingers. David, too, settles down to his business of explaining to Walther what a Mastersinger is and how the coveted distinction may be gained. Music in Nuremberg has become encrusted with a mass of rules, many of them absurdly pedantic, a knowledge of which is indispensable to anyone aspiring to the title of Mastersinger. As Walther knows nothing of all this, his informant goes into voluble detail, and a most entertaining dialogue ensues. David himself is apprenticed to Hans Sachs, the shoemaker, who teaches him cobbling and music at the same time, and his description of the technique of the Mastersinger's art is not made simpler by his frequent digressions on the subject of shoemaking. Long before he has finished our minds are in a whirl, and we heartily sympathize with Walther's despair at ever grasping the endless list of rules and formulas. There comes a time, however, when even David's eloquence is exhausted, and with a polite expression of goodwill he turns to help his fellows at their work.

It is midsummer eve and the Mastersingers are meeting in the church to make arrangements for the morrow's festival and to decide who shall be qualified to compete for the singer's prize. The nave of the church is cur-

tained off, benches are placed in position for the Mastersingers, a raised chair for the singer, and the 'Marker's'
cabinet is erected in the centre of the floor. This last is
a curious structure, in which the Marker (or Judge) is to
sit hidden from all eyes while the examination is in
progress.

Meanwhile two Mastersingers have come in—Pogner,
Eva's father, and Beckmesser, the elderly town clerk.
Beckmesser is a bachelor, and we soon gather that he
has pretensions to Eva's hand. But his conversation
with Pogner is interrupted by Walther, who greets the
goldsmith as an old friend, and announces that he has
come to compete for the prize. Pogner is surprised and
delighted, and undertakes to introduce him to the other
Mastersingers, who now begin to arrive. Soon the mus-
ter is complete; the Mastersinger Kothner calls the roll,
and the meeting proceeds to business. Pogner begs
leave to make an important announcement, and, rising
to his feet, explains his project for the festival. Being
a rich man, and filled with a desire to honour the art he
loves and to rebut the charge of avarice that has been
levelled against the burghers of the town, he has decided to offer as a prize for the contest of song his daughter Eva in marriage, together with the inheritance of
all his possessions. The Masters receive his words with
acclamation, but his qualification that the successful candidate must also win the maiden's favour gives rise to a
discussion, Beckmesser maintaining that the prize should
depend on something less fickle than a girl's fancy. However, this objection is overruled, as also is Hans Sachs'
plea that the people and not the Masters should be the
judges of the contest, and eventually Pogner's terms are
agreed to.

The goldsmith now formally introduces Walther as
an aspirant for admission to the Guild, and in spite of

the protests of Beckmesser, who scents a dangerous rival, his birth and standing are approved and he is allowed to enter for the preliminary test. Questions as to his teacher and the school at which he has studied elicit from him a lovely song of three stanzas, *Am stillen Herd,* in which he tells us that his teacher was Walther von der Vogelweide (a historical personage, some of whose poetic work still survives) and his school the school of nature. This strikes the Masters as very unorthodox, but they decide to allow him to sing his song. Beckmesser takes his place in the Marker's cabinet, the rules to be observed are read out, and the knight unwillingly seats himself in the singer's chair. The result, of course, is a foregone conclusion. The song, *Fanget an!* in praise of Love and Spring, is as fine an example as can be found of Wagner's lyrical gift, but it pays little regard to the laws of the Mastersingers, and gives Beckmesser all the opportunities he desires to vent his spite. Soon he is heard angrily scratching on the Marker's slate and doubtless his temper is not improved by the sly hit at the beginning of the second verse:

> Deep hid in thorny cover,
>   Consumed by wrath and hate,
> When now his reign is over,
>   Old Winter lies in wait.

He emerges from the cabinet, holds up the slate, all covered with chalk marks, and protests that the farce has gone far enough. The other Masters, who have been completely bewildered by the novel music, are of the same opinion. Sachs alone supports the singer and demands that he be heard to the end, but Beckmesser makes an angry retort and the proceedings speedily develop into an unseemly wrangle. Acting on a hint from Sachs ("Sing but to make the Marker sore") Walther finishes his song, but his voice is scarcely heard in the

330

rising clamour. At last the apprentices start dancing and singing round the Marker's cabinet and the meeting breaks up in confusion. Sachs alone remains awhile, lost in thought. Then he, too, leaves the stage.

Act II. It is evening in Nuremberg, and the apprentices are heard singing as they put up the shutters of their masters' houses. David is performing this duty for Sachs' home, a modest dwelling on the left of the stage with an elder-tree in front of it. On the right is Pogner's more pretentious abode, shaded by a lime-tree. Between the two a narrow street runs toward the back, and we have to imagine another one running at right angles to it across the proscenium. From Pogner's house there emerges Magdalene. She questions David eagerly about the morning's doings, only to retire disconsolately on hearing of Walther's failure. A moment later Sachs arrives, and he and David go into the house together, leaving the stage clear for Pogner and Eva, who come down the street on their return from an evening stroll. A short dialogue reveals that Pogner is somewhat doubtful of the wisdom of his project for the festival, but the goldsmith soon disappears through his own door, leaving Eva to speak for a moment with Magdalene. As soon as the girl hears the news of Walther she makes up her mind to seek further information from Sachs; but for the moment she goes indoors with her maid. Meanwhile Sachs has reappeared at his own door; David brings him his stool, table, and tools, that he may taste the evening air as he works, and is dismissed to bed.

Sachs arranges his materials, but he cannot work. Always there is running through his mind a lovely phrase from the song Walther sang in the morning, and leaning back he breaks into his famous monologue, *Wie duftet doch der Flieder.*

Secretly and gravely in the gathering darkness he gives

331

utterance to his longing for beauty, his sense of the inadequacy of his own artistic efforts, and his realization of the true genius with which capricious Fortune has endowed the careless, untutored knight. No sooner has he finished than Eva appears once more. She desires to learn the details of Walther's failure, but the wise shoemaker is not easily drawn, and she has to employ all her arts of seduction to coax the story out of him. The pathos of the scene lies in the fact that Sachs, who is a widower, is himself in love with Eva. He knows that she is not for him, and guessing how things stand between her and Walther he has schooled himself to an attitude of generous renunciation. But though his will is firm it cannot prevent his heart being wrung during this intimate conversation. Wagner has risen to the occasion, and his music here strikes a chord of delicate tenderness that we hardly find elsewhere in his work. But, moved though he is, Sachs does not lose his head. He allows himself to be cajoled into giving an account of the morning's doings, but cunningly pretends a hostility to the knight that he is far from feeling, and thus betrays Eva into a fit of anger that confirms his suspicions as to the true state of her affections. Her mission accomplished, the girl crosses the street once more, but is delayed at her own door by Magdalene, who informs her that Beckmesser is coming shortly to serenade her. Eva suggests that Magdalene should take her place, but before they have time to develop a plan footsteps are heard and Walther himself comes up the alley. Eva is soon in his arms, and in a brief but exquisite duet they declare their love. She agrees to fly with him at once, and is just returning to the house for suitable clothing when again there is an interruption. This time it is the Night Watchman on his round, and the girl has barely time to draw her lover behind the lime-tree and to disappear herself through Pogner's open door before he arrives, blows a blast on his absurd, discordant cow-horn, and goes on his way.

During all this Sachs had been sitting at his doorway, concealed from the lovers by the door itself. He has heard everything, and though he wishes them well he heartily disapproves of the proposed elopement, and sets himself to prevent it. Taking his lamp into the house he opens a shutter on the ground floor and brightly illuminates the alley in the middle of the stage just as Eva, who has returned in Magdalene's dress, is about to pass down it with Walther. Fearful of being observed the two draw back, and while they are hesitating fate again intervenes in the person of Beckmesser, who approaches, playing on his lute, by the very route they wish to take. They have no choice but to conceal themselves once more behind the lime-tree, where they remain throughout the forthcoming scene.

Beckmesser reaches Pogner's house, and having placed himself before Eva's window is about to begin his serenade when Sachs, who is now back in his doorway once more, strikes a resounding blow with his hammer and starts bellowing a cobblers' song at the top of his voice, *Jerum! Jerum!* His theme is Adam and Eve being driven shoeless from Eden, but the frequent recurrence of the name of Eva increases the anxiety of the lovers, while the whole song throws Beckmesser into a frenzy of rage. Knowing nothing of the evening's doings he supposes Eva to be at her window, and is desperately afraid of her mistaking Sachs' voice for his own. Deciding, however, that it is a case for diplomacy he comes up to the cobbler and bids him good-evening. Sachs pretends that he now observes his fellow-Master for the first time, tells him that he is working hard to have his (Beckmesser's) shoes ready for the festival, and goes on singing louder than ever. This is the moment that Magdalene chooses to appear at the window in her mistress's garments, and the sight of her causes the frantic Beckmesser to redouble his efforts to induce Sachs to stop. For some time he fails to produce the least impression, but at last he hits on an ingenious idea. He has composed his song for the festival, he says, and would be grateful for the cobbler's criticism. Sachs considers for a moment, and then declares that though he will readily hear the song, he must be allowed to cobble at the same time. This produces a deadlock, until Sachs makes the brilliant suggestion that Beckmesser should give him a lesson in the duties of a Marker: he will listen and mark the faults by a blow of his hammer. In despair the unhappy man agrees, but he has hardly got through a bar of his futile serenade before the sound of the hammer interrupts him. He tries to ignore it, but Sachs finds plenty to criticize, and soon he is brought to a standstill, and turns on the amateur Marker with a flood of angry recrimination. Still, remembering the figure at the window, he dare not waste time, and soon the serenade proceeds once more, to the irregular accompaniment of noisy hammer blows from Sachs and furious asides from the singer. The shoes are finished long before the song, and their maker lifts up his own voice in a pæan of triumph, while Beckmesser sings even louder to drown the din. At last the law-abiding Nurembergers can stand it no longer. One neighbour after another throws open his window and shouts to them to stop. David is awakened among the rest, looks out, and seeing his Magdalene being serenaded by Beckmesser rushes down into the street with a stick and administers a sound cudgelling.

By this time the neighbours also have reached the scene and are soon joined by journeymen and apprentices from all parts of the city who have been attracted by the growing clamour. Seeing David and Beckmesser at blows the rest fall to, and within a few moments there is a street fight in full swing. Everyone is shouting at once, and the volume of sound is increased by the women who by now are watching at their windows. The uproar is at its height when suddenly several things happen simultaneously. Walther comes forward from the lime-tree, sword in hand and with Eva clinging to him, resolved to cut his way through the crowd. Sachs, seeing this, makes a successful sally, catches Walther's arm, and pushes Eva in at the door of Pogner's house, where her father receives her under the impression that she is Magdalene. A well-aimed kick from Sachs deals effectively with David, and, still keeping a tight hold on Walther, the shoemaker follows his apprentice in at his door. The few seconds that this manœuvre has occupied have been well employed by the women in pouring quantities of cold water from the windows on the heads of the combatants below. Just as the flood descends a very loud blast on the cow-horn announces the imminent return of the Night Watchman. A sudden panic ensues, the mob melts as quickly as it collected, doors and windows are closed, and even the discomfited Beckmesser manages to limp away. The Watchman finds nothing but an empty street with silent shuttered houses, whose pointed roofs are just touched by the silvery light of the rising moon.

Act III. The grave, expressive phrase which opens the Introduction to the final Act makes it immediately clear that the mood of uproarious merriment that culminated in the street fight has given place to a more serene atmosphere. It is the *leit-motif* associated with Hans Sachs, and admirably suggests the poetic side of the Master's nature. A sudden change to the major key brings in the tune of the solemn chorale that we hear later in the Act, while snatches of the Cobbling Song remind us of previous events, though even this is now coloured by the prevailing thoughtfulness.

The rise of the curtain discloses Sachs in his living-room, seated by the window absorbed in a book. It is morning—the morning of the festival—and David appearing from the street with a basket full of flowers, ribbons, and dainties, is obviously intending to enjoy the general holiday. His naïve apology for his escapade of the night before gets no reply for some time, but when at last his master rouses himself and speaks, his voice has an unwonted gentleness. He bids David sing to him, and the lad stands up and dutifully repeats his lesson. He sings of St John baptizing in Jordan, of the German woman who brought her child to him to be christened by his name, and of how that name was changed in Germany from Johannes to Hans. A thought strikes him: "Hans? Hans? Why, Master! 'tis your name-day too!" Eagerly he offers the contents of his basket. Sachs is touched; he refuses the gift, which will be better appreciated by the giver, but sends the boy off to get himself ready for the festival. David joyfully departs, and Sachs loses himself once more in his thoughts. "Mad! mad! everyone's mad!" he murmurs, and there follows another great soliloquy, *Wahn, Wahn!*—a piece of writing so true, so tender, so expressive of the warm heart and wise head that are combined in the character of the shoemaker, that it easily and naturally takes its place among the greatest things in all opera. Musings on the spirit of mischief give way to a lyrical outburst of pride in his native Nuremberg. Yet even to this peaceful spot trouble has found its way: reminiscences of the night's doings bring an episode that has the delicacy of dew at sunrise, and then finally he pulls himself together:

336

> But now has dawned Midsummer day!
> We'll see now how Hans Sachs intends
> Turning this madness to his ends,
> That good may come of it. . . .
> For work hath never virtue in it
> Unless someone that's mad begin it!

And now a door opens and Walther enters and greets his host. Their attitude makes it clear that the two have reached a perfect understanding. Presently the young man's casual reference to a dream he has had "of beauty rare," and his reluctance to speak of it lest it fade, brings words full of wisdom from the shoemaker:

> My friend, just that is poet's work;
> To find in dreams what meanings lurk. . . .
> Perchance your dream may show the way
> To win the Masters' prize to-day.

It is some time before this wise counsel prevails with the young knight, still raw from his rejection by the Guild on the previous day. But Sachs is persistent and gets his way at last. The end of the discussion is worth quoting:

> WALTHER. Through all the rules that you have taught
> Meseems the dream hath come to naught.
> SACHS. The poet's art, then, try betimes;
> Lost words are often found in rhymes.
> WALTHER. Then 'twere no dream, but poet's art.
> SACHS. Good friends are they, ne'er far apart.
> WALTHER. But how by rules shall I begin?
> SACHS. First make your rules and keep them then.
> Think only on your vision's beauty,
> To guide you well shall be my duty.

He draws paper and ink toward him and prepares to write what he hears, while Walther, convinced at last, pours out the first lovely strain of the Prize Song, *Morgenlich leuchtend in rosigem Schein*. Prompted by his mentor, he matches it with a second, somewhat similar, and rounds off the whole with a rapturous 'after-song'

337

which wins generous approbation. Sachs elicits a second verse as well, but wisely refrains from pressing his demands for a third when the singer shows signs of restiveness. Master and pupil retire together to prepare for the festival, leaving the stage clear for the next comer. This is no other than Beckmesser, who hobbles in, still aching from the effects of David's stick, and finding the shop empty limps uneasily round, till suddenly his eyes fall on Sachs' copy of the Prize Song, which has been left on the table. He scans it hastily and then puts it in his pocket. So Sachs has been writing a trial song! He suspects a plot, and accuses the shoemaker, who now reappears from the inner room, of intending to enter for the contest of song and of having contrived the events of the previous night in order to discredit a dangerous rival. At first Sachs is puzzled by this outburst, but soon he notices the absence of the paper and puts two and two together. He meets Beckmesser's charge by a counter-accusation of theft, and then takes his breath away by offering him the song as a gift. Beckmesser well knows the value of Sachs' work, but at first he fears a trap. However, when the shoemaker promises to refrain from singing the song himself and to keep the secret of its authorship, suspicion and spite gradually give place to confidence and friendship in the town clerk's bosom, and eventually he departs jubilant, while Sachs looks after him with a thoughtful smile. He is not alarmed: he knows that Beckmesser's limitations will effectually prevent him from turning his good fortune to a profitable issue.

The sight of Eva diverts his mind into a new channel. He knows what has brought her and is not deceived when she excuses her visit by complaining that her shoes do not fit. A charming episode follows: Sachs places her foot on a stool in order to discover just where the shoe

338

pinches, and it is in this situation that they are found by Walther when he appears. Enraptured anew by Eva's beauty as she stands radiant in her festival finery he bursts spontaneously into the third verse of the Prize Song. Overcome by this and by the presence of her lover the girl falls weeping on Sachs' breast while Walther clasps him by the hand. It is more than he can bear, and turning moodily away he eases himself by singing a verse more of his Cobbling Song in a voice that is gruff with emotion. But Eva has at last seen into her old friend's heart, and tearing herself away from Walther she impulsively pours out her gratitude to the man to whom she owes her happiness. Yet, even as she speaks, her passion masters her again; gratitude gives way to the demands of a stronger feeling, and soon she is singing the praises of Love in a splendid outburst of ecstasy. The music, too, touches an oddly familiar chord, until presently the words of Sachs show whither it is that our steps have wandered:

My child,

Of Tristan and Isolde a grievous tale I know;
Hans Sachs is wise and would not endure King Marke's woe.
To find the man before too late
I sought—else that had been my fate.

In these few words lies the motive that has guided the shoemaker's actions, and the full depths of his generous nature are revealed. But now come David from his room and Magdalene from the street, and he puts aside his troubles that nothing may mar the happiness of the others. Drawing all around him he proceeds to 'christen' the newly created Prize Song. The scene culminates in the celebrated quintet, *Selig wie die Sonne,* which crowns it with a garland of incomparable beauty.

The curtain descends for a while, and the orchestra conducts us to the scene of the festival, an open meadow on the banks of the Pegnitz, with a raised platform on one side for the Mastersingers. When the stage becomes visible many of the people have already arrived, and the crowd is continually increased by the constant stream of journeymen and apprentices who advance in processions, guild by guild. The appearance of a boat-load of girls is naturally the signal for a dance, a merry interlude that is soon, however, cut short by the herald announcing the approach of the Mastersingers. Their procession comes slowly forward with Pogner and Eva in the midst, and the members take their places on the platform.

The proceedings open with a solemn hymn, the words of which are by the historical Hans Sachs, on whom Wagner's character is based, while the tune is the one we have already heard at the beginning of the Act. Sachs rises to his feet, and after acknowledging the acclamations of the crowd in a voice that trembles with emotion proceeds to set out the conditions of the contest. Then with a private word of encouragement for Pogner and a more enigmatic utterance for Beckmesser, he calls for the trial to begin.

As it happens, it is Beckmesser who has to sing first. No sooner has he begun than it becomes evident that Sachs had not misjudged his man. Beckmesser has utterly failed to grasp the song he tries to render, his memory forsakes him, and he only brings forth a stream of unintelligible balderdash. His efforts are received with shouts of mockery, and in a fury he rushes to Sachs, accuses him publicly of having written the song to bring about his discomfiture, and disappears in the crowd. Sachs picks up the fatal paper that Beckmesser has thrown down, and proceeds to explain. The song is not by him; such an achievement would be beyond him—as to its beauty, it must be properly sung before that can be appreciated. Beckmesser has proved his incompetence, and Sachs now summons anyone who may be able to stand forth and give the music the performance it deserves. Walther immediately steps forward amid the applause of the people, and a hush of excitement falls as he mounts the singers' platform. For the first few bars of the song several Mastersingers are busily engaged in scanning the paper which Sachs has passed to them, hoping to catch the singer tripping, but the spell of the melody quickly makes itself felt, and the 'score' is put aside. This is just as well, for the new version has several points of difference from the old, and though the changes are all improvements the detection of them might have given rise to difficulties. Long before the song is over it is plain that Sachs' stroke has succeeded, and at its conclusion the Mastersingers rise in a body and acknowledge the singer's right to the victor's wreath, which Eva shyly places on his brow. Once more the crowd hail Sachs as their chosen leader, while Pogner advances to invest Walther with the rank and insignia of a Mastersinger. But the knight petulantly refuses the honour, and it is left to Sachs to smooth away this last difficulty. He does so in his final oration, a musical masterpiece of amazing vigour and contrapuntal skill. The Prize Song and the theme of the Mastersingers are mingled in the music to symbolize the union of genius and tradition to which he urges that the efforts of all should be directed. We pass from climax to climax, the people join in to swell the chorus, and our last view of the stage shows us Hans Sachs receiving the homage of the folk he loves so well, their idol and their friend.

There is no doubt that *The Mastersingers* owes a great deal of its success to its plot, in which Wagner reveals a happy gift for comedy of which his other works give us no suspicion. The play is full of incident, and the action is so varied that it is safe to say that no other composer could have possibly welded the material into a satisfactory whole. Few people realize that the opera, if played without cuts, is considerably longer than *Tristan*. We become so absorbed in following the intricacies of the story presented to us in a series of ingenious and well-constructed situations that we lose count of the passage of time. Such a mass of detail would have ruined a more serious work, but here where the subject is comedy it is perfectly in place. Indeed, a more ideal libretto scarcely exists. The central idea of a contest of song offers unique opportunities to the composer, and the superb melodies and choruses that enchant our ears with each successive climax are not extraneous, but born out of the imperious demands of the drama itself.

And certainly Wagner has scattered his tunes with an ungrudging hand! Pogner's address and Walther's two songs in Act I; Sachs' monologue, his duet with Eva, and his Cobbling Song in Act II; and the Introduction, Sachs' second monologue, the Prize Song, the quintet, and numerous other things in Act III—all these selections enjoy a well-deserved popularity in the concert-hall, though lack of space renders it necessary to dismiss them here with a mere mention. Something, however, must be said of the Prelude. So compact and well-balanced is it that as a piece of orchestral music pure and simple it can stand beside the symphonies of Beethoven and Brahms, and yet at the same time it contains the very essence of the opera that is to follow. With the magnificent opening theme the sturdy Mastersingers rise up full of life and character and march in procession to the tune that is presently given out on the brass. The treatment of this section, diatonic, and full of ingenious counterpoint, suggests the old 16th-century fraternity with its traditional ideals, without a trace of any troublesome archaisms. But now the harmony assumes a richer and more subtle colouring, and a phrase or two taken from the

342

Prize Song form the basis of a movement that has for its subject Walther and his love for Eva. Again we return to the Mastersingers' theme, which now appears in a light and impertinent version, as though to remind us of the apprentices, the Mastersingers of the future. And then, as the music rises toward its climax, the supreme touch is added by the master-hand: the *motif* of the Master-singers is played simultaneously with the Prize Song (in anticipation of the conclusion of the opera). Here is the lesson Wagner desired to teach. Tradition is good and innovation is good, but it is in the blend of the two that Art reaches its highest manifestations. That this was the composer's own view is manifest from every page of the score, even if he had not given it such convincing expression in the mouth of the greatest of his characters, Hans Sachs. It is, of course, Hans who is the real hero of the piece, beside whom Eva appears a rather colourless young woman and Walther fades into little more than a lay figure. About the shoemaker-poet himself, the man who has looked life in the face and borne his burden uncomplainingly, there can be no two opinions. Lohengrin, Wotan, Siegfried, Tristan, Parsifal—the mighty creations of Wagner's genius—pass in stately review before the eyes of our imagination; but Hans Sachs dominates them all, just as he dominates the Nurembergers of the opera, by right of his mellow, gentle wisdom, and his triumphant humanity.

DER RING DES NIBELUNGEN

Words and Music by WAGNER.

1. DAS RHEINGOLD.   3. SIEGFRIED.
2. DIE WALKÜRE.   4. GÖTTERDÄMMERUNG.

*First complete production, Bayreuth, 1876; London, 1882;
New York, 1889.*
*("Das Rheingold" was produced at Munich in 1869, and
"Die Walküre" at Munich in 1870.)*

*T*HE RING OF THE NIBELUNG is not only one of the greatest of all musical works, it is also the longest, dwarfing by comparison any other single conception that the genius of a musician has ever sought to express with the aid of the art of sound. It consists of three complete operas and a Prologue, providing between them more than twelve hours' music, and it includes, besides its own complicated plot, sidelights and reflections on most of the things that occupied Wagner's busy mind from the time when, in 1848, he first occupied himself with the story of the hero Siegfried, in that day in 1874 which saw the completion of *The Dusk of the Gods*. To do full justice to such a monument of industry (to call it by no higher name) would require many volumes. Here it will be impossible even to allude to many of the interesting questions that are involved. But it would be unpardonable in a book of this kind to pass over such a masterpiece in complete silence. The bare outline of the story at least must be given; any who would probe deeper must refer to other works on the subject.[1]

[1] The general reader cannot do better than consult Mr. Ernest Newman's *Wagner* ("The Music of the Masters" series). If after reading this he is still eager for information, he will find at the end of Mr. Newman's book a bibliography that should satisfy all his requirements.

344

DER RING DES NIBELUNGEN

Those who have never considered the workings of a great creative mind, who picture Beethoven spending an afternoon in his study writing sonata after sonata, and who fondly imagine that a work like *The Ring* sprang complete in every detail from the mind of its maker, like Athene from the head of Zeus, would do well to pause a moment and examine the facts. It was in 1848, as already stated, that Wagner, still an official at the Dresden Court, first devoted his attention seriously to the Nibelung legends. He wrote the libretto of an opera entitled *Siegfried's Death,* and probably sketched a good deal of the music. Then followed the political troubles that led to his ignominious flight from Germany, and it was as an exile in Zurich that he took up the subject again three years later. Finding that the story of Siegfried's death required a vast amount of explanatory matter which it was difficult to incorporate in the drama, he solved the problem by writing the poem of "Young Siegfried." But still there was much that remained obscure, and the poems of "The Valkyrie" and "The Rhinegold" followed, in that order. Having thus written his tetralogy from the end backward he naturally found that "Young Siegfried" and "Siegfried's Death" required modification, and so they were recast and appeared eventually under the titles of *Siegfried* and *The Dusk of the Gods.* And now that the enormous libretto was completed he set to work upon the music, and by 1857 *The Rhinegold, The Valkyrie,* and the first half of *Siegfried* were finished. At this point, however, there came a break. Wagner was beginning to lose heart. He was still an exile from Germany, and the prospects of the ban upon him being raised appeared as remote as ever. *Tannhäuser* and *Lohengrin* were slow in winning their way to the hearts of the public, the chief obstacles to their success being the novelty of their style, the seriousness of

their aim, and their great length. If this was true of
these earlier works, what would be the fate of the immense tetralogy, even supposing the composer ever
brought his labours to a successful issue? The new work
was far more novel, far more profound, than anything
that had hitherto come from his pen, and he realized
only too well how small were the chances that these
'silent scores' would ever be brought to a hearing. Would
he not do better to abandon the whole thing and take up
some more practicable project? The story of how these
vague thoughts were crystallized by the coming of an
envoy from the Emperor of Brazil is told in the chapter
on *Tristan and Isolde*. The unfinished score of *The
Ring* was laid aside, and it was not until 1869, more than
ten years later, that he took it up again. The interven-
ing period had been eventful in more ways than one;
musically it had seen the creation of *Tristan and Isolde*
and *The Mastersingers,* in the practical affairs of life it
had witnessed the composer's return to Germany and the
wonderful piece of luck that had come to him in the
whole-hearted support accorded him by Ludwig, King of
Bavaria. There was no limit to the enthusiasm of this
eccentric monarch, which included, among other things,
the building of a theatre, at Bayreuth, specially to meet
the requirements of *The Ring*. Now, at last, the path
to a production seemed clear, and Wagner returned
eagerly to his neglected score. *Siegfried* was finished in
1871, and in 1874 the completion of *The Dusk of the
Gods* put the crown on the whole edifice. The foundation-
stone of the Bayreuth theatre had been laid on the 22nd
of May, 1872, and the building was, as it were, consecrated by the first performance of the entire *Ring* cycle,
which took place under the baton of Richter on the 13th,
14th, 16th, and 17th of August, 1876.

It will be seen from this short sketch that the composition of *The Ring of the Nibelung* was spread over a period that extended to more than a third of its author's lifetime. When we consider that this was also the period of his greatest creative activity and that a large part of that activity was spent on this very work, we shall not be surprised to find it packed with ideas, allegories, and philosophic reflections to a degree unusual even with this most philosophic of composers. It is not within the design of this book to discuss these matters or to add yet another to the many attempts that have been made to harmonize the inconsistencies that appear from time to time. It will be sufficient to point out that such inconsistencies, blemishes though they are, are very natural. In the course of twenty-five years a man modifies his ideas upon most subjects. The mature Wagner who completed *The Dusk of the Gods* was a very different man from the wild revolutionary who had first conceived the outlines of "Siegfried's Death." To eliminate all the incompatibilities would have involved rewriting the work entirely, a task from which the composer very naturally shrank. A more serious defect is the result of the haphazard order in which the libretti were completed. Each opera, it must be remembered, was intended originally to explain itself without the aid of a predecessor, and we consequently find in *The Valkyrie, Siegfried,* and *The Dusk of the Gods* many long sections devoted to the recapitulation of previous happenings with which we are already familiar from the earlier operas. Now that we have the complete tetralogy before us these sections are often extremely tedious and, doubtless, a further revision of the work would have led to their curtailment or excision. Against these defects we must set the breadth and power of the general conception, the sureness and ease of the execution, and the astonishing sense of progression that is preserved throughout. Above all there is the marvellous music. These things must be put to the credit side of the account. But before attempting to strike a balance we will turn for a while to the plot.

THE RHINEGOLD

The Rhinegold, which Wagner desires us to regard as a Prologue to the other three dramas, opens with one of the most imaginative scenes in the whole realm of opera. The orchestral Prelude is constructed on the simplest possible lines, being founded entirely on a single chord. A deep note on the horn, followed by chords on other low-pitched instruments, creates an impression of pregnant darkness, out of which is born a theme full of beauty and romance. The ebb and flow of this, and the ever-increasing agitation in the accompaniment, culminate in the rise of the curtain, which shows us the three Rhine Maidens swimming in the dark waters, immediately above the bed of the Rhine. Their lovely song is interrupted by the appearance of Alberich, the Nibelung dwarf, who has climbed hither from his home in the bowels of the earth. The Rhine Maidens easily elude his clumsy attempts to catch them and are going on to fool him to the top of his bent when a ray of sunlight from above strikes through the water on to the summit of a rocky pinnacle where a dull gleam betrays the presence of the magic Rhinegold. The maidens, swimming joyously around, sing of its powers; how, when fashioned into a ring, it will give to its owner the lordship of the world, but only he who forswears for ever the delights of love will hold the spell that will enable him to work the stubborn metal. Alberich has listened attentively, and now with hideous eagerness he scrambles up the pinnacle and seizes the gold. With a great oath he abjures love for ever, and disappears with his prize into the depths

348

whence he came. The curtain descends on the horror-struck cries of the Rhine Maidens.

It rises again on "an open space in a mountain height." Wotan, the father of the gods, is sleeping, his wife Fricka by his side. The dawning day lights up the glittering towers of Valhalla, the great castle seen in the background, which the giants have just completed for Wotan and the other gods. It soon transpires that the giants have not laboured without hope of reward: Freia, the goddess of youth and beauty, is the price that Wotan has agreed to pay. No sooner is he awake than Fricka reminds him of this rash promise. Wotan is relying on Loki, the god of fire and deceit, to extricate him from his difficulty, but Loki has not yet put in an appearance, and meanwhile Freia rushes on in full flight from the giants, Fasolt and Fafner, who arrive a moment later. Fasolt checks Wotan's attempts to evade the issue with the stern reminder that the god's power depends upon his keeping faith, and Freia's doom seems imminent, when at last Loki is seen approaching. Resourceful as ever, the fire-god tells the story of Alberich's rape of the gold, of the Ring that he has fashioned, and of the power of the Ring. The giants catch at the bait and offer to release Freia if Wotan can secure the prize and give it to them in exchange. Meanwhile she must remain with them as a hostage. Gloom and old age descend on the gods as the goddess of youth departs in the hands of the giants, and Wotan in desperation summons Loki to aid him in an attempt to steal the gold from Alberich.

This very ungodlike enterprise he successfully carries through in the grotesque scene that follows. Under the guidance of Loki he enters a cleft in the ground and begins his downward journey to Nibelheim. The orchestra gives a vivid picture of the progress of the celestial robbers till at last the clanging of innumerable anvils an-

349

nounces their arrival in the home of Alberich and the dwarfs.

Alberich has created sad confusion in Nibelheim through the power of the Ring, which he has used to enslave the dwarfs, compelling them to dig for him the precious metal and work it into ornaments. We see him first in converse with his brother Mime, the most cunning of the smiths. Mime has wrought for him a strangely fashioned helmet, the 'Tarnhelm,' that confers on its wearer many gifts, including invisibility, and the power to transform himself into any shape he likes. Alberich snatches it from him, and, disappearing suddenly by its help, gives him a sound whipping for his pains and goes off. Mime is still rubbing his back when the gods enter. Soon Alberich returns, driving before him his unwilling slaves, each of whom is loaded with some piece of gold or silver jewellery. They deposit their burdens in a heap, and then, obedient to the spell of the Ring, depart to fresh tasks under the supervision of Mime. Loki engages Alberich in conversation. The suspicions of the dwarf are allayed by the open admiration of his visitor, and presently he consents to satisfy Loki's curiosity about the powers of the Tarnhelm. He transforms himself first into a dragon, then into a toad. This is the moment Loki has been waiting for. A quick word to his companion and Wotan's foot is upon the crouching thing. Loki snatches the Tarnhelm from his head, and Alberich reappears in his own shape. Swiftly they bind him and carry him off by the way they came.

The final scene takes place in the upper regions once more. Alberich is compelled by his captors to give up his treasure. Summoned once more by the Ring, the Nibelungs appear from the cleft, make a pile of the hoard, and swiftly depart again. Loki throws the Tarn-

350

helm on to the heap, and finally Wotan wrenches the Ring itself from the finger of his prisoner, in spite of the dwarf's anguished protests. Then, and only then, do they untie him. Alberich raises himself in impotent fury; he can still curse his oppressors:

Am I now free? Really free?
Then listen, friends, to my freedom's first salute!
As at first by curse 'twas reached, henceforth cursed be this Ring!
Gold which gave me measureless might, now may its magic deal each
    owner death!
No man shall e'er own it in mirth, and to gladden no life shall its lustre
    gleam!
May care consume each several possessor, and envy gnaw him who
    feareth it not!
All shall lust after its delights, but none shall employ them to profit
    him!
To its master giving no gain, aye, the murderer's brand it shall bring!
To death he is fated, fear on him shall feed:
Though long he live, shall he languish each day,
The treasure's lord and the treasure's slave!
Till within my hand I in triumph once more behold it!

So, stirred by the hardest need, the Nibelung blesses his Ring:
I give it thee, guard it with care!
But my curse canst thou not flee![1]

With this frightful invocation of that strange power behind the gods called by the Hindus 'Brahma,' and by the Greeks 'Nemesis,' he disappears into the cleft.

Wotan is only just in time. The gods have hardly reassembled when Fasolt and Fafner return for their wages, bearing Freia with them. The gold is ready, but the giants will not be content till the pile is high enough to hide Freia from their sight. The hoard is heaped up, but even so it hardly suffices, and the giants, who in truth care little for the treasure, desiring only the Tarnhelm and the Ring, refuse to be satisfied till

[1] These extracts from the English version of *The Ring* are made by kind permission of Messrs Schott and Co.

the last fruits of Wotan's raid are added to the spoil. The Tarnhelm is willingly relinquished, but Wotan flatly refuses to part with the Ring till Erda, the primeval earth-goddess, appears and solemnly warns him that to retain it will only bring disaster and death to the gods. Awed by her words, he yields: the Ring is added to the heap and Freia is released. But immediately the curse of Alberich begins to work. The giants fall out over the division of the loot and Fafner strikes Fasolt dead with a blow of his staff. While he calmly makes off with the booty the gods stand horror-struck, dismayed at the web of evil that fate is weaving round them. Donner is the first to recover. Crying that he is sick of the gloom he mounts a crag and, swinging his hammer, summons the forces of the storm. The mists collect round him, completely hiding him from sight, till his hammer is heard falling on the rock with a crash. Immediately there is a flash of lightning and a terrific peal of thunder, the darkness is rent asunder, and behold! a rainbow bridge stretching across the valley to the castle. Full of mutual congratulations, the gods prepare to cross to their new and glorious home, Wotan especially feeling well satisfied with the issue of the day's work. But they are not to depart without a warning that the trouble is not yet over. The Ring in Fafner's hand is still a mighty power of evil, and with it goes the awful curse of Alberich. Wotan's own position, depending, as it does, on equity and fair dealing, has been gravely compromised by his surrender to Fafner of the Ring, the lawful property of the Rhine Maidens. And so, as the dignified procession moves across the bridge in triumph, there are wafted from the waters below the voices of the maidens calling for the return of their gold and crying out on the injustice of the gods.

352

THE VALKYRIE

Shortly before the end of *The Rhinegold* the orchestra announces very emphatically a new and striking *motif*, a phrase that we shall soon hear again associated with the magic sword. Its statement here is Wagner's method— a rather clumsy one—of telling us that there have arisen in Wotan's mind the outlines of a scheme by which he may free himself from the toils that threaten to destroy him. This plan he has begun to put into execution during the long interval that separates the close of *The Rhinegold* from the opening of *The Valkyrie*. To begin with, he has paid a long visit to Erda, who besides imparting much good counsel has borne him nine daughters, the Valkyries. These now roam over the world on their winged steeds; after every battle they collect the bodies of the slain warriors and carry them over their saddlebows to feast with the gods in Valhalla. Thus Wotan is gathering an army with which to face the hostile powers by which he is surrounded.

But this is not enough. There can be no peace for him until the terrible Ring is returned to the Rhine Maidens; only when that is done will its power and that of the curse that rests upon it be destroyed. He may not himself steal it nor take it in fight; he has given it to the giants as part of the ransom for Freia, and to take it from Fafner now would mean the abrogation of one of his own laws, those laws that are graven in runes on the shaft of his all-powerful spear, and which are the source of his own strength. But what if someone else, without his assistance, were to do the deed for him? With this idea in his mind he descends to earth as Wälse, a warrior, and proceeds to bring into existence the race of Wälsungs. Wedding a mortal woman he has by her a son and a daughter,

Siegmund and Sieglinde. Sieglinde is carried off one day by enemies while her menfolk are away, and married against her will to Hunding the Black. Some time later Siegmund loses his father also. The two are separated in the forest, and Siegmund's search for the missing Wälse leads only to the discovery of a discarded wolf-skin. Wotan has returned to his own place. Siegmund leads for some time the life of an Ishmaelite, his hand against every man and every man's hand against him.

Act I. In championing a distressed maiden Siegmund is outnumbered and overwhelmed by her enemies, and at last, his sword broken, compelled to seek safety in flight. Night falls. Stumbling on through the darkness he is overtaken by a terrific storm, graphically depicted in the orchestral Prelude to *The Valkyrie*. At length he spies a forest dwelling. Completely spent, he staggers in and falls almost unconscious by the hearth. The living-room of the hut is empty when he arrives, but soon Sieglinde —for it is to Hunding's house that he has unwittingly come—enters from the back. Seeing an exhausted and wounded man she attends to his needs. The brother and sister do not recognize one another, but their mutual interest is obvious by the time Hunding returns home. The laws of hospitality are sacred, but the host is suspicious of his unexpected guest and asks his name and story. Siegmund for his part is equally distrustful, and, though he tells his tale truly, he speaks of himself as 'Wehwalt' and his father as 'Wolfe.' Unfortunately, however, Hunding is allied to those with whom Siegmund fought during the day. The Wälsung's words betray this fact, and Hunding sternly tells him that in the morning they must meet in arms, although for the night his enemy is safe under his roof. He then retires with his wife, and Siegmund is left alone.

The light from the dying fire falls upon the great tree

354

whose trunk forms the main support of the hut. Something appears to glitter in the wood, something the nature of which is revealed by the frequent recurrence of the Sword *motif* in the orchestra, but Siegmund is heedless, lost in gloomy reflection. He is aroused by the return of Sieglinde—moved by sympathy for the outcast, she has come to help him in his difficulties, having drugged her husband with a sleeping-draught. She tells him of how at her marriage-feast a stranger appeared, none knew whence (though the orchestra informs us that it was Wotan). He carried a sword which he struck to the hilt in a tree, saying that none but the strongest should draw it forth. Siegmund takes heart again, and there follows a rapturous duet, one of the most lovely things in the whole tetralogy. Suddenly in the midst of it the door flies open and reveals the night without. The storm has passed and the forest is bathed in moonlight. Startled at the noise made by the door Sieglinde exclaims, "Who went?" Siegmund replies:

No one went—but one has come!
Laughing the Spring enters the hall!
Winter storms have waned in the moon of May,
With tender radiance sparkles the Spring;
On balmy breezes, light and lovely,
Weaving wonders on he floats.
O'er wood and meadow wafts his breathing,
Widely open laughs his eye:
In blithesome song of birds resounds his voice,
Sweetest fragrance breathes he forth:
From his ardent blood breathe all joy-giving blossoms,
Bud and shoot spring up by his might.
With gentle weapons' charm he forces the world;
Winter and storm yield to his strong attack:
Assailed by his hardy strokes now the doors are shattered
That, fast and defiant, held us parted from him.

They fall into one another's arms. But something in her lover's voice stirs a vague recollection in Sieglinde.

Explanations follow, and Siegmund's true origin is revealed; he is a Wälsung, as she is! In great exaltation he takes his stand before the tree and invokes the sword under the name of 'Needful.' Then with a mighty effort he draws it forth. Sieglinde hails him as lord and brother, and together they hasten away into the night.

This love-scene between brother and sister has brought upon Wagner a good deal of hostile criticism. No doubt the idea is repellent according to our modern notions; but such marriages were common enough in primitive communities, and indeed survived for long among civilized peoples, as is evidenced by such notable instances as those of the Pharaohs of Egypt and the Incas of Peru.

Act II. Another tempestuous Prelude, suggestive first of the lovers and later of the Valkyries on their galloping horses, introduces us to a rocky place among the mountains. Wotan, fully armed, addresses his favourite daughter, Brünnhilde the Valkyrie, and bids her hasten to assist Siegmund in his forthcoming fight with Hunding. Brünnhilde obediently departs, leaping lightly from rock to rock and uttering her wild Valkyrie cry. Before she disappears she warns Wotan that she can see his wife Fricka approaching. Fricka has come in her capacity of goddess of marriage to demand vengeance on Siegmund for carrying off Hunding's wife. The argument is long and tedious—it soon appears that Wotan is getting the worst of it. Fricka points out that if he were to help Siegmund he would once more be flouting those laws that are the mainstay of his rule, and when he pleads that Siegmund is the saviour who will extricate them all from their difficulties by securing the Ring without any assistance from the gods, she replies that Wotan has already rendered his assistance by providing him with the magic sword and sending Brünnhilde to aid him in the battle.

356

Wotan is compelled to yield. Brünnhilde re-enters as Fricka goes out, and he now turns to her. He pours his troubles into her sympathetic ear in another scene of considerable length, and eventually revokes his previous commands. It is Hunding she must protect, not Siegmund.

Brünnhilde finds this new commission (which she feels to be contrary to her father's real desires) extremely irksome, but Wotan breaks out in fearful wrath at the first suggestion of disobedience, and finally leaves her with strict injunctions to carry out his orders to the letter. Sadly she retires to a cave at the back, where she conceals herself to await Siegmund. Already he comes, and Sieglinde with him. The poor girl is worn out with hardship and anxiety; Siegmund is quite unable to soothe her, and after a hysterical outburst she falls senseless in his arms. Seating himself on the ground he pillows her head in his lap, and then bending over her presses a long kiss on her forehead. On raising his eyes again he perceives Brünnhilde, who advances slowly toward him. The musical and dramatic interest has flagged sadly in the earlier part of the Act, but from this moment it revives once more. Brünnhilde informs the Wälsung that she has come to bid him to Valhalla, to Wotan, the gods, and the heroes. Siegmund inquires whether Sieglinde is to accompany him. "No," comes the reply.

> Here on earth must she still linger;
> Siegmund will find not Sieglinde there.

"Then," says Siegmund,

> Greet for me Valhalla, greet for me Wotan,
> Greet for me Wälse and all the heroes,
> Greet too the beauteous wish-maidens:—
> To them I follow thee not!

It is Brünnhilde's sad task to convince him that the

choice does not lie in his hands. When this at last comes home to him and he realizes that even his magic sword will not avail him he draws the weapon in a mood of anguished despair. Even should it fail him against the foe it will at least serve for Sieglinde and his child that is to be:

> Two lives laugh to thee here:
> Take them, Needful, envious still!

At this Brünnhilde's resolution breaks down. Rather than witness such a tragedy she will disobey her father's commands. Calling to Siegmund that the decree is revoked, that he shall live and Hunding die, she rushes from the darkening stage. Overcome with joy, Siegmund kisses once more the sleeping Sieglinde and hurries himself into the gloom at the back, whence Hunding's horn-call can already be heard. Sieglinde awakes, and finds herself alone in the gathering storm. Hearing the angry voices of her husband and her lover she runs forward to separate them, but a fearful flash of lightning causes her to stagger back. By its gleam Siegmund and Hunding are seen in mortal combat. Brünnhilde appears hovering over Siegmund and protecting him with her shield, but just as he aims a mighty blow at Hunding there looms over the latter the form of Wotan, his redoubtable spear outstretched. Siegmund's sword is shattered on the spear, and Hunding plunges his weapon into his disarmed adversary's breast. The light goes out, and it is with difficulty that the eye follows Brünnhilde as she picks up the fragments of the broken sword, hurries to Sieglinde, and carries her off. Wotan is left alone with Hunding; his rage and grief are terrible.

> Go hence, slave! Kneel before Fricka:
> Tell her that Wotan's spear avenged what wrought her wrong.
> Go!—Go!

Hunding falls dead, and the god's anger is diverted into another channel:

> But Brünnhilde! Woe to the guilty one!
> Dire wage shall she win for her crime,
> If my steed overtake her in flight!

Act III. The celebrated 'Ride of the Valkyries' provides a terrific exordium for this Act. The storm is still raging, and above the turmoil of the elements can be heard the cries of the Valkyries, the sound of galloping hooves, and the frenzied whinnyings of the horses. The characteristic rhythm persists long after the curtain has risen, disclosing the Valkyries' Rock, a desolate mountain top. One by one the Valkyries arrive at the rendezvous, riding from the back on their winged steeds, which they tether in a neighbouring wood. Brünnhilde alone is missing. At last they catch sight of her, riding furiously, and a moment or two later she staggers in, supporting Sieglinde. Her sisters are amazed to find a living woman with her instead of the dead body of Siegmund, but their amazement turns to dismay as she breathlessly tells her story and begs the loan of a horse that she and Sieglinde may continue their flight from Wotan, whose relentless pursuit is already indicated by a persistent rhythm in the orchestra. None of the others dares to brave the fury of the angry god, and Sieglinde herself intervenes, begging to be allowed to await the death she deserves and desires. But the dauntless Valkyrie holds to her resolve. She appeals to Sieglinde in the name of Siegmund's child who is presently to be born to her, and who, she prophesies, will become "the world's most glorious hero." Now courage is kindled in Sieglinde's breast, and, obeying Brünnhilde, she flies eastward to the forest. Thither Wotan seldom goes: he leaves it to Fafner, who, transformed by the

Tarnhelm into a dragon, guards there the Ring and the Nibelung's hoard.

But Brünnhilde remains to face her father. Riding on the thunderstorm he has already reached the rock, and now he comes striding in. The Valkyries cower in terror before him, vainly endeavouring to shield their sister; he knows well she is with them and imperiously commands her to come forth. Meekly she obeys, and stands before him to receive her sentence. In mingled anger and sorrow he delivers it:

> Outcast art thou from the clan of the gods:
> For broken is now our bond;
> Henceforth from sight of my face art thou banned!
> He who wins thee robs thee of all!
> For here on the rock bound shalt thou be;
> Defenceless in sleep liest thou locked:
> The man shall master the maid
> Who shall find her and wake her from her sleep.

At this savage decree all shake in horror. But Wotan cares nothing for the feeble protests of the eight Valkyries; let them hasten from their doomed sister and never return, on pain of sharing her fate. Terrified they ride off, and Brünnhilde is alone with her father.

The concluding scene is matchless in its beauty and tenderness. Meekly but eloquently the Valkyrie pleads for mercy. She has disobeyed Wotan's spoken word, it is true, but in doing so she has fulfilled his dearest wish, and rescued Sieglinde, her child, and the broken sword. But the god is adamant, and seeing that her doom is irrevocable she makes a final appeal:

> By thy command enkindle a fire;
> With flaming guardians girdle the fell;
> To lick with tongue, to bite with tooth,
> The craven who rashly dareth
> To draw near the threatening rock!

Overcome by love and pity Wotan yields. It only

remains to put the sentence into execution. But before he does this he bids a tender adieu to his daughter:

> Farewell, thou valiant, glorious child!
> Thou once the holiest pride of my heart!
> Farewell!

> Thy brightly glittering eyes,
> That smiling oft I caressed, . . .
> On mortal more blessed once may they beam:
> On me, hapless immortal,
> Must they close now for ever.
> For so turns the god now from thee,
> So kisses thy godhead away.

Gently he kisses her eyes, and she sinks unconscious in his arms. He carries her carefully to the side of the stage, adjusts her helmet, and covers her with her great shield, while from the orchestra arise the strains of a celestial lullaby. Then, finally turning away, he summons Loki. Thrice with his spear he strikes the rock, and at the third stroke a flash of flame leaps forth which quickly spreads to a fiery ring, encircling the mountain-top. As he stretches out the spear to cast a final spell we hear on the brass the theme of Siegfried, prophetic of the awakening to come. And now all is accomplished, and the god slowly and reluctantly departs, leaving his daughter in utter loneliness to her long, fire-girt sleep.

SIEGFRIED

Act I. Sieglinde did not long survive her brother. She succeeded in escaping into the forest only to die in giving birth to her son, Siegfried. Eighteen or twenty years have now elapsed, during which the boy has been brought up by Mime, the Nibelung smith. We last saw Mime smarting under the lash of Alberich's whip in *The Rhinegold*; now he and Alberich both haunt the forest in which Fafner, transformed into a dragon, guards the

Ring. Mime inhabits a cave that he has fitted up as a smithy, and it is in this gloomy dwelling that the first Act of *Siegfried* takes place. The dark Prelude contains references to the Ring and Rhinegold *motifs,* elements in the drama that have rather fallen into the background during *The Valkyrie.* But the most prominent themes are those of Mime's Meditation (two chords with a big drop between them) and the Nibelung smith. Mime is evidently hard at work, and the object of his labours is revealed by a *pianissimo* reference to the Sword *motif.* Further explanation is provided by his opening soliloquy. In Siegfried he has found, he hopes, the champion who will slay Fafner and win for him the Ring. But for that deed a sword is required, and no sword that he can forge is strong enough to satisfy the young hero. There is indeed a blade that would serve— 'Needful,' Siegmund's weapon, the broken splinters of which he received from the dying Sieglinde. But these mighty fragments it is beyond his power to fashion anew.

A merry horn-call announces the advent of Siegfried. It is soon clear that the youth wastes no affection on the shifty dwarf who has nurtured him. He starts by scaring him out of his wits by means of a wild bear he has captured in the forest. Then, driving the beast away, he demands his sword. Mime timidly hands him the fruit of his labours, a weapon that Siegfried contemptuously smashes with a blow on the anvil. Then he turns to the Nibelung and questions him about his (Siegfried's) birth and parentage. The dwarf's attempts to persuade him that he is himself the hero's father Siegfried scornfully brushes aside. But the truth he will have, and he almost throttles Mime in his endeavour to force it out of him. He gets his way, and now at last he hears of Sieglinde. Mime withholds Siegmund's name, but the fragments of 'Needful' are produced as witness of the tale. Seeing

362

them, Siegfried exclaims joyfully, "And now these fragments straight shalt thou forge me!" A moment later
he rushes off to the forest again, leaving Mime to the
one task that is beyond his skill.

The dwarf's gloomy broodings are interrupted by the
appearance at the cave's mouth of 'the Wanderer,' an
old man with a large hat that hangs down over one side
of his face, thus hiding the fact that he has lost an eye.
This, we soon discover, is Wotan. Mime roughly refuses
his plea for shelter and bids him begone. But the
stranger is not so easily disposed of, and seating himself
by the hearth he wagers his head that he will answer any
three questions that the Nibelung chooses to ask him.
Having accomplished this he claims the right to question
his host in return. This part of the libretto must have
been written before Wagner had decided on the composition of the earlier operas. The game of question
and answer takes a long time and tells us nothing that
we do not already know, except the answer to the Wanderer's last question, "Who shall forge the splinters of
the sword?" Of this Mime is as ignorant as we are.
He cries out in despair, but the Wanderer only rises
from his seat and calmly prepares to go. At the cave's
mouth he stops and replies to his own question:

> He who the force of fear ne'er felt,
> 'Needful' shall he forge.
> Thy wily head ward from to-day!
> I leave it forfeit to him
> Who has never learned to fear.

And so with a smile he departs.

The interview has proved too much for Mime's nerves,
and he gives way to a fit of hysterics, fancying that
Fafner himself is after him. When Siegfried returns
he finds him hiding behind the anvil. He takes some
time to recover, and then begins to speak of fear. But

363

his talk only puzzles Siegfried, who accepts with naïve curiosity his offer to guide him to Fafner's den, there to learn what fear means. But first the sword must be forged, and Mime confesses that this is a task he cannot accomplish. With a scornful reproach Siegfried takes the pieces from him:

> My father's blade yields but to me!
> By me forged be the sword!

From here to the end the music proceeds with the utmost animation. Siegfried blows up the furnace and files the pieces of the sword into small fragments. These he melts in the fire, pours into a mould, and so gradually makes a new weapon out of the original metal, accompanying each step of the process with a stirring song. Mime sees that the sword will be forged, and even the dragon, he feels, will be unable to withstand the might of this boy; the Ring itself will fall into Siegfried's hands! He sets about, therefore, to prepare a poisonous brew. With this he will come forward as soon as the dragon is dead; the thirsty Siegfried will drink, and the Ring will be his at last! Siegfried pays little attention to what Mime is doing—already his work at the forge is nearing completion. Soon he puts the finishing touches, and swinging the newly fashioned sword before him, cries in triumph,

> Needful, Needful, conquering sword!
> Again to life have I woke thee!
> Dead layest thou in splinters here,
> Now shin'st thou defiant and fair. . . .
> See, Mime, thou smith:
> So sunders Siegfried's sword!

With a mighty blow he cleaves the anvil in two from top to bottom, and the curtain falls.

Act II. The curtain rises again on a clearing in the forest before Fafner's cave. A Prelude built mainly on the theme of the Giants—now distorted to represent Fafner in his dragon shape—and full of dark references to Alberich's curse, is a fit opening to the first scene. In a night of inky blackness Alberich keeps his tireless watch on the Ring and its grim guardian. The sudden rising of a storm and its equally sudden passing herald the approach of the Wanderer. Much of the dialogue that follows is superfluous for those who know the earlier operas, but the Wanderer breaks new ground when he tells Alberich of Fafner's imminent destruction at the hands of the young Siegfried. The Nibelung's thoughts fly at once to the Ring by which he still hopes to gain universal dominion, and, incidentally, vengeance on the lords of Valhalla. He even acts on the Wanderer's suggestion that he should awaken Fafner, warn him of his danger, and persuade him to deliver up the Ring. But the dragon is not to be frightened, and the Wanderer rides off on his storm-cloud, prophesying wonders to come. Alberich, too, vanishes into a cleft in the rocks, and now, as the dawn breaks, Siegfried, piloted by Mime, comes out into the clearing. Here, Mime tells him, shall he learn the meaning of fear. But Siegfried's loathing for Mime is unabated, and the dwarf's pratings of love and gratitude move him to scornful anger. Mime takes himself off to await the issue of the fight, muttering to himself,

> Fafner and Siegfried, Siegfried and Fafner:
> Would each the other might slay!

At this point there creep into the music the first strains of the lovely 'Forest Murmurs' which have made the Act famous. To begin with, Siegfried's thoughts wander to his dead mother, and are expressed in a tender soliloquy. But soon he is attracted by the song of a forest bird. His attempts to imitate this on a reed are a grotesque failure, as he readily admits, but he can do better on the horn, and placing this instrument to his lips he plays a rousing call. The effect of this is to wake Fafner, and after an interchange of compliments the battle begins. Wagner would have been better advised to place the slaying of the dragon off the stage; the clumsy machinery of the theatre is bound to make it ridiculous. Happily it does not last long; 'Needful' is duly planted in the monster's heart, and he dies with a half-uttered warning to his conqueror left unfinished.

In withdrawing his sword from the dragon's body Siegfried receives a drop of the blood upon his hand. It burns like fire, and involuntarily he carries his hand to his lips. The result of swallowing the blood is that he finds he can understand the song of the birds, and the bird who sang to him before now tells him clearly of the Tarnhelm and the Ring. With a word of thanks he disappears into the cave to seek these treasures. During his absence there is a short but wildly grotesque scene between Mime and Alberich, the latter of whom has just issued from his cleft. But their wrangling leads to no bargain and is brought to an abrupt end by the return of the hero bearing with him the objects of their greed. Once more the bird takes a hand in the game. He warns Siegfried of Mime's treachery: let him but listen to the dwarf's words; the dragon's blood that he has drunk will enable him to detect their true intent beneath the veneer of deceit. Here the stagecraft is again at fault. To friendly and seductive music Mime announces in set terms his intention to poison Siegfried. The suggestion is that the dwarf really uses cajoling words, but that, owing to the spell of the blood, Siegfried can see through his treachery. The effect, however, is childlike in the extreme, and it is a relief when the young hero puts an end to the episode by striking off Mime's head with a blow of the sword. He throws the corpse into the cave and pushes the dragon's body in the same direction, completely blocking the entrance. He feels no remorse, but he is acutely conscious of his loneliness and appeals again to the bird. His resourceful friend is ready with an answer in this difficulty too, and Siegfried learns of Brünnhilde, and the Rock whose girdle of fire none shall cross but him who knows not fear. Shouting with joy he begs that the way be shown him. The bird flutters off with Siegfried eagerly following, his whole mind bent on this new adventure.

Act III. It has already been said that the composition of *The Ring* proceeded interruptedly till 1857, and by that time Wagner had completed the libretto of the whole tetralogy and the music as far as the middle of *Siegfried*. The story goes that the end of the scene describing the death of Fafner marks the actual point when he laid down his pen. If that is so he proved himself a true artist when he started work again in 1869. During the interval both *Tristan* and *The Mastersingers* had been brought to birth, and the composition of these works represented an enormous addition to his experience and musicianship. Yet the score of the Second Act of *Siegfried* shows no signs of the twelve years' break: the style of the last part of it differs in no way from that of the rest. But when we reach Act III we immediately become conscious of a riper mastery, a more matured ease in the treatment. The stormy Prelude, based on various elemental ideas, such as the theme of Erda, that of Wotan's Spear, the Waters of the Rhine, and the End of the Gods, is the work of a man who treads with a firmer step, a greater assurance, than heretofore. And this remains true of the rest of the Act in spite of the manifest weakness of part of the libretto. The first scene, for example, is mostly redundant, immensely powerful though it is musically. It is placed in a wild spot at the foot of the mountain whose summit is crowned by the Valkyries' Rock. The Wanderer is at first the only figure on the stage; by potent spells he summons Erda, that her wisdom may help him in his perplexities. But when she appears her answers are so evasive that they are of no use to him—he does most of the talking himself, but we learn little from him, except that he has become a disciple of Schopenhauer. Realizing that there is no way out of the tangle in which he is involved, and that the doom of the gods is inevitable, he has found peace in accepting the situation and himself willing that which he knows must be. Erda descends "to endless sleep" and the Wanderer quietly awaits the coming of Siegfried.

The young man, when he arrives, is troubled at the sudden departure of his bird, which flew off (as we hear from the Wanderer a little later) to save its life from the ravens that always accompany Wotan. Siegfried asks the Wanderer to tell him the way to the Rock, and at first it seems that the god will help him. But Mime has not succeeded in teaching his foster-child good manners, and his rude jests at the Wanderer's appearance awake the divine anger, till at length the hallowed spear is stretched out to bar the path. Siegfried is no whit dismayed and, drawing his sword, breaks the spear in two with a single blow, thus, though he knows it not, raising the spell that surrounds Brünnhilde. The Wanderer picks up the pieces of his weapon and saying quietly, "Fare on: I cannot withstand thee," suddenly disappears. Siegfried joyfully proceeds to where the growing light of the fire beckons him on the mountain-side.

The scene is now changed. During the interval while the stage is hidden the orchestra plays a new and wilder version of the Fire music, through which we hear the theme of Siegfried and the call of his horn. The music rises to a climax and then dies down till the lovely strains of the Sleep theme tell us that the summit of the Rock has been reached. The curtain rises on the same scene as that at the end of *The Valkyrie*. Brünnhilde is asleep in the foreground.

No words can do justice to the magnificent music of this final portion of *Siegfried;* the reader must hear it for himself. Siegfried approaches, and, seeing what he imagines to be an armed knight asleep, he raises the shield, looses the helmet, and cuts through with his sword the rings on both sides of the breast-plate. This reveals Brünnhilde in woman's dress, and now for the first time he learns what it is to be afraid. His attempts to waken her are unsuccessful, till at last he yields to the temptation to kiss her on the lips. The spell is broken and Brünnhilde sits up, greets the world once more, and then turns to ask the name of her deliverer. On hearing that it is Siegfried she bursts into a cry of rapture, and the two voices join in a full Italian cadence—the first in the work:

> O mother, hail, who gave thee thy birth!
> Hail, O Earth, that fostered thy life!
> Thine eye alone might behold me,
> Alone to thee might I wake.

A flow of music follows hardly less wonderful than the duet in *Tristan*, although totally different in character. Siegfried's growing passion alarms Brünnhilde, who vainly attempts to lead his thoughts into other channels. Suddenly he embraces her. She flies terror-stricken to the other side of the stage:

> No god's touch have I felt!
> Low bent all heroes, greeting the maiden:
> Holy came she from Walhall.
> Woe's me! Woe's me!

The effect of the abrupt transition from the love-music to the majestic Valhalla *motif* is tremendous. But Siegfried's ardour is unabated, and already the woman in Brünnhilde is driving out the goddess. For a moment the issue sways in the balance while in a kind of vision she sees the awful shadow of Alberich's curse. But the cloud departs as swiftly as it came, and she pours out her happiness in a lovely lyrical song beginning,

> Ever lived I, ever live I,
> Ever in sweet longing delight—
> Yet ever to make thee blest!

The principal melody of which was also used prominently by Wagner in the tender "Siegfried Idyll." [The "Siegfried Idyll" is a composition for a very small orchestra, written by Wagner and played by a few of his friends as a tribute to his wife Cosima on her birthday—the first after their son Siegfried was born. Almost all the tunes in it are taken from the opera *Siegfried*.] A moment later she surrenders utterly, and the work rises to its last climax on the wings of love triumphant as, oblivious of her lost divinity, of the curse hanging over them, of everything but Siegfried, she throws herself into his arms.

THE DUSK OF THE GODS

Act I. Night reigns on the Valkyries' Rock. Brünnhilde and Siegfried have sought repose in the cave at the back, and the orchestral opening of the opera tells us that the place is given over to the shadowy elemental powers. The three Norns (or Fates) sit spinning, winding the rope of Destiny. Their talk is of Wotan, his history, and his approaching fall through the agency of the Ring and Alberich's curse. Suddenly the rope

370

breaks, and the three sisters descend to their mother Erda, their work for the world at an end.

Dawn begins to brighten the sky, and soon the sun rises, just as Brünnhilde and Siegfried enter from the cave. The joy of their newly won happiness finds vent in a duet no whit inferior to the one in *Siegfried*. Musically it serves to introduce to us three new *motifs*: the first of them, a strong, virile tune in march-time, is really nothing but a rhythmical metamorphosis of Siegfried's horn-call; the second, a tender strain containing a typical Wagnerian 'turn,' represents Brünnhilde and the change that love has wrought in her; the third is a cadence of singular beauty which recurs often in the course of the scene and of which considerable use is made hereafter. The lovers are radiant, but it is not their intention that their lives shall be spent in an endless idyll on this lonely Rock. There is work in the world for Siegfried to do! But before they part Siegfried gives Brünnhilde, as a pledge of his undying love, the Ring. She in return gives him her horse, Grane. Grane's supernatural attributes have been lost with those of his mistress, but his own equine courage and strength still remain to him, and these are put at the service of his new master. At length the farewells are said, and Siegfried and Grane quickly disappear from us over the edge of the hill, though they are watched by Brünnhilde till the curtain falls. Even after this the orchestra carries us with the hero on his journey down through the fiery belt till at last he reaches the banks of the Rhine. Here we notice a change: the music loses its exuberant vitality and the sinister Ring *motif* falls on our ears with a presage of evil to come. At this moment the curtain rises once more. All that has happened hitherto is but a prelude to the main action of the drama, and the First Act proper opens in the Hall of the Gibichungs.

371

These, we soon learn, are a noble race whose home is on the banks of the Rhine. Gunther, their chief, is disclosed in council with his sister Gutrune and his half-brother Hagen. Hagen takes the lead in the conversation. Referring to the fact that Gunther and Gutrune are still unmarried, he announces that he knows of fit mates for both of them, and tells of Brünnhilde and Siegfried. With the history of these two he is clearly well acquainted, but he maintains a discreet silence about Siegfried's ascent of the Rock, and the wooing and winning of his bride. Gunther's enthusiasm is for a moment somewhat damped when he hears that the fire is an obstacle he can never surmount, but Hagen asserts that Siegfried can achieve what Gunther cannot, and urges that the Wälsung be induced to undertake the task by the offer of Gutrune's hand. Should her beauty fail to subdue the hero's heart, he knows of a potion that can be relied on in matters of this kind. Gunther and Gutrune have hardly agreed to the plan when Siegfried's horn announces his impending arrival. He is warmly greeted by the Gibichungs, but Gutrune seizes an early opportunity to steal away, returning presently with a draught in which she has mixed some of Hagen's potion. Siegfried takes the drinking-horn and, pledging Brünnhilde, puts it to his lips. The orchestra accompanies the toast with the broad Italian cadence we heard in the love-duet of *Siegfried*. But the phrase is never finished: it stops on the penultimate note as the powerful drug takes effect, and after a moment's hesitation resolves unexpectedly on the theme associated with Gutrune, on whose form the hero's eyes have suddenly fixed themselves. There is no further difficulty; Brünnhilde is entirely blotted from Siegfried's memory, and he willingly undertakes to win her for Gunther if Gutrune be granted as guerdon of his toil. By the charm of the

Tarnhelm, whose use he now for the first time learns from Hagen, he will deceive Brünnhilde into believing that he is Gunther. Gunther and he swear a bond of blood-brotherhood and set out immediately for the Valkyries' mountain. Gutrune watches their departure, and then retires to her chamber. Hagen is left alone, and in a short monologue he gives us the first inkling of his true designs. It is not love of his half-brother that has led him to contrive his plot. The Ring alone is his object and with this in his possession he hopes to wield a power that will make both Gunther and Siegfried his obedient slaves.

The curtain falls for a short time, but the music goes on and quickly transports us to the Valkyries' Rock once more. Brünnhilde's love-dream is broken by the well-remembered sounds of the Valkyries' ride, and soon her sister Waltraute stands before her. The scene that follows is often tedious, but it can be saved by a good Waltraute. Driven by despair, the Valkyrie has braved her father's wrath and come to the forbidden Rock. She brings dark tidings from Valhalla, where Wotan sits in silence among the assembled gods, awaiting the doom that he cannot escape. One hope alone remains: let Brünnhilde return the Ring to the Rhine Maidens—then will the curse and its effects be removed for ever! It is in the hope of persuading her sister to make the sacrifice that Waltraute has now come. But as soon as Brünnhilde realizes that it is Siegfried's love-pledge that is in question she breaks out in scorn. Is her sister so mad as to think that her lover's gift is not more to her than Valhalla and all it contains? All Waltraute's pleadings are useless, and in the end she is compelled to return without accomplishing her mission.

No sooner has she gone than the flames grow brighter. For a moment Brünnhilde idly wonders what this may mean; then, guessing it is Siegfried returning, she springs up to greet him—only to recoil in dismay. Siegfried indeed it is, but Siegfried disguised by the Tarnhelm so as to resemble Gunther, and speaking in a feigned voice. Announcing that he is Gunther, the Gibichung, he tells her he has come to make her his bride. What follows is quickly told. Brünnhilde, terrified, seeks refuge in the power of the Ring; but this avails nothing against its rightful owner. After a short struggle he tears it from her finger, and then bids his fainting victim lead him to her cave. The vanquished Brünnhilde can do nothing but comply, and with trembling steps she goes to the cave-mouth and disappears. Siegfried, left alone for a moment, draws his sword. Let it be witness that it is for his blood-brother alone that he has wooed! Keeping it still unsheathed he, too, vanishes into the cave.

Act II. The First Act of *The Dusk of the Gods* plays for about two hours if we include the Prelude. Act II is shorter, but it gives the exhausted hearer little respite, its seriousness being unrelieved by any suggestion of a lighter or more lyrical mood. In an open space on the shore, in front of the Gibichungs' Hall, sits Hagen. He has set himself to watch through the night for the return of Siegfried and Gunther, but weariness has overcome him, and now he sleeps, his form barely distinguishable in the general obscurity. His rest is troubled by evil dreams: he seems to see the figure of Alberich crouching at his feet, and to hold converse with this grim nocturnal visitor. Their voices come to us from the heart of the shadows, and we learn for the first time of Hagen's kinship with the Nibelung. "Sleep'st thou, Hagen, my son?" whispers Alberich, and exhorts him to ceaseless vigilance and undying hate. Only so will he succeed in wresting the Ring from Siegfried and in gaining for his father and himself the heritage of the gods. For revenge on them Alberich is still burning, and his last thought as he disappears is to extract from Hagen an oath that he will exact this vengeance to the uttermost when the Ring is his.

The coming of day brings Siegfried with it. By the power of the Tarnhelm he has conveyed himself instantaneously from the Valkyries' Rock to the Hall of the Gibichungs, and now he cheerfully greets Hagen and calls for Gutrune. While Brünnhilde and Gunther are making by more toilsome methods the journey that he has so easily accomplished, he tells the story of how the bride was won. The tale of the doings on the Rock excites a passing pang of jealousy in Gutrune, but Siegfried easily allays her fears and goes on to speak of how in the morning he led Brünnhilde down the mountainside, and then, by the help of a fortunate mist, succeeded in changing places with Gunther without arousing her suspicion. Nothing remains to be done but prepare the wedding-feast, and he hastens with Gutrune into the Hall to speed the arrangements. Hagen, alone once more, puts a great cow-horn to his lips and blows a blast summoning the savage folk who follow Gunther's standard. From all sides they come with their rough weapons, and in a wild chorus demand wherefore they have been assembled. Hearing that it is a feast that is in prospect they burst into good-humoured laughter and accord a hearty welcome to Brünnhilde and Gunther, who at this moment reach the water's edge. Gunther leads his bride forward to meet Hagen, who has now been joined by Gutrune and Siegfried, and thus the Valkyrie finds herself confronted with her faithless lover. At first she is utterly bewildered, but soon, seeing the Ring on his finger, she begins to suspect something of the truth, and asks how it comes that the charm wrested from her by Gunther (as she believes) appears now on Siegfried's hand. This is more than Gunther can explain, and Brünnhilde, in an outburst of wild fury, calls for vengeance on them all for their treachery and especially on the traitorous Siegfried whose wife she swears she is.

By this time everyone is at cross-purposes. Brünnhilde believes that Siegfried, to gain Gutrune, has deliberately sacrificed his first love. Siegfried, forgetful of his previous happiness, knows only that he has been faithful to the truth reposed in him by Gunther. Gunther, for his part, is beginning to entertain grave doubts on this same point. Hagen alone knows the whole truth, and it is on his spear-point that Siegfried swears that he has kept faith, Brünnhilde that he has broken it. Among the whole company Siegfried alone maintains his cheerfulness. He assures Gunther that Brünnhilde's outburst signifies nothing but a fit of feminine petulance, and departs with Gutrune and the vassals to complete the preparations for the wedding. Hagen, alone with Brünnhilde and Gunther, cunningly works on their suspicions of Siegfried until at length a plot is hatched to murder him. Since none of them is strong enough to withstand him in fight he must die by a stab in the back from Hagen's spear, the weapon on which his false oath was sworn. With this plan of vengeance both Brünnhilde and Gunther declare themselves satisfied; the wedding procession with Siegfried and Gutrune appears from the Hall and as they join it the curtain falls.

Act III. The Third Act opens with a series of horn-calls indicating that a hunt is in progress. The stage shows us a wild valley; through it flows the Rhine, on whose waters the three Rhine Maidens are seen swimming. They have occupied the long interval since we last saw them at the beginning of *The Rhinegold* in composing and learning a new and exquisite song, with which they now delight our ears. Presently Siegfried

appears on the bank; in the course of the hunt he has
got separated from the rest, and has reached this spot
in search of his lost quarry. The Rhine Maidens offer
to find it for him if he will give them in return the golden
Ring on his finger. For a single moment he seems about
to grant their request, but they make the mistake of
threatening him with evils to come should he not comply
with their wishes. At this he calmly returns the talisman
to his finger; he cares little for the gold itself, and as for
the curse of Alberich, of which he now hears for the
first time, no one shall ever say that he has yielded from
fear. The Rhine Maidens swim slowly away prophesying that this very day he shall be slain. Brünnhilde will
inherit the Ring, to her will they go, and she will not
refuse to grant them their own.

The lyric loveliness of this scene provides a most
welcome relief from the general sombre mood of the
drama, but now the appearance of the hunting-party
brings us quickly to the tragic climax. They sit down to
eat and rest: Gunther is sunk in gloomy brooding and
Hagen preserves his usual grim aloofness. Siegfried be-
guiles the time with the tale of his adventures, and once
more we hear of Mime, of the slaying of Fafner, and the
winning of Tarnhelm and Ring. At this point Hagen
drops the juice of a herb into Siegfried's drinking-horn.
Suddenly and wonderfully there steal into the music the
notes of the cadence from the love-scene at the beginning
of the opera. The gates of Siegfried's memory have
been opened; he recalls once more the wooing and winning of Brünnhilde, and this story too he tells, quite
unconscious of the emotion his words are arousing in the
breast of Gunther. Hagen's moment has come. Two
ravens fly up from a bush in the background; he draws
Siegfried's attention to these and then, when the hero's
back is turned, plunges his traitor's spear deep into his

body. Siegfried rushes at him, raising his shield as though to bring it down and overwhelm him; but his strength fails him and he falls to the ground. Gunther is horror-struck when he sees the execution of the plot to which he has himself been a party, but the wounded warrior claims all his attention, and Hagen is suffered to depart unchallenged. Siegfried's dying thoughts fly back to his vanished happiness. He imagines that he is still on the Valkyries' Rock with Brünnhilde in his arms, and he dies with her name on his lips.

The interval required to change the scene is occupied by the tremendous 'Death March,' a piece which shows us the composer's genius in its loftiest aspect. It consists in reality of little but a series of *leit-motifs*, thrown into slow march-rhythm and so arranged as to bring before the eyes of our imagination the whole course of Siegfried's life. It is by no means long, but the epic quality of the themes themselves combined with the incomparable majesty of their setting creates an impression that is never to be forgotten. At length, when the heroic mood has exhausted itself, the march ends with a short but infinitely pathetic reference to Brünnhilde.

The curtain rises again on a moonlight night in the Gibichungs' Hall. Gutrune is alone, for Brünnhilde has gone down to the river and the hunting-party has not yet returned. Anxiously she awaits her Siegfried. But it is Hagen who appears first, Hagen in the wildest of spirits at the success of his villainy; brutally he breaks the news, just as the procession of death arrives at the Hall. All is horror and confusion. Gutrune casts on Gunther the blame for Siegfried's murder; Gunther accuses Hagen, who defiantly admits the deed and claims as his reward the Ring. Gunther refuses to give up Gutrune's dower, as he calls it, swords are drawn, and soon Gunther lies dead on the ground. With a cry of "Mime, the

378

Ring!" Hagen approaches Siegfried's body, but the dead man's hand raises itself threateningly, and horrified at the portent his murderer cowers away. And now with firm step Brünnhilde is seen making her way through the terror-stricken crowd to the front of the stage. Henceforth the interest is focused entirely on her. She begins quietly but with immense dignity:

> Silence your sorrow's clamorous cry!
> Whom ye all have betrayed,
> For vengeance cometh his wife.
> Children heard I whining to their mother, because sweet milk
>   had been spilled:
> Yet heard I not lament that befitteth the highest hero's fame.

Gutrune interrupts her with a shower of reproaches, but Brünnhilde, who has learnt all from the Rhine Maidens, quells her with a few words that reveal the whole plot, and with a wail of dismay at Hagen's treachery Gutrune falls senseless. Brünnhilde turns to the vassals, imperiously bidding them prepare a pyre and lift the body thereon. Others she sends to bring Grane, her faithful horse. Now she turns to Siegfried's body, and in a gentler voice pronounces his epitaph:

> Truer than his were oaths ne'er spoken;
> Faithful as he, none e'er held promise;
> Purer than his, love ne'er was plighted:
> Yet oaths hath he scorned, bonds hath he broken,
> The faithfullest love none so hath betrayed!
> Know ye why this was?
> O! ye, of vows the heavenly guardians,
> Turn now your eyes on my grievous distress!
> Behold your eternal disgrace!
> To my plaint give ear, thou mighty god!
> Through his most valiant deed, by thee so dearly desired,
> Didst thou condemn him to endure the doom that on thee had
>   fallen—
> He, truest of all, must betray me, that wise a woman might
>   grow!
> Know I now thy need?
> All things, all things, all know I,

All to me is revealed.
Wings of thy ravens wave around me;
With tidings long desired I send now thy messengers **home**,
Rest thou, rest thou, thou god!

She bends down and takes the Ring from Siegfried's finger:

My heritage yields now the hero.
Accursed charm! Terrible Ring!
My hand grasps thee—and gives thee away.

Soon the Rhine Maidens shall have their gold again, cleansed by the waters from the curse. Let them preserve it pure henceforth. Placing the Ring on her finger, she takes from a vassal a burning brand:

Fly home, ye ravens! . . .
To Brünnhilde's Rock first wing your flight.
There burneth Loki: straightway bid him to Wal'l
For the end of godhood draweth now near.
So cast I the brand on Wallhall's glittering walls.

She flings the torch on the pyre, and turns again to greet Grane, who has been led in. Does he know whither they are going on this last ride, and to whom?

Hei-a jo-ho! Grane!
Give him thy greeting!
Siegfried! Siegfried! See!
Brünnhilde greets thee in bliss.

She has mounted her horse and now urges it into the flames, in which it disappears with its rider. The fire blazes up till the Hall itself is alight and parts of the building come crashing down. But at this moment the Rhine suddenly overflows its banks, extinguishing the flames. On the bosom of the flood are borne the Rhine Maidens, who are seen circling over the place where the pyre has been. Hagen, who has been watching events in growing alarm, dashes into the water with a cry of "Give back the Ring!" But one of the Maidens already holds

380

the talisman, and the other two encircle the murderer with their arms and drag him with them into the depths. Meanwhile a glow in the sky betokens a new and mightier portent. The awestruck watchers raise their eyes, and behold, heaven itself is aflame! The stately pile of Valhalla is clearly visible for a moment with the gods and heroes seated in the great Hall. Then the whole is lost in a seething ocean of fire. The doom is accomplished, the struggle of ages ended at last.

Such is the massive grandeur of the 'Death March' that it seems impossible that the opera should continue without an anticlimax. But this last Scene takes us a step farther still. Wagner's genius rises easily on strong wings of inspiration and provides us with a *finale* that for sustained elevation of thought stands quite alone. The stagecraft may be clumsy and even childish, the poetry no more than second-rate, but these things matter little. It is the music that signifies, the music that, soaring above the petty limitations of the empyrean, grasps the whole universe in its invisible fingers. It is not a mere human tragedy that we have witnessed, it is the end of an Æon, of a dispensation, in which a whole heaven and earth have gone down in irretrievable catastrophe.

The music of *The Ring* shows, as has been already hinted, a steady progress throughout. *The Rhinegold* was the first opera that Wagner had written since *Lohengrin,* and in it we see the fruits of the years of thought that had intervened, since the completion of the earlier work. The *leit-motif* system which is applied only tentatively in *Lohengrin* appears in its completeness in *The Rhinegold.* The only defect is a slight awkwardness in the handling of the *motifs,* which occasionally degenerate into little more than labels. But in this and other respects the treatment becomes steadily firmer as the great work proceeds, until we reach the supreme mastery of the Third Act of *Siegfried*. The level of *The Dusk of the Gods* is not so consistently high. Wagner was handicapped by a libretto written years before, when his experience was much less than it had now become. We notice, too, that the new themes that are here introduced (chiefly in connection with the Gibichungs) are not always so distinctive as those with which we are already familiar, and a suspicion grows that some of the material for this opera has been taken straight from the old abandoned score of "Siegfried's Death." There is yet another point worth mentioning. The very number of the *motifs* constitutes a difficulty in *The Dusk of the Gods*. More than a hundred have been classified, and it is almost impossible for any of the characters to make a remark without evoking one of them. This *embarras de richesse* seriously interferes with the musical continuity, and there are times when we feel we are listening to something that is more like a catalogue of *motifs* than a connected work of art. On the other hand, the piece contains, as we have seen, moments of such stupendous power as to eclipse even the greatest things in the earlier scores.

Brünnhilde is surely the most glorious heroine in all opera. In Wagner's own work there is no one who can possibly be mentioned in the same breath with her, except, perhaps, Isolde—and Isolde is of the earth, earthy, compared with Brünnhilde. But the Valkyrie maiden is the only character in *The Ring* who really succeeds in arousing our sympathy, and, though we would do a great deal for her sake, it is surely too much to expect us to bear with all the large circle of her friends and relatives. A more exasperating collection of people it would be hard to find anywhere. Wotan, of course, is the worst offender; the length and prolixity of his egotistical discourses put him in a class by himself. But none of the party is really attractive. Which of us, for instance, would not gladly give one half of our worldly goods for an afternoon on the river with Brünnhilde, and as cheerfully surrender the other half to avoid the prospect of a round of golf with Siegfried? Of the terribly complicated tangle in which all these people get involved it is sufficient to say that this is not the stuff that plays are made of. Even Wagner got tired of unravelling it at last, so he effectually put an end to the story by getting rid of all his characters, human and divine, in one universal cataclysm—a simple but not very satisfactory solution.

The plain truth is that most of us find the drama as such a dreadful bore. No one would dream of bothering with *The Ring* if it were not for the music that accompanies it. Those portions of it where "the play's the thing"—or worse, where the dialogue's the thing—leave us quite unmoved, but the moment the music assumes the chief place our interest revives regardless of the dramatic situation. Those parts of the work with which the concert hall has made us familiar seem sure of immortality. Time alone can show whether the rest is aught more than the mortal coil. But if this indeed be so, it is a future generation that will attend its obsequies; upon us and upon our children the mighty shadow of the master still lies too heavily. We may criticize his work, but we dare not yet venture to tamper with it. The ultimate verdict we can be content to leave to posterity.

PARSIFAL

Words and Music by WAGNER.
Bayreuth, 1882; *New York,* 1903; *London,* 1912.

THE vicissitudes of *Parsifal*, Wagner's last great work, form one of the most interesting chapters in operatic history. Finished in January 1882, and produced on the 26th of July in the same year, it appeared at a time when the composer's reputation was fully established, and in the ordinary course of events would soon have found its way into all the principal opera houses of Europe and America. But this was not to be. The singular regulations by which it was protected forbade its performance at any other theatre save the Wagner theatre at Bayreuth (the scene of the original production) for a period of no less than thirty years. It thus became inaccessible, except in a few concert selections, to the musical world at large, and there quickly grew up round it a kind of legend, sedulously encouraged by the select band of pilgrims to Bayreuth, in the romantic light of which it soon came to be regarded as an almost supernatural revelation having little or nothing in common with ordinary operatic affairs. An unscrupulous impresario took advantage of the fact that the copyright did not include America to produce *Parsifal* in New York in 1903; but for the European public the veil of mystery was not lifted till the monopoly expired in 1912. Many of us can remember the excitement which this created and the thrill that went through Covent Garden Theatre on that memorable night as the violins took up the first strain of the Prelude and we settled ourselves to what was for most of us a new opera by Richard Wagner.

But though *Parsifal* had left its shrine and was here to be heard, seen, and criticized by everybody, the old atmosphere still clung about it. The absolute novelty of the subject as a theme for operatic treatment was itself an obstacle to the estimation of its real value, for there seemed at first to be no criterion by which it could be judged. It contained, moreover, certain elements that diverted attention from its æsthetic aspects, and the controversy which presently arose was as much concerned with religion and propriety as with the problems of music-drama. Even to-day the battle still rages fiercely as to whether or not the story of *Parsifal* is suitable for representation in the theatre, and in the midst of this fog of war it is difficult for the mere musician to see his way. But let us take heart. After all, one fog is much like another, and we may profit by the example of the prudent Londoner as he threads the murky thoroughfares of his smoke-shrouded city on a typical January afternoon. Being only concerned with the musical and dramatic side of the discussion let us keep strictly to the curb, refusing to be drawn into any digression, however enticing the prospect may appear.

Parsifal, then, is an opera based on the story of the Holy Grail. Its hero is the Sir Percival of Tennyson, and Wagner tells us of the adventures by which he rose to become the leader of the Knights of the Grail and guardian of the castle's treasure. The temptation to link the drama with *Lohengrin* is a strong one, but in reality the connexion is very slight. Lohengrin, it is true, claims Parsifal as his father, but there is no mention in *Parsifal* of Lohengrin, who could not have been born until long after the action of the play is finished. As to the music, the points in common are so few as to be negligible for our purpose.

The Prelude is constructed on the simplest possible

lines and makes use of only three themes, all of them associated with the Grail. The first (usually labelled 'The Love-feast of the Knights') is played four times, twice in the major, and twice in the minor. The second (familiar as 'The Dresden Amen') represents the Grail itself. The third (announced on the trombone and subjected to considerable development) is the theme of Faith. A return to the 'Love-feast' idea immediately precedes the rise of the curtain. This reveals a forest in the Grail's domain with a lake at the back. In the middle is a glade, on the floor of which the old hermit, Gurnemanz, and two esquires are lying asleep. Gurnemanz is awakened by a solemn call on the trombones; he rouses the esquires, and the three kneel and offer up their morning prayer. This done, they hasten to prepare for their King, who will soon be coming to take his morning bath in the lake and whose advent is even now heralded by the arrival of two of his knights. But here there is a weird interruption: a woman comes hurriedly in, unkempt and with dark, piercing eyes. In her hand she holds a small vial which she presses on Gurnemanz, bidding him offer it to the King—for the King, as all know, is afflicted by a grievous wound which defies every attempt to heal it. The woman, whose name is Kundry, then throws herself exhausted on the ground, just as the litter that bears King Amfortas is carried in and set down on the stage. Amfortas has almost ceased to hope for a cure—herbs and balsams from far and wide have been tried in vain. There is, indeed, a prophecy that help will come at last, at the hands of some mysterious visitant, a simple soul,

> Made wise through pity,
> And pure in heart,

but he has given up speculating what this obscure saying may signify. Gurnemanz offers him Kundry's vial, and

386

he turns painfully to thank her for it, but the strange woman only bids him begone to his bath, and wearily he gives the signal to proceed.

Kundry's behaviour has not inspired the esquires with confidence, and as soon as the King has gone they begin to abuse her openly, accusing her of bringing misfortunes upon them all by her wickedness. But Gurnemanz rebukes them, recalling the many occasions on which she has loyally helped them. He falls into a mood of reminiscence, in which he gradually unfolds the whole story of the Grail. The two treasures of the castle were the sacred Cup from which Our Lord drank at the Last Supper, and the Spear which pierced His side. These were delivered in a vision to Titurel, Amfortas' father, and it was he who built the castle to contain them and enrolled the band of knights for their defence. Among those who sought admission to the fraternity was Klingsor, but as he lacked the essential singleness of heart Titurel would have none of him. Enraged by his rejection, Klingsor turned to the black arts and raised by the power of sorcery a garden of fair women to lure the knights to their undoing. In time Titurel grew old and bequeathed his kingdom to his son, Amfortas. But Amfortas proved no match for Klingsor; he allowed himself to be enticed away by a woman of wondrous beauty, and in his absence Klingsor secured the Spear. He even succeeded in wounding the King with the stolen weapon, and it might have gone hard with him had not Gurnemanz himself been drawn to the scene by his master's cry. Amfortas' life was saved, but the wound, as they know, had refused to heal. Meanwhile the Spear remains in Klingsor's hands and the sorcerer is plotting to obtain the Grail itself.

Gurnemanz has no sooner finished than an outcry is heard from the lake. A wounded swan flutters weakly in and sinks dying on the stage, an arrow in its breast. All wild life is sacred in the domain of the Grail, and it is not long before the esquires have caught and brought in the author of the outrage. It is a young lad whose mien shows him to be utterly unconscious of having done anything wrong; but he is not lacking in sensibility, and at Gurnemanz's grave reproof his naïve pride in his archery turns quickly to remorse. His eyes fill with tears, and impulsively he breaks his bow and throws away his arrows. Questions elicit the astonishing fact that he knows neither his father's name nor his own. His mother he has but lately left, and after wandering through many wild places has come at last all unknowing to the holy mountain. His narrative rouses unexpected interest in Kundry, who betrays also a surprising acquaintance with his history. Now she startles him with the grievous news that his mother is dead; at this he exhibits the deepest emotion and seems about to faint, but she revives him with water and then herself sinks down as though overcome with emotion, while the sinister theme of Enchantment winds sinuously through the tissue of the music.

At this point the curtain usually descends, and it is left to the orchestra to lead us to the Hall or Temple of the Grail, in which the second Scene takes place. Wagner, indeed, directs that the stage itself should move, and that the young man and Gurnemanz should be seen walking, with a shifting panorama as a background, till they reach the castle. But in performance this device is horribly clumsy and most producers wisely leave it out.

The music has now assumed a grave and stately character, and the deep tones of bells increase the general feeling of solemnity. The Hall is empty when Gurnemanz and the boy first arrive, but it soon begins to fill with knights, who enter in dignified procession and take their places at tables ranged round the walls. It is the hour of the sacred rite. Amfortas is borne in to a choral accompaniment and assisted to a couch in front of the draped altar at the back. And now, when all is ready, there is heard from a recess behind Amfortas' couch the voice of the aged Titurel, speaking as though from the tomb. He bids his son reveal the Grail, the sight of which alone keeps him alive. But with an agonized cry the tortured Amfortas raises himself in vehement protest. The blessed spectacle which is joy and peace to them is torment unspeakable to him, the accursed, who must stand and minister to them while his tainted blood flows wildly through his veins till it escapes by the gaping wound. His magnificent outburst concludes with a prayer for pardon and death, and he sinks down exhausted. But his madness passes with his strength, and presently, rallying his forces, he bows to the inward call. The shrine is uncovered, revealing a crystal Cup, while a sudden darkness fills the Hall. Soon a dazzling ray falls from above, the sacred vessel glows with a soft light, and Amfortas lifts and waves it slowly from side to side, thus consecrating the bread and wine. Then he replaces it once more on the altar, the covering falls, and daylight slowly returns. The knights and esquires raise their voices in a solemn hymn while the consecrated elements are distributed; but Amfortas falls weakly back, and the movements of his attendants show that the wound has broken out afresh. Presently he is assisted to his litter and borne slowly from the Hall, the knights following behind.

Of all this scene Gurnemanz and his companion have been silent but attentive witnesses. At its conclusion the lad is so overwhelmed that he can offer no reply to the hermit's questions, and irritated by his seeming stupidity the old man pushes him angrily from the Hall, while a voice from above repeats the prophecy of him who is to come—the simple soul "made wise through pity, and pure in heart." There is a lovely choral cadence and the curtain falls.

Act II. It is in a very different atmosphere that the Second Act opens. The Prelude paints for us a horror of deep darkness, through which the coils of the Enchantment *motif* are ceaselessly writhing. At intervals, too, there is heard a descending *arpeggio,* like a shout of fiendish laughter. The stage, when we see it, is wrapped in profound gloom, and it is only with great difficulty that we discern the interior of the keep of Klingsor's magic castle, strewn with the apparatus of sorcery. The magician himself can just be distinguished at one side—half hidden in wreaths of strange, blue vapour, he is invoking some presence from the depths below. It is Kundry whom he summons and who seems to rise slowly from the shadows, her eyes closed as though in sleep. Waking suddenly, she utters a terrible cry and then a wail of misery and fear. Klingsor taunts her with her devoted service to the Knights of the Grail, and we learn that it was she who under his mighty spell lured Amfortas to his ruin. Now he calls her to a new task. Between him and the Grail, the object of his foul ambition, he sees but one obstacle, the youth who is even now approaching the castle walls—let her but rob him of his purity and the battle is won. Kundry refuses, and then ensues a mighty conflict of wills. But Klingsor's magic is strong, and at last with a shriek she vanishes, to carry out his behests. Already from his window the sorcerer has watched the new enemy scale the ramparts and disperse the castle's defenders. The time for the real trial of strength has arrived.

Suddenly the whole tower seems to sink into the earth,

390

Klingsor with it, and in its place appears an enchanted garden, filled with strange and lovely flowers. In it stands the young man, of whose ignominious ejection from the Hall of the Grail we were so lately witnesses. The contrast with the preceding Scene is complete, and it is heightened by the sudden irruption from all sides of groups of 'Flower-maidens,' clad in light, diaphanous garments. We need not follow these dainty creatures in their successive attitudes of fear, shyness, and ardour toward the comely stranger. He is willing enough to play with them, but he remains utterly unconscious of their efforts to seduce him. One of Klingsor's weapons has failed; now he employs another, the strongest in his armoury.

From out of the foliage is heard the voice of Kundry, and soon her form becomes visible through an opening. It is a transformed Kundry that we behold, reclining luxuriously on a couch. Gone are the wild garb and penitent mien, and in their place we perceive rich silks, soft outlines, and an attitude of voluptuous charm. Her advent puts an immediate end to the fairy-like episode of the Flower-maidens. They disappear as swiftly as they came, so that the bewildered lad, looking round the empty stage, is moved to murmur, "Of all this did I now but dream?" However, he has no time to waste in idle speculations—Kundry's first words have given him other food for thought. She has called him by his name, 'Parsifal,' and now she is telling him of his unknown history with an intimate familiarity that bespeaks a first-hand knowledge. He hears how his father was slain in battle, and how Heart-Sorrow (Herzeleid), his mother, reared him, far from the stormy ways of men. And then, too, he is reminded how he left her to languish and at last to die under a burden of grief too heavy to bear.

All this is part of a carefully laid plot. Parsifal is naturally moved by the tale, and it is while he is defenceless under the stress of emotion that Kundry, whispering that she comes to him as his mother's last gift, bends over him and presses a long kiss on his lips. For a moment her plan seems to have succeeded. But suddenly, with a loud cry, "Amfortas! the Spear-wound!" Parsifal starts up. That burning embrace and the pain it brings have shed a flood of light on his mind. He sees once more, as in a vision, the scene in the Hall of the Grail, and sees it for the first time with a full understanding of its significance. Kundry's attempts to lead his imagination back to thoughts of passion only serve to explain to him the exact nature of Amfortas' temptation, and he pushes her angrily away. But her resources are not yet exhausted, and she next appeals to his pity by telling him of the curse under which she labours. Back through the centuries her story takes her to that day, dim ages ago, when she watched a condemned Man staggering beneath His Cross on the road to Golgotha:

> Then laughed I!
> On me fell His look. . . .
> I seek Him now from world to world—
> Yet once more to behold Him.
> In darkest hour ween I that the hour is near,
> His eye on me doth rest;
> Then once more the accursed laugh outbreaketh,
> A sinner falls upon my bosom! [1]

But now, at long last, she has found one who will redeem her. Let her but for one hour bewail her sins upon his breast and all will be forgotten.

Parsifal, however, is by this time fully conscious of his mission and sees clearly how it is to be performed. He offers her not comfort but deliverance, and that is not

[1] These extracts from the English version are printed by kind permission of Messrs Schott and Co.

392

to be achieved by indulgence in a guilty passion. To all her burning words he replies only with a stern rebuke and a request to be shown the way back to Amfortas. At that she turns on him with all the fury of thwarted desire, curses his homeward road which she swears he shall never find, and calls Klingsor to come to her assistance. The sorcerer appears on the battlements grasping the Holy Spear, which he hurls with an angry taunt at Parsifal's unprotected form. But the weapon miraculously changes its course and remains suspended in the air over the young man's head. Seizing it in his hand, "he swings it in the sign of the Cross. The castle falls as by an earthquake; the garden withers to a desert; the ground is scattered with faded flowers; Kundry sinks down with a cry." Parsifal, turning to go, has but one word for the stricken woman,

> Thou knowest where thou canst meet with me again.

Act III. Once more we are in the domain of the Grail, close to Gurnemanz's hut, which is seen at the back of the stage. The pleasant freshness of spring is over the landscape, but there is no joy in the face of the hermit as he emerges from his door. A long time has elapsed since last we saw him, and he is now a very old man. His ear has caught the sound of groans, and, going to a thicket, he pulls aside the undergrowth and peers within. Then, bending forward, he pulls out the unconscious form of Kundry, stiff and cold. However, he is successful in his efforts to revive her, and presently she opens her eyes and sits up with a cry. She is dressed in the robe of a penitent, and the wildness has gone from her look. To the old man's inquiries she gives only two muttered words in reply, "Service! Service!"

There now appears striding slowly from the wood a

man encased from head to foot in black armour, a lowered spear in his hand. He seems worn and weary, and at first vouchsafes no answer to Gurnemanz's welcome. But when the hermit tells him it is Good Friday morning he lays down his weapons, raises his vizor, and kneels in silent prayer. His face is now visible, and the old man recognizes him as Parsifal returned. His devotions over, the wanderer greets him and acquaints him briefly with his story: how, driven from his path by the power of Kundry's curse, he has roamed the world over and encountered innumerable perils in defence of the sacred weapon he carries. Even now he scarcely dare hope that his journey is near its end.

Gurnemanz is overcome with a transport of joy at the thought that the Spear is recovered. He assures Parsifal that it is indeed the Grail's domain that he has reached, and gives him in his turn an account of how the brotherhood has fared. It is a gloomy tale. In the vain hope of winning death by denying himself the sight of the holy Cup Amfortas has refused to perform his office. For long the Grail has lain in its shrine, unseen by mortal eyes, while the strength of its knights has languished and the aged Titurel passed sadly to his grave. The emotion caused by this news is more than Parsifal's exhausted body can bear, and he sinks to the ground supported in Gurnemanz's arms. Aided by Kundry, the old man refreshes him with water from the holy spring and washes away the stains of travel. Soon he recovers and asks to be taken to Amfortas, who, he hears, is this day to officiate yet once more before the altar in honour of his dead father. But the others have not yet finished their ministrations, and he gazes in mild wonder at Kundry, who pours some of the contents of a golden vial over his feet and wipes them with her unbound hair. Taking the vial from her he bids Gurnemanz anoint his head, thus consecrating him King of the Grail and its people. This is duly done, and the first use he makes of his authority is to baptize Kundry, who falls weeping on the ground.

It is here that the sweet, celestial strains of the Good Friday music begin to be heard, throwing a gentle radiance over the score. The words of Parsifal and Gurnemanz celebrating the joy of nature in man's gratitude for his redemption have given its title to this tender intermezzo. But it is of the fresh purity of the trees and flowers decked in their spring garment of green that the music sings to us in a pastoral symphony whose idyllic beauty is untroubled by any hint of grief or suffering.

Parsifal is invested with the mantle of a Knight of the Grail, and with Gurnemanz and Kundry in attendance sets out for the castle. A transformation scene, similar to that in Act I, takes place, while the orchestra commemorates the death of Titurel in a gloomy march. When we reach the Hall, which is only dimly lighted, we find the ceremony just starting. The knights advance in two processions, the one bearing Amfortas and the shrouded Grail, the others the coffin containing the body of Titurel. In a solemn antiphonal hymn they heap their grave reproaches on their recreant ruler, and in reply Amfortas, raising himself on his couch, invokes the soul of his father in an appeal for death in which the dignity of suffering and passionate despair are finely blended. But the impatient knights break in on his soliloquy, bidding him perform his office. "Unveil the Grail! Thou must! thou must!"

With a mighty "No!" Amfortas rises to his feet. Maddened by pain and misery he rushes among them, tearing open his garments and bidding them bury their weapons in his sinful heart. His sudden movement and the wild light of ecstasy burning in his eyes fill the knights with consternation, and they shrink back in fear. We have reached the supreme climax of the work. Parsifal, who has entered unobserved, comes forward with quiet confidence and touches with the Spear-point the wound that Amfortas' gesture has revealed:

> Only one weapon serves:
> The Spear that smote must heal thee of thy wound.
> Be whole, absolved, and atoned!
> For I do hold thy office now.

Amfortas reels, his face transfigured with hope and holy joy, while Gurnemanz supports him in his arms. Parsifal moves toward the centre and displays on high the sacred Spear. Then he ascends the altar steps and firmly bids the esquires reveal the Grail. Amid murmurs of wonder and thanksgiving he takes in his hands the holy Cup, which shines softly in the growing darkness; the radiance descends from above, and in it a white dove is seen hovering over Parsifal's head. Whilst all are kneeling, wrapt in adoration, Kundry sinks lifeless to the ground, a look of divine peace lighting up her face. The curse is lifted, her expiation accomplished.

Whether Wagner has entirely succeeded in producing a masterpiece out of this material may be doubted. To many people the different elements in *Parsifal* appear not only diverse but actually incongruous. It is true that in mediæval times incidents from Holy Writ were often presented in dramatic form, and there seems no logical objection to a composer taking a sacred theme for an operatic work. But since the time of the liturgical dramas the Church and the Theatre have become more and more sharply differentiated when regarded from an æsthetic standpoint. By the end of the 17th century opera and oratorio were already distinct, and the tendency since has been to emphasize the contrast. Wagner's methods, with his direct appeal to the emotions and his

reliance on elaborate stage machinery, are utterly antag-
onistic to the restrained dignity that characterizes true
ecclesiastical music.

The result is that *Parsifal* falls between two stools.
In the Scenes in Acts I and III where the liturgical
element is strong, the intensely theatrical management
of the lighting (not to mention the appearance of the
dove) strikes a jarring note that is unpleasant. The
cathedral, we feel, and not the opera house, is the place
for this music. And yet when we hear parts of it in a
sacred building we are surprised to find how greatly it
suffers from the absence of the setting designed for it by
the composer.

We are thus faced at the outset by a serious dilemma
regarding the presentation of the work. This would not
greatly matter if the music were of the consistent excellence that we find in *The Mastersingers*. But, unfortunately, this is not so. There are moments in *Parsifal*
(such as the Prelude and the Grail Scene in Act I, all the
first half of Act II, and the Good Friday music and the
finale in Act III) which will bear comparison with anything that Wagner wrote, but the rest shows a fitfulness
of inspiration that is not without significance, perhaps,
when we remember that this is the composer's last work.
The arid wastes of Gurnemanz's discourses we may possibly pass over. There are things to match them elsewhere, notably in *The Ring*. But the lack of fertility in
the invention of new *motifs* that is apparent in the last
two Acts, and the scarcity of those great tunes that so
amply compensate for the dull patches in the earlier
works, are more difficult to account for on any supposition
but that of waning genius. It is not that the master has
lost his grip : his command of his material, his disposition
of his orchestral forces, remain unimpaired, and the Scene
in the Hall of the Grail and the Flower-maidens episode

are examples of supreme craftsmanship such as he alone could give us. But though his foot does not falter, his step seems, at times, to have lost its spring.

And yet, when criticism has done its worst, we are left with something that the world cannot possibly afford to lose—and the world has a way of sticking to its treasures in spite of the critics. The method by which it will preserve the nobler parts of *Parsifal* it is impossible to predict. But the popularity of the concert hall excerpts may, perhaps, afford a hint.

HÄNSEL UND GRETEL

Music by HUMPERDINCK. *Words by* FRAU A. WETTE.
Weimar, 1893; *London,* 1895; *New York,* 1895.

HÄNSEL UND GRETEL is a work that can safely be recommended to all opera-goers, young and old. The unsophisticated will enjoy the gentle, artless story and rich flow of easily grasped melodies, while the seasoned expert will find a rarer pleasure in seeing the Wagnerian method so happily adapted to such novel material. To a mind wearied by a sustained effort to grapple with the complications of Wagner's colossal masterpieces, nothing could be more refreshing than Humperdinck's little work. Anyone who goes once is sure to go again, and he will discover a new delight as he gradually realizes with what firm and cunning art the gossamer threads of the musical texture have been held and interwoven. But the atmosphere of freshness and innocent charm which struck him so pleasantly at the first hearing will still persist, as it is happily of a kind which does not soon grow stale.

It has been said that *Hänsel und Gretel* is the one successful opera based on a whole-hearted acceptance of Wagner's principles. The truth of this is too obvious to need discussion. Not only did Humperdinck openly avow his allegiance to Wagnerian methods and, in accordance with these, choose a story that is as much a part of Teutonic legend as the *Nibelungenlied,* but the music itself bears eloquent witness to his discipleship. The use he makes of the Prayer theme with which the Prelude opens, the way he builds up the whole of his first Scene on the little melody to which Gretel sings her opening song, are quite in the manner of Wagner. But the differences between the two writers are hardly less interesting than the similarities. Wagner could never have set *Hänsel und Gretel*; his methods were too heroic. Even in *Die Meistersinger* his laughter is that of a giant, and this fragile fairy-story of two children and a witch would have crumpled and collapsed under the weight of his prodigious genius; Humperdinck's gentler nature was far better suited to deal with such materials. For evidence of this we need look no farther than the tunes he uses. Nearly all of them are beautiful flowing melodies, many of considerable length, and as different from the short, pithy phrases that are characteristic of the Wagnerian *motifs* as can well be imagined. Occasionally, it is true, Wagner uses a more lyrical type of utterance—the Prize Song is a conspicuous example—but with him this is exceptional. Humperdinck's themes are almost all lyrical, as befits his subject, and two of them, Gretel's songs at the beginning of Acts I and II, are genuine folk-melodies.

The libretto is the work of Frau Adelheid Wette, the composer's sister, and was originally written for performance at a private gathering. Humperdinck provided music for it in this form, and was so charmed by the effect that he induced his sister to remodel it for a public production, himself rewriting the music, and the result is the opera as we know it.

The Prelude prepares us for what is to come, being constructed out of themes that play an important part later on. The first of these is the simple and touching Prayer theme to which I have already referred, and it defines at once the childlike atmosphere in which the opera is going to move. When the curtain goes up we see Hänsel and Gretel in their parents' cottage. The room is small and poorly furnished. By the door sits

400

Hänsel, making brooms. Gretel is knitting a stocking by the fireplace, and as she knits she sings an old song. It is about the geese; why have the poor geese no shoes? The cobbler has plenty of leather, but, alack, he has no last to fit a goose's foot. Hänsel takes up the same air, but changes the words and says how hungry he is, and this leads to a short dialogue on the subject of their poverty, in which we should notice the appearance of the Prayer theme to Gretel's words:

> When past bearing is our grief,
> God the Lord will send relief.[1]

She succeeds in chasing away her brother's fit of depression, and then tells him a great secret: a neighbour has brought them a jug of milk for their dinner! Hänsel is tempted to taste it, but is rebuked by his virtuous sister, who thinks they ought to get on with their work. This isn't Hänsel's idea at all—he would like to dance; to this suggestion Gretel succumbs, and there follows a charming duet and dance, to music that is closely related to the song with which the Act opened. At last in their excitement they tumble over one another and fall on the floor, and it is there that their mother finds them when she comes in a moment later. She is tired after a hard day's work and is naturally annoyed to find the children have been wasting their time. Unfortunately, while she is lecturing them, she knocks over the milk-jug. It falls with a crash, spilling the milk down her dress, and is broken to bits on the floor. Now what are they to have for supper? Despair is in her heart, but she pulls herself together and sends Hänsel and Gretel out into the wood to gather a basket of strawberries. As soon as they have gone she bursts into tears, overcome with misery. At the same moment the voice of the father outside is heard; he comes

[1] These extracts from the English version are printed by kind permission of Messrs Schott and Co.

in trolling a song, slightly tipsy, and in the highest spirits; he has had a most successful day, done a roaring trade selling his brooms, and brought home a whole load of delicacies for the family table. His wife is inclined to be sharp with him at first, but soon regains her temper when she hears his story and sees the contents of his basket. Then the conversation turns to the children, and the broom-maker indulges in a hearty laugh when he hears about the episode of the milk-jug. "But where are the children now?" he asks. "At the Ilsenstein for aught I know," replies his wife. "The Ilsenstein!" he repeats, horror-struck. What? Doesn't she know? That is where the witch lives, the 'Gobbling Ogress,' who catches little children, puts them into her oven, and bakes them into gingerbread! With a cry of dismay the mother, closely followed by the father, dashes out into the wood in search of Hänsel and Gretel.

Act II. The orchestra opens the Second Act with a very graphic picture of a witches' ride. This is quite an extended composition, but eventually the music becomes calmer and more pastoral in character until at last the curtain rises. We are in the heart of the forest; it is sunset; under a large tree sits Gretel, making a garland of wild roses, and singing another song from the treasure-house of German folk-lore. As soon as she has finished, Hänsel, who has been picking strawberries among the bushes, comes out, his basket nearly full. Playfully he crowns her Queen of the Wood, only admonishing her not to eat the fruit of his labours. The sound of a cuckoo is heard in the distance, and this gives them the idea of playing at being cuckoos who eat their neighbours' eggs. Unfortunately they pretend the strawberries are the eggs, and before they know where they are the basket is empty again. Their first idea is to gather some more, but suddenly they notice that it is already getting dark—

402

there is nothing for it but to go home. They prepare
to do so, but Hänsel is appalled to find that he has forgotten the way. For a moment he is horribly frightened,
but he pulls himself together and puts on an affected boldness to reassure his terrified sister. He gives a shout, as
much to keep up his own spirits as out of any hope of its
being answered, but only the echoes reply, and Gretel's
fears, which make her imagine that the shadows are
peopled by all sorts of evil shapes, begin to communicate
themselves to him. The climax is reached when there
actually does appear a little grey man with a tiny sack
on his back. However, he means them no ill. He is
the Sandman, the Sleep-fairy, and as he draws near he
soothes the children with friendly gestures and then,
scattering some sand upon their eyes, sings them his
lullaby of peace and security. By the time he has
finished they are both half asleep, but before they lie
down they fall on their knees and repeat their evening
prayer, beginning:

> When at night I go to sleep
> Fourteen angels watch do keep.

It is the most charming moment in the opera.

Their little act of worship over, the children go to sleep
in each other's arms, but the mists that have arisen at
the back of the stage are pierced by a beam of light, and a
stairway is revealed down which there come the fourteen
angels of the prayer. They group themselves round the
sleepers, while the light gets steadily brighter, and are
joined by other angels, till at length the curtain descends
upon a radiant scene of celestial glory.

Act III. It is in this final Act that most of the real
drama takes place. The first strains of the orchestra
give us the witch's theme, a concise phrase of seven notes,
more closely resembling a Wagnerian *motif* than anything

else in the opera. At the end of the Introduction we are shown the same scene as in the previous Act, only now it is early morning; the angels have vanished, and the background is wrapped in a mist, out of which there steps the Dew-fairy, singing a song not unlike the Sandman's, and shaking a dewdrop from a bluebell on to the children. Presently Gretel awakes, and rubbing her eyes looks round her sleepily. The Fairy has gone, and the girl is greeted by the song of the lark. Soon she rouses her brother; she has had a lovely dream of angels, she tells him, and is astonished when she hears that he has shared it. But at this moment Hänsel turns round and gives a cry of astonishment—the mist has cleared away, and in the background stands the witch's house, all made of tasty delicacies and surrounded by a fence of gingerbread children. On one side is a cage and on the other an immense oven. After a joyous duet they gain courage and trip forward to have a taste, while the trumpets in the orchestra give out a reference to the Prayer theme, as if to suggest that the children are still under invisible angelic protection. Soon the witch's voice is heard from the house, but they attribute the sound to their imagination and go on eating, so that she is able to steal up and throw a rope round Hänsel's neck before he realizes what has happened. To his horror he finds himself drawn close to her, Gretel following, and has to listen to her somewhat lengthy invitation to come and enjoy the delights that lie inside the house. But meanwhile he has managed to get clear of the rope, and he and Gretel suddenly start to run away, only to be stopped as the witch casts a spell upon them:

> Hocus pocus, witches' charm!
> Move not, as you fear my arm!

Hänsel is led into the cage, there to be fattened up,

while Gretel remains to do the witch's bidding. All the boy can do is to take advantage of the hag's momentary absence to warn his sister to keep her wits about her with a view to saving them both. The witch comes out, and in order that Gretel may help her to get things ready she disenchants her:

> Hocus pocus, elder-bush!
> Rigid body loosen!

and sends her off to the kitchen. While she is away the old woman relieves her feelings by a really horrible broomstick dance. She then takes a look at Hänsel to see whether he is fat enough to be eaten. Gretel must go first, she decides! At this moment the girl returns from the kitchen, and seizing her opportunity while the witch's back is turned, disenchants her brother with the counter-charm she has just heard used on herself. Presently the hag bids her have a look in the oven to see how the dough is getting on, but, warned by Hänsel, who perceives the danger, Gretel assumes a sham stupidity and thus persuades the witch to go and look for herself. The children come up behind, give her a push, and into the oven she goes while they hastily fasten the door upon her! Then, leaving her to bake, they dance the delightful 'Witch Waltz.' Suddenly with a loud bang the oven bursts, and a moment later Hänsel and Gretel see with astonishment that they are surrounded by children, whose disguise of gingerbread has fallen from them with the witch's death. The rest of the story is quickly told. Gretel awakes the children, Hänsel speedily disenchants them, and with a chorus of thanks they crowd round their rescuers. Soon the voice of the father is heard, and very shortly he and the mother appear on the scene. They are overwhelmed with joy to find their children, for whom they have been searching all night, safe and sound.

From the ruins of the oven the witch is dragged, baked to a gingerbread; and finally, as the curtain descends, all unite in a hymn of thanks for their deliverance.

There are many operas more impressive and more ambitious than *Hänsel und Gretel*, but none has caught so happily the simple charm of the fairy-story and the elusive freshness of childhood.

AÏDA

Music by Verdi. *Words by* du Locle *and* Ghislanzoni.
Cairo, 1871; New York, 1873; London, 1876.

THIS is perhaps the one work which can bear
without reproach the much-abused name of
Grand Opera. Grand, not grandiose, in conception, massive yet simple in structure, dealing with
heroic times and primitive passions, it calls for great
splendour of setting, great singing, and, in two at least
of the parts, for great acting. Musically it offers a
superb feast of pure melody such as none but Verdi could
have provided, offering a flexible medium for dramatic
expression, and orchestrated with a resourceful variety
of colour which the composer's previous works had but
faintly foreshadowed.

Nor in praising Verdi's masterpiece should the names
of the librettists be left unhonoured; Camille du Locle
and Antonio Ghislanzoni, collaborating, managed to produce in *Aïda* one of the finest 'books' ever written for
an operatic composer.[1]

The story of true love thwarted by destiny, betrayed
by jealousy, yet triumphant in death, has for its setting
the Court of the Pharaohs at a time when Egypt was at
constant strife with the neighbouring land of Ethiopia.
The reigning Pharaoh has a daughter, Amneris, who
numbers among her favourite waiting-women a beautiful
young Ethiopian, Aïda, brought from her native land
among the spoils of recent warfare. Although her slave,
Aïda is actually the equal of her mistress, for, unknown

[1] My thanks are due to Messrs G. Ricordi and Co. for permitting
me to use their text of the opera.

to all, she is the daughter of Amonasro, the reigning sovereign of Ethiopia. She is also her rival in love— the proud Amneris has long been on fire for Radames, the valiant Captain of the Egyptian Guards, but his heart is given to Aïda, who returns his love in secret. Amneris, tortured by jealous suspicion, bides her time. A fresh invasion of Egypt by the Ethiopians is a failure; King Amonasro is captured and brought with other prisoners to the Court of Pharaoh, where his identity is no more suspected than that of his daughter. Discovering Aïda's passion for Radames, now Chief of the Egyptian forces, he compels her to obtain from her lover a military secret of vital importance. Radames is overheard as he speaks the fatal words; though perfectly innocent in intention, he is convicted of treason and condemned to an awful death—to be entombed alive in the vaults beneath the Temple of Isis. But he does not die alone; Aïda contrives to gain an entrance to his dungeon, and the faithful lovers pass together through death to life, locked in each other's arms.

He who comes late to a performance of *Aïda* commits a grievous sin against himself and his neighbours. There must be perfect silence in the house if the first notes of the Prelude are to be heard, a heavenly love-song given out by the violins alone, *pianissimo,* and at a poignant height. After a short contrapuntal development of this theme, the heavy tread of destiny is heard in the bass, the march of the inexorable priests of Isis, to whom the lovers' piteous death is due. But again the song of love soars up, strong and triumphant, until the last notes seem to reach the stars and die away. Not even the most *blasé* of opera-goers, provided he still loves what is best in music, will willingly miss the Prelude to *Aïda.*

Act I. *Scene* 1. In the vast columned halls of the

royal palace of the Pharaohs, Ramphis the Chief Priest
and Radames, the young and valiant soldier, are in converse; the solemn swing of the orchestral phrases prepares us for heroic scenes and actions. The Ethiopians
once more have laid waste the Valley of the Nile—
the need is urgent; the Egyptian forces are already in
arms, and the oracle of Isis has declared the name of
the Captain who is to lead them to victory. "I go,"
says Ramphis, "to tell the King," whilst his significant
look assures Radames that he is the favoured man.

The young soldier is left alone to rejoice at his good
fortune, and his thoughts at once fly to Aïda—what bliss
to fight for her, to return victorious, to lay his crown of
laurels at her feet! No longer shall she suffer the indig-
nity of slavery, the woes of exile; to her own country he
will restore her, the greener, fairer land of Ethiopia,
where they will reign together. [*Celeste Aïda* is perhaps the most conventional number in the opera, and
certainly the most popular.]

The entrance of Amneris is heralded by a broad, insinuating melody in the orchestra, expressive of her
passion for Radames. The proud Princess of the Royal
House of Egypt notices at once the blaze of happiness
in his face, and demands the reason; he tells her of his
ambition and his dream of coming glory—his talk is all
of war, but hers, alas! of love. "And have you no
sweeter visions of your future?" she asks—"no tenderer
hopes?" Radames has nothing to reply, but the confusion of his manner wakens her suspicions, which are
confirmed at the agitated entrance of Aïda by the glances
which she intercepts between them.

[Amneris' jealousy is depicted in the restless melody
which now forms the orchestral background for the
voices—Aïda is brought on to the accompaniment of
the love-theme already heard in the Prelude.]

409

With all a woman's cunning Amneris gives her slave an affectionate welcome; calling her 'sister' and 'dearest,' she implores her to confide to her the reason for her obvious emotion. Aïda pleads her fear for the safety of her fatherland in the coming struggle, of which she has just heard the rumour, but the suspicions of the Princess grow apace; the jealousy *motif* continues to the end of the trio, while above the broken phrases of the tenor and mezzo Aïda's voice rings out in a really magnificent melody, in which she avows (though only for herself) her fervent love for Radames.

Now begins the first of the many fine *ensembles* to be found in this work. The King enters with his guards, priests, and courtiers, and in full council announces the outbreak of war; the news is at once confirmed by a messenger who brings tidings that the Ethiopians, led by their King Amonasro—Aïda shudders to hear her father's name—are even now marching upon Thebes. "Vengeance! Vengeance!" shout the infuriated Egyptians. The King assures them that all is prepared for battle, and that the Captain chosen to lead the army is Radames. King and priests now begin the impressive march-tune, *Su! del Nilo al sacro lido,* on which is built a magnificent chorus of patriotic ardour; Amneris hands to Radames the flag which is to lead him on to victory, and all voices are raised to acclaim him with the cry, *"Ritorna vincitor!"*

The excited multitude, the King, the priests, depart—only Aïda is left on the stage. She, too, has joined in the universal shout: "Go win the victor's crown!" Victor —over whom? Over her brother, her father, her own people! With a revulsion of feeling she calls on the gods to blot out so impious a prayer—for her own country, rather, would she invoke a victory. Yet—that must mean danger, perhaps death, to Radames, the man she

loves! Torn with these conflicting emotions the poor
girl breaks down, and, bowed to the earth, pours out her
soul in prayer (*Numi, pietà!*) :

> Look down, ye gods, on my despair!
> Turn where I will, no help is nigh!
> Almighty Love, hear thou my prayer!
> Come, end my anguish! Now let me die!

[This number, *Ritorna vincitor!* is a favourite piece
for the concert platform, where, unlike most operatic
extracts, it can be made almost as effective as on the
stage.]

Scene II. A strangely beautiful Scene is this, in which
Radames visits the Temple of Ptah, the God of War,
to obtain his blessing in the coming expedition. A vast
hall, with a double row of columns vanishing in the
darkness, is lit mysteriously from above, and filled with
clouds of incense from a score of golden tripods. In
the centre of the stage is an altar, and ranged between
the columns are the priestesses of the temple, who sing
a hymn of unearthly beauty, *Possente Ptah!* in which
they accompany themselves on the harp. Ramphis and
the priests interpose a few bars of solemn harmony and
the women's voices continue their solemn incantation,
which seems to hint the mysteries of a remote antiquity.
This, too, may be said of the sacred dance that follows.

Before it is ended Radames enters, divested of his
armour, and kneels before the altar. A veil of silver
tissue is placed upon his head, and Ramphis, as Chief
Priest, lays in his hands the sacred sword which shall
surely rout the enemies of Egypt. He then begins a
broad and solemn melody, *Nume, custode e vindice,* which
Radames repeats, the chorus of priests joining in, while
the full orchestra lends strenuous and brilliant support.
The weird strains from the women's voices are heard
again, in ever-quickening *tempo,* and a universal shout of

411

"Almighty Ptah!" brings to an end one of the most picturesque and impressive *finales* in Italian Opera. If it has a fault, it is the rare one of being possibly too short.

Act II. *Scene* 1. The whole of this long Act, which celebrates the triumphant return of Radames with his victorious army, might be described more particularly as "The Triumph of Amneris"; indeed, throughout the work the moments are not few when the spectator is inclined to ask whether the opera should not be named after the haughty Princess rather than her unhappy slave.

The short Scene with which the Act opens discovers Amneris among her tiring-women, busy with her toilette for the approaching festival; her slaves know well how to soothe and flatter her as they wave their feather fans and sing of the triumphs of Radames and the reward of love which awaits him. [*Chi mai fra gl'inni e i plausi* is a graceful yet vigorous choral duet for female voices to harp accompaniment.]

Amneris, lost in tender dreams of the future, breaks in with a long-drawn, voluptuous phrase, *Ah vieni, amor mio!* and admirable relief is provided by a grotesque dance of what are described as "young Moorish slaves," usually represented as so many tiny Petes and Topsies from "way down upon the Old Plantation."

Played softly by the 'cellos, the love-theme of the Prelude heralds the approach of Aïda, from whom Amneris is resolved to wring a confession of her secret. With unctuous affection she sympathizes with her grief at the slaughter of her countrymen: "But time, dear friend, will heal your sorrows—aye! and a greater power than time—the God of Love!"

Moved beyond endurance, Aïda breaks out into the ecstatic love-song *Amore, amore!*

O Love almighty, I bow before thee!
Giver of rapture, hope, and holy fear!
In pain and anguish I still adore thee!
Heaven lies around me when thou art near!

The melody, of which but a part is given in the Prelude, here finds its full development in a glorious outpouring of romantic passion.

A theme of insolent triumph is now heard in the orchestra: Amneris advances to the field on which her rival is soon to lie prostrate. "My sweet Aïda," she begins, "tell me thy secret trouble! Among the many heroes who fought for thy dear country, was there not one to whom thy heart was given? But take courage! A kindly fate perchance has spared him—not all, thou knowest, have perished. We too, alas! have heavy losses to mourn—our Captain Radames, I hear, is dead."

A piercing cry of anguish is Aïda's answer.

Amneris turns to fury: "And thou dost weep for him! Then—then—thou lovest him? I will know the truth!"

Seizing the unhappy girl by the arm, she brings her face to face: "Look at me, now, and listen! I told thee falsely! Radames still lives!"

Aïda falls on her knees with arms upraised to heaven: "Ye gracious gods, I thank you!"

"Then it is true! Thou lovest him! But hear me —I love him too! I am thy rival! *I, daughter of all the Pharaohs!*"

These words are uttered with a superb gesture of *hauteur*. Aïda replies with no less dignity of voice and manner: "My rival, sayest thou! A Princess, truly— and I no less than thou ——" She checks herself in time, for she must not reveal the secret of her birth. Falling at her rival's feet she pleads for pity in a song,

413

Pietà ti prenda del mio dolor, which, if rightly given, can move the theatre to tears.

" 'Tis true—I love him with measureless love! But thou—have mercy! Powerful and fortunate, pity my misery! Leave me my love—it is all I have!"

But Amneris is inexorable: she is the sovereign, Aïda the slave, whose fate is in the hands of her mistress. From outside is heard the noise of the approaching pageant, and the chorus of Act I, *Su! del Nilo al sacro lido!*

The Princess rises, awful in her exultation: "Listen! 'tis the song of victory! Now is the hour of my triumph! Follow me, and I will teach thee who thou art—no rival, but the meanest of my slaves! Radames is mine, and mine alone!"

Amneris sweeps from the stage, and the wretched Aïda is left, crushed and despairing, to cry to heaven for help: "Look down, ye gods, on my despair! Pity my agony! Now let me die!"

Scene II. A vast open space among the palms and temple of the city of Thebes; the people are gathering for the great pageant which is to honour the return of the victorious armies. On one side of the stage is a high daïs with a canopied throne, and a second seat of hardly less magnificence.

The royal procession enters: first the King, the officers of state, the captives, the priests, all the pomp and power of Egypt. Next comes Amneris, attended by Aïda and others of her slaves: a majestic figure, she takes her seat at the King's left hand.

The chorus, *Gloria all' Egitto,* begins with a great rhythmic shout of exultation over the mighty deeds of Egypt and Egypt's King. After a gentler passage for the women alone, the music takes on an entirely different colour as the solid phalanx of white-robed priests lift up

414

their voices in the significant phrases to which attention has already been drawn in the Prelude. There is something almost brutal about this massive theme, which is used throughout the opera, always with startling effect. "Glory give to the gods on high! 'Tis they who rule our destinies!"—such is the burden of their song; yet in it we seem to detect a sinister note which would suggest that it is the will of the priests rather than of the gods that must be done.

Excitement rises higher as an advance-guard of the Egyptian troops appears upon the scene, magnificent creatures with long silver trumpets on which they perform most manfully (though not always in tune with the orchestra) what is perhaps the most sonorous march ever written for a stage pageant. But Verdi has seen to it that there are no *longueurs* in Aïda. The soldiers soon cease to blare, and take up their ordered station to allow of the entrance of the dancing-women.

The ballet is a welcome diversion, gay and graceful, and delicately varied. But the height of the pageant is reached when the main body of the victorious troops enters, bearing aloft the statues of the gods with their different emblems, the bull, the sacred cat, the boat of Ra. The climax of sound is now reached as people, soldiers, priests, all unite in a repetition of the choral material from the beginning of the Act, but now much more elaborately orchestrated.

At last Radames himself appears, borne in a canopied litter on the shoulders of his officers. The King himself comes down from his throne to embrace and thank the saviour of his country; for him, too, a crown is waiting, the wreath of laurels which no hand but that of the King's daughter is worthy to place upon his brow. [What thoughts are in Amneris' heart the orchestra shows us—the insinuating melody associated with her

passion for Radames is played almost in its entirety.]
Yet the wreath is but the symbol of glory—what more
substantial reward does Radames desire? Let him ask
what he will, and, by all the gods, it shall be his! [Am-
neris' heart beats faster; but the victor's thoughts are
not of her.] His answer is unexpected: "First, O King,
let the prisoners of war be brought before thee!" The
order given, the sorrowful crowd of captives enters,
closely guarded—last of all Amonasro, King of Ethiopia,
but showing no sign of his royal rank. [It is interesting
to note here the sinister effect produced by the intervention of the priests, who, as their prisoners enter, repeat
their inexorable chant *pianissimo,* as if to protest against
any undue show of mercy to a fallen but still dangerous
foe.] Aïda springs forward into her father's arms; he
has just time to whisper a caution in her ear when the
King of Egypt bids him advance.

"Who art thou?"

"Aïda's father—one who fought for his country! We
were beaten—our King was slain—vainly I sought for
death." Then, with a gesture toward the prisoners,
"Yet, O King, do thou show mercy! Not for myself,
but for these I plead! Spare thy slaves here kneeling
before thee! So, in thine own hour of peril, may fate
be merciful to thee!"

[Amonasro's solo, *Ma tu Ré, tu signore possente,* so
splendidly worked into the *ensemble* that follows, is one
of the unforgettable things in the opera; like Aïda's
prayer, *Pietà ti Prenda,* in the preceding Scene, it expresses the dramatic emotion just as far as is possible
with a perfectly symmetrical melody in which formal
beauty is obviously the first object. It is not merely
the humble petition of a suppliant; a closer observation
will detect a hint of self-assertion, of veiled defiance even,
in the music as in the words.]

Now begins an *ensemble* of colossal structure and elaborate design: while the prisoners and the Egyptian people join together in the prayer for mercy, the priests, led by Ramphis, are sternly opposed to any such measure. There is something awful in the passage, *Struggi, o Ré, queste ciurme feroci,* in which they urge the King to devote the prisoners to death:

> Turn thy face from this treacherous nation!
> Be thou deaf to their pitiful tale!
> For the gods have decreed their destruction,
> And the will of the gods must prevail!

[Above the immense mass of choral sound no less than six solo voices strive to make themselves heard; Aïda, Amonasro, Ramphis, the King, are all interested in the petition for pardon, while Radames gives expression to his tender care for Aïda, and Amneris is muttering threats of vengeance.]

Radames now approaches the King to claim his promised reward: it is that all the Ethiopian captives should be set at liberty. The priests at once make violent opposition; Ramphis takes upon himself to point out to the King the danger of letting such implacable enemies escape. But Radames is firm: "There is no danger! Now that Amonasro their King is dead, further resistance on their part would be futile." His pleading wins the day: the prisoners shall be sent back to their own country, all with the exception of Amonasro, who, with Aïda, is to be kept as hostage.

But now the grateful King announces to his heroic General the magnificent reward he has reserved for him: "My daughter Amneris I give thee in marriage: when I am dead, thou shalt be King of Egypt."

This is the hour of Amneris' triumph: "Now," she cries, "Radames is mine indeed! Let the presuming slave try to take him from me if she dare!"

417

The Scene ends with another closely woven *ensemble,* in which the patriotic *Gloria all' Egitto* and the gloomy voices of the priests are well contrasted with the triumphant blare from the long trumpets of the soldiers on the stage. Amneris, too, has her song of triumph; Aïda and Radames are both in dejection; and Amonasro, noting the signs of their mutual love, already meditates a plan for the recovery of his fallen fortunes.

Thus ends an Act which for sheer magnificence can hardly be paralleled in opera. Pageant follows on pageant, effect upon effect, each contributing its due share to the perfection of the musical structure; nothing is introduced as mere ornament, each new spectacular element is part of an organic whole, and never was a lovelier ballet so fully justified. With grateful memories of *Il Trovatore* and *Rigoletto,* those "fair and flagrant things," we can only rub our eyes with amazement at the extraordinary advance the composer has made toward perfection in the way of dramatic expression. At the same time, we are thankful to find the essential Verdi still unchanged: there is still the old, generous flow of enchanting melody, only with the additional perfection that the formal beauty of the melodic curve is now enhanced by an entirely fresh wealth of orchestral colour.

Act III. If the previous Act was dramatically a triumph for Amneris, the present one belongs emphatically to the heroine, Aïda. It is richer in lovely melody than any other part of the work, while the tense interest of the drama never flags.

The scene is one of romantic beauty—we see the banks of the Nile in full moonlight, groves of palms to right and left, on one side the Temple of Isis almost hidden by the trees, though a bright light streams from the columned portico.

From within there comes the softest flutter of stringed

418

instruments at their highest pitch, to be followed by an unearthly sound of chanting voices. No passage in the opera is more striking than this short invocation, so plainly does the music speak of times and a people un-imaginably remote.

A boat now approaches, bearing Amneris and Ramphis the High Priest: the Princess is come to spend the night in prayer that the goddess may bless her union with Radames: as they enter the temple, the mystic chant rises to a wild *fortissimo,* then dies away as the doors are shut. But the moon is bright, and the murmur of the Nile is clearly heard in the orchestra, while above it soars the heavenly theme which symbolizes Aïda's faith-ful love, as a veiled figure enters with cautious step.

Aïda is despondent of the future. Radames will meet her here to-night—but for what purpose? "Oh, should he come only to take a last farewell"—she turns to the deep waters of the Nile—"then take me to thy bosom, thou dark and dreadful river! So shall I find peace at last—peace and oblivion."

Another longing, too, is heavy upon her—the longing for home and country. "Land of my fathers, ne'er shall I see thee more!" Her solo, *O cieli azzuri,* is one of the most exquisite things in the world of opera. Students of Verdi will find the old-remembered idiom here, as strongly marked as ever—but with a difference! The way in which he contrives by the distribution of the text to avoid monotony of rhythm, to give a new turn to a too familiar phrase, to enrich the sensuous charm of the melody by the delicate orchestral colouring—in all this we recognize the second spring of the composer's power-ful inspiration.

The song ends in a mood of resignation, a soft reverie, which is broken by the impetuous entrance of Amonasro, the royal captive. He can read his daughter's heart, her

419

love for Radames, her longing for her country; it is easy to work on her feelings. She, a Princess, to remain in the power of Amneris, her rival, and the bitter enemy of Ethiopia! Never! Her father is there to take her home! "*Rivedrai le foreste imbalsamate,*" he sings:

> Once again shalt thou see our leafy forests,
> Our fragrant valleys, our temples all of gold.

Radames, too, shall join her there to share her perfect bliss. The Egyptians—has she forgotten how they laid waste her own dear country?

> Burnt in fury our houses undefended—
> Old men, maidens, and children all were slain!

But the day of vengeance is at hand; even now the Egyptians are launching a new campaign; but this time his people are prepared, and will defeat them. One thing it is necessary for him to know—what route the enemy will choose for their march—and that Aïda must tell him. "But how?" she asks. "Radames!" is the answer. "He will meet you here! Does he not love you—and is he not the leader of the Egyptian army?"

Aïda recoils in horror: never will she tempt her lover to commit such treachery!

At once her father's wrath descends upon her in all its fury: she is no child of his: 'tis she who is a traitor to her country! He calls up to her imagination all the agony of war, the streams of blood, the groans of the dying—and worse than that:

> Horror! I see the dead arise,
> Hate in their eyeballs glowing,
> Pointing at thee with jeers and cries:
> "She hath betrayed us all!"

Aïda clings in terror to her father's arm, only to be thrown off in savage anger. "See!" he cries, "whose form is this that rises from the shadows? It is thy

420

mother, with curses on her lips: 'No child of mine art thou; nay, but the abject slave of the Egyptians!'" Aïda is conquered—she grovels at her father's feet—she will do all he wishes.

"But oh, my country!" she cries in agony. "What must I suffer for love of thee!"

Amonasro hides among the palms as the orchestra gives warning of the hero's approach in a striking, oft-repeated phrase; it is the jubilant cry of one sure of his triumph, in love as well as in battle. There is nothing now to bar him from Aïda; already high in the King's favour, he is to lead another army against the Ethiopians; he will return again victorious, and neither priests nor Princess will dare to oppose their union. Aïda feigns coldness and suspicion: let him go to Amneris, to whom he rightly belongs! In any case she, Aïda, can never be his: the King would not consent, and the fury of the powerful Amneris would overwhelm them both. Yet there is a way—one only—to fly the country!

Radames at first recoils, but Aïda has powerful means of persuasion: her beauty, his love for her, the prospect of a life of perfect freedom in her own fair land. Her air, *Là tra foreste vergini,* is enough to seduce the sternest from his duty:

> There is the forest's fragrant heart
> Laden with sweets uncloying,
> A perfect love enjoying,
> The world we'll soon forget!

She has won the day; under the influence of her spell Radames is wild to be gone. His impassioned outburst, *Sì! Fuggiam da queste mure!* is repeated by Aïda, and the two join in the theme of love triumphant with which Radames made his entry. They are hurrying off the stage when Aïda stops: "But tell me," she says, "what route are we to take? The passes will all be closed by the Egyptian forces."

"Nay, *one* will be open," is the reply; "the one chosen for our march on Ethiopia."

"And which is that?"

"The pass of Napata."

"The pass of Napata!"—a harsh, exultant voice repeats the words—it is Amonasro, who comes from his hiding-place among the palms. "Behold!" he cries, "Aïda's father—and the King of Ethiopia!"

The horror and despair of Radames are terrible to witness—his thrice-repeated cry, *"Io son disonorato!"* is unforgettable. Amonasro strives to reassure him: "Nay, there is no dishonour; 'tis Fate that willed it so! Come! and in my country shalt thou have both honour and power! There thou shalt reign, with Aïda for thy queen!"

But Fate works swiftly for the ending of all such dreams. "Traitor!"—the cry comes from the lips of a furious woman: it is Amneris, who has overheard them and now comes forward. Amonasro rushes at her with drawn dagger, but Radames puts himself between them. Amonasro has just time to drag Aïda away when Ramphis and his guards advance. Radames strides proudly toward him: "Priest! I am thy willing prisoner!"

Act IV. *Scene* 1. A lofty anteroom, dimly lighted; on one side the heavy portals of a prison, on the other the mouth of a broad stairway leading down into darkness. The orchestra preludes with the restless *motif* associated with Amneris' watchful jealousy; she is leaning against the prison doors, listening for any sound from within. She has good cause for gloomy reflection—her rival has escaped; the man she loves is in prison, expecting a traitor's death. No traitor he!—whatever he may have done, she loves him still—is it too late to save

422

him? She bids the guards bring Radames before her. Earnestly she pleads with him to save himself, and her peace of mind; if he will but confess his fault and appeal for mercy, she herself will kneel before the throne and obtain his pardon.

"Nay!" is his answer, "I am conscious of no crime; nor do I care to live, now that she I love is dead."

The Princess assures him that Aïda still lives—"but," she urges, "if I save thy life, promise me never to see her more!"

Radames chooses death rather than such real dishonour; he is led back again to his cell, and Amneris is left to all the tortures of her jealousy and hate. But her mood soon changes. Very softly in the lowest tones of the orchestra is heard the priests' *motif*, now like an awful march that speaks of doom and death; Amneris sees too clearly all that is to come. The white-robed priests file slowly across the stage and disappear into the vaults below. Despair seizes upon her—she hides her face in her hands: "Ah! let me not see that sight of terror—those dreadful ministers of death, who feel no pity. And it is I who have placed my beloved in their power—I, who might have saved him!" She sinks back in horror and remorse as Radames is brought once more from prison and led down to the subterranean hall of judgment.

Nothing could well be more impressive than the scene that follows. The stage is empty, save for the solitary figure of Amneris, half frantic with terror and remorse: clear and awful from below rises the chanting of the priests at their work of doom. The trumpet sounds; then the voice of Ramphis, the accuser: "Radames! thou hast betrayed thy country's secrets to the enemy. Answer the charge!" The last words are repeated by the rest of the priests in chorus; deep silence follows: Radames disdains to reply.

"Traitor! Traitor!" they thunder all together, while Amneris makes her frenzied appeal to heaven to save him. Thrice is the trumpet blown, thrice comes the accusing cry, and the silence that truly may be felt—but no word from Radames, no answer from the gods to Amneris' appeal. From the judgment hall below we hear the sentence delivered by the bass chorus: "Radames! thou art a traitor, and hast incurred the wrath of Osiris; hear then thy doom! In the vault beneath the altar of this temple thou must remain a prisoner till death shall set thee free!"

The fateful march is heard once more as the priests come from the crypt and cross the stage: Radames is not among them. Amneris makes her last frantic appeal: "Hear me, ye tyrants! Monsters of cruelty! Pause, ere ye murder an innocent man!" Then, turning to Ramphis: "Priest of Isis! I love this man! If by your act he dies, Heaven's curse be on you for evermore!"

For a moment they pause, implacable, to repeat their thunderous denunciation of the traitor, then go off, unmoved by the wild imprecations which Amneris hurls after them. "Race of devils! May the wrath of Heaven fall upon you! Be accursed for evermore!"

Scene 11. Verdi's device of showing us two independent groups of actors in one scene, which we find in *Rigoletto,* is here employed with even greater effect. We have two stages, an upper and a lower. Above is the interior of the Temple of Isis, ablaze with lights and wreathed in clouds of incense from many braziers; here are the white-robed priests, and the priestesses who move in the sacred dance—two of the priests are seen lowering a mighty slab of stone into its place in the centre of the stage—it is the ceremonial sealing of the tomb of Radames.

Below the vaulted roof, the pillars of the crypt are dimly seen; and Radames, resigned to his fate, knowing that Aïda is in safety—may she live on, and cease to sorrow for him! But even as he speaks he finds he is not alone: Aïda, learning of his awful doom, has found her way to his side! In the first rapture of this unlooked-for reunion the past, the present, are forgotten.

> At last united, all our troubles over,
> Ah, my beloved, let us die together!

So sings Aïda; but Radames is struck with horror to think that she too is now involved in his terrible doom. In a passage of true pathos, *Morir, si pura e bella!* he protests against such an end for one so young, so formed for love. As the mystic hymn is heard from the shrine above, he makes one last attempt to dislodge the fatal stone that seals their prison—but in vain. Aïda is already rapt above the earth in an ecstatic vision:

> Lo! where some angel hither flies
> From yonder azure dome!
> Ah yes, 'tis death in friendly guise
> Who comes to lead us home!

On the upper stage a figure, veiled in robes of mourning, advances to the centre of the stage, and bends low over the stone of death; it is Amneris, "daughter of all the Pharaohs." Broken-hearted, bowed to the dust, she can still pray: "O Isis, grant peace to the soul of my beloved: peace in thy heaven for evermore!"

Below, the faithful lovers, blessed in their death, are clasped in one another's arms. Amneris' prayer is answered.

OTELLO

Music by Verdi. *Words by* Boito, *from* Shakespeare.
Milan, 1887; *New York,* 1888; *London,* 1889.

WHEN *Otello* was first produced it was rapturously hailed by most of the critics as the composer's masterpiece, a verdict which would be stoutly challenged to-day. But in the late nineties the world of music was perhaps a little Wagner-mad: none but 'the Master's' methods were acceptable, and these were gulped down without discrimination; consequently it was considered a sign of grace that in this new score by the great Italian there was a comparative dearth of melody and very few separate numbers, while the musical interest was often to be found in the orchestra rather than on the stage. Certainly Verdi seems to have laid aside his Italian singing-robes for the time; you may call *Otello* music-drama if you like, a successful experiment along the lines laid down by Richard Wagner. Indeed, this opera and its still finer successor *Falstaff* show a development in method and technique which is nothing less than astounding in a composer already past his seventieth year; both works call forth our affectionate admiration, the latter gives us unqualified delight, yet it is open to question whether either is such a genuine expression of Verdi's peculiar genius as we find in the last Act of *Il Trovatore,* the close of *Rigoletto,* and Scene after Scene of *Aïda.*

Dramatically, *Otello* is apt to be dull, as any desiccated version of Shakespearean psychological tragedy is bound to be. The libretto is graced, but not saved, by the literary talent of the composer's lifelong friend, Arrigo

Boito; it is worth noting that two of the most striking passages, Iago's *Credo* and Desdemona's *Ave Maria* are interpolations by the librettist. The version of the Willow Song is taken from a very old Italian popular air, most beautifully treated.[1]

A century ago another *Otello,* by Rossini, was very popular, and became a showpiece for such artists as Pasta and Malibran; this work has long disappeared, though the Willow Song, *Assisa al piè d'un salice,* was heard frequently in the concert-room till the end of the last century. Verdi's Desdemona has been a favourite rôle with great vocalists—Albani, Eames, Melba; but the success of the opera depends upon the exponents of Othello and Iago. We are not likely soon to see the equals of the artists who created these parts, Tamagno, the brazen-throated, and the admirable Victor Maurel —the latter's Iago is still remembered as one of the most superb performances of the operatic stage.

Act I. A seaport in Cyprus; the Governor's castle near the shore. Without prelude the curtain rises on a stormy sea; a ship is seen in peril, but as the wind falls she comes safe to anchor, and Othello, Governor of Cyprus, steps on land. He tells the assembled people of the success of his expedition against the Turks, and passes to his castle, after giving orders for all to celebrate his return with music and feasting.

Iago now comes forward: in his heart the storms of envy and malice are never still. He confides to Roderigo how he hates Othello and despises Cassio, who has been made Captain over his head. To Cassio he now turns his attention; he plies him with wine, and by the aid of a drinking-song, *Inaffia l'ugola,* succeeds in making him drunk and embroiling him first with Roderigo and then

[1] My thanks are due to Messrs G. Ricordi and Co. for permitting me to use their text of the Opera.

with Montano, the ex-Governor. Finally he contrives to stir up a general tumult, which brings the indignant Othello on the scene. Desdemona presently follows; the thought that her rest has been disturbed by the uproar rouses her lord to fury; all the blame is laid upon Cassio, who is deprived of his captaincy. Iago, the evil spirit of the play, has scored his first triumph.

The Act ends with a love-duet of sustained lyric beauty. There are echoes here of the Shakespearean text—for instance, of the well-known lines:

> She loved me for the dangers I had passed,
> And I loved her that she did pity them;

but the words are mostly of Boito's invention. Special notice should be taken of the musical phrases accompanying the words *Un bacio! un altro bacio!*—we shall meet this *motif* again in a very different situation. For conclusion the voices mingle in a passage of exquisite tenderness: the Pleiades have set, the crescent moon is rising, the hour is late—but not too late for love, whispers Othello, as he draws Desdemona slowly up the castle steps.

As giving us the only glimpse of happy love to be found in the opera, we feel that this duet might well be longer.

Act II. In this scene the villainous Iago must be regarded, like Milton's Satan in *Paradise Lost,* as the real 'hero' of the piece. In a room with balconies opening on to the great garden of the castle we find him with Cassio, hypocritically condoling with his downfall, yet bidding him be of good cheer—his fortunes may be mended! Does not the fair Desdemona sway her lord Othello to her slightest wish? Let Cassio but gain her ear and induce her to plead for him, Othello will soon recall him to favour. The plot is laid with diabolical cunning, and the much-praised soliloquy for Iago, *Credo*

428

in un Dio crudel, in which Verdi certainly manages to suggest the ravings of a lost soul, is finely heralded by a great blast of trumpets such as might attend the clanging of the gates of hell. Man—so runs the sound and fury of the words—is the child of the Monster of cruelty who rules the world; in His own image He has created him. "I am vile," says Iago, "because I am a man—I feel the primal slime within my veins. He whom you call a just and honest man is but a lying hypocrite. Man is the plaything of malignant fate from the hour of his birth to the last day of his life; then comes death—and nothingness. Only a fool believes in heaven. That is my creed!"

This outburst over, he turns to spy on Cassio and Desdemona talking together in the garden; his poor dupe is bent on ingratiating himself with the lady, who is all gracious sympathy with his misfortune.

The approach of Othello from the castle hall gives Iago his opportunity; taking up his position behind a pillar he gazes fixedly and with a frown on the pair as Cassio is taking his leave. Just as Othello comes within hearing the villain shoots his first poisoned arrow in the words, *Ciò m'accora!* It is enough—Othello's peace is gone. To his demand for an explanation Iago replies with a feigned reluctance that serves to inflame suspicion: "My lord, before you were married, was Cassio acquainted with your lady? . . . Beware of jealousy, my lord. It is the green-eyed monster! Only—keep watch!"

This conversation is interrupted by a most welcome interval of pure beauty. Desdemona is seen advancing from the depths of the garden, surrounded by the fisherfolk with gifts of flowers and shells, while children strew lilies in her way; they accompany their delicious chorus with mandoline, cornemuse, and little hand-harps. As Desdemona joins in the closing cadences, even Othello is charmed for the time from his jealous brooding, but her very innocence plays into the enemy's hands. The crowd dispersed, she at once approaches her lord on Cassio's behalf, urging her request with such insistence that Othello can hardly control the growing fever of jealousy; Desdemona, supposing him to be unwell, offers her handkerchief, which he throws angrily to the ground, from which it is recovered by Emilia, in attendance on her mistress.

Now follows a quartet in which Iago manages to snatch from his wife Emilia the handkerchief on which so much depends, while Desdemona pleads tenderly for pardon if haply she has offended her lord. But the poison is working fiercely in Othello's brain—he dismisses her harshly, and the rest of the Act is filled by a long duet between the Moor and his evil genius.

Othello is provided with a solo, *Ora e per sempre addio* —a piece of pure old-fashioned Italian opera—before his fury breaks loose. In his frenzy he seizes Iago by the throat and flings him savagely to the ground—it is he who has awakened his master's suspicions, now let him furnish proof! Iago answers with a version of the well-known passage "I lay with Cassio yesternight," etc., and he describes the stolen handkerchief which he declares he has seen in Cassio's possession. Othello needs no further evidence; Desdemona is guilty beyond question in his eyes—blind eyes indeed that cannot see the arch-villain at his side.

It would be difficult to devise the right operatic ending for this scene; as it is we have to be content with an undeniably stagey duet, in which Iago and his victim join in a solemn vow that they will never rest till vengeance has been accomplished.

Act III. After a short Prelude, in which the 'green-eyed monster' motive of the previous Act is repeated,

430

the curtain rises on Othello and Iago in the hall of the castle. Iago, who by this time has his master under complete control, bids him remain while he fetches Cassio; then, in hiding, let him note the young soldier's behaviour, and he shall see that which will change suspicion to full certainty. Desdemona is seen approaching and Iago departs, pausing to hiss the words "The handkerchief!" into Othello's ear.

As the young girl advances, radiant with beauty, innocence, and wifely devotion, even Othello can hardly believe her capable of wrong. Alas, her innocence again destroys her; she comes, she says, to plead once more for Cassio—such great friends as they have been, will not her lord pardon and recall him? Othello is again in the raging furnace of jealousy. He asks her for a handkerchief—no, not that one—the one he gave her! Has she lost it—or given it away? Then woe betide her, for there is a curse attached to it! Even now the poor child fails to understand. "Ah!" she says, "you do but tease me, to keep me from plaguing you with my suit for Cassio!"

Othello loses his control: "The handkerchief! The handkerchief!" he thunders, and charges her to her face with guilt beyond the scope of her imagining. Her protestations, her tears, her prayers, are of no avail—the scene ends most cruelly. Taking her by the hand, he escorts her to the door with a frightful mockery of the courtesy he has shown on her entrance: "Give me once more that lily hand!"—here he breaks off: "But, nay— I ask your pardon!"—then shouting with the voice of a madman, "I did mistake you for that vile strumpet whom poor Othello took to wife!" he thrusts her violently from the scene.

His heart-broken lament for his lost love, *Dio! mi*

potevi scagliar, is interrupted by Iago, who bids him hide behind the pillars, for Cassio is coming.

Then follows the scene of Iago's jugglery with the handkerchief. The feather-headed Cassio is led on to jest and laugh over his amorous adventures, while Othello, who can see all, is yet not near enough to catch more than a word here and there, which his jealousy is quick to misinterpret. Yielding more and more to Iago's flattery, Cassio tells him a piquant little secret—how he has lately found in his bedroom a lady's handkerchief— dropped there by an unknown hand. "An unknown hand!" repeats Iago in derision, and loud enough for Othello to hear, "Show me the handkerchief!" Cassio produces it, Iago takes it from him and manages so to display it that Othello can identify it beyond all doubt as the one he had given Desdemona.

[The music of this scene, and especially of the trio, is masterly in its subtle differentiation of the various emotions—Cassio's levity, Iago's delight in the success of his devilish cunning, Othello's furious despair. Notable also is the melodious grace of Iago's bantering song about the handkerchief, *Questa è una ragna.*]

After Cassio's departure, Othello has but one thought —that Desdemona must die; by suffocation, Iago advises, that very night as she lies sleeping; he himself will see to the slaying of Cassio.

A long fanfare of trumpets announces the arrival of an embassy from Venice; Desdemona is summoned to help in the formal reception of the visitors, and even here some unhappy turn in the conversation leads her once more to speak kindly of her hope for Cassio's pardon— her old friend Cassio! Othello can endure no further; he commands her to be silent in so terrible a voice as to shock the whole assembly.

But still further blows await him; he reads the letter

432

from the Doge of Venice only to find that he is recalled to the capital, and that Cassio succeeds him as Governor of Cyprus. Desdemona weeps for pity to see her lord's distress, and he, supposing her to grieve for the approaching separation from Cassio, throws her brutally to the ground: "Lie there! Lie there, and weep!"

A long and most elaborate *finale* delays the dreadful end. Desdemona makes a heart-broken appeal for pity, and the rest join in a chorus of sympathy, when the Moor, who is no longer sane, for whom the very air is filled with blood, breaks in with an awful cry, "Flee, flee from Othello!" which sends them hurrying from the hall. Left alone with Iago, he raves more and more wildly, and falls at last unconscious to the ground.

From the street come the shouts of the people: "Long live Othello! Long live the Lion of Venice!" Iago dares to place his foot upon his master's neck and, pointing with scornful finger, cries out in fiendish exultation: "See where your lion lies!"

Act IV. The shortest and most perfect. The scene is Desdemona's bedroom; words and action follow Shakespeare with fair fidelity; the short Prelude is a mirror of the poor girl's sad and wistful thoughts.

While Emilia assists her to disrobe, Desdemona sings the lovely Willow Song, an old, old strain that tells of one who died because she loved too well. On her, too, is the shadow of death; Verdi shows us this with a touch of true dramatic genius. Her mistress has dismissed Emilia with a "Good night," sung quietly, on a low note; as the woman turns to leave her Desdemona realizes her own utter loneliness, her need of sympathy in the face of peril; with a poignant cry in the highest range of the voice she calls Emilia back, and clings to her as she takes what she feels will be her last farewell. Then, kneeling before an image of the Blessed Virgin, she says her Ave Maria, sings a quiet prayer, and lays her down to sleep.

The musical interest now passes to the orchestra, as the drama runs its familiar course swiftly to the end. Othello enters, puts out the light, and, parting the curtains of the bed, gazes long on the sleeping Desdemona; we hear the theme from the love-duet of Act I (*Un bacio! ancora un bacio!*) as he kisses her once, twice, thrice.

The brutal deed is hardly done when Emilia clamours at the door for admission; Desdemona is still able to reply to her question "Who has done this?" with "No one—myself! Commend me to my lord!"

Iago's villainy and Desdemona's perfect innocence are proved by Emilia and Cassio. Othello is frustrated in his first attempt at suicide, but he has another weapon at hand, and the orchestra for the last time plays with the tender love-*motif* as he falls dead beside the body of his innocent victim.

> I kissed thee e'er I killed thee—No way but this,
> Killing myself, to die upon a kiss.

CARMEN

Music by BIZET. *Words by* MEILHAC *and* HALÉVY
from MÉRIMÉE.
Paris, 1875; *London,* 1878; *New York,* 1879.

THE two most popular French operas are, beyond question, *Faust* and *Carmen,* but their popularity is the only thing they have in common; in most essentials they present a striking contrast. The plot of Gounod's opera, though but a faint and fragmentary echo of Goethe's mighty creation, has a certain ethical and philosophical basis; the atmosphere both of words and music is of the romantic-sentimental order, yet no one will deny that a first hearing of Gounod's *Faust* inclines the unspoilt mind to thoughtfulness. It is idle to look too closely into the ethics or psychology of *Carmen;* the best way is to give oneself up to the fascination of the realistic drama so boldly presented and clothed with music of such unfailing beauty and sincerity. *Carmen* is a rush of colour and action, of sensuous rhythm and delicious melody, but it is something greater than this—the music attains to heights of tragic expression which few composers have ever surpassed.

Faust saw the light in 1859, *Carmen* in 1875; each opera is undoubtedly its composer's masterpiece, yet how different were their immediate rewards! Gounod was 41 when he wrote *Faust;* he lived to see it take its place as the most popular opera in the repertory, and died in 1893, full of years and honour. *Carmen* was produced when Bizet was 37; he died three months after, brokenhearted at its failure. But if Paris rejected it, other capitals were quick to recognize a work of so rare a quality; it reached London in 1878, New York a year later; but not till 1883 was tardy justice done to it in the city that had shown herself so unworthy of its first production.

It is difficult for us to conceive how *Carmen* could have failed with any audience—only political rancour and the prejudices of musical pedantry can account for it. Its score is full of arresting melodies, its libretto must rank with the very best. MM. Meilhac and Halévy took the well-known tale by Prosper Mérimée, and, with many a deft alteration and addition, managed to build a drama that well preserves the spirit of the original. Nevertheless, the story of *Carmen* hardly attains to the importance of a plot; it is rather "a streak of life," actual, crude and highly coloured; we recognize it as the begetter of *Cavalleria Rusticana, Pagliacci,* and many another degenerate offspring. The gipsy-heroine is hardly more than a splendid animal, irresistible in her sensuous beauty, superb in her physical courage, knowing no law higher than her own desires: Carmen's amours, we are told, are rarely of more than six months' duration. At the beginning of the play we find her making a fresh conquest, of a young soldier, Don José, who forsakes his sweetheart, Micaela, and sullies his military honour, at her call. He is even imprisoned, on her account; immediately after his release Carmen's fancy for him burns itself out; she flings herself into the arms of Escamillo, a handsome bull-fighter, and so drives her former lover mad with jealousy. The last scene is at the entrance of the bull-ring in which Escamillo is winning fresh victories; as Carmen is about to pass in to share his triumph Don José intercepts her and stabs her to death. The crowd pour out of the arena, and the last tableau shows us the lifeless body of Carmen between her two

436

lovers, one of whom is doomed shortly to die, the victim of a heartless woman's caprice.

Act I. We are in Spain before the curtain rises. The overture starts off with a clash and blare of rhythmical jingle that sets us at once in the midst of the arena where a crowd is assembled for the bull-fight, the national pageant of the Spanish people. We are made a part of the coloured scene, the shouts of the fighters, the hoof-beats of the animals, the ever-growing excitement; then, without preparation, we seem to pass into a lurid dark-ness as the brass gives out a sinister theme that is partly the voice of judgment, partly a wail of despair, that speaks unmistakably of some dreadful doom to come. The overture ends in a discordant crash, and the curtain rises at once on a square in Seville, all brightness and animation (*Sur la place*).

> See, the square is like a fair,
>   And high and low come and go!
> Droll is the sight, a motley show!

There is a lofty bridge, reached by a flight of steps, up and down and over which the people go; there is also a cigarette factory, and, to the front of the stage, a guard-house, with Captain Morales and his men on duty.

The crowd having cleared away, a young girl comes timidly down the steps and stands in hesitation, a country girl, it is plain, not used to cities and their ways. Still, she can speak to the Captain; she is looking for a corporal, José by name—does the Captain know him? He does—José will come on duty shortly, when the guard is changed. Micaela hurries away, preferring to put herself beyond the reach of the soldier's too gallant attentions.

The sound of fifes and drums is heard, and a little band

of urchins marches solemnly across the stage, in droll imitation of the relieving guard that now arrives. José is informed of his pretty visitor; it must be Micaela, he says, his old playmate and sweetheart. At this moment a noisy bell is heard, and from the gates of the cigarette factory issues a stream of bold-eyed beauties, enough to unsettle a whole company of brigadiers. Lining up in the centre of the stage they lose no time in showing off their charms, while they sing a chorus of truly delicious quality, in which the melody seems to soar and mingle with the wreaths of smoke from the cigarettes the girls are holding.

A vivid flash from the orchestra, and Carmen appears on the bridge, hurries down the steps, and challenges the world to produce her equal in the way of seductive womanhood. The type was new to the stage of 1875 as *La Traviata* had been in 1853, but whereas Violetta, the soulful courtesan, almost set a fashion in operatic heroines, the full-blooded wanton of Mérimée and Bizet has found no imitators. Carmen stands for wild, un-trammelled freedom: she must be free, above all in the matter of love, to bestow her favours where, when, and for just as long as she pleases.

The amorous soldiers are naturally all desirous of her flaming beauty: "Tell us, Carmen," they cry, "when are you going to choose a new lover?" She surveys them coldly, with a slight contempt: "As I don't know myself, how can I tell you? To-morrow, maybe—perhaps not at all! But one thing is sure—not to-day!"

Then follows the most famous of all operatic songs begotten in the last fifty years, known as the *Habañera,* the name of the slow, swinging dance to which Carmen moves about the stage, *L'amour est un oiseau rebelle*:

Love must ever be wild and free,
A mountain-bird that none can snare.

438

CARMEN

She sings of the waywardness of love, how none can tell the season of his coming nor the reason for his going; love cannot be lured, cannot be bound; 'tis not the man who tells his love that is always the chosen one—the maid will sometimes give the preference to one who never speaks a word. The refrain—"You love me not—but I love you! And when *I* love—why, then, beware!"—is evidently directed at José, who sits stolidly astride a chair, busy with some trifling task, and pretending to take no notice. At the end of her song Carmen takes a crimson flower from her dress, flings it with sure aim in the soldier's face, and runs off the stage, followed by her companions, amid peals of laughter.

That flower has given José his death-wound, though he knows it not; he stops to gather it and hide it near his heart just as Micaela returns, all modesty and maidenly affection. She brings him a letter from his mother, and the music takes on a great tenderness that speaks of happier days, and of the simple village pleasures they had known together in childhood.

Micaela's solo, and the duet that follows, *Ma mère, je la vois,* are delicious passages of a quiet lyrical quality in happiest contrast to what has gone before. Micaela cannot stay long, but it is clear that José's love for her has been revived by her visit. When she is gone he takes the crimson flower from his tunic and is about to throw it away when shrill cries are heard from the factory, and the girls come tumbling out in wild confusion. Carmen, it appears, has had a quarrel with another girl and has drawn her knife upon her; the chorus is divided into two parties, one laying the blame on the gipsy, the other defending her, with such vehemence that it ends in a free fight, in which the soldiers have to interfere. Meanwhile the Captain, who is accustomed to Carmen's dangerous outbursts, sends José with a couple of men to arrest her.

The gipsy is dragged out, a prisoner, but unsubdued; to all questions put to her she answers merely with a jaunty "Tra-la-la!" sung as it were for her own amusement. Her hands are now bound behind her back, and she is given over into Don José's custody, while the others retire. Now is Carmen's opportunity; she has already taken the measure of the young corporal, and at once sets to work to enslave him. The charm works quickly; there is no need of a *pas de fascination*—the mere sound of her voice, a glance from under those dark lashes, is sufficient. She moves to the other side of the stage singing softly to herself, though the words are a spell to steal José's heart and senses away. *Sur les remparts de Séville,* sings Carmen, "I have a friend called Lillas Pastia; he keeps a tavern where the wine is good, and where one can sing and dance most gaily. It is there I am going—and I know who's going with me! None of your haughty glittering officers—no! he is just a poor corporal—but he loves me, and that is enough!" José is an easy conquest for so accomplished a charmer; at the end of the second verse she sidles up to him and makes a gesture with her tied hands. José, no longer master of himself, cuts the cords, and Carmen, free once more, dances wildly about the stage to the tune of the *Seguidilla* she has just been singing. But this is no time for dancing; José arranges the cords around her wrists so that she may still seem to be a prisoner; and only just in time, for now the Captain and his men return with a written warrant for her imprisonment, and a crowd has gathered to see the fun. Carmen is being led off between two guards when she makes an unexpected dash for liberty, up the steps and across the bridge, where she turns to fling the rope that had bound her into the midst of the astonished people, who have certainly had better entertainment than they had bargained for.

The construction of this Act compels our admiration. It is a vivid panorama of fresh and unexpected incidents, where nothing is forced, but all is knit together in a most natural sequence. Against the picturesque background the crimson-lipped gipsy stands out in bold relief, the others being merely accessory; although Micaela, the timid country girl, assumes some importance as an excellent foil to the flamboyant figure of Carmen. Micaela is an invention of the librettists; although apt to be dramatically tedious, the character is useful not only by way of contrast, but also as serving to develop the rather colourless psychology of José. Musically she is of the highest importance; on the two short scenes in which she appears Bizet has lavished his most exquisite melodies, so graceful, so appealing, that great singers have not disdained to appear in what is only a subordinate part. As to the rest, there is not a dull or negligible page in all the score, while the *Habañera* and the *Seguidilla* have definitely helped to raise the level of popular taste in operatic melody.

Act II. At the not too reputable tavern "close by the ramparts of Seville" we find Carmen in all her glory, among the gipsies, soldiers, smugglers, for whom the obliging host, Lillas Pastia, provides good accommodation. There has been feasting and drinking, and some of the gipsies have already begun to amuse the company with song and dance. Carmen cannot resist the familiar lure; leaping to her feet she rattles her tambourine and works up the frenzy as only she can do; this number, *Les tringles des sistres tintaient,* reaches almost the limit of rhythmical excitement.

She has good reason for her high spirits; José will soon join her here; for eight weeks he has been in prison for conniving at her escape, and has only that day been released. Carmen's vanity is gratified at the thought of

441

her conquest, and she thinks tenderly of the lover who has suffered for her sake.

But now the shouts of those outside announce the coming of one whom we may consider the real hero of the play: "Long live Escamillo!" is the cry, "Long live the Toreador!" A magnificent personage swaggers on to the stage, obviously conscious of his right to the applause that greets his appearance; one of the best bull-fighters in Spain, the idol of the people, there is no tavern that would not feel honoured by a visit from Escamillo.

It would be difficult to imagine a more vivid musical impression of such a figure than that which Bizet has given us in the famous Toreador's Song, *Votre toast,* with its picturesque description of the crowded arena, the exciting contest, and the daring spirit of the fighters. Of one thing only a Toreador is, and must be, afraid— the fire that flashes from a woman's eyes. Escamillo is at no pains to hide his admiration for Carmen, nor can she help being attracted toward him for the moment; indeed, they are a handsome pair of animals, and would be well mated, one thinks. The bull-fighter soon takes his departure—but that short encounter is enough; their eyes have mingled, and destiny has bound them fast together.

José still tarries. Carmen, however, is not alone, and the time is filled by some lively argument between her, Mercedes and Frasquita, her two friends, and the two smugglers Remondado and El Dancairo. The men are eager to be off on the adventure of the night, and insist that the girls shall accompany them—women's help is invaluable on such occasions! The quintet that follows is a little masterpiece of sparkling humour, *En matière de tromperie*:

442

CARMEN

When there is cheating to be done,
One thing is clear, clear as the sun,
Women can always give good aid,
Women are cheats, born to the trade!

The girls must come along, say the smugglers, in order to throw dust into the eyes of the excisemen; her two companions are all for the adventure, but Carmen refuses to budge. She is quite frank with her reason—she is in love, head over heels in love, and she is expecting her lover shortly.

So the others go off with mocking laughter, just as a man's voice is heard singing a snatch of a song outside: "Halt there! Who goes there?" "'Tis a Spanish Brigadier!" It is José, and for the time being Carmen wants nothing more—he is sufficient for her passionate nature; she lavishes all her love upon him, she will dance for him as no one has ever seen her dance before—dance for him alone!

José sits entranced as Carmen moves slowly round to a measure that is full of seductive grace, to the accompaniment of castanets and the sound of her own voice. She has become thoroughly absorbed into the spirit of the dance, as her lover is lost in watching her, when the call of a distant bugle breaks the spell—it is the signal for José to return to barracks. All the soldier in him responds to that sound—he rises to go. Carmen at first can hardly believe he is in earnest, she throws herself into the dance with greater vigour than before; but the martial music grows more and more insistent, and at last José calls upon her to stop—for he must leave her.

The dancing gipsy is instantly transformed to a figure of sullen anger—she turns on José with violent reproaches: "So this is my reward—and all my trouble wasted on a man who loves a bugle better than me! Go then! You shall not deceive me twice! No, no! you never loved me!"

Never loved her! The distracted lover takes from near his heart the crimson flower she flung him at their first encounter—he had treasured it ever since, his consolation, his pledge of hope. Does not that mean love at first sight, and love for ever? José's Flower Song, *La fleur que tu m'avais jetée*, has become a favourite with the public, but hardly with the race of operatic tenors—in spite of its great lyrical charm, it is not easily made effective on the stage.

Carmen, relenting, now suggests that he shall fly with her "over the hills and far away," to share the roving life of absolute freedom for which she is best fitted. [The music of this passage may well be compared with the soprano air *Là tra foreste vergini* in *Aïda*, Act II, Scene 1, where the situation is very similar.] The handsome gipsy brings all her fascinations into play, and José is almost vanquished, but in the end the soldier in him triumphs, and he prepares to go. Defeated, humiliated, Carmen becomes a flaming fury. Reaching for his helmet, sword, and belt, she flings them noisily at him: nay, he shall not stay another minute, she herself will drive him away!

A knocking is heard at the door, and Morales breaks into the room. Although it has hardly been made clear hitherto, the Captain has long been under the spell of Carmen's opulent beauty; on this occasion he expected a *tête-à-tête* with her, and is naturally enraged to find a common soldier preferred before him. There is a quarrel, and José is betrayed into drawing his sword on his superior officer. Carmen calls in her friends to part the two men, and Remandado and El Dancairo make Morales their prisoner. As for José, it is plain that his career as a soldier is at an end; there is nothing now to

444

prevent him from following Carmen and the smugglers, who welcome the new recruit, and so he is borne off, an incongruous figure among that lawless crew, to their haunts in the mountain fastnesses.

Act III. The action here requires careful watching, as so many small incidents occur which, while essential to the understanding of the plot, do not always succeed in making the right impression.

The scene is wildly picturesque; a rocky hollow in some high mountain pass, the smugglers' secret haunt, accessible only by two narrow defiles carefully guarded. It is hardly dawn as yet, and men and women are still asleep among the packs and bales that strew the ground; they awake to join in a chorus which is singularly happy in expressing the fresh out-of-door atmosphere of the scene; to its swinging rhythm many of them move away to their different tasks, and we are aware of Carmen with her two girl friends, Frasquita and Mercedes, and of José, a restless, gloomy figure. He, the seasoned soldier, is badly out of place among this vagrant company; his moody fits have already gone far to kill the gipsy's passion for him, to say nothing of the fact that the more imposing figure of Escamillo has taken full possession of her heart. She taunts her lover with his dejected air, and hints that it might be better for him to go back to his old way of life. That his mistress can even suggest that they should part fills the infatuated José with a blind jealousy, and he threatens to kill her; but Carmen is not afraid. She is a born fatalist—when her time comes she must die, and not before; it is all written in the book of Fate—each must abide the appointed hour.

Yet when Frasquita and Mercedes decide, half in jest, to tell their fortunes by the cards, Carmen feels impelled to follow their example. The two young girls make merry over the bright fortunes they find predicted for them, but when Carmen begins to lift the veil all is darkness and horror—she draws a spade, the symbol of death. "Yes! 'tis death!" she cries. "First come I—afterwards he—both of us doomed to die!"

This trio of the cards, *Coupons! mêlons!* is one of the fine dramatic strokes of the opera. The graceful duet for the two young girls sparkles and ripples its vivacious course, to be succeeded by the tragic gloom of Carmen's solo, the latter part of which is overlaid by the return of the lighter melody. The situation is unique in opera, and Bizet may be said to have exhausted its musical possibilities.

All now go off, with the exception of José, who is set to guard the pass on the opposite side to that by which the others have left. On the empty stage Micaela now makes an entry even more timid and furtive than in the first Act. She has come to seek her lover, and she knows well in what company she may expect to find him.

The character of Micaela is too vague and colourless to raise much sympathy—we even find her a little tiresome —but the music assigned to her must always rank among the best things in French opera. The present solo *Je dis que rien ne m'épouvante,* is one of the loveliest of romantic lyrics, and there have been performances of *Carmen* in which some fresh-voiced *débutante* has made it the outstanding success of the opera. It has no dramatic significance; the young girl merely expresses her resolve to overcome her natural fears, and her pious trust in Heaven's protection—but it has the lovely effect of a momentary patch of liquid blue in the midst of a stormy sky.

Though there is no one in sight, Micaela is soon frightened into hiding by the sound of a carbine shot; it is José, who has fired at a figure he sees descending the rocky path that leads to the encampment. But the

446

man still advances—it is Escamillo. He boldly tells José his business: he has come to try his luck with Carmen—he hears she has grown weary of her latest lover. A fight with knives ensues, which would have ended fatally for Escamillo had not the gang of smugglers returned in time to separate the two men.

The resourceful Toreador manages to make his peace, and invites them all to witness his triumph at the coming bull-fight at Seville. All joyfully accept the offer, and it is plain from Carmen's manner that Escamillo is, for the present at least, the man of her choice.

The Toreador goes carelessly on his way. Micaela is discovered and dragged from her hiding-place; her love for José gets the better of her fears, and before them all she earnestly entreats him to return with her to their native village, where his old mother is lying at the point of death. From such an appeal José cannot turn away; he is about to let Micaela lead him off when Escamillo's voice is heard outside singing the gallant refrain of the Toreador's song. Carmen, fascinated, is actually hastening after her latest lover when José stops her—there is murder in his look as he points his ugly knife at her heart. Carmen turns back with a mocking laugh, but in those eyes she has read her fate more plainly than any cards can tell her.

Act IV. A short scene suffices for the tragic *dénouement*; Carmen herself plays into the hands of Fate, as if desirous of hastening the inevitable end.

We are again in Seville, and ready for the bull-fight. The great square, at the back of which is the entrance to the arena, is filled with the gayest of crowds, joyfully impatient for the coming show. As the ceremonial procession passes up the steps and through the gates the excitement grows and grows, until the climax is reached at the entrance of Escamillo, victorious in love as in the

447

combat. For Carmen is with him; they are all in all to each other now; it is her applause that will nerve him for the most splendid triumph of his career, and it is she who will share in its reward.

It requires skilful stage management to make possible, in the midst of such a crowd, the intimate leave-taking which follows between the lovers, yet it is one of the most valuable dramatic touches in the play. This tender, passionate good-bye is only for a brief moment, as Escamillo thinks; but Carmen knows that it is farewell for ever—the cards can never lie—and with this last good-bye she feels that her good days are done. In this short passage a great actress can win more sympathy for the heroine than in all the rest of the play.

[The little duet *Si tu m'aimes, Carmen,* is one of the 'points' of the opera; the few bars of formal melody are perhaps the only banal thing in the score, but they are undeniably effective, and never fail to grip the house.]

Escamillo passes in to the scene of his glory—Carmen remains. Her smuggler friends surround her, and Frasquita takes her aside to warn her of her danger: she implores her to save herself while there is yet time; she has seen José lurking in the crowd, and there is murder in his face. But Carmen is unmoved: she is a fatalist and does not know fear. She bids them all go in to the show: for herself, she will remain, to face her destiny. The crowd disappears through the gates; Carmen waits till she is alone on the stage, then prepares to follow them. She is already up the steps and at the gates—but Fate is there before her; José bars her path, desperately in love, and half mad with jealousy.

Carmen rises to her greatest height; coldly, boldly, she tells him the truth. Her love for him is dead. She is not afraid of him, he may kill her if he will, but never again will she be his.

448

CARMEN

José strives to keep down the madman within him; piteously he implores her to fly with him, to follow him (as once she had besought him) to some ideal retreat "over the hills and far away"—there his devotion, his worship, will win back her love; there they will be happy once more together. Shouts of wild excitement are heard from the bull-ring—Escamillo's triumph is at its height. Carmen makes a rush toward the gate, when José again intercepts her, this time with his knife drawn: "Back!" he cries, "you shall not go to your new lover! Confess! 'tis Escamillo you love!"

"Yes!" is the fearless answer, "I love him, and would gladly die for him! *Viva! Viva Escamillo!*"

But her end is near; José is a madman now; there are still a few moments of horror as he pursues Carmen from corner to corner of the stage, waiting his best opportunity to strike. At last she makes another wild attempt to escape through the gates; she is already up the steps when José stabs her brutally between the shoulders, and Carmen staggers backward, falling lifeless in the middle of the stage, just as the people pour out from the arena, shouting for the victorious Escamillo.

José, a soldier to the end, gives himself up to an officer, then falls grief-stricken beside the body of his victim; his is the last voice we hear: "Carmen, Carmen, I love you! Speak to me, Carmen!"—and the curtain falls to the impressive theme of doom which we heard in the overture and which throughout the opera has served to invest the rather brazen figure of the heroine with the dignifying shadow of tragedy.

SAMSON ET DALILA

Music by SAINT-SAËNS. *Words by* F. LEMAIRE.
Weimar, 1877; *New York,* 1895; *London,* 1909.

THE custom which once forbade the representation of Biblical subjects on the English stage
must account for the fact that Saint-Saëns' best-
known opera was over thirty years old before it was seen
at Covent Garden, though it had previously been heard
in the concert-room. It is still very popular, largely on
account of Dalila's famous air *Mon cœur s'ouvre à ta
voix*; in fact it is the musical presentment of the Philistine
enchantress that gives distinction to the opera. For the
rest, the score is what we might call 'safe'—always
musicianly, with plenty of solid choral-writing, picturesque orchestration, and a flow of graceful *cantilena*
for the solo voices, thoroughly typical of the French
school as influenced by Gounod.

The drama is extremely simple, admitting of little
action outside the three chief incidents—the slaying of
Abimelech by Samson, his betrayal by Dalila, and the
final tragedy in the Temple of Dagon. The background
is the racial struggle between Israelites and Philistines,
but the central interest lies in the age-old story of the
strong man, unconquerable in fight, vanquished at last by
a beautiful woman—"terrible as an army with banners."

Act I. Gaza, a stronghold of the Philistines. "At that
time the Philistines had dominion over Israel"; thus
much we learn from the Book of Judges; otherwise the
events of this Act are without Scriptural authority.

Before the rise of the curtain an invisible chorus of
Israelites is heard bewailing their bondage, and imploring

450

Jehovah's aid to free them from the Philistine yoke. When the scene is disclosed, a dejected crowd is dimly seen—for it is night—still engaged in lamentation and prayer. The choral work here, with its fugal passages, has that flavour of oratorio which is characteristic of this opera.

Samson comes forward to reproach his countrymen for their want of faith, and urges them to renew the struggle against their oppressors. He has hard work to rouse them from their dejection, but after his vigorous solo *Implorons à genoux* the crowd is caught by the fire of his inspiration: "It is the Lord who speaks through him! Let us follow Samson, and Jehovah be our guide!"

The ringing shouts of "Jehovah!" bring on to the scene Abimelech, the Satrap of Gaza, with a guard of Philistine soldiers. He taunts the Israelites with their helpless position. What avails it to call upon their God Jehovah? Did he deliver them in the day of battle? Let them rather turn to Dagon, who is above all other gods! At this blasphemy Samson asserts himself as the inspired leader of Israel; he sees the heavens opened, and Jehovah's armies gathering to their aid. "The hour is come!" he cries. "Lift up thy head, O Israel, and break the chains that bind thee!" The crowd are now ready to follow wherever he may lead. Abimelech, seeing the danger, draws his sword on Samson, who disarms him and kills him with his own weapon; still brandishing his sword, he scatters the panic-stricken Philistines right and left, and leads the Israelites off to victory.

The High Priest of Dagon, attracted by the uproar, comes from the temple and tries in vain to rally his demoralized people, whose only thought is to flee to a place of safety; he then proceeds to deliver a solemn curse on Samson, the Israelites, and the God they wor-

451

ship, and so departs, with the body of Abimelech borne before him.

There are situations in Italian Opera where the flight of time must be disregarded. As the dead Satrap is carried out, the Israelites return victorious: it has taken little more than the length of a High Priest's curse for Samson to destroy the army of the Philistines. The night is over, a splendid sun has risen—in the orchestra as on the stage—when the basses intone, unaccompanied, a solemn hymn of thanksgiving for victory, *Hymne de joie, hymne de délivrance,* which by its monotonous cadence and compass limited to five notes gives an effective touch of Eastern colour; this is relieved by a bass solo for a Hebrew Elder, and the short but impressive scene ends with the resumption of the chant.

But all sober thoughts are swept away before the flood of beauty which fills the stage as the portals of Dagon's temple unfold, and Dalila advances with her flower-maidens, bringing garlands of roses to crown the victors' brows. We are left in some doubt as to Samson's previous relations with the Philistine woman; she addresses him as *"Mon bien-aimé,"* and it is plain that he is already in her toils, but no reason is suggested for his determined rejection of her present advances. She has come, she says, to greet the conqueror—the conqueror of her heart: in phrases suggested by the Song of Songs she offers him the honied wine of her love, and hints at the bliss in store for him at her home in the Valley of Sorek—let him follow her thither!

But Samson resolutely turns his face away and prays Heaven to keep him from the snare, while the Hebrew Elder is at his side to strengthen his resolve by solemn warnings.

The weakness of the drama at this point is obvious.

452

After the apparent failure of her effort there is really nothing more for Dalila to do; any direct encounter with Samson at this point would be premature: she merely sings at him, and he continues to avoid her. Saint-Saëns has to fall back upon a ballet, in which the temptress bears a part, and the Act closes with a seemingly artless ballad, *Printemps qui commence,* and the return of Dalila to the temple with many a backward glance at Samson, who plainly shows by the trouble in his face that all his struggles have been in vain.

Act II. Outside Dalila's dwelling in the Vale of Sorek. A sultry night; the air is heavy with the scent of flowers, and there is a presentiment of coming storm. [Saint-Saëns is as careful as Dickens to enlist the sympathies of Nature for the emotional situation.]

Dalila is seated on a couch beneath a vine-covered trellis. In the previous Act we may have taken her for merely a splendid courtesan, anxious to make a conquest of the hero of the hour; but her character is developed on quite other lines—she is now seen to be of the race of Jael and Deborah, an instrument of the gods for her country's welfare. The armies of Philistia have fled before the power of Samson; she, Dalila, ere this night be over, will make him bond-slave to her beauty and deliver him helpless into their hands. In the air *Amour, viens aider ma faiblesse,* she invokes the God of Love to strengthen her, and she has no fear for the issue.

The High Priest of Dagon now arrives, despondent and anxious; the town of Gaza is in the hands of the rebel Israelites—all resistance has broken down—the nation's only hope is in Dalila. The High Priest is aware that Samson was at one time in thrall to her charms; if her influence has waned, can she not renew it? Let her but discover and destroy the secret sources of his giant strength, and she may demand of her country what reward she pleases.

But Dalila is not moved by the promise of riches; all she desires is to revenge herself on Samson. "For know," she cries, "that, like you, I abhor him!" Hitherto she has exhausted all her store of flattery and fond caresses to win his secret from him, but in vain; to-night she will try a surer way to victory—even Samson himself will not be able to hold out against her tears!

Dalila, left alone, looks out into the pitchy darkness, and listens anxiously for footsteps; but there is no sound except the rising wind which foretells the coming storm, and she goes into the house.

Distant lightning shows up the blackness of the night as Samson enters, his heart in wild commotion. He is drawn hither against his will—he feels that for him the place is accursed; even now he would retreat, but Dalila comes flying from the house and smothers him with her caresses.

Still Samson holds her off—he must not stay with her, he has only come to say farewell; the Lord has chosen him to be the deliverer of his people, and he must obey the call.

Dalila knows the strong man's heart only too well; Samson has strength to resist her blandishments, her merely sensuous appeal, but, with the outbreak of her tears, the victory is in her hands.

The lightning is nearer now, more frequent, and more vivid, but the storm has to wait while the temptress draws her captive to the couch beneath the vines and sings the song on which the existence of the opera depends, *Mon cœur s'ouvre à ta voix*. The words are nothing, but as an expression of purely voluptuous allurement the music could hardly be surpassed. It is difficult, indeed, to realize that Dalila is merely acting a part—if this be

454

only a feigned emotion, in what form would this woman voice her real passion, as

Vénus toute entière à sa proie attachée?

But not even her tears can wrest his secret from Samson. He dare not disobey the word of God: is not the storm now breaking a sign of His wrath? With a cry of rage, with words of bitter scorn, she leaves him, and sweeps into the house. Samson can endure no longer: raising his hands to heaven as if entreating pardon for his weakness, he follows after her, while the storm bursts in all its fury.

Toward the end of the descriptive orchestral passage which ensues, some Philistine soldiers are seen stealthily approching the house; there is a crash of thunder as Dalila appears on the terrace, holding aloft the hero's shorn locks, the symbol of her victory. She calls to the soldiers to enter and finish the ruin she has begun: Samson, against whom no man living could stand; Samson, the slayer of thousands, lies blinded, bound, and helpless at a woman's feet.

Act III. This Act is, musically, the most satisfactory of the three; the interest is worked up by a steady crescendo to the climax—there is nothing superfluous; Saint-Saëns, relying largely on chorus and ballet, is at his best.

Scene I shows us Samson in prison, yoked like a beast of burden to the pole of the mill, around which he is laboriously plodding. Blinded, shorn of his strength, he compels our sympathy throughout. No insult, no humiliation, is spared him as the Act proceeds: he bears them all with the patience of Job; he is a penitent, who desires nothing better than to suffer.

The Israelites, his fellow-captives, are heard, without, reproaching him for betraying his country's cause: his only answer is to pray for their deliverance, and to offer his life as atonement for his transgressions.

So in *Scene* II, in the Temple of Dagon, whither the helpless giant has been summoned to make sport for the Philistines, Samson is proof against all provocation—nothing can distract him from his fervent prayers.

Some of the music here is a repetition of what has gone before. The elaborate ballet, with its Oriental colour, is preceded by the strains in which the flower-crowned maidens sang of spring on their first appearance; when Dalila offers Samson the wine-cup and mockingly invites him to drink to the memory of their past delights, she plays with the very phrases of the great love-song in the previous Act. But nothing, not even the blasphemous insults of the High Priest, can move Samson to reply: he continues to pray, with growing fervour, that it may please Jehovah to give him back his strength, to be used for His honour and glory.

The coming catastrophe is finely imagined, and gives the composer his greatest opportunity. It is the hour of the morning sacrifice to Dagon, and an occasion of special thanksgiving for Samson's overthrow and the triumph of Philistia. The High Priest and Dalila lead off the hymn with broad, impressive phrases, sung in canon, *Gloire à Dagon vainqueur!* Glory to Dagon, who giveth his servants the victory! Let the name of Dagon be exalted above all other gods! All the people join in prayer and adoration: Samson too must do homage to Dagon and pour a libation in his honour: let him be brought forward that he may be seen of all! By the High Priest's command he is led to take his stand between the two massive pillars of stone that support the central dome.

Meanwhile the attention of all is turned to the ritual of the sacrifice. The Priest pours wine upon the altar fires, which, after dying down, are seen again to leap heavenward, and with a brighter flame—it is a sign that the god himself has descended. The worshippers are moved to tense excitement—Dalila and the High Priest join in a shrill, inarticulate cry—we almost expect the 'knives and lancets' of the priests of Baal. "Glory to Dagon, who is god above all other gods!"

But it is a vain thing that the people have imagined. Samson has never ceased from praying, and at last his prayers are answered—he feels his strength return. Unnoticed by any, he clasps either pillar with a mighty arm —they sway, they crash, and all is over—Samson once more has slain his thousands, and himself lies buried with them beneath the ruins of Dagon's temple.

LES CONTES D'HOFFMANN

Music by OFFENBACH. *Words by* BARBIER.
Paris, 1881; *New York,* 1882; *London,* 1910.

*T**ALES OF HOFFMANN*—for it is in its English form that it is best known in this country —is one of the surprises, the oddities, of operatic history; it is the only regular 'opera,' in the conventional sense, of a composer whose immense, if ephemeral, reputation was gained in a very different field. Jacques Offenbach (1819-1880) might well be described as the King of *Opéra bouffe.* Throughout the Second Empire he dominated Paris, without a rival in his own peculiar realm. Nearly eighty operettas stand to his credit, all of the lightest possible texture, but exactly calculated to please the taste of that frivolous, cynical period. Some critics have compared them to the sparkling exhilaration of champagne, to others they have seemed merely a carrion corruption. Nor was their fame confined to the Gay City; *Orphée aux Enfers, La Belle Hélène, La Grande Duchesse,* went the round of the European capitals. Works of this calibre, however, are naturally short-lived, and not long after the composer's death Offenbach's name ceased to be one to conjure with. So far as England is concerned, a partially successful revival of *The Grand Duchess* toward the end of the last century rang down the curtain. When, therefore, in 1910, an opera entitled *Tales of Hoffmann* was staged at Covent Garden, the younger generation was, not unnaturally, puzzled. "Who is this Offenbach?" many might easily ask, and, with still more reason, "Who was Hoffmann?" The title, it must be confessed, is a clumsy one, and requires explanation.

E. T. W. Hoffmann was a real personage, a shining light of the Romantic Movement in Germany at the beginning of the 19th century; part musician, part author, he wrote an opera, *Undine,* to which Weber gave enthusiastic praise; but he is best known for his fantastic romances, which may be compared with Poe's *Tales of Mystery and Imagination.* Both Hoffmann and Poe were in high favour with the literary circles of Paris, and in 1851 MM. Barbier and Carré produced at the Odéon a play called *Les Contes d'Hoffmann,* which seems to have made an indelible impression on Offenbach, then a young man of thirty. When in later life he determined to show the public that he was capable of something far better than the flummery with which he had so long delighted them, he turned to Hoffmann for the subject of a three-act opera, to which he devoted many years of loving care. He left it still unfinished at the time of his death (1880), but E. Girard supplied what was wanting, and *Les Contes d'Hoffmann* was produced at the Opéra Comique in 1881.

It was given in New York, without much success, in 1882, and revived in 1907. Introduced to London in 1910, it has been ever since one of the most popular operas, and has meant the resurrection of a composer whose life's work was almost forgotten in this country.

Offenbach called his work a Fantastic Opera, and the epithet is of the greatest importance toward a right appreciation of the very strange libretto. Between a Prologue and an Epilogue are unfolded three distinct stories, entirely disconnected, except as forming episodes in the life of the same person. The authors hit upon the original idea of taking the actual Hoffmann, the fantastic writer, as the central figure of certain weird adventures, such as he himself delighted to imagine. These adventures, concerned with three different love affairs, he relates to his boon companions as they sit drinking round the tavern table—or is supposed to relate, for the various scenes are really enacted for our benefit on the stage.

Hoffmann himself is the only character who appears in all the scenes, though Nicklaus his friend and fellow-student (a part assigned for the sake of vocal balance to a mezzo-soprano) bears him company up to the end of Act II. It will be noticed, however, that in each Act there is one mysterious figure for whom it is not easy to account, and that there is a strong family resemblance between the three: Coppelius, maker of magical glasses, Dapertutto, dealer in men's shadows, Dr. Miracle with his unholy spells—all these do, in fact, represent the same personality, *i.e.,* the Devil himself, or, if you prefer, Hoffmann's Evil Genius, the cause of his disasters. The action of the piece is fantastic in the highest degree, and puts perhaps too great a strain upon our powers of make-belief, but the underlying idea is perfectly clear. *Tales of Hoffmann* is a somewhat cynical exposure of the vanity of love's young dream; the hero's first love turns out to be merely a mechanical doll, his second a heartless courtesan, while the third is snatched from him by the hand of death—and Hoffmann turns for consolation to his old friend the punch-bowl.

The Prologue introduces us to a beer-cellar in Nuremberg, kept by one Luther, and attached apparently to an opera house: the students present are discussing a performance of *Don Giovanni,* of which they have just heard the first Act; indeed, the entrance of Hoffmann (with Nicklaus his friend) is heralded by the first bars of Leporello's air in that opera, *Notte e giorno faticar.* The appropriateness of the quotation lies in the fact that the real Hoffmann is known to have had an intense enthusiasm for Mozart; he actually adopted one of the composer's names, and was in the habit of signing himself 'Amadeus.'

The stage is filled by a crowd of noisy young Bohemians, intent upon spending a merry evening. Hoffmann, though moody and quarrelsome at first, dominates the assembly—he is 'the master,' 'the poet.' After they have coaxed a song from him—the ballad of the little dwarf Kleinzack—no one thinks of returning to the theatre for the rest of *Don Giovanni;* they all settle down, pipe and glass, to enjoy Hoffmann's account of his adventures with the three goddesses who, from time to time, have reigned in his heart—Olympia, Giulietta, and Antonia.

Act I. The delicious minuet that serves as *intermezzo* prepares us for a gay gathering at the house of Spalanzani, a somewhat shadowy personality, with a mania for experimenting in certain curious bypaths of what he is pleased to call 'science.' "Science, my friends!" he repeats grandiloquently, "science is everything!" At any rate it has enabled him to invent a wonderful automaton, a beautiful doll as large as life, that can walk, dance, sing, and say a good deal more than "Yes!" and "No!"—so well equipped, in fact, as to pass for a human being except under the closest inspection. This very evening he is to present his creation to his friends as, "Olympia, my daughter!" He has just placed his 'child' on a couch in a curtained recess and left the room when Hoffmann enters, lifts the curtain, and at once falls in love with the beautiful sleeper. Now comes on the scene the mysterious Coppelius ('Mephisto No. 1' we may call him), a purveyor of scientific instruments, and, especially, of magic spectacles which enable the wearer to see things in a particularly rosy light. [The capital song, "I have glasses that sparkle and shine," has unmistakable affinity to the more genial aspects of Gounod's Mephistopheles.]

Hoffmann falls into the snare, and Olympia, seen through those wondrous glasses, at once becomes the loveliest vision in all creation.

Spalanzani now returns. Coppelius has a bone to pick with him: Olympia, he says, belongs as much to himself as to her actual inventor, for did not he, Coppelius, provide the eyes, which constitute the most irresistible of her attractions? Spalanzani had anticipated this claim; to meet it he gives Coppelius a cheque —which he knows to be worthless—on Elias the banker. To the strains of the lovely minuet the guests now arrive, prepared to pay homage to the fair *débutante,* though whether they are initiated into the secret is not apparent. Spalanzani leads in Olympia, whose sparkling eyes and elegant figure win instant admiration, while her mechanical bowings and an occasional squeaky "Oh!" and "Yes!" are sufficient to satisfy the requirements of society. When to a harp accompaniment she 'obliges' with a high-pitched and tinkly solo, "Every grove," the wonder knows no bounds. Whatever conclusions the company may arrive at, we cannot fail to notice the careful way in which Spalanzani directs his 'daughter's' movements, nor to hear an alarming whirring noise at such times as he contrives secretly to wind up the run-down machinery. Hoffmann, however, has no misgivings; thanks to the magic spectacles, Olympia is living flesh and blood to him, the loveliest creature he has ever seen.

The guests go in to supper, and the amorous youth is left alone with his beautiful doll. His most impassioned pleadings elicit nothing more than a colourless "Yes!" or "Ah!" but when at last he ventures to squeeze her hand some fresh machinery is set in motion; the fair automaton runs aimlessly up and down the stage and glides through the curtains into another room, to which Hoffmann follows her.

The mystery-man, Coppelius, now returns in a furious rage; he has discovered that Elias' bank has failed, and Spalanzani's cheque is worthless. Vowing vengeance, he rushes from the room.

The guests return from supper, and the dance begins; Hoffmann leads out Olympia for the valse. It is soon plain that all is not well with the dancing doll—something has gone wrong with the works; Olympia gets out of all control, and dances wildly hither and thither, off the stage and on again, dragging her partner along with her, until Spalanzani manages at last to stop her. Hoffmann sinks exhausted on a sofa; his magic spectacles are broken, and there is no more spirit in him. Olympia has still vitality enough to execute a few more weird gyrations before she dances off the stage for the last time. Almost immediately a tumult springs up in the orchestra; there is a cry behind the scenes: "The man with the glasses is here!" and a noise is heard as of machinery being shattered into a thousand pieces. Coppelius has had his revenge. Hoffmann, already half disillusioned, realizes the truth at last—and the company offer him as much sympathy as is usual on these occasions:

> Ha! ha! ha! the farce is over!
> To a doll he played the lover!

Act II. This scene is in most effective contrast to what has gone before. Instead of the mechanical doll and her rather tawdry surroundings we have Giulietta, the splendid courtesan, her voluptuous charms enhanced by all the beauty of a moonlight *fête* in Venice. The shimmer of lamps and torches is reflected in the waters of the Grand Canal, which lap, lap ever against the marble walls of her palace. The music, too, takes on a richer colouring. Austere indeed or wholly insensible must he be who does not yield to the seduction of the *barcarolle*, "Lovely night, O night of love!"; on its own level it is one of the perfect things in the music of the theatre, a piece of beauty which no amount of familiarity has yet been able to deflower. Played before the curtain rises, it is first sung by Giulietta and Nicklaus, who land from a gondola. Hoffmann, it seems, is in one of his cynical moods and rather contemptuous of the softer passions; his spirited drinking-song, "When love is but tender and sweet," is a protest against such follies. Nicklaus, however, who knows his friend—and Giulietta —warns him against remaining in such dangerous company, but Hoffmann is rooted in his false security, and trouble soon begins.

Enter 'Mephisto No. 2,' in the guise of one Dapertutto ('Mr All-over-the-place,' 'Mr Ubiquitous'—what you please); he has overheard the young man's boasts, and marks him for an easy victim. Dapertutto, perhaps the most fantastic figure in the play, deals in human souls; those of women, he knows, can always be snared by the glitter of diamonds—Giulietta's has long been his; men's souls he catches by means of a certain magic mirror in his possession; let a man but look therein, he is deprived at once of his reflection, his shadow, and his soul.

Hoffmann is to be the next victim, and it is Giulietta who is to hold up the mirror for his undoing, and add his soul to Dapertutto's collection: that mysterious personage explains his intentions in the solo "As jewels divine," in which he makes effective play with a hand-mirror and a splendid diamond which he has brought as an inducement for his fair accomplice. Giulietta has already been successful in the case of one Schlemihl— the name is taken from one of Chamisso's best-known

464

stories—a sketchy character introduced to strengthen the
slender thread of the plot; it is an easy matter to captivate the amorous Hoffmann, to awaken Schlemihl's
jealousy, and then to play off one against the other.
Schlemihl, she tells Hoffmann, has a key to her boudoir—
her new lover may have it if he can secure it. For such
a prize what will he not do! He challenges the other
to a duel in which, thanks to the sword provided by
'Mephisto No. 2' (in imitation of his great original in
Gounod's opera), he kills his rival. Snatching the key
from the lifeless body, he rushes to Giulietta's room—
to find it empty. The air is filled with the sound of many
voices, chanting the lovely *barcarolle,* but the 'night of
love' is not for Hoffmann; leaning from the balcony,
he sees a gondola move slowly away—in it is Giulietta,
reclining in the arms of some more favoured lover. Our
poor hero has lost his shadow, his soul, his mistress—it
is fortunate that Nicklaus, his friend, is at hand to drag
him away and so save him from being arrested for the
murder of his rival.

[Quite apart from the famous *barcarolle,* which dominates it, the music of this Act is well worthy of close
attention; it is surprisingly fresh, vigorous, and original,
while the duet (No. 10) and the following septet attain
to a distinction beyond the reach of many a composer
with a reputation far greater than Offenbach's.]

Act III. In this Act the spirit of romantic fantasy
runs wild. The mysterious personage whom we have
seen in Act I as Coppelius, and as Dapertutto in Act II,
throws off all disguise, and as Dr Miracle is obviously our
old friend Mephistopheles himself.

The curious blend of the weird, the pathetic, and the
picturesque from which the scene is woven has certainly
called forth the highest powers of the composer. If it

fails of its right effect, as is too often the case, it is because of the difficulty in finding singers at once able and willing to bring to the music that serious artistic treatment which it undoubtedly deserves and demands.

The story is of a certain Antonia, daughter of Councillor Crespel, a widower; her mother, it appears, was a prima donna of renown, from whom the girl has inherited voice and ambition, but not the strength to follow in her footsteps. Antonia is consumptive, and it is her father's unhappy duty to dissuade her as much as possible from the exercise of the talent she undoubtedly possesses. Hoffmann, with whom she is in love, joins his influence to that of her father, and she promises to sing no more; but Miracle, the Devil as Doctor, contrives that she shall break her vow. By conjuring up a phantom of her dead mother he induces her to give one more exhibition of her powers; the effort is too much for her, and she sinks lifeless to the ground.

A delicate art is needed to maintain the atmosphere of pleasing if rather morbid fantasy proper to this scene. Antonia is discovered seated at a harpsichord in a music-room "oddly furnished," to quote the stage directions; there are violins on the wall, and a large portrait of Antonia's mother. Her opening romance, "Thou art flown," has a curious quality of faded beauty well in keeping with the sad state of the consumptive girl, whose thoughts are partly of her mother, partly of Hoffmann, her long-absent lover. Her father enters and gently reproves her; she knows that all singing is forbidden, because of the danger to her health. Antonia promises obedience and leaves the room dejectedly. Crespel, full of fears for the future, gives orders to his servant Franz that no visitors are to be admitted that day, and goes out. [This Franz, stupid and almost stone-deaf,

gives the one touch of humour to this scene; it seems a
pity that the amusing solo, "Night and Day," which
Offenbach has assigned him is always omitted in the
English performance.]

Thanks to Franz's stupidity, Hoffmann finds his way
into the room, and his duet with Antonia, " 'Tis but a
song of love," is one of the outstanding attractions of the
opera. At its close Hoffmann, who is not yet aware of
the girl's unhappy secret, is alarmed to see her in evident
distress after the exertion of singing, but his inquiries
are cut short by the voice of Crespel, and he conceals
himself in the room as the father enters. The stupid
Franz now announces the arrival of Dr Miracle, and the
atmosphere of sentiment is changed to one of weird
mystification.

Crespel, it is plain, is haunted by the fear of this so-
called Dr Miracle—"No doctor!" he cries; "say, rather,
assassin and gravedigger! He killed my wife, and would
kill my daughter! Already I hear the clinking of his
deadly flasks!" And with the conventional "Ha! ha!
ha!" the Devil-Doctor makes a sudden and glittering
appearance on the stage. As in Act I our Mephistopheles
carried magic spectacles, and in Act II the fatal mirror,
as symbols of his uncanny powers, so here he brandishes
certain glass phials of sparkling fluid which he clinks
together with an air of triumph. In this scene, indeed,
the Satanic nature of this personage is fully emphasized:
he comes and goes at will through walls and floors, is
invisible at times to all but the audience, and is constantly
attended by a green light which throws his sneering
features into horrible prominence.

He has come, he says, to begin the cure of Antonia;
will his good friend Crespel take him to her room?
Crespel will throw him out of the window if he stirs a

step in that direction! "Never mind!" says the amiable Doctor, "I will treat your daughter from a distance!"

Placing two armchairs in the middle of the room he seats himself in one and begins to put forth his spell of waving hands in the direction of Antonia's room: Crespel and Hoffmann (still in hiding) seem fixed in their places and look on with horror as the door slowly opens: no material form is seen, but Miracle rises, takes an invisible Antonia by the hand, and seems to seat her in the chair beside him. He then goes through the pantomime of feeling her pulse, and questions her as to her symptoms: finally he commands her to sing, and, from the wings, Antonia's voice is heard in a chromatic cascade of two octaves. The Doctor now apparently dismisses his patient, and, shaking his head over her sad condition, turns to the father, jingling in his face the glittering phials with which he proposes to effect a cure. Crespel indignantly turns him out of the room and locks the door. But the Devil is not so easily disposed of; in a minute he is back again, entering through the wall this time, and jingling his phials as before in the face of the infuriated Crespel, who once more drives him away and himself accompanies him.

Hoffmann now comes from his hiding-place and Antonia from her apartment. Her lover, at last awake to the danger that threatens her, exacts from her a solemn promise to sing no more; fearing her father's return, he hurries away, and Antonia sinks exhausted into a chair. In a moment the Tempter is at her side; invisible to his victim, we see Mephisto, with glittering eyes, gleaming teeth, and a face of sickly green, as he bends over Antonia and pours poison into her soul. What! sing no more! Beauty, youth, such wonderful talent, are all to be wasted—buried in dull domesticity? Let her think of the career that is hers for the taking—to be the greatest

468

singer of the day! Think of the joys of such a life as that—the artistic triumphs, the applause of the crowded theatre—and then the diamonds! But Antonia is proof against such allurements; she will be true to Hoffmann and to her promise, and she turns toward her mother's picture imploring her help. This is Miracle's great opportunity. By his magic art the picture comes to life, and a voice is heard, her mother's voice it seems, urging her daughter to follow her on the path of glory: "Sing on, sing on!" it seems to say. Antonia yields to the illusion; to Miracle's wild accompaniment on the violin she gives out her voice in all its power and to the full extent of its compass; the strain is more than she can bear— she falls, dying, on the stage, while Mephisto vanishes through the floor with a peal of fiendish laughter.

[This number, "Dearest child, 'tis thy mother," is perhaps the most distinguished achievement in the whole opera; Antonia's feverish ecstasy, the insidious persistence of the Tempter, the effective melody of the ghostly mother's voice, combine in a trio which, while making the strongest possible popular appeal, must inspire all musicians with admiration and respect, mingled with regret that so singular a talent should have found in this opera the sole opportunity for its proper exercise.]

To compensate the unlucky hero for his three disastrous adventures in the field of love, the original libretto has a short scene (*Intermezzo* and *Romance*) in which the Muse appears, to console the wild poet with the assurance that she alone is his true mistress, who will always be faithful to him. This number, however, is never given to-day. In the short *finale* Hoffmann is shown once more in Luther's cellar with his fellow revellers. Olympia, Giulietta, Antonia, have diverted them all exceedingly, but it has been thirsty work for narrator and listeners alike, and 'the master' calls loudly for a

steaming bowl of punch, which is brought in to the noisi-
est of welcomes.

> If any pain or care remain,
>   Let's drown it in the bowl!

is the prevailing sentiment; yet Hoffmann has fallen back
into his sad reverie before the curtain falls.

MANON

Music by MASSENET. *Words by* MEILHAC *and* GILLE.
Paris, 1884; *London,* 1885; *New York,* 1885.

THE story from which the libretto is taken was
written by Antoine Prévost, a renegade monk,
in the first half of the 18th century. Massenet
is not the only composer who has been attracted by it. A
setting by Auber (1856) is still recalled by virtue of a
single number, the "Laughing Song" (*L'éclat de rire*),
which prima donnas seem determined to keep alive, while
Puccini's *Manon Lescaut* (1893) has been placed by
competent judges among his best work. The Abbé
Prévost's story has always had a great popularity in
France; indeed, it ranks as a classic, the peculiar merit
claimed for it being the success with which it points "the
contrast of unworthy conduct and exalted sentiment";
but the 'book' of an opera can scarcely be expected to
deal in such fine distinctions, and in *Manon* we have
merely the story of a very charming wanton,

> Fond of a kiss and fond of a guinea,

who, after throwing over her true love for a richer man,
succeeds later in inducing him to forsake the religious
life to which he had dedicated himself, and, after many
adventures, dies in his faithful arms.

Act I. The curtain rises on the courtyard of an inn
at Amiens. It is a really old-fashioned coaching hostelry,
with galleries and ample stables, promising good accommodation for man and beast. The court is filled with a
noisy throng—swaggering Guardsmen, elaborately
dressed beaux, coiffed girls in flowered gowns—all await-

471

ing the arrival of the stage-coach from Arras, an event which never fails to afford infinite entertainment to the townsfolk. Prominent in the crowd is Lescaut, a Guardsman—bluff and careless and not over-subtle—who is expecting his young cousin Manon.

Intending passengers, with porters carrying their luggage, come on the scene just as the coach arrives.

Among the passengers who alight Lescaut notices a young and extremely pretty girl standing apart from the crowd and, hazarding that it is his cousin, introduces himself. She is delighted to find a friend among so many strangers, but his clumsy elegance embarrasses her, fresh from country ways. Her charming aria, *Je suis encore étourdie,* expresses her delight, mingled with shyness, at all the new and lovely things she has beheld that morning for the first time.

The coach takes in new passengers and departs, the townspeople gradually disperse, and Lescaut goes off to look after Manon's modest luggage, leaving her to gaze around in admiration at the gay life of the town, so different from the quiet surroundings to which she has been accustomed. Town manners, too, she soon discovers, are very different from those of the country, for an old *roué,* Guillot, coming out on to the balcony of a pavilion overlooking the courtyard, sees Manon and is instantly captivated by her beauty. He appears incredibly old to Manon, who is more amused than disturbed by his advances; but he is serious enough to suggest an elopement. Lescaut returns in time to hear the end of the whispered conversation, and takes the opportunity to give his cousin some rather pompous advice on the folly of talking to strangers (*Regardez-moi bien dans les yeux*).

Manon is soon left alone again, for Lescaut, excusing himself on the plea of momentary business, suffers him-

472

self to be drawn to the nearest tavern by some of his boon companions. She endeavours to follow her cousin's advice, but her romantic nature is spurring her to wild, ambitious dreams. Three gaily dressed ladies—the not over-virtuous friends of old Guillot—appear on the balcony and are greatly admired by the simple girl. Those dresses, those jewels, that brilliant, careless way of life— alas, they are not for Manon! Her family have destined her for the grey austerities of the convent, to which she is even now on her way. [Manon's little snatch of song, *Hélas, Manon,* is an admirable example of Massenet's graceful way of expressing a sort of boudoir pathos, which charms but hardly touches us.]

However, Destiny now appears in the form of the handsome young Chevalier des Grieux. After a few platitudes about the joy of soon seeing his father again— notice the 'heavy father' *motif* in the 'cellos!—he suddenly catches sight of Manon, and the fate of both is decided. [The orchestra here gives out a graceful theme in nine-eight time, expressive of nothing in particular, which will haunt us to the end of the opera, and may be labelled 'Des Grieux's love-*motif*.']

Not in any opera does the flower of love-at-first-sight —without the aid of a love-philtre—blossom so suddenly as here. Without a moment for reflection Des Grieux pours out his passion in spoken words, and then asks pardon for his boldness. "What is there to forgive," answers Manon, "when every word you say fills me with delight?" She is just a simple village maiden, she explains, on her way to the gloom of the cloister. Nay, but that, says Des Grieux, will never happen now; henceforth she is the mistress of his heart for evermore, and they must never part. Manon enters with enthusiasm into this proposal, and when the carriage ordered by old Guillot drives into the courtyard she sees in it the guiding hand of Providence. "How lucky!" she exclaims. "Let us take it and go to Paris!" And off to Paris they go!

The scene ends with a noisy quarrel between Guillot and the now tipsy Lescaut, each blaming the other for the mischief of the elopement; the others thoroughly enjoy the *fracas,* while from the balcony we hear the malicious tittering of the three gay ladies, Poussette, Javotte, and Rosette.

Act II. The scene is the apartment in Paris to which Des Grieux has brought his simple country maiden. He is discovered writing a letter, the nature of which is suggested by the 'heavy father' *motif* in the orchestra. Manon peeps over his shoulder and will give him no rest until he consents to her reading it—aloud, of course, for our edification. Yes! it is to his father, extolling the charms of his beloved with all a lover's extravagance, and asking the parental consent to their union. Des Grieux is evidently very deeply in love, Manon apparently the same, though we, as onlookers, may have our doubts on that head. As the Chevalier is going out to despatch his letter, he notices for the first time a handsome bouquet of hothouse flowers, and questions Manon as to the sender. Ah! she cannot even guess; someone threw them in at the window!

The maid who now enters the room lets us into the secret; she comes to announce that two Guardsmen desire to speak with Des Grieux; one is a relation of Madame's (Lescaut, of course), the other, she whispers in her mistress's ear, "is a wealthy lord, who adores you!" Manon's instant exclamation "De Brétigny!" leaves us in no doubt as to the sender of the bouquet.

Lescaut and De Brétigny make a noisy entrance; the former has come, in the interests of the honour of his family, to demand of Des Grieux whether he intends to marry Manon; his behaviour is purposely offensive, and

474

there is every prospect of a lively quarrel, but the reading of part of the Chevalier's recently written letter soon leads to a friendly understanding. Lescaut's motives throughout are not altogether clear, but it is plain that he has come in order to back up De Brétigny in the plot of which we are now to learn.

Lescaut, under pretext of reading the letters in a better light, manages to draw Des Grieux to the window, thus leaving Manon and De Brétigny together. There is obviously a very good understanding between the two already, and the object of his present visit is frankly this—to induce her to forsake her present love for the sake of the far greater luxury she would enjoy under the protection of a great nobleman like himself. As a cogent argument in favour of his proposal, he informs her that the Chevalier's father has arranged to seize and carry off his son that very night.

The effect of this announcement on Manon is difficult to determine. Although she is insistent all through the scene on expressing her devotion to Des Grieux, she makes no attempt to acquaint him with the plot of which she has just heard—though she seems to waver, her mind is apparently made up, she is not proof against the 'guilty splendour' that De Brétigny is able to offer her. When Des Grieux has at last gone out to send off his letter, Manon sings the most pathetic little song imaginable, *Adieu, notre petite table!*—nothing less than a farewell to the little supper-table laid for two, at which she and her lover are about to take their last meal together.

Des Grieux, on returning, has a rather sickly but very 'favourite' number, in which he paints a picture of Manon, as he would like to see her, installed in a 'home, sweet home' cottage, with the regulation birds and all the usual accessories.

But Fate will have its way. There is a knocking without—and Manon, visibly affected and affectionate, lets her lover go out of the door through which she knows he will never re-enter. She runs to the window, however, to see him driven away, and then falls into a chair "overcome with grief."

[The amount of spoken dialogue introduced into this Act is thoroughly justified, but no device can make us accept the dramatic development. It is an attempt to depict the conflict between the worse and better instincts in Manon's character; but a psychological problem which requires page after page of good prose for its proper unfolding can hardly be compressed into one short Act of an operatic libretto. The incidents we have just witnessed, so far from winning sympathy for our heroine, merely convince us that she is *capable de tout*.]

Act III. *Scene* 1. Massenet can always be relied on for a courtly dance-measure in the olden style, and the minuet which forms the *entr'acte* with the gavotte which follows are two of his most charming examples.

The scene is a delightful one. We are in the Cours-de-la-Reine in Paris, on the day of a popular fête. There are booths, a dancing pavilion, shouting hawkers, and flocks of people. Enter the gay companions of old Guillot—Poussette, Javotte, and Rosette. They sing a little puff of a trio, and are gone in a moment. Lescaut comes next, followed by a crowd of hawkers. It appears that he is in love, for he delivers, with ludicrous sentimentality, a song in praise of a charmer. *O Rosalinde* is an excellent piece of fooling.

De Brétigny now appears. He has succeeded in retaining the affections of Manon, but it is clear from the conversation between him and Guillot that the latter will make an attempt to outbid him; for he who would hold Manon must not deny her any fancy, however costly.

Manon herself now comes on the scene, and the admiring crowd, surging round her, hazards that this must be a duchess at the very least. She has indeed changed from the simple country miss that alighted from the Arras coach; she is now a great lady, sumptuously attired, and fully aware of her powers of fascination. And yet, despite her paint and powder and profusion of jewels, she is a pathetic figure. Indeed, the only real merit of the book is the portrait of this butterfly creature, capable of a great love, yet led through the most polluted places in her insatiable quest after pleasure and jewels, ever more dazzling jewels. There is a hint of this in the famous vocal gavotte which she now sings: *Obéissons quand leur voix appelle. Carpe diem!*—snatch at the passing hour while youth is yours.

Enter the old Count des Grieux, who engages De Brétigny in conversation. Manon, drawing near, overhears that her former lover is about to renounce the world and enter the seminary of Saint-Sulpice. She contrives to manœuvre De Brétigny out of the way and introduces herself to the Count. The old gentleman then commits a fatal mistake. Thinking that he has taken the full measure of her he insinuates that his son is no longer thrall to her charms, and has in fact quite forgotten her.

Forgotten her!—that is clearly impossible, reasons Manon, and impulsive as ever she captures Cousin Lescaut there and then and bids him take her to Saint-Sulpice at once.

The spoken dialogue at the close of this Scene has been accompanied by the graceful minuet which we have already heard, but as the main characters depart the people renew their song and dance to the loud strains of the gavotte.

Scene II. The seminary of Saint-Sulpice. There is no doubt as to where this scene is laid, for the music is charged with operatic ecclesiasticism. Two *dévotes* are speaking rapturously of Des Grieux's eloquence as a preacher, and they reverently withdraw as the young seminarist enters with his father. The latter is under no illusion as to his son's vocation; he bids him go and marry a girl worthy of his rank and station; but the boy is resolute, and so with a few words of kind irony the father leaves him.

Fuyez, douce image, sings the unhappy lover, striving hard to efface the memory of Manon from his mind. But he is destined to succumb. No sooner has he left the scene than Manon herself appears, treading warily and much oppressed by the gloom of her surroundings. From within the building comes the chant of the *Magnificat.* A flood of religiosity invades Manon, and quite oblivious of the irony of her request she fervently prays to Heaven for the return of her lover.

Then Des Grieux, re-entering, comes face to face with her. He is struck dumb by this unexpected apparition: she is tearfully suppliant. Though adamant at first, he is no proof against her enchantments and flees to her arms in the end, throwing all his clerical ambition to the winds.

It is strange that other librettists omit this Scene, which is the strongest in the whole opera. Massenet, however, has made full use of the dramatic possibilities of the spectacle of earthly love, in arms, forcing the priestly citadel, and reclaiming the object of its desires.

Act IV. *Scene* 1. After a Prelude of a few bars the curtain rises on a fashionable gaming-house in Paris. Here we find a great many of our old friends—Lescaut, of course, and Poussette, Javotte, and Rosette, who though scarcely deserving of such considerate treatment, are nevertheless blessed with most charming trios throughout the piece. There are also present gay gentle-

478

men of fashion, old *roués,* professional sharpers, and hangers-on of every description, grouped about the tables.

After a terse chorus of sharpers (which might have come from *Rigoletto*) and some concerted music between Lescaut and the three merry ladies, Manon and the retrieved Des Grieux appear.

The Chevalier is in very low spirits; and well he might be, for in his blind love for Manon he has allowed himself to be drawn into very unsavoury company. But Manon is the same as ever. The clink of gold is as music in her ears, and she easily persuades her lover to try his luck at the tables, for, as a matter of fact, their own supplies are running low and Manon cannot bear poverty. The young man begins to play with old Guillot for heavy stakes, while Manon, aided by Pousette, Javotte, and Rosette, spurs him to fresh efforts by her song. With all the luck of a beginner Des Grieux manages to win heavily until old Guillot, in a rage, swears that he is cheating. A general hubbub ensues, and the old gentleman leaves the room vowing that he will be avenged. He is back in no time with the night-watch and bids them arrest the young sharper and his female accomplice. Des Grieux is overcome with shame at the charge, and the sudden entrance of his father completes his disgrace. The music now swells to a climax, reinforced by all the voices. Manon and the young man are both taken in charge by the officers, and we learn what their fate is to be. The Count's influence will procure his son's release, but Manon will go . . . "to where many of her sort have gone"—she will be deported to the West Indies.

Scene II. A short and mournful Introduction ushers in the last Scene. It is a lonely place on the road to Havre, along which the convict-gang will pass on their way to the ship. The whole scene is one of utter dreariness and hopelessness. Huddled by the roadside sits Des Grieux, bemoaning the terrible fate that has over-taken his Manon. Even at this last hour he entertains a wild hope of falling upon the escort with a body of men procured by Lescaut, and rescuing the unhappy girl. But even that hope is shattered; Lescaut, appear-ing, announces that his men have deserted him.

The soldiers' marching-song is heard in the distance; Des Grieux, driven almost to madness, proposes to at-tack them single-handed, but is persuaded in the end by Lescaut to hide behind some bushes and await develop-ments.

The marching-song draws nearer and nearer, till the soldiers debouch on the scene, escorting a motley crowd of prisoners, and plainly ashamed of their inglorious charge. From his hiding-place Des Grieux, to his ter-rible distress, learns that one of the women, Manon in fact, is already half dead.

It is now time for Lescaut to act. Accosting the sergeant, he easily bribes him to allow Manon to be left behind, on the condition that she is brought in to a neighbouring village before nightfall. Convicts and es-cort are soon on their way again, and their song gradually fades in the distance.

Once again are the two lovers united; she exhausted and remorseful, Des Grieux deliriously happy at holding her once more in his arms. He beseeches her to cease reproaching herself; the past is past and a future full of happiness is before them. But Manon knows that she is dying. With fast-waning strength she recalls the vari-ous stages of their love—the coaching inn, Paris, and Saint-Sulpice—the orchestra, meanwhile, playing softly the love-music of their first meeting.

Her whole nature seems to be purified of all its dross and tinsel by the swelling torrent of love which she draws from her lover's embrace. She can even smile at her own foibles: on Des Grieux's bidding her look up at the evening star which has just appeared, she smiles and says: "Yes! the sky is hung with jewels—and thou knowest how I always loved them!"

But the end has come. With one last kiss she cries, "I die! Better so, better so," and sinks back lifeless in the arms of her lover. A single phrase of her air in Act I, *Hélas, Manon,* is heard in the orchestra before the curtain falls on the sad story of Manon Lescaut.

THAÏS [1]

Music by MASSENET. *Words by* L. GALLET, *from* ANATOLE
FRANCE'S *romance.*
Paris, 1894; New York, 1908; London, 1911.

WE have here a striking example of the difficulty
inseparable from any attempt to turn a piece
of literature into an opera libretto. Egypt in
the fourth century of our era; the contrast between the
unbridled luxury of Alexandria and the austere asceticism
of the Cenobites or monks of the desert; a story of a holy
man who succeeded in converting the most celebrated
courtesan of the age, but nearly lost his own soul in the
effort—such are the picturesque elements from which
Anatole France evolved his famous romance of *Thaïs*.
Massenet was right in seeing in it an excellent subject for
operatic treatment, but the delicate irony of the original
has necessarily evaporated in the course of adaptation,
nor was the composer's talent of the calibre necessary to
recreate in music the spirit of Roman Egypt. Still, he
has written a picturesque opera containing much that is
attractive; there is plenty of easy-flowing melody, and
his orchestral episodes, though often simple to the point
of *naïveté*, are frequently effective.

Act I. After a short orchestral Introduction, descriptive of the quiet life of the Cenobites, the curtain rises
on the Thebaïd, the desert home of those Christian
ascetics. The old Palemon and twelve of his brother-
monks are seated at their evening meal. After a short
while the conversation turns to Athanaël (the 'Paph-
nuce' of the novel), and one gathers that he is absent

[1] This analysis is contributed by Mr. Peter Latham.

482

upon a journey. Almost immediately, however, he appears, walking slowly as though overcome by fatigue. He is greeted by the brethren and offered food, but he pushes it away, saying that his heart is too full of sorrow for him to eat. He has been to Alexandria and found it entirely given over to wickedness under the influence of Thaïs.

"Who is this Thaïs?" ask the monks.

"A vile priestess of the cult of Venus," replies Athanaël. He had known her, he goes on, in his unregenerate days, when only the grace of God had kept him from sinning with her. But now—if only he could win her soul for Christ!

Palemon gives him some wise advice against meddling with the affairs of the outside world, and the brethren, after their evening prayer, separate for the night.

Athanaël is left alone on the darkened stage, asleep in front of his cell. In his dreams he sees a vision of the theatre at Alexandria, the crowd, and Thaïs herself, representing the wanton goddess whom she serves. Starting up in horror he utters an impassioned prayer: he understands; it is God's Will that he should return to Alexandria and rescue Thaïs. Raising his voice he summons the monks, tells them of his resolve, and, disregarding the advice of Palemon, starts off again into the desert. The rest fall on their knees in prayer.

In the second Scene we are overlooking Alexandria from the terrace of the house of Nicias the philosopher. After an orchestral Prelude representing the splendour and magnificence of the city, we see Athanaël slowly approaching. The servant is at first disinclined to admit him, but soon, struck by his bearing, goes off to tell his master.

Athanaël, left alone, apostrophizes the city of his birth. "Alexandria," he says, "from thy love I have turned away my heart. For thy riches I hate thee! Ye Angels, purify with the beating of your wings the tainted air that surrounds me."

Nicias appears, accompanied by two beautiful slaves, Crobyle and Myrtale. He had known Athanaël well before the latter became a monk, and now hastens forward to welcome him. Athanaël soon acquaints him with the reason of his visit, and asks him if he knows Thaïs and where she may be found. Yes, Nicias can tell him; she is his mistress, and is to be one of his guests that very evening. He willingly agrees to Athanaël's suggestion that he, too, should be of the party, and to his request to be provided with suitable garments. But let him beware of offending Venus!

There follows an amusing scene as Crobyle and Myrtale deck out the monk in some of their master's finery, laughing the while and paying him mocking compliments. Nicias joins in, urging him to take their jesting in good part, and Athanaël completes the quartet with earnest prayers for strength.

No sooner is the toilette finished than the guests begin to arrive. They enter, Thaïs among them, to the strains of a *bizarre* march, are greeted by Nicias, and pass on to the banqueting-hall. Nicias and Thaïs are left alone, and in a short and delicate scene they agree to enjoy the evening to the full as to-morrow they are to part for ever. Athanaël soon returns and exhorts Thaïs to penitence, but she is in no mood to listen to such talk, and in an air full of grace and lascivious charm she tells him, "There is no truth but in loving—open your arms to love!" Athanaël will accept no rebuff, and tells her he will seek her again in her own house; Thaïs and Nicias, who have now been joined by the other guests, drown his voice in a repetition of the previous air, and with a gesture of horror he flies from the scene.

Act II. The house of Thaïs. She is seen surrounded by a gay company of actors and actresses, but soon dismisses them. Left alone, haunted by a fear that her beauty is on the wane, she turns for reassurance to her mirror, and in a dainty song implores Venus for the gift of everlasting youth. But she cannot stifle the inward voice that cries: "Thaïs, Thaïs, you too will grow old!" Turning round, she perceives Athanaël, who has entered quietly. Breathing a prayer against temptation he starts on his task of conversion. At first he fails to make any impression and himself almost falls a victim to her charms, for she takes him for a magician and is ready to offer herself to him in return for the secret of that eternal life of which he speaks.

"First," he cries, "leave the living death which you call life, and which destroys you, body and soul! Arise, arise! flee to the desert!"

Terrified at last, she begs him to do her no harm, but he only renews his appeal, and at length she begins to yield. At this moment, however, the voice of Nicias is heard calling for admittance, and all her self-control gives way to an outburst of petulant anger. She will not surrender to the pleading of either man. "Tell him," she says to Athanaël, "that I am not for him—nor will I follow you! I am Thaïs—Thaïs I will remain—Thaïs, who believes neither in him, nor in you, nor in your God!" She breaks down in hysterical laughter and tears as the curtain falls.

Athanaël, in no way discouraged, but taking her rejection of her former lover as a good omen, resolves to wait outside on her threshold until the morning light.

The music that follows suggests the gradual change that takes place in Thaïs' mind. The storm that has arisen does not die down immediately, but presently she becomes calmer, and, her thoughts recurring to what

485

Athanaël has said, she resolves to do as he wishes. Her conversion is symbolized by the well-known "Meditation," which has established an independent fame as a concert-piece.

Scene II. An open place in front of Thaïs' house. From across the way come sounds of music and revelry; it is Nicias and his nightly crew. The moon is low in the west, and a lamp by Thaïs' door throws a flickering light on the figure of Athanaël stretched on the pavement. After a few moments Thaïs appears and, recognizing Athanaël, tells him she is willing to obey him. What are his commands? Not far from Alexandria, he tells her, there is a community of holy women; thither he will take her. But first she must prove the sincerity of her resolve—she must burn her house and all that it contains. This she will do; she pleads only for a little statue of Eros; it is so beautiful; may it not be spared? But Athanaël, hearing that it is a gift from Nicias, dashes it angrily to the ground, where it is shattered to fragments. He and Thaïs then enter the house to set it alight.

No sooner have they disappeared than Nicias and his friends come out from the house opposite. They are in high spirits and express their determination to keep up the revels till long after sunrise.

Here, appropriately enough, Massenet has inserted the ballet which at that time was essential to any work that aspired to a performance at the Paris Opéra. On other stages, however, this is often omitted and the play goes straight on.

Athanaël reappears at Thaïs' door and is recognized by the revellers. At first they misconstrue his appearance at such a place and such a time, but very soon his words and the appearance of Thaïs in a rough dress ready for the journey reveal to them the true state of affairs. At the same moment a wisp of smoke from the house shows that Athanaël has been as good as his word. At once a shout of protest is raised: Thaïs must not be allowed to leave them; as for Athanaël, to the gallows with him! The group of revellers, now enlarged to a crowd by the advent of a number of people who have been attracted by the noise, becomes more and more angry, and stones are thrown; it is Nicias who, by the ingenious device of scattering the contents of his purse upon the ground, succeeds in distracting their attention, and, lit by the flames of the burning house, Thaïs and Athanaël make good their escape.

Act III takes us to an oasis in the desert. The sight of some women who come in silence to draw water from the well suggests that the religious house mentioned by Athanaël is not far off. The music portrays alternately the cool waters of the oasis and the heat of the sun through which Thaïs and her guide are struggling on their toilsome journey. Presently they appear, Thaïs half-dead with fatigue, and Athanaël pitilessly urging her onward; only when she stumbles and he has to catch her to prevent her falling does he consent to call a halt. And now a sudden change manifests itself in him. From hurling curses on her past iniquities he turns to blessing her present attitude—their journey's end is near, he says, but for a while she must rest. He departs to fetch some water and gather fruit, and on his return they join in a duet of pious rejoicing as they eat their meal. Immediately after, voices are heard intoning a Paternoster, and the holy women appear, led by their abbess, Albina. Athanaël briefly explains to her the situation, and with a few tender words of farewell entrusts Thaïs to her care. "Farewell," replies Thaïs, "farewell for ever!" Athanaël starts. "For ever?" he exclaims. But the procession has already moved away. Once more we hear the music of the "Meditation" as Athanaël, left alone, gives way to words of passionate regret in no wise suitable to his monkish habit.

With *Scene* II we return to the Thebaïd. A storm is threatening, and the monks, having supped, are already preparing to disperse to their cells, when Athanaël appears. Since his return from his journey he has neither eaten nor drunk, in a vain attempt to drive out by his austerities the pride he feels at his success and the vision of Thaïs by which he is haunted. Flinging himself at the feet of Palemon he confesses his temptation and invokes his aid. But Palemon has no counsel to give him—he must fight his own battle. He sleeps, and in a vision he sees Thaïs as she appeared to him at Nicias' banquet. Suddenly she disappears, and he hears a voice—"Thaïs of Alexandria is about to die!" Rising in a frenzy of passion and despair he abjures his hopes of Heaven and rushes off into the gathering storm.

Scene III. The music calms down and it is to the quiet strains of the "Meditation" that the curtain rises for the last time on the garden of Albina's convent. In the middle, under a fig-tree, lies Thaïs, dying. Round her are assembled the nuns praying for her soul. Albina speaks of her virtues: "For three months she has watched, wept, prayed, without ceasing—cruel penances have marred the beauty of her body, but her soul is washed clean of every stain."

Soon a tumult in the orchestra heralds the arrival of Athanaël. Albina greets him, but at the sight of Thaïs he forgets all else and throws himself down by her bed. She opens her eyes, recognizes him, and speaks of their journey together, while the orchestra once again plays the melody of the "Meditation." But it is only earthly love that he now desires, and in strangled accents he begs her to live—for him. Thaïs is deaf to all his appeals.

She is beyond earthly things, and in great soaring phrases sings of the angels whom she sees coming to take her soul. The heavens open, and, stretching out her arms toward the celestial vision, she expires. Athanaël gives a wild cry, "She is dead!" and the curtain falls.

CAVALLERIA RUSTICANA

Music by MASCAGNI. *Words by* TARGIONI-TOZZETTI *and*
MENASCI.
Rome, 1890; *London,* 1891; *New York,* 1891.

AT the time of its production this short, realistic
opera, with its straightforward story of love and
revenge, its swinging rhythm, and the irresistible
Intermezzo, had an enormous success, and great hopes
were entertained of the composer's future. These have
never been fulfilled. Although he has written many
other operas, Mascagni is known the world over merely
as the composer of *Cavalleria Rusticana.*

The plot of the opera is taken from a Sicilian tale by
Giovanni Verga, out of which the librettists have woven
a sordid but effective drama of love, hate, jealousy, and
revenge. Turiddu, a Sicilian peasant, on returning from
army service, finds that his old love, Lola, has married
a young carter, Alfio. He consoles himself by making
love to Santuzza, and his advances meet with more than
adequate response. As is the way of human nature,
however, Turiddu tires of his easy conquest and hankers
after his old allegiance. Lola, delighted to have an opportunity of revenging herself upon Santuzza, of whom
she is wildly jealous, encourages him. Santuzza, when it
dawns upon her that Turiddu is tired of her and, crowning insult, is making love to Lola again, very naturally
enlightens Alfio. Alfio kills Turiddu, and the curtain
falls upon general woe and lamentation.

Very effective is the temporary interruption of the
orchestral Prelude by a tenor solo sung behind the curtain by Turiddu, *O Lola, bianca come fior di spino;* this

490

was an absolutely new idea at the time, and one which the composer's rival, Leoncavallo, did not hesitate to imitate two years later in *Pagliacci*.

The curtain rises to disclose a picturesque market square in a Sicilian village bathed in sunlight. On the right a church lends an air of additional peace to a naturally tranquil scene. The natural complement of the church, the village inn, stands on the left-hand side next to a little cottage.

Festivity is in the air—for it is Easter Day—as one may gather from the little parties of men and women, gaily dressed, who hurry across the square to church, and from the joyous ringing of the bells. To complete the picture, a band of peasants passes by, singing the praises of youth and spring—it is well-nigh impossible to believe these happy surroundings are to be the setting of a tragedy. But now Santuzza, entering, makes her way over to the tavern where Lucia, Turiddu's mother, lives. Her suspicions at once begin to darken the scene. At first only vague, they are strengthened by Lucia's innocent report of her son's doings; she says that he went the night before into a neighbouring hamlet for wine, but Santuzza replies that he was seen that very night in the village. Their conversation is interrupted by the entrance of Alfio, a cheerful young carter, with a crowd of peasants. He sings a rollicking song of the road, *Il cavallo scalpita*, which certainly clears the atmosphere. When the crowd have melted away, Alfio, friendly and talkative, unwittingly discloses the fact that he saw Turiddu near his cottage that morning, thus confirming Santuzza's worst suspicions. But now the organ sounds, so, bidding them go to Mass without him, Alfio departs.

The action is interrupted by the entry of the chorus, who, ranging themselves across the stage, sing the *Regina Cœli* to a strain which is repeated in the first part of the famous *Intermezzo.* This is followed by the Easter Hymn *Inneggiamo, il Signor non è morto,* led by Santuzza. The hymn finished, the peasants again enter the church, leaving Santuzza and Lucia alone. The former relates the story of Turiddu's faithlessness in the aria *Voi lo sapete, o mamma,* almost breaking down in the agony of her emotion. Lucia, failing in her attempts to comfort, goes into church to pray for her.

The inevitable collision between Santuzza and Turiddu now occurs. In reply to his protests that he did, indeed, go to Francofonte, the village, for wine, Santuzza retorts that he was seen at dawn stealing from Lola's, or rather Alfio's, cottage. She has evidently hit upon the truth; able at last to give expression to long suppressed grievances, Santuzza works herself into a pitch of frenzy. The more Turiddu urges he has ceased to care for her, the more violently she affirms her love for him. Then comes a dramatic moment. Lola is heard without, singing a charming *stornello*—one of those short snatches of song so popular in Sicily—*Fior di giaggiolo.* On her entry she understands the situation at a glance, and takes a malicious pleasure in aggravating it. Lola feels quite sure of her position—she can safely jeer at her discarded rival. What! Santuzza! neighbour Turiddu! still lingering to gossip! Why are they not at Mass? "Lola," says Santuzza, "this is Easter Day—our Lord is risen— He is with us, and sees all things. Only those whose conscience is clear dare go to Mass to-day." "Then," replies Lola, "I thank the Lord that *I* dare!" and with a toss of the head and a challenging glance to Turiddu, she enters the church.

The unequal combat between the other two is renewed in the duet *No, no, Turiddu,* which works up to a climax where the exasperated man flings Santuzza brutally to the ground, and hurries to join Lola in the church.

Crushed, exhausted, the girl does not stir until the arrival of Alfio puts new life in her—the life of hate, the desire of revenge. She has only to tell the young Sicilian the bare facts of Lola's relations with Turiddu, and the tragic sequel becomes inevitable; Alfio is changed to a madman, thirsting for vengeance without delay (*Ad essi non perdono, vendetta avrò*).

Now follows the famous *Intermezzo* which from the first made such a sensational and universal success as has not since been equalled. Yet it is doubtful whether its real merit is generally appreciated. To countless thousands, who may or may not have seen the opera, it appeals as a series of luscious melodic phrases with a rhythmic swing that is irresistible—in fact as 'a rattling good time.' But it is much more than this—the *Intermezzo* is an essential part of *Cavalleria Rusticana*, and loses half its value when detached from its proper environment. The manner of its introduction is masterly. We have been listening to a tale of passion and wrong, of fiery love and hate—a broken-hearted girl has just left the stage, and a jealous madman crying out for blood—we know that tragedy is close at hand. Now the stage is empty, but the curtain is not lowered; we are left to the contemplation of the inanimate scene before us while the *Intermezzo* is begin played.

It has been said that the function of the orchestra in Wagnerian music-drama is, like that of the chorus in Greek tragedy, to afford a running commentary on the action of the piece; that is undoubtedly Mascagni's intention in the *Intermezzo*. We see before us the quiet village, the small white houses glowing golden in the sunlight under a pure Sicilian sky. There is the tavern, for refreshment and good-fellowship—there is the church for prayer and adoration, where all the homely joys of every life are blessed and sanctioned, and where the weary body is brought to welcome rest at last. As we gaze and listen we pass into a dream of peace and beauty—it is a scene where "all but the spirit of man is divine"—and we wake to realize what a sorry mess man is prone to make of it.

It is a sense of this violent contrast that Mascagni's music should convey to us. At the same time it is obvious that the art of the scene-painter is here raised to a quite unique importance; not the most elaborate and costly setting for *Parsifal* or *The Ring* can ever have a tithe of the artistic significance contained in this simple picture which we absorb, as it were, through two senses while we listen to the *Intermezzo*.

Mass is over and the people come out of church, Turiddu with Lola at his side; he invites them all to join him at his mother's tavern across the square. His drinking-song, *Viva il vino spumeggiante,* is barely ended when Alfio comes up; one look at his face is enough to drive the women off the stage. Turiddu offers him a cup of wine; Alfio dashes it aside and challenges him to a duel, which is accepted in the Sicilian fashion, by an embrace and a bite of the ear. Alfio goes off while Turiddu remains to take a pathetic farewell of his mother; he is leaving home for a time, he tells her, and commends Santuzza to her care, if he should not return. [Musically this is one of the most effective moments of the opera.] The poor woman is not left long in bewilderment—Santuzza enters and falls weeping on her neck; the others wander back in twos and threes, uneasy with a presentiment of coming trouble. The orchestra prepares us for the climax with a succession of arresting chords and a mutter of drums; then shrieks are heard outside, and a woman rushes on with the cry, "Turiddu is dead! Someone has killed poor Turiddu!" The curtain falls on the horrified crowd closing round the senseless forms of Santuzza and Mother Lucia.

Cavalleria Rusticana has held the stage for thirty-five years, and its popularity to-day is hardly diminished; it has outlived the excessive laudation with which it was first received, as well as the many severe criticisms that have since been passed upon it. Like the story, the music is generally too melodramatic, occasionally violent, in its method, and truth of expression is often sacrificed to the impulse of a too insistent rhythm. Yet when the composer can resist this tendency—as, for example, in Santuzza's song, *Voi lo sapete, o mamma,* and Turiddu's farewell to his mother—he is truly and powerfully dramatic. His gift of fresh, spontaneous melody never fails him; above all, from first to last he is passionately sincere. Of the many Italian operas written since the death of Verdi, *Cavalleria Rusticana* is the one that would seem to have the best chance of survival.

PAGLIACCI

Words and Music by LEONCAVALLO.
Milan, 1892; London, 1893; New York, 1893.

LEONCAVALLO'S tense and vivid musical drama shares with Mascagni's *Cavalleria Rusticana* the distinction of having founded the modern Italian school of *verismo* (realism), which Mr Krehbiel trounces so soundly in his *Second Book of Operas*. The composer has told us that the plot was suggested by incidents in real life which had deeply impressed him as a boy. The realistic note is boldly insisted upon at the very outset by the famous Prologue, which, though imitating Mascagni in the interruption of the orchestra by a vocal solo, contains an idea that is quite original.

As a rule the Prologue to a play is either a short *résumé* of the plot, or an apologetic reminder of the fact that, after all, it is 'only play-acting.' But here, when the Clown suddenly thrusts his whitened face through the curtain to beg a word with us, it is something very different that he has to say. "Our story," he declares, "is a true one—the incidents are real, and, what is more, we people on the stage are real men and women, with passions like yourselves; often we are cast for parts for which we are but little in sympathy at the moment—so be sorry for us, since, as you know, it is hard to have to play the clown when one's heart is breaking. And one thing more: the saying that 'all the world's a stage' may also be read backward, if you please; sometimes the real tragedies of life are played out on the stage, as you will shortly see. Up with the curtain!"

People are accustomed to enjoy the fine dramatic stuff

of the Prologue to *Pagliacci,* much as they do the "Star of Eve" song in *Tannhäuser,* without troubling to understand its precise meaning: that meaning is certainly not quite clear, but the above paraphrase, we think, conveys its true intention.

The opera is a play within a play; the incidents of the First Act result in the crude farce that is presented in Act II being turned into an actual tragedy. *Pagliacci* is the Italian name for those strolling players, or mountebanks, who are a feature of village festivals all over Italy; the little play around which Leoncavallo's tragedy turns is a typical example of the entertainment they have to offer. The characters are the conventional ones that have been handed down for centuries—Columbine, Harlequin her lover, Pagliaccio (or First Clown, we may here call him) her husband, and Taddeo (Second Clown). Harlequin makes love to Columbine, Taddeo catches them at it, and runs to fetch Pagliaccio; in the regular sequel the husband's part is to be held up to ridicule, and chased off the stage by Harlequin, but in the opera this little knockabout show is not allowed to run its natural course, and the end is very different. However, all this occurs in the Second Act, to which the First is in the nature of a prelude.

Act I. A blazing afternoon in an Italian village. It is the Feast of the Assumption, so there can be no question of work for anyone; the peasants are all out to welcome the troupe of *pagliacci,* whose theatre is seen set up already in a field, with a hunchback to guard it. This is Tonio, who has just sung the Prologue; in the little play he takes the part of Taddeo. The others now arrive, almost mobbed by the excited people, who have to be called to silence by the loud beating of a drum; the drummer is Canio, the proprietor of the show, and the Pagliaccio of the little play. With him are Nedda the Columbine, who is his wife off the stage as well as on, and Beppe, who plays Harlequin. Canio invites them all to come and see the show at seven that evening, and, as the church bell rings, the peasants troop off to Vespers, singing a very charming chorus, *Din don! suona vespero.*

By this time an incident has occurred that throws light on the relations between Canio and his pretty wife, Nedda. On her arrival Tonio has stepped forward to help her to descend from the cart in which she is seated, but Canio sends him back with a box on the ear, and lifts his wife down himself. The peasants roar with laughter, regarding it as a foretaste of the fun to come, but Tonio slinks away muttering threats of vengeance, and Nedda has seen a look in her husband's face which frightens her. Canio goes off to the tavern with some villagers, and Nedda believes herself to be alone.

We soon learn that her husband has good cause for his jealousy; she is afraid of him; but, light of heart as she is light of love, she can give herself up wholly to the charm of the glorious sunshine. A passing flight of birds attracts her fancy, and she addresses them in the popular 'ballatella,' *Stridono lassù.* These "feathered *zingari* of the air," whither do they journey? What seek they? They know not; only their vague desires lead them to wander, and Fate directs their course: in them she sees a symbol of herself.

The words of this song are contrived with considerable skill to fit the situation; the melody, unfortunately, is frankly banal, though helped by some graceful and effective orchestration.

Tonio, who has been in hiding, now comes forward to plead his cause with Nedda. The hunchback is madly in love with her, and in spite of her contemptuous refusal his passion grows more and more violent until, at

498

last, she is obliged in self-defense to strike him with a whip. The blow is her own death-warrant.

The music is not adequate to the strong situation. Tonio's monologue, *So ben chè difforme*, was the favourite 'sob-stuff' of sentimental baritones for many a year; the English version, though not very close to the original, conveys a just impression of the quality of the music:

> I know that you hate me, and laugh in derision—
>   For what is the Jester? He plays but a part;
> Yet he has his dream and his hope and his vision—
>   The Clown has a heart!
> And ah, when you pass me, uncaring, unseeing,
>   You know not my sorrow, so cruel and sweet;
> I give you my spirit, my life, and my being,
>   I die at your feet!

After the maddened hunchback is gone, Nedda's accepted lover appears—Silvio, a young farmer, who has been for some time smitten with the pretty Columbine, and has now come to urge her to fly with him. Their long duet is effectively varied, but the leading love-*motif*, with its perpetual triple rhythm, is too much in the vein of the solo we have lately had from Tonio, and it must be remembered that both the parts are for baritone.

The lovers have just agreed to meet at midnight when Canio, guided by Tonio, rushes on in time to hear his wife's words: "To-night, and for ever, I am thine," but the man to whom they are addressed is already out of sight. Canio goes in frenzied pursuit, but returns baffled. Nedda, of course, will not disclose her lover's name: maddened by her refusal, her husband rushes at her with a knife, and is stopped only just in time by Beppe and Tonio. The latter persuades Canio to postpone his vengeance till after the show; Nedda's lover will probably be among the spectators, and means may be found to make him betray himself. Meanwhile all must go and dress for the evening performance.

Canio is left alone on the scene; yet he too must follow the rest, plaster his face with white and red, and put on the comical garments of the Clown. The people pay him to make them laugh, and he must laugh with them —laugh, though his love is faithless, laugh, though his heart is broken.

This soliloquy, known as *Vesti la giubba,* is in a way the complement of the famous Prologue; both are excellent examples of the purely emotional type of music by virtue of which this opera makes its strong popular appeal.

Act II. Our mountebanks are preparing for the little crowd that is hurrying up from all sides to see the show. Tonio beats the big drum and does the shouting, while Beppe looks after the women and tries to keep them from quarrelling. When enough people have assembled, Nedda goes round from bench to bench to take the money; Silvio is already in the front row, and as he pays for his place he reminds her of their assignation for to-night. So all is ready for the tragedy which we know must follow.

But, first, the unsuspecting peasants must enjoy the fun for which they have paid—the curtains of the tiny stage are parted, and the simple farce begins.

The music now takes on a welcome change. Instead of long, cloying phrases of violent passion or clammy sentiment, we are glad to listen for a time to clean dance-music and airs with an old-fashioned grace. Columbine (Nedda) is alone on the stage, but not for long; though her husband, as she tells us, is away for the night, someone else is evidently expected. The minuet which serves for her short solo stops as the sound of a guitar is heard outside. Columbine listens with rapture to the voice of Harlequin (Beppe), who sings a serenade which belongs to that delightful world of music from which passion is excluded. But she does not admit him yet. Taddeo (Tonio) has first to appear—he has been to market, and proceeds to lay his basket and his heart at Columbine's feet. The first part of the scene is pure burlesque, but when Columbine, weary of his nonsense, tells him to be off, we get a dramatic surprise. In order to remind us that it is really Tonio, not poor Taddeo, with whom Nedda has now to reckon, the music of the scene in Act I where the hunchback pleads and is rejected in similar fashion is repeated note for note. But when Harlequin jumps in at the window, we are back again in the world of unreality—he kicks poor Taddeo out of the room, and the audience roars with laughter.

Harlequin and Columbine now sup together to the strains of an intimate little gavotte, and all goes merrily until Taddeo rushes in to warn them that Columbine's husband, Pagliaccio, has returned before his time—he knows all, and is on their track. The spectators are delighted at Taddeo's droll manner, and the way in which the plot is developing.

Harlequin leaps out of the window, and Canio, as Pagliaccio, enters just in time to hear his wife call after her stage-lover the very words she had used in the real situation in the First Act: "This night, and for ever, I am thine, love!" He strives hard to keep within the spirit of his part, but the question which he has to put to Columbine: "Who has been with thee? Tell me his name!" and her stubborn refusal force him back into the world of reality. He will act no more: "No!" he cries, "I'll play the Clown no longer! I am a man again, and my poor bleeding heart calls out for blood— blood to wipe out your shame and mine, accursed woman!"

The spectators are quite carried away by excitement, and wildly applaud what they consider a splendid piece of acting. Nedda, as Columbine, makes a brave effort to get back to the play; to the tune of the recent gavotte she assures him, coquettishly, that the man who has just left her was only Harlequin—poor, harmless Harlequin!

But the tension is too great—the storm of passion breaks loose. After one more terrible "Tell me your lover's name!" and one last cutting "No!" from Nedda, the audience wake up to the truth—there is murder in Canio's words and looks. Some of the women leave in terror. Silvio is on the alert; he has drawn his knife, but is held back by those around him. Nedda tries to escape into the audience, but Canio is too quick for her— she falls to the ground, his knife between her shoulders. In her death-agony she calls instinctively on her lover: "Help, Silvio!"

So Tonio was right! In an instant Canio has leapt from the stage and stabbed Silvio to the heart.

It is all over. The knife drops from his listless hands as the poor Clown turns, in dazed fashion, to the audience and addresses them for the last time: "The play is finished."

Pagliacci and *Cavalleria Rusticana* were for a long time the Tweedledum and Tweedledee of the operatic world; dispute would grow hot as to their relative merits. Leoncavallo's work is obviously the more subtle conception of the two, and shows a far greater talent for orchestration: moreover, we must not forget that Leoncavallo was fortunately able to write his own words, and the 'book' of *Pagliacci* is no mean achievement.

In *Cavalleria Rusticana,* on the other hand, Mascagni excels by a constant flow of broad, spontaneous, vocal melody, in which his rival was conspicuously lacking, and

502

this, when combined with a strong libretto, such as we have here, is the best guarantee of a long life for any opera. At the present time it seems probable that both these works, in spite of their many weaknesses, will survive all the many imitations that have succeeded them.

LA BOHÈME

Music by Puccini. *Words by* Illica *and* Giacosa,
from Murger's *romance.*
Turin, 1896; *London,* 1897; *New York,* 1898.

LOVERS of Henry Murger's *Scènes de la vie de
Bohème,* a series of brilliant sketches of student-
life in Paris's *Quartier Latin* toward the middle
of the last century, were inclined to look askance at any
attempt to consolidate such slight material into a four-
Act opera libretto. The book, while possessing a fantastic charm and a definite literary quality, was entirely
lacking in dramatic interest, and yet Puccini was assuredly justified in his choice; the subject was well suited
to his picturesque methods, and with the aid of two
skilful librettists [1] he has contrived a very pretty entertainment. Of all his operas *La Bohème* is the most pleasing, and will probably prove the most enduring.

The work is divided into four short Acts; each one
is prefaced in the vocal score with a quotation from the
novel; the *leit-motif* to the whole, in a literary sense, is
to be found in the phrase, "A gay life but a terrible
one," which the librettists have taken from the French
writer's admirable preface. Certain incidents susceptible
of musical or dramatic treatment have been detached
from the lengthy original and are connected by a sufficiently coherent thread of interest. The music is beautifully orchestrated at all points, and catches exactly the
spirit of each scene, grave or gay.

Act I. (*In the Attic.*) The curtain rises almost im-

[1] My thanks are due to Messrs G. Ricordi and Co. for permitting
me to use their text of the opera.

mediately and discloses a typical Bohemian studio of a poverty-stricken aspect. Though it is Christmas Eve there is no fire in the stove. Two of the 'faithful,' Rudolf the poet and Marcel the painter, are seen; the one looking pensively out of the window, as is the way of poets, and the other at work on his masterpiece, "The Passage of the Red Sea." We hear a vigorous phrase in the orchestra which stands for the whole of the Latin Quarter brood, with their "gay and terrible" life: it often reappears in the course of the opera.

Marcel complains of the cold, and Rudolf answers with a charming phrase from his big aria in the scene with Mimi later in this Act. Naturally the conversation soon turns to love, but even this fiery topic does not suffice for warmth, so Rudolf, in a fit of abnegation, sacrifices the manuscript of his latest tragedy to provide fuel. While they warm themselves, Colline, a philosopher, enters, frozen with cold, and in no good humour: he throws a large bundle of books tied up in a handkerchief on the table—volumes which he has been unsuccessful in pawning. A trio follows, as more of the manuscript goes to feed the flames, when, unexpectedly, two boys come in bearing food, wine, cigars, and fuel for the fire which they set down before the astonished eyes of the three. Schaunard, a musician, who completes the Bohemian quartet, enters triumphantly; he has been playing to an English *milord,* who naturally is fabulously wealthy, and the musician, faithful to tradition, has incontinently spent his reward. But he refuses to allow his comrades to eat indoors on the night of the Christmas vigil, and puts away the provisions in a cupboard. "You may drink here," he says, "but you must dine in the Latin Quarter!" As they are filling their glasses a knock is heard: it is the landlord, a person of benevolent aspect,

505

come to collect the rent. The quartet manage with wine and jest to divert him from his purpose, and finally bundle the befuddled old man out of the room. The whole of this scene is treated with the greatest vivacity. Marcel, Colline, and Schaunard now propose going out; the poet has an article for a new journal to finish; he promises to join them later.

Rudolf has not been long at work before there is a timid knock, and a female voice is heard, complaining that her candle has been blown out. It is Mimi, the little seamstress who lives on the floor above; immediately on her entrance she is seized with a fit of coughing, and—how the word dates her!—'swoons'! Rudolf, helpless after the manner of his sex, sprinkles a little water on her face, and she revives on hearing him comment audibly on her charms. Whether this determines her subsequent manœuvres it is hard to say, but she makes for the door, only to find that she has left her key behind: her candle again goes out: then his: and the two are left in darkness hunting for the key. Rudolf finds it but secretes it in his pocket, and perjures his immortal soul in emphatic denial of its whereabouts. Soon, as will have been guessed, the hands of these two young people touch and Rudolf gives voice to the famous aria *Che gelida mannina*. Mimi, who, for a prima donna, has listened with commendable silence, now feels it is time the poet gave way to her, so she follows with the equally famous aria, *Mi chiamano Mimi*.

The moon (ah, faithful, punctual moon!) has risen and brightens the room: in the courtyard Rudolf's friends are calling out to him to come down: their voices fade into the distance, and Rudolf, turning from the window, sees Mimi encircled by the moonlight. The theme of the poet's big song is played very softly on

506

the orchestra and marks the beginning of the short scene which Caruso and Melba used to make so memorable.

Mimi tells Rudolf to go off and join his friends, but coyly suggests that she too might come. The infatuated poet does not, apparently, read in this request the sign-manual of the coquette; so they go out into the night together.

Act II. (*In the Latin Quarter.*) "Christmas Eve: a square flanked by shops of all sorts; on one side a café. A vast motley crowd: soldiers, serving-maids, children, students, work-girls, gendarmes, etc. Shop-keepers are crying their wares." Such are the stage directions. Rather apart from this bustling scene Rudolf and Mimi are walking up and down together, and the other Bohemians can be recognized here and there. Puccini has built up an excellent concerted piece at the beginning of the Act, a Scene which is a pleasure both to eye and ear.

Mimi displays a distinctly acquisitive instinct, and makes straight for the milliner's, where the unfortunate Rudolf has to purchase a bonnet for her: then she art-lessly admires a necklace in a jeweller's shop, but this time the poet will not be drawn.

Presently Colline, Schaunard, and Marcel come out of the café carrying a table, and are at once noted by the eagle-eye of Mimi, who insists on joining them: she is formally introduced by Rudolf.

A charming little interlude is provided by the entrance of Parpignol the toymaker, with a gaily painted little barrow festooned with foliage and flowers and painted lanterns, followed by a crowd of merry urchins: unfor-tunately for the young rascals their mothers are in the vicinity, so they are bundled off to bed.

An extremely pretty girl, followed by a pompous, over-dressed old gentleman, now comes in: this is Musetta, a lady of light virtue but great charm, with her latest admirer, whom she treats like a dog. She is well known to the Bohemians and particularly to Marcel, an early flame of hers: the oddly matched couple sit down at a table opposite to the others, and the lady proceeds to give an exhibition of histrionics, mainly with the idea of attracting Marcel's attention: the poor man is doing his best to resist the fascination of the heartless little wretch, but when she sings the best-known tune in the opera, *Quando men vo soletta per la via,* he has to be restrained by force from rushing over to her. Alcindoro, the aged beau, is scandalized! Colline, as befits a philosopher, and Schaunard also are deeply interested in the psychology of the scene, and their comments as well as the conversations of Mimi and Rudolf are all woven into the texture of the music with great skill.

Finally Musetta hits on an old ruse—the manœuvre of the tight shoe—and screams the place down until Alcindoro rushes off to buy another pair: as soon as he disappears, Marcel and Musetta embrace with much fervour.

But we are not done with excitement yet: drums in the distance herald a tattoo, and the people run here and there, not knowing from which direction the soldiers will come. They enter on the left, headed by a gigantic drum-major, dexterously wielding a baton. The Bohemians calmly tell the waiter that Alcindoro will settle *both* the bills, and prepare to leave, in such a way as to draw the attention of all around them. Musetta, being without her shoe, cannot walk, so Marcel and Colline must carry her: they are given an ovation by the crowd, who proceed to follow after the soldiers. Alcindoro now returns and is confronted with the two bills—one of a prodigious length. He subsides into a chair as the curtain

falls. So ends what is one of the merriest scenes in the
whole range of modern Italian Opera.

Act III. (*The Barrière d'Enfer.*) A cheerless dawn
over a snow-covered landscape toward the close of Feb-
ruary—conditions that temporarily justify such a description as the 'gateway of hell' for the toll-gate on the
Orleans road leading to Paris.

Marcel and Musetta now live together in a tavern near
by and earn their living, one by painting signboards, and
the other by teaching singing. A light burns in the
tavern, from which sounds of joviality are heard coming
even at this late hour: Musetta strikes in with a few
bars of her waltz-song.

The coldness and dreariness of the scene are cleverly
painted in the music. Men and women on their way to
work pass through the toll-gate, and as the light grows
Mimi comes in looking anxiously about her: she is seized
with a violent fit of coughing, but, recovering herself,
asks a serving-woman who has come out of the inn to
tell Marcel she is there. As she waits, a bell in a convent near by rings for Matins. Marcel is very surprised
to see her; he tells her how Musetta and he have been
earning their living, and diffidently adds that Rudolf is
asleep in the tavern. Poor Mimi bursts into tears, she
declares that she cannot go to him, for though he loves
her he is madly jealous—with cause, one suspects. Marcel suggests a separation and promises his help. Mimi
is again shaken with coughing, and then, as Rudolf is
waking, Marcel advises her to hide behind a tree and
hear what passes. Rudolf comes out and at once says he
wants a separation from Mimi on account of her heart-
lessness and constant flirtations: then suddenly the poet
retracts his hard words, and works himself into a passion
of tender solicitude—he loves her still, and fears she is

dying from the awful cough which never leaves her. This upsets the poor girl behind the tree so much that she forgets her concealment and betrays her presence by her sobbing. The lovers are swept into each other's arms; and Marcel, whether from tact or necessity, rushes into the tavern.

Releasing herself from Rudolf's embrace Mimi sings the beautiful little aria which is founded on her song in the First Act: very softly a solo violin rises above the rest of the orchestra with one of the phrases heard under such different conditions before, and then the music swells into a passionate climax which merges into the final quartet. The two sing tenderly of past joys, but their reminiscences are rudely broken into by a sound of breaking plates and glasses from the tavern: Musetta runs out pursued by Marcel: she has been caught flirting! The two have a pretty quarrel, unheeded by Mimi and Rudolf. Calling each other by abusive names they go back into the inn; the other two, oblivious to all the world in the new joy of reconciliation, move away arm in arm and are heard singing in the distance as the curtain falls.

Act IV. (*In the Attic.*) The scene is the same as in the First Act: Marcel and Rudolf are pretending to work—a usual state of affairs—but are really trying to draw information from each other about their respective mistresses, who, it seems, have once more deserted them. Rudolf has seen Musetta in a *coupé,* Marcel has caught a glimpse of Mimi in a carriage, apparelled like a duchess. Both men pretend not to care, but the duet which follows shows that they are longing for reunion. Rudolf even gets maudlin over Mimi's rose-pink bonnet, which he fondles as he sings.

Schaunard and Colline coming in now, with four rolls

510

and a herring, reveal the poverty-stricken condition of the commissariat: the four try to imagine their poor fare is, in reality, a fine dinner. To keep up their spirits they indulge in some rather obvious foolery which takes the form of a mock dance and fight: when this is at its height the door suddenly opens and Musetta enters in a state of great agitation: Mimi, she says, is there, but scarcely strong enough to climb the staircase. The poor little consumptive is brought in by Rudolf, and, with the help of the others, is put into the bed. Musetta relates how she had found her (having left her old viscount) almost dying—but longing to be near Rudolf. The orchestra plays the tune of her first song, which colours the whole scene. The Bohemians are in a fix—no food, no warmth for the dying girl, who for the moment is better and glad to be with her friends.

Musetta determines to pawn her ear-rings and Colline his coat, to which he bids an emotional farewell. They all go out leaving Mimi and Rudolf alone: the orchestra now plays a phrase of the poet's song and, as the scene progresses, snatches of tunes before heard are played or sung with pathetic significance. Mimi, with the old instinct of coquetry still strong in her, bids Rudolf tell her if she is still pretty; she recalls their first meeting, the ruse of the key, sings very softly his words, "Your tiny hand is frozen! let me warm it into life!" Then a sudden spasm shakes her, terrifying Rudolf! But she recovers as the others come in, Musetta with the muff the poor little creature so longs for, and Marcel with a phial: the doctor will follow as quickly as he can. Childishly happy with the muff, Mimi gently falls asleep. Musetta, busied in preparing the medicine, murmurs a prayer for her companion, and the others whisper together in a corner.

Schaunard is the first to see that Mimi is dead; he tells

511

Marcel, but they dare not break the news to Rudolf, until their strange looks and sunken voices force him to realize what has happened; he flings himself on Mimi's bed sobbing, while the others stand round, grief-stricken, as the curtain falls.

MADAMA BUTTERFLY

Music by PUCCINI. *Words by* ILLICA *and* GIACOSA.
Milan, 1904; *London,* 1905; *New York,* 1906.

PUCCINI had achieved two great successes in the operatic world with *La Bohème* (1896) and *La Tosca* (1900), and therefore might reasonably have expected to add to his laurels upon the first production of *Madama Butterfly* (1904). But the Italian public is not, like the British, a respecter of persons, however celebrated, and evidences of displeasure were manifest soon after the rise of the curtain at the Scala: these gave way later to hoots and hisses in the best Italian style.

The curious thing is that no one appears to know why these things occurred. Some put forward the unfamiliarity of the stage setting as a reason, others (which seems more probable) the inadequacy of the singers; it has also been suggested that playing the opera in only two Acts provoked resentment.

Whatever the cause, when the work, revised, slightly shortened, and with Act II played in two parts, was given at Brescia only a few months after, it obtained a brilliant reception, and has since gone the round of all the opera houses with unvarying success.

The plot is drawn from a play by David Belasco which is actually a heavily sentimentalized version of Pierre Loti's *Madame Chrysanthème*. It is, for an opera, very simple and straightforward, and is founded on the time-honoured tradition that a sailor has a wife in every port.[1]

[1] My thanks are due to Messrs G. Ricordi and Co. for permitting me to use their text of the opera.

513

The situation before the curtain rises is quickly told. Pinkerton, a young U.S. naval lieutenant stationed at Nagasaki, has determined to make 'a Japanese marriage' with a pretty young *geisha,* Cho-Cho-San, with whom he fancies himself to be in love.

Having bought a house for the honeymoon, he has come to inspect it on the wedding day.

Act I. A Japanese house, terrace, and garden. Below, in the background, the bay, the harbour, and the town of Nagasaki.

A short and vigorous Prelude opens the First Act, during which, as well as at other times in the opera, fragments of Japanese tunes give effective touches of local colour. On the rise of the curtain we behold B. F. Pinkerton—radiant in the uniform of a lieutenant in the U.S. Navy, with Goro, euphemistically described as a marriage-broker. This egregious personage is explaining, "obsequiously and with much bowing and scraping," cleverly suggested in the music, the many advantages of the house that Pinkerton has hired for his temporary ménage, and which is full of the most ingenious contrivances. The inspection over, Goro claps his hands, and two men and a woman enter and prostrate themselves before the embarrassed Pinkerton; they are Suzuki, Cho-Cho-San's hand-maid, the cook, and the servant. The first-named betrays a loquacity which fortunately has little opportunity to display itself in the course of the opera. As Pinkerton is frankly bored, Goro bundles them off. It is significant that the gallant sailor regards their charming soubriquets—Miss Gentle-Breeze-of-Morning, Ray-of-the-Golden-Sunbeam, and Sweet-scented-Pine-Tree, as foolish; he is evidently a person of little artistic sensibility.

Presently the U.S. Consul, Sharpless, appears, breathless from climbing the hill.

[Pinkerton's aria at this point, *Dovunque al mondo,* addressed to Sharpless, is preceded by a few bars of the *Star-spangled Banner,* an air for which one may claim, without being 'a hundred per cent. American,' that it can at least hold its own with any melody in the opera.]

Pinkerton breaks off, to have a drink with the Consul before continuing the ingenuous exposition of nautical morality that constitutes the basis of his song, concluding with a toast, "America for ever!" in which Sharpless, and the brass of the orchestra, join with much fervour.

Now that the social amenities have been observed, the Consul feels it his duty to warn Pinkerton of what may be the consequence of his impulsive action, but the heedless youth merely replies with a charming expression of his passion for Cho-Cho-San, *Amore o grillo.* The men drink again; this time to Pinkerton's new friends and relations to be, though Pinkerton at the same time unashamedly toasts the *real* wife from America he will one day marry.

Goro runs in to say that Butterfly and her friends are coming; indeed, their shrill voices are already heard in the distance, one soaring like a lark above the rest—it is Butterfly. Her entrance, just as the climax of her song (*Ancora un passo*) is reached, is an effective moment, vocally and dramatically, while the brightly coloured kimonos and sunshades of the heroine and her companions make a charming stage picture.

Butterfly explains in the ensuing dialogue that her people were once wealthy but lost their money, so that she was compelled to earn her living as a *geisha.* Sharpless very naturally asks where her father is—her mother is with her—but the innocent question has a most depressing effect on the assemblage, which nervously fans itself as Butterfly answers shortly, "Dead." A rather humorous incident now takes place. "What might your age be?" asks Sharpless. "Try to guess!" coquettes Butterfly. "Ten!" hazards the gallant gentleman. "Guess higher!" the lady replies. "Twenty, then!" "Guess lower!—Fifteen exactly! I am old, am I not?" she adds—a statement which may be variously interpreted!

The High Commissioner, the Official Registrar, and a crowd of relations now come on to the scene, excitedly discussing the two Americans, while refreshments are brought. Puccini manages the bustle of this scene cleverly, and it makes an effective concerted piece. Butterfly introduces her relatives; then, taking Pinkerton on one side, she shows him her few girlish possessions (which she produces from her sleeves)—silk handkerchiefs, a fan, a mirror, a knife, held sacred because the Mikado had sent it to her father for the purpose of committing *hara-kiri*—thus is the mystery of this parent explained—and finally the souls of her ancestors; but Pinkerton shows not the slightest sympathy with this rather pathetic little exhibition.

Butterfly tells him confidentially how she has become a Christian to please him, and, to prove her sincerity, incontinently throws away the souls of her unfortunate forefathers!

At length they are married: Cho-Cho-San is now Madame Pinkerton. The Consul takes his leave, and the relatives are drinking the health of the newly married couple to a delightful tune, *O Kami, O Kami*, when the peace of the scene is rudely interrupted by strange cries coming from the path up the hill. It is the Bonze, Cho-Cho-San's uncle, a High Priest of the Buddhist faith. "Abomination!" he cries to the frightened girls now huddled together, while Butterfly remains alone in a corner. "She has renounced her true religion!"

After consigning Butterfly's soul to everlasting torment and inducing all the relations to disown her, the Bonze is bundled out by the enraged Pinkerton, the rest following with cries of *"Hou! Hou! Hou! Cho-Cho-San!"*

Pinkerton endeavours to comfort his terrified little bride. He scarcely realizes, being what he is—a very ordinary, unobservant young man—what her change in belief has meant to Butterfly. He, not Christianity, is now her religion. But the faith of her ancestors cannot easily be uprooted—and Suzuki, muttering her prayers before the Buddhist shrine, is a further reproach to her.

Twilight is beginning to fall as Pinkerton leads his bride toward the house. A beautiful theme wells up out of the orchestra, scored with Puccini's almost unfailing instinct for the right thing. Suzuki helps Butterfly into her white wedding garment and retires for the night; the two lovers are left alone.

From here to the end is a long love-duet (*Viene la sera*), broken only by sinister reminiscences of the Bonze's theme. The night gradually falls, the stars come out, and the music glows with lyric fervour. Finally the tune heard on Butterfly's first appearance takes possession of both orchestra and singers.

As the curtain falls Pinkerton vanishes into the house with Butterfly clasped in his arms.

Act II. *Part 1.* Inside Butterfly's house. After a few bars of prelude, in which the Bonze's theme is prominent, the curtain rises to disclose a barely furnished interior. The curtains are drawn, leaving the room in semi-darkness, but Suzuki can just be seen praying before the image of Buddha; from time to time she rings the prayer bell. Butterfly is standing rigid and motionless near a screen—it is three years since she entrusted her life and soul to the care of Pinkerton—and she is a mother.

Presently Suzuki draws up the curtains and slides back the partition giving on to the charming little garden. "How soon," asks Butterfly half jokingly, "shall we be starving?" They have only a few coins left, but Butterfly is confident Pinkerton will come back, in spite of Suzuki's scepticism. Did he not have locks put on the doors to keep out her relations and give her protection? She sings the theme of the first song with passionate emphasis, but Suzuki is still unconvinced. "Did ever a foreign husband yet return to his nest?" Butterfly, furious, seizes hold of her, cries: "Silence! or I'll kill you!" and then, calming down, she relates with much charm Pinkerton's last words to her—his promise to come back "when the robins nest again." The violins in the orchestra set up a realistic twittering, followed by what is probably the most famous aria in the opera, *Un bel dì,* so often heard on the concert platform. As she finishes, Butterfly, overcome with emotion at the picture she has imagined of her husband's return, casts herself into Suzuki's arms.

Suddenly Goro and Sharpless appear in the garden and presently the Consul comes in. "Madame Butterfly?" he asks. "No! Madame Pinkerton," she answers: then, turning round, she recognizes him, claps her hands with pleasure, and orders Suzuki to bring cigarettes and cushions. Sharpless is anxious to explain the reason of his visit, which weighs not a little on his mind, but the little lady constantly interrupts and will not allow him more than a few words for some moments. At last he manages to say, "I've a letter from Mr. Pinkerton," and shows it to her. The poor little creature is overjoyed: "I am the happiest woman in Japan," she cries. Then, "When do the robins nest in America?" she asks. The Consul is surprised at the apparently irrelevant question, so she explains. Then he understands too well and hesitatingly confesses his ignorance of ornithology—a word which puzzles Butterfly. She tells him how Goro—who was presumably in the habit of receiving a commission on marriage contracts—had come to her soon after Pinkerton's departure and tried to persuade her with arguments and presents to remarry, and that he is now pressing the claims of the wealthy Yamadori, a mentally deficient plutocrat! Indeed, at this moment the gentleman appears with his retinue and again presses his suit. Butterfly refuses him—she is already married, as she thinks. A discussion as to grounds of divorce follows. "In my country, the United States," the little Japanese 'wife' says, "desertion does not give the right of divorce"; and she appeals to Sharpless to support her. Goro whispers to the Consul, "Pinkerton's ship is already signalled." Yamadori takes his pompous farewell, and Sharpless settles down to the difficult task of reading Pinkerton's letter to Butterfly, a scene which has been delightfully treated by Puccini with the lightest of touches.

Inevitably Butterfly misunderstands the purport of Pinkerton's words to the Consul, "On you I am relying to act discreetly, to prepare her with tact and caution."

"He's coming," she cries and is enraptured. The Consul tries another way. He asks her what she would do if he never came back. "Two things I might do," she answers, while the orchestra gives out low chords of heavy portent—"become again a *geisha*—or die." Sharpless is much moved and, in his longing to help, urges her to accept Yamadori. This mortally offends Butterfly. She tells Suzuki to show him the door—then, repenting, runs into the room on the left, to return carrying her baby, which she exhibits to the Consul, proudly pointing out his American features.

The big dramatic aria, *Sai cos' ebbe cuore,* if sung as

it deserves, is really touching. The poor little mother breaks down at the end and hugs the child passionately; even Sharpless cannot restrain his tears. "The child's name is 'Trouble' now," Butterfly says, "but it shall be 'Joy' when the father returns."

The theme of *Un bel dì* is heard again in the orchestra. The Consul goes, but there is no rest for Butterfly, for Suzuki rushes in dragging Goro by the ear. She has found that he was going about the town saying that no one knows who the child's father is, a statement that makes Butterfly nearly kill him as she pushes him out of the house. Worn with emotion her thoughts fly to the child. She tells him his avenger will soon be here; indeed at this moment a cannon-shot is heard from the harbour. Very softly the strings play the *Un bel dì* theme as Butterfly, running to the window with her telescope, reads the name of the man-of-war which has just come into harbour—"Abraham Lincoln." Now all her hopes are justified: "My love and my faith have triumphed!" she cries; "he's here! He loves me!"

The entrancing flower-duet, *Scuoti quella fronda,* follows, during which the two women deck the house so profusely with flowers that the garden is stripped bare. Then Suzuki brings in the baby, while Butterfly touches up her white face with carmine, dreading lest Pinkerton should find her changed. She puts on her white kimono so that he may see her as on her wedding day, and even the baby is dressed up in festal garments for the occasion.

Night has fallen. Suzuki brings in some Japanese lanterns, which she puts on the flower-strewn floor. Butterfly intends to watch at the window for the husband who is coming back to her; she makes three holes in the paper screen through which they may peep; and so, like sentinels, the wife, the child, the faithful servant, take up their posts—Butterfly remaining rigid and motionless as a statue.

Puccini has secured a very beautiful effect for the end of this scene. The chorus, out of sight, hums softly a tune heard previously during the reading of Pinkerton's letter, supported by a very light and delicate orchestral accompaniment. It intensifies the pathos of the stage picture. Suzuki and the baby are already dropping off to sleep as the curtain falls—Butterfly alone stands upright and tragically awake.

Act II. *Part* II. There is no change of scene. When the curtain rises Butterfly is standing, still motionless, by the window; the other two are fast asleep. As it is now daylight, Butterfly wakes up Suzuki and takes the baby in her arms; she is still confident of Pinkerton's return. With the baby clasped to her bosom she goes up the staircase singing a simple little lullaby, while Suzuki mourns for her "poor Madame Butterfly." The orchestra now announces the arrival of Sharpless and Pinkerton, who are soon heard knocking at the door; Suzuki cannot restrain her surprise when she lets them in, but they motion her to be silent and creep in cautiously on tiptoe.

She tells them how eagerly Butterfly has examined every ship that came into the harbour, and how, confident that Pinkerton is returning to her, she has decorated the house with flowers; how, too, she has been up all night watching. Then she catches sight of a figure in the garden. "Who is that?" she says fearfully. Sharpless tells Suzuki that the strange lady is Pinkerton's wife— his real American wife. A trio follows, in which Sharpless insists that the baby must be cared for. Pinkerton expresses futile remorse, and Suzuki wonders how she can ever break the news to Butterfly. When she is gone, Pinkerton, after giving Sharpless money for the deserted little wife, sings a most unconvincing "Farewell, O happy home; farewell, home of love," while Sharpless reminds him of his repeated warning, only too well justified. So the contemptible creature goes out, leaving Sharpless to face the music.

Kate, the American wife, who has surely the most thankless part in all opera, comes in with Suzuki from the garden. Butterfly calls from the room above, "Suzuki, where are you?" and appears at the head of the staircase. The faithful maid tries to stop her mistress coming down, but Butterfly runs into the room, sure that Pinkerton is hiding somewhere. A sinister reminiscence of the Bonze's curse-theme comes out of the orchestra. Suddenly Butterfly sees Kate, who is crying quietly. The scene that follows is of almost unbearable poignancy, and Puccini has treated it only too convincingly. Butterfly, who is trying not to understand what is only too obvious, drags the admission from Suzuki that Pinkerton is alive but will come no more to her. Kate tells her, as kindly as possible, who she is—she was married a year ago—and asks if she may do something for the child. She is certainly more broad-minded than most wives would be in similar circumstances! "Can he have his son?" she asks. "Yes, if he comes here half an hour from now," replies Butterfly; so Kate and Sharpless go. Butterfly almost collapses, but under Suzuki's tender care gradually recovers; she tells the maid to shut out the sunlight so that the room may be in almost total darkness.

"Go and play with my child," Butterfly commands poor Suzuki, who is very reluctant to leave her, so unnaturally calm is she. At length the maid goes, and Butterfly crosses to the shrine, lifts the white veil from it, throws this across the screen, and takes down the dagger hanging near the image of Buddha. This she kisses softly, while reading the words inscribed upon it:

Death with honour is better than life with dishonour.

As she points the knife at her throat the door on the left opens and the child runs in, holding out his arms toward his mother. She lets the dagger fall, and clasps him to her heart. "You! You! You!" she cries. "Though you must never know it, 'tis for you, my love, I'm dying!"

When her fit of sobbing is over Butterfly bandages the child's eyes, and gives him two American flags to play with, then seizes the dagger and goes behind the screen.

Tottering out with the white scarf round her throat, she gropes her way to the child, falls to the ground beside her son with just enough strength left to embrace him. Pinkerton is heard calling from outside, "Butterfly, Butterfly!" and rushes into the room with Sharpless, as Butterfly, pointing feebly to the child, who is still waving his little flags, draws her last breath.

Pinkerton falls on his knees beside her, and Sharpless, picking up the child, turns from the tragic scene.

The opera ends with an enigmatic chord which has no suggestion of finality in it. Can it be intended to indicate that Kate also will have to suffer for the most despicable of all operatic heroes?

TOSCA

Music by PUCCINI. *Words by* ILLICA *and* GIACOSA,
from SARDOU'S *drama.*
Rome, 1900; *London,* 1900; *New York,* 1901.

WHILE *Tosca*[1] after a prosperous career of a
quarter of a century still holds a prominent
place on the operatic stage, Sardou's drama
from which it was taken seems to have fallen out of the
repertory, possibly because no actress has cared to follow
the great Sarah Bernhardt in the title part written
especially for her. In the case of the opera, however, it
is probably the sensational character of the drama rather
than the lure of the music that is the vital element, since,
apart from the two numbers *Vissi d'arte* and *E lucevan le
stelle,* so dear to patrons of the gramophone, Puccini's
score contains little of the melodic charm which has
secured for *Bohème* and *Butterfly* so wide a popularity.

Tosca may perhaps be described as a fashionable
rather than a popular opera; the feast of horrors it supplies is not altogether to the general taste, whereas the
central character makes a very special appeal to a more
sophisticated audience. The part of Floria Tosca, the
brilliant, voluptuous *diva,* swayed by alternate fits of
passion and piety, capable of daring all things for her
lover, demands for its interpretation an artist who is at
once beautiful, distinguished, in the highest degree 'tem-
peramental,' and powerful enough to convey to us three
of the biggest thrills to be found in any opera.

Apart from the commanding figure of the heroine, it

[1] My thanks are due to Messrs G. Ricordi and Co. for permitting
me to use their text of the opera.

524

is as a highly coloured melodrama that *Tosca* makes its effect. The scene is Rome in the year 1800, a time when the name of Bonaparte was a terror to the monarchy, and anyone suspected of Republican tendencies stood in deadly peril. The tragedy turns upon the rivalry between Scarpia, the Chief of the Police, and Mario Cavaradossi, a young painter of Republican sympathies, for the possession of Floria Tosca, the beautiful singer and faithful mistress of Mario. Scarpia, on discovering that his rival has given shelter to Angelotti, a fugitive political prisoner, condemns him to torture and to death. Tosca, to save her lover, consents to yield to the desires of Scarpia, who accordingly gives orders to his officer, in Tosca's presence, to arrange for merely a mock execution. When he turns to claim his share of the bargain at Tosca's hands, she stabs him to the heart, and hurries off to acquaint her lover with the news. She is allowed to be present while the firing party arrives, does its duty, and departs. But Mario does not rise. Bending over his body, the horrified woman realizes the truth—Scarpia's agents had understood their orders in accordance with that villain's real intention. Mario is dead.

Meanwhile Scarpia's body has been found, and the guard arrives to arrest his murderers. Before they can take her, Floria Tosca has thrown herself from the walls of the castle of Sant' Angelo.

Act. I. There is no overture: after a few *fortissimo* chords, ominous in their harsh progression, the curtain rises on the interior of the Jesuit church of Sant' Andrea in Rome. Raised on a platform to the left is a large canvas, with the painter's materials at hand; on the right a private chapel, guarded by an image of the Blessed Virgin.

Some hurried syncopation in the orchestra brings on the dishevelled figure of the fugitive Angelotti, still in

the prison garb in which he has just escaped from Sant'
Angelo. Making straight for the shrine of the Madonna,
he searches eagerly and finds at last a key with which
he unlocks the door of the chapel and disappears inside.
(This key has been placed there by his sister, the
Marchesa Attavanti, the holder of the chapel, who has
assisted in his escape.)

The orchestra now passes to a swinging rhythm in
six-eight time for the shambling entrance of the Sacristan,
the only comedy character in the opera; so anxious is
Puccini to make the most of him that he even uses a
special sign to mark the various bars at which the good
man is to give a nervous twitch to his shoulders. The
Sacristan is busy with a sheaf of brushes that he is clean-
ing for the painter, Mario Cavaradossi, but breaks off at
the sound of the Angelus bell. His prayer is hardly over
when Mario enters and resumes work on his canvas—
a representation of the Magdalen. Glancing at the picture, the Sacristan is surprised to find that it is a portrait
of a lady whom he has lately noticed kneeling long in
prayer before the Virgin's shrine. Mario, it seems, struck
by her beauty, has given his saint the blue eyes and golden
hair of this lady—none other than the Marchesa Attavanti, who has come hither to invoke the aid of Heaven
on her brother's behalf. Puccini has found room here
for one of the few purely lyrical pieces in the opera;
Mario takes from his pocket a miniature of Floria Tosca,
and in the aria *Recondita armonia* contrasts the blonde
beauty on his canvas with the darker, more compelling
charm of Tosca, to whom all his love is given. The
Sacristan is shocked at such unsuitable reflections, and,
after a muttered denunciation of the painter as a "dog
of a Voltairean" and a foe to the Government, leaves
him alone.

Angelotti, supposing the church to be empty, now

comes from his hiding-place, and is greeted as a friend and fellow by Cavaradossi, who has hardly time to lock the door of the church and press food and wine upon him from the basket the painter had brought for himself when Tosca's voice is heard outside, and the fugitive retires again to the chapel, taking the basket with him.

Floria Tosca now makes her entrance, in the *directoire* costume, the long stick, and large sheaf of flowers so familiar to a former generation from the many portraits of Bernhardt in one of her most famous parts. The long-drawn phrases on the violins convey to us the softer, more gracious side of Tosca's nature, while the scene that follows serves rapidly to develop some other aspects of her character—a not too pleasing mixture of sensuous passion and sentimental piety. The flowers she brings are for the Virgin's altar; these disposed of, she lays amorous siege to the willing Mario in the long solo *Non la sospiri, la nostra casetta;* although her lover responds with equal warmth, her mood soon changes to furious jealousy on recognizing in Mario's painting the likeness of the Attavanti, whom she at once imagines to be her rival. It requires a passage of tender protest on Mario's part, *Qual'occhio al mondo,* and a lengthy duet to calm Tosca's suspicions; at last she leaves him to his work, with the parting words: "Paint your saint with black eyes, not blue—black, like mine!"

Angelotti now ventures out again, and it is arranged that he shall go at once to the painter's villa, where he can lie safely hidden for the time in a secret chamber leading from a well in the garden. A noise outside alarms them, and Mario hurries the fugitive away through a door at the back of the chapel.

The orchestra, which has been almost superfluous during the dialogue, now wakes up as the Sacristan enters, out of breath, with the report of the defeat of Bonaparte and all the Powers of Darkness; he has counted on annoying Mario by his news, since, according to his peculiar theology, "To vex an infidel is deserving of a big Indulgence." However, he has to content himself with the sympathy of the crowd of choristers and altar-boys who now rush into the church and rejoice noisily at the good tidings—there is to be a *Te Deum* that very evening, for which they will be paid extra, while at the Farnese Palace will be given a grand new cantata, and Floria Tosca is to sing.

The excitement is at its height when the stern figure of Scarpia is seen at the door of the church; the boys steal meekly away, leaving the Sacristan alone with the Chief of the Police. Once more the music sinks necessarily into abeyance during the close dialogue which follows. Scarpia has reason to believe that Angelotti is hidden in the church. He questions the Sacristan, notes the half-finished portrait of the Marchesa Attavanti, then searches her private chapel; here he discovers a fan with the Attavanti coat of arms, and the empty food basket—the property, as the Sacristan tells him, of Mario Cavaradossi. He concludes that Angelotti has certainly been in the church, and that Mario and the Marchesa have together assisted him to some safe hiding-place.

With the re-entrance of Tosca the musical interest rises in a steady *crescendo* to the final climax. She has come, expecting to find her lover, to tell him of her unforeseen engagement to sing at the Palace that evening—Scarpia at once sees his way to profit by Mario's absence and Tosca's disappointment.

To the subdued dingdong of bells the villain, like another Iago, proceeds to pour his poison into Tosca's jealous heart. With suave flattery he compliments her on her fervent piety—she, the darling of the stage, can always find time for her devotion; many women, indeed, come to church, but not all of them to pray—nay (with a glance at the portrait), some come merely to wanton with their lovers! Tosca's suspicious nature at once takes fire—Scarpia has but to show her the fan with the Attavanti coronet to convince her of Mario's faithlessness. She bursts into a passion of jealous rage—it is obvious that on leaving the church she will go straight to her lover in the hope of surprising him with her rival. Scarpia conducts Tosca to the door with grave courtesy— and gives orders to his officer, Spoletta, to follow her instantly and report to him without delay. Meanwhile the church has been filling with a devout and eager throng; as the Cardinal and his train proceed up the aisle to the high altar the boom of cannon is heard without, and the organ floods the building with the strains of triumph. Scarpia has good reason to exult; Cavaradossi and Tosca, fate has thrown them both into his power— the one he destines for the scaffold, the other for his own amorous arms. The mingled lust and hate that make up his long soliloquy stand out clearly against the background of the solemn *Te Deum* which fills the church and in which he finally joins. The whole *finale* is an undeniably fine piece of theatrical effect—it was very fitting that it should be repeated on the occasion of its first performance.

Act II. In spite of the necessary predominance of the heroine, it is a question whether the figure of the villain of the piece is not the finer operatic achievement. In the previous Act we have his character firmly outlined— Baron Scarpia, Chief of the Police, a name to tremble at—a man made up of lust and craft and inexorable hate—here we see him expanding in the hour of his expected triumph. He is seated in his apartment at the Farnese Palace; through the open window come the sounds of a gavotte, for, on the floor below, the Queen of Naples has a grand entertainment to celebrate the defeat of Bonaparte; it is here that the new cantata is to be given, in which La Tosca will take the leading part. (It will help us to realize the period if we recall that, in Sardou's drama, Paisiello is the composer of the music, which he conducts in person.)

All promises well for Scarpia, both in love and war; the Republican forces have received a check, and two of their supporters, Angelotti and Mario Cavaradossi, will soon be in his power; with the removal of the latter the path is clear to the attainment of his great desire—Mario gone, Tosca surely cannot long resist him!

Scarpia, it will be remembered from the last Act, by arousing her jealousy, had driven Tosca to hurry to Mario's villa in the expectation of finding him with the Marchesa Attavanti, and had ordered Spoletta to follow and spy upon her actions. That officer now returns with his report. Tosca had stayed but a short time at the villa; search has been made for Angelotti, but in vain; Mario Cavaradossi, denying all knowledge of the fugitive, has been arrested, and is now at Scarpia's disposal.

Having written a short note to be handed to Tosca so soon as the cantata should be ended, the Chief of the Police orders Mario to be brought before him. The *diva's* powerful voice is heard from the royal halls below as Scarpia sternly accuses the young painter of aiding and sheltering Angelotti, an enemy to the State; Mario haughtily denies the charge, and disclaims all knowledge of the fugitive's movements.

The cantata now over, Tosca hastens into the room, surprised but not yet alarmed to find Mario present. From her affectionate greeting to her lover Scarpia argues that she had found at the villa not the Marchesa Attavanti but Angelotti, and had assisted at his concealment—

530

he resolves to try a plan by which he hopes to obtain from Tosca the information which Mario may still persist in withholding.

The scene that follows is without doubt the most gruesome, the most harrowing, to be found in the whole of opera; whether the situation is fit for artistic treatment is a matter of question—it is certainly a potent attraction for a certain section of opera-goers, and a favourite with the singers. Though the tenor's opportunities are comparatively slight, it is a great scene for the soprano and the baritone, both of whom must have exceptional dramatic power to enable them to carry it through with success.

Mario Cavaradossi is led into an adjoining room, where, as Scarpia puts it, his deposition will be taken; the latter then proceeds to question Tosca as to her knowledge of Mario's dealings with Angelotti. Her first answers are given with haughty indifference; she knows nothing—it is quite useless to question either her or Mario. "We shall see!" says Scarpia—then, with an awful change of demeanour, he tells her the truth. In the next room, behind those doors, lies her lover, bound hand and foot—round his head an iron band with terrible claws which, at the turn of a screw, can tear the tender flesh, make blood gush from his temples, or crush the skull, if nothing else will serve. As Scarpia pauses the victim's groans begin, and the wretched woman is thus made to share each pang of the beloved, yet remains powerless to soothe or help him. Nay, says Scarpia, her lover's fate is in her own hands; will she not shorten his agony by confessing all she knows? She will not, dare not—she has pledged her word to Mario.

The torture is renewed with greater violence—a door is opened that she may more plainly hear the sufferer's groans—she is even allowed to see and speak with him.

531

Cavaradossi is heroic in his agony, he is resolved to keep the secret to the end, and exhorts Tosca to equal firmness—he can even shout defiance at his enemy. A fine musical climax is here attained in a passage between Scarpia—with his ever more thunderous demand, "Say, where is Angelotti? Where have you hidden him?"—and Tosca with her growing frenzy of denial and refusal. This is succeeded by a short lull, as the exhausted woman gives way to a fit of quiet sobbing, and Spoletta mutters a verse of the *Dies iræ*.

But Scarpia, impatient of further delay, gives orders for a still sharper turn of the screw—the appalling cry wrung from the tortured man is too much for Tosca's weakened resistance; indeed, she has hardly strength to gasp out: "The well in the garden—Angelotti is hidden there."

At a word from Scarpia, Mario is brought in, bleeding, unconscious, and is laid on the sofa. Tosca flings herself beside the senseless form, covering it with tears and kisses. On regaining consciousness Mario's first fear is whether, in his delirium, he may have betrayed the secret of Angelotti's hiding-place; Tosca has hardly time to assure him to the contrary when Scarpia, with diabolical intention, turns to Spoletta with the words: "*Go! Search the well in the garden!*"

Mario knows that Tosca must have given the information; he curses, but has scarcely strength to cast her from him, when a messenger arrives with tidings that galvanize the young Republican into new life. To-day's rejoicings have been premature; Napoleon has retrieved his fortunes by a decisive victory at Marengo. Now comes one of the finest moments in the opera. With a great shout of "Victory!" Mario contrives to stagger from the couch, confront his enemy Scarpia, and hurl insults and defiance at him in his share of the short trio

L'alba vindice appar', a vigorous piece of vocal writing, doubly welcome after the prolonged melodrama which has been the only possible accompaniment of the previous action.

Mario is led away to execution; Tosca makes a wild but futile attempt to cling to him—she is thrust violently back by the guard, and the door is closed. She is alone with the cruel and lustful Scarpia.

The rest of the Act, with the exception of Tosca's one lyrical passage, is really Scarpia's. With the suavity peculiar to the stage villain in his most deadly mood, he invites Tosca to join him at the table where supper is waiting—at least she will taste a glass of wine? Fie! so fair a lady should not so distress herself! Doubtless in a little talk together they will be able to arrange some plan for setting Mario at liberty. Tosca only partly grasps his meaning. "How much do you demand for his release?" she asks. "Name your price!" But it is not money that will satisfy this man, who now shows her his real nature. He has always loved her, always desired her, but what he has seen to-day has increased his passion tenfold. In a fiery passage, *Già mi struggea l'amor della diva*, he tells her how her tears and caresses for her lover, her scorn and hatred of himself, have fanned the flame of his desire—he has sworn to possess her! Horrified and desperate, Tosca answers with words of anger and loathing that serve merely to whet his lust. "I hate you! I hate you!" she cries, "villain and coward!" "What matter!" he replies; "love and hate are all one to me when once I have you safely in my arms!" He pursues her round the room, she shrieking wildly for help—when both are arrested by the throbbing of a drum; it is the guard escorting a party of doomed men to the scaffold. Mario, says Scarpia, has but an hour to live—but Tosca may save him yet. This prolonged passage of repose, where nothing is heard but the ominous tap of the drum, blending with the faint suggestion of a funeral march in the orchestra, is certainly one of the happiest ideas in the opera—it prepares us admirably for Tosca's famous solo, *Vissi d'arte, vissi d'amore*. Although the effect is pathetic, it cannot be said that the melody here is either novel or distinguished; in the second section, *Sempre con fè sincera*, good use is made in the orchestra of the suave theme that heralds Tosca's appearance in the church in Act I. The song is a wail of self-pity; Tosca, who, with all her faults, has done many deeds of kindness and preserved some fervour of religion, finds it hard that she herself should be left to suffer such cruelty from another.

At the end she kneels to Scarpia, imploring him to spare her lover's life. He is beginning again to press her for the only price he will accept, when Spoletta enters the room: Angelotti has been found, but has succeeded in taking his own life. "Then," says Scarpia, "let his dead body hang on the gallows!" "And the other— Mario Cavaradossi?" asks Spoletta. Scarpia looks at Tosca: "What say you now?" he whispers.

Her lover's peril is too imminent—Tosca signifies her willingness to pay the price, provided that Mario is at once set free. That, says Scarpia, is impossible—it is necessary that the mere form of execution shall first be gone through. He turns to Spoletta: "The prisoner Cavaradossi will not be hanged—he must be shot—but only blank cartridges are to be used, *as was done in the case of Count Palmieri*—a mock execution—you understand me?" Yes—Spoletta understands quite well what his master intends. Tosca is satisfied, the more as she herself will be allowed to be present, and will tell Mario what to do—furthermore, she demands a safe conduct for herself and Mario, who will leave Rome at once.

During the long passage of melodrama that accompanies the writing and sealing of the necessary passport Tosca manages to get possession of a sharp knife from the supper-table. Scarpia has finished writing, and advances on her with arms open to embrace her: "At last, my Tosca! Mine at last!" "At last!" she cries, "here is my kiss!"—and stabs him to the heart. Escaping the clutches of the dying man, she mocks him in his agony: "Yes! Look at me! I am Tosca—and there lies Scarpia, slain by a woman's hand!" She bends over him, listening greedily for the death-rattle: "Die, then, with God's curse upon you!"

Then her mood changes. Now Scarpia is dead, Tosca must forgive him—nay, even say a prayer for his sin-stained soul. She takes two candles from the table and places them on either side his head—the large crucifix from the wall she lays upon his breast. But for these lights the stage is in darkness as Tosca leaves the room.

The torture scene of this Act, as given in the opera, though sufficiently harassing for most tastes, is but a modification of the horrors of Sardou's drama as produced at the Porte-Saint-Martin theatre in 1887. The realistic treatment then adopted was, in fact, too much for the first-night audience, and some considerable retrenchment of the blood-curdling details had to be made for subsequent performances; the Fat Boy, it was felt, had gone too far in his desire to make our flesh creep. Of the critics, the judicious Jules Lemaître did not hesitate to utter a vigorous protest: "M. Sardou," he wrote in the *Journal des Débats,* "a soif de sang. Il est le Caligula du drame."

Act III. In a melodrama of this kind, which depends largely on a cumulative series of harrowing incidents, it is not always easy for the composer to find sufficient opportunities for the necessary periods of relief. In the preceding Act the audience has been kept on the rack even more continuously than the tortured Mario; Puccini must have felt that we should all be glad of a rest, and he deserves our gratitude for the opening of Act III.

After a short but impressive theme has been given out by the horns, our eyes and ears are soothed on the rising of the curtain. We see a platform on the roof of the castle of Sant' Angelo, under a starry sky—in the distance, though hardly visible as yet, are the Vatican and the dome of St Peter's; the quiet beauty of the scene is enhanced by the distant tinkle of sheep-bells, and some snatches of an antique song from a shepherd in the valley below. But now the dawn begins to break, and from far around comes the clear sound of matin-bells from church and convent. As the light grows, we notice the details of the stage setting; we are aware of a sort of chamber in the wall in which are chairs and a table, with heavy registers upon it, and a crucifix above; also in a corner of the platform the head of a stairway leading to the floor below. From this a gaoler presently appears, to prepare for the arrival of the firing party with the prisoner. He has just lit the lamp in front of the crucifix when Mario is brought in under escort.

He is informed that he has just an hour to live. The proffered services of a priest are rejected by this sturdy Voltairean—he has only one request, to be allowed to write a letter. The gaoler is bribed by the offer of a costly ring to supply him with paper and pen, and Mario is left alone.

But it is obvious that the tenor cannot be allowed to waste the precious moments in selfish silence—very soon the pen is laid aside, and Mario indulges in sweet, sad memories of his first meeting with her for whom the letter is intended—the beloved Tosca, whom he will never see again. The result is the well-known air *E lucevan le stelle,* a picturesque romance memorable for its sonorous climax on the words *"e muoio disperato."*

Tosca now enters; too excited to speak, she merely thrusts the order for their safe conduct into his hands; but the necessary explanation is soon given in the vigorous movement *Il tuo sangue o il mio amore,* a fine piece of straightforward declamation with just sufficient support from the orchestra, which supplies an echo of the drum-taps and the funeral march that were the features of the scene described above.

Tosca alternately shudders and exults at the thought of her fearful experience—"These hands of mine," she says, "were steeped in Scarpia's blood!" This gives occasion for Mario's amorous outburst, *O dolci mani, mansuete e pure,* and a long duet follows, in which they picture the perfect happiness that awaits them in the future.

It is doubtful at first whether Mario is quite convinced—he seems almost to have a presentiment of the awful truth; but Tosca's exuberant confidence prevails with him, and the two join in a fine outburst of hope and love triumphant, *Trionfal di nova speme,* to the melody given out by the horns at the beginning of the Act. But the hour will soon be over—there is still much to be arranged.

The poignant pathos of the remainder of this Act, achieved as it is by quite legitimate means, has a certain artistic value far superior to the crude horrors that have gone before. Tosca is excited to the point of gaiety; Mario has a part to act, and she will coach him in the "business"; as soon as the muskets go off, he must be sure to drop flat on the ground, just like a dead man— Tosca, the actress, is of course familiar with the trick, and can show him how an effective stage fall is managed. The two can even laugh together over their little piece of play-acting; yet, somehow, we feel that Mario is acting merely for Tosca's sake—he himself is certain what the end will be. The situation is finely conceived and really touches us to pity and terror.

The clock strikes four, and the sun is rising, when the firing party lead Mario to the spot where the sentence is to be carried out—" a mock execution, *just as in the case of Count Palmieri.*" Spoletta has not forgotten how that nobleman died.

Tosca waits impatiently for the farce to be ended; she has no misgivings—but must stop her ears when the muskets go off; she is delighted with the way in which Mario manages his fall: "Like a true artist!" she comments. Then, as the soldiers disappear down the stairway, she moves warily toward the spot where Mario lies—covered over with a cloth. She cautions him not to move yet —they might return! She listens at the stairs until the footsteps have quite died away—then she flies to her lover: "Mario! Mario! Get up! 'Tis time now!"

But Mario does not stir—neither did the Count Palmieri.

Tosca raises the cloth—

Fortunately she has but little time to suffer. The body of Scarpia has been discovered, and Spoletta with his men are heard approaching, on the track of the murderess.

As they pour on to the stage, Floria Tosca takes the only way—she mounts the parapet, and finds her death below the walls of the castle of Sant' Angelo.

LOUISE [1]

Words and Music by CHARPENTIER.
Paris, 1900; *New York*, 1908; *London*, 1909.

THIS work has probably had a greater success upon the English stage than any French opera since *Carmen*. No doubt this is largely due to the performance of Madame Edvina in the title rôle, where she scored a triumph that will not be forgotten by those who witnessed the first London productions of Charpentier's work. But the piece itself contains novel qualities that account for much of its attraction, and at the same time make it difficult to fit into any definite category. *Louise* is one of the few operas that deal with contemporary life. This by itself might incline us to class it with Puccini's *La Bohème,* especially as in both cases the scene is laid in Paris, but Charpentier's libretto shows a more vivid sense of the picturesque side of Parisian life than is to be found in the work of the Italian composer. The style of the music, too, is completely different. Limpid, light, and unmistakably French, it nevertheless exhibits a closely woven texture into which are introduced constantly running fragments of tune that remind us in spite of ourselves of the Wagnerian *leitmotif.* And yet *Louise* is almost as remote from Wagner as it is from Puccini. Seldom or never do these fragments assume the supreme importance that is theirs in the work of the German master, where they are at once the structural framework of the opera and the elements from which long melodies and even complete tunes are evolved. Here they are rather bubbles that from

[1] This analysis is contributed by Mr Peter Latham.

time to time float to the surface of the orchestral river. They have no history, they are seen and they disappear, only to reappear again. Or they are like the sounds that detach themselves at intervals from among the dull murmurs of a great city, sounds insignificant enough taken singly, but containing in their sum the very spirit of the place and its inhabitants.

Thus it is that in the short, epigrammatic Prelude we are transported at once to Paris, Paris the gay and careless, the paradise of young artists, and the very home of freedom. And thus, when the curtain goes up and shows us Louise in the humble living-room of her parents' house we are not in the least surprised to see a young man standing outside his studio opposite and pouring out his love with a passion and a vehemence that in London would bring a couple of policemen on the scene before he had finished a dozen bars. This is Julien, and it soon appears that Louise is not indifferent to his advances. She goes to the window and there follows a duet, in the course of which it becomes clear that, like other lovers, they have their difficulties. Louise's parents, it seems, do not entirely trust unattached young artists. Her mother, in particular, has assumed an attitude which the young couple are inclined bitterly to resent. But what matter? They have managed to meet none the less! Unfortunately the mother, entering quietly, has overheard the last part of the conversation, and when Louise turns from the window the situation is distinctly awkward. The mother, naturally annoyed, mocks at her daughter's transports and gives her a good scolding. Louise imprudently allows herself to be drawn into a discussion which only makes things worse. "Shameless girl!" exclaims the mother, "instead of hiding your face you dare to boast of your lover!" "My lover!" cries Louise, "he is not that yet; but, really, one would think

540

that you wished him to become it!" "Little wretch," says the incensed parent, "be careful that I don't tell the whole story to your father."

At this moment the father's step is heard on the stairs. He enters, a letter in his hand. Louise takes heart again, for Julien, before they were separated, had shown her a letter that he was sending to her parents, telling her that it contained a request for her hand. During the meal which follows the conversation comes mainly from the father, who is in philosophic mood. He is a poor man and has to work hard for his living. But are the rich any better off than he is? All a man wants is good health, a happy home, and a loving family. These he has got, and he asks no more. After dinner the matter of the letter is introduced. The father is inclined to be reasonable; his idea is to make some inquiries about the young man, and ask him in one evening. But the mother, stung by the memory that Julien has laughed at her, will not hear of it, and Louise, attempting to defend her lover, only receives a smack for her pains. Her father tries to comfort her. If they are thwarting her, they are doing it for her good; choosing a husband is not an easy business; she lacks experience, and love is proverbially blind. He has not yet made up his mind about Julien, but what he has heard of him so far has not been very encouraging. If he separates them now, Louise may live to thank him some day. She loves her father, does she not? Very well; he also loves her. But she must obey him.

Louise is in despair. In compliance with his request she takes the evening paper and starts to read to him. But her voice is stifled with sobs; she stops and breaks down in tears.

Act II opens with a graphic orchestral picture, "Paris awakes." The curtain then rises on an open space in front of the house at which Louise works. It is five o'clock in the morning. We need not concern ourselves with the sociological lessons which Charpentier wished to teach in *Louise*. All we need to know is that this very picturesque scene is designed to show the dangers of the girl's position. Freedom is all very well, but daughters who refuse to take good advice, however distasteful it may be, are apt to get into serious trouble and bring nothing but misery on themselves and those who love them.

Dotted about the stage are various figures typical of the Paris streets at dawn. To them enters the "Noctam-bule," a young man in evening dress. He plays no part in the general action of the play, and like the rest is rather a type than a character. He is the very essence of the gay night-life of Paris, the thoughtless, irresponsible 'Night Wanderer.' Blessed with the gift of youth and riches he goes about in the pursuit of pleasure, ignorant, or at least careless, of the suffering around him. A social parasite and an egotist to the core, he can be cruel in the satisfaction of his whims. Should they cause ruin to his victims, so much the worse for them. The attractive but rather sinister figure is thus the very embodiment of the temptations that beset Louise.

Gradually the light increases and these strange characters disappear. A band of Bohemians arrives, Julien among them. It soon appears that he is bent on carrying off Louise. She will come to work as usual, escorted by her mother, but the mother will leave her at the door and Julien will rush forward and persuade her to run away with him. One by one the Bohemians depart, wishing him good luck, and saying they will make Louise their Muse, a phrase that is explained later. All falls out as arranged, but Julien finds it more difficult than he anticipated to persuade Louise to elope. She loves him, yes! but she is frightened, and evading his ardent appeals

542

she slips back into the workshop. Throughout the scene there is a constant stream of typical Parisian characters passing across the stage at the back.

Scene II shows the interior of the workroom. The girls are all at work, chattering and gossiping the while. Louise alone, sitting a little apart from the rest, sews in silence. They suspect her of being in love, and start to tease her, but are distracted by the sound of music in the street. It is Julien with his guitar. At first they are charmed and throw him coppers and kisses, to the annoyance of Louise, who begins to wish she had gone off with him as he suggested. But they soon tire of his persistent eloquence and call to him to change his song. Suddenly Louise gets up and puts on her hat. She is not well and is going home. No, she requires no escort. As soon as the door has closed behind her, the girls, suspecting something of the truth, crowd to the window. Louise appears in the street, and—walks off with Julien! The girls turn back into the room amid peals of laughter.

Act III. The scene now changes to a little rustic house and garden in the Butte Montmartre. In the background, over the hedge, Paris appears like a panorama. It is evening, some time after the events of the preceding Scene. A Prelude, entitled *Vers la cité lointaine,* prepares us for the rising of the curtain, which shows us Julien, a book in his hand, seated in a chair in the garden. Behind him is Louise, her face radiant with happiness. She comes forward and tells him of her love and the joy of surrender in a song, *Depuis le jour,* a lyric inspiration of real beauty that has become as well known on the concert platform as on the operatic stage. The dialogue that follows is a good deal too long. The memory of the objections raised by her parents to her union with Julien leads Louise to ask if love should really be guided by experience. This gives him the opportunity for some

543

shallow philosophizing, while the night falls, and in the distant city lights begin to appear. Turning toward it the lovers deliver an invocation praying it to protect them, its children. Paris seems to respond with a promise of freedom, and after an ecstatic outburst of passionate song they go slowly into the house.

A change in the music, which begins to glitter with strange orchestral effects, announces a fresh development. Outside in the road appears a Bohemian. He jumps the hedge, looks carefully round, and seeing that the coast is clear, beckons to another. They open the gate to yet three more who enter staggering under a huge burden. This turns out to consist of Venetian lanterns, streamers, and other decorations with which they hastily adorn the façade and door of the cottage. A fresh crowd of Bohemians, men and girls, arrives, followed by the good people of the neighbourhood, who have considerable misgivings about what is going to happen next. Finally the "Noctambule," dressed up as *Le Pape des fous,* comes in with mock dignity. The stage, which has assumed an exceedingly picturesque aspect, is now ready. A Bohemian who has climbed to the roof of the house points to Louise, who has appeared with Julien, and in a short speech announces that they have assembled to instal her as the "Muse of Montmartre." This they proceed to do. There is plenty of shouting and dancing and a *danseuse* executes a *pas seul,* after which, as representative of all the Bohemians, she presents Louise with a crown made of roses that the girls have brought with them. There are speeches from the *Pape des fous* and from an old Bohemian, and Louise, who has shyly signified her acceptance of their homage, is hailed with acclamations. Then comes the *dénouement.* There is a sudden interruption of the revels. The brightly dressed crowd parts asunder and there in the background is a single veiled figure, dressed all in black. It is Louise's mother. Timidly she starts to come forward. Some Bohemians make a half-hearted attempt to stop her, but the crowd quickly melts away and she is left alone with Louise and Julien. She has a message to deliver: Louise's father has been prostrated by grief at her elopement and is now very ill. Will she come? The lovers are deeply moved, but Julien is distrustful. His fears are somewhat allayed, however, when the mother promises to let the girl return to him, and reluctantly he gives his consent. Louise embraces him and then slowly and regretfully follows her mother from the scene.

Act IV brings us back to the house of the parents. The houses opposite have been pulled down and a view of Paris has thus been opened up. Otherwise nothing is changed. Louise is visible in her room, at work. Her father is seated near the table in the living-room. He has almost recovered from his illness, but is sunk in gloomy thoughts from which his wife vainly endeavours to distract him. Gone now is his contentment with his lot; he has loved his daughter and believed that she loved him, but the call of young blood has been too strong, and all his efforts for her sake have only resulted in estranging her from him. The memory of all they have done for her has been blotted out by the mere glance of a stranger. Curses on him! The mother goes to Louise in the next room and begs her to come and soothe her father. Unfortunately she cannot resist the temptation to scold her, and allows it to slip out that they have no intention of letting her return to Julien, promise or no promise. The girl comes into the living-room, goes to her father, and meekly but coldly wishes him good-night. In a pitiful attempt to win her over he takes her on his knee and rocks her as he had done when she was a child. It is her loving parents who are with her; all they desire is her happiness. But the inevitable answer comes at once: "If you desire my happiness you have only to make a sign." And so the useless discussion goes on once more, till at last, in answer to another appeal, her father exclaims, "Ah, she that speaks is not my daughter! my only joy! my hope! my beauty!" "My beauty!" How sweet these words had sounded on her lover's lips. Distant echoes from the town seem to repeat the phrase, and forgetful of all else she turns to the window and invokes Paris, in the name of freedom, to come to her rescue. Her father, who is beginning to lose his temper, closes the window, but this only has the effect of directing her thoughts to Julien. To him she will return! And with words of passionate love on her lips she makes for the door. Her father blocks the way and she turns back. But her resolution is unshaken: Julien will soon come and take back his love. This is too much for the old man; in a transport of rage he flings open the door! "Go then! Go and enjoy yourself! Go to the city! They are waiting for you—go!" Louise, terrified by his change of tone, hesitates. But he picks up a chair as though to throw it at her, and with a cry of fright she rushes from the room. Immediately his anger cools. He follows her on to the staircase and his voice is heard calling "Louise!" But it is too late: she has gone. Slowly he comes back, and stops, listening to the sounds of the city.

Then, raising his fist and shaking it, he cries despairingly "Oh Paris! ! !" as the curtain falls.

PELLÉAS ET MÉLISANDE

Music by DEBUSSY. *Words by* MAETERLINCK.
Paris, 1902; *New York,* 1908; *London,* 1909.

IT is exceedingly difficult to give a description of
this amazing work that shall be at once just and
sympathetic, or even to convey any definite impression of its quality, so remote is it from all other operas.
Everything in it is different; of drama there is the least
possible allowance; scene after scene passes in which
the characters do nothing but talk, and their talk is of a
strange, unintelligible nature. The dialogue is carried
on largely in the language of every day, lapsing at times
into a childish simplicity which can hardly fail to irritate,
while we are often puzzled to understand exactly what
bearing it has upon the situation. So with the scanty
and disjointed action. Great emphasis is laid on incidents
whose significance is not apparent; the importance of
the actors seems dwarfed at times by that of the scenic
surroundings, which assume here and there almost the
place of a protagonist; the climax is already reached in
Act IV, and the last Act, like the first, is almost wholly
given over to vague dialogue.

As for the music, it is impossible in so short a compass
to give any but the sketchiest outline of the methods by
which Debussy works his lovely magic; all is so new, so
strange at first, that it may well bewilder, but we end by
acknowledging that it lights up, interprets, and tran-
scends the text with the sure intuition of genius in a way
that no other composer has ever approached.

The vocal part consists largely of an unfettered recitative that follows with remarkable fidelity the inflex-

547

ions of the speaking voice, except in moments of exalted passion, where certain lyrical passages are introduced that seem to spring naturally from the situation. This is obviously the only treatment possible for Maeterlinck's peculiar dialogue, and Debussy has applied it with perfect success; there are passages in *Pelléas et Mélisande* which come very near to realizing the ideals of the Renaissance scholars who in 1600 set out to restore the methods of Greek Tragedy, though the apter comparison would be with the Gregorian Chant of the Roman Church, in the study of which the composer is known to have been deeply immersed.

But the real interest lies in the orchestra, and here again both structure and texture are so peculiar that it is hardly possible to give any idea of the music except by actual quotation. Two striking features, however, must be noted. First there are the startling harmonies, almost revolutionary it would seem in their novelty, yet based, as the composer maintained, on the fundamental principles of acoustics, combined with a reverential study of the voices of Nature. The second feature is absolutely original; in each Act, although the dramatic action may be interrupted by several changes of scene, the music forms a continuous symphonic poem, never admitting of a full close until the end.

After these very imperfect indications of what is to be expected of this unique musical drama, we will proceed to give some account of its development.

The story resembles in outline that of Paolo and Francesca. Golaud, who has been a widower for some years, takes a young girl, Mélisande, for his second wife; she is drawn by an irresistible affinity to the love of Pelléas, his younger brother; Golaud discovers the secret, and kills Pelléas.

The other characters are the aged King Arkel, grand-

548

father of the two brothers, Geneviève their mother, and Yniold, the little son of Golaud. The whole atmosphere is unmistakably Poesque; the scenery has its psychology as well as the men and women, on whom it exercises a powerful influence; the domain of Allemonde, where the action takes place, is assuredly not far distant from

> . . . the dim lake of Auber
> In the misty mid region of Weir.

We will analyse the first Act in some detail, in order to show the general manner in which the drama is conducted.

Act I. *Scene* I. Golaud, while on a hunting expedition far from home, comes upon a young girl, Mélisande, sitting by a well in a wood and sobbing bitterly. Drawn by her beauty and her distress, he questions her, but with little result—she will only say that she comes from a far land from which she has fled, and that she has lost her way. "From whom, then, hast thou fled? Who hath done thee wrong?" asks Golaud. "All men!" is the reply.

At the bottom of the well he spies the glitter of a crown, evidently fallen from her head, and proposes to recover it for her. But no—she will not have it—it was the crown "he" gave her, she says, and offers no further word of explanation.

Mélisande is beautiful, and very young—Golaud's hair, as she frankly tells him, is already turning grey; nevertheless she lets him lead her out of the wood. We hear no more of the crown, nor of him who gave it to her. "Where are we going?" asks the girl. "I know not," is Golaud's answer; "I too have lost my way."

Scene II. The interior of Arkel's castle, where we find the aged, half-blind king with his daughter Geneviève, the mother of Golaud and Pelléas. She reads him a let-

549

ter that Golaud has written to Pelléas announcing his
return in three days' time, accompanied by the youthful
Mélisande, his six months' bride. He has not informed
them of his marriage—the girl is from a strange and
far-off country, and he is doubtful as to the feeling of his
family; if they are willing to receive her, let them hang
from the castle turret a light that may be seen from the
ship on which he is returning. To Pelléas, who makes a
very brief appearance, this task is assigned.

Scene III. Borne as it were on the stream of the
orchestra we pass to the gardens of the castle. A gloomy
region this, hidden in the midst of vast forests, so dense
in parts that the sun is never seen; only toward the sea
is there any open sky. Geneviève and Mélisande are
gazing toward the light, when Pelléas enters from that
direction. The talk now is all of the sea. 'Tis to the
sea, says Geneviève, that they must look for their light,
but now even the sea is darkling. There will be a storm
to-night, thinks Pelléas. As he speaks, the voices of
sailors are heard, putting out to sea; as the ship sails
into the light Mélisande recognizes it as the one which
had brought her to Allemonde—ah! why should that
ship put out to sea in the face of a tempest?

The night falls suddenly. Geneviève turns to go home,
leaving Pelléas to show Mélisande the way. He offers to
lead her by the hand—but both her hands are full of
flowers—then he must take her arm in his, so steep is the
path, so dark the night.

"To-morrow," he says, "I may be going away!"
"Ah!" cries the girl, "why should you go?"

So ends the first Act: the remaining four preserve a
consistent similarity of treatment. It is plain that by this
flat, bald dialogue, this languid trickle of action, something more is intended than is at first apparent. The
truth is that all must be interpreted by the light of sym-

bolism; certain words, for instance, as light and darkness, forest and sea, must be understood in their symbolic values; read in this way, each phrase, each incident,
will be found to have its full significance. But such
specialized discernment is not for all of us; it is to the
orchestra that we must turn for enlightenment, and few
can fail to be impressed by the marvellous art with which
Debussy succeeds in creating an atmosphere which conveys the very spirit of the scene, as well as the vague
emotions of the shadowy figures before us.

It seems advisable in the case of *Pelléas et Mélisande*
to depart from our usual custom of giving a detailed
analysis of each Act—this would entail quoting passage
after passage of the symbolist dialogue, which, when
divorced from the music, is generally tedious. We must
content ourselves with disentangling the thin thread of
the drama from the many scenes which consist of little
but talk.

Act II. *Scene* I shows us Pelléas and Mélisande sitting
by the fountain in the castle grounds at midday. The
girl is playing with her wedding-ring, which falls into the
well and is seen no more. Some mysterious connexion
is evidently intended between this scene and the opening
episode of the opera where Golaud firsts meets Mélisande by the well, into which her crown has fallen.

Consequently in *Scene* II we are not surprised to find
that Golaud has been telepathically affected by Mélisande's action. He is lying injured, on a couch, tended
by his young wife; while hunting on the previous day he
was thrown from his horse while the bells were sounding
for midday, the precise time at which the ring was lost;
as he fondles Mélisande's fingers he notices its absence
and demands an explanation. Mélisande lies to him: she
dropped the ring, she says, in a cave by the sea when
she was gathering shells, and it is still there. Golaud

sternly bids her go at once and recover it. She is afraid to go alone? Then let Pelléas accompany her.

Scene III. The entrance to the sea-cave. The two stand hand-in-hand in the darkness, waiting for the moon to light them—they have come, apparently, in order to be able to describe the spot at which the ring is supposed to have been dropped. When at last the moon shines out it shows, within the cave, the forms of three old men with long white hair, asleep. "There is famine in the land," is Pelléas' comment. [While we faithfully record such incidents, we must leave it to the reader's ingenuity to explain them.]

Act III. *Scene* I. This is the first real love-scene in the opera. Mélisande is combing her hair at the window of her bower in the turret. Though it is near midnight Pelléas happens to be passing by, and begs Mélisande to reach him her hand that he may kiss it. As she leans far out of the window the whole mass of her long hair— "longer than myself," is her own description—falls over Pelléas, hiding him for the moment in a cloak of rippling gold. Passion awakes in him, and he requires many words and images to express his lover's ecstasy while he holds her captive by her hair. After Mélisande's white doves have flown out from her tower—"never again to return," she says—Golaud comes upon them thus entangled. "Such children! Such children!" he remarks—"laughing nervously," as the stage direction has it—and walks off with Pelléas.

Scene II. The atmosphere here is that of "The House of Usher." Golaud has brought Pelléas down to the mouldering caverns underneath the castle—there are pools of stagnant water, and the whole place reeks of death. The elder man takes Pelléas by the arm and makes him lean over a projecting rock: "Do you see the gulf on the edge of which you are standing, Pelléas?"

PELLÉAS ET MÉLISANDE

But Golaud's arm is shaking ominously—Pelléas rises: "It is stifling here," he says; "let us go!"

The change from the gloom to a sunlit terrace in the gardens gives Debussy occasion for one of his loveliest tonal pictures, which Pelléas accompanies by a vocal rhapsody on the beauty of the scene. Golaud then proceeds in the baldest possible language to tell his brother that he has noticed there is something between him and his wife. "I know, of course," he says, "that there is no harm in it—nothing but childish folly. But Mélisande is about to become a mother, and we must be careful not to upset her; so, for the present, it will be best for you to keep away from her."

Scene IV. This is the Scene which has given such great offence to many—and, indeed, it is difficult to defend it.

Golaud and his little son Yniold are seated below the window of Mélisande's room in the turret. Knowing that the child is often with Mélisande, he questions him closely as to what he has seen pass between her and Pelléas. At last, suspecting his brother to be even now in her room, he lifts the child up to the level of the window, to play the spy and report on what he sees.

"They are silent," says Yniold; "they are standing apart, and both are looking at the light."

The Scene is frankly unpleasant, both in conception and detail—its object, apparently, is to establish Mélisande's innocence.

Act IV. *Scene* I. A short scene for the lovers in which they agree to meet that evening for the last time—Pelléas leaves on the morrow. Incidentally he mentions the strange recovery of his father, who has been lying ill for a long time in the castle; this event Pelléas looks upon as the happiest of omens for the future.

Scene II. The aged King Arkel harps also on this theme. In a long monologue for the benefit of Mélisande he expresses his sympathy with her obvious unhappiness, and hints that now sickness has at last been banished from the castle all things else will take a turn for the better. Unfortunately for his theory, Golaud enters at this moment, his long-pent jealousy in flood at last. The innocent testimony of the child Yniold, the memory of Pelléas and Mélisande bound together in the meshes of her long golden hair—these things have fermented in his brain, and now the boiling torrent of passion is poured out upon his young wife. Harsh words lead to brutal action: seizing her by the long hair he drags her up and down the stage until old Arkel interferes. "Absalom! Absalom!" shouts the madman, as he hauls the wretched girl along. "Is he drunk?" asks Arkel. "No!" replies Mélisande, "but he does not love me any more—and I am not happy!"

Scene III. We are again by the fountain. The child Yniold is provided with a solo in which he laments his inability to move a boulder behind which he has lost his golden ball; he is also interested in the distant bleating of some sheep which are being driven to the slaughterhouse. [Here once more we appeal to the reader's interpretative powers!]

Scene IV. The last meeting of Pelléas and Mélisande. In the moonlight by the fountain, under shelter of the linden-tree, they make the first definite mutual avowal of their love. The language here is fortunately purged to a great extent of symbolism, and goes no farther than the usual extravagance of lovers' talk.

> PELLÉAS. Come into the light! Here 'tis too dark for us to see our happiness.
> MÉLISANDE. Nay, let us stay here! I feel I am closer to you in the darkness!

Alas! their time is short. A harsh grating sound is heard—it is the closing of the castle gates for the night.

554

The lovers find a positive happiness in the thought that
fate has decided for them. "All is lost now—yet all is
won!" Their passion rises to the height of ecstasy—
they know, they feel that someone is coming, that death
is nearing, yet they only hold each other in a closer
embrace.

Then Golaud steals behind them, unseen—his sword
descends, and Pelléas falls dead beside the fountain's
brim.

Act V. Mélisande's chamber. She has been delivered
before her time of a little girl, and now lies at the point
of death.

Golaud, filled with remorse, asks pardon of Mélisande,
which she freely grants. But his worst torment comes
from the doubt which he still entertains as to her relations with Pelléas. He asks her plainly, "Was her love
for Pelléas a guilty passion?" Her simple "No!" fails
to satisfy him: again he implores her, under the shadow
of death, to tell the truth. She still persists in her
former answer—how can he suppose the contrary? But
Mélisande is soon past questioning, and Golaud's doubts
are still unsolved, when she passes away with her little
child beside her—seeming herself so small, so innocent,
that, as old Arkel says, she might well be, not its mother,
but an elder sister.

A more thankless task could hardly be imagined than
to attempt such a skeleton analysis of Maeterlinck's text,
to which Debussy has only too faithfully adhered; yet,
vague, elusive, even meaningless, as it must seem at a first
approach, it has the one supreme merit of having inspired
the composer with a musical masterpiece. The talent of
Maeterlinck is happily merged in the genius of Debussy.
If we find the drama difficult of comprehension, it is to
the orchestra, as we said before, that we must look for

enlightenment. Here Debussy holds up for us the seer's crystal globe in which before us pass the thoughts and emotions of the characters, the scenes in which they move, and, behind all, the shadows of "vast, formless things" that weave their inevitable destinies. All is like

Chases in arras, dreams in a career—

but, however fleeting the vision, Debussy has contrived that it shall be invariably lovely in colour and design.

It is probable that the opera of *Pelléas et Mélisande* will long outlive the play of that name; yet what lover of Debussy but must wish that the composer could have had for his partner, not Maeterlinck, the experimental symbolist, but that "august master of beauty," Edgar Allan Poe!

BORIS GODOUNOV

Music by MOUSSORGSKY. *Words from* PUSHKIN.
St Petersburg, 1874; *London,* 1913; *New York,* 1913.

THE widespread popularity of this opera is not
easy to account for at first sight. It is hardly a
play at all in the generally accepted sense of the
word; several of its many scenes are entirely taken up
with elaborate *tableaux* that do nothing to forward the
action of the drama, while others are occupied with picturesque incidents which, though interesting in themselves, bear little or no relation to the main outlines of
the plot. Even the story itself, when we have succeeded
in discovering it among the mass of irrelevant detail,
appears extraordinarily austere. The love element which
might have been used to lighten it is thrust remorselessly
into the background, and the heroine (if such she can be
called) is a lady with whom Moussorgsky has made it
impossible for us to feel the slightest sympathy. We
turn in dismay from the play to the music, only to
encounter the same uncompromising sternness; no overture, no orchestral interludes, grave, sparkling, or tender, as the occasion demands—nothing to break the
monotony of the continuous recitative to which the dialogue is set but a few songs of the simplest possible kind,
pleasant enough, no doubt, but entirely inadequate to
leaven the huge mass in which they are embedded.
Finally, we discover that the whole thing is marred by an
angularity in the writing that often amounts to down-
right clumsiness. It must be a sovereign merit that can
compensate for such an accumulation of defects. Where
does it lie?

To answer this question fully would require a more elaborate argument than there is space for in a book of this kind. But a few observations may not come amiss. In the first place let us remember that the main political events described in the opera actually took place much as Moussorgsky described them. Boris Godounov did in fact reign as Czar of Russia from 1598 to 1605. Modern research has, indeed, established that he was not implicated in the murder of Czarevitch Dimitri, for which the composer makes him responsible. But his guilt was widely believed at the time and for long afterward. We are thus witnessing a drama that is true in all but one of its main essentials.

This would signify little were it not for the peculiar cast of Moussorgsky's mind. The creator of *Boris Godounov* was, according to his lights, an ardent patriot, and a holder of democratic views, and a vehement believer in artistic realism. Beauty for beauty's sake meant little to him; truth was his ideal, and in music and drama he identified truth with accurate representation. For a man of this sort the stock-in-trade of romantic opera possessed no attraction. The theme he sought must be true, or at least credible; its material must be connected in some way with his beloved country; and it should provide him with an opportunity for a display of that sympathy with an oppressed people that was one of the mainsprings of his character.

In the story of the Czar Boris as told by Pushkin he found what he wanted, and, undismayed by the vastness of his canvas or by the slenderness of his technical equipment, he set to work with all the eagerness of an enthusiast. But it would not do to treat it in the manner of conventional opera with overture, chorus, aria, and the rest: that would be artificial and unworthy of an honest artist. The play must begin at once with the minimum

558

of orchestral prologue, and the instruments must confine themselves throughout to supporting the tones of the voice. The singers themselves must employ a recitative approaching as near as may be to the modulations of spoken speech. Set songs and choruses may be interpolated on occasion (as in a Shakespeare play), but only when the dramatic situation permits. Nor must the story itself be allowed to degenerate into a romantic eulogy of a bloodthirsty tyrant; the real hero of the piece must be the suffering, persecuted people, downtrodden and harried, hopeless, without a leader, and yet the one solid reality amid the welter of contending and ephemeral faction. Crowded scenes will thus become an important element in the work. As to the music, it will maintain a distinctively Russian element throughout; such songs as there are will generally be folk-songs or composed in the folk style, while the choruses will consist of well-known songs or hymns, except on such occasions as it is desired to represent the wild shoutings of an undisciplined crowd.

Except in the Third Act, which takes place in Poland, and where, as we shall see, a more formal element crept in, Moussorgsky was unswervingly faithful to his convictions. But his uncompromising honesty, while it accounts for the character of the work, does not of itself explain its greatness. To understand that we must realize first that he was so saturated in the Russian folk music that its idiom was to him, at least, as natural as the general language of musical Europe. This in itself gives a unique character to *Boris*. But there is something more: Moussorgsky was a dramatic genius of the first order. Not only does he share with other Russian composers that gift for colour which enables him to deal effectively with those scenes in which the crowd figures prominently; he is just as successful when there are only one or two characters on the stage. His recitative is so original, so powerful, that it never wearies us, even when labouring under the disadvantages inevitable to translation, and in the great moments, such as that of Boris' death, he rises to heights where he stands, in his own sphere, alone.

It has just been said that he was unswervingly faithful to his convictions. A single exception must be made. Moussorgsky seems to have been captivated to a certain extent by his tyrant, and Boris looms like a Titan over the whole drama. We may be grateful for this concession, since it provides a unifying element that is badly needed. But it has done more than this; it has provided an unparalleled opportunity to any singer who was great enough to act the part as well as sing it. How that opportunity was taken by Chaliapin many of us can remember. Certainly no one who saw his performance will ever forget it.

Prologue. The curtain rises on the courtyard of the monastery of Novodievich, near Moscow. Boris is supposed to be within the building. A bewildered crowd cries to him to have pity on his children, to accept the crown which is being offered to him and ascend the steps of the Russian throne. But there is no spirit in the singing at this 'officially arranged' demonstration, and it is only the vigilant eyes of the police that keep things going. As to why they have been brought together or what it is they are praying for the poor folk have no idea. At last the clerk of the Duma comes out and announces that Boris has rejected the proffered honour. A band of pilgrims passes into the monastery. The curtain falls. When it rises again the people are once more assembled, this time in the courtyard of the Kremlin. Boris has now accepted the throne and his coronation is proceeding in the cathedral. The crowd are awaiting the conclusion of the ceremony and the return of the royal procession. Presently Boris appears, but the acclamations of his people are powerless to cheer the lonely, troubled heart of the new Czar. He offers up a short but impressive prayer for divine guidance, and passes on.

These two opening Scenes contain nothing in the nature of dramatic action and remind one more of episodes in a historical pageant than of the beginning of an opera. But they fulfil, nevertheless, the purpose that Moussorgsky had in view, and create a background that is never quite forgotten as the piece proceeds.

Act I. *Scene* I. A cell in a monastery. Pimen, an old monk, is at work by lamplight, writing the last page of his chronicle, an account of the troubled times in which he has lived. A steadily moving, tortuous phrase in the orchestra represents his laborious penmanship. The silence of the night is unbroken but for some faint sounds from a choir that are heard for a moment in some distant wing of the building. In a corner of the room lies Gregory, a young monk, asleep. Suddenly he wakes, disturbed by an evil dream. Pimen calms him, and he questions the old man about his chronicle, about the past, and, above all, about the murdered Czarevitch, Dimitri. "He was about thy age—and would be reigning now," replies Pimen, "but God hath overruled it." The matin-bell begins to sound, and taking his staff the old man totters out. But his words have fired Gregory's imagination, and his last words before he follows his teacher are charged with import in view of what follows:

> Boris! Boris! Princes may bow before thee,
> And none so bold as to rebuke thee for
> The death of that unhappy child.
> Yet from the darkness of this lonely cell
> A humble monk shall cry aloud thy secret!

Thou shalt not long escape from human justice,
And God from Heaven shall smite thee in his wrath![1]

Scene II.   An inn on the Lithuanian frontier.   The
Hostess is sitting alone.   To pass the time she sings a
song:

> I have caught a drake
> With feathers of the blue!
> Ah, what a joy to see
> Is my little drake to me, etc.

She is interrupted by the entrance of two wandering
friars, Missail and Varlaam.   One must use the word
friars, for there is no other that is appropriate; but the
reader must not be misled.   The vagabond ruffians who
roamed about Russia at this time calling themselves
friars had little in common with the often saintly products of Western monasticism.   Turbulent, unruly, and
often actually criminal in their dispositions, they were
one of the many scourges that flourished in a time when
the government of the country was unsettled and the
hand of authority weak.   With them is Gregory.   The
young man has now definitely embarked upon his great
adventure.   He has left his monastery and is now on his
way to Poland, where he intends to declare himself to be
Dimitri the Czarevitch, escaped from the clutches of
Boris and eager to unseat the usurper and regain the
throne of his father.

The influence of the good wine which the Hostess sets
before them makes Varlaam talkative.   He was a soldier
once and served with the army of Ivan the Terrible at
the siege of Kazan.   The song in which he describes the
capture of the city is a vigorous piece of work that enjoys
a well-deserved popularity.   But the revels are presently
brought to a sudden conclusion.   A knock is heard her-

alding the arrival of the police, who have been warned of Gregory's escape and have orders to apprehend him. He is only saved by his quickness of wit. Taking advantage of the fact that no one else can read, he takes the warrant and so misrepresents its contents that suspicion is momentarily diverted to Varlaam. Then, while all are crowding round the friar, he makes a sudden dash for the window and escapes into the night.

Act II. The interior of the Czar's apartments in the Kremlin. Feodor and Xenia, Boris' son and daughter, are shown in the charge of their old nurse. Xenia is bewailing the loss of her affianced lover, and the nurse, finding her attempts at consolation unavailing, tries to distract her with a song. A charming interlude follows. The nurse's song—a lot of absurd nonsense about a midge, set to a lively tune—is capped by Feodor with a 'clapping song,' in which the nurse soon joins.

But now the little scene is brought abruptly to an end by the entry of the Czar. Boris speaks a word of sympathy to Xenia, and, bidding her seek solace among her young companions, sends her to her chamber. Then he turns to the Czarevitch. He is delighted to find that Feodor has been studying a map; the knowledge he is acquiring will be useful to him some day—sooner, perhaps, than he imagines. This train of thought leads to a magnificent monologue beginning, "My power is absolute," in which regret, remorse, terror, and an overwhelming sense of guilt strive together in his tortured soul. He is interrupted by a sudden noise without and sends his son to see what is the matter. The boy soon returns and relates the cause of the disturbance: it was only a parrot that flew at one of the nurses. But again the tender scene between father and son is broken into, this time by Prince Shouisky. He is the bringer of bad news: not only is there a revolt of Boyars, but a Pretender has arisen in Poland who calls himself Dimitri. At that name Boris sharply orders his son to withdraw. When they are alone he asks the Prince if he is quite sure the real Dimitri is dead. Shouisky reassures him on that point; he actually saw the body of the murdered child and willingly describes the whole scene. But Boris, whose agitation is visibly increasing, cuts him short and dismisses him. The Czar is alone, and his overwrought nerves conjure up before him a hideous apparition of the boy he has so foully done to death. He starts back, clutches at his throat in an agony of terror, and then suddenly falls on his knees:

> God Almighty! Thou that seekest not the death of a sinner,
> O spare thy servant. Have mercy on my guilty soul!

Act III transports us to Poland, and the curtain rises on the boudoir of Marina Mnishek, daughter of the Palatine of Sandomir. Her maidens attempt to amuse their Princess with a song, but she dismisses them abruptly when it is over and, left to herself, indulges in a long and rather tedious soliloquy. This is delivered to the rhythm of a mazurka, and in the course of it we learn that Gregory (who now calls himself Dimitri) is being sheltered by Marina's father and that the girl herself is inclined to look favourably upon him. This is in no way due to the promptings of her heart—Marina's hard nature is entirely incapable of any weakness of that kind. It is not on Dimitri himself that her desires are fixed, but on the throne of Moscow that he aspires to win.

And now comes a strange episode. Marina's agreeable reflections are put an end to by the sudden entrance of Rangoni, a Jesuit priest. He too has observed the fascination which Marina exerts upon Dimitri, and is determined to make use of it for his own purposes.

564

Speaking with all the authority of his holy office he bids her use all her woman's wiles to captivate the Pretender, even to the sacrifice of her honour, and then, when she has brought him to the condition of being unable to refuse her anything, to extort from him a promise to bring heretic Russia into the Roman fold. This audacious scheme does not appeal to the pleasure-loving Marina and she refuses to have anything to do with it. But she is afraid of the Jesuit in spite of herself, and when he lets loose upon her all the thunders of the Church, threatening her with everlasting damnation, she is speedily cowed into submission.

Scene II. Dimitri is awaiting Marina in the moonlit garden of the castle. But there is no sign of the proud Princess, and it is Rangoni who presently steals out from the shadow of the wall. As soon as he hears that it is from his beloved that the priest has come, Dimitri plies him earnestly with requests to bring her to him. The Jesuit sees another chance of advancing his project: he will willingly assist the intrigue if the Czarevitch will grant him a boon in return. He wishes to become his intimate counsellor, watch over his comings and goings, and be the guardian of his inmost thoughts. Dimitri is well aware whither all this is tending, but his passion will brook no delay and reluctantly he agrees. At this moment a company of lords and ladies come out from the castle, Marina among them, to the strains of a polonaise, and for a while Dimitri withdraws. The guests, however, do not stay long, and as soon as they have gone he returns and is shortly joined by Marina. The girl has learnt her lesson well. While he speaks of love as the only object worth striving for she remains quite unmoved and taunts him with his baseness; but when, stung by her reproaches, he talks of Russia and the crown he will win, she yields at once, and the Act ends with a short love-duet.

This is undoubtedly the weakest portion of the opera. It is said that it did not form part of the composer's original plan and was only inserted by him when his friends complained of the lack of feminine interest in the piece. Be this as it may, Moussorgsky's genius certainly flags here; the soil of Poland is less congenial to it than that of his native Russia, and his mazurka and polonaise contrast very unfavourably with the Russian tunes he employs elsewhere. The historical Marina is a hard, unsympathetic character with whom he found it impossible to do much. The most successful scene is that between her and the Jesuit, and here for a moment the music lives. But, dramatically, the introduction of the Roman priest is unwarranted, for we hear no more of him and very little of his schemes after the end of the Act.

The final Act, however, makes full amends for the weakness of its predecessor. We have done with the Polish interlude, and back in his own country the composer finds his feet again at once. The first Scene is laid in a woodland clearing. A road runs across the stage. The frenzied whirling figures of the short introduction suggest the wild, tumultuous nature of the scene to come. The curtain goes up, and in there rushes a crowd of people dragging with them a captive Boyar of Boris' faction. Seating him on a log they proceed to mock and taunt him. After a while the Village Idiot shambles up, pursued by a crowd of urchins who tease him and filch from him his jealously guarded penny. The next arrivals are the friars, Missail and Varlaam, who are now loud in their praise of Dimitri and their curses of Boris. They join the crowd, which welcomes them gladly. A pair of Jesuits who appear a little later are

566

not so fortunate. Neither the friars nor the people desire interference from Rome, and the Jesuits are quickly bound and led off to be hanged. A procession of troops goes by; Dimitri himself crosses the stage, and on his departure the crowd follows him. Snow has begun to fall. The idiot boy, alone amid the fluttering snowflakes, searches vainly for his lost penny, his clouded mind gazing hopelessly out into the future. He is the very symbol of the oppressed, despairing people.

> Trickle, trickle, tears! Bitter, bitter tears!
> Weep and mourn, ye true believers!
> For the foe will come with sword in hand,
> And a doom will fall on a darkened land!
> Then woe to the land, and woe to the folk,—
> Poor starving folk!

This last Scene was originally placed by Moussorgsky at the very end of his score, and he could hardly have hit upon a more finely artistic conclusion to his work. But producers were nervous about a *finale* in which the leading character did not appear at all, and so in the Rimsky-Korsakoff edition, the one generally followed, the death-scene of Boris, which we are about to describe, was placed last.

We are in the Kremlin at a special meeting of the Duma. The Boyars are assembled and engaged in futile discussion. Presently Shouisky enters and describes how Boris is haunted by visions of the murdered Dimitri. He is in the middle of his narrative when Boris himself reels in, crying, "Avaunt! Avaunt!" But he collects himself quickly and allows Shouisky to summon an old monk who is waiting for an audience. It is Pimen, who has come to relate to the Czar the story of a miracle wrought at Dimitri's tomb. Boris hears him to the end and then falls fainting into the arms of the Boyars. Once more he recovers himself, but now he feels that his end is near. Dismissing the Duma he sends for his son and then, tenderly and with words of wise advice, takes his farewell of him, bidding him protect his sister and commending them both to the care of the God who has deserted their father. The funeral knell is heard and the Boyars re-enter in procession. Feodor makes an attempt to cheer his royal parent, but Boris gently stops him: "Nay, nay, my son, my hour has come." His agony is upon him, but he has strength left for the one supreme effort. Summoning all his ebbing forces the dying lion rises for the last time to his full height, a king even in his mortal weakness, and cries aloud, "While I have life I still am Czar!" But Death is at his throat and even as he speaks he sways, stumbles, and sinks back into his chair gasping a broken, incoherent prayer for mercy. A moment later all is over. The horror-struck Boyars whisper, "He is dead!" and the curtain falls.

LE COQ D'OR

Music by RIMSKY-KORSAKOFF. *Words by* BIELSKY,
from PUSHKIN.
Moscow, 1910; *London,* 1913; *New York,* 1918.

ALTHOUGH the number of operas composed by Rimsky-Korsakoff in the course of his long life runs well into double figures, it is only the first and the last of them that are at all familiar to English audiences. The first, *The Maid of Pskoff,* has become remarkable from the performance of Chaliapin in the rôle of Czar Ivan during the great 1913 season of Russian opera in London, and this same season also saw the production of *Le Coq d'Or,* the composer's last work, which has since received a number of performances in England at the hands of various companies. It is in many ways a remarkable piece. With the single exception of Moussorgsky, Rimsky-Korsakoff is probably the finest operatic composer that Russia has produced, while as a master of orchestration he can stand comparison with the greatest names in music. This is the work of his old age, the matured vintage of a vast experience, and his touch throughout is singularly sure. The story by its very nature presents peculiar problems of musical and dramatic characterization, but he solves them all with that ease and assurance that only come from a complete mastery of his medium.

Realizing, however, that his work might easily be misinterpreted, he has published some "Remarks" at the beginning of the score, from which it is worth quoting an extract or two:

The composer does not sanction any 'cuts.'

The composer desires that the singers in all his works keep strictly to the music written for them.

An opera is first and foremost a musical work.

But even with hints like these *Le Coq d'Or* is difficult to produce in the right way. Not only is the music for the singers of a most exacting nature, demanding vocal and interpretive gifts of the highest order, but the artists who take the leading parts must also be actors of a kind rarely met with on the operatic stage, and skilful dancers to boot, otherwise the work will lose much of its point. So great have these difficulties appeared in the eyes of some people, that the experiment has actually been made of presenting *Le Coq d'Or* with a double cast, each character being represented by a singer standing in the orchestra or elsewhere and an actor or dancer upon the stage. This novel attempt to solve one of the stock problems of opera was never sanctioned by the composer, and is not likely to be widely followed, if only on account of the expense involved.

The story is adapted from a tale by Pushkin. It is described as a "fable," and such it certainly is; but certain elements in the plot are left so obscure that one is almost compelled to accept the theory propounded in many quarters that it has a symbolical or satirical meaning. What that meaning may be it is hard to say, but it has been suggested that the clue is to be sought among the obscure pages of Russian political history. The preface by the author of the libretto does not really throw much light on the subject. He says (to quote from the translation): "The principal charm of the story lies in so much being left to the imagination, but, in order to render the plot somewhat clearer, a few words as to the action on the stage may not come amiss.

"Many centuries ago, a wizard, still alive to-day,

570

sought by his magic cunning to overcome the daughter
of the Aerial Powers. Failing in his project, he tries
to win her through the person of King Dodôn. He is
again unsuccessful, and, to console himself, he presents to
the audience in his magic lantern the story of heartless
royal ingratitude."

A muted trumpet opens the proceedings with a phrase
whose reference to the title of the work is unmistakable.
It is soon joined by other instruments, and a curious,
sinuous theme is heard whose wayward rhythm and
strange intervals suggest the music of the East. This
theme plays an important part in the opera and is associated with the Queen of Shémakâ; presently it gives
place to another, hardly less peculiar, which is first heard
on the bells, and represents the Astrologer, who now appears in front of the curtain. In a few words he tells us
that by his magic he will bring before our eyes an ancient
fable, then suddenly he disappears and the curtain rises.

King Dodôn sits in state in his spacious audience-
chamber. Beside him are his two sons, Afrôn and
Guidôn. A crowd of counsellors and courtiers is present,
among whom we recognize General Polkân, whose long
beard and military bearing make him a conspicuous
figure. At the doors stand sentries, fast asleep, while
at the back we catch a glimpse of the strange city over
which King Dodôn rules.

The King is troubled. In spite of the fact that he is
not as young as he was, neighbouring nations will still
insist on attacking him. He could weep with vexation.
What is to be done? Guidôn suggests that they lay in
a store of provisions and vintage wines and entrench
themselves in the capital. Afrôn inclines toward giving
the whole army a month's leave, then suddenly assembling
it and marching out to battle.

The King and his courtiers are full of admiration for

both these plans, but the military soul of Polkân stirs him to angry speech, and he expresses his contempt in forcible language. This leads to a slight disturbance, while the courtiers catch Polkân and give him a good beating, but it is soon over and they return to their deliberations.

Suddenly there is seen approaching the old Astrologer of the Prologue. He kneels before King Dodôn and tells him that he comes with a solution of his difficulties. He has a Golden Cock which he will give the King; the moment anything happens that is likely to disturb the tranquillity of the kingdom this bird will cry out, "Cock-a-doodle-doo! Danger lies in wait for you!" Until it does that everyone can rest in security. So saying he produces the bird, which immediately crows, "Cock-a-doodle-doo! Peace and quietness for you!"

The King is delighted. Let the Cock be placed on a high point of vantage and start on his duties at once. He thanks the Astrologer, and at first offers him any reward he likes to name, but when the old man tries to extract from him a written promise to this effect, duly witnessed, he backs out hastily. The Astrologer bows and departs, the King dismisses the courtiers, stretches himself in the sun, and says he feels sleepy. His housekeeper, Amelfa, who has just come in, summons the servants, who appear bearing a huge bed. But first the King must take some refreshment. She offers him a dish of dainties. Before he eats he sends for his parrot to amuse him; but his drowsiness soon overcomes him, the parrot is removed, the King climbs into bed, and the orchestra lulls him to sleep with a soothing *berceuse*, while Amelfa keeps the flies off his face.

Presently we hear the theme of the Queen of Shémakâ, indicating the nature of the royal dreams, but this is

572

rudely interrupted by the voice of the Golden Cock calling his warning. A crowd assembles and Polkân, rushing in, shakes his reluctant master into wakefulness. The King gets up, addresses the people, and then turns to his sons, who have come in fully armed. They are each to take half the army and start at once. Unwillingly they depart, and their father returns quietly to bed. But what was it he was dreaming about? Amelfa eventually guesses and he goes happily to sleep.

Again the warning voice of the Cock is heard, and again the people assemble. But the King sleeps on, and once more it is Polkân who has to rouse him. This time Dodôn will take the field himself. His armour is brought; it is very rusty and he has difficulty in donning it as he has increased in girth since last he wore it. At length he is ready, a horse sufficiently quiet for him to ride has been provided, and with Polkân and the remaining troops he passes from the stage followed by words of good advice from the people.

Act II. It is night. By the faint light of the moon we can discern a dark and gloomy gorge. On the hillside lie the bodies of fallen warriors, and in the centre of the stage those of King Dodôn's two sons. The background is shrouded in mist, and the atmosphere of horror is heightened by the sound of the orchestra, which discourses strange and sombre music. Presently we catch the martial air to which the troops had marched off at the end of the previous Act, but now it is heard in the minor key, muffled and pregnant with foreboding. Two at a time, the soldiers of Dodôn appear coming along the gorge, only to halt in grief and terror at the sight before them. Their laments are cut short by the arrival of the King himself with Polkân. In the darkness he stumbles over the bodies of his sons, recognizes them, and breaks into a song of woe. They have quarrelled, he supposes, and this is the result. Polkân is beginning to rally the troops, who have all burst into tears, when the mist rolls away and in the increasing light of dawn there is seen in the background a gorgeously decorated tent. "This, then, is the treacherous enemy!" cries the general. "Forward with the artillery!" A large cannon is brought up and all is ready for its discharge, when the folds of the tent are seen to tremble, the soldiers run away, and there emerges, richly dressed and radiant with beauty, the Queen of Shémakâ, who from this moment onward dominates the action. She starts by singing her "Hymn to the Sun," a magnificent example of modern *coloratura* writing. The King and Polkân are astonished.

> DODON. 'Tis amazing for a woman!
> POLKAN. Execution superhuman!
> She is fair and full of wit,
> Let us join her for a bit!

They do so. The Queen receives them graciously, though she makes no secret of her desire to 'subdue' Dodôn. Polkân opens a conversation on conventional lines, but after a while she takes objection to his manners and he is sent away behind the tent, to stay there till the King says, "One!" Then she moves her cushion nearer to Dodôn and begins her task of conquest in earnest. It is an easy matter. The poor old man is bewildered by her beauty, her strangeness, and the brilliance of her singing, for she pours forth song after song in an abundance that speaks much for the fertility of the composer and makes the highest demands on the powers of the singer. But at last she grows tired. Will not the King sing a song now? Dodôn protests that he has long given up singing, but she presses him, and at last in despair he rises to his feet and bawls:

> Lady fair, through thick and thin,
> I will strive thy love to win,

to an air even more ridiculous than the words set to it. She soon tires of this form of amusement, sings another song herself, and then asks him to dance for her. Again he protests, but she overcomes his opposition by threatening to call back Polkân. Then, removing his helmet and breastplate, and thus leaving him in an absurd costume, she ties a handkerchief round his head, puts a fan in his hand, and bids her retinue come and see the fun. Desperately he dances, faster and faster grows the music, till at last he falls to the ground panting for breath. Presently he recovers a little and manages to summon up enough courage to make his clumsy proposal. She hesitates, and only yields on his promise that Polkân shall be condemned to death! The King's carriage is brought, he and the Queen get into it, and the procession starts off for home, but not before the Queen's retinue have had time to make some caustic remarks about the unsuitability of the match.

Act III. We are back in the capital. The street is crowded with people asking for news, and sounds of crowing in the orchestra show us that the Golden Cock is still at his post. Amelfa appears, and in answer to questions announces that the King and his army have been victorious and are shortly returning with a Queen whom they have rescued. Very soon the procession arrives, and the Queen's retinue, which includes giants, dwarfs, and other oddities, presents a spectacle much appreciated by the people. Finally the King himself appears with the Queen, both still sitting in the carriage, and is loyally welcomed by his subjects. A sudden diversion, however, is produced by the appearance of the old Astrologer. He acknowledges the royal greeting, and announces that he has come to claim the fulfilment of the King's promise to reward him. He asks for —the Queen! Amid the general amazement Dodôn attempts to reason with him, offering him state appointments or anything else he likes. But he utterly fails to move him, and finally, losing his temper, strikes him dead with a blow of his sceptre. The Queen laughs, but the King already regrets his rash act, and turns to her for comfort. She rebukes him curtly, "Nay, the sorry jest is ended," and suddenly there rises the voice of the Cock. The bird flies off its perch, hovers over the crowd, and then, descending suddenly, pecks Dodôn violently on the head and kills him. A clap of thunder is heard, and in the sudden darkness that falls the Queen can be heard laughing. When it grows light again she has disappeared and the people have nothing else to do but weep over the death of their beloved ruler. But on the descent of the curtain the Astrologer appears for a moment in front of it, just as he did at the beginning of the opera. "Let no one be distressed at the tragic ending of the story," he says. "Of all the figures on the stage only two were real—the Queen and I." And so he bows and disappears, leaving us to make what we can of it. The whole-hearted admirers of *Le Coq d'Or* evidently agree with the composer's theory: "An opera is first and foremost a musical work." In other words: "Take care of the sounds and the sense will take care of itself."

DER ROSENKAVALIER

Music by RICHARD STRAUSS. *Words by* H. VON
HOFMANNSTHAL.
Berlin, 1911; *London,* 1913; *New York,* 1913.

EACH of the three principal operas by Richard
Strauss, *Salome, Elektra,* and *Der Rosenkavalier,*
has in turn been condemned in certain quarters
as being *contra bonos mores*; on such a judgment in
connexion with the first two works we shall offer no
opinion, but all musicians must rejoice that the third
and best of the three has already passed beyond the
sphere of irrelevant censure into the world of accepted
successes.

The description on the title-page—"A comedy for
music by H. von Hofmannsthal. . . . Music by Richard
Strauss"—is an indication that poet and composer must
be considered as of equal rank—if, indeed, the former
be not entitled, like his own Baron Ochs, to walk three
paces in advance of the latter. In any case it is certain
that no composer ever had so distinguished a col-
laborator.

As poet, dramatist, and prose essayist, Hugo von
Hofmannsthal has long been a prominent figure in Con-
tinental literature; he is less widely known in England
than in the United States, where Mr Charles Wharton
Stork's admirable translations of the lyrical poems have
drawn attention to a very important aspect of his genius.
Hofmannsthal is before all things a symbolist, and this
fact must be kept in mind in estimating even the fantastical manner of *Der Rosenkavalier.*

("The Rose-bearer" is the not very happy title of

577

the English version. "The Silver Rose" would, perhaps, better convey the idea, since it is around such a Rose that the story is woven, and this Rose is the symbol of Love.)

This drama is many things in one; it is a comedy of intrigue, after the Beaumarchais model, a comedy of manners, *à la* Congreve, it has grim touches of Hogarthian satire; but all is permeated by the spirit of Hofmannsthal the poet, with his symbol of the Silver Rose— not to be denied his moments of tenderness and pathos, lifting a squalid situation into the realm of fantastic humour, intent often on showing us beauty even in the waste places. Through all these moods Strauss has followed the poet in complete sympathy, with the result that *Der Rosenkavalier* stands next to Humperdinck's *Hänsel und Gretel* in the direct line of the Wagnerian succession.

Act I. We must imagine ourselves in the great world of Vienna at the time when Maria Theresa was Empress —a world of elegant gallantry, into the atmosphere of which the dramatist plunges us at once, without preliminary or reserve. The scene is a large *salon* communicating with others in the private apartments of the Princess von Werdenberg, the most impressive and convincing figure of a *grande dame* to be found on the operatic stage.

The situation disclosed at the rising of the curtain is unusual, and what is generally described as 'piquant.' It is early morning, and the birds sing cheerily, yet the general impression is not so much that day is just beginning as that a happy night is hardly ended.

Stretched on a sofa, in elegant *déshabillé,* is the Princess von Werdenberg, while at her feet reclines Octavian, her boy-lover, still adoring the white arm she allows him to retain.

578

"Bichette!" says the boy.

"Quinquin!" says the Princess, as she strokes his hair. Octavian is in deadly earnest and too young to know better—this great and gracious lady is for him the immortal goddess, ever young and ever fair. But the Princess—'Marie Thérèse' she has been named, after a still greater lady—is a married woman of vast experience, and with a clear eye for the inevitable future. In the midst of the boy's too ardent worship, his little fits of jealousy, his protestations of a lifelong devotion, she realizes only too well that they are living in a fool's paradise; his youth has just begun, her prime is nearly over; the day will come—to-morrow, maybe—when he will leave her, to find his true affinity.

No need to speak of Octavian's indignant denial of such a possibility. One fact, however, cannot be gainsaid—the Princess has a husband, who may return at any moment from his hunting expedition. A commotion without suggests that her fears are realized, and Octavian takes refuge in a curtained alcove. Fortunately it turns out to be nothing worse than a certain country cousin of the Princess, a formidable bore, indeed, but not dangerous. Baron Ochs von Lerchenau—Squire Bull of Darksmead, we might render it in English—is the dominating personage in the opera, and a masterly creation. He has a certain likeness to the booby-squires of our eighteenth-century fiction, in some points he resembles the Falstaff of *The Merry Wives*—like Sir John he is a very mountain of lechery—while in the matter of pompous self-complacency he sets a standard of his own.

The Baron has come, it appears, on a matter of the highest family importance. He is about to be married. He has decided to bestow the overwhelming honour of his hand, with all the solemn dignity attaching to his lengthy pedigree, upon the daughter of a certain worthy citizen Faninal, who has only lately succeeded in adding the indispensable 'von' to his name, thanks to the vast fortune he has made as an army-contractor. The Baron is full of apologies for such a *mésalliance,* but, as he says, the fellow owns an immense property—and his health, he hears, is none of the best. As for the girl, she is charming, and only just come from a convent-school. In any case, his mind is made up, and he has come to ask his cousin's assistance in a very delicate matter. It is the custom, it seems, among families of the highest rank, that the prospective bridegroom, before visiting his *fiancée,* should send her a silver rose as the symbol of his love; this must be presented in person by a member of his family—can the Princess von Werden-berg suggest a suitable ambassador for the present occasion?

As the Scene develops the Princess has need of all her breeding to enable her to bear with the liberties in which her too blue-blooded relation thinks fit to indulge. The foregoing voluble statement of the Baron's errand has been constantly interrupted by his shameless flirtation with the pretty serving-maid in attendance on the Princess—none other, in fact, than Octavian, who has taken advantage of his concealment in the alcove to assume this disguise, and now passes for 'Mariandel,' a country girl, new to her Highness's service. At the first sight of the strapping wench the lustful Ochs is all on fire and, in spite of the Princess's endeavours to get her out of the room, persists in detaining her, and takes every opportunity of whispering proposals into her ear. The Princess can only resign herself to the situation, while Octavian enjoys the fun and leads the Baron on to commit himself still further.

At last the Princess hits upon a device by which to get 'Mariandel' out of the room; she sends her to fetch a miniature of a certain kinsman of the family who might possibly act as the bearer of the Silver Rose. The portrait with which Octavian returns is actually one of himself—the Princess has prepared a satisfactory explanation—and the Baron is well pleased that Count Octavian Rofrano, younger brother of the Marquis, should be his ambassador.

Now follows the most diverting scene of the opera— the Princess's *levée*. The folding-doors are thrown open and at once the stage is crowded by a clamorous mob of candidates for her Highness's favour. A dressing-table is brought prominently forward, at which the Princess submits herself to the operations of her *perruquier* and at the same time endeavours to take some courteous notice of each of her noisy petitioners. Among these we may notice a French milliner (with a *chapeau Paméla*), an Italian tenor with his flautist, a dealer in parrots and monkeys, a scholar, a widow 'lady of quality' with her three 'quality' orphans, to say nothing of what the major-domo describes as "the usual pack of rubbish." [We must keep an eye on two very suspicious-looking Italians, man and woman, who would seem to be always lurking, for some dark purpose of their own, in places where they are least likely to be noticed; their names are Valzacchi and Annina, and their function is to add a touch of grotesque fantasy to the action.]

While all these enact their little parts—the tenor has a charming Italian song, and the four ladies a delicious little quartet that irresistibly recalls Mozart—the Baron Ochs is busy with an attorney over the marriage settlement. Their business over, the Princess dismisses the crowd, courteously retaining the scholar for a few minutes' conversation. The mysterious Italians seize the opportunity to commend themselves to the Baron's notice; he is about to take a young and lovely bride;

their business is to supply secret information—who knows how soon he may require their services? Ochs dismisses them, without the expected *douceur*, and turns, to present the Silver Rose to the Princess, who now hurries him also out of the room—she must dress, or she will be late for Mass.

Whether her Highness ever gets so far as the confessional we do not know, but the rest of the Act is given up to a self-revelation on her part which would be invaluable to her spiritual director. She begins with an indignant denunciation of her unspeakable kinsman, Baron Ochs von Lerchenau; she feels an intense loathing at the thought of the approaching alliance between such a brute with a young girl fresh from school. And yet, was not her own fate much the same? What remains of the innocent child she herself can call to mind—how many years ago!—where is she now? Alas, she died so young! —but what of the years since then? And soon they will be speaking of "the old Princess Theresia." . . .

It is in this mood that the boy Octavian finds her when he returns, dressed as himself once more. He cannot move her from her sadness—she is obsessed by the thought of

Time's wingèd chariot hovering near

—soon it will overtake them, and bear him away from her: "Now, or to-morrow—if not to-morrow, very soon." She soothes his passionate protests as best she may, and dismisses him—they will meet again that evening in the Prater.

Octavian leaves her—and, for the first time, without a kiss. Instantly she summons her footmen and orders them to call him back, but he has already galloped out of sight. Finally she rings for her little black boy, to whom she confides the Silver Rose, the symbol of love, to be delivered into the hands of the Count Octavian—he will understand.

The curtain falls on the Princess, with bowed head, gazing sadly into the darkening future.

From this mere summary of an extraordinarily complicated Scene much has necessarily been omitted; but attention must be drawn to Ochs' long and unctuous disquisition on the various kinds of women and the way to trap them: *Macht das einen lahmen Esel aus mir?* It might be called "The Profligate's Vade-mecum," so rich is it in the advice that can only come from a varied experience. Strauss, in his musical commentary, has not missed a single point of interest; so elaborate indeed is the orchestration, so rapid and emphatic the delivery of the vocal part, that it would seem to matter little whether it be sung or spoken. The words must be heard—the musical interest lies with the orchestra. Vocal compensation, however, is made in the delightful trio for Ochs, Octavian, and the Princess, *Nein, Er agirt mir gar zu gut,* which closes the episode.

It seems futile to compare Ochs' monologue, as some have done, with the famous *Madamina* of Leporello in *Don Giovanni,* since the two conceptions belong to entirely different worlds. Nor is much to be gained by suggesting that Octavian is a sort of grown-up Cherubino; the latter is a purely ideal figure, while "Mignon" is altogether too actual, and for this reason can never be a sympathetic figure on the operatic stage—he is better appreciated in the subtle pages of von Hofmannsthal's libretto.

That the composer had Mozart constantly in his mind is clear from many a passage, such as the little quartet already alluded to, and the breakfast-scene, in which Strauss, wisely eschewing comparison, gives us a charming waltz where Mozart might have written a minuet.

583

But perhaps the loveliest thing in the whole Act is the Princess's soliloquy toward the end, *Kann mich auch an ein Mädel erinnern,* and that is Strauss' very own.

Act II.   The present Act is comparatively simple after the crowded confusion of Act I; it is really a passionate love-duet against a background of excellent comedy, with some splashes of rather biting satire.   We are in the mansion of the newly ennobled Herr von Faninal, a very perfect snob indeed, but hardly so diverting a figure as the outrageous Ochs.

The family has been apprized of the coming visit of the young Count Octavian as the bearer of the Silver Rose to Sophie, the daughter of the house, and the bride-elect of Baron Ochs von Lerchenau.   Faninal is just going out, for, as the major-domo reminds him, it is contrary to etiquette that he should be found on the premises when the ambassador arrives.   Marianne, the duenna—a worshipper of rank—is at the window, in excited anticipation.   Sophie's excitement takes another form.   She, a young girl, with the influence of the convent still upon her, is about to be united in the holy state of wedlock with "the virtuous and noble Lord of Lerchenau," as Marianne describes him; she is overwhelmed by the honour, she is dazzled by the splendour of the bridegroom she has never seen; from a full heart she prays Heaven to keep her from the deadly sin of pride, and from loving too much the pomps and vanities of this world.

Outside we hear a noise of cheers and shouting that comes always nearer; already they are calling, "Room for the Count Rofrano!" beneath her windows.   "And will they so call out all the grand titles of my husband-to-be when he comes to claim me?" she wonders.   That husband she has not yet seen, and even her imaginary portrait of him begins to fade from the moment that she

584

sets eyes on the glittering apparition who now enters the room—not an angel from Heaven, as Marianne suggests, but the young Octavian, the bearer of the Silver Rose of love.

It is a beautiful and impressive scene as the young Count in silver and white advances with the Rose, like a pale silver flame, in his hand; his retinue are in green and white, and prominent among them are his Hungarian bodyguard, with their big fur caps and crooked sabres; Faninal's household forms the background.

With an embarrassed reverence Octavian offers the flower to the girl, who stands entranced at the wonderful vision before her. The Rose would seem to exhale an influence as powerful as Isolde's love-potion; it requires a long passage of great lyrical beauty to express their first fantastic rapture. The fragrance, says Sophie, when first she bends over the silver filagree, is that of real roses; yet no; this is a gift from Heaven; only the roses of Paradise can smell so sweet. Octavian, too, feels that this is no earthly rose that can work such miracles in him; he has found himself at last: "I was a boy, until I saw her face!" Toward the end of the duet, though each is singing 'aside' they are allowed to use the same words: "There was once a time when I was blest like this—but where can it have been?" Henceforth, at any rate, this blessed memory will never fade.

The first mysterious ecstasy is over; the servants leave the room, and only Marianne remains while the two sit side by side, and Sophie discusses, with childish innocence, the subject of her approaching marriage, from which she promises herself such happiness. Does Octavian never long to marry? But with him, of course, it is different; a man is always a man—but a woman is nothing until she is married; what does she not owe to her husband!

This dialogue, *Ich kenn' Ihn schon recht wohl,* is sung throughout to one of the many waltz-measures which, though a bone of contention among the critics, are an unquestionable factor in the popularity of this opera; the present simple and elegant example of the form seems peculiarly appropriate to the situation.

The waltz changes to a march as the husband to whom Sophie is to owe so much is ushered into the room. A greater contrast between this procession and the one we have lately witnessed could hardly be imagined. The Baron, a gross and overbearing animal, is followed by some loutish retainers, apparently fresh from the plough and squeezed into ill-fitting liveries; the obsequious Faninal, in attendance, seems the more respectable figure of the two.

Sophie's illusions are shattered at a glance, and every movement of the Baron but heightens her disgust. His first attempt at compliment is enough; carefully examining her hand as he kisses it, he remarks approvingly on the delicate wrist, "a thing," he adds, "rarely found in persons of your station." ("This might be some low horse-dealer!" is Sophie's comment.) As he proceeds to put her through her paces, the poor girl grows hot with shame and anger, but her restiveness only excites the baser part of the Baron's nature. "That's just how I like 'em!" he chuckles. "Egad! I have the luck of all the Lerchenaus!" Once they are married, he feels sure, she will make the most devoted of wives!

[It is here that we have the one really popular passage in the opera, the facile waltz-tune (*Mit mir, mit mir!*) to which Ochs expresses his maudlin sentiments; it is exactly the sort of music that would make the fortune of any 'musical comedy,' and the composer of *Elektra* evidently wrote it to show how well able he was to carry

586

on the old Strauss tradition and provide the Viennese public with its favourite fare.]

All this while Octavian has been boiling with indignation, and even the duenna (who is enchanted with the Baron's "easy ways") begins to feel nervous at the turn things are taking, when Faninal fortunately enters with the notary, and the three men withdraw into the next room, Ochs leading the way and taking good care that his future father-in-law shall keep not less than three paces behind him.

An uproar among the Baron's drunken servants calls the duenna from the room, and the pair are left alone. Lovers at first sight, their recent experience has brought them closer together. All tumult dies away in the orchestra as we begin the long love-duet that works up to its climax in the passage *Mit Ihren Augen voll Tränen*. By this time the boy and girl are in each other's arms, and blind to all else, though for some time their actions have been watched by others. These are the Italian spies, Valzacchi and Annina, who have made a noiseless entry through secret panels on opposite corners of the room, and, choosing their moment, rush on their victims, hold them fast, and shout loudly for Baron Ochs von Lerchenau.

The Baron is rather amused than seriously annoyed when he grasps what he imagines to be the situation; but Octavian is in a very different mood—he has something that the Baron must hear without delay. "This young lady ——" he begins, but Ochs will not listen—he affects to regard it all as a mere boyish freak—besides, Sophie is wanted in the next room. The girl flatly refuses to follow him, and Octavian stands in front of the door to bar the Baron's passage. "This lady," he says firmly, "has decided that under no circumstance will she marry you—and for my part I may tell you that

I consider you a thief, a liar, a dowry-hunter, and a dirty clodhopper." [At this crisis we find ourselves once more away on the wings of the waltz-measures which pursue us throughout this Act.] The noble Ochs' reply is to whistle for his men, who appear at the folding-doors. But Octavian's blood is up; he forces the Baron to draw, and, closing with him, inflicts the slightest of wounds on his arm.

The Baron's cries of pain and alarm bring the whole household on the scene, and a very enjoyable *ensemble* follows (still in the liveliest waltz-time), while the booby is helped on to a couple of chairs, and fussed over by his attendants, the duenna, and Faninal. The latter now becomes the centre of interest; besides condoling with the Baron and expressing his pious horror at Octavian's audacity, he has Sophie also to deal with. Her quiet statement that she has no intention of proceeding with the match drives him to distraction—she *shall* marry the Baron, dead or alive! He will drive her to church himself—what! she will say "No!" at the altar! Then a convent, nay, a prison-cell, shall be her lot for the rest of her life.

Sophie makes her escape, Octavian has already left, Faninal hurries out to order the choicest of wines for the wounded man, who is now in the hands of a physician. Thanks to his attention, the Baron soon begins to feel quite at his ease again; under the influence of some generous Tokay he hums his favourite waltz, *Mit mir,* and gives himself up to the agreeable imaginings which the words suggest.

The future glows with a still rosier light when the mysterious Annina enters and hands him a letter from —Mariandel! This non-existent personage writes to say that she will be free to-morrow evening, and entirely at his lordship's disposal. The Baron is in the highest of spirits: "Did I not say I have the luck of all the Lerchenaus?" he chuckles, as he lumbers off to bed, filled with delicious anticipations of to-morrow's assignation with the Princess's servant-maid.

Only one thing Ochs has forgotten; when the go-between hands us a mysterious letter on the stage, we are expected to reply by pressing a purse of gold into her hand—this the Baron has, most unfortunately, omitted to do.

Act III. After a brilliant and elaborate introduction —a *fugato* in six parts—the curtain rises on a scene in dumb show which puzzles us sorely as to its purpose; it is plain, however, that we must be prepared for any amount of trickery and illusion in the events which are to follow.

In semi-darkness and perfect silence mysterious figures move to and fro, apparently rehearsing for one of Messrs Maskelyne and Cooke's entertainments or a bogus spiritualist *séance*. Apparitions rise through trap-doors, faces peer out suddenly from panels which revolve noiselessly, while a 'blind' window is shown to be highly 'practicable.' The directors of these manœuvres are the two Italians, Valzacchi and Annina; the latter is in widow's weeds, and is seen making-up her face and otherwise altering her appearance. Octavian, too, in his Mariandel disguise is here, but only for a short time; the purse of gold he gives Valzacchi on leaving makes it plain in whose interest, and against whom, the two intriguers are "maturing their felonious little plans."

The silent conspirators having departed, servants come and light the candles; we now see a large room in an old-fashioned hostelry, with a curtained recess and a table laid for two. We need hardly say that the expected guests are Ochs and Mariandel.

The Baron's first act on entering is to extinguish most

of the candles; he declines the help of the officious waiters, and, left alone, proceeds to ply his companion with wine, in order to overcome the shyness which 'she' affects to feel. We soon begin to be thankful for the arrangements, of which we had glimpses at the beginning of the Act, whereby the room has been transformed into a sort of cabinet of mysteries; we see that this is one of many ingenious devices by which the threatened unpleasantness of the scene is constantly averted.

The first thing to awaken the Baron's uneasiness is the startling likeness between Mariandel's features and those of the young Count under whose punishment he is still smarting—he cannot banish Octavian from his thoughts. But more definite fears soon assail him. In the very act of embracing his Mariandel he is conscious of a face scowling at him from a corner of the room: the opposite wall seems alive with leering eyes: he turns just in time to see a man's form vanish through the floor. He is beside himself with fright when the situation takes on a more broadly comic aspect. The blind window opens, and a funereal figure with outstretched arms shrieks, "My husband! 'tis he!" and vanishes, only to reappear through the door, followed by four small children, deserted like herself, she explains, by the heartless Baron! The woman storms, the children bawl "Papa!" in chorus; the Baron demands that they should be thrown out of the room, but meets with little sympathy from the landlord, who talks darkly of bigamy, and complains bitterly of the scandal that threatens his respectable establishment. The tumult grows, until Ochs rushes to the window and shouts for the police.

This is the Baron's fatal mistake—he has overestimated his own importance. The Commissary of Police who comes in answer to his call knows nothing of Ochs von Lerchenau—a provincial nobody—he merely sees an

590

irate and pompous personage in a compromising position. Who is he, pray? And who is this young woman? He must know that such things are not permissible in Vienna!

(At this juncture Octavian dispatches a secret messenger to Faninal, and the Baron's valet sends to implore the assistance of the Princess von Werdenberg.)

Driven into a corner, the Baron declares that the lady with him is his affianced bride, the daughter of that well-known citizen the noble Herr von Faninal. Unfortunately for the Baron, Faninal arrives at the moment to give an indignant denial to such a statement—his daughter Sophie is waiting down below. Before she can come up, the alleged widow with her abandoned brood renew their whining accusations, to which Faninal is quite ready to listen. Sophie arrives on the scene, only to express her joy at the turn events have taken—for her part she is glad to be definitely rid of the man she has no intention of marrying. These successive shocks, which mean the ruin of his dearest hopes, are too much for poor Faninal, who collapses and is taken to an adjoining room.

This prolonged series of fantastic events now culminate in a scene of the wildest farce. The Baron is about to leave, taking Mariandel with him; that personage, however, strongly objects, and claims the protection of the Commissary. A few whispered words are sufficient to fill that officer with amused surprise, as he hands the cheeky 'girl' to the curtained recess, into which she disappears. The furious Baron has to be restrained while a complete set of female garments are flung out one by one into the room, to be made into a bundle by the smirking officer, while Octavian pushes a dubious head from time to time between the curtains.

The entrance of the Princess von Werdenberg clears the atmosphere and brings with it a welcome repose. A

591

great lady by birth and tradition, a woman of the world by long experience, 'Marie Thérèse' appears like the 'goddess from the car' who is to unravel the tangled intrigue. The Commissary is well known to her, and after a short 'aside' with him she is *au fait* with all that has happened. Anxious to avoid scandal, to hurt no one's feelings, she endeavours to make light of the whole affair: "It is just one of those trifling masquerades," she says, "of which we Viennese are so fond." Even with the Baron she is courteous, though firm. If he is wise, she hints, he will retreat without more ado. But the Ochs' hide is of a prodigious thickness; even after Sophie has delivered a message from her father to the effect that never again will the Baron be allowed to darken his doors, he still fails to realize his true position. The Princess's patience is marvellous, but at last she tells him plainly that he must renounce all pretensions to the Faninal alliance, and had better not show his face in Vienna for some time to come.

The Baron's final discomfiture, played to the briskest of waltz-tunes, is a most joyous affair. As he turns toward the door the whole pack are on him—landlord, waiters, coachmen, boots, all crowd around with clamorous demands for money; the brats, still wailing for "Papa!" get between his legs, while Annina (her old self again) dances in front of him, maliciously repeating his favourite boast, "Egad! I have the luck of all the Lerchenaus!" At last the Baron makes an ignominious bolt, with his pursuers at his heels.

Purged by so much hearty laughter of its grosser elements, the action proceeds leisurely to a tranquil close. On the stage are left Octavian, Sophie, and the Princess —grave, serene, and a great lady, she commands our sympathy. Face to face with the trial she had foreseen "now or to-morrow—if not to-morrow, very soon," she meets it bravely and with perfect dignity. But she is much more than a woman of the world; she had vowed always to put Octavian's happiness before her own, and she will do so—it is her duty to smooth the way for the boy and girl she sees before her. She finds a way to soften Octavian's painful embarrassment—"Go, and do all that your heart commands!" she bids him—she contrives to set even Sophie at her ease with words of commendation, and, as a crowning act of courtesy, undertakes to pacify her father by offering to drive him home in her own carriage. What the effort has cost her may be gathered from her share in the fine trio *Hab' mir's gelobt ihn lieb zu haben.*

She goes into the next room to speak with Faninal. With her departure all problems and complexities have vanished both from stage and orchestra, and the opera is vignetted off with a formal duet of Mozartian sweetness and simplicity, in which Octavian and Sophie enter upon that dream of a never-ending love which the Princess dreamed so long ago, and which she still retains among her most sacred memories.

The two most significant operas that have appeared within the last thirty years are Debussy's *Pelléas et Mélisande* and Strauss' *Rosenkavalier,* and in each case the words demand a more than usual amount of consideration. In the first-named work a drama of some literary pretensions has served as admirable material for a composer whose musical genius conceals the weakness of the text by making it an integral part of something far greater. With *Der Rosenkavalier* the case is very different. Hugo von Hofmannsthal belongs to the authentic race of poets, Richard Strauss ranks with the greatest of symphonic composers—the conjunction of the two results in a conflict of fairly equal forces in which the poet comes off the loser.

Von Hofmannsthal's work has in it so fine a literary quality that *Der Rosenkavalier,* if expanded for the stage, might well take its place among the classic comedies. His Baron Ochs is, as we have said, a great creation; the Princess von Werdenberg, on a smaller scale, hardly less so; on the stage Octavian might be made convincing, and Sophie would be seen in the right perspective. The whole conception of the play is a happy mingling of satirical comedy with delightful fantasy, not without passages of tender beauty, while the dialogue and the situations are contrived throughout with the most delicate subtlety.

All this, of course, the composer has absorbed and striven faithfully to express, but the matter is too complex for musical treatment, and Strauss' vigorous and exuberant methods seem particularly ill-suited to the task. Accustomed for so long to make thunder and lightning with his orchestra, he forgets that there are situations in which

> it is excellent
> To have a giant's strength, but tyrannous
> To use it like a giant.

Even in the quieter passages Strauss' orchestration too often resembles that favourite economy of our mid-Victorian ancestors, the 'crossed' letter, which it required both time and patience to decipher; in neither case can the meaning be apprehended at a cursory encounter, and in the traffic of the stage this must always prove a serious handicap. And far too often is the ocean of sound lashed to a fury which beats the life out of the poor singers struggling to make themselves heard. As we have already pointed out, this is generally the fate

594

of Ochs—for him to trouble to learn his 'notes' would almost seem to be labour thrown away; he can only win through by means of the most strenuous declamation and an unremitting attention to by-play.

But one of the most striking instances of this overweening tyranny of the instruments is to be found at the end of the First Act. The Princess has just dismissed Octavian, who has gone quietly from the room, when we are lifted almost out of our seats by such a hullabaloo in the orchestra as suggests nothing less than an immediate catastrophe—say the outbreak of a revolution, or the fall of Dagon's Temple. And what does it actually signify? Why, that "Mignon" has gone off without embracing his mistress! Although the poor lady is trying to express that fact, and her consequent emotions, through the ordinary dramatic channels, not only are we unable to hear what she says, but our attention is distracted from the figure on the stage by the unaccountable uproar in the orchestra.

Confronted with such a lack of proportion, and recalling by what simple means and with what beautiful effect Gluck or Mozart, or Verdi in his maturity, would have expressed an equivalent situation, we are inclined to question whether Opera in these latter days has not gone somewhat astray. Surely it would be better to leave the emotional revelation to the singer's art, supported, not crushed, by the orchestra; while in the case of a 'character' part like Ochs' it seems as if a welcome return might be made to the old *recitativo secco,* or even the device of speaking the words to music.

Indeed, Strauss himself appears to have realized that, after all, the orchestra was not the only means of expression at his command; in no other opera has he paid such attention to the voice, or given us so much genuine melody. For this we owe him a great debt of gratitude, and for much else besides—for not having hesitated to shock the 'serious' with the frivolity of his waltzes —for offering incense so freely at the shrine of Mozart, least 'serious' of musical divinities—and, more particularly, for the quiet and lovely close of the final scene. In writing *Der Rosenkavalier* Strauss seems to have paused for a while on the path he had so long pursued, resolved to look back and ponder over the past before proceeding farther. If our young composers will consent to profit by the ripe experience of so great a genius and imitate his example, the welcome day cannot be far distant when the tyranny of the orchestra in the domain of opera will at last be ended.

INDEX

603

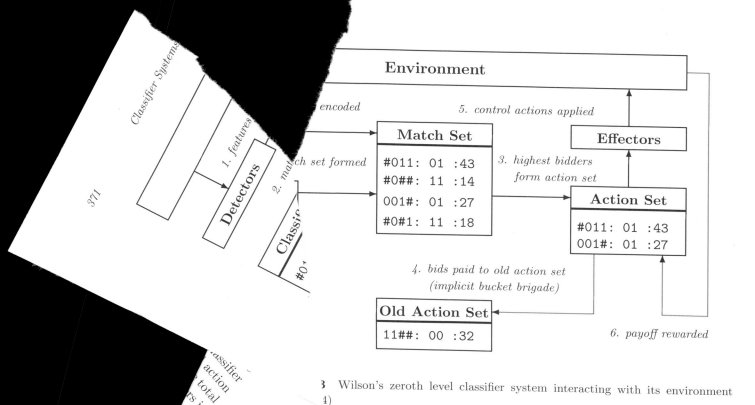

3 Wilson's zeroth level classifier system interacting with its environment
4)

Figure 21.3 shows a ZCS system with its environment. A single cycle of a ZCS can be described as follows:

1. The features in the visible portion of the environment are encoded by the detectors. The result is a binary string (not shown in the figure, but equal to "0011") that is matched to the classifiers in the next step.

2. The match set is formed by comparing the condition of every classifier against the binary string returned by the detector. If no such classifier exists, then a special step (called "covering") is taken to add a new matching classifier to the ZCS.

3. Using a random roulette selection method on the strengths of all classifiers in the match set (identical to the roulette selection method described in Chapter 20), a single classifier is chosen. All classifiers in the match set that advocate the same action are then placed in the action set.

4. Every classifier in the action set pays a portion of its strength to every classifier in the previous action set (if it exists).

Symbol	Meaning
β	learning rate for strength updates in im
γ	discount factor for payments made to pr
τ	tax rate for strength reduction on classifi
ρ	probability of invoking the GA in a given
ϕ	covering parameter; covering occurs if $s(M$

Table 21.1   Summary of ZCS parameter

5. The control action is applied by the effectors.

6. Any reward received by the ZCS is evenly distributed to all
   action set.

After the final step, the current action set replaces the old action set,
begins anew.

The previous description omits a few details concerning how payoff is
to the classifiers. To further explain things, we need to use some symbols
the various sets and some other special values. Let P refer to the entire
population, M refer to the match set, A to the action set, and O to the ol
set. Also, for any of the sets (A, for example), let the notation $s(A)$ refer to th
strength of every classifier of the set and let $|A|$ refer to the number of classifi
the set.

We can now more rigorously describe the credit assignment as follows. All
the system parameters are summarized Table 21.1. To start, a fraction, β, of th
strength of each classifier in A is deducted from all members of A. This total
amount, $\beta s(A)$ is stored for a later step in a temporary holding place, which we
will refer to as the "bucket" or b. Next, if the ZCS receives a reward of r after
taking the action, then the strength of each member of A is increased by $\beta r/|A|$.
Afterward, if O is not empty, then the strength of each member of O is increased
by $\gamma b/|O|$, where b is the "bucket" used in the first step. Finally, all members of M
that are not part of A have their strength reduced by τ, which can be thought of
as a penalty or tax for having advocated a non-winning strategy.

The process of changing the strengths of the classifiers can be intuitively described by the following. Each classifier that contributes toward a specific action
pays a portion of its strength to the classifiers that helped the ZCS get into the state
that activated the action. That is why credit is passed from the current action set
to the old action set. Next, each of the classifiers in the action set evenly shares in
any reward received. Also note that at the next time step they will receive a share
of the rewards at that time, but discounted by γ. Thus, classifiers pay those that
help them and receive payment from those they help. The final step of the credit

assignment, that is, the taxation step, makes the ZCS eventually more decisive. Wilson explains that the taxation reflects an explore/exploit tradeoff: A lower tax rate allows different actions to be tried while a higher tax rate encourages a specific action to be exploited.

The reinforcement algorithm can be combined with a GA as follows. Using a biased coin, the GA can be invoked at each cycle of the simulation with probability ρ. When the GA is invoked, exactly two parents are selected, via roulette selection on their strengths, that will have offspring that replace two other members of the population that are chosen by roulette selection on the inverse of their strengths. Thus, the strongest classifiers are most likely to reproduce and replace the weakest classifiers, but the whole process is stochastic, so anything can happen. This procedure is especially convenient because it keeps the population size constant and operates with a trivial amount of overhead at each cycle of the ZCS. As in the previous chapter, new offspring can be crossed and/or mutated. If they are crossed, then the average of the parents' strengths is used as the strength of the offspring.

In the second step of the performance cycle of the ZCS, it is possible for there to be no classifiers that match the current state returned by the detectors. When this happens, a special operation is invoked. The current state is used as a template to create a new classifier condition, "#" symbols are randomly sprinkled on the condition, the action of the new classifier is randomly set, and the strength of the classifier is set to the average strength of the population. The new classifier replaces an existing classifier that is chosen by roulette selection on the inverse of the strengths. Wilson refers to this as the "covering operation" and compares the process to rote memorization. Covering is also used if $s(M)$ is less than some fraction of the population's average strength, which occurs when every member of the match set is relatively week.

21.4   Experiments with ZCS

We are now ready to put together everything from the last section to see how classifier systems can learn to solve problems. We will consider three problems in this section, all of which require us to simulate an artificial environment for the classifier system to interact with. The first two problems are test cases proposed by Wilson. The last problem is a standard test problem from the reinforcement learning community whose solution requires that the ZCS be augmented with a form of memory.

Woods1   Figure 21.4 shows an environment known as Woods1 that defines a rectangular grid world that a virtual creature (or "animat") is allowed to roam through. All of the actions of the creature are dictated by a ZCS. The ZCS can "see" only the eight cells that immediately surround it in its current location, and it is permitted to move only one step in one of the four compass directions at each time

```
.....................................................
.OOF..OOF..OOF..OOF..OOF..OOF..OOF..OOF..OOF..OOF..OOF.
.OOO..OOO..OOO..OOO..OOO..OOO..OOO..OOO..OOO..OOO..OOO.
.OOO..OOO..OOO..OOO..OOO..OOO..OOO..OOO..OOO..OOO..OOO.
.....................................................
.....................................................
.OOF..OOF..OOF..OOF..OOF..OOF..OOF..OOF..OOF..OOF..OOF.
.OOO..OOO..OOO..OOO*.OOO..OOO..OOO..OOO..OOO..OOO..OOO.
.OOO..OOO..OOO..OOO..OOO..OOO..OOO..OOO..OOO..OOO..OOO.
.....................................................
.....................................................
.OOF..OOF..OOF..OOF..OOF..OOF..OOF..OOF..OOF..OOF..OOF.
.OOO..OOO..OOO..OOO..OOO..OOO..OOO..OOO..OOO..OOO..OOO.
.OOO..OOO..OOO..OOO..OOO..OOO..OOO..OOO..OOO..OOO..OOO.
.....................................................
```

Figure 21.4 Environment of Wilson's Woods1: Shown are rocks ("O"), food ("F"), empty spaces ("."), and the ZCS's current position ("*")

step. The grid world wraps around so that as soon as the ZCS steps off one side, it is transported to the opposite edge; thus the grid world is infinite in size as far as the ZCS is concerned.

Grid cells in Woods1 either are empty ("."), contain food ("F"), or contain a rock ("O"). The ZCS can walk through empty space but cannot walk through rocks. If the ZCS lands on food, it receives a reward of 1000. The detector of the ZCS works by mapping the eight nearest cells into a binary string of sixteen characters. Food has a sensor code of "11," rocks are coded by "10" and a blank is represented by "00." The first two characters in the detector string correspond to the cell just north of the ZCS, and all other character pairs correspond to the remaining cells, working clockwise from the northern cell. Thus, for the displayed ZCS position in Figure 21.4, the detector would return the sixteen-bit string "0000000000101011."

Since the ZCS is rewarded only when it lands on a piece of food, its goal is to get food as quickly and as often as possible. The ZCS is trained by running several trial problems. A single problem consists of placing the ZCS at a random location in the grid world. The ZCS produces an action, and if it corresponds to moving to anything other than a rock, then the move is allowed. If the ZCS lands on food, then it receives its reward, the world is reinitialized to the initial configuration, and the ZCS is randomly relocated. In this way, the ZCS can experiment by trying many different actions under several different circumstances.

If the ZCS performed nothing more complicated than a random walk, then from a random starting position we could expect it to take approximately twenty-seven

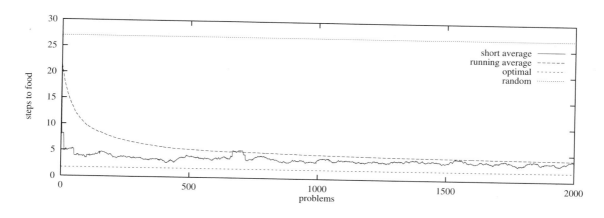

Figure 21.5   ZCS performance in Woods1: The "short average" plot is an average over the 50 most recent trials. The running average curve is over all past trials.

steps to find food.   If the ZCS behaved perfectly and always proceeded by the shortest path to the nearest food, then it would require only about 1.7 steps on average.   Using a population of 400 classifiers and parameter values described in Section 21.5, the ZCS starts off close to random and does very poorly, but after less than 100 trials it gets down to four steps.   After several hundred more steps the performance is improved a bit more.

The overall performance for a single experiment is shown in Figure 21.5.   As can be seen, the performance is far better than random, not quite as good as a perfect system but not so bad, considering that the solution was found automatically.   Looking back to Figure 21.4, we can perform some hindsight analysis to see why the problem of traversing Woods1 is solvable.   Woods1 has the property that no matter where one is located in it, it is always possible to tell where the nearest food is, based solely on the eight adjacent cells.   This is due to two facts.   First, Woods1 is perfectly periodic, so once you know what a small portion of the world looks like, you know the whole world.   Second, regardless of where one stands in Woods1, there is always at least one observable feature that tells you exactly where you are standing relative to the rocks.   This means that Woods1 is a relatively easy problem.

Woods7   Figure 21.6 shows Wilson's Woods7 environment, which is much more complicated than Woods1.   From the map, it is pretty clear that it has neither of the two properties that made Woods1 an easy problem.   Not only is it possible to get lost in Woods7, that is, there are many areas that look similar with limited perception, but the food and rocks are arranged in a nonuniform manner.

```
..........O.............................OO.........O........
.OFO......F..........F..........O.......F.........FO........
..........O.........OO......F...............................
....................................O......O........F......O.....
...F......OFO.......OFO..........F.........OO......F....
...OO..................................O..................O...
..........OO.......O........OO.....................O.......
.OFO......F......OF.......F........OFO.......F......
........................................................O.......
...OO.......O..................O.......OO.......O......
..F......F......O........FO......F........OF....OFO.
..........O.....OF..........................................
..O.....................O..........O......O.......O....
..F......F...........F.........FO......F......OF...
..O.......OO..........O...................O.......
.................O....................O..............
..F.......OFO.....F.........F.........F.....OF......
...OO...............O........OO.......O.......O.......
```

Figure 21.6   Environment of Wilson's Woods7: Shown are rocks ("O"), food ("F"), and empty spaces (".")

The experimental results for a typical run using an identical setup for training a ZCS to traverse Woods7 as was used in Woods1 are shown in Figure 21.7. Once again, the ZCS does far better than random but not quite as well as the optimal solution. To be fair, the ZCS really doesn't stand a chance of coming close to the optimal solution because the ZCS has no memory and cannot, therefore, tell where it is located on the map. If you had memory, then after passing several distinctive features it would be possible to find your exact location; hence, the ZCS is really at a disadvantage.

In general, the ZCS will wander around in some general direction when it can see only blanks. When it comes directly adjacent to some food, it will eat it. But when the ZCS sees a rock, it will move around the rock, apparently looking for the expected morsel of food. Sometimes the ZCS gets confused and makes a bad turn, which accounts for some of its inefficiency. Nevertheless, it is impressive that the ZCS can learn the general pattern of the map that food always occurs near a rock.

The Cups Problem   Our final experiment involves what is known as the "cups problem," which seems like a silly problem at first but turns out to be quite challenging (Whitehead & Lin, 1995). In the cups problem, a robot is placed on a linear

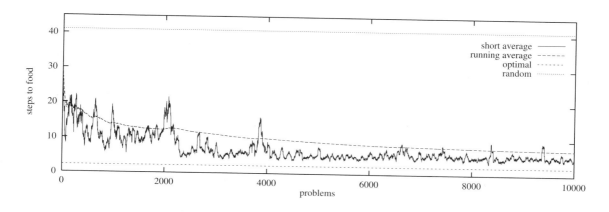

Figure 21.7 ZCS performance in Woods7: The "short average" plot is an average over the 50 most recent trials. The running average curve is over all past trials.

grid. The robot can do one of three things: It can move left, move right, or attempt to pick up a cup if it is standing above one. The sensory abilities of the robot are quite limited and are restricted to exactly four bits of information:

- Is there a cup to the immediate left of the robot?

- Is there a cup to the immediate right of the robot?

- Did the robot collide with a wall on the left?

- Did the robot collide with a wall on the right?

The robot cannot "see" walls. It knows that it is near one only if it runs into it. To make things worse, the robot cannot see what is directly beneath it, so to successfully pick up a cup, it must see it to one side, move on top of it, remember that it is on top of it, and pick it up.

The robot doesn't really know what any of these signals that it is receiving mean. It doesn't even know what the three possible control signals are. It just receives inputs and can send some output. The goal that the robot must achieve sounds amazingly simple: It must pick up two cups. But wait, it gets worse. The robot never receives any sort of feedback until it picks up the second cup. Thus, in order for the robot to know that it has done the right thing, it must go through an extremely complex and specific sequence of actions.

The exact configuration of the robot's world looks like

```
W..C*..CW
```

where the "W" characters stand for walls, the "C" characters represent the cups, and the "*" is the robot's initial location. For simplicity (and to keep the experiment consistent with the setup used by other researchers) the robot always starts out at the same location.

Since the ZCS needs some form of memory in order to solve the problem, we will augment Wilson's ZCS by incorporating a memory register into each classifier. This idea is similar to maintaining a message list, but is somewhat more compact in that we can specify the exact number of bits of memory to use in advance. The general scheme modifies the ZCS classifiers by making each have the form

$$condition: register: action: new\ register: strength.$$

What this means is that the classifier is considered a match only if the condition matches the environment description returned from the detector and the current register value matches *register*. If this classifier is acted upon, then *action* is performed by the effector, and the register is given the new value of *new register*. Thus, the classifiers can now be conditioned upon a certain memory being present and can also set the memory to a new value.

We could have made the problem easier for the ZCS by having the detector return twice as much information: one string for the current state and another string for the previous state. Encoding the information in this way is exactly the information that the ZCS needs to solve the problem (i.e., is it now on top of a cup?). But by being given only the current state and a single bit of memory, the ZCS must actually learn what feature is important to remember. Thus, *how* to remember is built into the system but *what* to remember is entirely up to the ZCS.

While it would be easier for the ZCS if we just gave it the information that it needs, it is educational to use the memory register instead. Why? For many problems, human designers simply do not know what information is required to solve a problem. By giving the ZCS the ability to form its own memories, we have removed one more design decision from the human. In a sense, we are forcing the ZCS to learn what to learn.

For this experiment I used 100 classifiers and a single bit for the register. As stated earlier, the problem requires four bits for the detector, and two bits for a control action ("10" means move left, "01" means move right, and "11" means pick up). Every experiment consisted of many trials, where a trial consists of starting the robot in the initial configuration and letting the whole thing run until both cups are picked up. In a typical experiment, the first 100 or so trials were extremely inefficient and often took hundreds of steps before the robot managed to pick up both cups simply by dumb luck. Afterward, the ZCS would eventually find a relatively efficient technique. Sometimes the ZCS could only learn how to pick up cups that were approached from the left side. Other times, the ZCS would only pick up the rightmost cup after running into the wall. Overall, the ZCS could usually be counted on to find a solution that took around ten steps or so.

Every now and then, the ZCS would manage to discover the optimal solution that takes exactly seven steps. This solution, as learned by the ZCS, can be implemented with four classifiers that roughly correspond to:

- If there is a cup to the left, then move to the left and turn the register on.

- If there is a cup to the right, then move to the right and turn the register on.

- If there is nothing to the left or right and the register is on, then pick up and turn the register off.

- If there is nothing to the left or right and the register is off, then move right.

Thus, the ZCS learned to associate the register with the fact that the robot was on top of a cup.

For all three example problems, the ZCS essentially had to learn a detailed path through a feature space. Somewhat counterintuitive is that each step in the path is learned in reverse order. When the ZCS just happens to find itself near a goal and when it just happens to make the right move to get to that goal, then that single classifier is reinforced. This has the effect of strengthening one classifier so that if the ZCS is in a similar situation, then it will be more likely to take the right path. But the bucket brigade algorithm (both implicit and explicit versions) will share strength with other classifiers that assist in getting the system back to the state that was near the goal. In this way, a classifier system learns how to make the very last step of a journey, followed by the next-to-last step, then the third-to-last step, and so on, ultimately learning as many partial solutions as possible in order to get to the final goal.

21.5   Further Exploration

Two programs were used for all experiments in this chapter. The first one is named simply zcs, and it can be used to train a classifier system to find food in an arbitrary environment. The second program, zcscup is a slight modification of the first program that I wrote especially for the cups problem. Both programs take identical options, as shown in Table 21.2.

The -specs option is used to specify a file that describes what the ZCS's world looks like. The specification files have a very simple text format that is obvious once you look at some of the examples. For the ZCS parameters described in Table 21.1, -lrate corresponds to β, -drate to γ, -trate to τ, -grate to ρ, and -cover to ϕ. All of the other options have the same meaning as they had in the GA examples from the previous chapter.

For all three experiments reported, the parameters used were the same as the default values for the programs. In fact, these values are identical to values reported

Option Name	Option Type	Option Meaning
-specs	STRING	file with world specs
-steps	INTEGER	number of simulated steps
-seed	INTEGER	random seed for initial state
-size	INTEGER	population size
-sinit	DOUBLE	initial classifier strength
-lrate	DOUBLE	BB learning rate
-drate	DOUBLE	BB discount rate
-trate	DOUBLE	tax rate for strength reduce
-crate	DOUBLE	GA crossover rate
-mrate	DOUBLE	GA mutation rate
-grate	DOUBLE	GA invocation rate
-cover	DOUBLE	covering factor
-wild	DOUBLE	probability of # in cover
-avelen	INTEGER	length of windowed average
-inv	SWITCH	invert colors?
-xmag	INTEGER	magnification factor for X Windows
-term	STRING	how to plot points

Table 21.2 Command-line options for `zcs` and `zcscup`

by Wilson. The only notable setting is that **zcscup** required a lower crossover rate (`-crate 0.1`) to solve the cups problem. This is most likely due to the "brittleness" of the problem, since crossing in this case will improve solutions only under extremely rare conditions.

21.6   Further Reading

Awad, E. M. (1996). *Building expert systems: Principles, procedures, and applications.* Minneapolis/St.Paul: West/Wadsworth.

Clark, W. R. (1995). *At war within: The double-edged sword of immunity.* New York: Oxford University Press.

Farmer, J. D., Packard, N. H., & Perelson, A. S. (1986). The immune system, adaptation & learning. *Physica D*, 22(1–3): 187–204.

Holland, J. H. (1976). Adaptation. In R. Rosen & F. M. Snell (Eds.), *Progress in theoretical biology IV* (pp. 263–293). New York: Academic Press.

Holland, J. H. & Holyoak, K. J. (1989). *Induction: Processes of inference, learning and discovery.* Cambridge, Mass.: MIT Press.

Kaelbling, L. P. (Ed.). (1996). *Recent advances in reinforcement learning.* Boston: Kluwer Academic.

Lumsden, C. J. & Wilson, E. O. (1981). *Genes, mind, and culture: The coevolutionary process.* Cambridge: Harvard University Press.

Wesson, R. (1991). *Beyond natural selection.* Cambridge, Mass.: Bradford Books/MIT Press.

Whitehead, S. D. & Lin, L.-J. (1995). Reinforcement learning of a non-Markov decision process. *Art. Intell.*, 73(1–2): 271–306.

Wilson, S. W. (1994). ZCS: A zeroth level classifier system. *Evol. Comp.*, 2(1): 1–18.

22 Neural Networks and Learning

As a net is made up of a series of ties, so everything in this world is connected by a series of ties. If anyone thinks that the mesh of a net is an independent, isolated thing, he is mistaken. It is called a net because it is made up of a series of interconnected meshes, and each mesh has its place and responsibility in relation to other meshes.
— Buddha

If the brain were so simple we could understand it, we would be so simple we couldn't.
— Lyall Watson

I bet the human brain is a kludge.
— Marvin Minsky

A SHORT LIST of some mundane tasks that humans can effortlessly perform includes recognizing faces, understanding and speaking in a native language, walking upright while chewing gum, and manipulating objects with one or both hands. All of these tasks are easy to ignore, even when we do them simultaneously, most likely because we can do them without too much conscious thought involved. Despite this fact, "simple" tasks such as these represent some of the most challenging problems in computer science. Much has been spoken and written of how tasks that are "machine easy"—performing precise and complicated symbolic manipulation—are "human hard." The flip side to this is that many "human easy" tasks are "machine hard" since it is difficult to algorithmically describe such everyday skills.

Consider the hardware involved. Typical home computers can perform hundreds of millions of operations in a single second, while a single neuron can merely oscillate at a fraction of the same speed. Individual transistors that make up a CPU can propagate signals at speeds limited only by the speed of light and the physical distances between them, which is why silicon chips etched on smaller scales can be driven to higher clock speeds. On the other hand, neurons propagate electrical signals through a chemical medium that is sluggish in comparison. In fact, a single neuron can look clumsy compared with a pocket calculator.

How is it, then, that brains can easily do things that defy the abilities of the most sophisticated computers? The real power of the brain lies in massive parallelism. While a typical CPU has around 5 million transistors and a typical home computer around 100 million (10^8) transistors, the human brain has a staggering 10^{11} neurons, each of which may be connected to thousands of other neurons for a total of 10^{13} to 10^{14} synaptic connections. It is through this massive parallelism and connectivity that the human brain is able to perform such impressive feats of computation.

Using the brain as inspiration, researchers are now designing new types of computing devices that have many of the qualities contained in natural networks of neurons. Such devices, known as *artificial neural networks* or "neural nets," possess many simple processing units that are massively interconnected with each other. This departure from more traditional computer science methods has many potential benefits. First and foremost, neural nets are not programmed in the usual sense of the word but instead are trained with a *learning algorithm* that modifies neural connections based on the net's experience. Changing the way a neural net is wired changes the way it responds to inputs. Thus, the solutions to many different problems may differ only in the specifics of how a neural net is connected. By automating the whole process with a learning algorithm, researchers have been able to train neural nets to do tasks that have previously defied traditional approaches.

The second major benefit of using neural nets resides in massive parallelism. In a neural net, each neuron is conceptually identical. Each receives inputs and produces an output. The output response of a single artificial neuron is typically so simple that it can be computed with a hand-held calculator. If we think of each artificial neuron as a grossly simplified computer, it becomes possible to build hardware versions where all calculations are performed in parallel. This way, instead of simulating the same operation thousands of times in succession, each artificial neuron can perform its own calculation in parallel with all others in the network, thus reaping the same benefit that the brain does by doing many simple things at once.

In Chapter 18 we examined feedback neural networks whose weights were determined according to simple rules and left fixed. In this chapter, we will be considering *feedforward neural networks* having the property that no sequence of connections among neurons forms a loop, which means that no neuron can feed back directly or indirectly to itself. This architectural simplification makes it easier to design algorithms for automatically changing the weights. For example, in the case of Hebbian learning (see Section 18.2 on page 312), it was possible to set weights according to how the neurons were supposed to interact with each other. This chapter will highlight more general rules that extend the basic idea. The result is a technique for performing *supervised learning* that allows weights to be dynamically modified as new information is acquired by the neural network.

The history of neural networks is actually quite interesting, since the topic as a research area has had many high and low points. We will begin this chapter

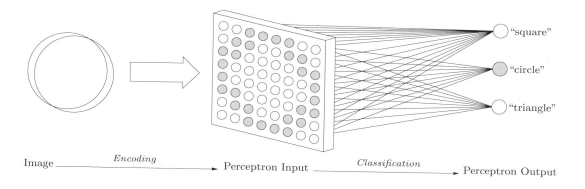

Figure 22.1   A stylized picture of a perceptron

with an introduction to the first feedforward neural network ever used, examine the problems that exposed its weaknesses, rediscover an extension that solved many of the earlier problems, consider some numerical examples, explore how neural networks can form internal representations of an input pattern, and finish off with some example applications.

22.1   Pattern Classification and the Perceptron

To summarize our exposure to the history of artificial neural networks so far, Chapter 18 introduced the McCulloch-Pitts neuron, originally proposed in the 1940s, and the Hopfield-Tank feedback neural network, an invention of the 1980s. Obviously there are some holes in this history. One of the greatest periods of activity in neural network research was in the 1960s. During this time, research was centered on Frank Rosenblatt's *perceptron*, a type of pattern classification device based on Rosenblatt's model of visual perception.

The basic idea behind the perceptron is illustrated in Figure 22.1, which shows that a perceptron can consist of multiple inputs and multiple outputs. Perceptrons are an example of feedforward networks because, unlike feedback networks, the activation of the network always propagates in one direction, starting from the inputs and ending at the outputs. The inputs are typically understood to represent visual information that is presented to an eyeball-like device, while the outputs represent the perception of the visual stimulus. For example, as seen in the figure, when the perceptron inputs are presented with a circular shape, the output with the label "circle" becomes activated, indicating the content of the input. This general type of problem goes by the name of *pattern classification* since the goal is to label or classify many different patterns into a smaller number of classes. The problem can be conceptually simplified by reducing the number of classes to two. A perceptron that needs to classify all objects into two classes needs only a single output. When activated, the output indicates that the inputs form a member of the one class, such as the class of circles, while inactivity indicates that the inputs did not form a member, that is, the input is a member of the class of non-circles. Thinking of the perceptron in this way allows us to simplify things considerably by breaking the multiple-output perceptron in Figure 22.1 into three separate perceptrons, each of which has a single output for its respective class.

Mathematically, with multiple inputs and a single output (all of which take 0/1 binary values), the output of a simple perceptron is described by the function

$$y = \Theta \left(\sum_{i=1}^{n} w_i x_i + b \right),$$

where x_i is a binary input, $\Theta(x)$ is the unit step function that is equal to 1 if $x > 0$ and 0 otherwise, w_i represents the synaptic strength of the connection from input i to the output, and b is a threshold or bias term.[1] For convenience, you can think of the w_i terms as being the lines in Figure 22.1 that connect the inputs to the outputs. The perceptron "fires" with a nonzero output whenever the weighted sum of the inputs multiplied by the weights is greater than the negation of the threshold.

"Neurons" in the perceptron consist of the outputs. We don't consider the inputs to be neurons because they simply pass information forward without processing it in any way. By way of comparison, the outputs form a weighted sum of the incoming signals and pass it through activation functions, thus performing a simple type of computation.

Clearly, a perceptron is a special type of function that maps binary inputs to a single binary output. To better understand how functions are represented by a perceptron, we will now consider some general features of binary functions and one simple example function in particular. If a perceptron has n inputs, then there are exactly 2^n different binary patterns that could be presented as input to the perceptron. For example, with two inputs there are four different input patterns: $(0, 0)$, $(0, 1)$, $(1, 0)$, and $(1, 1)$. With 2^n patterns, there are exactly 2^{2^n} functional mappings from the input pattern space to the space of binary numbers because each of the 2^n patterns can be labeled with either a 1 or a 0. With the two-input example, one such mapping could be the binary AND function, which is equal to 1 if and only if both inputs are 1.

Figure 22.2 shows three different ways of looking at a perceptron that represents the AND function. In Figure 22.2a we see weights and bias values that result in a perceptron behaving like an AND circuit, which you can check by verifying that $x_1 + x_2 - 1.5 > 0$ only when both binary inputs are 1. In Figure 22.2b, the gray

---

[1] The equation above is nearly identical to the McCulloch-Pitts neuron described in Figure 18.2 on page 310.

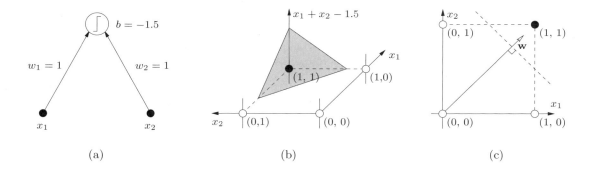

(a)   (b)   (c)

Figure 22.2 Three views of a perceptron solving the AND problem: (a) the perceptron with weights and bias shown; (b) the decision plane shown in three dimensions; (c) the decision line shown in two dimensions. Figure adapted from (Hertz et al., 1991)

region is a portion of the plane defined by $x_1 + x_2 - 1.5$, which we will refer to as the decision plane. Notice that the decision plane intersects the (x_1, x_2) plane, forming a diagonal line. The gray section of the decision plane corresponds to the region where $x_1 + x_2 - 1.5 > 0$ is true, while the region on the other side of the diagonal line (i.e., moving closer to $(0, 0)$) corresponds to where $x_1 + x_2 - 1.5 < 0$. Exactly on the diagonal line is where $x_1 + x_2 - 1.5 = 0$ is true, which is more clearly seen in Figure 22.2c. This diagonal line in two dimensions forms a linear decision boundary such that everything on one side belongs to one class and everything on the other side forms another class. Hence, having a perceptron compute the AND function is simply a matter of setting the weights such that a line separates (1,1) from the other three points. Implementing a perceptron that computes another function simply puts the decision boundary somewhere else.

In addition to the diagonal decision boundary, Figure 22.2c shows a vector labeled **w** that is formed by taking the two weights and the bias term to make a three-dimensional vector with components $[1, \ 1, \ -1.5]^T$. The decision boundary displayed in Figure 22.2c can be seen to be perpendicular to **w**. Unfortunately, Figure 22.2c can show only two of the three dimensions, so the third component of **w** is essentially lost in the image. Nevertheless, it is often useful to visualize the decision boundary in this way.[2] In particular, when considering how small changes in the weight vector change the input-output response of a perceptron, it is crucial to think of all of the weight and bias terms of a perceptron as one composite object.

Now that we have seen how mappings can be represented by a perceptron, we can now look at the more interesting issue of how to automatically find a set of weights that implements a mapping of our choice. In the usual case, we may not

---

[2]Section 13.3, starting on page 207, gives a geometrical interpretation of the inner product, which may be helpful in visualizing the effect that weight vectors have on inputs.

Neural Networks as Universal Computers | Digression 22.1

A network of McCulloch-Pitts neurons can form a universal computer if wired correctly. The proof is actually quite simple. We know that home PCs with infinite memory are universal computers as well. If we can show that a neural network can emulate a home PC, then the proof is complete.

Every modern computer is made from silicon chips that have millions of transistors etched onto them. The transistors form logical digital gates such as the AND and OR functions. The NOT operation is another logical function that turns 1s to 0s and 0s to 1s. With only AND and NOT gates, or just OR and NOT gates, it is possible to emulate any conceivable digital circuit. (Figure 22.6 on page 393 should give you a taste of how this can be done.) Therefore, if we can just show that a neural net can emulate AND and NOT or OR and NOT, then we know that a neural network is computationally universal.

We have already seen in this chapter how an AND circuit can be implemented as a perceptron. Emulating an OR circuit requires that a perceptron decision boundary separate (0, 0) from the other points. To compute a NOT gate, one only needs a weight of -1 and a threshold of $\frac{1}{2}$ in a simple perceptron. Therefore, a McCulloch-Pitts neural network or a multilayer perceptron with feedback connections could be wired up to emulate any conceivable digital circuit, including a home computer. This proves that neural networks are computationally universal, with the one caveat that total memory will be finite if we are limited to a finite number of neurons.

---

have a specific function like the AND function in mind, but will instead have a number of example inputs and target values that we want the perceptron to classify correctly. Our goal is to find some way of changing the behavior of a perceptron when it works incorrectly. In other words, we want it to learn based on feedback that a teacher would give it. In this setup, if you want a perceptron to recognize squares, then you would present the perceptron with labeled data that consist of images along with the correct class. The squares will be labeled as squares and circles, triangles, and other shapes as non-squares. With enough examples, in time the perceptron could learn to distinguish squares from non-squares on its own. And if things go truly well, your perceptron may even be able to generalize by correctly recognizing squares that it has never seen before.

The perceptron learning algorithm is more rigorously described by the following procedure, which is performed repeatedly until all patterns in a training set are correctly classified. The first step is to apply the input pattern to the perceptron. If the output of the perceptron is equal to the target value, t, then we move on to the next pattern. But if the perceptron's output differs from the target output, then we adjust the weights by

$$w_i^{\text{new}} = w_i^{\text{old}} + \eta(t - y)x_i \text{ and}$$
$$b^{\text{new}} = b^{\text{old}} + \eta(t - y),$$

where η is a very small constant referred to as the *learning rate*.[3] The effect on the weights is relatively simple to understand. Assume for the moment that x_i is equal to 1 (if it is equal to 0, then the learning rule will not change the weight). The weight change is always proportional to $(t - y)$. If t is 1 and y is 0, then the weight is increased; otherwise the weight is reduced. In other words, if we want the output to be on when it is off, then making the weights more positive will help make that happen the next time around. But if the output is on when it is supposed to be off, pushing the weight in a more negative direction will reduce the perceptron's ability to fire.

As a disclaimer, the biological plausibility of the perceptron learning rule is somewhat debatable, since the idea of all biological neurons having target values is somewhat suspect. Nevertheless, the perceptron learning rule does resemble a form of behavioral adaptation, with the error term $(t - y)$ representing a form of negative feedback.

Another way of visualizing how the weights change over time is to think about how a perceptron can make mistakes. If the perceptron misclassifies a pattern, then it is natural to describe the error by $E = (t - y)^2$, which gets larger the more y differs from t. Ignoring for the moment the fact that both y and t are supposed to have binary values, the function $E = (t - y)^2$ is a quadratic function that defines a single valleylike surface in a multidimensional space. Since y is a function of the weights in the perceptron, we can look at how E changes when the weights are changed. Figure 22.3 shows the error surface with the optimal weight vector corresponding to the lowest point of the surface. The perceptron learning algorithm is a special case of a more general algorithm, known as *steepest descent*, that attempts to minimize error functions by always moving in a downhill direction. By thinking of the perceptron learning rule in this way, we can see how the weight changes correspond to taking a small step toward the bottom of the error valley. The step size is determined by η and the direction is determined by the negative feedback in $(t - y)$. Later on in this chapter, when we examine more complicated feedforward neural networks, you should keep this image in mind because it applies to the most complicated types of networks.

Rosenblatt and others showed that if a set of weights existed that solved a problem, then the perceptron learning algorithm would always find the correct weights in a finite number of steps. This positive result caused a sense of euphoria among neural researchers in the 1960s because it seemed to imply that perceptrons

---

[3]This learning rule actually was independently discovered many times and, as a result, it is known by several different names, such as the *delta rule*, the adaline rule, the Widrow-Hoff rule, and the LMS rule.

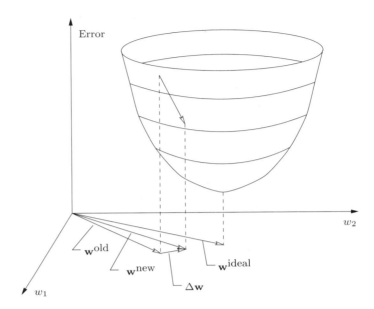

Figure 22.3 The delta rule as a steepest descent step in the error surface. Figure adapted from (Caudill & Butler, 1990).

could be used to magically solve all types of previously intractable problems. Think about it: Distinguishing circles from squares is one thing, but imagine that one could automatically distinguish dogs from cats, people you know from people you don't, or enemy aircraft from friendly aircraft. With this kind of discriminatory power all sorts of tasks that require human intervention could be automated. The problem with this conclusion is that success of the perceptron learning algorithm is conditioned on the existence of a solution in the first place. As it turns, out there are many extremely simple problems that can be proved to be beyond the powers of a perceptron.

22.2   Linear Inseparability

The most famous example of a simple problem that cannot be solved by a perceptron is the exclusive-or (XOR) problem. In the simplest version there are two binary inputs. The target output response is equal to 1 if and only if exactly one of the inputs is a 1. XOR is equivalent to the notion that the sum of the inputs is odd. A more general version of this problem is known as the n-bit parity problem, where the goal is to classify inputs according to whether they have an even or odd number of 1s; thus, the XOR problem is just a two-bit odd parity problem.

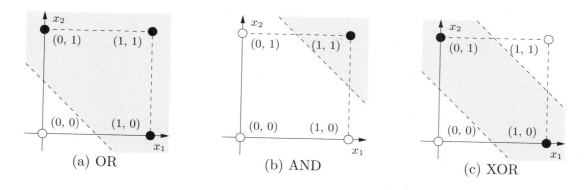

Figure 22.4   Three decision boundaries: Only the first two are linearly separable.

Figure 22.4 shows three different binary mappings and their associated decision boundaries. The first two problems, OR and AND, can be solved by a perceptron precisely because it is possible to draw a single line that divides the black points from the white points. For the XOR problem this is clearly not possible. OR and AND have the property that they are *linearly separable* while XOR is said to be *linearly inseparable*.

While Figure 22.4c shows that the patterns in the XOR problem cannot be correctly divided by a single line, thus making the point that perceptrons are ill-suited for some problems, it is still instructive to consider the more general n-bit parity problem to get an appreciation for some of the issues involved. The parity problem has the property that if you flip a single bit in an n-bit string, then the resulting string will always be in the opposite class from the first string. Why? Well, if the first string had an even number of 1s, then flipping a 0 to a 1 or a 1 to a 0 is going to change the number of 1s to an odd number. In other words, input patterns that are close to each other in a Euclidean sense are far away from each other in terms of their class. This means that in order to classify parity strings correctly, you can't just look at the inputs as individual bits; instead, you must look at the whole input string as one object in order to detect the higher-order patterns.

As mentioned earlier, the 1960s saw an almost reckless optimism in the faith that some practitioners had for perceptrons. Toward the end of the decade there was something of a backlash as many researchers began to voice skepticism. In 1969, Marvin Minsky and Seymour Papert published a book, entitled *Perceptrons*, that dealt the final blow to perceptrons as a research topic. In their book, they demonstrated that whole classes of problems were insolvable by any simple perceptron with any learning algorithm. Minsky and Papert also added some much-needed mathematical rigor to the area by giving detailed proofs for their claims. The effect

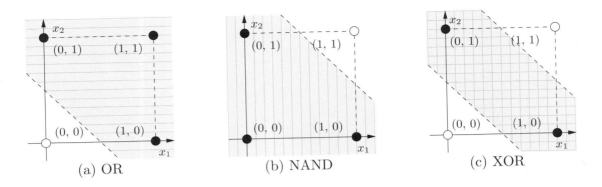

(a) OR   (b) NAND   (c) XOR

Figure 22.5 Forming XOR as a composition. The XOR set in (c) can be defined as the intersection of the sets in (a) and (b)

on the neural network community was nearly instantaneous. Research into neural networks would still continue, but it would take the area almost two decades to recoverer.

22.3   Multilayer Perceptrons

The fact that perceptrons cannot compute an XOR function clearly indicates that they have limited use in application areas; however, as a theoretical tool, perceptrons serve a useful role as the simplest example of what is now generally referred to as a feedforward neural network. We will see that the outright dismissal of neural networks in the late 1960s was in fact premature and a case of throwing out the baby with the bathwater. But first, let's look back to the XOR problem so that we can come up with a way to solve it with a more complicated type of perceptron.

Figure 22.5 shows another way of thinking about what it means for a point to be in the set for which XOR is true. If NAND is the set of all points that are not in AND, then XOR can be seen as the intersection between the sets defined by OR and NAND. This is an important clue to how a neural network should solve this problem. We know that a perceptron can compute the OR function, and NAND appears to be linearly separable as well. Hence, one perceptron could be wired to compute OR while another is used to compute NAND. If both of these perceptrons fire at the same time when given the same input, then we know that the input pattern belongs in the set defined by XOR.

Figure 22.6a shows a diagram for a digital circuit that computes XOR by first computing OR and NAND. In Figure 22.6b we see the same circuit, but this time it is realized as a *multilayer perceptron* (MLP) that computes intermediate values in order to compute the final value. Using multiple layers is the key to making

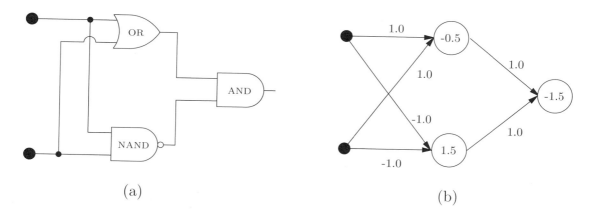

Figure 22.6 A two-layer perceptron solves XOR: (a) the solution as a digital circuit, and (b) weight and bias values for a perceptron that emulates the XOR circuit

perceptrons compute more powerful functions since multiple perceptrons can be composed through one another. Many researchers knew in the 1960s that this was the way to go in order to form more complicated neural nets. The problem was that no one knew how to train the things. Training the weights to an output neuron was never a problem, since the delta rule could always be used to compute appropriate weight changes. But how should one go about changing the weights that go into the "hidden neurons" in the middle of the network? The delta rule makes changes to the weights that are proportional to the difference between the target output value and the actual output value. We know what the actual output is for these hidden neurons, but we have no idea what the target values should be. In fact, it's not even clear what it means for hidden neurons to have target values.

22.4   Backpropagation

The solution to the problem of how to train hidden neurons had to be rediscovered several different times before the bulk of the research community took notice. The problem was solved somewhat independently by several individuals and groups: A. E. Bryson and Y.-C. Ho; Paul Werbos; D. B. Parker; and David Rumelhart, G. Hinton, and R. Williams. Rumelhart and his collaborators published a two-volume book that gained widespread attention and was largely responsible for ushering in a renaissance of research. The key to the solution is twofold: Replace the unit step function with a smooth sigmoidal function and generalize the delta rule so that error signals are passed backward through the hidden nodes. The resulting method for

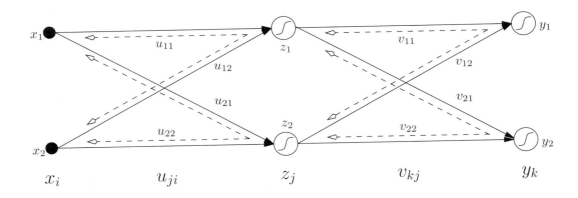

Figure 22.7   A labeled multilayer perceptron

computing weight changes is known as *backpropagation*[4] (or "backprop") because of the manner in which the error signals are passed backward through a network.

Before we look into the learning algorithm, we need to get some notational conventions out of the way. Figure 22.7 shows a multilayer perceptron with a single hidden layer. As before, the inputs into the system are denoted by the x_i terms and the outputs by the y_k terms, but this time there are hidden neurons whose outputs we will annotate with z_j terms. Each of these neurons computes a weighted sum and passes it through a sigmoidal activation function, $g(x)$.

To simplify the notation even further, we are going to ignore the threshold terms that were used earlier.[5] Since we have multiple layers of weights, it is notationally just easier to refer to them by two different base variables, u_{ji} and v_{kj}. But also note that there is no reason why you can't use a three- or thirty-layer perceptron as well. We are using the two-layer example (i.e., two layers of weights) of an MLP just because it is the simplest network with multiple layers. With these rules and caveats in place, the feedforward pass of a two-layer MLP is compactly described by

$$y_k = g\left(\sum_j v_{kj} z_j\right) = g\left(\sum_j v_{kj} g\left(\sum_i u_{ji} x_i\right)\right).$$

---

[4]Some practitioners of neural networks refer to the "backpropagation learning algorithm" or "backpropagation networks." Both terms are slightly incorrect since "backpropagation" really just refers to the method for computing the error gradient of a network. If you don't know what that last sentence means, don't worry about it. The point is that backpropagation is neither a type of network nor a learning algorithm, but a mathematical operation.

[5]We can do this without losing any mathematical details because the threshold term can be simulated by having an extra input that always has the value of 1. The weights coming from this auxiliary neuron play the same role that the threshold did in the earlier sections.

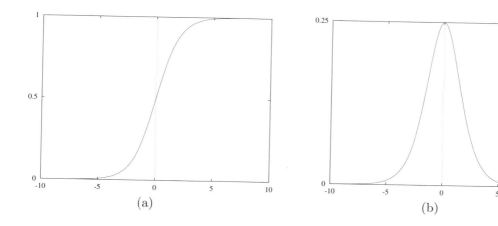

Figure 22.8   A sigmoidal activation function (a) and its derivative (b)

As for the activation function, $g(x)$, Figure 22.8a shows a plot of the sigmoid function that we first saw in Figure 18.5 (page 320). In this chapter we need to consider the mathematical properties of the sigmoid function in greater detail. In Figure 22.8b, the first derivative[6] of the sigmoid is shown. Notice that the tails of the derivative, where it goes to 0, correspond exactly to where the sigmoid saturates at either 0 or 1. Moreover, the highest point of the derivative is where the rate of change in the sigmoid is at its greatest. The sigmoid function is mathematically described by $g(x) = 1/(1 + \exp(-x))$. Computing the derivative of $g(x)$ turns out to be very easy because for this case it just happens to be equal to $g'(x) = g(x)(1 - g(x))$. Since this derivative is always computed with respect to a particular neuron, for example, an output neuron y_k or a hidden neuron z_j, it is more convenient to refer to it as $y'_k = y_k(1 - y_k)$ or $z'_j = z_j(1 - z_j)$, respectively.

We are now finally ready to see how backprop works. Our goal here is to fill in the blanks in the equations below:

$$u_{ji}^{\text{new}} = u_{ji}^{\text{old}} + \eta \Delta u_{ji} \text{ and}$$
$$v_{kj}^{\text{new}} = v_{kj}^{\text{old}} + \eta \Delta v_{kj}.$$

That is, we need to come up with a way for specifying how to calculate weight changes so that learning can occur. The problem is: What should Δu_{ji} and Δv_{kj} be? The derivation of backprop can be a bit intimidating at first, but understanding it requires nothing more than knowledge of how summations and derivatives work. In the derivation that follows, I will primarily attempt to give an intuitive feel for how it works, and only then will we make things more mathematically rigorous.

---

[6]For an introduction to derivatives see Section 11.2 (page 165) or refer to a good calculus text.

Let's start with Δv_{kj} since these are the weights that connect to the output neurons that have target values. Earlier, we saw that the weight changes for a simple perceptron were calculated as the product of the input to the neuron, x_i, and an error term, $(t - y)$. Calculating Δv_{kj} is very similar except that we now need to account for the fact that the activation function, $g(x)$, is continuous instead of discrete. In the case of the step function, $\Theta(x)$, knowing the value of the output tells you almost nothing about what the input was, that is, if $\Theta(x)$ is 1, then we know only that x is positive. But in the case of the sigmoid function, $g(x)$, knowing its output tells you a lot about its input. To see why, recall that the derivative of a function yields information about how the output changes when the input changes. If the derivative, $g'(x)$, is large, then we know that the input was near the threshold boundary and that changing x just a little could change $g(x)$. But if $g'(x)$ is very close to 0, then $g(x)$ is saturated near one of the extremes—producing something close to 0 or 1.

In this light, the expression $g'(x)(t - y)$ contains many pieces of information. If it is close to 0, then we know that t is very close to y, $g'(x)$ is close to 0, or both of these conditions are true. In the first case, we don't want to change the way that the neuron fired because it gave the correct response. In the second case, the output may or may not be correct, but the weights are such that they would have to be changed a great deal in order to change the neuron's response; thus, perhaps it is better to leave them alone, since drastic changes could adversely affect other portions of the network. In the last case, with both terms close to 0, the neuron has fired correctly and is doing so unambiguously.

Now consider the opposite case, when $g'(x)(t - y)$ is far from 0. This tells us two important pieces of information. First, we know that the neuron fired incorrectly. The sign of $g'(x)(t - y)$ will tell us which way the neuron was wrong. (Did it output something close to 1 when it was supposed to yield a 0, or the other way around?) And with $g'(x)$ far from 0, we know that the neuron is firing near the middle of its activation area, that is, near $\frac{1}{2}$. This is very important. It means that changing the weights just a little bit can yield a dramatic improvement.

Putting all of this together, we can think of $g'(x)(t - y)$ as supplying us with the error correction information. As such, for an output neuron y_k, we will use the Greek letter delta with a subscript to represent the error correction information for output k, $\delta_{y_k} = y_k'(t_k - y_k)$, with the k subscript being used on all of the terms to indicate that we are talking about a specific output neuron with a specific target value. The weight change, Δv_{kj}, is now computed very similarly to the way the perceptron update rule worked. We set Δv_{kj} equal to $z_j \delta_{y_k}$, because z_j is the input connected to y_k via v_{kj}. Intuitively, this is very similar to the perceptron update rule, $x_i(t - y)$, but now all of the error correction information is in δ_{y_k} instead of just $(t - y)$.

We now turn our attention to the more difficult question of how to compute the updates for the hidden weights, Δu_{ji}. The short answer is that we will ultimately

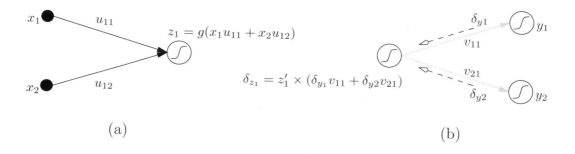

Figure 22.9   The MLP (a) feedforward pass compared with (b) the backpropagation pass

compute another delta term, δ_{z_j}, for the hidden neurons, which lets us set Δu_{ji} equal to $x_i \delta_{z_j}$, but this requires us to figure out what δ_{z_j} should be. Since each hidden neuron, z_j, sends its output to the y_k neurons via the v_{kj} weights, each hidden neuron can potentially contribute something to all of the y_k neurons. In other words, a hidden neuron's error correction term needs to be a function of the error correction terms that were calculated for the neurons that it connects to. The value of this term is equal to

$$\delta_{z_j} = z_j' \sum_k v_{kj} \delta_{y_k}.$$

Once again, the z_j' portion of the expression comes from the fact that we need to know how changing the net input into z_j changes its output. The summation takes all of the error correction terms from the output layer and sums them, weighted by the connection strengths.

Figure 22.9 shows both the forward and backward calculations for a single hidden neuron. We are already familiar with the forward pass in Figure 22.9a; however, the backward pass shown in Figure 22.9b illustrates how backprop is actually a reversed form of the forward pass. In the forward pass we are computing activation values, while in the backward pass we are computing correction terms. The forward pass goes left to right while the backward pass goes right to left. In each case, the value is calculated as part of a weighted sum of the terms that were computed in the earlier stage. The neat thing about backprop is that it is an efficient way to compute the error correction terms. It takes the same number of calculations as the forward pass, which is a surprising fact, considering that the values of the error correction terms are not as "obvious" to us as the activation values. Putting everything together, we now have

$$u_{ji}^{\text{new}} = u_{ji}^{\text{old}} + \eta x_i \delta_{z_j} \quad \text{and} \quad v_{kj}^{\text{new}} = v_{kj}^{\text{old}} + \eta z_j \delta_{y_k}, \quad \text{with}$$

$$\delta_{y_k} = y_k'(t_k - y_k) \quad \text{and} \quad \delta_{z_j} = z_j' \sum_k v_{kj} \delta_{y_k},$$

which completes the update rule. Because of the generic way in which the δ terms are computed, backpropagation is also referred to as the generalized delta rule.

The error surface of an MLP can look like a rugged landscape with many peaks and valleys. The peaks correspond to high error values where the MLP is producing incorrect outputs, while the valleys correspond to lower error rates and better output response. The backpropagation algorithm always adjusts the weights such that a very small step is taken in a downhill direction. Referring back to Figure 22.3 on page 390, given enough time and with a small enough step size, the weight updates suggested by backprop will always find a *local minimum* of the error surface that is a valleylike region having the property that any small adjustment of the weights can only hurt the MLP's performance. We know that a minimum will always be reached because each of the weight changes is always in the direction of the opposite of the error gradient. In other words, backprop is an efficient method for calculating how a change in each of the weights will change the error of its performance.

Unfortunately, the error surface of a complicated MLP trained to approximate a complicated function will almost always have many local minima that are suboptimal. Finding the *global minimum*, that is, the best minimum in the error surface, is the ultimate goal, but there is no guarantee that backprop will actually find it. In Section 22.9 we will discuss some of these issues in greater detail. None of this means that MLPs are poor at solving problems. In fact, as we will see in the next section, MLPs can solve some interesting problems. We simply need to recognize that there is no such thing as a free lunch. Perceptrons can be proved to converge to the best solution possible precisely because they are capable of forming only a very limited set of approximations. MLPs are much more powerful from a function approximation point of view and lack global convergence because each MLP can approximate many different types of functions.

22.5   Function Approximation

We are now ready to see how multilayer perceptrons can be trained to mimic other functions by looking at three simple problems. In the first example we will use an MLP with two hidden neurons to learn the XOR problem. In the second example we will train an MLP to emulate the logistic map, a chaotic system first discussed in Chapter 10. For the third example, we will build a model of the Hénon map, a more complicated chaotic system that was introduced in Chapter 11. Afterward, we will constructively see how it is possible for an MLP to approximate any function.

XOR   For the XOR problem, we want the output of the MLP to correctly classify all possible input pairs. We start the MLP with random initial weights selected

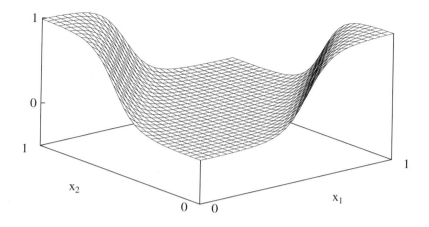

Figure 22.10 Output response surface of an MLP trained on the XOR data

from a -1 to 1 range. Random initialization is necessary because starting an MLP with all weights 0 can cause learning to proceed very slowly or not at all. Using backpropagation (plus some minor improvements discussed in Section 22.9), we train the network by randomly picking one of the four training patterns, adjusting the weights, then randomly picking another pattern, and so on, until the error drops to something close to 0. The total modeling error in this case is equal to the average of the partial errors produced for each pattern,

$$\text{Error} = \frac{1}{4} \sum_{p=1}^{4} (t^p - y^p),$$

where t^p represents the target value for pattern p and y^p is the MLP's output response when it is passed the inputs for pattern p.

After around 1000 or 2000 training iterations (which takes less than a second for my home PC to compute), the MLP has learned the correct mapping. Figure 22.10 shows the output response of the trained MLP. The x- and y-axes of the plot are labeled x_1 and x_2 for the two inputs, while the z-axis shows the MLP's output. As can be seen, the MLP has an output response that is elevated at the (0, 1) and (1, 0) corners but is depressed at the (0, 0) and (1, 1) corners. In between the four corners, the MLP interpolates things with a smooth, basinlike depression.

Logistic Map In the next example, the logistic map, we have a time series generated from the system while it is in the chaotic regime. We will train an MLP with one input and one output. The input to the MLP will be some point from the generated time series, labeled x_t, that has the target output of x_{t+1}. In other

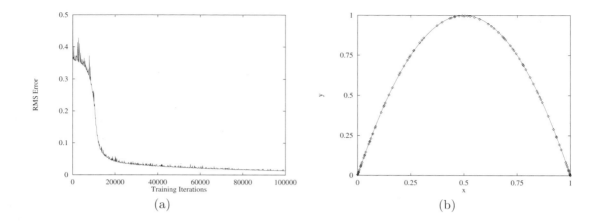

Figure 22.11   Training an MLP on chaos: (a) the training error as a function of the number of training iterations and (b) the target function (the logistic map) and the MLP's output response

words, given one point of the current portion of the chaotic series, we want the MLP to predict what the next point will be. Notice that our target values are no longer binary but may instead range anywhere from 0 to 1. Because of this, it is no longer appropriate to use a sigmoidal activation function on the output. Instead, we will simply use the identity function as a pseudo-activation function, that is, $g(x) = x$. This requires us to modify the backpropagation procedure slightly, by using $g'(x) = 1$ for the output neuron. The resulting values for the deltas are actually simpler than they were before, since δ_{y_k} is now equal to $(t_k - y_k)$. Other than this one change, everything stays the same.

Using two hidden neurons and 100 training patterns, Figure 22.11a shows the root mean squared error as related to the number of training iterations. It takes slightly more than 10,000 iterations to drop the error to an acceptable size, but I allowed the training to continue for a solid 1 million iterations just to illustrate the fact that learning slows down after a while.[7] The output response of the trained MLP is shown in Figure 22.11b. The solid line shows the actual target function, $x_{t+1} = 4x_t(1 - x_t)$, and the predicted points from the data set. As can be seen, the predictions are extremely accurate.

---

[7]This example also illustrates that MLPs may learn very slowly at times. In terms of rate of convergence, simple backprop is about the worst training procedure in existence. More sophisticated techniques like quasi-Newton's method or conjugate gradient offer learning speeds hundreds or even thousands of times faster. But these techniques are way beyond the scope of this book. Readers wishing to know more about advanced optimization routines should consult one of the neural network or numerical analysis texts in the bibliography.

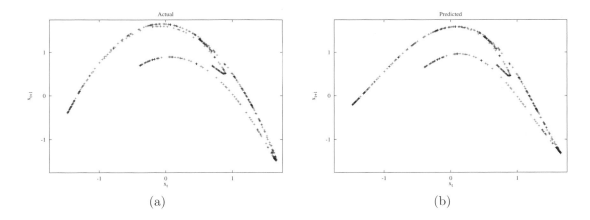

Figure 22.12 The reconstructed Hénon map: (a) the actual attractor plotted from the training points; (b) the attractor as approximated by an MLP

Hénon Map Our last example is a more complicated time series generated from the Hénon map. (See Section 11.1 on page 160 for an introduction to the Hénon map.) For this problem we must use two inputs that use two successive points from the time series, (x_t, x_{t+1}), while the target output is the next point, x_{t+2}. Since this time series is more complicated than any of the other examples, we will need more hidden neurons to increase the approximation power of the MLP. I used ten hidden neurons.

After 3000 training iterations the error drops considerably. The error could be reduced further with more training, but I would like this example to illustrate how an MLP could be slightly under-trained. Figure 22.12 shows the phase space of the actual Hénon map and the reconstructed attractor from the MLP. The approximation is very close, but some subtle differences are noticeable. The map in time series form is shown in Figure 22.13, which again reveals that the fit is very close but not perfect. Finally, Figure 22.14 shows the training error for the entire 3000 iterations.

All of these examples demonstrate that MLPs can learn mappings by just looking at training examples. What is not clear, however, is how the MLPs can form the correct output response. Multilayer perceptrons have a property known as *universal approximation*, which means that given any functional mapping, there exists an MLP that can approximate the mapping to an arbitrary accuracy. This does not necessarily mean that we can always find the weights to build that particular MLP; it just means that some values for the weights exist. MLPs with a single hidden layer of sigmoidal neurons are universal, but the proof of universality for this class

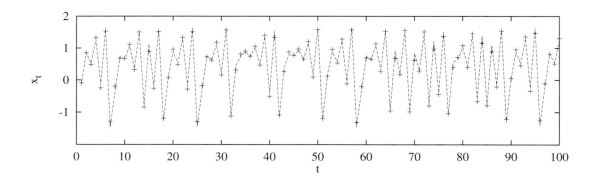

Figure 22.13   An actual and predicted portion of the Hénon map in time-series form: The lines are for the actual series and the points are the predicted values

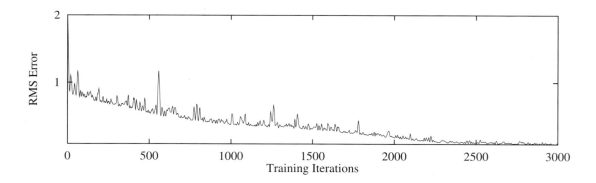

Figure 22.14   Training error for the Hénon map as a function of the number of training iterations

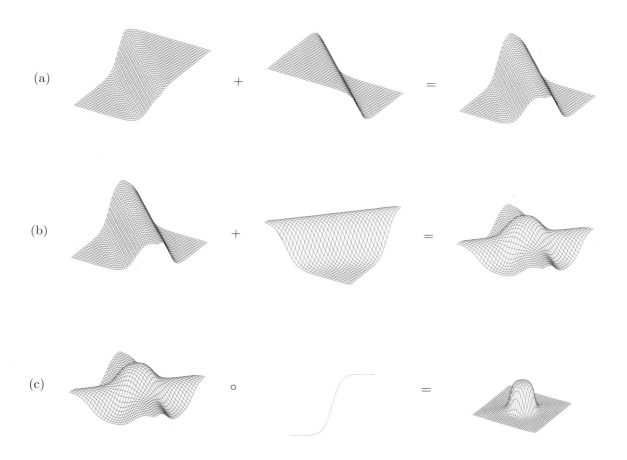

Figure 22.15   Forming bumps with $4 + 1$ neurons: (a) two parallel but opposite sigmoids add up to form a single ridge; (b) two ridges form an elevated cross pattern with a peaked center; (c) the cross pattern is composed through a fifth sigmoid that filters out all but the peak, leaving a single local bump

of networks is not simple. With two hidden layers and a linear output, there is an elegant geometric proof for showing that MLPs are universal. The basic idea was first shown by Alan Lapedes and Rob Farber, and works as follows.

Suppose you have a continuous function that you want to approximate. The function may take any number of inputs. All we need is that the output of the function be well-defined for any legal input. The key idea is that a function of this type can always be approximated by adding up a large collection of localized bumps. If one legal input-output pair for this function is (x, y), then you will want to place a local bump at position x with a height of y. For other point pairs, you will place more bumps. You only need to make sure that the bumps are thin enough that they do not interfere with each other too severely, and wide enough that they allow for smooth interpolation between the bumps.

Universality is guaranteed if we can show that an MLP can place a bump with an arbitrary width and height at an arbitrary location. Figure 22.15 shows how a single bump can be formed with five hidden neurons in a two-dimensional input space. In the first stage, a single ridge is formed by adding up two sigmoids that are reflections of one another. Two more sigmoids are used to form a second ridge that is perpendicular to the first. Adding up the ridges yields a cross pattern that is elevated in the middle. The cross pattern was formed from four hidden neurons in the first hidden layer. The highest point in the cross pattern has a height of 4, the lowest points are near 0, and the ridges have a height of 2. The last step needed to form the bump is to pass the cross pattern through yet another hidden neuron in the second hidden layer of neurons. This final neuron acts as a filter. The weights coming into it squelch anything below 3.5, and amplify anything above 3.5. This has the affect of removing everything but the peak in the middle of the cross pattern, thus forming a bump.

By adjusting the weights, we can place this bump in any location and give it any height or width that we wish. For the general case of having n inputs, we need $2n + 1$ nodes to form a bump in an n-dimensional space. And by adding up many such bumps, it is possible to represent any conceivable input-output mapping with a multilayer perceptron.

22.6   Internal Representations

Since we have seen that MLPs can represent arbitrary functions, we will now consider a final example that shows how backpropagation can be used by an MLP to form an internal representation of a set of input patterns. This is a very subtle and important point, for if we are to expect a neural network to do something that seems intelligent, then it is necessary that a neural network can learn and exploit patterns within a set of data.

For example, suppose that we wish for a neural net to perform some task, be it function approximation, pattern classification, or some other generic type of prob-

Input Patterns							Target Patterns						
R	**S**	**S**	**S**	**S**	**F**	**F**	**R**	**S**	**S**	**S**	**S**	**F**	**F**
0	1	0	0	0	1	0	0	1	0	0	0	1	0
0	0	1	0	0	1	0	0	0	1	0	0	1	0
0	0	0	1	0	1	0	0	0	0	1	0	1	0
0	0	0	0	1	1	0	0	0	0	0	1	1	0
0	1	0	0	0	1	0	1	1	0	0	0	1	0
0	0	1	0	0	1	0	1	0	1	0	0	1	0
0	0	0	1	0	1	0	1	0	0	1	0	1	0
0	0	0	0	1	1	0	1	0	0	0	1	1	0
1	1	0	0	0	1	0	0	1	0	0	0	1	0
1	0	1	0	0	1	0	0	0	1	0	0	1	0
1	0	0	1	0	1	0	0	0	0	1	0	1	0
1	0	0	0	1	1	0	0	0	0	0	1	1	0
1	1	0	0	0	1	0	1	1	0	0	0	1	0
1	0	1	0	0	1	0	1	0	1	0	0	1	0
1	0	0	1	0	1	0	1	0	0	1	0	1	0
1	0	0	0	1	1	0	1	0	0	0	1	1	0
x_1	x_2	x_3	x_4	x_5	x_6	x_7	t_1	t_2	t_3	t_4	t_5	t_6	t_7

Table 22.1   Random, structured, and fixed data mixed into one data set: Columns labeled **R**, **S**, and **F** are effectively random, structured, and fixed, respectively

lem. Furthermore, let's also assume that the input data to the neural network contain things that are random, perfectly regular, and structured in some way. Our hope will be that the neural network will learn to ignore the randomness and regularity, but also discover the hidden order in the structured input data and be able to internally represent it in a more meaningful manner.

Put another way, the neural network and learning algorithm's task is a lot like what many people have to go through in order to pick a movie that they will like with high probability, based only on what a fixed set of movie reviewers say about the movie. Some reviewers seem to like everything ever put on film, so what they say about any movie is useless, in that it tells you nothing at all about whether or not you will like a movie. Other movie reviewers have such complex tastes that you may be hard pressed to ever guess what kind of movie they would like or dislike. However, if you find that your taste in science fiction films is similar to one particular critic's, or that your preferences for comedy films are exactly opposite to those of another critic, then these are both useful pieces of information for you to use when picking a movie.

To illustrate these issues further, Table 22.1 shows sixteen input and target patterns that we would like a neural network to reproduce (meaning that given

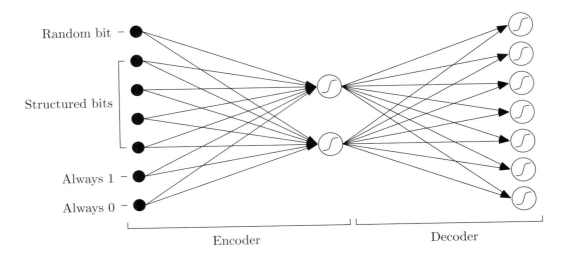

Figure 22.16 An encoder-decoder MLP that compresses a seven-bit input pattern into two bits, then decodes it with minimal information loss

an input vector from one row, we would like the neural network to reproduce the corresponding target vector from the same row). For the moment, we will ignore the neural network and just concentrate on the data in the table. The most obvious thing about the data is that inputs x_6 and x_7, along with targets t_6 and t_7, are perfectly regular in that they never change. This means not only that t_6 and t_7 are perfectly predictable, but also that x_6 and x_7 contain no information that would allow us to infer other things about other portions of the input or target vectors.

Note, however, that this is not the case for inputs x_2 through x_5 and targets t_2 through t_5. As with the fixed portions of the data set, the structured inputs are equal to their corresponding targets, but within the subset of these four inputs (or targets) there is a pattern, in that exactly one of the four inputs (or targets) is always on. Thus, if you know only which of the four inputs is on, you also know the value of the remaining three inputs as well as of the four targets.

Things are quite different for x_1 and t_1 which are labeled as "effectively random." For these two values there is no pattern to their values, since every combination of values is contained in the data set. For example, if you were to make any hypothesis concerning when or why x_1 or t_1 is 1 or 0 (as a function of the other inputs or targets), your hypothesis would have to be wrong, because whatever rule you try to construct could be disproved by a counter-example from another portion of the data set.

Putting this all together, we would like a neural network to discover the hidden order in the structured data but learn to ignore the fixed and random portions.

Moreover, our neural network will never "see" all of the data set at once, but only individual rows in isolation.

Figure 22.16 shows a special type of neural network that will be used for this problem. The network has seven inputs and targets that correspond to the dimensionalities of the data set. But also notice that there are only two hidden neurons. These two hidden neurons form an information bottleneck in that the network must learn to compress the information from the inputs into two values that can be decompressed by the right half of the network. The left portion of the network is an encoder because it encodes the seven inputs into two values, while the right half acts as a decoder that attempts to invert the encoding performed earlier.

While you and I have had the benefit of looking at the data set in its entirety beforehand, we also know that there is a structured pattern in four of the inputs and the targets. Since the neural network is randomly initialized, it has no preconceived notion about anything concerning the training data. It does not know what is regular, irregular, compressible, or incompressible. It has only one goal, and that is to reproduce the target values with the highest amount of accuracy. But to do this, it must learn to ignore the randomness and regularity because it is constrained to pass all of the information through only two hidden neurons. Thus, while we have explicitly constructed the network to minimize the redundancy of the input vectors, it must learn to do so almost as an implicit goal.

Training the network from Figure 22.16 on the data from Table 22.1 proceeds fairly rapidly for this problem. After only a few thousand training cycles it produces the output shown in Table 22.2 to within 10 percent. As can be seen, the structured and fixed target values are accurately reproduced while the random data are only statistically described by their mean. Things get interesting when we consider the hidden activation values that are produced for particular input values. What we find is that the network produces four distinct pairs of activation values that depend only on the structured data; thus, the network has learned to ignore both the fixed and the random data under all circumstances. The four distinct activation pairs for the hidden neurons represent the four types of input patterns for the structured data. The decoder portion of the network has learned to recover the structured data from the compressed versions in the hidden nodes, while the outputs corresponding to the fixed and random data are hardcoded in that they are produced independent of the hidden nodes. It is also interesting that the network settles on the mean of the data for both the random and the fixed data. For the fixed data this happens to be a perfect representation, but for the random data the mean is a slightly imperfect representation.

We should also note that the particular method of encoding and decoding the input vectors is somewhat arbitrary. For example, instead of the four activation pairs being (0, 1), (1, 0), (1, 1), and (0, 0), they could have just as easily been (1, 1), (0, 1), (0, 0), and (1, 0). The specifics of the encoding are not important. What is important is that the encoder and decoder agree on the representation.

Input Patterns							Hidden Units		Output Patterns						
R	S	S	S	S	F	F			R	S	S	S	S	F	F
0	1	0	0	0	1	0	0	1	0.5	1	0	0	0	1	0
0	0	1	0	0	1	0	1	0	0.5	0	1	0	0	1	0
0	0	0	1	0	1	0	1	1	0.5	0	0	1	0	1	0
0	0	0	0	1	1	0	0	0	0.5	0	0	0	1	1	0
0	1	0	0	0	1	0	0	1	0.5	1	0	0	0	1	0
0	0	1	0	0	1	0	1	0	0.5	0	1	0	0	1	0
0	0	0	1	0	1	0	1	1	0.5	0	0	1	0	1	0
0	0	0	0	1	1	0	0	0	0.5	0	0	0	1	1	0
1	1	0	0	0	1	0	0	1	0.5	1	0	0	0	1	0
1	0	1	0	0	1	0	1	0	0.5	0	1	0	0	1	0
1	0	0	1	0	1	0	1	1	0.5	0	0	1	0	1	0
1	0	0	0	1	1	0	0	0	0.5	0	0	0	1	1	0
1	1	0	0	0	1	0	0	1	0.5	1	0	0	0	1	0
1	0	1	0	0	1	0	1	0	0.5	0	1	0	0	1	0
1	0	0	1	0	1	0	1	1	0.5	0	0	1	0	1	0
1	0	0	0	1	1	0	0	0	0.5	0	0	0	1	1	0
x_1	x_2	x_3	x_4	x_5	x_6	x_7	z_1	z_2	t_1	t_2	t_3	t_4	t_5	t_6	t_7

Table 22.2   Results of training an encoder-decoder neural network: the network compresses the structured data, statistically describes the random data, and hard-codes the regular data. The shown values are only approximate

The key point to all of this is that the neural network learned to form an internal representation of the input patterns that ignored regularity and randomness, and compressed whatever could be compressed. It is never guaranteed that a neural network can do the same thing for any data set, but it is pleasing, nonetheless, that our network does the right thing for this example.

Forming internal representations is arguably one of the most important characteristics of any type of model. If we wish to train a neural network to perform pattern classification or to model a physical process, an internal representation for the data is useful in that it can often represent that which is truly important about the data. For the case of pattern classification, some patterns may be invisible to humans because they are visible only in some higher-dimensional space or they may exist only with respect to millions of individual data points. Having a model and a learning method that can automatically discover such hidden order is crucial to the goal of more compactly describing the phenomenon. Similarly, for the case of modeling a physical process, sometimes the most predictive part of state space does not reside in any individual input, but is instead some function of multiple inputs. Discovering the hidden function is, again, another facet of forming an internal representation.

22.7   Other Applications

The four example problems from the previous sections only scratch the surface of what it is possible to do with neural networks. Moreover, the multilayer perceptron is only one of many different types of neural networks in current use; it just happens to be the most popular type. In this section I will briefly list some applications in the hope of conveying the broad applicability of neural networks.

Pattern Recognition   The general problem of pattern recognition can be applied to a nearly infinite number of problem areas. Some current applications include optical character recognition for human handwriting, facial recognition, sonar classification, credit card fraud detection, and electrocardiogram classification. In this application area the inputs to a neural network can consist of any digital form of information, such as an image, sound, spending record, or heartbeat.

Function Approximation   Included here are all forms of time-series prediction, which include predicting the stock market and the weather. There are also many industrial processes that are not well understood analytically. Neural networks have been used to build data-based models that surpass in accuracy models built from physical first principles. Because a neural network has a well-defined structure, it is possible and often helpful to perform sensitivity analysis on a neural network trained to emulate a physical process. Doing so allows researchers to find out what measurements in a process have predictive power, which gives engineers greater insight into how a physical process works.

Signal Processing   Many audio signals are continuously corrupted with noise. In a hearing aid, for example, background conversations, miscellaneous white noise, and spurious events like a loud bang can cause trouble for people who are wearing a device that amplifies these sounds as well as normal conversations. Neural networks are being used to selectively filter out different types of noise, thus enabling hearing aid users to perceive their environment more accurately. Similar applications can be found in cellular telephones and speaker phones.

Control   Building models of processes can be difficult, but an even more challenging problem is controlling a process. Using techniques from reinforcement learning, neural networks have been trained to control many different systems. Current applications include neural networks that can drive a car down a highway, control chemical processes, or a manipulate a robot arm. There are many different ways to build controllers with neural networks. One way is to model an ideal controller already in existence. The neural network controller essentially learns to duplicate the actions taken by another controller (say, a human). In other situations a technique known as model inversion can be used. Model-based control is a third technique that trains a controller to manipulate a second neural network that models some process. This last technique has been used to build controllers for processes that humans are incapable of controlling.

Compression and Correction   Many data streams coming from sensors contain redundancy that can be exploited. In some cases it is possible to exploit this property by building an auto-associative neural network (similar to the encoder-decoder from the previous section) that merely produces an output vector that is equivalent to an input vector. The usefulness in this is that a hidden layer can be made to have fewer neurons than there are inputs or outputs. This means that the neural network must learn an efficient way to compress the data through the bottleneck of the hidden layer. In so doing, a neural network not only may compress the information into a more usable form, but also can correct for missing values in the input vector.

Soft Sensors   From an engineering point of view, it is seldom possible to put as many sensors on a system as we would like. Consider detecting illegal emissions from an automobile engine. Installing complicated sensors on every car would contribute greatly to production costs. Researchers are working on building neural networks that can infer a difficult but needed measurement from readily available measurements. A neural network for this application would have things like engine temperature, gas consumption, and engine misfires as inputs and would output an approximation of the desired measurement, toxic emissions.

Anomaly Detection   In this application area, a neural network is used to build a model of "typical" states of some system. Despite the fact that the network sees only the normal states, it is possible for a network to recognize anomalous conditions simply because they differ from the normal state. Automatically recognizing when anomalies occur can prevent component failures before they are too serious (say, in a helicopter), or even distinguish abnormal heartbeats from normal ones.

Because neural networks is such an active area of research, it is quite possible for this list to be out of date by the time this book is published. Nevertheless, as computing power increases and more data become available, it is likely that neural networks will be applied to hundreds of different applications.

22.8   Unifying Themes

Part of the opening discussion was unfair in its characterization of a single neuron. Much has been learned over the past thirty years about how neurons work, but there are still many puzzles to be solved. Sophisticated models of a single neuron that go way beyond the ideas in a perceptron neuron may contain hundreds of coupled nonlinear differential equations that can be only coarsely simulated in real time on a computer. While the research community is somewhat split as to how complete our understanding of a single neuron can ever be, the possibility remains that we may never have a perfect understanding of how a neuron works. But this does not stop us from using the things that we already know about how real neurons work. In fact, some have suggested that perfect knowledge of how biological neurons work is not strictly necessary for us to exploit them in simulations. This seems to be a reasonable hypothesis when we consider that computer scientists can safely ignore the quantum-level events that occur in real digital circuitry without losing any of the important details of how computation works in principle.

One of the more important parts of an artificial neuron is the nonlinear activation function. We were able to build more powerful neural networks by having intermediate hidden neurons produce values that were used by neurons further down the network. If a linear activation function were used, the resulting output of a multilayer perceptron would be yet another linear function of the inputs. In other words, an MLP with all linear activation functions can produce only the same class of functions that a single-layer linear perceptron can. This means that there would be no advantage in having multiple layers in a network. Thus, nonlinearity in a neuron is a a critical part of its power.

Also note that most researchers do not believe that the brain performs anything like backpropagation at the level of a neuron. A natural learning phenomenon that most closely resembles backprop is probably related to simple behavioral adaptation, which is a feedback process that adjusts behaviors to account for an environment.

We also know that human intelligence emerges from multiple levels of complexity. On the topmost level, intelligence may consist of many interacting yet partially modular components such as memory, feature recognition, and language processing, to name a few. On the lowest level lies the behavior of a single neuron. In between these two extremes lies the massive interconnectedness that glues the lower-level functions to higher-level functions. Intelligence may be an emergent phenomenon that can be best appreciated from a higher-level viewpoint, while neural interactions occupy the lower rung of the ladder. Because of this, researchers in learning must often attempt to straddle reductionist and holistic viewpoints simultaneously.

22.9   Further Exploration

A single program, `mlp`, was used for the four experiments in this chapter. The command-line options are summarized in Table 22.3. The program simulates an MLP with a single hidden layer of neurons. The number of neurons in the MLP is determined by the values used with the `-numin`, `-numhid`, and `-numout` options. The training data file is specified with the `-dfile` option. Data files should begin with a single number to indicate the number of training patterns, which is then followed by all of the patterns given as (input, target) vector pairs.

Option Name	Option Type	Option Meaning
-dfile	STRING	data file name
-numin	INTEGER	number of inputs
-numhid	INTEGER	number of hidden nodes
-numout	INTEGER	number of outputs
-lrate	DOUBLE	learning rate
-mrate	DOUBLE	momentum rate
-winit	DOUBLE	weight initialization factor
-linout	SWITCH	use linear outputs?
-steps	INTEGER	number of simulated steps
-seed	INTEGER	random seed for initial state
-pdump	SWITCH	dump patterns at end of run?
-gdump	SWITCH	dump gnuplot commands at end?
-freq	INTEGER	status printout frequency

Table 22.3   Command-line options for mlp

The -winit option specifies how big the initial weights will be. If w is the value passed to this option, then all weights will be randomly initialized in the $-w$ to w range with a uniform distribution. The -seed option is helpful if you wish to rerun an experiment with a different set of initial weights. If real-valued outputs are needed (as with the logistic map), the -linout switch should be set. The program trains the MLP for the number of iterations specified by -steps. With the -freq option, the printout frequency of the training can be controlled. Each of these printouts consists of the average error of the MLP computed over the entire training set.

With the -pdump option set, the program will print each input along with the MLP's output at the end of training. And with the -gdump option set, the program will create a file called mlp.gnp that contains specifications for the trained network represented as a gnuplot function. This is convenient if you want to plot the surface that represents the MLP's response to two inputs.

Finally, the learning rate or step size is controlled by the -lrate option. There is also an option called -mrate that controls a momentum factor that is used in the training. We did not talk about momentum prior to this section, but it is a simple modification to backprop that greatly increases performance. To explain how it works, for weight vector $\mathbf{w}$ with momentum rate μ, let the weight change determined by plain backprop be denoted by $\Delta\mathbf{w}^{\text{bp}}$. The update rule used by backprop with momentum is

$$\Delta\mathbf{w}^{\text{new}} = \mu\Delta\mathbf{w}^{\text{old}} + \eta\Delta\mathbf{w}^{\text{bp}} \text{ and}$$
$$\mathbf{w}^{\text{new}} = \mathbf{w}^{\text{old}} + \Delta\mathbf{w}^{\text{new}},$$

with μ taking a value between 0 and 1. This allows the program to retain a little bit of the previous step direction. If the MLP proceeds down an error surface like a ball rolling down a hill, momentum allows the ball to speed up over long downhill stretches as well as to jump over little potholes.

Those wishing to try their hand on more sophisticated neural architectures and learning algorithms should consult one of the texts listed in the next section or the bibliography.

22.10   Further Reading

Caudill, M. & Butler, C. (1990). *Naturally intelligent systems.* Cambridge, Mass.: MIT Press.

Haykin, S. (1994). *Neural networks: A comprehensive foundation.* New York: MacMillan.

Hertz, J., Krogh, A., & Palmer, R. G. (1991). *Introduction to the theory of neural computation.* Reading, Mass.: Addison-Wesley.

Minsky, M. & Papert, S. (1988). *Perceptrons* (expanded ed.). Cambridge, Mass.: MIT Press.

Nilsson, N. J. (1965). *Learning machines: Foundations of trainable pattern classifying systems.* New York: McGraw-Hill.

Press, W. H., Flannery, B. P., Teukolsky, S. A., & Vetterling, W. T. (1986). *Numerical recipes.* Cambridge: Cambridge University Press.

Rumelhart, D. E., Hinton, G. E., & Williams, R. J. (1986). *Parallel distributive processing.* Cambridge, Mass.: MIT Press.

23 Postscript: Adaptation

The sciences do not try to explain, they hardly even try to interpret, they mainly make models. By a model is meant a mathematical construct which, with the addition of certain verbal interpretations, describes observed phenomena. The justification of such a mathematical construct is solely and precisely that it is expected to work.
— John von Neumann

Breadth-first search is the bulldozer of science.
— Randy Goebel

The most extensive computation known has been conducted over the last billion years on a planet-wide scale: it is the evolution of life. The power of this computation is illustrated by the complexity and beauty of its crowning achievement, the human brain.
— David Rogers

IN THIS FINAL postscript we will dissect the general form of an adaptive system into three subsystems that are all deserving of study in their own right: an environment, a model of the environment, and a search procedure that attempts to adapt the model to the environment. We will see that all three components of an adaptive system are highly dependent on each other, in that each partially determines the other two. Our goal for this postscript is to see how this interdependence can be viewed from a computational viewpoint. As a consequence, all sophisticated adaptive procedures, including scientific methodology, are subject to the paradoxical attributes associated with self-reference and computability.

We will first compare and contrast learning, evolution, and cultural adaptation to examine the relationship between models and search methods, and also to see how all three processes are similar in their generality. We will then look at how an environment limits the types of feasible search procedures. This means that search methods can be adapted to tune models more effectively. This is followed by an examination of the relationship between models and environments that will highlight coadaptive processes that tune models and environments in a recursive manner. Putting all of these facts together, we will then consider how adaptation can be a "bootstrap" process by which adaptive systems spawn increasingly more sophisticated adaptive systems.

In the final section of this chapter, we will consider how the recursive framework of adaptive systems relates to Gödel's incompleteness and Chaitin's generalization of Turing's Halting Problem. In the end, we will find that these two computational results bring forth severe limitations on how well we can know and understand the universe.

23.1 Models and Search Methods

The term *model* can mean different things in different contexts, but for our purposes we will use a definition that is somewhat connected to the topics from this book part. With this in mind, we will use the term to mean a well-defined process that maps inputs to outputs but also happens to be parameterized in such a way that the model can be tuned by changing the parameters. The parameters may be discrete or continuous, but in either case they act as knobs that can be adjusted to change the input-output mapping that the model produces. As a simple example, we could model a periodic process by the equation

$$f(x; a, b, c) = a \sin(bx - c),$$

which has an output, a single input, x, and three parameters, a, b and c, that correspond to the amplitude, frequency, and phase of the sine wave, respectively. With this equation, we could adjust the three parameters to build a rough approximation of a frictionless pendulum, the average seasonal temperature, or the lunar cycle.

A *search procedure* is a method for choosing parameter values so that a model is made to closely approximate an environment. For the sine wave example, the model is so simple that for any environment, there is a best solution that can be found with a deterministic procedure. In this case, the simplicity of the model has simplified the search procedure for the parameters.

For most real-world systems that one could imagine modeling, a simple sine wave is completely inadequate as a representation of the environment. On the other hand, in principle classifier systems and neural networks can be used to model anything, because they are so general that virtually any process can be approximated with them.[1] But approximation power is somewhat of a curse as well. By using a more complicated model, we lose the bonus of having a search procedure that is guaranteed to work under all circumstances. Things are so bad that the general

---

[1] Including GAs in this statement is a little problematic, since GAs are really a type of search procedure, as we shall see shortly.

problem of optimizing a neural network or a classifier system is known to be NP-complete under many reasonable cases and intractable under some special cases.

This double-sided result is partially due to the modular nature of the models. Both classifier systems and neural networks derive their power from the fact that they are composed of many simple units that can be combined to form complex patterns. Doyne Farmer and others have made a more profound observation by noting that the similarities of these adaptive systems actually run quite deep. The following discussion is mostly inspired by Farmer's "Rosetta Stone" paper, which compares the aforementioned adaptive systems with immune and autocatalytic networks. Here, I will just give a summary of the comparison for neural networks and classifier systems, but afterward I will attempt to expand on the comparison to bridge the idea for evolution, culture, and learning.

Since the output of both a neural network and a classifier system is a composition of values computed at intermediate stages, both models need a form of working memory that allows these auxiliary values to be stored. For a neural network, this is simply a neuron that holds some value that is later passed to another neuron. The equivalent structure for a classifier system is a little more subtle because we haven't been in the habit of drawing classifier systems as networks. However, a message in a classifier system serves the same purposes despite the fact that it does not directly correspond to a tangible structure like a neuron. Messages are posted by classifiers on the message list, where they remain for a single time step. At the beginning of the next time step, the active messages trigger other classifiers; thus, the messages serve the role of holding an intermediate piece of information and triggering the production of other information.

Synapses in a neural network serve the role of transporting information from a source to a destination. They may also be associated with a strength. Classifiers serve a similar role since they are paired with a condition and a message, which act as a source and a destination, respectively. A synapse's strength is analogous to a classifier's strength; both strengths increase the probability that a message or signal will have a consequence when propagated further.

The net input of a neuron is computed as a weighted sum of other neuron activation values. In a classifier system, identical messages may be posted by more than one classifier. This is identical to having multiple neurons propagating signals to a single destination. Where a neural network uses a weighted sum to combine the signals, a classifier system will usually combine all of the identical messages into a single message that has an intensity proportional to the sum of the strengths of the original messages. Thus, both systems combine multiple signals into one in a weighted manner.

A neural network will additionally pass the net input of a neuron through a sigmoidal activation function, which has the effect of limiting the activation value to a well-defined range. Likewise, classifier systems do not propagate all messages on the message list at each iteration. Instead, only the strongest messages are able to trigger classifiers on the next time step. This selection method effectively treats a group of the strongest messages as active and thresholds all others to an inactive state. Hence, both systems pass information through thresholds that allow only a portion of the information to propagate.

One could continue this comparison to the point of showing that it is always possible to have these two model types mutually emulate one another in an efficient manner. However, the model types differ most in how they are tuned to their environment. For neural networks, a learning-like procedure is used to slightly change weights according to a error gradient measure, that is, if an error measure decreases in some direction of the weight space, then a small step is taken in that direction. Classifier systems use a related method for adjusting weights (the bucket brigade algorithm, or implicit bucket brigade) that assigns credit from one classifier to another in the form of payments. But also note that classifier systems additionally depend on a genetic algorithm to introduce new classifiers into the system. Thus, classifier systems are adapted with a learning-like procedure as well as an evolutionary-like procedure.

In the real world, cultural breakthroughs are made on time scales that are slow relative to learning but fast relative to evolution. In the simplest case, cultural adaptation is merely a process of imitation, as is the case with many animals. For humans, cultural adaptation has become far more significant because of the invention of language. For culture, language serves much the same role that far-reaching synapses do in a brain. Whenever an innovation can be passed only via imitation, propagation of the innovation can occur only at a very slow and localized rate. However, language, in particular writing, enables innovations to spread both far and wide. Whereas neurons serve the role of information holders in a neural network, humans act as the basic information repository in a cultural system. Under this view, synaptic strength starts to resemble the number and total influence of the holders of a particular idea. Individuals modify ideas with learning by incrementally improving on an idea that was acquired elsewhere. For example, Catholicism is an idea that has been around for quite a while. It is typically passed from parent to child, but on occasion it is transferred in a more evangelical manner. Influential members of the faith have incrementally modified the religion through their own efforts, as in the case of Thomas Aquinas, whose philosophical writings changed the way many Catholics interpreted the Bible. In other cases, the changes in Catholicism have resembled evolution more closely, as when the church accommodated new members by incorporating (memetic crossover?) pagan festivals as official holidays.

On a global scale, biological evolution starts to resemble culture and learning if we consider the species to be the basic type of information holder. Species are connected to each other through a web of interactions that may be competitive or cooperative. The population or total amount of genetic material resembles what we have been thinking of as the unit strength in the other models. Evolution performs a type of parameter search that stochastically samples nearby points in the genome. Genetic shifts that result in a more fit individual can move the entire species in a specific genetic direction. While this is not the same as a gradient-based search, stochastic sampling and gradient ascent are both examples of the hill-climbing search method.

All of this will be relevant in the next section, where we will see how search methods relate to environments and search spaces.

23.2 Search Methods and Environments

Since adaptive systems have parameters that can be modified, the space of all possible parameter settings defines a *search space*. For evolutionary systems, the search space consists of all conceivable DNA sequences, while for a neural network with n weights, the search space is equal to an n-dimensional hyperspace of weight settings. The purpose of adaptation is to move through the space from a region of poor fitness to one of good fitness. However, since fitness is a measure of how successfully a model is matched to its environment, the difficulty of the search problem is intimately tied to the environment. In this section, we will see that search methods may be adapted to an environment. In other words, we will see that phrases such as "learning to learn" or "evolving evolution" may refer to real processes.

To explain what is meant by a "search method," imagine that you have a very important meeting that is going to start promptly at midnight on the highest point of a mountain range. There is no way of getting to this point except to climb, and to make things worse, you do not have a map of the region nor do you have any idea where the peak is located. You have a flashlight to light your way, but there is a dense fog surrounding the mountain that permits you to see only about one foot in front of you. You have only three things working in your favor. First, this mountain range happens to be on a small planet with very low gravity, so you can make large leaps if you are certain that there is firm ground where you will land. Second, there are lots of little pebbles lying about, and being the current world champion in darts, you can throw the pebbles with perfect accuracy. Third, you have an altimeter and a compass to help you navigate.

You start at the base of the mountain. Since you can see only very small localized regions, your first move is to try to walk uphill. This works for a while, but eventually you reach a small peak. Your companions are not there, so you know that this is not the tallest peak. Scooping up a handful of pebbles, you methodically throw several pebbles in various directions, in an attempt to find a region that has a higher peak. At some point, one of your pebbles makes a sound that clearly indicates it has hit a peak that is higher than your current location. You then take

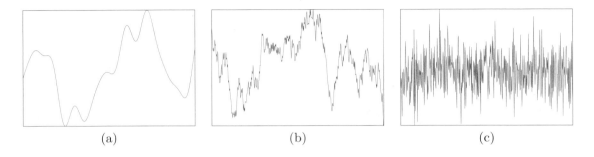

(a)   (b)   (c)

Figure 23.1   Three types of search spaces: (a) smooth, (b) neither smooth nor strictly random, and (c) random

advantage of the low gravity and leap to this new location. Once there, you start to climb in an uphill direction. This continues for some time, but you are running short of time. Fortunately, just before midnight, your friends hear your silly efforts, throw you a rope, and pull you up to your destination.

This little scenario illustrates how adaptation and search procedures must often proceed in a nearly blind manner, making tentative probes until progress is made. But there are other useful comparisons that can be made between search methods and this scenario. First, search methods can work in different ways. Sometimes a localized search makes sense. Other times, you are better off probing more distant areas with pebbles. Learning in artificial neural networks takes smooth steps, while genetic algorithms perform a very structured type of probing.

Figure 23.1 illustrates three types of search spaces. In Figure 23.1a we have a nice and smooth surface that lends itself to a learning-like procedure that makes small steps in an uphill direction. Some minor probing with the pebbles is necessary in order to find the largest peak, but one would expect to take more small steps than large probes for this search space. On the other hand, Figure 23.1c shows a surface that is completely random. Small and local steps are useless in a space such as this. The best search strategy for this surface is to randomly probe the entire region. Figure 23.1b shows a surface that is somewhat between the two extremes. While the surface has many irregular bumps, it contains a certain amount of continuity in that the height of a region is usually close to the height of nearby points. In a search environment such as this, you would need a mixture of local search steps and distant but structured probes to find the peak.

Knowing the type of search space that you may encounter is a huge advantage if you are limited to a fixed search method. But what should you do if the search space changes? There is much evidence that search methods in natural systems are adapted according to environments. As a first example, consider the different types of search probes that a fit population would make versus those of an unfit population. In biological systems "search probe" can be thought of as a mutation rate, with large and small mutations corresponding to large and small probes, respectively. Fit individuals have little to gain and much to lose from large mutations. Fit individuals are far better off taking small steps so as not to undo earlier progress. However, for an unfit population, small steps are usually useless. When your house is on fire, drinking some iced tea may make you momentarily feel better, but is clearly a case of the right idea applied in too small a proportion. Unfit individuals are better served by attempting large probes, for in times of trouble, big changes are needed. If the change makes things worse, well, things were bad already.

Biological systems have some sophisticated cellular machinery devoted to correcting replication errors in DNA. The level of sophistication varies between single-cell and multicellular animals as well as between the species, but it is present to some degree in all organisms. When bacteria are dangerously close to starving, the error correction machinery is inhibited to the degree that more drastic mutations are permitted. The advantages for bacteria in this case are significant: If a new mutation permits a bacterium to metabolize a new food source, then starvation can be avoided (Wills, 1989). Other examples of how evolution is evolved include the invention of sex in single-cell animals and sexual selection in the higher animals.

Human culture has experienced several major innovations that have altered the way in which information is passed through the generations. Many animals can communicate in ways such that information important to survival is passed from individual to individual. Birds declare territory and warn of predators with songs and chirps. Bees do a cute little jig that describes the location of a nectar cache. Otters teach their young how to smash open shells. But humans have taken communication to the unique extreme that our languages can express an infinite number of ideas. This innovation opened the door to a method of symbolically passing on information in a way that is distinct from imitation.

Another major milestone in human culture is the advancement of written language. The alphabet and the printing press have enabled us to make more or less permanent records of important knowledge. And of comparable importance was the invention of the scientific method. By defining a systematic way to ask and answer questions about nature, the scientific method has enabled humans to propel themselves to the point that human culture now far outweighs evolution in its affect on the world as a whole.

While evolution has produced increasingly complex animals, it has also adapted the process of adaptation. Hence, we have not only an advancement of physical structures but also an advancement of the functional structures of adaptation. Evolution produces simple adaptation, which allows for learning, which permits imitation, which spawns culture, which brings forth language, which gives birth to science, by which evolution is rediscovered.

23.3   Environments and Models

We have been speaking of models and environments as if they were two very distinct things that one could separate with a line. In reality, one creature's model is another creature's environment, which is to say that biological systems must adapt to other adapting biological systems. When multiple creatures simultaneously adapt to each other, the fitness of an organism becomes a function of how other organisms are behaving. The usual idea of evolution proceeding up a fitness landscape is no longer true in this case, for if a species stays still, that is, does not genetically change, and other species change, then the fitness landscape of the static species is altered despite its determination to stay still. This means that organisms often will have to continuously adapt just to stay at a comparable level of fitness. This is why Stuart Kauffman has often referred to fitness landscapes as being squishy: Taking a step deforms the terrain.

Coevolution encourages Red Queen scenarios that often result in biological arms races (as discussed in Chapter 20) that spawn adaptations that would never come about on their own. Danny Hillis and others have exploited coevolution as a means for improving the evolutionary optimization of genetic algorithms. But it is the mutual adaptation that changes both models and environments that is our main interest in this section.

Coadaptation relates to the search problem in a very unusual way. To see why, consider the No Free Lunch (NFL) theorem of David Wolpert and William Macready. Because there are so many different methods of performing search and optimization, one hot topic among researchers is the relative efficiency of the different methods. If one method could be clearly identified as being better than the others, then computer scientists could use the best method on any problem and no longer worry about finding a better technique. The NFL theorem states that over all possible search spaces, all methods perform equally well, including the simple technique of randomly guessing. Wolpert and Macready proved the NFL theorem by averaging a search score over every possible search space, which will contain well-behaved surfaces like Figure 23.1a as well as many random surfaces like Figure 23.1c.

At first glance the NFL theorem seems to be very disappointing in its implications. Under a strict interpretation it means that gradient-based learning and genetic algorithms are no better than a random guess. But Wolpert and Macready (as well as Stuart Kauffman) have pointed out that it may actually imply something far more interesting. Specifically, we know that evolutionary fitness landscapes are far from random. Kauffman has suggested that the NFL theorem actually highlights the importance of coadaptation. When an animal and its environment are mutually adapting to one another, the fitness landscapes (that is, the evolutionary search spaces) are molded to one another. Coadaptation squeezes the search spaces in such a way that they become highly nonrandom. One implication of this is that search methods may be optimally adapted for the space that they are used in. In other words, evolution may be evolved.

A similar property can be seen in learning systems as well. Training feedforward neural networks on a fixed set of input-output patterns is a relatively well-defined problem. Although finding the best weights for a feedforward network is known to be an NP-complete problem, there are many encouraging results that indicate that good solutions to challenging problems can be found. Parallel to the ideas in coevolution there are more complicated types of neural networks having recurrent connections that couple the network's output (or some internal states) to the network's input. Networks of this type are far more powerful than strictly feedforward nets (they are, in fact, capable of universal computation); however, the newly gained power comes at considerable expense. Specifically, finding the best set of weights for a recurrent network turns out to be an incomputable problem in the worst case, since the individual artificial neurons must adapt not only within the context of other neurons in the network but also in the context of the previous states of the neurons, making the whole problem hopelessly recursive. So, again, we find that once a system becomes self-referential, it must border a boundary between computability and incomputability. This means that no general technique can be used to solve the problem of training a recurrent neural network. Partial solutions must in some ways be adapted to the specifics of the problems. For systems of this type, "learning to learn" may be a more promising method.

23.4   Adaptation and Computation

In speaking of adaptation as a process of model-building, we have really been talking about ideas very central not just to computer science but to all of science.

In the end, scientific research is about building models. When we try to characterize a phenomenon by a set of equations or a program, it is a model that we are building. We interact with nature in many ways, but from a scientific perspective our interactions are characterized in two ways. First, we manipulate and observe nature so as to gather data. With this data we attempt to describe how nature works. For the second way, we use our descriptions of nature to make predictions of what nature will do at a later time. Our models are continuously adapted by new discoveries. And over time our models and our methods for adapting them become more sophisticated.

Curiously, the theory of computation has a lot to say about the limits of what we can do with science. As discussed in Chapters 9 and 14, Gregory Chaitin's extension of the Halting Problem proves that finding the smallest program (that is, a model) that explains a set of data (or observations) is in the general case undecidable. Considering that Occam's Razor is one of the foundations of the way we build our models, Chaitin's result implies that there may be phenomena that cannot be described more compactly than themselves.

From the opposite direction, Gödel's incompleteness and Turing's incomputability results (discussed in Chapters 4 and 3) tell us that even if we have a perfect model for some phenomenon, there are many interesting questions concerning the real phenomena that cannot be answered by looking at the model.

Is this a gloomy view of how far science can go toward describing the universe? I don't think so. To see why, read on.

23.5   Further Reading

Casti, J. L. (1989). *Alternate realities: Mathematical models of nature and man.* New York: John Wiley & Sons.

Farmer, J. D. (1990). Rosetta stone for connectionism. *Physica D*, 42(1–3): 153–187.

Hillis, W. D. (1992). Co-evolving parasites improve simulated evolution as an optimization procedure. In C. G. Langton, C. Taylor, J. D. Farmer, & S. Rasmussen (Eds.), *Artificial life II*, volume 10 of *Sante Fe Institute Studies in the Sciences of Complexity* (pp. 313–324). Redwood City, Calif.: Addison-Wesley.

Kauffman, S. (August 1991). Antichaos and adaptation. *Sci. Am.*, 265(2): 64–70.

Sarle, W. S. & Net Poohbahs (1994). Kangaroos and training neural networks. FAQ list available from `ftp://ftp.sas.com/pub/neural/kangaroos`.

Wills, C. (1989). *The wisdom of the genes.* New York: Basic Books.

Wolpert, D. H. & Macready, W. G. (1995). No free lunch theorems for search. Technical Report SFI-TR-95-02-010, The Santa Fe Institute, Santa Fe, N.M.

Epilogue

Recursion, which is the hallmark of computation, is an integral part of the structural and functional self-similarity of fractals and chaos. Parallel collections of simple things possess a similar form of recursion that comes about from local interactions. When interactions are permitted to change, systems can display collective behavior that is computationally profound.

The line between computability and incomputability defines a spectrum in which all natural phenomena exist. Things that reside at either of the two extremes are usually uninteresting because they are either too ordered or too disordered. Things in between the two operational extremes display a stunning variety of sophistication, complexity, and beauty that is directly related to the computable properties of these systems.

Because of the power of computation and the ubiquity of computational-like features in natural systems, a mixture of computability and incomputability forms an interface between the hierarchical partitions of natural systems. This, in turn, has deep implications for how closely humanity can understand nature.

24   Duality and Dichotomy

When two texts, or two assertions, perhaps two ideas, are in contradiction,
be ready to reconcile them rather than cancel one by the other; regard them as two
different facets, or two successive stages, of the same reality, a reality convincingly
human just because it is complex.
— Marguerite Yourcenar

To see a World in a grain of Sand,
And a Heaven in a Wild Flower,
Hold Infinity in the palm of your hand,
And Eternity in an hour.
— William Blake

IN THE VARIOUS contexts of philosophy, religion, and science, humans have shown a fondness for classifying things in terms of absolutes, such as, black and white, good and evil, order and chaos, yin and yang, and so on. Absolutes are easy to comprehend and comfortable to our minds because they remove ambiguities and reinforce a sense of understanding. To be sure, there clearly exist domains in which binary rules not only work but also capture the essence of that which is being described. But for many things—and perhaps most things—reality blends the black-and-white absolutes into a beautiful melody of gray.

Just as life depends on an environment that allows water to exist in solid, liquid, and gaseous forms, so nature's most amazing and beautifully complex creations must exist at the juncture between computability and incomputability. On these two extremes scientific understanding is best pursued in the form of theory and experimentation, respectively. But at the interface between the two, both extreme approaches must give way to the grayness of reality.

In this final chapter, we will pull together all of the loose threads from the earlier chapters and attempt to reconcile conflicting themes into a single message. We will first consider issues of Chapter 1 and reexamine some of the commonalities that can be found in the diverse topics that have been covered in this book. Afterward, we

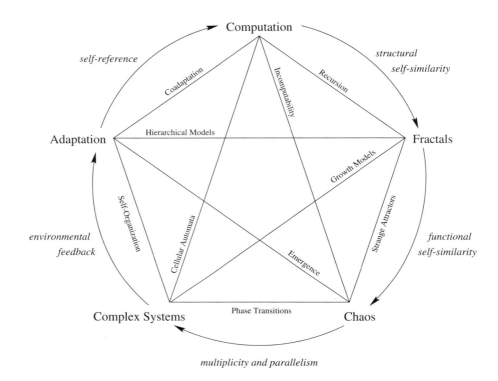

Figure 24.1   The relationships among computation, fractals, chaos, complex systems, and adaptation

will consider the boundary between computability and incomputability as it applies to the contents of this book and, in particular, the topics covered in the postscript chapters. We will then finish with a speculative discussion on how the grayness of this fundamental boundary is an integral part of the beauty of nature.

24.1   Web of Connections

Continuing with some of the themes first introduced in Chapter 1, the properties of recursion, parallelism, and adaptation play an interesting role as attributes of natural systems. For example, in order for the universe to move coherently from one state to the next, the universe must "remember" previous states, which means that recursion (and its close cousins, feedback and iteration) exists as a form of memory that binds locally occurring moments in time. Multiplicity and parallelism play a similar role that has to do with binding locally occurring points in space.

With this in mind, we can see how mixtures of recursion and multiplicity partially define and differentiate computation, fractals, chaos, complex systems, and adaptation. Figure 24.1, is a slightly revised version of Figure 1.1 that has a couple of extra labels to illustrate some of the relationships uncovered between the book parts. Starting from a computational framework, fractals are special "programs" that build self-similar structures. Chaotic systems are similar to fractals but also contain functional self-similarity that occurs at different scales. By adding multiplicity and parallelism to nonlinear systems, complex systems can be formed with only local interactions. And when complex systems are coupled to their environment with a feedback mechanism, systems can form implicit models of the environment, which is the basis of adaptation. Finally, when an adaptive system becomes so complex that it receives feedback from itself, a self-referential system is created that can potentially have all of the strengths and weaknesses of the computational basis that we started out with.

In this way, primitive computational systems can beget more sophisticated computational systems that build on previously built pieces. Looking at the organization of nature, we find that most interesting things are composed of smaller interesting things. This is evident when we consider that societies, economies, and ecosystems are made of animals, humans, and species, which are made of cells that consist of amazingly complicated organelles, which are themselves composed of an elaborate ensemble of autocatalytic chemical reactions. Each level is nearly a universe in itself, since all of them use and support types of structural and functional self-similarity, multiplicity and parallelism, recursion and feedback, and self-reference. Nature, then, appears to be a hierarchy of computational systems that are forever on the edge between computability and incomputability.

24.2 Interfaces to Hierarchies

We have seen in many examples that the novelty of a system is related to the indeterminacy of the computation that it performs. Static systems are boring because they settle down to steady-state behavior. Overactive systems lack the coherence to retain consistent patterns from one time step to the next. In between are systems that are forever changing but have a consistent underlying structure or function. Such nonequilibrium systems are analogous to a whirlpool of water; while the molecules of a whirlpool are forever moving and changing, the motion of the whirlpool contains a sufficient amount of constancy that it has functional persistence.

This behavior, which is best seen as being on the border between computability and incomputability, acts as an interface between the components of hierarchically organized structure. Tables 24.1 and 24.2 summarize some of the phenomena that can be characterized in this way. As can be seen in the table, this interface between computability and incomputability is relevant to mathematical, fractal, chaotic,

	Computable	Partially Computable	Incomputable
Sets	recursive	RE and CO-RE	not RE and not CO-RE
Numbers	rational	computable irrational	incomputable
Programs	trivially (never) halt	possibly halt	—
Proofs	true or false	profound statements	unprovable
NP-Complete Problems*	underconstrained	critically constrained	overconstrained

	Computable	Partially Computable	Incomputable
Deterministic Geometry	Euclidean	deterministic fractal	—
Stochastic Geometry	—	stochastic fractal	pure noise
AC	compressible	possibly incompressible	incompressible
Mandelbrot Set	white regions	border regions	black regions

	Computable	Partially Computable	Incomputable
Continuous Dynamics	fixed point or periodic	chaotic	high-dimensional chaos or stochastic
Discrete Dynamics	regular from over-sampling	complex at mid-sampling	irregular from under-sampling
Attractors	integral dimensions	strange	infinite dimensional
Mater*	solid	liquid	gas

Table 24.1 "Novelty" as a function of computability, part 1: Entries with a ⋆ are merely analogous. Not all entries listed as being "Partially Computable" are themselves technically incomputable, but instead represent a region between overly simple things and overly complex things.

complex, and adaptive systems. In each case, the most interesting types of behavior fall somewhere between what is computable and what is incomputable.

This raises an interesting point regarding the levels at which science tries to discover patterns in nature. The bottom-up reductionist approach is to describe the functions of the lowest-level structures and to infer the structure and function of higher-level things based on the known rules. This is a perfect approach when things are computable and can be described in a closed analytical form. In such simple systems, all higher-level behaviors can be predicted from a basic set of rules.

The top-down and somewhat holistic approach is to describe things from the opposite direction. Experiments are made and observations are noted. From this

	Computable	Partially Computable	Incomputable
Wolfram CA	class I or II	class IV	class III
Langton's λ	$\lambda < 1/3$	$\lambda \approx 1/2$	$\lambda > 2/3$
Agent Interactions	globally coordinated or always cooperative	locally coordinated or competitive and cooperative	uncoordinated or always competitive
NK Nets	$K = 1$	$K = 2$	$2 < K \leq N$
Sandpiles	flat and stable	critical	tall and unstable
Economics[*]	communism	free but regulated	unrestrained
Governments[*]	dictatorial	democracy	anarchy

Patterns	consistent	hidden order	inconsistent
Models	not self-referential	coadaptive or recurrent	hopelessly self-referential
Search Methods	local or greedy	hybrid	exhaustive
Search Spaces	smooth	complex structured	pathological

Table 24.2 "Novelty" as a function of computability, part 2: Entries with a ⋆ are merely analogous. Not all entries listed as being "Partially Computable" are themselves technically incomputable, but instead represent a region between overly simple things and overly complex things.

point, one is faced with the difficult task of deriving lower-level rules from upper-level behaviors. While both methods of investigation have a role in science (and in all scientific domains), the interface between levels of organization may be such that neither method is really up to the job. For novel phenomena, simulation becomes a crucial form of investigation.

24.3   Limitations on Knowledge

Figure 24.2 illustrates how science interacts with the universe. On the left side of the figure are natural processes that are recurrently coupled to themselves. On the right is human understanding that attempts to model the natural world. Experimentation consists of manipulating the environment and observing the changes that come about. Theorizing is the process of manipulating models to see if they make accurate predictions of future observations. Simulation resides between the two, and manipulates both models and environments.

As stated in the last postscript, Gödel's incompleteness result tells us that no theory or model can be used to make all of the predictions that we would like.

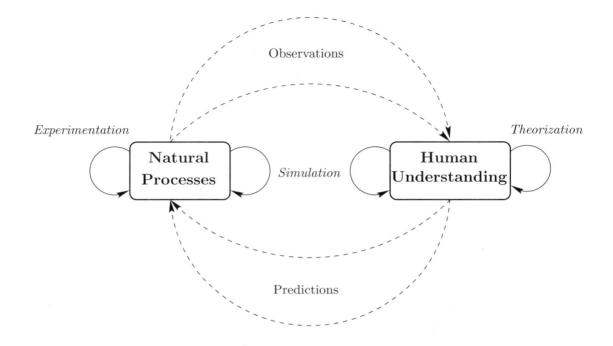

Figure 24.2   The universe of natural processes related to scientific understanding

Chaitin's extension of Turing's Halting Problem proves that there is no reliable way to build theories and models. Turing's incomputability shows us that simulations and natural processes may never halt, but also that we may never be able to prove this fact. Together, these three results rigorously prove that there are many things about nature that we will never be able to know with any amount of effort via experimentation, theorization, and simulation. This is truly wonderful.

Think back to Chapter 8, where we first constructed the Mandelbrot set. White pixels, that is, the background portions, correspond to points that we know must diverge under the Mandelbrot iterations, while black pixels correspond to points that we *suspect* will never diverge. While every white point corresponds to something that we are certain about, there are some black points (i.e., the main kidney-shaped section) that we can also color with certainty. On the border are black points that we merely suspect are colored correctly. It is impossible for us to determine the correct color of these points with perfect certainty. It is this region, between computability and incomputability, that contains all of the novelty and beauty of the M-set. If the rules for determining the colors of the M-set points lacked this pathological quality, the M-set would not be what it is. Instead, it would repeat itself, or worse yet, simply stop yielding any patterns. But as it is, the M-set contains an infinite amount of complexity and beauty that can never be exhausted.

We could make similar arguments about all of the other topics covered in the book. For example, these issues, as they pertain to mathematics and the theory of computation, mean that there is an infinite supply of programs and mathematical statements that will forever be just on the threshold of being understood. As soon as we understand them, there will remain a newly discovered and infinite collection of mysterious programs and mathematical statements. For the case of dynamical systems, while we may always make further progress in understanding particular systems, there will always be some processes that lie just beyond our abilities to predict. Similarly, for complex systems, parallel collections of simple nonlinear objects will always be able to produce behavior that is emergent and novel from the point of view that the collective behavior is far more interesting than the individual behaviors. And for adaptive systems, as long as perfect stability is never achieved, adaptation will build more complex models of environments, which further increases the complexity of the environments as well as the methods of adaptation.

Nature, being composed of all of these things, will always have novelty, richness, and beauty that can never be exhausted. As with the M-set, we can appreciate nature's beauty precisely because we can simulate it, but only to limited accuracy. If all natural phenomena were either perfectly describable or absolutely indescribable, not only would they be uninteresting, but life would be impossible.

Source Code Notes

The process of preparing programs for a digital computer is especially attractive, not only because it can be economically and scientifically rewarding, but also because it can be an aesthetic experience much like composing poetry or music.
— Donald E. Knuth

W HILE READING this book, you will have the opportunity to duplicate almost all of the figures and results by experimenting with the supplied programs. A link to an FTP site that contains the source code for the programs can be found at this book's homepage, located at:

```
http://mitpress.mit.edu/0262062003.html
```

The source code is written entirely in C and is known to work under Solaris, Linux, and Windows NT. This appendix gives a brief introduction on how to use the programs, tells where to find additional documentation, and gives a brief description of each program.

Input Interface   In general, all programs have a command-line interface, meaning that all runtime parameters for the programs are specified on the same line in which the command name is typed. Command-line options will usually take a value that is either INTEGER, DOUBLE (a double precision floating-point number), or a STRING. An option that is a SWITCH takes no value since specifying the option on the command-line toggles an internal value in the program between "on" and "off." For example, the command:

```
prog -val 3.1415 -name "PI" -number 5 -flip
```

executes the program named **prog** and sets three value options (**-val**, **-name** and **-number**) to three values appropriate to their type and directly following the options on the command-line. The final option, named **-flip**, is a SWITCH and, therefore, takes no value.

-term	Driver	Notes
vga	Linux VGA	for Linux systems without X Windows
x11	X Windows	for most UNIX systems
win	Windows NT	may also work under Windows 95
ps	PostScript	best for line plots saved to a file
pgm	PGM	best for pixel plots saved to a file
none	—	inhibit all graphics
raw	—	outputs (x, y, color) triplets in ASCII

Table 25.1   Program terminal drivers

In no case does any program take interactive input. Some programs may need to operate on an entire set of input data (such as patterns to be remembered by a Hopfield network), in which case, the data is specified by a STRING option that denotes the input data filename.

Output Interface   The output of a program is either plain text or graphical. If a program displays graphics (as most of them do), then you need to specify a value for the -term option that is appropriate for your computer system. This option tells the program which of the graphic terminal drivers to use. Table 25.1 contains a list of possible values to use with the -term option. Most programs that display graphics will have two more options named -width and -height that are used to specify the size of the graphics device. Additionally, the -inv SWITCH option will force reverse video, and -xmag can be used to increase the size of the X Windows display without increasing the resolution.

The PostScript and PGM graphic drivers do not actually display graphics but write the contents of the graphics in the specified file format. To save the output, the standard output of the program should be redirected to a file.

For programs that do not display graphics, some output may be sent to the standard output and standard error text streams. Periodic text output (such as the current error level of a neural network being trained) is usually sent to standard error and the final output of the program (such as the data points for a generated chaotic time series) is sent to standard output. Thus, by redirecting the standard output stream, the periodic output will still be displayed while the final output of the program can be stored in a file.

Documentation   A minimal program description is given at the end of the chapters where the programs are mentioned. Detailed documentation is in the software distribution in the format of UNIX-style manual pages and HTML web documents. Moreover, programmers may wish to inspect the source code itself, since all of the documentation is automatically derived from the source code.

Program Descriptions   The programs below are listed in the order in which they appear in the text.

stutter   interprets simple lisp and only understands `car`, `cdr`, `cons`, `if`, `set`, `equal`, `quote`, and `lambda`, but is still Turing-complete. Uses stop-and-copy garbage collection and has an adjustable heap size. Examples that implement integer and floating-point arithmetic are provided. There is even an example `stutter` function to compute the square root of a floating-point argument with nothing but the primitives listed above.

diffuse   Generates diffusion limited aggregate growth that looks like coral.

lsys   Builds L-system fractals. Accepts multiple rules so that complicated fractals (such as a Penrose tiling) can be expressed. Great for generating plantlike fractals.

mrcm   Uses the Multiple Reduction Copy Machine algorithm to generate affine fractals. Accepts an arbitrary number of transformations. Good for making snowflakes and mosaic patterns.

ifs   Similar to `mrcm` but uses Iterated Functional Systems for finer granularity.

mandel   Plots the famous Mandelbrot set. There are options for the displayed coordinates, zoom level, coloring schemes, etc.

julia   Generates Julia sets, which are related to the Mandelbrot set. Has options similar to `mandel`.

gen1d   Generates a time series from a one-dimensional map. Nothing fancy; it just shows how chaos can be seen in simple systems.

bifur1d   Plots a bifurcation diagram for a one-dimensional map to illustrate how a change in a single parameter can move a system from fixed-point behavior, to periodic, and finally to chaos. Different regions can be zoomed in on.

phase1d   Plots the phase space and trajectories of a one-dimensional map. Showing trajectories in the phase space more clearly illustrates why fixed-points and limit cycles occur. This can also be used to show the exponential divergence of nearby trajectories.

henon   Plots the phase space of the Hénon map, a two-dimensional system with a fractal shape. Different regions can be zoomed in on.

henbif   Plots a bifurcation diagram for the Hénon system. This is similar to **bifur1d** but shows that bifurcations apply to multidimensional systems as well.

henwarp Takes a square of a specified area and "warps" it a fixed number of times by the Hénon system. This illustrates the stretching and folding motion of chaotic systems as well as shows how points within an attractor's basin of attraction are eventually forced into a strange attractor.

lorenz   Plots the phase space of the Lorenz system, a three-dimensional system described by differential equations with a fractal shape. Both plain phase-space plots and delayed state-space plots are possible.

rossler Similar to **lorenz**, but uses the Rossler system.

mg   Plots a two-dimensional embedding of the phase space of the Mackey-Glass system, a delay-differential system, with arbitrary parameters.

gsw   Simulates an individual-based three-species predator-prey ecosystem according to the specified parameters. The three species consist of plants, herbivores, and carnivores (grass, sheep, and wolves; hence the name, **gsw**). Updates are done synchronously, and each species has several parameters which can control their life cycles, from the ability to give birth, to the likelihood of starvation. Population statistics of the three species can be calculated over a subset of the entire grid.

predprey Plots the phase space of a three-species predator-prey system (described by differential equations) which may be fractal in shape. Both plain phase-space plots and delayed state-space plots are possible.

lotka   Simulates the two-species Lotka-Volterra predator-prey system with a second-order Euler's method. This program serves as a simple introduction to differential equations.

hencon   Controls the Hénon system with the OGY control law for arbitrary choices of the system parameters. The control law is analytically calculated based on the system parameters. The user can select times in which control is turned on and off so that time-to-control and transients can be observed. Gaussian noise can be injected into the system.

ca   Simulates arbitrary one-dimensional cellular automata with an arbitrary choice of simulation parameters. Random rules can be generated and used with a desired lambda value.

life   Simulates Conway's Game of Life with an arbitrary set of initial conditions. Input files need to be in the PBM file format.

hp   Simulates and plots the time evolution of the hodgepodge machine according to specified parameters. With a proper choice of parameters, this system resembles the Belousov-Zhabotinsky reaction which forms self-perpetuating spirals in a lattice.

termites   Simulates a population of termites which do a random walk while possibly carrying a wood chip. Under normal circumstances, the termites will self-organize and move the wood chips into piles without a global leader. The termites' behavior is dictated by the following set of rules: If a termite is not carrying anything and it bumps into a chip, then it picks it up, reverses direction, and continues with the random walk. If it is carrying a chip and bumps into another, it drops the chip, turns around, and starts walking again. Otherwise, it just does a random walk whether it is carrying a chip or not.

vants   Simulates and plots a population of generalized virtual ants (vants). The behavior of the vants is determined by a bit string with length equal to the number of states that each cell in the vants' grid world can take. If a vant walks on a cell in state s, then the vant turns right if the s'th bit of the rule string is 1 and left if it is 0. As it leaves the cell the vant changes the state of the old cell to $(s + 1)$ modulo the number of states.

boids   Simulates a flock of boids according to rules that determine their individual behaviors as well as the "physics" of their universe. A boid greedily attempts to apply four rules with respect to its neighbors: It wants to fly in the same direction, be in the center of the local cluster of boids, avoid collisions with boids too close, and maintain a clear view ahead by skirting around others that block its view. Changing these rules can make the boids behave like birds, gnats, bees, fish, or magnetic particles.

sipd   Simulates and plots the spatial iterated Prisoner's Dilemma over time according to the specified parameters. Each cell in a grid plays a specific strategy against its eight neighbors for several rounds. At the end of the last round, each cell copies the strategy of its most successful neighbor, which is then used for the next time step. Possible strategies include "Always-Cooperate," "Always-Defect", "Random," "Pavlov," and "Tit-for-Tat."

eipd   Simulates the ecological iterated Prisoner's Dilemma over time according to the specified parameters. At every time step the population of each strategy is calculated as a function of the expected scores earned against all strategies weighted by the populations of the opponents. Possible strategies include "Always-Cooperate," "Always-Defect," "Random," "Pavlov," and "Tit-for-Tat."

assoc   Attempts to reconstruct a corrupted image with a McCulloch-Pitts feedback neural network that acts as an associative memory. The weights of the network are determined via Hebb's rule after reading in multiple patterns. Weights can be pruned either by size, by locality, or randomly.

hopfield Solves a task assignment problem via a Hopfield neural network while plotting the activations of the neurons over time. The program uses the k-out-of-n rule for setting the external inputs and synapse strength of the neurons.

gastring Uses a genetic algorithm to breed strings that match a user-specified target string. This program illustrates how GAs can perform a type of stochastic search in a space of discrete objects. Reproduction of strings entails crossover and mutation with strings being selected based on fitness.

gabump   Uses a genetic algorithm to find the maximum of a single-humped function that is centered at a user-specified location. This program serves as an example of how GAs can be used to optimize functions which take a floating-point argument.

gasurf   Uses a genetic algorithm to find the maximum of a multi-humped function. This program serves as an example of how GAs can be used to optimize functions which take multiple floating-point arguments.

gatask   Uses a genetic algorithm to solve a task assignment problem with user-specified costs. This program illustrates how GAs can perform combinatorial optimization. Reproduction of strings entails special crossover and mutation operations which preserve constraints on the form of feasible solutions.

gaipd   Uses a genetic algorithm to evolve iterated Prisoner's Dilemma (IPD) strategies according to user-specified constraints. This program illustrates how GAs can demonstrate coevolution since IPD strategies can only be successful within the context of their likely opponents.

zcs   Adapts a zeroth level classifier system (ZCS) with the implicit bucket brigade algorithm and a genetic algorithm so that the ZCS can traverse a two-dimensional terrain, avoid obstacles, and find food. At the beginning of each step the ZCS is placed at a random location of its world. It interacts with its environment until it finds food, which yields a reward. The simulation then restarts with the ZCS placed at a new random location. The progress of the ZCS is continuously plotted, while the statistics on the time to find food are calculated and displayed. At the end of the simulation the classifiers that make up the final ZCS are saved to a log file.

zcscup   Trains a zeroth level classifier system (ZCS) to solve the cups problem with the implicit bucket brigade algorithm and a genetic algorithm. Solving this problem requires the ZCS to learn to remember important features from previous states, which makes this problem very challenging. The ZCS always starts in the same initial position. It interacts with its environment until it finds both cups, which (only at that point) yields a reward. The simulation then restarts with the ZCS placed at the original location. The progress of the ZCS is continuously plotted, while the statistics on the time to find both cups are calculated and displayed. At the end of the simulation the classifiers that make up the final ZCS are saved to a log file.

mlp   Trains a multilayer perceptron with a single hidden layer of neurons on a set of data contained in a file using the backpropagation learning algorithm with momentum. Output units can be linear or sigmoidal, allowing you to model both discrete and continuous output target values.

Glossary

A

Activation The time-varying value that is the output of a NEURON.

Activation Function A FUNCTION that translates a NEURON'S NET INPUT to an ACTIVATION value.

Adaptive Subject to ADAPTATION; can change over time to improve fitness or accuracy.

Adaptation An internal change in a SYSTEM that mirrors an external event in the system's ENVIRONMENT.

Affine An equation that can be written in terms of MATRIX-VECTOR multiplication and vector addition.

Agent See AUTONOMOUS AGENT.

AI An abbreviation for ARTIFICIAL INTELLIGENCE.

Algorithm A detailed and unambiguous sequence of instructions that describes how a COMPUTATION is to proceed and can be implemented as a PROGRAM.

Algorithmic Complexity The size of the smallest PROGRAM that can produce a particular sequence of numbers. Regular patterns have low algorithmic complexity and RANDOM sequences have high algorithmic complexity.

Always Cooperate A PRISONER'S DILEMMA STRATEGY that cooperates with its opponent under all circumstances (the exact opposite of ALWAYS DEFECT).

Always Defect A PRISONER'S DILEMMA STRATEGY that never cooperates with its opponent under any circumstance (the exact opposite of ALWAYS COOPERATE).

Analog Having a CONTINUOUS value.

Analytical Can be symbolically represented in a closed form that does not require any of the complex aspects of a PROGRAM such as an ITERATIVE sum.

Analytical Solution An exact solution to a problem that can be calculated symbolically by manipulating equations (unlike a NUMERICAL SOLUTION).

Arms Race Two or more species experience ADAPTATION to one another in a COEVOLUTIONARY manner. This often seen in PREDATOR-PREY SYSTEMS.

Artificial Intelligence The science of making computers do interesting things that humans do effortlessly.

Artificial Life The study of life processes within the confines of a computer.

Associative Memory Memory that can be referenced by content, as opposed to location. HOPFIELD NETWORKS will act as associative memories when trained with the HEBBIAN LEARNING rule.

Asynchronous Describes events that occur independently of each other but on a similar time scale.

Attractor A characterization of the long-term behavior of a DISSIPATIVE DYNAMICAL SYSTEM. Over long periods of time, the STATE SPACE of some DYNAMICAL SYSTEMS will contract toward this region. Attractors may be FIXED POINTS, PERIODIC, QUASIPERIODIC, or CHAOTIC. They may also be STABLE or UNSTABLE.

Autonomous Agent An entity with limited perception of its ENVIRONMENT that can process information to calculate an action so as to be goal-seeking on a local scale. A BOID is an example of an autonomous agent.

Axiom A STATEMENT that is assumed to be true and can later be used along with THEOREMS to prove other theorems. Also, the starting configuration of an L-SYSTEM.

B

Backpropagation An ALGORITHM for efficiently calculating the error GRADIENT of a NEURAL NETWORK, which can then be used as the basis of LEARNING. Backpropagation is equivalent to the DELTA RULE for PERCEPTRONS, but can also calculate appropriate WEIGHT changes for the HIDDEN LAYER weights of a MULTILAYER PERCEPTRON by generalizing the notion of an error correction term. In the simplest case, backpropagation is a type of STEEPEST DESCENT in the SEARCH SPACE of the network weights, and it will usually CONVERGE to a LOCAL MINIMUM.

Basin of Attraction A region of STATE SPACE in which all included states of a DYNAMICAL SYSTEM ultimately lead into the ATTRACTOR.

Bias See THRESHOLD.

Bifurcation The splitting of a single mode of a SYSTEM'S behavior into two new modes. This usually occurs as a FUNCTION of a CONTINUOUSLY varying CONTROL parameter. A cascade of bifurcations will usually precede the onset of CHAOS.

Binary Written in a form that uses only 0s and 1s. A STRING of BITS.

Bit The smallest unit of information; the answer to a yes/no question; the outcome of a coin toss; a 0 or a 1.

Boid An AUTONOMOUS AGENT that behaves like a simplified bird but will display flocking patterns in the presence of other boids.

Boolean Taking only 0/1, true/false, yes/no values.

Bottom-Up A description that uses the lower-level details to explain higher-level patterns; related to REDUCTIONISM.

Brown Noise/Brownian Motion A form of RANDOMNESS that is the result of cumulatively adding WHITE NOISE, to yield a RANDOM WALK pattern.

Bucket Brigade Algorithm A LEARNING ALGORITHM that is a method for adjusting the STRENGTHS of the CLASSIFIERS of a CLASSIFIER SYSTEM. "Winning" classifiers pay a portion of their earnings to other classifiers that assisted them in being activated, similar to an economic SYSTEM.

Byte Eight BITS. In programming, often used to store a single text character.

C

Cantor Set A simple FRACTAL SET composed of an UNCOUNTABLE INFINITY of dust-like points, but that also has 0 measure (meaning that the sum width of all points is 0). The Cantor set is constructed by removing the middle third of a unit line segment, and then RECURSIVELY removing the middle third of any remaining line segments, for an infinite number of steps.

Cellular Automaton (CA) A DISCRETE DYNAMICAL SYSTEM that is composed of an array of cells, each of which behaves like a FINITE-STATE AUTOMATON. All interactions are local, with the next state of a cell being a FUNCTION of the current state of itself and its neighbors. CONWAY'S GAME OF LIFE is a CA.

Chaos/Chaotic Irregular motion of a DYNAMICAL SYSTEM that is DETERMINISTIC, SENSITIVE to initial conditions, and impossible to predict in the long term with anything less than an infinite and perfect representation of ANALOG values.

Chomsky Hierarchy Four classes of languages (or computing machines) that have increasing complexity: regular (FINITE-STATE AUTOMATA), context-free (push-down automata), context-sensitive (linear bounded automata), and RECURSIVE (TURING MACHINES).

Classifier A rule that is part of a CLASSIFIER SYSTEM and has a condition that must be matched before its MESSAGE (or action) can be posted (or effected). The STRENGTH of a classifier determines the likelihood that it can outbid other classifiers if more than one condition is matched.

Classifier System An ADAPTIVE SYSTEM similar to a POST PRODUCTION SYSTEM that contains many "if . . . then" rules called CLASSIFIERS. The state of the ENVIRONMENT is encoded as a MESSAGE by a DETECTOR and placed on the MESSAGE LIST from which the condition portion of the classifiers can be matched. "Winning" classifiers can then post their own messages to the message list, ultimately forming a type of COMPUTATION that may result in a message being translated into an action by an EFFECTOR. The STRENGTHS of the classifiers are modified by the BUCKET BRIGADE ALGORITHM, and new rules can be introduced via a GENETIC ALGORITHM.

Coevolution Two or more entities experience EVOLUTION in response to one another. Due to FEEDBACK mechanisms, this often results in a biological ARMS RACE.

Complement A SET composed of all elements that are not members of another set.

Combinatorial Optimization A class of problems in which the number of candidate solutions is combinatorial in size. Each possible solution has an associated cost. The goal is to find the solution with the lowest cost. Because of the vast numbers involved, explicit SEARCH an entire SEARCH SPACE is not always possible.

Complete Describes a FORMAL SYSTEM in which all STATEMENTS can be proved as being true or false. Most interesting formal systems are not complete, as proved in GÖDEL'S INCOMPLETENESS THEOREM.

Complex Number A number that has a REAL component and an IMAGINARY component and is characterized as a point on a plane (instead of the REAL NUMBER line).

Complex System A collection of many simple NONLINEAR units that operate in PARALLEL and interact locally with each other so as to produce EMERGENT behavior.

Complexity An ill-defined term that means many things to many people. Complex things are neither RANDOM nor regular, but hover somewhere in between. Intuitively, complexity is a measure of how interesting something is. Other types of complexity may be well defined; see the index for other references.

Compressible Having a description that is smaller than itself; not RANDOM; possessing regularity.

Computable Expressible as a yes/no question that can be answered in any case by a computer in finite time.

Computation The realization of a PROGRAM in a computer.

Connectivity The amount of interaction in a SYSTEM, the structure of the WEIGHTS in a NEURAL NETWORK, or the relative number of edges in a GRAPH.

Conservative System A DYNAMICAL SYSTEM that preserves the volume of its STATE SPACE under motion and, therefore, does not display the types of behavior found in DISSIPATIVE SYSTEMS.

Consistence In FORMAL SYSTEMS, having the property that all STATEMENTS are either true or false.

Continuous Taking a REAL value, i.e., not DISCRETE. DYNAMICAL SYSTEMS may operate in continuous time or space.

Control Exerting actions to manipulate a SYSTEM or ENVIRONMENT in a goal-seeking manner.

Convergence For computers, halting with an answer; for DYNAMICAL SYSTEMS, falling into an ATTRACTOR; for SEARCHES (e.g., BACKPROPAGATION and GENETIC ALGORITHMS), finding a location that cannot be improved upon; for infinite summations, approaching a definite value.

Conway's Game of Life A CELLULAR AUTOMATON rule set that operates on a two-dimensional grid. Each cell changes its state according to the states of its eight nearest neighbors: dead cells come alive with exactly three live neighbors, and cells die if they have anything but two or three neighbors. The Game of Life can display complex patterns such as GLIDERS, FISH, and GLIDER GUNS, and is also capable of UNIVERSAL COMPUTATION.

Co-Recursively Enumerable (CO-RE) The COMPLEMENT of a SET that can be RECURSIVELY ENUMERATED.

Countable Infinity Having the same number of objects as the SET of NATURAL NUMBERS.

Crossover A genetic operator that splices information from two or more parents to form a composite offspring that has genetic material from all parents.

D

Darwinism The theory of EVOLUTION as proposed by Charles Darwin, which combined VARIATION of INHERITABLE traits with NATURAL SELECTION. After the discovery of the physical mechanism of genetics, this was further refined into NEO-DARWINISM.

Delta Rule The PERCEPTRON LEARNING rule that specifies that WEIGHT changes should be proportional to the product of a weight's input and the error (or delta) term for the perceptron.

Derivative An expression that characterizes how the output of a FUNCTION changes as the input is varied. Unlike INTEGRALS, derivatives can be calculated in an ANALYTICAL manner very easily.

Decision Problem A problem in which all questions take the form "Is something a member of a particular SET?" and all answers are either "yes" or "no."

Detector A sensor that translates the state of a CLASSIFIER'S ENVIRONMENT into a MESSAGE that is suitable for posting to the MESSAGE LIST of the CLASSIFIER SYSTEM.

Determinant A quantity of a MATRIX that characterizes the amount of expansion or contraction that the matrix inflicts on a VECTOR when that vector is multiplied by the matrix.

Deterministic Occurring in a non-RANDOM manner such that the next state of a SYSTEM depends only on prior states of the system or the ENVIRONMENT. Perfect knowledge of previous states implies perfect knowledge of the next state.

Diagonal Matrix A MATRIX that has 0 entries along all nondiagonal entries, i.e., only the main diagonal may have non-zero values.

Difference Equation An equation that describes how something changes in DISCRETE time steps. NUMERICAL SOLUTIONS to INTEGRALS are usually realized as difference equations.

Differential Equation A description of how something CONTINUOUSLY changes over time. Some differential equations can have an ANALYTICALLY SOLUTION such that all future states can be known without SIMULATION of the time evolution of the SYSTEM. However, most can have a NUMERICAL SOLUTION with only limited accuracy.

Differentiation The act of calculating a DERIVATIVE; the inverse operation of calculating an INTEGRAL.

Diffusion Limited Aggregation A type of STOCHASTIC FRACTAL formed by particles floating about in a RANDOM manner until they stick to something solid.

Discrete Taking only non-CONTINUOUS values, e.g., BOOLEAN or NATURAL NUMBERS.

Dissipative System A DYNAMICAL SYSTEM that contains internal friction that deforms the structure of its ATTRACTOR, thus making motion such as FIXED POINTS, LIMIT CYCLES, QUASIPERIODICITY, and CHAOS possible. Dissipative systems often have internal structure despite being far from EQUILIBRIUM, like a whirlpool that preserves its basic form despite being in the midst of constant change.

Diverge For ALGORITHMS or computers, to run forever and never halt; for ITERATIVE SYSTEMS (like the equations for the MANDELBROT SET), reaching a state such that all future states explode in size.

Dot Product The INNER PRODUCT of two VECTORS.

Dynamical System A SYSTEM that changes over time according to a set of fixed rules that determine how one state of the system moves to another state.

Dynamics/Dynamical Pertaining to the change in behavior of a SYSTEM over time.

E

Ecology The study of the relationships and interactions between organisms and ENVIRONMENTS.

Ecosystem A biological SYSTEM consisting of many organisms from different species.

Edge of Chaos The hypothesis that many natural SYSTEMS tend toward DYNAMICAL behavior that borders static patterns and the CHAOTIC regime.

Effector The part of a CLASSIFIER SYSTEM that can translate MESSAGES into actions that can manipulate a SYSTEM or an ENVIRONMENT.

Eigenvalue The change in length that occurs when the corresponding EIGENVECTOR is multiplied by its MATRIX.

Eigenvector A unit length VECTOR that retains its direction when multiplied to the MATRIX that it corresponds to. An $(n \times n)$ matrix can have as many as n unique eigenvectors, each of which will have its own EIGENVALUE.

Embedding A method of taking a SCALAR TIME SERIES and using delayed snapshots of the values at fixed time intervals in the past so that the DYNAMICS of the underlying SYSTEM can be observed as a FUNCTION of the previously observed states.

Emergent Refers to a property of a collection of simple subunits that comes about through the interactions of the subunits and is not a property of any single subunit. For example, the organization of an ant colony is said to "emerge" from the interactions of the lower-level behaviors of the ants, and not from any single ant.

Usually, the emergent behavior is unanticipated and cannot be directly deduced from the lower-level behaviors. COMPLEX SYSTEMS are usually emergent.

Entropy A measure of a SYSTEM'S degree of RANDOMNESS or disorder.

Environment If that which is under study is a SYSTEM, then the rest of the world is the environment.

Equilibrium A state of a SYSTEM that, if not subjected to PERTURBATION, will remain unchanged.

Ergodic The property of a DYNAMICAL SYSTEM such that all regions of a STATE SPACE are visited with similar frequency and that all regions will be revisited (within a small proximity) if given enough time.

Euclidean Pertaining to standard geometry, i.e., points, lines, planes, volumes, squares, cubes, triangles, etc.

Euler's Method The simplest method of obtaining a NUMERICAL SOLUTION of a DIFFERENTIAL EQUATION. There are many other numerical techniques that are more accurate; however, an ANALYTICAL SOLUTION (i.e., a closed form of an INTEGRAL) is always preferred but not always possible.

Evolution A process operating on populations that involves VARIATION among individuals, traits being INHERITABLE, and a level of FITNESS for individuals that is a FUNCTION of the possessed traits. Over relatively long periods of time, the distribution of inheritable traits will tend to reflect the fitness that the traits convey to the individual; thus, evolution acts as a filter that selects fitness-yielding traits over other traits.

Evolutionary Stable Strategy (ESS) In GAME THEORY and biology, a STRATEGY that, when possessed by an entire population, results in an EQUILIBRIUM such that MUTATION of the strategy can never result in an improvement for an individual. ALWAYS DEFECT is an ESS, while ALWAYS COOPERATE is not.

Excitatory Refers to a neural SYNAPSE or WEIGHT that is positive such that activity in the source NEURON encourages activity in the connected neuron; the opposite of INHIBITORY.

Experimentation One process by which scientists attempt to understand nature. A phenomenon is observed and/or manipulated so that changes in the phenomenon's state can be seen. The resulting data can be used to derive new MODELS of a process or to confirm an existing model. Experimentation is the complement of THEORIZATION. See also SIMULATION.

Expert System A special PROGRAM that resembles a collection of "if ... then" rules. The rules usually represent knowledge contained by a domain expert (such as a physician adept at diagnosis) and can be used to SIMULATE how a human expert would perform a task.

F

Feedback A loop in information flow or in cause and effect.

Feedback Neural Network A NEURAL NETWORK that has every NEURON potentially connected to every other neuron. The ACTIVATIONS of all neurons are updated in PARALLEL (SYNCHRONOUS or ASYNCHRONOUS order), unlike a FEEDFORWARD or RECURRENT NEURAL NETWORK.

Feedforward Neural Network A NEURAL NETWORK that is organized with separate layers of NEURONS. Connections in such a network are limited to one direction such that the ACTIVATIONS of the input neurons are updated first, followed by any HIDDEN LAYERS, and then finished with the outputs.

Feigenbaum Constant A constant number that characterizes when bump-like MAPS such as the LOGISTIC MAP will BIFURCATE.

Finite-State Automaton (FSA) The simplest computing device. Although it is not nearly powerful enough to perform UNIVERSAL COMPUTATION, it can recognize REGULAR EXPRESSIONS. FSAs are defined by a state transition table that specifies how the FSA moves from one state to another when presented with a particular input. FSAs can be drawn as GRAPHS.

Fish A simple object in CONWAY'S GAME OF LIFE that swims vertically or horizontally.

Fitness A measure of an object's ability to reproduce viable offspring.

Fitness Landscape A representation of how MUTATIONS can change the FITNESS of one or more organisms. If high fitness corresponds to high locations in the landscape, and if changes in genetic material are mapped to movements in the landscape, then EVOLUTION will tend to make populations move in an uphill direction on the fitness landscape.

Fixed Point A point in a DYNAMICAL SYSTEM's STATE SPACE that maps back to itself, i.e., the system will stay at the fixed point if it does not undergo a PERTURBATION.

Formal System A mathematical formalism in which STATEMENTS can be constructed and manipulated with logical rules. Some formal systems are built around a few basic AXIOMS (such as EUCLIDEAN geometry) and can be expanded with THEOREMS that can be deduced through PROOFS.

Fractal An object with a FRACTAL DIMENSION. Fractals are SELF-SIMILAR and may be DETERMINISTIC or STOCHASTIC. See also CANTOR SET, DIFFUSION LIMITED AGGRE-GATION, IFS, JULIA SET, L-SYSTEMS, MRCM, MANDELBROT SET, and STRANGE ATTRACTOR.

Fractal Dimension An extension of the notion of dimension found in EUCLIDEAN geometry. Fractal dimensions can be non-integer, meaning that objects can be "more than a line but less than a plane" and so on. There is more than one way of computing a fractal dimension, one common type being the Hausdorff-Besicovich dimension. Roughly speaking, a fractal dimension can be calculated as the quotient of the logarithm of the object's size and the logarithm of the measuring scale, in the limit as the scale approaches 0. Under this definition, standard Euclidean objects retain their original dimension.

Function A mapping from one space to another. This is usually understood to be a relationship between numbers. Functions that are COMPUTABLE can be calculated by a UNIVERSAL COMPUTER.

Function Approximation The task of finding an instance from a class of FUNCTIONS that is minimally different from an unknown function. This is a common task for NEURAL NETWORKS.

G

Game Theory A mathematical formalism used to study human games, economics, military conflicts, and biology. The goal of game theory is to find the optimal STRATEGY for one player to use when his opponent also plays optimally. A strategy may incorporate RANDOMNESS, in which case it is referred to as a MIXED STRATEGY.

Gaussian Normally distributed (with a bell-shaped curve) and having a MEAN at the center of the curve with tail widths proportional to the STANDARD DEVIATION of the data about the mean.

Generalized Delta Rule Another name for BACKPROPAGATION.

Genetic Algorithm (GA) A method of SIMULATING the action of EVOLUTION within a computer. A population of fixed-length STRINGS is evolved with a GA by employing CROSSOVER and MUTATION operators along with a FITNESS FUNCTION that determines how likely individuals are to reproduce. GAs perform a type of SEARCH in a FITNESS LANDSCAPE.

Genetic Programming (GP) A method of applying simulated EVOLUTION on PRO-GRAMS or program fragments. Modified forms of MUTATION and CROSSOVER are used along with a FITNESS function.

Glider A simple object in CONWAY'S GAME OF LIFE that swims diagonally through the grid space.

Glider Gun An object in CONWAY'S GAME OF LIFE that builds and emits GLIDERS, which can then be collided in purposeful ways to construct more complicated objects.

Global Minimum (Maximum) In a SEARCH SPACE, the lowest (or highest) point of the surface, which usually represents the best possible solution in the space with respect to some problem.

Gödel Number A NATURAL NUMBER computed via a GÖDELIZATION procedure that uniquely corresponds to a STRING.

Gödelization A method for mapping arbitrary STRINGS to NATURAL NUMBERS such that the process is ONE-TO-ONE and INVERTIBLE. The process usually exploits the properties of PRIME NUMBERS. Since Gödelization can be defined as a COMPUTABLE FUNCTION, and since functions can be Gödelized, some functions (or PROGRAMS) can assert STATEMENTS about other functions or programs, or themselves.

Gödel's Incompleteness Theorem Any sufficiently interesting FORMAL SYSTEM can express true STATEMENTS for which there can be no PROOF in the original formal system.

Gödel's Statement Given the formal STATEMENT "There does not exist any PROOF for the statement with GÖDEL NUMBER x applied to x," which has it own Gödel number, g, Gödel's statement paraphrased is "There does not exist a proof of the statement with Gödel number g applied to itself." Gödel's statement is true, but cannot be proven true in the FORMAL SYSTEM in which it is constructed, which leads to GÖDEL'S INCOMPLETENESS THEOREM.

Gradient A VECTOR of partial DERIVATIVES of a FUNCTION that operates on vectors. Intuitively, the gradient represents the slope of a high-dimensional surface.

Graph A construct that consists of many nodes connected with edges. The edges usually represent a relationship between the objects represented by the nodes. For example, if the nodes are cities, then the edges may have numerical values that correspond to the distances between the cities. A graph can be equivalently represented as a MATRIX.

H

Halting Problem The problem of determining if a PROGRAM halts or doesn't halt on a particular input. This is an INCOMPUTABLE problem.

Halting Set The RECURSIVELY ENUMERABLE SET of GÖDEL NUMBERS that correspond to PROGRAMS that halt if given their own Gödel number as input.

Hebbian Learning A rule that specifies that the strength of a SYNAPSE between two NEURONS should be proportional to the product of the ACTIVATIONS of the two neurons.

Hénon Map A CHAOTIC SYSTEM (defined by the two equations $x_{t+1} = a - x_t^2 + by_t$ and $y_{t+1} = x_t$) that has a FRACTAL STRANGE ATTRACTOR and operates in DISCRETE time.

Hidden Layer In a FEEDFORWARD or RECURRENT NEURAL NETWORK, a layer of NEURONS that is neither the input layer nor the output layer but is physically between the two.

Hill-Climbing One of the simplest SEARCH methods that attempts to find a LOCAL MAXIMUM by moving in an uphill direction. It is related to STEEPEST ASCENT. Hill-climbing may use GRADIENT information, or RANDOM sampling of nearby points, in order to estimate the uphill direction.

Holism The idea that "the whole is greater than the sum of the parts." Holism is credible on the basis of EMERGENCE alone, since REDUCTIONISM and BOTTOM-UP descriptions of nature often fail to predict complex higher-level patterns. See also TOP-DOWN.

Hopfield Network A type of FEEDBACK NEURAL NETWORK that is often used as an ASSOCIATIVE MEMORY or as a solution to a COMBINATORIAL OPTIMIZATION problem.

I

IFS An iterated functional system; it constructs a FRACTAL by ITERATING a VECTOR quantity through an AFFINE equation that is RANDOMLY selected on each iteration.

Imaginary Number The square root of a negative number. The square root of -1 is often denoted as i for the purpose of writing out COMPLEX NUMBERS.

Implicit Parallelism The idea that GENETIC ALGORITHMS have an extra built-in form of PARALLELISM that is expressed when a GA SEARCHES through a SEARCH SPACE. Implicit parallelism depends on the similarities and differences between individuals in the population. The theory posits that GAs process more SCHEMATA than there are STRINGS in a population, thus getting something of a free lunch. See also NO FREE LUNCH.

Incomputable Something that cannot be characterized by a PROGRAM that always halts. SETS that are incomputable may be RECURSIVELY ENUMERABLE (like the HALTING SET), CO-RECURSIVELY ENUMERABLE (e.g., the halting set's COMPLEMENT), or NOT RECURSIVELY ENUMERABLE (which, if also not CO-RE, is a RANDOM set).

Incomputable Number A REAL NUMBER with an infinite decimal (or BINARY) expansion that cannot be enumerated by any UNIVERSAL COMPUTER.

Inheritable Refers to a trait that can be genetically passed from parent to offspring.

Inhibitory Refers to a neural SYNAPSE or WEIGHT that is negative such that activity in the source NEURON encourages inactivity in the connected neuron. The opposite of EXCITATORY.

Inner Product For two VECTORS of the same dimensionality, the sum of the pairwise products of the two vector components, $\sum_i x_i y_i$.

Integral The cumulative CONTINUOUS sum of a FUNCTION. The integral of a DIFFERENTIAL EQUATION represents the future state of a DYNAMICAL SYSTEM; however, most integrals do not have an ANALYTICAL SOLUTION, which means that they may only have NUMERICAL SOLUTIONS, an admittedly inexact process.

Integration The act of calculating an INTEGRAL, by either a NUMERICAL or an ANALYTICAL SOLUTION; the inverse operation of DIFFERENTIATION.

Invertible A FUNCTION is invertible (with a unique inverse) if the output uniquely determines the input (i.e., it is ONE-TO-ONE) and the set of legal outputs is equal to the set of legal inputs. The function x^2 is not strictly invertible, while x^3 has an inverse. For operations the definition is slightly looser. While INTEGRATION and DIFFERENTIATION are considered to be inverse operations, there are an infinite number of INTEGRALS that are valid results for integrating any function; thus, the process is not one-to-one.

Irrational Number A REAL NUMBER that cannot be represented as a fraction.

Iterated Prisoner's Dilemma The PRISONER'S DILEMMA game played in an ITERATIVE manner for a number of rounds that is unknown to both players.

Iterate/Iterative Doing something repeatedly. Doing something repeatedly. Doing something repeatedly. Doing something repeatedly. Doing something repeatedly.

J

Julia Set A SET of COMPLEX NUMBERS that do not DIVERGE if ITERATED an infinite number of times via a simple equation. The points form an extremely complex FRACTAL. There is an UNCOUNTABLE INFINITY of Julia sets, each of which corresponds to a particular complex number that appears as a constant in the iterative procedure. Julia sets are similar to CO-RECURSIVELY ENUMERABLE sets because only points that are not a members of the set can actually be identified as such. All of the Julia sets are related to the MANDELBROT SET.

K

Koch Curve A FRACTAL curve that looks like the edge of a snowflake. It has no DERIVATIVE at any point.

L

Lamarckism A method of heredity that does not apply to genetics but is applicable to social ADAPTATION. Lamarckism posits that acquired traits can be passed from parent to offspring.

Lambda Calculus A MODEL OF COMPUTATION that is capable of UNIVERSAL COMPUTATION. The LISP programming language was inspired by Lambda calculus.

Learning A process of ADAPTATION by which SYNAPSES, WEIGHTS of NEURAL NETWORK's, CLASSIFIER STRENGTHS, or some other set of adjustable parameters is automatically modified so that some objective is more readily achieved. The BACKPROPAGATION and BUCKET BRIGADE ALGORITHMS are two types of learning procedures.

LIFE See CONWAY'S GAME OF LIFE.

Limit Cycle A PERIODIC cycle in a DYNAMICAL SYSTEM such that previous states are returned to repeatedly.

Linear Having only a multiplicative factor. If $f(x)$ is a linear FUNCTION, then $f(a + b) = f(a) + f(b)$ and $cf(x) = f(cx)$ must both be true for all values of a, b, c, and x. Most things in nature are NONLINEAR.

Linearly (In)separable Two classes of points are linearly separable if a LINEAR FUNCTION exists such that one class of points resides on one side of the hyperplane (defined by the linear function), and all points in the other class are on the other side. The XOR mapping defines two SETS of points that are linearly inseparable.

Lisp A programming language designed to manipulate lists that was inspired by LAMBDA CALCULUS and was the inspiration for STUTTER.

Local Minimum (Maximum) The bottom of a valley or the top of a peak; a point in a SEARCH SPACE such that all nearby points are either higher (for a minimum) or lower (for a maximum). In a CONTINUOUS search space, local minima and maxima have a 0 GRADIENT VECTOR. Note that this particular valley (or peak) may not necessarily be the lowest (or highest) location in the space, which is referred to as the GLOBAL MINIMUM (MAXIMUM).

Logistic Map The simplest CHAOTIC SYSTEM that works in DISCRETE time and is defined by the MAP $x_t = 4rx_t(1 - x_t)$. FEIGENBAUM'S CONSTANT was first identified for this map.

Lorenz System A system of three DIFFERENTIAL EQUATIONS that was the first concrete example of CHAOS and a STRANGE ATTRACTOR.

Lotka-Volterra System A two-species PREDATOR-PREY SYSTEM that in its simplest form can display only FIXED POINTS or LIMIT CYCLES. More complicated versions with three or more species can yield CHAOS.

L-System A method of constructing a FRACTAL that is also a MODEL for plant growth. L-systems use an AXIOM as a starting STRING and ITERATIVELY apply a set of PARALLEL string substitution rules to yield one long string that can be used as instructions for drawing the fractal. One method of interpreting the resulting string is as an instruction to a TURTLE GRAPHICS plotter. Many fractals, including the CANTOR SET, KOCH CURVE, and PEANO CURVE, can be expressed as an L-system.

M

Mackey-Glass System A delay DIFFERENTIAL EQUATION $(dx/dt = (ax(t - \tau))/(1 + x^{10}(t - \tau)) - bx(t))$ that can display a wide variety of behaviors via an adjustable delay term, τ. Even though this system generates a single SCALAR TIMES SERIES, it can be extremely CHAOTIC because its value at any time may depend on its entire previous history.

Mandelbrot Set An extremely complex FRACTAL that is related to JULIA SETS in the way that it is constructed and by the fact that it acts as a sort of index to the Julia sets. Like the Julia sets, the Mandelbrot set is calculated via an ITERATIVE procedure. Starting conditions that do not DIVERGE after an infinite number of iterations are considered to be inside the set. If, and only if, a COMPLEX NUMBER is in the Mandelbrot set, then the Julia set that uses that complex number as a constant will be connected; otherwise, the corresponding Julia set will be unconnected.

Map A FUNCTION that is usually understood to be ITERATED in DISCRETE time steps.

Matrix A rectangular two-dimensional array of numbers that can be thought of as a LINEAR operator on VECTORS. Matrix-vector multiplication can be used to describe geometric transformations such as scaling, rotation, reflection, and translation. They can also describe the AFFINE transformation used to construct IFS and MRCM FRACTALS.

Mean The arithmetical average of a collection of numbers; the center of a GAUSSIAN distribution.

Meme A unit of cultural information that represents a basic idea that can be transferred from one individual to another, and subjected to MUTATION, CROSSOVER, and ADAPTATION.

Message The basic unit of information in a CLASSIFIER SYSTEM that is stored in the MESSAGE LIST. A message may correspond to an external state of an ENVIRONMENT or an internal state of the classifier system.

Message List The portion of a CLASSIFIER SYSTEM that retains information in the form of MESSAGES.

Mixed Strategy In GAME THEORY, a STRATEGY that uses RANDOMNESS by employing different actions in identical circumstances with different PROBABILITIES.

Model In the sciences, a model is an estimate of how something works. A model will usually have inputs and outputs that correspond to its real-world counterpart. An ADAPTIVE SYSTEM also contains an implicit model of its ENVIRONMENT that allows it to change its behavior in anticipation of what will happen in the environment.

Model of Computation An idealized version of a computing device that usually has some simplifications such as infinite memory. A TURING MACHINE, the LAMBDA CALCULUS, and POST PRODUCTION SYSTEMS are all models of computation.

Monotonic The property of a FUNCTION that is always strictly increasing or strictly decreasing, but never both. The SIGMOIDAL ACTIVATION function of a MULTILAYER PERCEPTRON is monotonically increasing.

MRCM The Multiple Reduction Copy Machine ALGORITHM, which can be used to make AFFINE FRACTALS. MRCM fractals are related to IFS fractals in that they both use the same types of affine transformations. The MRCM algorithm performs several affine transformations of a seed image in PARALLEL to yield a secondary seed image. The output of the MRCM is RECURSIVELY passed back through to its input multiple times, to yield the fractal.

Multilayer Perceptron (MLP) A type of FEEDFORWARD NEURAL NETWORK that is an extension of the PERCEPTRON in that it has at least one HIDDEN LAYER of NEURONS. Layers are updated by starting at the inputs and ending with the outputs. Each neuron computes a weighted sum of the incoming signals, to yield a NET INPUT, and passes this value through its SIGMOIDAL ACTIVATION FUNCTION to yield the neuron's ACTIVATION value. Unlike the perceptron, an MLP can solve LINEARLY INSEPARABLE problems.

Mutation A RANDOM change in any portion of genetic material. For a GENETIC ALGORITHM, this means that a value in a BIT STRING is randomly set.

N

Nash Equilibrium In GAME THEORY, a pair of STRATEGIES for a game such that neither player can improve his outcome by changing his strategy. A Nash equilibrium sometimes takes the form of a SADDLE structure. Under some cases, when a strategy is at a Nash equilibrium with itself, the strategy resembles an EVOLUTIONARY STABLE STRATEGY.

Natural Number Any of the standard counting numbers; a positive integer.

Natural Selection The natural filtering process by which individuals with higher FIT-NESS are more likely to reproduce than individuals with lower fitness.

Neo-Darwinism A synthesis of DARWINISM with the mechanisms of genetics; the idea that ADAPTATION equals a combination of VARIATION, heredity, and selection. See also EVOLUTION, INHERITABLE, and NATURAL SELECTION.

Net Input The weighted sum of incoming signals into a NEURON plus a neuron's THRESH-OLD value.

Neural Network (NN) A network of NEURONS that are connected through SYNAPSES or WEIGHTS. In this book, the term is used almost exclusively to denote an artificial neural network and not the real thing. Each neuron performs a simple calculation that is a FUNCTION of the ACTIVATIONS of the neurons that are connected to it. Through FEEDBACK mechanisms and/or the NONLINEAR output response of neurons, the network as a whole is capable of performing extremely complicated tasks, including UNIVERSAL COMPUTATION and UNIVERSAL APPROXIMATION. Three different classes of neural networks are FEEDFORWARD, FEEDBACK, and RECURRENT NEURAL NETWORKS, which differ in the degree and type of CONNECTIVITY that they possess.

Neuron A simple computational unit that performs a weighted sum on incoming signals, adds a THRESHOLD or bias term to this value to yield a NET INPUT, and maps this last value through an ACTIVATION FUNCTION to compute its own ACTIVATION. Some neurons, such as those found in FEEDBACK or HOPFIELD networks, will retain a portion of their previous activation.

Newton's Method An ITERATIVE method for finding 0 values of a FUNCTION.

Niche A way for an animal to make a living in an ECOSYSTEM.

No Free Lunch (NFL) A THEOREM that states that in the worst case, and averaged over an infinite number of SEARCH SPACES, all SEARCH METHODS perform equally well. More than being a condemnation of any search method, the NFL theorem actually hints that most naturally occurring search spaces are, in fact, not RANDOM.

Nonlinear A FUNCTION that is not LINEAR. Most things in nature are nonlinear. This means that in a very real way, the whole is at least different from the sum of the parts. See also HOLISM.

Not Recursively Enumerable (not-RE) An infinite SET that cannot be RECURSIVELY ENUMERATED. SETS of this type that are also not CO-RECURSIVELY ENUMERABLE are effectively RANDOM.

NP Nondeterministic polynomial time problems; a class of computational problems that may or may not be solvable in POLYNOMIAL time but are expressed in such a way that candidate solutions can be tested for correctness in polynomial time. See also TIME COMPLEXITY and NP-COMPLETE.

NP-Complete A problem type in which any instance of any other NP class problem can be translated to in POLYNOMIAL time. This means that if a fast ALGORITHM exists for an NP-complete problem, then any problem that is in NP can be solved with the same algorithm.

Numerical Solution A solution to a problem that is calculated through a SIMULATION. For example, solving the THREE BODY PROBLEM is not possible in the worst case; however, with the DIFFERENTIAL EQUATIONS that describe the motions of three bodies in space, one could simulate their movements by simulating each time step. Nevertheless, numerical solutions are usually error-prone due to SENSITIVITY and, therefore, can be used to estimate the future for only relatively short time spans, in the worst case.

O

Occam's Razor The principle that when faced with multiple but equivalent interpretations of some phenomenon, one should always choose the simplest explanation that correctly fits the data. Occam's Razor is useful for selecting competing MODELS for some phenomena.

One-to-One A FUNCTION or MAP that for every possible output has only one input that yields that particular output; if $f(a) = f(b)$, then $a = b$.

Optimization The process of finding parameters that minimizes or maximizes a FUNCTION.

Outer Product An operation on two VECTORS that yields a MATRIX. Given two vectors with the same dimensionality, the outer product is a square symmetric matrix that contains the product of all pairs of elements from the two vectors, i.e., $A_{ij} = x_i y_j$.

P

Parallel/Parallelism Many things happening at once.

Pattern Classification A task that NEURAL NETWORKS are often trained to do. Given some input pattern, the task is to make an accurate class assignment to the input. For example, classifying many images of letters to one of the twenty-six letters of the alphabet is a pattern classification task.

Payoff In GAME THEORY, the amount that a player wins, given the player's and his opponent's actions.

Peano Curve A FRACTAL SPACE-FILLING curve that can fill a plane even though it is a line of infinite length. Oddly enough, it has an integer FRACTAL DIMENSION of 2.

Perceptron The simplest type of FEEDFORWARD NEURAL NETWORK. It has only inputs and outputs, i.e., no HIDDEN LAYERS.

Periodic Refers to motion that goes through a finite number of regions, returns to a previous state, and repeats the same fixed pattern forever.

Perturbation A slight nudge.

Phase Space In this book, another name for STATE SPACE. In the scientific literature, "phase space" is used to denote the space of motion in a DYNAMICAL SYSTEM that moves in CONTINUOUS time, while STATE SPACE is often used for DISCRETE time SYSTEMS.

Phase Transition In physics, a change from one state of matter to another. In DYNAMICAL SYSTEMS theory, a change from one mode of behavior to another.

Planning In computer science, and particularly in ARTIFICIAL INTELLIGENCE, the task of determining a stepwise plan to accomplish a very specific task.

Polynomial A FUNCTION in which the output is the sum of terms that are the products of constant values and the input raised to some integer power. The polynomial of a polynomial is another polynomial. From a TIME COMPLEXITY point of view, polynomials are well-behaved.

Post Production System A MODEL OF COMPUTATION that resembles a collection of "if . . . then" rules and is capable of UNIVERSAL COMPUTATION.

Predator-Prey System An ECOSYSTEM in which one portion of the population consumes another. With three or more species, simple predator-prey interactions can lead to CHAOS and biological ARMS RACES. See also LOTKA-VOLTERRA SYSTEM.

Prime Number A NATURAL NUMBER that can be evenly divided only by itself and 1.

Prisoner's Dilemma A non-ZERO-SUM GAME in which both players have incentive not to cooperate under any circumstances. Thus, the optimal GAME THEORY STRATEGY of ALWAYS DEFECT has the paradoxical property that both players would have a higher PAYOFF if they ignored the advice of game theory.

Probability The likelihood that a RANDOM event will occur.

Program An ALGORITHM that is written in a programming language for execution on a physical computer.

Proof A sequence of STATEMENTS in which each subsequent statement is derivable from one of the previous statements or from an AXIOM of a FORMAL SYSTEM. The final statement of a proof is usually the THEOREM that one has set out to prove.

Q

Quasiperiodic Refers to a form of motion that is regular but never exactly repeating. Quasiperiodic motion is always composed of multiple but simpler PERIODIC motions. In the general case, for motion that is the sum of simpler periodic motions, if there exists a length of time that evenly divides the frequencies of the underlying motions, then the composite motion will also be periodic; however, if no such length of time exists, then the motion will be quasiperiodic.

R

Random/Randomness Without cause; not COMPRESSIBLE; obeying the statistics of a fair coin toss.

Random Walk A walk in one or more dimensions that is dictated by the outcome of a coin toss. The direction of each step of the walk is specified by the coin toss. The resulting RANDOM motion is often referred to as BROWNIAN MOTION.

Rational Number A number that can be expressed as a fraction.

Real Number Any number that can be represented with a potentially infinite decimal expansion to the right of the decimal point. NATURAL, RATIONAL, IRRATIONAL, and INCOMPUTABLE numbers are all real numbers.

Recurrent Neural Network A network similar to a FEEDFORWARD NEURAL NETWORK except that there may be connections from an output or HIDDEN LAYER to the inputs. Recurrent neural networks are capable of UNIVERSAL COMPUTATION.

Recursive Strictly speaking, a SET or FUNCTION is recursive if it is COMPUTABLE; however, in the usual sense of the word, a function is said to be recursive if its definition make reference to itself. For example, factorial can be defined as $x! = x \times (x - 1)!$ with the base case of 1! equal to 1. See also SELF-REFERENTIAL.

Recursively Enumerable (RE) A potentially infinite SET whose members can be enumerated by a UNIVERSAL COMPUTER; however, a universal computer may not be able to determine that something is not a member of a recursively enumerable set. The HALTING SET is recursively enumerable but not RECURSIVE.

Reductionism The idea that nature can be understood by dissection. In other words, knowing the lowest-level details of how things work (at, say, the level of subatomic physics) reveals how higher-level phenomena come about. This is a BOTTOM-UP way of looking at the universe, and is the exact opposite of HOLISM.

Regular Expression A definition for a class of STRINGS that can be recognized by a FINITE-STATE AUTOMATON. An example of a class of strings that is regular would be legal mathematical expressions using only "+" and digits. An example that is not regular is the same legal mathematical expressions as before, but with properly nested parentheses.

S

Saddle A type of surface that is neither a peak nor a valley but still has a 0 GRADIENT. Saddle points are situated such that moving in one direction takes one uphill, while moving in another direction would be downhill. Hence, saddles look like the things that cowboys ride on.

Scalar A single number, as opposed to a multidimensional VECTOR or MATRIX.

Schema/Schemata A similarity template used to analyze GENETIC ALGORITHMS. By using wild-card characters, a schema defines an entire class of STRINGS that may be found in a population.

Search/Search Method A method for finding a region of interest in a SEARCH SPACE. Usually, the interesting regions correspond to solutions to a specific problem. HILL-CLIMBING, STEEPEST DESCENT (ASCENT), SIMULATED ANNEALING, and GENETIC ALGORITHMS are all search methods.

Search Space A characterization of every possible solution to a problem instance. For a NEURAL NETWORK the search space is defined as all possible assignments to the network WEIGHTS; for a GENETIC ALGORITHM, it is every conceivable value assignment to the STRINGS in the population.

Selection See NATURAL SELECTION.

Self-Organization A spontaneously formed higher-level pattern of structure or FUNCTION that is EMERGENT through the interactions of lower-level objects.

Self-Organized Criticality (SOC) A mathematical theory that describes how SYSTEMS composed of many interacting parts can tune themselves toward DYNAMICAL behavior that is critical in the sense that it is neither STABLE nor UNSTABLE but at a region near a PHASE TRANSITION. SOC systems display events in a power-law distribution and are never quite at EQUILIBRIUM. See also EDGE OF CHAOS and SELF-ORGANIZATION.

Self-Referential Referring directly back to oneself through information flow, influence, or cause and effect. See SELF-REFERENTIAL.

Self-Similar An object that is structurally RECURSIVE in that a part will look like the whole. See also FRACTAL.

Sensitivity The tendency of a SYSTEM (sometimes CHAOTIC) to change dramatically with only small PERTURBATIONS.

Set A collection of things, usually numbers. Sets may be infinite in size.

Shadowing Lemma Implies that a numerical SIMULATION of CHAOS may "shadow" a real trajectory of a real CHAOTIC SYSTEM.

Sigmoidal An "S" shaped FUNCTION that is often used as an ACTIVATION FUNCTION in a NEURAL NETWORK.

Simulate/Simulation EXPERIMENTATION in the space of theories, or a combination of experimentation and THEORIZATION. Some numerical simulations are PROGRAMS that represent a MODEL for how nature works. Usually, the outcome of a simulation is as much a surprise as the outcome of a natural event, due to the richness and uncertainty of COMPUTATION.

Simulated Annealing A partially RANDOM method of SEARCH and OPTIMIZATION usually used for COMBINATORIAL OPTIMIZATION problems. The technique is modeled on how the molecular structure of metals is disordered at high temperatures but very ordered and crystalline at low temperatures. In simulated annealing, a problem instance is reformulated so that it loosely resembles disordered material. Gradually, the temperature is lowered such that the ordered states correspond to good solutions to a problem.

Space Complexity A FUNCTION that describes the amount of memory required for a PROGRAM to run on a computer to perform a particular task. The function is parameterized by the length of the program's input. See also TIME COMPLEXITY.

Space-Filling Refers to a curve that manages to twist and turn in such a way that it actually fills a space or volume. All space-filling curves are FRACTAL.

Special Function In LISP or STUTTER, a built-in FUNCTION that may or may not fully evaluate its arguments, such as the `if` primitive.

Stable Having a BASIN OF ATTRACTION that is non-zero in size; an ATTRACTOR that can withstand some form of PERTURBATION.

Standard Deviation A measure of the spread of a SET of data. For a GAUSSIAN distribution, the standard deviation hints at the width of the tails of the distribution FUNCTION.

Statement In a FORMAL SYSTEM, a STRING of characters that is formed according to well-defined rules such that it is legal for the language that is the formal system.

For example, in the formal system of arithmetic, the expression "$5 + 3 \times (2 - 4)$" is a valid and well-formed statement, but "$5+)3 \times \times (2(-4)$" is not.

State Space In this book, another name for the PHASE SPACE of a DYNAMICAL SYSTEM. Roughly speaking, if the DYNAMICS of a dynamical system can be described by n values, then the state space is the n-dimensional volume that the system moves through. SYSTEMS that are CONTINUOUS in time will form a smooth trajectory through this volume, while DISCRETE systems may jump to different locations on subsequent time steps. In either case, if a system ever returns to a previously visited location in the state space, then the system is in either a FIXED POINT or a LIMIT CYCLE. For CHAOTIC systems, or for PROGRAMS that never halt, the system will always be at a previously unvisited portion of the state space.

Steepest Descent (Ascent) A SEARCH METHOD that uses the GRADIENT information of a SEARCH SPACE and moves in the opposite direction from the gradient until no further downhill (or uphill) progress can be made. See also HILL-CLIMBING.

Stochastic Something that is RANDOM.

Strange Attractor An ATTRACTOR of a DYNAMICAL SYSTEM that is usually FRACTAL in dimension and is indicative of CHAOS.

Strategy In GAME THEORY, a policy for playing a game. A strategy is a complete recipe for how a player should act in a game under all circumstances. Some policies may employ RANDOMNESS, in which case they are referred to as MIXED STRATEGIES.

Strength For a CLASSIFIER SYSTEM, a CLASSIFIER's relative ability to win a bidding match for the right to post its MESSAGE on the MESSAGE LIST.

String Any sequence of letters, numbers, digits, BITS, or symbols.

Stutter A silly programming language used in this book that is based on LISP and is capable of UNIVERSAL COMPUTATION.

Symmetric Matrix A MATRIX with the lower-left half equal to the mirror image of the upper-right half.

Synapse The junction between two NEURONS in which neural activity is propagated from one neuron to another. See also EXCITATORY, INHIBITORY, and WEIGHT.

Synchronous Acting in a lockstep fashion, with each event occurring in a precise order, or in such a way as to eliminate the notion of order entirely.

System Something that can be studied as a whole. Systems may consist of subsystems that are interesting in their own right. Or they may exist in an ENVIRONMENT that consists of other similar systems. Systems are generally understood to have an internal state, inputs from an environment, and methods for manipulating the environment or themselves. Since cause and effect can flow in both directions of a system and environment, interesting systems often posses FEEDBACK, which is SELF-REFERENTIAL in the strongest case.

T

Theorem A STATEMENT in a FORMAL SYSTEM that has PROOF.

Theorization A process by which scientists attempt to understand nature; it is the complement to EXPERIMENTATION. Theorization is the process of building mathematical MODELS for how things work. Scientists always desire theories that are simpler than the data they explain. See also OCCAM'S RAZOR and SIMULATION.

Three Body Problem The problem of determining the future positions and velocities of three gravitational bodies. The problem was proved unsolvable in the general case by Henri Poincaré, which forshadowed the importance of CHAOS. Although no ANALYTICAL SOLUTIONS are possible in the worst case, a NUMERICAL SOLUTION is sometimes sufficient for many tasks.

Threshold A quantity added to (or subtracted from) the weighted sum of inputs into a NEURON, which forms the neuron's NET INPUT. Intuitively, the net input (or bias) is proportional to the amount that the incoming neural ACTIVATIONS must exceed in order for a neuron to fire.

Time Complexity A FUNCTION that describes the amount of time required for a PROGRAM to run on a computer to perform a particular task. The function is parameterized by the length of the program's input. See also SPACE COMPLEXITY.

Time-Reversible A property of DYNAMICAL SYSTEMS that can be run unambiguously both forward and backward in time. The HÉNON MAP, LORENZ SYSTEM, and VANT CELLULAR AUTOMATA are all time-reversible, while the LOGISTIC MAP, the MACKEY-GLASS SYSTEM, and most other CELLULAR AUTOMATA are not. Time-reversible systems are described by FUNCTIONS that are INVERTIBLE.

Time Series A sequence of values generated from a DYNAMICAL SYSTEM over time. CHAOTIC SYSTEMS can be analyzed by examining the time series generated by a single portion of the SYSTEM. See also EMBEDDING.

Tit-for-Tat An effective STRATEGY for playing the ITERATED PRISONER'S DILEMMA. Tit-for-Tat starts by cooperating, and then does whatever its opponent did in the previous round of play.

Top-Down A method of examining things that first looks at higher-level phenomena and then tries to explain lower-level patterns in terms of the higher-level observations. This is the exact opposite of BOTTOM-UP. See also HOLISM and REDUCTIONISM.

Transpose An operation that flips a MATRIX about the main diagonal.

Turing Machine A MODEL OF COMPUTATION that uses an underlying FINITE-STATE AUTOMATON but also has an infinite tape to use as memory. Turing machines are capable of UNIVERSAL COMPUTATION.

Turtle Graphics A simple language for drawing graphics in which a "turtle" is used to make strokes on a plotting device. Typical commands include "move forward," "draw forward," and "turn left."

U

Uncountable Infinity An order of infinity that is larger than the number of NATURAL NUMBERS. The number of REAL NUMBERS is uncountably infinite.

Universal Approximation Having the ability to approximate any FUNCTION to an arbitrary degree of accuracy. NEURAL NETWORKS are universal approximators.

Universal Computation Capable of computing anything that can in principle be computed; being equivalent in computing power to a TURING MACHINE, the LAMBDA CALCULUS, or a POST PRODUCTION SYSTEM.

Universal Computer A computer that is capable of UNIVERSAL COMPUTATION, which means that given a description of any other computer or PROGRAM and some data, it can perfectly emulate this second computer or program. Strictly speaking, home PCs are not universal computers because they have only a finite amount of memory. However, in practice, this is usually ignored.

Unstable Having a BASIN OF ATTRACTION that is 0 in size; being such that the slightest PERTURBATION will forever change the state of a SYSTEM. A pencil balanced on its point is unstable.

V

Value Function A built-in FUNCTION in LISP or STUTTER that evaluates all of its arguments prior to being executed, e.g., `car`, `cdr`, and `cons`.

Vant A virtual ant; a type of CELLULAR AUTOMATON that vaguely emulates the activity of one or more ants.

Variation Genetic differences among individuals in a population.

Vector A one-dimensional array of numbers that can be used to represent a point in a multidimensional space.

Weight In a NEURAL NETWORK, the strength of a SYNAPSE (or connection) between two NEURONS. Weights may be positive (EXCITATORY) or negative (INHIBITORY). The THRESHOLDS of a neuron are also considered weights, since they undergo ADAPTATION by a LEARNING ALGORITHM.

White Noise Noise that uniformly distributed in the frequency domain; RANDOMNESS that is uniformly distributed; thus, a white noise process with a range of 0 to 1 would yield a random number in this range with PROBABILITY equal for all possible values. BROWN NOISE is a result of cumulatively adding white noise.

X

XOR The exclusive-or FUNCTION; given two BOOLEAN inputs, the output of XOR is 1 if and only if the two inputs are different; otherwise, the output is 0.

Z

Zero-Sum Game In GAME THEORY, a game in which a win for one player results in an equal but opposite loss for the other players.

Bibliography

Abelson, H., Sussman, G. J., & Sussman, J. (1996). *Structure and interpretation of computer programs.* Cambridge, Mass.: MIT Press.

Arbib, M. A. (1966). Self-reproducing automata—some implications for theoretical biology. In C. H. Waddington (Ed.), *Towards a theoretical biology*, volume 2 (pp. 204–226). Edinburgh: Edinburgh University Press.

Arneodo, A., Coullet, P., & Tresser, C. (1980). Occurrence of strange attractors in three-dimensional Volterra equations. *Phys. Lett. A*, 79A(4): 259–63.

Ashby, W. R. (1966). *An introduction to cybernetics.* New York: John Wiley & Sons.

Awad, E. M. (1996). *Building expert systems: Principles, procedures, and applications.* Minneapolis/St.Paul: West/Wadsworth.

Axelrod, R. (1984). *The evolution of cooperation.* New York: Basic Books.

Axelrod, R. & Hamilton, W. D. (1981). The evolution of cooperation. *Science*, 211(4489): 1390–1396.

Bai-Lin, H. (Ed.). (1984). *Chaos.* Singapore: World Scientific.

Bak, P. (1996). *How nature works: The science of self-organized criticality.* New York: Springer-Verlag.

Bak, P. & Chen, K. (January 1991). Self-organized criticality. *Sci. Am.*, 264(1).

Bak, P., Tang, C., & Wiesenfeld, K. (1988). Self-organized criticality. *Phys. Rev. A*, 38(1): 364–374.

Barlow, C. (1991). *From Gaia to selfish genes: Selected writings in the life sciences.* Cambridge, Mass.: MIT Press.

Barnsley, M. (1988). *Fractals everywhere.* New York: Academic Press.

Barnsley, M. (1989). Iterated function systems. In *Chaos and Fractals: The Mathematics Behind the Computer Graphics*, volume 39 of *Proc. Symposia Appl. Math.*, Providence, R.I. American Mathematical Society.

Beckmann, P. (1977). *A history of π* (Fourth ed.). Boulder, Colo.: Golem Press.

Benhabib, J. (Ed.). (1992). *Cycles and chaos in economic equilibrium.* Princeton: Princeton University Press.

Bennett, C. H., Gács, P., Li, M., Vitanyi, P. M. B., & Zurek, W. H. (1993). Thermodynamics of computation and information distance. In *Proceedings of the twenty-fifth annual ACM symposium on theory of computing*, (pp. 21–30)., San Diego. ACM Press.

Bennett, C. H. & Landauer, R. (July 1985). Fundamental physical limits of computation. *Sci. Am.*, 253(1): 48–56.

Berlekamp, E., Conway, J. H., & Guy, R. (1982). *Winning ways for your mathematical plays*. London: Academic Press.

Blum, L., Cucker, F., Shub, M., & Smale, S. (1995). Complexity and real computation: A manifesto. Technical Report TR-95-042, International Computer Science Institute, Berkeley, Calif.

Blum, L., Shub, M., & Smale, S. (1988). On a theory of computation over the real numbers; NP completeness, recursive functions and universal machines (extended abstract). In *29th annual symposium on foundations of computer science*, (pp. 387–397)., White Plains, N.Y. IEEE.

Bowler, P. J. (1996). *Charles Darwin: The Man and his influence*. Cambridge: Cambridge University Press.

Boyd, R. & Richerson, P. J. (1985). *Culture and the evolutionary process*. Chicago: University of Chicago Press.

Breder, C. M. (1951). Studies in the structure of the fish school. *Bull. Am. Mus. Nat. Hist.*, 98(3): 7ff.

Bremmerman, H. J. (1962). Optimization through evolution and recombination. In M. C. Yovits, G. T. Jacobi, & G. D. Goldstein (Eds.), *Self-organizing systems* (pp. 93ff). Washington, D.C.: Spartan Books.

Bryson, A. E. & Ho, Y. C. (1969). *Applied optimal control*. New York: Blaisdell.

Burks, A. W. (1961). Notes on John von Neumann's cellular self-reproducing automaton. Technical Report 108, Department of Computer Science, University of Illinois, Urbana.

Burks, A. W. (1974). Cellular automata and natural systems. In Keidel, W. D., Händler, W., & Spreng, M. (Eds.), *Cybernetics and bionics*, (pp. 190–204)., Munich. R. Oldenbourg.

Cairns-Smith, A. G. (1966). The origin of life and the nature of the primitive gene. *J. Theor. Biol.*, 10(1): 53–88.

Cairns-Smith, A. G. (1985). *Seven clues to the origin of life*. Cambridge: Cambridge University Press.

Capra, F. (1996). *The web of life: A new scientific understanding of living systems*. New York: Doubleday.

Casti, J. L. (1989). *Alternate realities: Mathematical models of nature and man*. New York: John Wiley & Sons.

Casti, J. L. (1994). *Complexification: Explaining a paradoxical world through the science of surprise*. New York: HarperCollins.

Caudill, M. & Butler, C. (1990). *Naturally intelligent systems*. Cambridge, Mass.: MIT Press.

Chaitin, G. J. (1966). On the length of programs for computing finite binary sequences. *J. ACM*, 13(4): 547–569.

Chaitin, G. J. (1969). On the simplicity and speed of programs for computing infinite sets of natural numbers. *J. ACM*, 16(3): 407–422.

Chaitin, G. J. (January 1970). To a mathematical definition of "life". *ACM SIGACT News*, 4: 12–18.

Chaitin, G. J. (1975). A theory of program size formally identical to information theory. *J. ACM*, 22(3): 329–340.

Chaitin, G. J. (1997). *The limits of mathematics: A course on information theory & limits of formal reasoning*. Singapore: Springer-Verlag.

Charles-Edwards, D. A. (1986). *Modelling plant growth and development*. New York: Academic Press.

Cheeseman, P., Kanefsky, B., & Taylor, W. M. (1991). Where the really hard problems are. In Mylopoulos, J. & Reiter, R. (Eds.), *Proceedings IJCAI-91*, (pp. 331–336)., Sydney.

Chomsky, N. (1956). Three models for the description of language. *IRE Trans. Info. Theory*, 1: 113–124.

Chomsky, N. (1959). On certain formal properties of grammars. *Info. and Control*, 2(2): 137–167.

Chomsky, N. & Miller, G. A. (1958). Finite state languages. *Info. and Control*, 1(2): 91–112.

Church, A. (1936). A note on the Entscheidungsproblem. *J. Symbol. Logic*, 1: 40–41 and 101–102.

Church, A. (1951). *The Calculi of Lambda-Conversion*, volume 6 of *Annals of Mathematical Studies*. Princeton: Princeton University Press.

Clark, W. R. (1995). *At war within: The double-edged sword of immunity*. New York: Oxford University Press.

Conrad, M. & Pattee, H. H. (1970). Evolution experiments with an artificial ecosystem. *J. Theor. Biol.*, 28(3): 393–409.

Cook, S. A. (1971). The complexity of theorem-proving procedures. In *Conference record of third annual ACM symposium on theory of Computing*, (pp. 151–158)., Shaker Heights, Oh. ACM.

Cowan, G., Pines, D., & Meltzer, D. (Eds.). (1994). *Complexity: Metaphors, models, and reality*, volume XIX of *Santa Fe Institute Studies in the Sciences of Complexity*. Reading, Mass.: Addison-Wesley.

Crutchfield, J. P. (1994). The calculi of emergence: Computation, dynamics and induction. *Physica D*, 75(1–3): 11–54.

Crutchfield, J. P. & Young, K. (1989a). Computation at the onset of chaos. In W. Zurek (Ed.), *Complexity, entropy and the physics of information*. Reading, Mass.: Addison-Wesley.

Crutchfield, J. P. & Young, K. (1989b). Inferring statistical complexity. *Phys. Rev. Lett.*, 63(2): 105–108.

Darwin, C. (1859). *On the origin of species.* London: John Murray.

DasGupta, B., Siegelmann, H., & Sontag, E. (1994). On the intractability of loading neural networks. In V. Roychowdhury, K.-Y. Siu, & A. Orlitsky (Eds.), *Theoretical advances in neural computation and learning.* Boston: Kluwer.

Dauben, J. W. (1990). *Georg Cantor: His mathematics and philosophy of the infinite.* Princeton: Princeton University Press.

Davis, M. (Ed.). (1965). *The undecidable.* New York: Raven Press.

Dawkins, R. (1976). *The selfish gene.* Oxford: Oxford University Press.

Dawkins, R. (1983). *The extended phenotype: The gene as a unit of selection.* Oxford: Oxford University Press.

Dawkins, R. (1986). *The blind watchmaker.* New York: W. W. Norton.

Dennett, D. C. (1978). *Brainstorms: Philosophical essays on mind and psychology.* Cambridge, Mass.: Bradford Books/MIT Press.

Derrida, B. & Pomeau, Y. (1986). Random networks of automata: A simple annealed approximation. *Europhys. Lett.,* 1(2): 45–49.

Descartes, R. (1987). *Méditations on first philosophy.* Cambridge: Cambridge University Press.

Dewdney, A. K. (1984). Computer Recreations: Sharks and fish wage an ecological war on the toroidal planet wa-tor. *Sci. Am.,* 251(6): 14–22.

Dewdney, A. K. (1985). Computer Recreations: Exploring the field of genetic algorithms in a primordial computer sea full of flibs. *Sci. Am.,* 253(5): 21–32.

Dewdney, A. K. (August 1988). The hodgepodge machine makes waves. *Sci. Am.,* 225(8): 104–107.

Dewdney, A. K. (1989). *The Turing omnibus: 61 excursions in computer science.* Rockville, Md.: Computer Science Press.

Dewdney, A. K. (1993). *200 percent of nothing: An eye-opening tour through the twists and turns of math abuse and innumeracy.* New York: John Wiley & Sons.

Doyle, J. C., Francis, B. A., & Tannenbaum, A. R. (1992). *Feedback control theory.* New York: MacMillan.

Edelman, G. M. (1987). *Neural darwinism: The theory of neuronal group selection.* New York: Basic Books.

Eigen, M. & Winkler, R. (1982). *The laws of the game: How the principles of nature govern chance.* New York: Harper Colophon.

Esbensen, B. J. & Davie, H. K. (1996). *Echoes for the Eye: Poems to celebrate patterns in nature.* New York: HarperCollins.

Faltings, G. (1995). The proof of Fermat's Last Theorem by R. Taylor and A. Wiles. *Notices Amer. Math. Soc.,* 42(7): 743–746.

Farmer, D. & Kauffman, S. (1988). Biological modelling: What's evolving in artificial life. *Nature,* 331(6155): 390–391.

Farmer, D., Toffoli, T., & Wolfram, S. (Eds.). (1983). *Cellular Automata: Proceedings of an Interdisciplinary Workshop*, Amsterdam. North-Holland.

Farmer, J. D. (1990). Rosetta stone for connectionism. *Physica D*, 42(1–3): 153–187.

Farmer, J. D., Lapedes, A., Packard, N. H., & Wendroff, B. (1986). *Evolution, games and learning*. Amsterdam: North-Holland.

Farmer, J. D., Ott, E., & Yorke, J. A. (1983). The dimension of chaotic attractors. *Physica D*, 7(1–3): 153–180.

Farmer, J. D., Packard, N. H., & Perelson, A. S. (1986). The immune system, adaptation & learning. *Physica D*, 22(1–3): 187–204.

Feigenbaum, M. J. (1978). Quantitative universality for a class of nonlinear transformations. *J. Stat. Phys.*, 19(1): 25–52.

Feigenbaum, M. J. (1979). The universal metric properties of nonlinear transformations. *J. Stat. Phys.*, 21(6): 669–706.

Field, R. J. & Noyes, R. M. (1974). Oscillations in chemical systems. V. Quantitative explanation of band migration in the Belousov-Zhabotinskii reaction. *J. Am. Chem. Soc.*, 96(7): 2001–2006.

Fogel, L. J., Owens, A. J., & Walsh, M. J. (1966). *Artificial Intelligence through Simulated Evolution*. New York: Wiley.

Forrest, S. & Mayer-Kress, G. (1991). Using genetic algorithms in nonlinear dynamical systems and international security models. In L. Davis (Ed.), *The genetic algorithms handbook* (pp. 166–185). New York: Van Nostrand Reinhold.

Fowler, D. R., Meinhardt, H., & Prusinkiewicz, P. (1992). Modeling seashells. *Comp. Graphics*, 26(2): 379–387.

Fredkin, E. & Toffoli, T. (1982). Conservative logic. *Int. J. Theor. Phys.*, 21(3–4): 219–253.

Gale, D. & Propp, J. (1994). Further ant-ics. *Math. Intell.*, 16(1): 37–42.

Gardner, M. (1961). *More mathematical puzzles and diversions*. New York: Penguin.

Gardner, M. (October 1970). Mathematical Games: The fantastic combinations of John Conway's new solitaire game 'Life'. *Sci. Am.*, 223(4): 120–123.

Gardner, M. (1971). Mathematical Games: On cellular automata, self-reproduction, the Garden of Eden and the game of "Life". *Sci. Am.*, 224(2): 112–117.

Gardner, M. (April 1978). Mathematical Games: White and brown music, fractal curves and 1/f fluctuations. *Sci. Am.*, 238: 16–32.

Gardner, M. (1983). *Wheels, life, and other mathematical amusements*. New York: W. H. Freeman.

Garey, M. R. & Johnson, D. S. (1979). *Computers and intractability: A guide to the theory of NP-completeness*. New York: W. H. Freeman.

Garfinkel, A., Spano, M. L., & Ditto, W. L. (1992). Controlling cardiac chaos. *Science*, 257(5074): 1230.

Gell-Mann, M. (1995). *The quark and the jaguar: Adventures in the simple and the complex*. New York: W. H. Freeman.

Gerhardt, M., Schuster, H., & Tyson, J. J. (1991). A cellular automaton model of excitable media IV. Untwisted scroll rings. *Physica D*, 50(2): 189–206.

Gleick, J. (1987). *Chaos*. New York: Viking.

Gödel, K. (1931). Über formal unentscheidbare Sätze der Principia mathematica und verwandter Systeme I. *Monats. für Math. und Phys.*, 38: 173–198.

Gödel, K. (1932). Ein spezialfall des entscheidungsproblem der theoretischen logik. *Ergebn. math. Kolloq.*, 2: 27–28.

Gödel, K. (1965). On intuitionistic arithmetic and number theory. In M. Davis (Ed.), *The undecidable* (pp. 75–81). New York: Raven Press.

Gödel, K. (1986). On completeness and consistency. In S. Feferman, J. W. Dawson, Jr., S. C. Kleene, G. H. Moore, R. M. Solovay, & J. Van Heijenoort (Eds.), *Kurt Gödel: Collected works*, volume 1 (pp. 235–237). Oxford: Oxford University Press.

Goldberg, D. E. (1989). *Genetic algorithms in search, optimization, and machine learning*. Reading, Mass.: Addison-Wesley.

Goldstine, H. H. (1993). *The computer from Pascal to von Neumann*. Princeton: Princeton University Press.

Gonick, L. & Smith, W. (1993). *The cartoon guide to statistics*. New York: HarperCollins.

Grebogi, C., Ott, E., & Yorke, J. A. (1987). Chaos, strange attractors, and fractal basin boundaries in nonlinear dynamics. *Science*, 238(4827): 632–638.

Hall, N. (Ed.). (1991). *Exploring chaos: A guide to the new science of disorder*. New York: W. W. Norton & Co.

Hamilton, W. (1964). The genetical evolution of social behavior. *J. Theor. Biol.*, 7: 1–31.

Haykin, S. (1994). *Neural networks: A comprehensive foundation*. New York: MacMillan.

Hebb, D. O. (1949). *The organization of behavior*. New York: Wiley & Sons.

Hènon, M. (1976). A two-dimensional mapping with a strange attractor. *Comm. Math. Phys.*, 50(1): 69–77.

Hertz, J., Krogh, A., & Palmer, R. G. (1991). *Introduction to the theory of neural computation*. Reading, Mass.: Addison-Wesley.

Hillis, W. D. (1992). Co-evolving parasites improve simulated evolution as an optimization procedure. In C. G. Langton, C. Taylor, J. D. Farmer, & S. Rasmussen (Eds.), *Artificial life II*, volume 10 of *Sante Fe Institute Studies in the Sciences of Complexity* (pp. 313–324). Redwood City, Calif.: Addison-Wesley.

Hirst, B. & Mandelbrot, B. (1995). *Fractal landscapes from the real world*. New York: Distributed Art Publishers.

Hodges, A. (1983). *Alan Turing: The enigma*. New York: Simon and Schuster.

Hofstadter, D. R. (1979). *Gödel, Escher, Bach: An eternal golden braid*. New York: Basic Books.

Hofstadter, D. R. (1985). *Metamagical themas: Questing for the essence of mind and pattern*. New York: Basic Books.

Hogeweg, P. (1988). Cellular automata as a paradigm for ecological modelling. *App. Math. & Comp.*, 27(1).

Hogg, T., Huberman, B. A., & McGlade, J. M. (1989). The stability of ecosystems. *Proc. Royal Soc. of London*, B237(1286): 43–51.

Hogg, T., Huberman, B. A., & Williams, C. P. (1996). Phase transitions and the search problem. *Art. Intell.*, 81(1–2): 1–15.

Holland, J. H. (1962). Outline for a logical theory of adaptive systems. *J. ACM*, 9: 297–314.

Holland, J. H. (1967). Nonlinear environments permitting efficient adaptation. In J. T. Tou (Ed.), *Computer and information sciences II*. New York: Academic Press.

Holland, J. H. (1975). *Adaptation in natural and artificial systems*. Ann Arbor: University of Michigan Press.

Holland, J. H. (1976). Adaptation. In R. Rosen & F. M. Snell (Eds.), *Progress in theoretical biology IV* (pp. 263–293). New York: Academic Press.

Holland, J. H. & Holyoak, K. J. (1989). *Induction: Processes of inference, learning and discovery*. Cambridge, Mass.: MIT Press.

Holldobler, B. & Wilson, E. O. (1990). *The ants*. Cambridge, Mass.: Belknap Press of Harvard University Press.

Hopcroft, J. E. & Ullman, J. D. (1979). *Introduction to automata theory, languages, and computation*. Reading, Mass.: Addison-Wesley.

Hopfield, J. J. (1982). Neural networks and physical systems with emergent collective computational abilities. *Proc. Nat. Acad. Sci.*, 79(8): 2554–2558.

Hopfield, J. J. & Tank, D. W. (August 1986). Computing with neural networks: A model. *Science*, 233(4764): 625–633.

Hornik, K., Stinchcombe, M., & White, H. (1989). Multilayer feedforward networks are universal approximators. *Neural Networks*, 2(5): 359–366.

Isenberg, C. (1978). *The science of soap films and soap bubbles*. Avon, U.K.: Tiero.

Judd, J. S. (1990). *Neural network design and the complexity of learning*. Cambridge, Mass.: MIT Press.

Kaelbling, L. P. (Ed.). (1996). *Recent advances in reinforcement learning*. Boston: Kluwer Academic.

Kauffman, S. (August 1991). Antichaos and adaptation. *Sci. Am.*, 265(2): 64–70.

Kauffman, S. (1995). *At home in the universe: The search for laws of self-organization and complexity*. Oxford: Oxford University Press.

Kauffman, S. A. (1969). Metabolic stability and epigenesis in randomly constructed genetic nets. *J. Theor. Biol.*, 22(3): 437–467.

Kauffman, S. A. (1984). Emergent properties in random complex automata. *Physica D*, 10(1–2): 145–56.

Kauffman, S. A. (1986). Autocatalytic sets of proteins. *J. Theor. Biol.*, 119(1): 1–24.

Kauffman, S. A. (1993). *Origins of order: Self-organization and selection in evolution.* Oxford: Oxford University Press.

Kauffman, S. A. & Smith, R. G. (1986). Adaptive automata based on Darwinian selection. *Physica D*, 22(1–3): 68–82.

Kirchgraber, U. & Stoffer, D. (1990). Chaotic behaviour in simple dynamical systems. *SIAM Review*, 32(3): 424–452.

Kohonen, T. (1977). *Associative memory.* Berlin: Springer-Verlag.

Koiran, P., Cosnard, M., & Garzon, M. (1994). Computability with low-dimensional dynamical systems. *Theoret. Comp. Sci.*, 132(1): 113–128.

Kolmogorov, A. N. (1965). Three approaches to the quantitative definition of information. *Prob. Info. Trans.*, 1(1): 1–7.

Kolmogorov, A. N. (1968). Some theorems on algorithmic entropy and the algorithmic quantity of information. *UMN: Uspekhi Matematicheskikh Nauk*, 23.

Koza, J. R. (1992). *Genetic programming: On the programming of computers by natural selection.* Cambridge, Mass.: MIT Press.

Kuang, Y. (1993). *Delay differential equations with applications in population dynamics.* New York: Academic Press.

Langton, C. (1984). Self-reproduction in cellular automata. *Physica D*, 10(1–2): 135–144.

Langton, C. (1986). Studying artificial life with cellular automata. *Physica D*, 22(1–3): 120–149.

Langton, C. G. (Ed.). (1989). *Artificial Life*, volume 6 of *Santa Fe Institute studies in the sciences of complexity*, Reading, Mass. Addison-Wesley.

Langton, C. G., Taylor, C., Farmer, J. D., & Rasmussen, S. (Eds.). (1992). *Artificial Life II*, volume 10 of *Santa Fe Institute studies in the sciences of complexity*, Reading, Mass. Addison-Wesley.

Lapedes, A. & Farber, R. (1987). Nonlinear signal processing using neural networks: Prediction and system modelling. Technical Report LA-UR-87-2662, Los Alamos National Laboratory, Los Alamos, N.M.

Lapedes, A. & Farber, R. (1988). How neural nets work. In D. Z. Anderson (Ed.), *Neural information processing sytems* (pp. 442–456). New York: American Institute of Physics.

Levy, S. (1992). *Artificial life: A report from the frontier where computers meet biology.* New York: Vintage Books.

Li, T. Y. & Yorke, J. A. (1975). Period three implies chaos. *Am. Math. Monthly*, 82(10): 985–992.

Li, W., Packard, N., & Langton, C. G. (1990). Transition phenomena in CA rule space. *Physica D*, 45(1–3): 77–94.

Lin, L.-J. & Mitchell, T. M. (1992). Memory approaches to reinforcement learning in non-Markovian domains. Technical Report CMU//CS-92-138, Carnegie Mellon University, School of Computer Science, Pittsburgh, Pa.

Lindenmayer, A. (1968). Mathematical models for cellular interactions in development, I & II. *J. Theor. Biol.*, 18: 280–315.

Lindenmayer, A. & Rozenberg, G. (1972). Developmental systems and languages. In *Conference record, fourth annual ACM symposium on theory of computing*, (pp. 214–221)., Denver, Colorado.

Lorenz, E. N. (1963). Deterministic nonperiodic flow. *J. Atmos. Sci.*, 20: 130–141.

Lotka, A. (1910). Zur theorie der periodischen reaktionen. *Z. phys. Chemie*, 72: 508.

Lovelock, J. E. (1983). Daisy World: A cybernetic proof of the Gaia hypothesis. *CoEvol. Quart.*, 38(summer): 66–72.

Lumsden, C. J. & Wilson, E. O. (1981). *Genes, mind, and culture: The coevolutionary process*. Cambridge: Harvard University Press.

Mackey, M. C. & Glass, L. (1977). Oscillation and chaos in physiological control systems. *Science*, 2(4300): 287–289.

MacRae, N. (1992). *John von Neumann: The scientific genius who pioneered the modern computer, game theory, nuclear deterrence, and much more*. New York: Pantheon Books.

Mandelbrot, B. (1978). *Fractals: Form, chance, and dimension*. New York: W. H. Freeman.

Mandelbrot, B. (1983). *The fractal geometry of nature*. New York: W. H. Freeman.

March, R. H. (1995). *Physics for poets*. New York: McGraw-Hill.

Margolus, N. (1984). Physics-like models of computation. *Physica D*, 10(1–2): 81–95.

Margulis, L. (1981). *Symbiosis in cell evolution*. San Francisco: W. H. Freeman.

May, R. M. (1972). Limit cycles in predator-prey communities. *Science*, 177: 900–902.

May, R. M. (1974). Biological populations with nonoverlapping generations: Stable points, stable cycles, and chaos. *Science*, 186(4164): 645–647.

May, R. M. (1976). Simple mathematical models with very complicated dynamics. *Nature*, 261(5560): 459–467.

Mayer-Kress, G. (1992). Nonlinear dynamics and chaos in arms race models. In L. Lam & V. Naroditsky (Eds.), *Modeling complex phenomena* (pp. 153–183). Berlin: Springer.

Maynard Smith, J. (1975). *The theory of evolution* (third ed.). New York: Penguin.

Maynard Smith, J. (1982). *Evolution and the theory of games*. Cambridge: Cambridge University Press.

Maynard Smith, J. (1986). *The problems of biology*. Oxford: Oxford University Press.

McCarthy, J. (1960). LISP 1 programmer's manual. Technical report, Computation Center and Research Laboratory of Electronics, MIT, Cambridge, Mass.

McCulloch, W. S. & Pitts, W. (1943). A logical calculus of the idea immanent in nervous activity. *Bull. Math. Biophys.*, 5: 115–133.

Meinhardt, H. (1995). *The algorithmic beauty of sea shells*. New York: Springer.

Michalewicz, Z. (1996). *Genetic algorithms + data structures = evolution programs*. New York: Springer-Verlag.

Minsky, M. (1972). *Computation: Finite and infinite machines*. London: Prentice-Hall.

Minsky, M. (1979). The society theory of thinking. In P. H. Winston & R. H. Brown (Eds.), *Artificial intelligence: An MIT persective* (pp. 423–450). Cambridge, Mass.: MIT Press.

Minsky, M. (1987). *The society of mind*. London: Heinemann.

Minsky, M. & Papert, S. (1988). *Perceptrons* (expanded ed.). Cambridge, Mass.: MIT Press.

Mitchell, M. (1996). *An introduction to genetic algorithms*. Cambridge, Mass.: MIT Press.

Moore, C. (1990). Unpredictability and undecidability in dynamical systems. *Phys. Rev. Lett.*, 64(20): 2354–2357.

Moore, C. (1991a). Generalized one-sided shifts and maps of the interval. *Nonlinearity*, 4(3): 727–745.

Moore, C. (1991b). Generalized shifts: Unpredictability and undecidability in dynamical systems. *Nonlinearity*, 4(2): 199–230.

Moore, C. (1996). Recursion theory on the reals and continuous-time computation. *Theor. Comp. Sci.*, 162(1): 23–44.

Nicolis, G. & Prigogine, I. (1977). *Self-organization in nonequilibrium systems*. New York: John Wiley & Sons.

Nijhout, H. F. (November 1981). The color patterns of butterflies and moths. *Sci. Am.*, 245(5).

Nilsson, N. J. (1965). *Learning machines: Foundations of trainable pattern classifying systems*. New York: McGraw-Hill.

Nowak, M. & Sigmund, K. (1993). A strategy of win-stay, lose-shift that outperforms Tit-for-Tat in the Prisoner's Dilemma game. *Nature*, 364(6432): 56–58.

Nowak, M. A. & May, R. M. (1992). Evolutionary games and spatial chaos. *Nature*, 359(6398): 826–829.

Nowak, M. A., May, R. M., & Sigmund, K. (June 1995). The arithmetics of mutual help. *Sci. Am.*, 272(6): 76–81.

Omohundro, S. (1984). Modelling cellular automata with partial differential equations. *Physica D*, 10D(1–2): 128–134.

Ore, O. (1988). *Number theory and its history*. New York: Dover.

O'Rourke, J. (1994). *Computational geometry in C*. Cambridge: Cambridge University Press.

Ott, E., Grebogi, C., & Yorke, J. A. (1990a). Controlling chaos. *Phys. Rev. Lett.*, 64(11): 1196–1199.

Ott, E., Grebogi, C., & Yorke, J. A. (1990b). Controlling chaotic dynamical systems. In D. K. Campbell (Ed.), *Chaos—Soviet-American perspectives on nonlinear science* (pp. 153–172). New York: AIP.

Ott, E., Sauer, T., & Yorke, J. A. (1994). *Coping with chaos.* New York: Wiley.

Papert, S. (1980). *Mindstorms: Children, computers, and powerful ideas.* New York: Basic Books.

Peitgen, H.-O., Jürgens, H., & Saupe, D. (1992). *Chaos and fractals.* New York: Springer-Verlag.

Penrose, R. (1989). *The emperor's new mind.* Oxford: Oxford University Press.

Pickover, C. A. (1991). *Computers, pattern, chaos and beauty: Graphics from an unseen world.* New York: St. Martin's Press.

Poincaré, H. (1890). Sur les équations de la dynamique et le problème de trois corps. *Acta Math.*, 13: 1–270.

Póincare, H. (1952). *Science and hypothesis.* New York: Dover.

Poundstone, W. (1985). *The recursive universe.* New York: William Morrow.

Poundstone, W. (1992). *Prisoner's Dilemma.* New York: Doubleday.

Press, W. H., Flannery, B. P., Teukolsky, S. A., & Vetterling, W. T. (1986). *Numerical recipes.* Cambridge: Cambridge University Press.

Prusinkiewicz, P., Lindenmayer, A., Hanan, J. S., et al. (1990). *The algorithmic beauty of plants.* New York: Springer-Verlag.

Rand, D. A. (1994). Measuring and characterizing spatial patterns, dynamics and chaos in spatially extended dynamical systems and cologies. *Philos. Trans. Roy. Soc. A*, 348(1688): 497–514.

Rand, D. A. & Wilson, H. (1995). Using spatio-temporal chaos and intermediate-scale determinism to quantify spatially-extended ecosystems. *Proc. R. Soc. Lond. B*, 259(1355): 111–117.

Rapoport, A. & Chammah, A. M. (1965). *Prisoner's Dilemma.* Ann Arbor: University of Michigan Press.

Rechenberg, I. (1973). *Evolution strategy: Optimization of technical systems by means of biological evolution.* Stuttgart: Fromman-Holzboog.

Resnick, M. (1988). LEGO, logo, and life. In C. Langton (Ed.), *Artificial life* (pp. 397–406). Reading, Mass.: Addison-Wesley.

Resnick, M. (1994). *Turtles, termites, and traffic jams: Explorations in massively parallel microworlds.* Cambridge, Mass.: Bradford Books/MIT Press.

Reynolds, C. W. (1987). Flocks, herds, and schools: A distributed behavioral model. *Comp. Graph.*, 21(4): 25–34.

Ribenboim, P. (1991). *The little book of big primes.* New York: Springer-Verlag.

Richardson, L. F. (1961). The problem of contiguity: An appendix of statistics of deadly quarrels. *General Systems Yearbook*, 6: 139–187.

Ridley, M. (1995). *The red queen: Sex and the evolution of human nature.* New York: Macmillan.

Rosenblatt, F. (1962). *Principles of neurodynamics: Perceptrons and the theory of brain mechanisms*. Washington, D.C.: Spartan Books.

Rucker, R. (1995). *Infinity and the mind: The science and philosophy of the infinite*. Princeton: Princeton University Press.

Ruelle, D. (1980). Strange attractors. *Math. Intell.*, 2(3): 126–137.

Ruelle, D. (1993). *Chance and chaos*. Princeton: Princeton University Press.

Ruelle, D. & Takens, F. (1971). On the nature of turbulence. *Comm. Math. Phys.*, 20(3): 167–192.

Rumelhart, D. E., Hinton, G. E., & Williams, R. J. (1986). *Parallel distributive processing*. Cambridge, Mass.: MIT Press.

Sarle, W. S. & Net Poohbahs (1994). Kangaroos and training neural networks. FAQ list available from `ftp://ftp.sas.com/pub/neural/kangaroos`.

Schrödinger, E. (1944). *What is life?* Cambridge: Cambridge University Press.

Schroeder, M. (1991). *Fractals, chaos, power laws*. New York: W. H. Freeman.

Schwefel, H.-P. (1977). *Numerische optimierung von computer-modellen mittels der evolutionsstrategie*. Basel: Birkhäuser.

Shaw, E. (1962). The schooling of fishes. *Sci. Am.*, 206: 128–138.

Shinbrot, T., Ditto, W., Grebogi, C., Ott, E., Spano, M., & Yorke, J. A. (1992). Using the sensitive dependence of chaos (the "butterfly effect") to direct trajectories in an experimental chaotic system. *Phys. Rev. Lett.*, 68(19): 2863–2866.

Siegelmann, H. T. & Sontag, E. D. (1991). Turing computability with neural networks. *Appl. Math. Let.*, 4(6): 77–80.

Solomonoff, R. J. (1964a). A formal theory of inductive inference: Part I. *Info. and Control*, 7(1): 1–22.

Solomonoff, R. J. (1964b). A formal theory of inductive inference: Part II. *Information and Control*, 7(1): 224–254.

Stanley, H. E. & Ostrowsky, N. (Eds.). (1985). *On growth and form: Fractal and non fractal patterns in physics*. Kluwer Academic.

Sterman, J. D. (1984). Instructions for running the beer distribution game. Technical Report D-3679, System Dynamics Group, MIT, Cambridge, Mass.

Sterman, J. D. (1988). Modeling managerial behavior: Misperceptions of feedback in a dynamic decision making experiemnt. *Management Sci.*, 35(3): 321–339.

Stewart, I. (1990). *Does God play dice?: The mathematics of chaos*. Oxford: Blackwell.

Stewart, I. (July 1994). Mathematical Recreations: The ultimate anty-particles. *Sci. Am.*, 271(1): 104–107.

Stewart, I. (1995). *Nature's numbers: The unreal reality of mathematical imagination*. New York: Basic Books.

Stewart, I. (1996). *From here to infinity*. Oxford: Oxford University Press.

Stinson, D. R. (1995). *Cryptography: Theory and practice*. Boca Raton: CRC Press.

Strang, G. (1980). *Linear algebra and its applications*. San Diego: Harcourt Brace Jovanovich.

Strogatz, S. (1994). *Nonlinear dynamics and chaos*. New York: Addison Wesley.

Tagliarini, G. A. & Page, E. W. (1987). Solving constraint satisfaction problems with neural networks. In *Proceedings of the first international conference on neural networks*, San Diego.

Takens, F. (1980). Detecting strange attractors in turbulence. In D. A. Rand & L. S. Young (Eds.), *Dynamical systems and turbulence* (pp. 366–381). New York: Spinger-Verlag.

Tank, D. W. & Hopfield, J. J. (December 1987). Collective computation in neuronlike circuits. *Sci. Am.*, 257(6): 104–114.

Toffoli, T. (1977). Computation and construction universality of reversible cellular automata. *J. Comp. Sys. Sci.*, 15(2): 213–231.

Toffoli, T. (1984). Cellular automata as an alternative to (rather than an approximation of) differential equations in modeling physics. *Physica D*, 10(1–2): 117–127.

Toffoli, T. & Margolus, N. (1987). *Cellular automata machines*. London: MIT Press.

Tomita, K. & Tsuda, I. (1979). Chaos in Belousov-Zhabotinskii reaction in a flow system. *Phys. Lett. A*, 71(5–6): 489.

Tu, P. N. V. (1992). *Dynamical systems: An introduction with applications in economics and biology*. Berlin: Springer-Verlag.

Turing, A. M. (1936). On computable numbers, with an application to the Entscheidungsproblem. *Proc. London Math. Soc.*, 2(42): 230–265.

Turing, A. M. (1950). Can a machine think? *Mind*, 59(236): 433–460.

Turing, A. M. (1952). The chemical basis of morphogenesis. *Phil. Trans. Roy. Soc. London*, B(237): 37–72.

Turing, A. M. (1963). Computing machinery and intelligence. In E. A. Feigenbaum (Ed.), *Computers and Thought*. New York: McGraw-Hill.

Ulam, S. M. (1962). On some mathematical problems connected with patterns of growth of figures. *Proc. Symposia Appl. Math.*, 14: 215–224.

Ulam, S. M. & von Neumann, J. (1947). On combinations of stochastic and deterministic processes. *Bull. Am. Math. Soc.*, 53: 1120.

Vanecek, A. & Celikovsky, S. (1996). *Control systems: From linear analysis to synthesis of chaos*. New York: Prentice-Hall.

von Neumann, J. (1958). *The computer and the brain*. New Haven: Yale University Press.

von Neumann, J. (1966). *Theory of self-reproducing automata*. Urbana: University of Illinois Press.

von Neumann, J. & Morgenstern, O. (1944). *Theory of games and economic behavior*. Princeton: Princeton University Press.

Waldrop, M. M. (1992). *Complexity: The emerging science at the edge of order and chaos.* New York: Simon & Schuster.

Wang, H. (1987). *Reflections on Kurt Gödel.* Cambridge, Mass.: MIT Press.

Wassermann, G. D. (1997). *From Occam's Razor to the roots of consciousness: 20 essays on philosophy, philosophy of science and philosophy of mind.* Avebury.

Watson, J. D. (1991). *The double helix: A personal account of the discovery of the structure of DNA.* New York: New American Library.

Weinberg, R. (1970). Computer simulation of a primitive, evolving eco-system. Technical Report 03296-6-T, University of Michigan, Ann Arbor.

Werbos, P. (1974). *Beyond Regression: New Tools for Prediction and Analysis in the Behavioral Sciences.* PhD thesis, Harvard University, Cambridge, Mass.

Wesson, R. (1991). *Beyond natural selection.* Cambridge, Mass.: Bradford Books/MIT Press.

Whitehead, A. N. & Russell, B. (1910). *Principia mathematica.* Cambridge: Cambridge University Press.

Whitehead, S. D. & Lin, L.-J. (1995). Reinforcement learning of a non-Markov decision process. *Art. Intell.*, 73(1–2): 271–306.

Wickler, W. (1968). *Mimicry in plants and animals.* New York: World University Library.

Wiener, N. (1948). *Cybernetics, or control and communication in the animal and the machine.* New York: John Wiley.

Wills, C. (1989). *The wisdom of the genes.* New York: Basic Books.

Wilson, E. O. (1971). *The insect societies.* Cambridge, Mass.: Belknap Press of Harvard University Press.

Wilson, E. O. (1975). *Sociobiology: The new synthesis.* Cambridge, Mass.: Belknap Press of Harvard University Press.

Wilson, S. W. (1994). ZCS: A zeroth level classifier system. *Evol. Comp.*, 2(1): 1–18.

Wolfram, S. (1983). Statistical mechanics of cellular automata. *Rev. Mod. Phys.*, 55(3): 601–644.

Wolfram, S. (1984a). Cellular automata as models of complexity. *Nature*, 311(4): 419–424.

Wolfram, S. (1984b). Computation theory of cellular automata. *Comm. Math. Phys.*, 96(1): 15–57.

Wolfram, S. (1984c). Universality and complexity in cellular automata. *Physica D*, 10(1–2): 1–35.

Wolfram, S. (Ed.). (1986). *Theory and applications of cellular automata.* Singapore: World Scientific.

Wolfram, S. (1994). *Cellular automata and complexity.* Reading, Mass.: Addison-Wesley.

Wolpert, D. H. & Macready, W. G. (1995). No free lunch theorems for search. Technical Report SFI-TR-95-02-010, The Santa Fe Institute, Santa Fe, N.M.

Index

---

*Numbers in bold refer to glossary entries.

Production Notes

It would have been impossible to write this book without the vast collection of excellent software used by the author. In fact, this book was produced entirely with free software. Production and software development took place over three-plus years on a number of Intel-based personal computers running Linus Torvold's Linux operating system, which had the X window system providing all GUI services. The bulk of the user-level commands under Linux were written as part of the GNU project. All editing was done with Richard Stallman's `emacs` editor. All programs were written with Stallman's `gcc` compiler. Additionally, Larry Wall's `perl` scripting language was extensively used for automating boring tasks.

Line drawings were made with `xfig`, all edited bit-mapped images were drawn with either `xpaint` or the `gimp` editor, and all plots were produced with `gnuplot`. A few figures derived from royalty-free clip art collections or royalty-free data sources. The book was typeset with LaTeX using BibTeX to produce the bibliography and `makeindex` for the index.

The author gratefully thanks and acknowledges the community of hackers who have made such excellent software available for free; without it producing this book would have been impossible.